S0-ALH-045

CCDA Self-Study: Designing for Cisco Internetwork Solutions (DESGN)

Diane Teare

Cisco Press

800 East 96th Street, 3rd Floor
Indianapolis, IN 46240 USA

CCDA Self-Study: Designing for Cisco Internetwork Solutions (DESGN)

Diane Teare

Copyright© 2004 Cisco Systems, Inc.

Published by:
Cisco Press
800 E. 96th Street
Indianapolis, IN 46240 USA

All rights reserved. No part of this book may be reproduced or transmitted in any form or by any means, electronic or mechanical, including photocopying, recording, or by any information storage and retrieval system, without written permission from the publisher, except for the inclusion of brief quotations in a review.

Printed in the United States of America   6 7 8 9 0

Sixth Printing   June 2006

Library of Congress Cataloging-in-Publication Number: 2003104996

ISBN: 1-58705-141-9

Warning and Disclaimer

This book is designed to provide information about Designing for Cisco Internetwork Solutions (DESGN). Every effort has been made to make this book as complete and as accurate as possible, but no warranty or fitness is implied.

The information is provided on an "as is" basis. The authors, Cisco Press, and Cisco Systems, Inc., shall have neither liability nor responsibility to any person or entity with respect to any loss or damages arising from the information contained in this book or from the use of the discs or programs that may accompany it.

The opinions expressed in this book belong to the author and are not necessarily those of Cisco Systems, Inc.

The Cisco Press self-study book series is as described, intended for self-study. It has not been designed for use in a classroom environment. Only Cisco Learning Partners displaying the following logos are authorized providers of Cisco curriculum. If you are using this book within the classroom of a training company that does not carry one of these logos, then you are not preparing with a Cisco trained and authorized provider. For information on Cisco Learning Partners please visit:www.cisco.com/go/authorizedtraining. To provide Cisco with any information about what you may believe is unauthorized use of Cisco trademarks or copyrighted training material, please visit: http://www.cisco.com/logo/infringement.html.

Feedback Information

At Cisco Press, our goal is to create in-depth technical books of the highest quality and value. Each book is crafted with care and precision, undergoing rigorous development that involves the unique expertise of members from the professional technical community.

Readers' feedback is a natural continuation of this process. If you have any comments regarding how we could improve the quality of this book or otherwise alter it to better suit your needs, you can contact us through e-mail at feedback@ciscopress.com. Please be sure to include the book title and ISBN in your message.

We greatly appreciate your assistance.

Corporate and Government Sales

Cisco Press offers excellent discounts on this book when ordered in quantity for bulk purchases or special sales.
For more information, please contact:
U.S. Corporate and Government Sales 1-800-382-3419 corpsales@pearsontechgroup.com

For sales outside of the U.S. please contact:
International Sales international@pearsoned.com

Trademark Acknowledgments

All terms mentioned in this book that are known to be trademarks or service marks have been appropriately capitalized. Cisco Press or Cisco Systems, Inc. cannot attest to the accuracy of this information. Use of a term in this book should not be regarded as affecting the validity of any trademark or service mark.

Publisher	John Wait
Editor-in-Chief	John Kane
Executive Editor	Brett Bartow
Cisco Representative	Anthony Wolfenden
Cisco Press Program Manager	Sonia Torres Chavez
Manager, Marketing Communications, Cisco Systems	Scott Miller
Cisco Marketing Program Manager	Edie Quiroz
Managing Editor	Patrick Kanouse
Development Editor	Ginny Bess
Project Editor	Marc Fowler
Copy Editor	Bridget Collins
Technical Editors	Matthew H. Birkner
	Shawn Boyd
	Keith Hutton
Team Coordinator	Tammi Barnett
Book Designer	Gina Rexrode
Cover Designer	Louisa Adair
Compositor	Mark Shirar
Indexer	Eric Schroeder

CISCO SYSTEMS

Corporate Headquarters
Cisco Systems, Inc.
170 West Tasman Drive
San Jose, CA 95134-1706
USA
www.cisco.com
Tel: 408 526-4000
    800 553-NETS (6387)
Fax: 408 526-4100

European Headquarters
Cisco Systems International BV
Haarlerbergpark
Haarlerbergweg 13-19
1101 CH Amsterdam
The Netherlands
www-europe.cisco.com
Tel: 31 0 20 357 1000
Fax: 31 0 20 357 1100

Americas Headquarters
Cisco Systems, Inc.
170 West Tasman Drive
San Jose, CA 95134-1706
USA
www.cisco.com
Tel: 408 526-7660
Fax: 408 527-0883

Asia Pacific Headquarters
Cisco Systems, Inc.
Capital Tower
168 Robinson Road
#22-01 to #29-01
Singapore 068912
www.cisco.com
Tel: +65 6317 7777
Fax: +65 6317 7799

Cisco Systems has more than 200 offices in the following countries and regions. Addresses, phone numbers, and fax numbers are listed on the
Cisco.com Web site at www.cisco.com/go/offices.

Argentina • Australia • Austria • Belgium • Brazil • Bulgaria • Canada • Chile • China PRC • Colombia • Costa Rica • Croatia • Czech Republic
Denmark • Dubai, UAE • Finland • France • Germany • Greece • Hong Kong SAR • Hungary • India • Indonesia • Ireland • Israel • Italy
Japan • Korea • Luxembourg • Malaysia • Mexico • The Netherlands • New Zealand • Norway • Peru • Philippines • Poland • Portugal
Puerto Rico • Romania • Russia • Saudi Arabia • Scotland • Singapore • Slovakia • Slovenia • South Africa • Spain • Sweden
Switzerland • Taiwan • Thailand • Turkey • Ukraine • United Kingdom • United States • Venezuela • Vietnam • Zimbabwe

Copyright © 2003 Cisco Systems, Inc. All rights reserved. CCIP, CCSP, the Cisco Arrow logo, the Cisco *Powered* Network mark, the Cisco Systems Verified logo, Cisco Unity, Follow Me Browsing, FormShare, iQ Net Readiness Scorecard, Networking Academy, and ScriptShare are trademarks of Cisco Systems, Inc.; Changing the Way We Work, Live, Play, and Learn, The Fastest Way to Increase Your Internet Quotient, and iQuick Study are service marks of Cisco Systems, Inc.; and Aironet, ASIST, BPX, Catalyst, CCDA, CCDP, CCIE, CCNA, CCNP, Cisco, the Cisco Certified Internetwork Expert logo, Cisco IOS, the Cisco IOS logo, Cisco Press, Cisco Systems, Cisco Systems Capital, the Cisco Systems logo, Empowering the Internet Generation, Enterprise/Solver, EtherChannel, EtherSwitch, Fast Step, GigaStack, Internet Quotient, IOS, IP/TV, iQ Expertise, the iQ logo, LightStream, MGX, MICA, the Networkers logo, Network Registrar, *Packet*, PIX, Post-Routing, Pre-Routing, RateMUX, Registrar, SlideCast, SMARTnet, StrataView Plus, Stratm, SwitchProbe, TeleRouter, TransPath, and VCO are registered trademarks of Cisco Systems, Inc. and/or its affiliates in the U.S. and certain other countries.

All other trademarks mentioned in this document or Web site are the property of their respective owners. The use of the word partner does not imply a partnership relationship between Cisco and any other company. (0303R)

Printed in the USA

About the Author

Diane Teare is a consultant in the networking, training, and e-learning fields. Diane has over 20 years of experience in design, implementation, and troubleshooting of network hardware and software, and has also been involved in teaching, course design, and project management. Diane was the course director/master instructor for the Designing Cisco Networks (DCN) and Building Scalable Cisco Networks (BSCN) courses at one of the largest authorized Cisco Learning Partners and was recently the Director of e-Learning for the same company, where she was responsible for planning and supporting all of the company's e-learning offerings in Canada, including Cisco courses. Diane has a bachelor's degree in applied science in electrical engineering and a master's degree in applied science in management science. Diane was a Cisco Certified Systems Instructor (CCSI) and currently holds her Cisco Certified Network Professional (CCNP) and Cisco Certified Design Associate (CCDA) certifications. She edited *Designing Cisco Networks* (ISBN 1-57870-105-8) and coauthored *Building Scalable Cisco Networks* (ISBN 1-57870-228-3) and *Building Scalable Cisco Internetworks* (ISBN 1-58705-084-6), all from Cisco Press. Diane is currently updating *Building Scalable Cisco Internetworks*, which will be published in 2004.

About the Technical Reviewers

Matthew H. Birkner, CCIE No. 3719, is a Technical Leader at Cisco Systems, where he specializes in IP and MPLS network design. He has influenced multiple large carrier and enterprise designs worldwide. Matt has spoken at Cisco Networkers on MPLS VPN technologies in both the U.S. and EMEA over the past few years. Matt, a double CCIE, wrote the Cisco Press book *Cisco Internetwork Design*. Matt holds a BSEE from Tufts University, where he majored in electrical engineering.

Shawn Boyd is a Senior Network Consultant for ARP Technologies Inc. Shawn is active in course development and is a Certified Cisco Systems Instructor (CCSI) with Global Knowledge and is responsible for teaching most of the CCNP, CCDP, and security courses. His background is in network security and design at a service provider level. Shawn has worked for Canada's largest Telco providers, for whom he performed network designs and implementations and was the lead contact for many large government contracts.

Keith T. Hutton holds the following certifications: CCSI, CCNP, CCDP, MCP, and A+. For the past 13 years, Keith has been involved in the communications industry in both the private and public sector. Prior to his employment at Global Knowledge, he provided consulting services to the telecommunications industry in Canada. Keith is a graduate of Queen's University and has 10 years of prior service as a Communications and Electronics Engineering Officer for the Canadian Forces Primary Reserves.

Dedication

This book is dedicated to my wonderful husband, Allan Mertin, who is always encouraging me to follow my dreams; to our delightful son Nicholas, who lights up our lives each day; and to my parents, Syd and Beryl, for their warm thoughts and support. Thank you.

"The better part of one's life consists of his friendships."

—Abraham Lincoln

Acknowledgments

I would like to thank the many people who helped put this book together, including:

The Cisco Press team—Brett Bartow, the Executive Editor, was the catalyst for this project; he coordinated the team and ensured that sufficient resources were available for the book's completion. Tammi Barnett was instrumental in organizing the logistics and administration. Ginny Bess, the Development Editor, has been invaluable in producing a high-quality manuscript. I would also like to thank Patrick Kanouse and Bridget Collins for their excellent work in shepherding this book through the editorial process.

The Cisco Systems team—Many thanks to the members of the DESGN course development team.

The technical reviewers—I would like to thank the technical reviewers of this book, Matt Birkner, Shawn Boyd, and Keith Hutton, for their thorough, detailed review and very valuable input.

My family—Of course, this book would not have been possible without the constant understanding and patience of my family. They have lived through the many weekends and nights it took to complete it. Special thanks to Nicholas for telling me many times: "Mummy, go back in your office!" Although it was a bit heartbreaking, it did the job!

Contents at a Glance

Introduction xxvi
Foreward xxvii

Chapter 1   Internetworking Technology Review   3

Chapter 2   Applying Design Principles in Network Deployment   29

Chapter 3   Structuring and Modularizing the Network   117

Chapter 4   Basic Campus Switching Design Considerations   181

Chapter 5   Designing WANs   255

Chapter 6   Designing IP Addressing in the Network   319

Chapter 7   Selecting Routing Protocols for a Network   373

Chapter 8   Designing Networks for Voice Transport   441

Chapter 9   Evaluating Security Solutions for the Network   545

Chapter 10   Applying Basic Network Management Design Concepts   607

Chapter 11   Review and Case Study   681

Appendix A   IPv4 Addressing Job Aids   715

Appendix B   References   751

Appendix C   Open System Interconnection (OSI) Reference Model   759

Appendix D   Summary of ICND Router and Switch Commands   773

Appendix E   Common Requests For Comments   793

Appendix F   Network Address Translation   799

Appendix G   Answers to Review Questions, Case Studies, and Simulation Exercises   815

Glossary   903

Index   977

Contents

Introduction   xxvi

Foreward   xxvii

Chapter 1   Internetworking Technology Review   3

The OSI Model   3

LANs   5

LAN Physical Network Access   6

LAN Data Transmission Types   6

WANs   6

WAN Categories   7

WAN Virtual Circuits   7

WAN Dialup Services   7

WAN Devices   8

Internetwork Addressing   8

Media Access Control (MAC) Addresses   9

Network Layer Addresses   9

Network Devices   9

Hubs   9

Bridges and Switches   10

Bridging Protocols   11

Spanning Tree Protocol   12

Bridges Versus Switches   12

Virtual LANs   13

Routers   13

Routing   15

TCP/IP Protocol Suite   16

TCP/IP Network Layer   16

TCP/IP Transport Layer   17

TCP/IP Application Layer   18

IPv4 Addressing   18

TCP/IP Routing Protocols   22

Resource Reservation Protocol   23

NetWare Protocol Suite   24

AppleTalk Protocol Suite   25

IBM SNA Protocols   26

Traditional SNA Environments   26

IBM Peer-based Networking   26

Data-link Switching (DLSw)   26

Chapter 2   Applying Design Principles in Network Deployment   29

Identifying Organizational Network Policies and Procedures   29

Network Organizational Model   29
  Traditional Organizational Model   30
  Modern Organizational Model   31
  Benefits of a Networked Organization   32
Network Organizational Architecture   33
  Architecture Components   33
  Implementing the Network Organizational Model   34
  Network Organizational Architecture Example   35
Organizational Policies   36
  Defining Policies   37
  Policy Makers   38
Organizational Procedures   39
  Organizational Structure   39
  Information Flows   40
Using Networking to Accomplish Organizational Goals   42
  Flexible Network Infrastructure Features   43
  Flexible Network Example   43
Network Design Methodology   44
  Design as an Integral Part of the PDIOO Methodology   45
  Design Methodology   47
Identifying Customer Requirements   49
  Assessing the Scope of the Network Design Project   49
  Identifying Required Information   50
    Extracting Initial Requirements   51
    Identifying Network Requirements   52
  Organizational Goals   53
  Organizational Constraints   55
  Planned Applications and Network Services   57
  Technical Goals   60
  Technical Constraints   62
  Cisco Network Investment Calculator for IP Telephony   63
Characterizing the Existing Network   64
  Identifying the Existing Infrastructure and Its Features   65
  Customer Input   65
    Example 1: OSI Network Layer Topology Map   65
    Example 2: Data Link Layer (Layer 2) Topology Map   66
    Example 3: Network Services Map   67
    Example 4: Network Applications Map   67
    Example 5: Modularizing the Network   69
  Auditing the Existing Network   70
  Tools for Auditing the Network   71
    Manual Auditing   72
    Network Health Checklist   76

Analyzing Network Traffic and Applications   77
Tools for Analyzing Traffic   79
NBAR   79
NetFlow   80
Analysis Tools Examples   81
Summary Report   84
Creating a Draft Design Document   85
Designing a Topology and Network Solution Using Structured Design Principles   86
Top-down Approach to Network Design   87
Structured Design   87
Top-down Design Compared to Bottom-up Approach   89
Top-down Design Example   90
Decision Tables in Network Design   91
Network Design Tools   94
Planning a Design Implementation   95
Building a Prototype or Pilot Network   97
Documenting the Design   97
Implementing and Verifying the Design   98
Monitoring and Redesigning the Network   99
Summary   99
References   100
Case Study and Simulation Exercise   101
DJMP Industries Case Study Scenario   101
Company Facts   101
Current Situation   102
Plans and Requirements   103
Case Study: Network Upgrade   105
Simulation: New Applications   105
Scenario   105
Initial Traffic   106
New Applications Introduced   108
HTTP Traffic   109
Increased Link Speed Between Houston and San Jose   110
Review Questions   111

Chapter 3   Structuring and Modularizing the Network   117
Network Hierarchy   117
Hierarchical Network Model   117
Hierarchical Network Design Layers   118
Hierarchical Model versus Open System Interconnection (OSI) Model   120
Access Layer Functionality   120
The Role of the Access Layer   120
Layer 2 and Layer 3 Switching in the Access Layer   121

Distribution Layer Functionality   123
    The Role of the Distribution Layer   123
    Distribution Layer Example   124
Core Layer Functionality   125
    The Role of the Core Layer   125
    Design Consideration: Layer 2 Versus Layer 3 Switching in the Core   126
Using a Modular Approach to Network Design   127
    Enterprise Composite Network Model   128
        Evolution of Enterprise Networks   128
        Enterprise Composite Network Model Overview   128
        Functional Areas of the Enterprise Composite Network Model   129
        Guidelines for Creating an Enterprise Composite Network   131
    Enterprise Campus Modules   132
        Campus Infrastructure Module   133
        Network Management Module   134
        Server Farm Module   134
        Edge Distribution Module   135
        Enterprise Campus Example   135
        Enterprise Campus Guidelines   136
    Enterprise Edge Modules   137
        E-commerce Module   139
        Internet Connectivity Module   139
        VPN/Remote Access Module   140
        WAN Module   140
        Enterprise Edge Guidelines   141
    Service Provider Edge Modules   141
        Internet Service Provider Module   142
        PSTN Module   143
        Frame Relay (FR)/ATM Module   143
        Service Provider Edge Guidelines   144
Network Services and Solutions Within Modular Networks   145
    Intelligent Network Services in an Enterprise Composite
    Network Model   145
        Intelligent Network Services   145
        Intelligent Network Services Example   147
    Security in Modular Network Design   148
        Understanding the Threats   148
        External Threats   152
    High Availability in Modular Network Design   155
        Designing High Availability into a Network   155
        High Availability in the Server Farm   156
        Designing Route Redundancy   159
        Designing Link Redundancy   161

Network Solutions in an Enterprise Composite Network Model   163
    Network Solutions   163
    Voice Transport in Modular Network Design   164
        Two Voice Implementations   164
        IP Telephony Components   165
        Modular Approach in Voice Network Design   165
        Evaluating the Existing Data Infrastructure for Voice Design   167
    Content Networking in the Modular Network Design   168
        Content Delivery Network (CDN) and Content Networking (CN)   168
        Content Networking Example   173

Summary   174

References   175

Review Questions   176

Chapter 4   Basic Campus Switching Design Considerations   181

Campus Design Methodology   181
    Designing an Enterprise Campus   181
    Network Geography   182
        Intra-Building Structure   183
        Inter-Building Structure   183
        Distant Remote Building Structure   184
        Network Geography Considerations   184
    Network Application Characterization   185
        Client-Client Applications   185
        Client-Distributed Server Applications   186
        Client-Server Farm Applications   187
        Client-Enterprise Edge Applications   188
        Application Requirements   189
    Data Link Layer Technologies   191
        Shared Technology   192
        Switched LAN Technology   192
        Comparing Switched and Shared Technologies   192
    Layer 2 and Layer 3 Switching Design Considerations   194
        Spanning-Tree Domain Considerations   195
        Load Sharing Guidelines   198
        Layer 2 Versus Layer 3 Switching   199
    Transmission Media   201
        Unshielded Twisted-Pair (UTP) Cables   201
        Optical Cables   202
        Copper Versus Fiber   203
        Cabling Example   205

Campus Design   206
    Introduction to Enterprise Campus Design   206
        Enterprise Campus Module Requirements   207

Enterprise Campus Design Considerations   208
Network Traffic Patterns   209
    80/20 Rule in the Campus   209
    20/80 Rule in the Campus   209
    Network Traffic Pattern Example   210
Multicast Traffic Considerations   211
QoS Considerations for Delay-sensitive Traffic   213
    QoS Categories   214
    QoS in LAN Switches   214
    QoS Example with Voice Traffic Across a Switch   215
Building Access and Distribution Layers Design   216
    Building Access Layer Considerations   216
    Building Access Design Examples   218
    Building Distribution Layer Considerations   219
    Building Distribution Layer Example   220
Campus Backbone Design   221
    Layer 2 Campus Backbone Design   221
    Split Layer 2 Campus Backbone Design   222
    Layer 3 Campus Backbone Design   223
    Dual-path Layer 3 Campus Backbone Design   225
    Network Management Module Integration   226
Server Placement   226
    Local Server in a Building Access Module   226
    Server in a Building Distribution Module   226
    Server Farm   227
    Server Connectivity Options   229
    The Effect of Applications on Switch Performance   229
Designing Connectivity to the Remainder of the Enterprise Network   230
    Design Guidelines for the Edge Distribution Module   231

Summary   232

References   233

Case Study and Simulation Exercise   234
    Case Study: Enterprise Campus Design   234
    Simulation 1: Shared Versus Switched LAN   235
        Scenario   235
        Client Accessing Server in Unloaded Shared Ethernet   235
        Client Accessing Server in Loaded Shared Ethernet   238
        Introducing Switched Ethernet   240
    Simulation 2: Layer 2 Versus Layer 3 Switching   241
        Scenario   242
        Initial Traffic   242
        Layer 2 Only Design   243
        Layer 3 Switching in Distribution   244
        Layer 3 Switching in Core and Distribution   247
        Layer 3 Access Switch   248
        IP Routing Process on the Server   249

Review Questions   250

Chapter 5   Designing WANs   255

   Enterprise Edge WAN Design Methodology   255

      Introduction to WANs   256

      WAN Technologies in the Enterprise Edge   256

         Traditional WAN Technologies   257

         Emerging WAN Technologies   258

         Internet Service Provider Networks   259

         Types of WAN Interconnections   260

      WAN Design Methodology: Planning and Designing   260

         Application Requirements of WAN Design   262

         Technical Requirements: Maximum Offered Traffic   263

         Technical Requirements: Bandwidth   264

         Evaluating Cost-effectiveness of WAN Ownership   265

         Comparing WAN Technologies   267

      WAN Design Methodology: Implementation   268

         Redundant Links in an Enterprise Edge Network   268

         Optimizing Bandwidth in a WAN   268

         Data Compression   269

         Window Size   271

         Queuing to Improve Link Utilization   272

         Traffic Shaping and Policing to Rate-limit Traffic Classes   275

   Selecting WAN Technologies   276

      Technologies for Remote Access   277

         Evaluating Detailed Networking Requirements   278

         On-Demand Connections: ISDN Versus Analog Modem   280

         Always-on Connections: TDM Versus Packet Switching   280

         Always-on Connections: Frame Relay Versus X.25   281

         Packet-Switched Network Topologies   281

         Design as a Never-ending Process   283

      WAN Backup Technologies   283

         Dial Backup Routing   284

         Permanent Secondary WAN Links   285

         Shadow PVC   287

      Connecting Dispersed Enterprise Sites   288

         Point-to-Point Connection   288

         Synchronous Optical Network (SONET) and Synchronous Digital Hierarchy (SDH) as a Point-to-Point Alternative   289

         Dense Wavelength Division Multiplexing   289

         Dark Fiber   290

      IP Connectivity and Emerging WAN Technologies   290

         DSL Technologies   291

         LRE Technology   294

         Cable Technology   295

         Wireless Technologies   298

         Broadband Fixed Wireless Example   299

Point-to-Point or Point-to-Multipoint Wireless Connections   299
Benefits of Using Wireless Solutions   300
MPLS   300
Virtual Private Networks   303
VPN Applications   303
VPN Connectivity Options   304
Benefits of VPNs   308
Internet as a WAN Backup Technology   308
IP Routing without Constraints   308
Layer 3 Tunneling with GRE and IPSec   308
Summary   311
References   312
Case Study   312
Case Study: WAN Upgrade and Backup   313
Review Questions   314

Chapter 6   Designing IP Addressing in the Network   319
Designing IP Addressing   319
IPv4 Addresses   319
IPv4 Address Structures   320
IPv4 Address Format   321
Subnet Mask   322
Number of Host Addresses   322
IPv4 Address Classes   323
Subnets   325
Determining the Size of the Network   325
Determining the Network Topology   326
Size of Individual Locations   327
Network Size for IP Addressing   328
Private Versus Public Addresses   329
Private IPv4 Addresses   330
Public IPv4 Addresses   330
When to Use Private or Public IPv4 Addresses   330
Private Versus Public Address Selection Criteria   331
Requirements for Private and Public IPv4 Address Types   332
How Private Address and Public Address Network Parts Interconnect   332
Guidelines for the Use of Private and Public Addresses in an Enterprise Network   333
Implementing IP Addressing Hierarchy   334
Route Summarization   334
IP Addressing Hierarchy Criteria   336
Determining the Summarization Groups   336
Impact of Poorly Designed IP Addressing   338
Impact of Route Aggregation   339
When to Use Fixed or Variable Subnet Masking   339
IP Addressing Plan and Routing Protocol Considerations   341

Methods of Assigning IP Addresses   343
Static Versus Dynamic IP Address Assignment Methods   344
When to Use Static and Dynamic Address Assignment   345
Guidelines for Assigning IP Addresses in the Enterprise Network   345
Using DHCP to Assign IP Addresses   346
Name Resolution   347
Static Versus Dynamic Name Resolution   348
When to Use Static or Dynamic Name Resolution   348
Using DNS for Name Resolution   349
Introduction to IPv6   350
IPv6 Address Structure   351
IPv6 Features   351
IPv6 Address Format   351
IPv6 Datagram Structure   352
IPv6 Address Types and Scopes   354
IPv6 Address Scope Types   354
IPv6 Unicast Addresses   354
IPv6 Address Assignment Strategies   358
Static IPv6 Address Assignment   358
Dynamic IPv6 Address Assignment   358
Dynamic IPv6 Renumbering   359
IPv6 Name Resolution   360
Static and Dynamic IPv6 Name Resolution   360
IPv4- and IPv6-Aware Applications and Name Resolution   360
IPv4 to IPv6 Transition Strategies and Deployments   361
Differences Between IPv4 and IPv6   361
IPv4 to IPv6 Transition   362
Dual-Stack Transition Mechanism   362
Tunneling Transition Mechanism   363
Translation Transition Mechanism   365
IPv6 Routing Protocols   366
RIP New Generation   366
Open Shortest Path First Version 3   367
Integrated IS-IS Version 6   367
BGP4+   367
Summary   368
References   369
Case Study   369
Case Study: Network Addressing Plan   370
Review Questions   370

Chapter 7   Selecting Routing Protocols for a Network   373

Routing Protocol Selection Criteria   373
   Static Versus Dynamic Routing   374
      Static Routing   374
      Dynamic Routing   375
   Distance Vector Versus Link-State Versus Hybrid Protocols   376
      Distance Vector Example   378
      Link-State Example   379
      Choosing Between Distance Vector and Link-State Protocols   380
   Interior Versus Exterior Routing Protocols   380
      IGP and EGP Example   381
   Routing Protocol Metrics   382
      What Is a Routing Metric?   382
      Metrics Used by Routing Protocols   383
   Routing Protocol Convergence   385
      RIPv2 Convergence Example   386
      Comparison of Routing Protocol Convergence   387
   Flat Versus Hierarchical Routing Protocols   388
      Flat Routing Protocols   388
      Hierarchical Routing Protocols   389
      Deciding Which Routing Protocol Is Best for Which Network   389
      Comparison of Routing Protocols   389
      When to Choose RIPv1 or RIPv2   390
      When to Choose IGRP   391
      When to Choose EIGRP   391
      When to Choose OSPF   391
      When to Choose Integrated IS-IS   392
Routing Protocol Features   392
   On-Demand Routing (ODR)   392
      Example: ODR Usage in Hub and Spoke Topology   393
   RIPv2 to RIPv1 Comparison   394
   EIGRP   395
      EIGRP Characteristics   397
   OSPF   398
      OSPF Hierarchical Design   398
      OSPF Characteristics   399
   Integrated IS-IS   400
      An Integrated IS-IS Network   401
      Integrated IS-IS Characteristics   402
   Choosing the Appropriate Interior Routing Protocol   403
   Border Gateway Protocol   404
      BGP Implementation Example   405
      External and Internal BGP   406

Routing Protocol Deployment   407
  Hierarchical Network Structure and Routing Protocols   407
    Routing in the Core Layer (Backbone)   408
    Routing in the Distribution Layer   409
    Routing in the Access Layer   409
    Remote Access and Internet Connectivity   410
  Route Redistribution   411
    Route Redistribution Possibilities   412
    Route Redistribution Planning   413
    Core and Access Layer Route Redistribution   413
    Remote-access and Internet Route Redistribution   414
  Route Filtering   414
    IGP Filtering   415
  Integrating Interior Routing Protocols with BGP   416
    IBGP   417
  Route Summarization   419
    The Value of Route Summarization   419
    Route Summarization Example   419
    Summarization in the Enterprise Composite Network Model   420
Summary   421
References   422
Case Study   423
Case Study: Routing Protocol Selection   423
  Simulation: Network Convergence   424
    Network Convergence Scenario   424
    Initial Traffic   424
    Layer 2 (Bridged) Network Convergence   424
    Convergence in Mixed Layer 2/Layer 3 Network   428
    Network Convergence in a Layer 3 Network   432
Review Questions   436

Chapter 8   Designing Networks for Voice Transport   441
Traditional Voice Architectures and Features   441
  Analog and Digital Signaling   442
  Private Branch Exchanges (PBXs) and the PSTN   444
    Differences Between a PBX and a Public Telephone Switch   444
    PBX Features   446
    PSTN Switch Features   447
  Local Loops, Trunks, and Interswitch Communications   448
  Basic Telephony Signaling   449
    Telephony Signaling   450
    Analog Telephony Signaling   451
    Analog and Digital Trunk Signaling   452
    ISDN Digital Signaling   452
    QSIG Digital Signaling   453
    SS7 Digital Signaling   453

PSTN Numbering Plans   454
  Numbering Plans   454
  Voice Routing   454
  North American Numbering Plan   455
PSTN Services   456
  Centrex   457
  Virtual Private Voice Networks   458
  Voice Mail   459
  Call Center   459
  Interactive Voice Response   460
Integrating Voice Architectures   460
  Voice over IP Introduction   461
    Drivers for Integrating Voice and Data Networks   461
    Time-division Multiplexing in PSTN   461
    Open Standards Are Drivers for Converged Networks   463
  H.323   466
    An Introduction to H.323   466
    Key Benefits of the H.323 Protocol   466
    H.323 Components   467
  IP Telephony Introduction   470
    IP Telephony Design Goals   472
    Single Site IP Telephony Design   472
    Centralized IP Telephony Design   473
    Internet IP Telephony Design   474
  Voice Routing   475
    Voice Ports   475
    Dial Peers   476
    Relationship Between Dial Peers and Call Legs   477
  Voice Issues   477
    Packet Delays   477
    Jitter   482
    Packet Loss   483
    Echo   483
  Voice Coding and Compression   485
    Coding and Compression Algorithms   485
    Voice Coding Standards (Codecs)   486
    Codec Mean Opinion Score   486
    Codec Design Considerations   487
  VoIP Control and Transport Protocols   487
    Voice Conversation   488
    Call Control Functions   489
  Bandwidth Considerations   489
    Reducing the Amount of Voice Traffic   490
    Voice Bandwidth Requirements   490

QoS Mechanisms and Their Impact on Voice Quality   492
Designing Voice QoS   492
QoS Mechanisms   493
AutoQoS for Voice over IP   497
Voice over Frame Relay   498
VoFR Implementations   499
VoFR Design Guidelines   500
Voice over ATM   502
ATM Introduction   502
ATM Classes of Services   502
ATM Adaptation Types   503
VoATM Design Guidelines   504
Capacity Planning Using Voice Traffic Engineering Concepts   505
On-net and Off-net Calling   505
Considerations When Migrating to an Integrated Network   507
GoS   508
Grade of Service Introduction   508
Erlang Tables   509
Trunk Capacity Calculation Example   512
Off-net Calls Cost Calculation Example   512
DSP Resources for Voice Coding   514
WAN Capacity Planning   515
WAN Capacity Calculation   516
Combining GoS with WAN Capacity Calculation   517
Call Admission Control   518
Campus IP Telephony Capacity Planning   519
Planning Cisco CallManager Processing Requirements   520
Planning for Network Capacity and Performance   520
Planning Trunking Capacity   521
Summary   522
References   524
Case Study Simulation   525
Simulation: Voice Transport over IP Network   526
Voice Transport over IP Network Scenario   526
Testing the Data Load   527
VoIP Pilot   530
VoIP in Production   532
Voice and Data Network with QoS   534
Review Questions   537

Chapter 9   Evaluating Security Solutions for the Network   545
Identifying Attacks and Selecting Countermeasures   545
Security as a Network Service in Modular Network Design   545
Basic Security Assumptions   546
Basic Security Requirements   546
Integrity and Confidentiality Threats   546
Availability Threats   548

Network Devices as Targets   550
Network Device Security Guidelines   551
Networks as Targets   553
Reconnaissance Attacks Against Networks   553
DoS Attacks Against Networks   554
Hosts and Applications as Targets   557
Host and Application Protection Guidelines   558
Identifying Security Mechanisms for a Defined Security Policy   559
Security Policy   559
The Security Wheel   559
Documenting the Security Policy   560
Security Policy Example   561
Physical Security   561
Physical Threats   561
Physical Security Guidelines   562
Authentication   563
Access Control Mechanisms   563
Network Authentication   564
Network Authentication Guidelines   566
Authorization and Network Filtering   567
Network Authorization Guidelines   569
Transmission Confidentiality   570
Encryption   571
Transmission Confidentiality Guidelines   572
Maintaining Data Integrity   572
Transmission Integrity Guidelines   574
Secure Management and Reporting   575
Audit Trails and Intrusion Detection   575
Secure Management and Monitoring Guidelines   577
Selecting Security Solutions within Network Modules   577
Cisco SAFE Blueprint   578
Securing the Internet Connectivity Module   580
Risks at the Internet Connectivity Module   580
Guidelines for Securing Internet Connectivity Module   581
E-commerce Module Security   583
Risks in the E-commerce Module   583
Guidelines for Securing the E-commerce Module   583
Remote Access and VPN Module Security   585
Risks in the Remote Access and VPN Module   585
Guidelines for Securing the Remote Access and VPN Module   586
Wireless Security   587
WAN Module Security   591
Risks in the WAN Module   592
Guidelines for Securing the WAN Module   592

Securing the Network Management Module   593
Risks in the Network Management Module   593
Guidelines for Securing the Management Module   594
Securing the Server Farm Module   595
Guidelines for Securing the Server Farm Module   596
IP Telephony Security   597
Voice Network Vulnerabilities and Solutions   597
IP Telephony Risks and Mitigation Strategies   599
Auto Update Server   599
Summary   600
References   602
Review Questions   603

Chapter 10   Applying Basic Network Management Design Concepts   607
Network Management Protocols and Features   607
Network Management Architecture   608
Protocols and Standards   609
SNMP   609
SNMP Message Types   610
SNMP Version 2   611
SNMP Version 3   612
MIB   613
MIB-II   615
Cisco MIB   616
MIB Example   617
RMON   617
RMON1   618
RMON1 Groups   619
RMON1 and RMON2   620
RMON2   621
CDP   623
CDP Information   623
How CDP Works   624
NetFlow   625
NetFlow Activation and Data Collection Strategy   627
NetFlow Versus RMON Information Gathering   629
Syslog Accounting   629
Syslog Distributed Architecture   631
Functional Areas of Network Management   632
Fault Management   632
Fault Management Architecture   633
Events   634
Event Processing   634

Configuration Management   635
Configuration Management Practices   636
Network Configuration Standards   638
Configuration Challenges   640
Configuration Tools   641
Accounting Management   642
Accounting Tools   643
IP Accounting   643
Accounting Using the AAA Framework   644
NetFlow Accounting   645
Performance Management   646
Performance Practices   648
Performance Data Reporting   650
Performance Collection Challenges   651
Performance Information Collection Solutions   652
Performance Solution Tools   653
Security Management   654
Security Management Examples   655
Managing Service Levels in a Network   657
The Importance of SLAs   657
SLA Requirements   659
Challenges of Managing SLAs   659
Requirements in SLAs   660
SLA Metrics   661
SLM as a Key Component for Assuring SLAs   662
End-to-End SLM Challenges   663
High-level and Detailed Reporting   663
SLM Example   664
SLM Planning   665
Service Assurance Agent   666
SAA Deployment   668
Network Response and Availability Applications   670
IPM   671
Service Management Solution   674
Summary   675
References   677
Review Questions   678

Chapter 11   Review and Case Study   681
Review of Key Topics   681
Applying Design Principles in Network Deployment   681
Structuring and Modularizing the Network   684
Basic Campus Switching Design Considerations   687
Designing WAN Networks   688

Designing IP Addressing in the Network   691

    IPv4   692

    IPv6   693

Selecting Routing Protocols for a Network   695

Designing Networks for Voice Transport   697

Evaluating Security Solutions for a Network   701

Applying Basic Network Management Design Concepts   703

Comprehensive Case Study: MCMB Corporation Network Redesign   706

    Scenario: MCMB Corporation Network Redesign   707

        Company Facts   707

        Current Situation   707

        Plans and Requirements   710

    Exercise: Propose Your Network Redesign   710

        Campus Redesign   710

        WAN Backup Design   711

        IP Addressing Redesign   712

        Routing Campus Redesign   712

        Extranet Design   713

Appendix A   IPv4 Addressing Job Aids   715

Appendix B   References   751

Appendix C   Open System Interconnection (OSI) Reference Model   759

Appendix D   Summary of ICND Router and Switch Commands   773

Appendix E   Common Requests For Comments   793

Appendix F   Network Address Translation   799

Appendix G   Answers to Review Questions, Case Studies, and Simulation Exercises   815

Glossary   903

Index   977

Foreword

CCDA Self-Study: Designing for Cisco Internetwork Solutions (DESGN) is a Cisco-authorized, self-paced learning tool that helps you understand foundation concepts that are covered on the CCDA exam. This book was developed in cooperation with the Cisco Internet Learning Solutions group, which is the Cisco team that is responsible for developing the CCDA exam. As an early-stage exam preparation product, this book presents detailed and comprehensive coverage of the tasks that network engineers must perform to design routed and switched network infrastructures that involve LAN, WAN, and dial access services. Whether you are studying to become CCDA certified or are simply seeking a better understanding of the products, services, and policies that enable you to gather customer requirements, identify solutions, and design network infrastructures, you will benefit from the information presented in this book.

Cisco Systems and Cisco Press present this material in text-based format to provide another learning vehicle for our customers and the broader user community, in general. Although a publication does not duplicate the instructor-led or e-learning environment, we acknowledge that not everyone responds to the same delivery mechanism in the same way. It is our intent that presenting this material via a Cisco Press publication enhances the transfer of knowledge to a broad audience of networking professionals.

Cisco Press presents other books in the Certification Self-Study Series on existing and future exams to help achieve Cisco Internet Learning Solutions Group's principal objectives: to educate the Cisco community of networking professionals, and to enable that community to build and maintain reliable, scalable networks. The Cisco Career Certifications and classes that support these certifications are directed at meeting these objectives through a disciplined approach to progressive learning.

To succeed with Cisco Career Certifications and in your daily job as a Cisco certified professional, we recommend a blended learning solution that combines instructor-led training with hands-on experience, e-learning, and self-study training. Cisco Systems has worldwide authorized Cisco Learning Partners who can provide you with the most highly qualified instruction and invaluable hands-on experience in lab and simulation environments. To learn more about Cisco Learning Partner programs that are available in your area, please go to www.cisco.com/go/authorizedtraining.

The books that Cisco Press creates in partnership with Cisco Systems meet the same standards for content quality that is demanded of our courses and certifications. It is our intent that you will find this and subsequent Cisco Press certification self-study publications of value as you build your networking knowledge base.

Thomas M. Kelly

Vice President, Internet Learning Solutions Group

Cisco Systems, Inc.

August 2003

Introduction

Modern networks are both extremely complex and critical to business success. As organizational processes continue to increase the requirements for bandwidth, reliability, and functionality from their networks, network designers are challenged to rapidly develop and evolve networks that use new protocols and technologies. Network designers are also challenged to stay current with the internetworking industry's constant and rapid changes. Designing robust, reliable, scalable networks is a necessary skill for network operators and designers in the modern organizational environment.

CCDA Self-Study: Designing for Cisco Internetwork Solutions (DESGN) teaches you how to design enterprise networks. You will learn about the criticality of the enterprise network using the Enterprise Composite Network Model. Network complexity and methods to simplify your design are important aspects of this book. Specific topics include local-area network (LAN) and wide-area network (WAN) designs, Internet Protocol (IP) addressing, routing protocol selection, designing voice networks, including security in your designs and network management design.

DESGN is the first step in the design certification track, and this book provides in-depth information to help you prepare for the DESGN exam and start you down the path to attaining your CCDA certification. CCDA is the first step that is necessary for accomplishing the CCDP certification.

Objectives of This Book

When you complete the readings and case studies in this book, you will be able to describe the principles of network design and present the guidelines for building a network design solution. You will also be able to describe how the Enterprise Composite Network Model simplifies the complexity of today's networks. You will be able to design the Enterprise Campus in a hierarchical modular fashion, design the Enterprise WAN network, design a network addressing plan, and select optimal routing protocols for the network. You will also be able to evaluate network security solutions and assess the design implications of voice transport across the network.

The book is divided into 11 chapters, 7 appendixes, and a glossary:

- Chapter 1, "Internetworking Technology Review," reviews key internetworking technology information.

- Chapter 2, "Applying Design Principles in Network Deployment," introduces the principles of network design and presents guidelines for building an effective network design solution.

- Chapter 3, "Structuring and Modularizing the Network," introduces the Enterprise Composite Network Model, which is a modular hierarchical approach to network design.

- Chapter 4, "Basic Campus Switching Design Considerations," introduces general campus switching design considerations and describes modularity in switching designs.

- Chapter 5, "Designing WANs," discusses the wide-area network technologies in the Enterprise Edge functional area of the Enterprise Composite Network Model.

- Chapter 6, "Designing IP Addressing in the Network," discusses IP addressing design and provides guidelines for building an efficient IP addressing solution.

- Chapter 7, "Selecting Routing Protocols for a Network," describes considerations for selecting the most appropriate routing protocol for a network.

- Chapter 8, "Designing Networks for Voice Transport," introduces voice design principles and provides guidelines for a successful integrated network deployment.

- Chapter 9, "Evaluating Security Solutions for the Network," introduces Cisco's Security Architecture for Enterprise (SAFE) Blueprint that employs a modular approach to designing network security.

- Chapter 10, "Applying Basic Network Management Design Concepts," introduces network management protocols, the functional areas of network management, and design guidelines for each functional area.

- Chapter 11, "Review and Case Study," reviews key topics in this book and presents a comprehensive case study.

- Appendix A, "IPv4 Addressing Job Aids," contains job aids to provide some background information on IPv4 addressing.

- Appendix B, "References," lists the websites and other external readings referred to in the text by chapter.

- Appendix C, "Open System Interconnection (OSI) Reference Model," is a brief overview of the Open System Interconnection seven-layer model.

- Appendix D, "Summary of ICND Router and Switch Commands," contains a listing of some Cisco router IOS and Catalyst switch commands that you might find in the Cisco Press book *CCNA Self-Study: Interconnecting Cisco Network Devices*, organized in various categories.

- Appendix E, "Common Requests for Comments," lists some common Requests for Comments (RFCs).

- Appendix F, "Network Address Translation," contains information about Cisco's network address translation feature.

- Appendix G, "Answers to Review Questions, Case Studies, and Simulation Exercises," contains the answers to the review questions, case studies, and simulation exercises that appear at the end of the chapters.

- The glossary provides definitions for networking terms and acronyms that are used throughout the book.

Review Questions, Case Studies, and Simulation Exercises

Some chapters conclude with a case study on DJMP Industries, a fictitious manufacturer of portable speed bumps, to help you evaluate your understanding of the concepts presented. In each task of the case study, you act as a network design consultant and make creative proposals to accomplish the customer's business needs. The final goal of each case study is a paper solution; you do not have to provide specific product names.

The case study also presents some simulations of various scenarios that are related to DJMP. The included exercises are a paper-only version of the simulation that was actually performed by a simulation tool and include the simulation tool's results. You can review the scenario and the simulation results and answer the questions.

At the end of each chapter, you will have an opportunity to test your knowledge by answering review questions on the subjects covered in the chapter.

To find out how you did and what material you might need to study further, you can compare your answers to those provided in Appendix G, "Answers to Review Questions, Case Studies, and Simulation Exercises." Note that for each of the case study tasks, Appendix G provides a solution based on the assumptions made. There is no claim that the provided solution is the best or only solution. Your solution might be more appropriate for the assumptions you made. The provided solution allows you to understand the author's reasoning and offers you a means of comparing and contrasting your solution.

Who Should Read This Book

This book is intended for pre-sales and post-sales network engineers who are involved in network design, planning, and implementation, and for those who plan to take the DESGN exam toward the CCDA certification. This book provides in-depth study material for that exam.

To fully benefit from this book, you should have the prerequisite skills obtained from the following:

- Holding a Cisco Certified Network Associate (CCNA) certification, which can best be achieved by completing the Introduction to Cisco Networking Technologies (INTRO) course or the book *CCNA INTRO Exam Certification Guide* (Wendell Odom, Cisco Press, 2003), and completing the Interconnecting Cisco Network Devices (ICND) course or the book *CCNA ICND Exam Certification Guide* (Wendell Odom, Cisco Press, 2003). (Refer to Appendix D for a listing of some of the Cisco router IOS and Catalyst switch commands that you might find in ICND, organized in various categories.) (Note that other Cisco Press books that are related to ICND and INTRO are also available.)

- Having practical experience deploying and operating networks based on Cisco network devices and the Cisco IOS.

Having CCNP or an equivalent level of knowledge and experience is an advantage.

Cisco Systems Networking Icon Legend

Cisco Systems, Inc., uses a standardized set of icons to represent devices in network topology illustrations. The icon legend that follows shows the most commonly used icons that you might encounter throughout this book.

 Access Point
 CallManager
 Router
 Bridge
 Hub
 DSU/CSU
 Cisco IP Phone 7960

 H.323 Device
 PBX
 Catalyst Switch
 Multilayer Switch
 ATM Switch
 ISDN/Frame Relay Switch
 Content Switch

 Voice-Enabled Router
 Router with Firewall
 Communication Server
 Gateway
 Access Server
 Phone
 Netflow Router

 VPN Concentrator
 PIX Firewall
 Network Management Appliance

 PC with Software
 Terminal
 File Server
 Web Server
 Cisco Works Workstation
 Modem
 Sun Workstation

 PC
 Printer
 Laptop
 IBM Mainframe
 Front End Processor
 Cluster Controller
 Macintosh

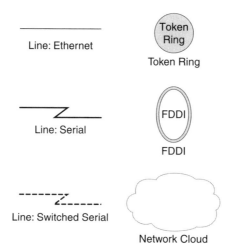

Line: Ethernet

Token Ring

Line: Serial

FDDI

Line: Switched Serial

Network Cloud

Command Syntax Conventions

The conventions that are used to present command syntax in this book are the same as those used in the Cisco IOS Software Command Reference. The Command Reference describes these conventions as follows:

- Vertical bars (l) separate alternative, mutually exclusive elements.

- Square brackets ([ ]) indicate optional elements.

- Braces ({ }) indicate a required choice.

- Braces within brackets ([{ }]) indicate a required choice within an optional element.

- **Boldface** indicates commands and keywords that are entered exactly as shown.

- *Italics* indicate arguments for which you supply values.

NOTE   The commands and configuration examples presented in this book are based on Cisco IOS Release 12.0.

This chapter reviews key internetworking technology information and covers the following topics:

- The OSI model
- LANs
- WANs
- Internetwork addressing
- Network devices
- Routing

CHAPTER 1

Internetworking Technology Review

An *internetwork* is a collection of individual networks that are connected by intermediate networking devices and that function as a single large network. *Internetworking* refers to the industry, products, and procedures that meet the challenge of creating and administering internetworks.

The first networks were time-sharing networks that used mainframes and attached terminals. Both IBM's System Network Architecture (SNA) and Digital's network architecture implemented such environments.

Local-area networks (LANs) evolved around the PC revolution. LANs enabled multiple users in a relatively small geographical area to exchange files and messages and access shared resources, such as file servers.

Wide-area networks (WANs) interconnect LANs across normal telephone lines (and other media), thereby interconnecting geographically dispersed users.

Today, high-speed LANs and switched internetworks are widely used to support high-bandwidth applications, such as voice and videoconferencing.

Computers must agree on a set of traffic rules for successful communication. This set of rules is known as a *protocol*. Two computers use the same protocol if they wish to communicate. Two computers trying to use different protocols would be like speaking French to someone who only understands German—it would not work.

Many different networking protocols are currently in use. In the past, each networking vendor would invent its own protocol; today, standard protocols exist so that devices can communicate with each other. For example, the Internet Protocol (IP) is the most widely used routed protocol, but Novell's Internetwork Packet Exchange (IPX) and Apple Computer's AppleTalk can also be used in some cases.

The OSI Model

Because sending data, such as an e-mail, involves doing so many things, a standards committee— the International Organization for Standardization (ISO)—compiled a list of functions that can occur on the network and divided them into seven categories. These categories are collectively known as the *Open System Interconnection (OSI) seven-layer model*. It represents everything that must happen in order to send data. It does not say how these things are to be done, just what needs to be done. Figure 1-1 illustrates the OSI model's seven layers.

Figure 1-1   *Each Layer of the Seven-layer OSI Model Represents a Function That Is Necessary When Devices Communicate*

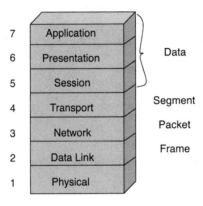

NOTE   For additional OSI model details, refer to Appendix C, "Open System Interconnection (OSI) Reference Model."

Different vendors implement the functions differently at these layers. For example, there are different implementations of the physical layer—copper wires and fiber optic cables are two common ones.

The OSI model's upper layers—Layers 5, 6, and 7—manage application issues. The application layer is the OSI layer that is closest to the end-user; both the OSI application layer and the user interact directly with the software application. The presentation layer provides a variety of coding and conversion functions that are applied to application layer data. The session layer establishes, manages, and terminates communication sessions between presentation layer entities.

As data passes through the functions at each of the layers, information is added to allow the data to proceed through the network. The data is encapsulated, or wrapped, in the appropriate information. This encapsulated information includes addressing and error checking.

At Layer 4 (the transport layer), the data (comprised of the information from the application, presentation, and session layers) is encapsulated in a segment.

At Layer 3 (the network layer), this segment is then encapsulated in a packet or datagram. At Layer 3, routed protocols are used to send data through the network. There are different types of packets for each of the routed protocols at Layer 3; examples include IP and IPX packets.

At Layer 2 (the data link layer), this packet is then encapsulated in a frame. The type of LAN or WAN to which you are connected determines the data link layer. There are different types of frames for each type of LAN or WAN. For example, the frames sent out on Ethernet are different from those sent out on Frame Relay because they are different protocols.

At Layer 1 (the physical layer), the frame is sent out on the wire in bits.

When data is received at the other end of the network, the additional information must be removed. The data is therefore decapsulated (sometimes referred to as *un-encapsulated*), or unwrapped, until the original sent data arrives at its destination.

LANs

A LAN typically has the following characteristics:

- Interconnects devices over a short distance (hence the term local-area)
- Is relatively fast
- Belongs to you
- Is there all the time

NOTE   These characteristics are relative to those mentioned for WANs in the following section.

Many different LAN technologies exist. Ethernet, which runs at 10 megabits per second (Mbps), is the most common. Newer versions, which are known as Fast Ethernet and Gigabit Ethernet, run at 100 Mbps and 1 gigabit per second (Gbps), respectively.

Other LAN technologies include Token Ring, and Fiber Distributed Data Interface (FDDI) and Wireless LANs (WLANs). Token Ring is an IBM invention that is primarily found on IBM sites and typically runs at 4 or 16 Mbps. FDDI is based on optical fiber and runs at 100 Mbps. WLANs are becoming more prevalent in modern networks; the current standard IEEE 802.11b discusses speeds of 1 to 11 Mbps, while the IEEE 802.11a standard enables speeds up to 54 Mbps.

LAN protocols function at the lowest two layers of the OSI reference model: the physical layer and data link layer.

LAN Physical Network Access

LAN protocols typically use one of two methods to access the physical network medium:

- In the *carrier sense multiple access collision detect (CSMA/CD) scheme*, network devices contend for the use of the physical network. CSMA/CD is sometimes called *contention access*. Examples of LANs that use the CSMA/CD media access scheme are Ethernet networks.

- In the *token passing media access scheme*, network devices access the physical medium based on possession of a token. Examples of LANs that use the token-passing media access scheme include Token Ring and FDDI.

LAN Data Transmission Types

LAN data transmissions fall into three classifications:

- In a *unicast transmission*, a single packet is sent from the source to a destination on a network. The source node uses the destination node's address to address the packet. The source node then sends the packet to the network, which finally passes the packet to its destination.

- A *multicast transmission* consists of a single data packet that is copied and sent to a specific subset of nodes on the network. The source node uses a multicast address to address the packet. The source node then sends the packet to the network, which makes copies of the packet and sends a copy to each node that is part of the multicast address.

- A *broadcast transmission* consists of a single data packet that is copied and sent to all nodes on the network. In these types of transmissions, the source node uses the broadcast address to address the packet. The source node then sends the packet to the network, which makes copies of the packet and sends a copy to every node on the network.

WANs

A WAN interconnects devices that have different geographical locations. A WAN typically has the following characteristics:

- Interconnects devices over a long distance (hence the term wide-area)
- Is slow (compared to a LAN)
- Belongs to someone else (the service provider)
- Is there only when you want to send something

WAN protocols function at the lowest two layers of the OSI reference model: the physical layer and data link layer. (X.25, which also functions at layer 3, is an exception.)

WAN Categories

WANs can be categorized as follows:

- **Point-to-point links**—Provide a single, pre-established WAN communication path from the customer premises, through a carrier network (such as the telephone company), to a remote network. A point-to-point link is also known as a *leased line* because its established path is permanent and fixed for each remote network that is reached through the carrier facilities.

- **Circuit switching**—A WAN switching method in which a dedicated physical circuit is established, maintained, and terminated through a carrier network for each communication session. Used extensively in telephone company networks, circuit switching operates much like a normal telephone call. Integrated Services Digital Network (ISDN) is an example of a circuit-switched WAN technology.

- **Packet switching**—A WAN switching method in which network devices share a single point-to-point link to transport packets from a source to a destination that is located across a carrier network. Statistical multiplexing is used to enable devices to share these circuits. Asynchronous Transfer Mode (ATM), Frame Relay, Switched Multimegabit Data Service (SMDS), and X.25 are examples of packet-switched WAN technologies.

WAN Virtual Circuits

Virtual circuits are logical circuits that are created to ensure reliable communication between two network devices. Two types of virtual circuits exist:

- **Switched virtual circuits (SVCs)**—Virtual circuits that are dynamically established on demand and terminated when transmission is complete. Communication over an SVC consists of three phases: circuit establishment, data transfer, and circuit termination.

- **Permanent virtual circuits (PVCs)**—Permanently-established virtual circuits that consist of one mode: data transfer.

WAN Dialup Services

Dialup services offer cost-effective methods for connectivity across WANs. Following are two popular dialup implementations:

- **Dial-on-demand routing (DDR)**—A technique whereby a router can dynamically initiate and close a circuit-switched session when transmitting end-stations demand. The router is configured to consider certain traffic *interesting* (such as traffic from a particular protocol), and other traffic *uninteresting*. When the router receives interesting traffic that is destined for a remote network, a circuit is established and the traffic is transmitted normally. If the router receives uninteresting traffic and a circuit is already established, that traffic also is transmitted normally. The router maintains an idle timer that is reset only when it receives interesting traffic. If the router does not receive any interesting traffic before the idle timer expires, the circuit is terminated. Likewise, if it receives uninteresting traffic and no circuit exists, the router drops the traffic.

- **Dial backup**—A service that activates a backup serial line under certain conditions. The secondary serial line can act as a backup link that is used when the primary link fails, or as a source of additional bandwidth when the load on the primary link reaches a certain threshold.

WAN Devices

The following devices are used in WAN environments:

- **WAN switch**—A multiport internetworking device that is used in carrier networks. These devices typically switch such traffic as Frame Relay, X.25, and SMDS, and operate at the data link layer.

- **Access server**—Acts as a concentration point for dial-in and dial-out connections.

- **Modem**—A device that interprets digital and analog signals, thereby enabling data to be transmitted over voice-grade telephone lines.

- **Channel service unit/digital service unit (CSU/DSU)**—A digital-interface device (or sometimes two separate digital devices) that adapts the physical interface on a data terminal equipment (DTE) device (such as a terminal) to the interface of a data circuit-terminating (DCE) device (such as a switch) in a switched-carrier network. The CSU/DSU also provides signal timing for communication between these devices.

- **ISDN terminal adapter (TA)**—A device that is used to connect ISDN Basic Rate Interface (BRI) connections to other interfaces, such as EIA/TAI-232. A terminal adapter is essentially an ISDN modem. (TA functionality is now incorporated into many ISDN routers.)

Defining the type of WAN, the specifications, and the desired options is called *provisioning the network*.

Internetwork Addressing

Internetwork addresses identify devices separately or as members of a group. Addressing schemes vary depending on the protocol family and the OSI layer.

Media Access Control (MAC) Addresses

MAC addresses identify network entities in LANs. MAC addresses are unique for each LAN interface on a device. MAC addresses are 48 bits in length and are expressed as 12 hexadecimal digits. The first 6 hexadecimal digits, which are administered by the Institute of Electrical and Electronics Engineers (IEEE), identify the manufacturer or vendor and are called the Organizational Unique Identifier (OUI). The last 6 hexadecimal digits indicate the interface serial number, or another value administered by the specific vendor. MAC addresses are sometimes called burned-in addresses (BIAs) because they are burned into read-only memory (ROM); the address is copied into random-access memory (RAM) when the interface card initializes.

Network Layer Addresses

A *network layer address* identifies an entity at the OSI network layer. Network addresses usually exist within a hierarchical address space and are sometimes called *virtual* or *logical addresses*.

Network layer addresses have two parts: the network on which the device is located, and the device (or host) number of the device on that network. Devices on the same logical network must have addresses with the same network part; however, they have unique device parts.

Network layer addresses are analogous to postal addresses: one part indicates the street, city, province/state, and so on, and the other part identifies the building number on that street. For example, a building at 27 Main Street is on the same "network" as a building at 35 Main Street. The "network" portion of their addresses, Main Street, is identical, but the "device" portions are unique.

Network Devices

Following are the main devices used in networking:

* Hubs
* Bridges and switches
* Routers

Hubs

As shown in Figure 1-2, a *hub* is used to connect devices so that they are located on one LAN. The cables that are usually used for Ethernet have RJ-45 connectors. Because only two devices can be connected with these cables, you need a hub if you want to interconnect more than two devices on one LAN.

Figure 1-2   *A Hub Connects Devices on One LAN*

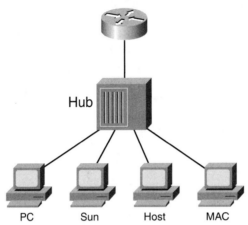

A hub is not a smart device. It sends all the data from a device on one port to all the other ports. When devices are connected via a hub, all devices hear everything the other devices send, whether it was meant for them or not. This is like being in a room with many people—if you speak, everyone hears you. If more than one person speaks at a time, there is only noise. Rules must be put in place if real conversations are to happen; in networking, these rules are the protocols.

Bridges and Switches

To improve performance, LANs are usually divided into smaller, multiple LANs, which are then interconnected by a LAN bridge, or a switch, as shown in Figure 1-3.

Figure 1-3   *LANs Are Split into Many Smaller LANs, Using Switches to Improve Performance*

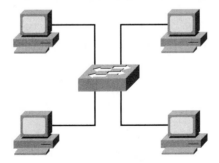

Switches and bridges have some intelligence. When devices are connected via a switch or a bridge, a device only hears the following:

- Everything that the other devices on its port send
- Any information from devices on other ports that was meant for everyone (a broadcast)
- Any information from devices on other ports that was meant for devices on its port

A device that is connected to a switch or bridge does not hear any information that was meant only for devices on other ports of the switch.

Upper-layer protocol transparency is a primary advantage of both bridging and switching. Because the devices operate at the data link layer, they are not required to examine upper-layer information. They can therefore rapidly forward traffic representing any network layer protocol. It is not uncommon for a bridge to move AppleTalk, DECnet, IP, Xerox Network Systems (XNS), and other traffic between two or more networks.

By dividing large networks into self-contained units, bridges and switches provide several advantages. Because only a certain percentage of traffic is forwarded, a bridge or switch diminishes the traffic experienced by devices on all connected segments. Bridges and switches extend the effective length of a LAN, permitting the attachment of distant stations that were not previously permitted.

Bridging Protocols

Switches and bridges can communicate with each other by using a bridging protocol. Cisco routers (acting as bridges) and switches support several types of bridging protocols, including the following:

- **Transparent bridging**—Found primarily in Ethernet environments.
- **Source-route bridging (SRB)**—Found primarily in Token Ring environments.
- **Translational bridging**—Translates from Ethernet bridging to Token Ring bridging.
- **Encapsulating bridging**—Allows packets to cross a bridged backbone network.
- **Source-route transparent (SRT) bridging**—Allows a bridge to function as both a source-route and transparent bridge.
- **Source-route translational (SR/TLB) bridging**—Allows a bridge to function as both a source-route and transparent bridge, and to bridge between the two.

NOTE   In source-route bridging terminology, Layer 2 frames are also known as *packets*.

Spanning Tree Protocol

The *Spanning Tree Protocol (STP)* is a Layer 2 link management protocol; Cisco switches use the IEEE 802.1d STP.

The purpose of STP is to maintain a loop-free network topology in networks that include redundancy. A loop-free topology is accomplished when the switch or bridge recognizes a loop in the topology and logically blocks one or more redundant ports automatically. This prevents problems such as broadcast storms, which occur when broadcasts continuously circle the network.

Switches send Bridge Protocol Data Unit (BPDU) frames to each other to build and maintain a spanning tree, so they can respond to a failure or addition of a link, switch, or bridge. When the network topology changes, the switches and bridges that run STP automatically reconfigure their ports to avoid connectivity loss or loop creation.

As illustrated in Figure 1-4, ports that use STP transition through four states: blocking, listening, learning, and forwarding. A port can take up to 50 seconds to transition to the forwarding state; the port can only send and receive data in the forwarding state.

Figure 1-4   *STP Requires Ports to Transition Through States*

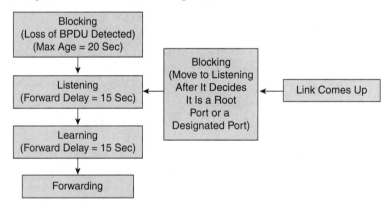

Bridges Versus Switches

Although bridges and switches share most relevant attributes, several distinctions differentiate these technologies. While switches are significantly faster because they switch in hardware, bridges switch in software. Switches can interconnect LANs of unlike bandwidth; for example, a switch can connect a 10-Mbps Ethernet LAN and a 100-Mbps Ethernet LAN. Switches also can support higher port densities than bridges. Some switches support cut-through switching, which reduces latency and delays in the network; bridges, on the other hand, only support store-and-forward traffic switching. Switches also support virtual LANs (VLANs).

Cisco switches are known as *Catalyst switches* (because Cisco bought a company called Catalyst). Examples of Catalyst switches include the following series: Catalyst 2950, Catalyst 3550, Catalyst 4500, and Catalyst 6500. Generally, the bigger the series number, the more LAN ports the switch has.

Virtual LANs

A *VLAN* is a logical, rather than physical, grouping of devices. The devices are grouped using switch management software so they can communicate as if they were attached to the same wire—when, in fact, they might be located on a number of different physical LAN segments.

You can design a VLAN to establish stations that are segmented logically by function, project team, or application without regard to the physical location of users. You can assign each switch port to only one VLAN. Ports in a VLAN share broadcasts; ports in different VLANs do not share broadcasts. This setup improves the network's overall performance.

A VLAN can exist on a single switch or span multiple switches, as illustrated in Figure 1-5. It can include stations in a single building or multiple-building infrastructures, or it can connect across WANs.

Figure 1-5   *VLANs Can Span Multiple Switches*

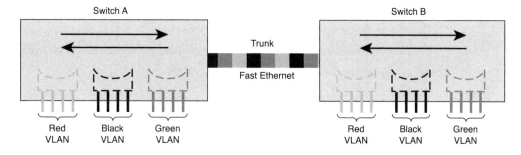

Each VLAN configured on the switch is like a separate physical bridge that implements address learning, forwarding/filtering decisions, and loop avoidance mechanisms. Trunks carry data for multiple VLANs.

Layer 3 functionality (routing) is required for passing data between VLANs.

Routers

As shown in Figure 1-6, a *router* connects devices on LANs to devices on other LANs, usually via WANs.

Figure 1-6 *A Router Connects Devices on LANs to Devices on Other LANs, Usually Via WANs*

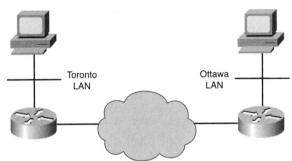

A router is much more intelligent than hubs and switches. Soon after companies started deploying PCs and connecting them via LANs, they wanted to take it one step further and interconnect LANs and PCs that are located at geographically separate locations. A router provides this facility. It connects to a local LAN and then over a longer distance to another router, which in turn connects to a remote LAN. Two PCs that are located hundreds of miles apart can now exchange data.

A router's job includes the following tasks:

- Segments LANs and WANs
- Determines the best way to send data to its destination
- Communicates with other routers to learn from them and tell them what it knows
- Sends the data the best way, over a LAN or a WAN

NOTE The route that the router determines is the best depends on the routing protocol in use. For example, some routing protocols define best as the least number of hops, while others define best as the highest bandwidth.

When devices are connected via a router, a device hears only the following:

- Everything that the other devices on its port send
- Any information from devices on other ports that was meant for devices on its port

A device that is connected to a router does not hear any of the information that is only meant for devices on other ports, or any information from devices on other ports that was meant for everyone.

Cisco has a large selection of routers, including the following series: Cisco 1700, 2600, 3700, 7600, and 12000. In general, the higher the series number, the more LAN and WAN ports the router has and the better performance it provides.

Routing

Routing is the act of moving information across an internetwork from a source to a destination. At least one intermediate node is typically encountered along the way. Routing occurs at Layer 3, the network layer.

Cisco Press's *Introduction to Cisco Routers* provides the following definitions of routed protocols and routing protocols:

- A *routed protocol* contains enough network layer addressing information for user traffic to be directed from one network to another network. Routed protocols define the format and use of the fields within a packet. Packets that use a routed protocol are conveyed from end-system to end-system through an internetwork.

- A *routing protocol* supports a routed protocol by providing mechanisms for sharing routing information. Routing protocol messages move between the routers. A routing protocol allows the routers to communicate with other routers to update and maintain routing tables. Routing protocol messages do not carry end-user traffic from network to network. A routing protocol uses a routed protocol to pass information between routers.

A *metric* is a standard of measurement, such as path length, that routing algorithms use to determine the optimal path to a destination. To aid the process of path determination, routing algorithms initialize and maintain routing tables, which contain route information. Route information varies depending on the routing algorithm used.

Routing algorithms can be classified by type. Key differentiators include the following:

- **Static versus dynamic**—Static routing algorithms are not really algorithms at all, rather, they are table mappings the network administrator establishes before the beginning of routing. These mappings do not change unless the network administrator alters them. Dynamic routing algorithms dynamically adjust routing tables as a network changes. Rather than the network administrator, the routers change the routing table mappings.

- **Single-path versus multipath**—Some routing protocols support multiple paths to the same destination.

- **Flat versus hierarchical**—In a flat routing system, the routers are peers of all other routers. In a hierarchical routing system, some routers form a routing backbone. Routing systems often designate logical groups of nodes, which are called domains, autonomous systems, or areas.

- **Host-intelligent versus router-intelligent**—Some routing algorithms assume that the source end-node determines the entire route. This is usually referred to as *source routing*. Other algorithms assume that hosts know nothing about routes. In these algorithms, routers determine the path through the internetwork based on their own calculations.

- **Intradomain versus interdomain**—Some routing algorithms work only within domains; others work within and between domains.

- **Link-state versus distance vector versus hybrid**—Link-state algorithms (also known as *shortest path first algorithms*) flood routing information to all nodes in the internetwork. However, each router sends only the portion of the routing table that describes the state of its own links. Distance vector algorithms (also known as *Bellman-Ford algorithms*) call for each router to send all or some portion of its routing table, but only to its neighbors. In essence, link-state algorithms send small updates everywhere, whereas distance vector algorithms send larger updates to only neighboring routers. Hybrid, or advanced, routing protocols have attributes that are associated with both distance vector and link-state protocols; hybrid protocols send small updates to only neighboring routers.

Many *suites of protocols* define various protocols that correspond to the functions defined in the OSI seven layers, including routed protocols, a selection of routing protocols, applications, and so forth. Protocol suites are also known as *protocol stacks*. The following sections provide a brief overview of some of these protocol suites.

TCP/IP Protocol Suite

TCP/IP is the most widely used protocol suite by far; it is the only one used in the Internet. TCP/IP is short for Transmission Control Protocol/Internet Protocol, named for two of the protocols in the suite. It was not invented by any single vendor, but evolved as the Internet grew.

TCP/IP Network Layer

The TCP/IP network layer (Layer 3) includes the following protocols:

- **IP**—Defines a set of rules for communicating across a network. IP contains addressing information and some control information that enables packets to be routed. IP has two primary responsibilities: providing connectionless, best-effort delivery of datagrams through an internetwork, and providing fragmentation and reassembly of datagrams to support data links with different maximum transmission unit (MTU) sizes. IP version 4 (IPv4) is currently used in the Internet; IP version 6 (IPv6) is an emerging protocol.

- **Address Resolution Protocol (ARP)**—Allows a host to dynamically discover the MAC address that corresponds to a particular IP network layer address. For two devices on a given network to communicate, they must know the other device's physical addresses.

- **Reverse Address Resolution Protocol (RARP)**—Used to map MAC addresses to IP addresses. Diskless workstations that do not know their IP addresses when they boot might use RARP, which is the logical inverse of ARP. RARP relies on the presence of an RARP server with table entries of MAC-to-IP address mappings.

- **Internet Control Message Protocol (ICMP)**—Used to report errors and other information regarding IP packet processing to the source.

TCP/IP Transport Layer

Two transport protocols are defined at the TCP/IP transport layer (Layer 4):

- **TCP**—Provides connection-oriented, end-to-end reliable transmission of data in an IP environment. TCP performs connection establishment using a *three-way handshake* mechanism. A three-way handshake synchronizes both ends of a connection by allowing both sides to agree upon initial sequence numbers. This mechanism also guarantees that both sides are ready to transmit data and know that the other side is also ready to transmit. This is necessary so that packets are not transmitted or retransmitted during session establishment or after session termination.

- **User Datagram Protocol (UDP)**—A connectionless protocol that acts as an interface between IP and upper-layer processes. Unlike TCP, UDP does not add reliability, flow-control, or error-recovery functions to IP. Because of UDP's simplicity, UDP headers contain fewer bytes and consume less network overhead than TCP.

TCP and UDP use protocol port numbers to distinguish multiple applications (described in the next section) running on a single device from one another. The *port number* is part of the TCP or UDP segment and is used to identify the application to which the data in the segment belongs. Well-known, or standardized, port numbers are assigned to applications so that different implementations of the TCP/IP protocol suite can interoperate. Examples of these well-known port numbers include the following:

- **File Transfer Protocol (FTP)**—TCP port 20 (data) and port 21 (control)
- **Telnet**—TCP port 23
- **Trivial File Transfer Protocol (TFTP)**—UDP port 69

TCP/IP Application Layer

In the TCP/IP protocol suite, the OSI model's upper three layers are combined into one layer, which is called the application layer. This suite includes many application layer protocols that represent a wide variety of applications, including the following:

- **FTP and TFTP**—To move files between devices.
- **Simple Network Management Protocol (SNMP)**—Used for network management, to report anomalies on the network, and to set network threshold values.
- **Telnet**—A terminal emulation protocol.
- **Simple Mail Transfer Protocol (SMTP)**—Provides e-mail services.
- **Domain Name System (DNS)**—Translates network node names into network addresses.

IPv4 Addressing

As mentioned, network layer addresses have two parts: the network on which the device resides and the device's device (or host) number on that network. Devices on the same logical network must have addresses with the same network part; however, they have unique device parts.

As shown in Figure 1-7, IPv4 addresses are 32 bits. The 32 bits are grouped into four sets of 8 bits (octets), separated by dots, and represented in decimal format; this is known as *dotted decimal notation*. Each octet bit has a binary weight (128, 64, 32, 16, 8, 4, 2, 1). The minimum value for an octet is 0, and the maximum decimal value for an octet is 255.

Figure 1-7   *IPv4 Addresses Are 32 Bits, Written in Dotted Decimal Format*

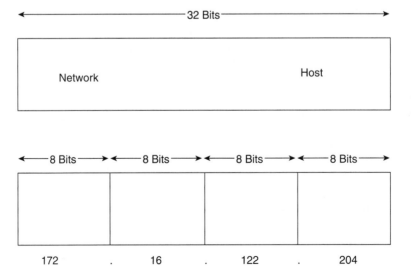

IPv4 Address Classes

IPv4 addressing defines five address classes: A, B, C, D, and E. Only Classes A, B, and C are available for addressing devices; Class D is used for multicast groups, and Class E is reserved for experimental use.

The first octet of an address defines its class, as Table 1-1 illustrates for Class A, B, and C addresses. This table also shows the format of the addresses in each class as defined by the network bits (N) and host bits (H).

Table 1-1   *IP Address Classes A, B, and C Are Available for Addressing Devices*

Class	Format (N = network number, H = host number)	Higher-order Bit(s)	Address Range
Class A	N.H.H.H	0	1.0.0.0 to 126.0.0.0
Class B	N.N.H.H	10	128.0.0.0 to 191.255.0.0
Class C	N.N.N.H	110	192.0.0.0 to 223.255.255.0

Reference: RFC 1700, available at www.cis.ohio-state.edu/cgi-bin/rfc/rfc1700.html

NOTE   Class D addresses have higher-order bits 1110 and are in the range of 224.0.0.0 to 239.255.255.255. Class E addresses have higher-order bits 1111 and are in the range of 240.0.0.0 to 255.255.255.255.

IPv4 Subnets

IPv4 networks can be divided into smaller networks, called *subnetworks* (or *subnets*). Subnetting provides several benefits for the network administrator, including extra flexibility, more efficient use of network addresses, and the capability to contain broadcast traffic (a broadcast does not cross a router).

Subnets are under local administration. As such, the outside world sees an organization as a single network and does not have detailed knowledge of the organization's internal structure.

A subnet address is created by borrowing bits from the host field and designating them as the subnet field. A *subnet mask* is a 32-bit number that is associated with an IP address; each bit in the subnet mask indicates how to interpret the corresponding bit in the IP address. In binary, a subnet mask bit of 1 indicates that the corresponding bit in the IP address is a network or subnet bit; a subnet mask bit of 0 indicates that the corresponding bit in the IP address is a host bit. The subnet mask then indicates how many bits have been borrowed from the host field for the subnet field.

An address's *default subnet mask* depends on its address class. Referring to Table 1-1, Class A addresses have one octet, or 8 bits, of network and three octets or 24 bits of host; therefore, the default subnet mask for a Class A address is 255.0.0.0. This indicates 8 bits of network (binary 1s in the mask) and 24 bits of host (binary 0s in the mask). Similarly, the default subnet mask is 255.255.0.0 for a Class B address and 255.255.255.0 for a Class C address.

Subnet mask bits come from the high-order (leftmost) bits of the host field.

When all of an address's host bits are 0, the address is for the wire (or subnet); when all of an address's host bits are 1, the address is the broadcast on that wire.

For example, a Class B network 172.16.0.0 with 8 bits of subnet would have 8 of the available 16 host bits borrowed for subnet bits, and the subnet mask would be 255.255.255.0. With these 8 subnet bits, there are $2^8 = 256$ subnets; each subnet has 8 host bits, so $2^8 - 2 = 254$ hosts are available on each subnet. (The two hosts are subtracted in these calculation because of the subnet address and the broadcast address.) The subnets would be 172.16.0.0, 172.16.1.0, 172.16.2.0, and so on. On the first subnet, the available host addresses would be 172.16.0.1, 172.16.0.2, 172.16.0.3, and so on.

NOTE   This book's formula for obtaining the number of subnets differs from that of some earlier courses and books. Previously, the same formula that was used to count hosts, $2^n - 2$, was used to count subnets. Now the formula 2^n is used for subnets (where n is the number of bits by which the default mask was extended) and $2^n - 2$ is used for hosts (where n is the number of host bits). The 2^n rule for subnets has been adopted because the all-1s subnet has always been a legal subnet according to the RFC, and subnet 0 can be enabled by a configuration command (the **ip subnet-zero** global configuration command) on Cisco routers (in fact, it's on by default in Cisco IOS release 12.0 and later). Note, however, that not all vendors' equipment supports the use of subnet 0.

Tables 1-2 and 1-3 indicate the number of subnetting bits, the associated subnet mask, and the resulting number of subnets and hosts that are available for Class B and C networks, respectively.

Table 1-2   *Class B Subnetting*

Number of Subnet Bits	Subnet Mask	Number of Subnets	Number of Hosts
2	255.255.192.0	4	16382
3	255.255.224.0	8	8190
4	255.255.240.0	16	4094
5	255.255.248.0	32	2046

Table 1-2   *Class B Subnetting (Continued)*

Number of Subnet Bits	Subnet Mask	Number of Subnets	Number of Hosts
6	255.255.252.0	64	1022
7	255.255.254.0	128	510
8	255.255.255.0	256	254
9	255.255.255.128	512	126
10	255.255.255.192	1024	62
11	255.255.255.224	2048	30
12	255.255.255.240	4096	14
13	255.255.255.248	8192	6
14	255.255.255.252	16384	2

Table 1-3   *Class C Subnetting*

Number of Subnet Bits	Subnet Mask	Number of Subnets	Number of Hosts
2	255.255.255.192	4	62
3	255.255.255.224	8	30
4	255.255.255.240	16	14
5	255.255.255.248	32	6
6	255.255.255.252	64	2

The same subnet mask is usually used for all subnets within the same *major network* (a Class A, B, or C network). Using *variable length subnet masking* (*VLSM*) means using a different mask in some parts of the network.

How Subnet Masks Are Used to Determine the Network Number

To determine the network (or, more specifically, the subnetwork) address to which a packet should be forwarded, the router first extracts the IP destination address from the incoming packet and retrieves the internal subnet mask. Next, it performs a logical AND operation to obtain the network number. This causes the removal of the host portion of the IP destination address, while the destination subnetwork number remains. The router then looks up the destination subnetwork number in its routing table and matches it with an outgoing interface. Finally, it forwards the frame toward the destination IP address (routers typically have a default path to which to forward data for unknown destination addresses).

Following are three basic rules that govern logically ANDing two binary numbers:

- 1 ANDed with 1 yields 1
- 1 ANDed with 0 yields 0
- 0 ANDed with 0 yields 0

The truth table (a table used to define results of logical operations) in Table 1-4 illustrates the rules for logical AND operations.

Table 1-4   *Rules for Logical AND Operations*

Input	Input	Output
1	1	1
1	0	0
0	1	0
0	0	0

Here are two simple guidelines for remembering logical AND operations:

- Logically "ANDing" a 1 with any number yields that number
- Logically "ANDing" a 0 with any number yields 0

Table 1-5 illustrates an example of the logical ANDing of a destination IP address and the subnet mask. The subnetwork number, which the router uses to forward the packet, remains.

Table 1-5   *Sample Calculation of Subnet Number*

		Network	Subnet	Host	Host
Destination IP address	172.16.1.2	10101100	00010000	00000001	00000010
Subnet mask	255.255.255.0	11111111	11111111	11111111	00000000
Subnet number	172.16.1.0	10101100	00010000	00000001	00000000

TCP/IP Routing Protocols

The TCP/IP suite defines the following selection of routing protocols:

- **Routing Information Protocol (RIP)**—A distance-vector protocol that uses hop count as its metric. RIP is widely used for routing traffic and is an interior gateway protocol (IGP), which means it performs routing within a single autonomous system (AS). (An *AS* is a collection of networks under a common administration that share a common routing strategy.) The latest enhancement to RIP is the RIP version 2 (RIPv2) specification, which allows more information to be included in RIP packets and provides a simple authentication mechanism.

- **Interior Gateway Routing Protocol (IGRP)**—Cisco developed this routing protocol in the mid-1980s to provide a robust protocol for routing within an AS. IGRP is a distance vector interior gateway protocol. It uses a combination (vector) of metrics; delay, bandwidth, reliability, and load are all factored into the routing decision.

- **Enhanced Internet Gateway Routing Protocol (EIGRP)**—Represents an evolution from its predecessor, IGRP. EIGRP is a hybrid routing protocol that integrates the capabilities of link-state protocols with distance vector protocols. EIGRP incorporates the Diffusing Update Algorithm (DUAL). Key capabilities that distinguish EIGRP from other routing protocols include fast convergence, support for VLSM, support for partial updates, and support for multiple network layer protocols (in addition to IP, EIGRP supports IPX and AppleTalk).

- **Open Shortest Path First (OSPF)**—A link-state routing protocol that calls for the sending of link-state advertisements (LSAs) to all other routers within the same hierarchical area. OSPF LSAs include information about attached interfaces, metrics used, and other variables. As OSPF routers accumulate link-state information, they use the shortest path first (SPF) algorithm to calculate the shortest path to each node. Unlike RIP, OSPF can operate within a hierarchy. The largest entity within the hierarchy is an AS. Although it is capable of receiving routes from and sending routes to other autonomous systems, OSPF is an interior gateway routing protocol. An AS can be divided into a number of areas, which are groups of contiguous networks and attached hosts.

- **Border Gateway Protocol (BGP)**—An exterior gateway protocol (EGP), which means that it performs routing between multiple autonomous systems or domains and exchanges routing and reachability information with other BGP systems. BGP was developed to replace its predecessor, the now-obsolete Exterior Gateway Protocol (EGP) (note the dual use of the EGP acronym), as the standard exterior gateway routing protocol used in the global Internet. BGP solves serious problems with EGP and scales to Internet growth more efficiently.

Resource Reservation Protocol

The *Resource Reservation Protocol* (*RSVP*) is a network control protocol that enables Internet applications to obtain special quality of service (QoS) for their data flows. RSVP is not a routing protocol; instead, it works in conjunction with routing protocols and installs the equivalent of dynamic access lists along the routes that routing protocols calculate. RSVP occupies the place of a transport protocol in the OSI seven-layer model.

In RSVP, a *data flow* is a sequence of messages that have the same source, destination (one or more), and QoS. QoS requirements are communicated through a network via a flow specification, which is a data structure that internetwork hosts use to request special services from the internetwork. A flow specification often guarantees how the internetwork will handle some of its host traffic.

RSVP supports three traffic types: *best effort*, *rate-sensitive*, and *delay-sensitive*. The type of data flow service that is used to support these traffic types depends on the QoS features implemented. These traffic types are described as follows:

- **Best-effort traffic**—Is traditional IP traffic, including file transfer and mail transmissions. The service supporting best-effort traffic is called best-effort service.

- **Rate-sensitive traffic**—Is willing to give up timeliness for guaranteed rate. For example, rate-sensitive traffic might request 100 kbps of bandwidth. If it actually sends 200 kbps for an extended period, a router can delay traffic. An example is H.323 videoconferencing, which requires a constant transport rate. *Guaranteed bit-rate service* is the RSVP service that supports rate-sensitive traffic.

- **Delay-sensitive traffic**—Requires timeliness of delivery and varies its rate accordingly. For example, MPEG-II video averages about 3 to 7 Mbps, depending on the amount of change in the picture. MPEG-II video sources send key and delta frames. Typically, one or two key frames per second describe the whole picture, and 13 or 28 delta frames describe the change from the key frame. Delta frames are usually substantially smaller than key frames. As a result, rates vary quite a bit from frame to frame; a single frame requires delivery within a frame time, however. A specific priority must be negotiated for delta frame traffic. RSVP services that support delay-sensitive traffic are referred to as *controlled-delay service* (non-real-time service) and *predictive service* (real-time service).

RSVP data flows are generally characterized by sessions, over which data packets flow. A session is a set of data flows with the same unicast or multicast destination, and RSVP treats each session independently.

In the context of RSVP, QoS is an attribute specified in flow specifications that is used to determine how participating entities (routers, receivers, and senders) handle data interchanges. Both hosts and routers use RSVP to specify the QoS. Hosts use RSVP to request a QoS level from the network on behalf of an application data stream. Routers use RSVP to deliver QoS requests to other routers along the data stream path(s). In doing so, RSVP maintains the router and host state to provide the requested service.

NetWare Protocol Suite

NetWare is a network operating system (NOS) that provides transparent remote file access and numerous other distributed network services, including printer sharing and support for various applications (such as electronic mail transfer and database access). NetWare specifies the upper five layers of the OSI reference model and, as such, runs on virtually any media-access protocol (Layer 2). In addition, it runs on virtually any kind of computer system, from PCs to mainframes. Introduced in the early 1980s, NetWare was developed by Novell, Inc. It was derived from XNS, which was created by Xerox Corporation in the late 1970s, and is based on a client/server architecture. Clients (sometimes called *workstations*) request services, such as file and printer access, from servers.

IPX is the original NetWare network layer (Layer 3) protocol that is used to route packets through an internetwork. IPX is a connectionless datagram-based network protocol and, as such, is similar to the Internet Protocol found in TCP/IP networks.

As with other network addresses, Novell IPX network addresses must be unique. These addresses are represented in hexadecimal format and consist of two parts: a network number and a node number. The network administrator assigns the IPX network number, which is 32 bits long. The node number, which is usually the MAC address of one of the system's network interface cards (NICs), is 48 bits long.

The Sequenced Packet Exchange (SPX) protocol is the most common NetWare transport protocol at Layer 4 of the OSI model. SPX resides on top of IPX in the NetWare Protocol Suite. SPX is a reliable, connection-oriented protocol that supplements the datagram service provided by the IPX protocol.

AppleTalk Protocol Suite

AppleTalk, which is a protocol suite Apple Computer developed in the early 1980s, was developed in conjunction with the Macintosh computer. AppleTalk's purpose was to allow multiple users to share resources, such as files and printers. The devices that supply these resources are called *servers*, and the devices that use these resources (such as a user's Macintosh computer) are called *clients*.

AppleTalk was designed with a transparent network interface. That is, the interaction between client computers and network servers requires little user interaction. In addition, the actual operations of the AppleTalk protocols are invisible to end users, who see only the result of these operations. Two versions of AppleTalk exist: AppleTalk Phase 1 and AppleTalk Phase 2.

AppleTalk uses addresses to identify and locate devices on a network in a manner similar to the process utilized by protocols such as TCP/IP and IPX. These addresses, which are assigned dynamically, are composed of the following three elements:

- **Network number**—A 16-bit value that identifies a specific AppleTalk network.

- **Node number**—An 8-bit value that identifies a particular AppleTalk node that is attached to the specified network.

- **Socket number**—An 8-bit number that identifies a specific socket that runs on a network node.

AppleTalk addresses are usually written as decimal values separated by a period. For example, 10.1.50 means network 10, node 1, socket 50. This might also be represented as 10.1, socket 50.

IBM SNA Protocols

Today, IBM networking consists of two separate architectures that branch from a common origin. Before contemporary networks existed, IBM's SNA ruled the networking landscape; it is therefore often referred to as traditional or legacy SNA.

With the rise of personal computers, workstations, and client/server computing, IBM addressed the need for a peer-based networking strategy with the creation of Advanced Peer-to-Peer Networking (APPN) and Advanced Program-to-Program Computing (APPC).

More recently, Data-Link Switching (DLSw) has emerged to transport SNA data over IP networks.

Traditional SNA Environments

SNA was developed in the 1970s with an overall structure that parallels the OSI reference model. With SNA, a mainframe running Advanced Communication Facility/Virtual Telecommunication Access Method (ACF/VTAM) serves as the hub of an SNA network. ACF/VTAM is responsible for establishing all sessions and for activating and deactivating resources. Resources in this environment are explicitly predefined, thereby eliminating the requirement for broadcast traffic and minimizing header overhead.

IBM Peer-based Networking

Changes in networking and communications requirements caused IBM to evolve (and generally overhaul) many of SNA's basic design characteristics. The emergence of peer-based networking entities (such as routers) resulted in a number of significant changes in SNA. Internetworking among SNA peers hinges on several IBM-developed networking components.

APPN represents IBM's second-generation SNA. By creating APPN, IBM moved SNA from a hierarchical, mainframe-centric environment to a peer-based networking environment. At the heart of APPN is an IBM architecture that supports peer-based communications, directory services, and routing between two or more APPC systems that are not directly attached.

Data-link Switching (DLSw)

As IP networks became more prevalent, the need to transport SNA data over these networks became apparent.

DLSw provides a means of transporting SNA and network basic input/output system (NetBIOS) traffic over an IP network. DLSw is an alternative to SRB, which is a protocol for transporting SNA and NetBIOS traffic in Token Ring environments that was widely deployed before the introduction of DLSw. DLSw addresses some of SRB's shortcomings, particularly in WAN environments.

Data-Link Switching Plus (DLSw+) is Cisco's implementation of the Data Link Switching standard. The end-systems can attach to the network over Token Ring, Ethernet, Synchronous Data Link Control (SDLC), Qualified Logical Link Control (QLLC), or FDDI. DLSw+ switches between diverse media and locally terminates the data links, keeping acknowledgments, keepalives, and polling off the WAN.

This chapter introduces the principles of network design and presents the guidelines for building an effective network design solution. It includes the following sections:

- Identifying Organizational Network Policies and Procedures
- Network Design Methodology
- Identifying Customer Requirements
- Characterizing the Existing Network
- Designing a Topology and Network Solution Using Structured Design Principles
- Planning a Design Implementation
- Building a Prototype or Pilot Network
- Documenting the Design
- Implementing and Verifying the Design
- Monitoring and Redesigning the Network
- Summary
- Case Study and Simulation Exercise
- Review Questions

CHAPTER 2

Applying Design Principles in Network Deployment

This chapter begins with an overview of the organizational network policies and procedures a network designer should know before participating in the design process, and then it describes each phase of the network design process. It also explains how to gather customer requirements and identify business and technical constraints. Because many customers build on an existing network, this chapter also presents methods of characterizing the existing network. It presents structured design principles and concludes with a discussion of planning a design implementation, prototyping, implementing, and verifying the design solution.

After reading this chapter, you should be able to identify organizational network policies and procedures, and the phases of the network design process. You should also be able to document the customer's network requirements, characterize an existing network, and identify how to implement a network design.

Identifying Organizational Network Policies and Procedures

Understanding an organization's procedures is a prerequisite for determining its network requirements. The following sections present a Network Organizational Model and discuss how to identify organizational network policies and procedures that might affect an organization's networking decisions.

Network Organizational Model

The *Network Organizational Model* opens the corporate information infrastructure to key stakeholders (including prospects, customers, partners, suppliers, and employees) by leveraging both networking and competitive advantages.

NOTE   The words *stakeholders* and *constituencies* are used interchangeably in this book. They represent all of the entities that have some stake in the organization, including prospects, customers, partners, suppliers, owners, and employees.

Before introducing the Network Organizational Model, we review how organizations have traditionally been viewed.

Traditional Organizational Model

The pace of business worldwide is accelerating rapidly. Product cycles are shrinking, just-in-time manufacturing is common, and decisions are only made when challenges arise. In such an environment, access to relevant information is essential. For many organizations, remaining competitive can mean the difference between survival and extinction.

A traditional corporation is frequently built on a model that presents a closed infrastructure and provides limited integration with external organizations. The vertical integration model of intra-organizational communication externally presents so-called *raw network connections*, which offer only very limited services to those users.

Many people still cling to an outdated, traditional information technology model that builds walls around corporate information and systems, thereby limiting access to a select few. Even when internal systems and information are shared, this is often limited to point-to-point applications. The traditional organizational model, which is depicted in Figure 2-1, is characterized by the following:

- The organization is integrated vertically.

- Partnering is difficult and costly.

- Most of the production (organizational processes) is done internally.

Figure 2-1   *Traditional Organizational Model*

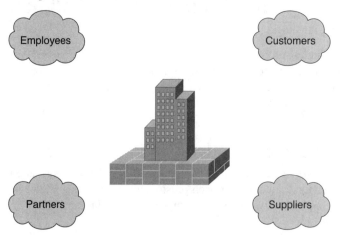

The level of competition has increased in the current global, networked market. Businesses that fail to take advantage of what networking has to offer are missing opportunities and allowing competitors to gain important economic advantages. Companies must foster interactive relationships with their stakeholders by opening up internal systems (including production) and the flow and accessibility of information.

Modern organizational processes and applications that are based on a Network Organizational Model can overcome many obstacles of the traditional, vertical design.

Modern Organizational Model

Internetworking introduces another method of organizational communication. Additionally, the Internet presents an open market with almost unlimited allocation of goods, resources, and people. With such a market approach, Internet applications offer the potential to dramatically increase service availability.

A new approach was developed to overcome the obstacles of vertical integration. This approach is based on horizontal integration and is represented by the Network Organizational Model, which is based on the following three core assumptions:

- The relationships a company maintains with its key stakeholders can be as much of a competitive differentiator as its core products or services.

- The manner in which a company shares information and systems is a critical element in the strength of its relationships.

- Being connected is no longer adequate; organizational relationships and the communications that support them must exist in a networked fabric.

Key Point: Vertical Versus Horizontal Integration

An vertically integrated organization includes all expertise and functions that are required to produce its product or service in-house. There is little need for information sharing outside of the organization. These traditional organizations also tend to limit access to information internally.

In contrast, a horizontally integrated organization partners with other organizations that have the expertise that is required to help them produce their product or service in a more efficient and effective manner. Sharing information, both internally and externally, is key to these modern organizations.

The Network Organizational Model builds on a system that integrates all the participating entities into an organizational Ecosystem. Ecosystems can be created both internally, within an organization, and/or externally, with partners and suppliers. A prerequisite for such an Ecosystem is a flexible and scalable network infrastructure, which is provided by both the Internet and enterprise networks.

A Network Organizational Model provides an open, collaborative environment that transcends many traditional barriers to organizational relationships and between geographies, thereby allowing diverse constituents to access information, resources, and services in a way that works best for them. Tight integration of all key constituencies is a result of a modern Ecosystem Model.

As shown in Figure 2-2, the following entities form the modern organizational Ecosystem:

- **Employees**—Information must be readily available to employees for organizations to function most effectively. Intranet applications provide the backbone for immediate access to current information and services.

- **Customers**—Using online support services, customers receive more convenient services more quickly; also, any customer, large or small and located virtually anywhere, can access these services. An additional advantage of online support services is their lower cost compared to that of traditional services.

- **Partners**—Successful partnerships leverage the resources of each partner.

- **Suppliers**—The purchasing function (ordering, delivery, and billing) can be time- and labor-intensive, not to mention expensive. Organizations can leverage their networks to create links to their suppliers, which results in less-costly transactions that can happen just in time.

Figure 2-2   *Modern Organizational Ecosystem Model*

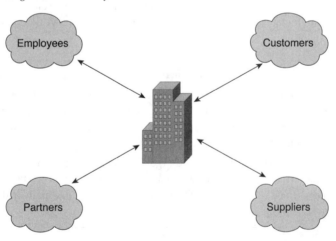

Benefits of a Networked Organization

Organizations want scalable and manageable systems that allow them to accomplish more with less. The leaders in any endeavor are those who effectively employ network technology to reach the goals of improved productivity, reduced time to market, greater revenue, lower expenses, and stronger relationships.

Key Point: The Importance of Effective Network Design

Having the best networking technology is only part of the solution. An organization's network must be designed and deployed to effectively support the organization's requirements. A networked organization views the network as a means of supporting applications that generate revenue, reduce costs, and improve customer/supplier relationships.

A modern automobile manufacturer is an example of an Ecosystem. Rather than producing every car component, the company contracts with partners that specialize in particular components and technologies. For example, a partner that has expertise in materials can produce the engine chassis; with the cooperation of other component partners, the automobile manufacturer assembles only the completed engine. If all partners are online, the transactions have minimal cost, just-in-time manufacturing can be accomplished, and it is easier to plan around component shortages. These relationships and the ability to share information save the automobile manufacturer and its partners time and money.

Network Organizational Architecture

The modern organizational model is built around a modular architecture that reflects the Network Organizational Model. This architecture supports applications that are built on common network solutions using shared network services over an appropriately-scaled network infrastructure.

Architecture Components

Modern organizations require a flexible, scalable, and robust infrastructure built on a network architecture that addresses current and future organizational growth. Modern organizations are able to streamline operations for two major reasons:

- They use technology that is aligned with their organizational needs
- They establish a technology foundation that allows them to build critical applications more easily

Figure 2-3 depicts the Network Organizational architecture.

Figure 2-3 *Network Organizational Architecture*

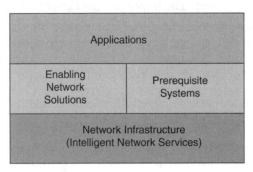

This architecture is divided into several layers, making the organizational processes easier to implement or expand. Each layer has special tasks that contribute to the success of the organizational processes:

- **Applications**—Address organizational goals directly. They offer a discrete set of functions, which are accessed via the network, for authorized users such as employees, customers, suppliers, or partners.

- **Enabling network solutions (such as voice transport or content networking)**— Make modern networks more intelligent so they can support applications.

- **Prerequisite systems**—Are combinations of structured data and business logic, sometimes wrapped in an application that exposes information as requested or directed.

- **Network infrastructure**—Includes network platforms and links, coupled with intelligent network services, which provide a highly available and secure network.

Key Point: Network Organizational Model Architecture

The Network Organizational Model architecture combines applications with enabling network solutions, prerequisite systems, and network infrastructure with intelligent network services to provide a foundation for organizational policies and procedures that support organizational goals.

Implementing the Network Organizational Model

Here are some guidelines to follow when implementing the Network Organizational Model:

- The implementation should be incremental and logical, starting small and growing as success builds. For example, many companies implement select customer support first because they foresee the network's potential for developing closer relationships with their customers.

- An organization's network architecture must reflect its logical structure and the processes conducted within the organization and its ecosystem.

- Soliciting constant input from users ensures that the network is usable and that the resulting architecture brings the perceived benefits to the organization.

- Open access to information, resources, and services through a network organizational environment sets new standards for relationships with customers, clients, partners, suppliers, and employees. Therefore, a level of control and manageability is desired on all levels of the networked architecture.

An organization should begin the implementation by selecting the most critical application, or one that has the greatest impact on organizational processes. Keep in mind that this model is not about incremental improvements in existing tasks; rather, it looks for breakthrough methods of sharing information, tools, and systems to build stronger organizational relationships.

Once the application is selected, its requirements are analyzed, and the necessary network solutions, prerequisite systems, and intelligent network services should be provided and deployed. For example, if the application requires a secure data search in a repository, the appropriate database and search engine must be provided and the adequate security mechanisms deployed.

Network Organizational Architecture Example

Figure 2-4 is an example of an architecture that supports mechanisms for the faster and easier announcement of new or modified products to corporate users, partners, or customers.

Figure 2-4 *Architecture Example*

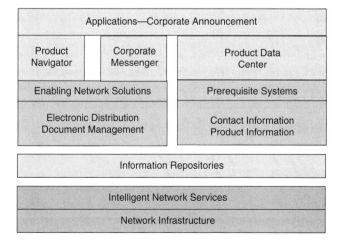

Figure 2-4 illustrates three different business applications. The applications are simple to use, and users can obtain all necessary data directly from each application. Details of the applications include the following:

- **Product navigator**—With this application, customers do not need to call the company to receive detailed information about a product. The product navigator application helps customers find specific information on products, depending on their needs.

- **Corporate messenger**—A customer uses the messaging application to receive all announcements for the given products—for example, a new software version. This application automatically dispatches information to customers without any manual intervention from the corporate administrator.

- **Product data center**—This application retrieves product information from the central storage in the format the customer demands. For example, the customer can choose a document to be displayed on the web, or downloaded in Acrobat or another format.

For these applications to work, the enabling network solutions (electronic distribution and documentation management) and prerequisite systems (contact information and product information) must be provided. Coupled with the supported databases, these solutions and systems allow the applications on the upper layer to more quickly and easily access the information requested by the user. For example, when a user requests the data sheet for a particular device, the application accesses the repository and searches for an answer with the help of the document management technology.

Organizational Policies

Every organization implements specific policies to achieve its organizational goals. A network designer must discuss and understand these policies before designing or redesigning a customer's network.

Policies are the rules and guidelines an organization follows to achieve its organizational goals. Policies are understood, implemented, and maintained at all levels of an organization. Many sets of internal documents explain an organization's operation policies, procedures, and standards. Organizational policies fall into two categories:

- Common legal and regulatory policies
- Organizationally specific policies

Common policies are general policies that the majority of organizations implement, usually in response to legal, regulatory, or contractual requirements. Common policies define the rules an organization follows to achieve its organizational goals. For example, Generally Accepted Accounting Principles (GAAP) drive many accounting policies in the United States. In some countries, governmental institutions such as the Post, Telephone, and Telegraph (PTT) organizations can limit the available network equipment choices.

Organizationally specific policies require an understanding of the organization's goals, mission, and desired outcomes. If a network designer does not understand the organizationally-specific policies, a project can fail because the design might not meet the customer's requirements. Understanding specific policies might also require sensitivity to an organization's tolerance of risk.

Some policies that are relevant to building a network infrastructure include technology, vendor orientation, and preference policies. For example, if an organization already uses equipment from a certain vendor, the network maintenance organization has existing knowledge of the equipment operation and therefore is less inclined to change vendors. In another example, an organization might have a policy to use routers that support a standard protocol, such as Open Shortest Path First (OSPF). Equipment that violates this policy is not purchased without executive intervention.

Defining Policies

As shown in Figure 2-5, policies within an organization can vary over time, thereby affecting the organizational procedures, processes, workflows, and outcomes.

Figure 2-5   *Policy Cycle*

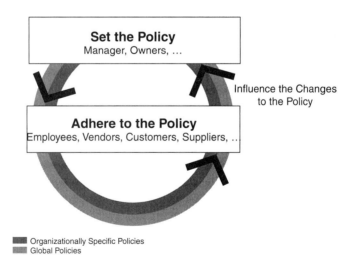

Management sets the policy and must also monitor its implementation, measure its subsequent impact on the organization, and redefine the policy as necessary to align with organizational goals.

The typical goals of organizational policy, which is often defined and implemented by senior management, are to direct and align the efforts of all players under a common goal.

Therefore, employees, partners, customers, and suppliers must align with an organization's specified policies to maintain business relationships.

Evolving market demands or organizational operations can drive policy changes. Small companies can change their internal policies to meet the requirements of partner companies' network specifications, or to accept new solutions that do not align with the current policy.

For example, Company B might decide to use a new application with partnering Company A, but finds that the application is not compliant with Company A's policy. Company A's management might then decide to redefine the partnership with Company B because of the noncompliance in policies.

Top management usually defines and changes policy because of evolving organizational demands. However, exceptions can occur, such as when a vendor or a network designer proposes a solution that requires policy change for proper implementation. Otherwise, employees, customers, or partners are expected to adhere to the predefined policies. Anyone in the organization can propose policy changes if it appears that a policy is no longer aligned with the organization's objectives or external requirements. Management must act to implement these proposals before they become effective as policy.

For example, Organization X requires secure communication with Organization Y; however, neither communication nor network security policies exist within Organization X. This situation requires that Organization X develop a new policy that defines how secure communication with Organization Y will be achieved.

Policy Makers

Organizations are divided into numerous levels, each with its own responsibilities and policies; every level needs to manage its own responsibilities. For example, an organization can include three core levels:

- **Executives and senior managers**—Make major strategic business decisions and direct overall policies. This level forms the top of an organizational hierarchy.

- **Departmental or unit managers**—Manage and control organizational projects and activities and assign tasks to nonmanagerial employees. In many companies, one manager might oversee a number of subordinate managers within a department; these subordinate managers, in turn, provide direction to nonmanagerial employees. However, in a small company, a single manager might control all activities within a single department.

- **Employees**—Perform the work by contributing effort, ideas, and knowledge. Employees help realize the tasks their supervisors assign. Employees are specialists in many organizations. For example, workers on an automobile assembly line are specialists in assembling specific parts of a car. Using the appropriate specialists enables an organization to complete complex and highly demanding tasks.

The organization chart in Figure 2-6 illustrates a sample hierarchical structure for a small to mid-sized sales organization.

Figure 2-6   *Example of Hierarchy in an Organization*

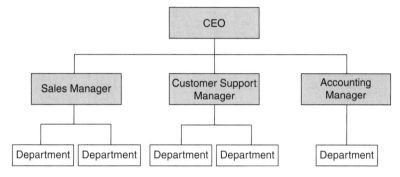

In Figure 2-6, the Chief Executive Officer (CEO), who might also be the owner, resides at the top of the hierarchy. The CEO and senior executives decide which projects they will undertake, identify the benefits these projects will bring to the organization, and address the obstacles they need to overcome for the project to succeed.

Figure 2-6 also identifies the following three upper managers, who oversee their own departments:

- **Sales manager**—Manages and controls the domestic and international sales department.

- **Customer support manager**—Controls the customer support department and any other department that is involved in customer relations (such as a customer support help desk).

- **Accounting manager**—Controls the finance department, which is responsible for carrying out financial transactions.

Organizational Procedures

Organizational procedures significantly influence network design. The following sections describe the importance of determining the customer's organizational structure and its procedures.

Organizational Structure

Typical organizations are comprised of one or more divisions or departments, which are interrelated and together form an integrated structure.

NOTE The terms *organization*, *institution*, *enterprise*, and *company* are used interchangeably in this book. These terms all refer to an entity that participates in an organizational process.

Organizational structure can vary, depending on the size of the organization. Small organizations can consist of only a few departments, while large corporations can be integrated with many smaller organizations or departments.

A typical business organizational structure includes several departments, such as Manufacturing, Accounting, Marketing, and Management.

Each department in this structure has its own functions and tasks. The number and functions of departments might vary, depending upon the size and type of organization. Each department performs different tasks and has particular responsibilities in the overall organization.

In a successful company, all departments must work together to achieve the best results. Every department has an assigned role in the organizational procedures. Well-structured organizations can react more quickly and compete more effectively in a rapidly changing environment.

Information Flows

Figure 2-7 illustrates a sample organizational structure and the procedural relationships among its various components.

Typical departments, such as manufacturing, accounting, marketing, and management, are synergistically interconnected. Departments are linked internally through information flows that help achieve organizational goals. External links to partners, customers, and suppliers also exist. Most organizational procedures affect a number of departments and external entities.

The network designer must determine the major processes and procedures within an organization and identify the involved departments and their communications to the external partners, suppliers, or customers. For example, suppliers communicate with production more often than with marketing, and partners often relate more directly to marketing and management than to production; however, the communication flow can vary.

Figure 2-8 illustrates the communications that occur when a customer buys an organization's product (presented in Figure 2-7) and how information technology can enhance the relationships and procedures within the organization. The underlying information technology provides the services for all departments. Using this infrastructure, business can be conducted so that data is available to all involved participants, without being entered more than once.

Figure 2-7   *Sample Organizational Information Flow*

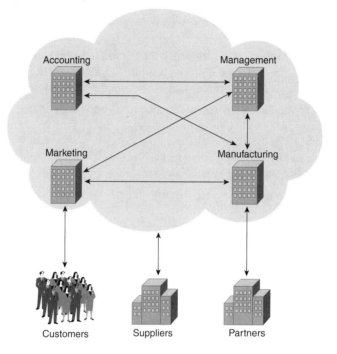

Figure 2-8   *Sales Order Process Example*

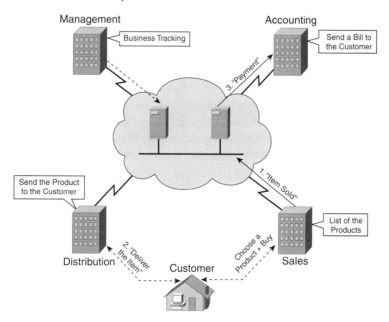

In this example:

- The customer chooses one of the products from a list, based on sales and marketing data that is available in the system.

- When the selection is completed, the application stores the data collected from the customer, requests the delivery, and initiates the payment process. Business system applications detect these processes and inform the impacted divisions.

- The distribution division ensures that the product will be delivered to the customer's address. At the same time, the application informs the remaining departments about the status of the purchase. The application updates the database information and proceeds with any additional tasks, if necessary (for example, if the product is out of stock and new supplies are needed).

- The accounting department controls the payment process, including such tasks as generating the invoice.

Using Networking to Accomplish Organizational Goals

During the past decade, people have become increasingly reliant on networks and the Internet for fulfilling business strategies and for personal use. Networks are now considered strategic assets. Today, common organizational applications include e-commerce, customer service, supply-chain management, and online training. The integration of the Internet with the organization offers new opportunities for improvements to network organizational processes and procedures, while challenging traditional policies. Organizational goals can only be achieved by using the network infrastructure effectively.

As previously discussed, a traditional network is limited in many ways. Most traditional networks provide only limited (if any) external access to important organizational applications. Today, few companies can survive without carefully established partnerships that require open, yet controlled, access.

In addition, many traditional networks are focused on internal connectivity only, rather than on reliability and manageability. A modern network that is based on the Network Organizational Model overcomes these issues by creating a more flexible, more responsive, and highly available open network.

Network technology that is based on the Network Organizational Model can dramatically increase efficiency, productivity, and customer satisfaction. For example, in the past, a bank customer was required to be physically present to carry out complex financial transactions with a bank. Now the Internet supports most financial transactions from the home or office.

Flexible Network Infrastructure Features

Business networks allow organizations to stay current on the latest industry trends and developments, thereby resulting in a competitive advantage. A flexible network infrastructure that can scale to constant change is a key for successful deployment of network applications that support organizational processes.

Organizational goals cannot be achieved without a complete understanding and integration of the following network features:

- **Functionality**—Organizational applications require a fully functional network to support the organization's defined goals. The network must be able to support the applications that are required for conducting the organizational processes.

- **Scalability**—Constant growth and expansion of the organizational tasks and processes require the network infrastructure to support the same scalability as the organization, with a goal of easy and inexpensive investment in the infrastructure.

- **Availability**—Critical business applications require networks to be highly available and provide services on a 24/7 basis. All network infrastructure components must be built with redundancy and resiliency to provide this service anywhere, anytime.

- **Performance**—Organizational applications require a certain level of network performance. Networks must be able to identify users and applications and provide the required responsiveness and throughput while maintaining economic utilization levels.

- **Manageability**—Management systems play an important role in today's organizational processes. They improve control, capacity management, performance monitoring, and fault detection for professionals who are not necessarily technical experts in all applicable disciplines. For example, a management system can provide case-tracking or statistical analysis of critical business events. The network must be proactively managed as a critical asset.

- **Efficiency**—The efficiency of the organization's network infrastructure provides optimum service results with reasonable operational costs and appropriate capital investment. For example, converging voice and data on a single integrated network can lead to enhanced efficiency and cost effectiveness.

Flexible Network Example

Figure 2-9 illustrates a sample network infrastructure with an emphasis on the features necessary for accomplishing specific organizational goals.

Figure 2-9 *Flexible Network Implementation Example*

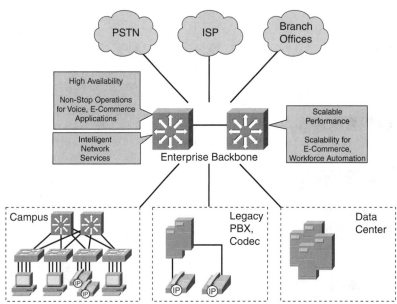

In Figure 2-9, a high-speed connection and fast network devices in the enterprise network backbone (supporting a Network Organizational Model) can achieve the required performance. The devices in this network design are based on versatile, scalable platforms that can provide further functionality with minimal additional investment. Such scalability can provide enough capacity to run an organizational application, such as e-commerce, without immediately replacing the existing infrastructure. This network configuration can also support the high availability, reliability, and manageability required by an e-commerce application, which must be available 24 hours a day to support users all over the world. The sample network transports both data and voice, thereby increasing the efficiency of the network while reducing costs (installation, ongoing operations, and management costs).

Network Design Methodology

The network design methodology presented in this section is derived from Cisco's Plan-Design-Implement-Operate-Optimize (PDIOO) methodology, which reflects a network's life cycle. The following sections describe the PDIOO phases and their relation to the network design methodology. Subsequent sections explain the design methodology in detail, beginning with customer requirements and concluding with the design verification.

Design as an Integral Part of the PDIOO Methodology

The PDIOO methodology reflects the phases of a standard network's life cycle. Every network encounters these phases during operation.

Figure 2-10 illustrates the PDIOO network life cycle. As shown in this figure, the PDIOO life cycle phases are separate, yet closely related.

NOTE   As shown in Figure 2-10, the PDIOO network life cycle actually contains six phases—the sixth is Retirement. Although this final phase is not incorporated into the name of the life cycle (PDIOO), it is nonetheless an important phase.

Figure 2-10 *PDIOO Network Life Cycle Influences Design*

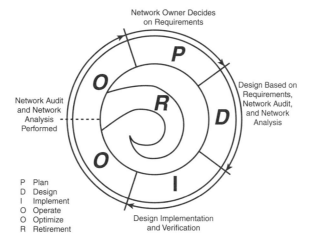

The following describes each PDIOO phase:

- **Plan phase**—This phase identifies the network requirements, which are based on goals, where the network will be installed, who will require which network services, and so forth. The output of this phase is a set of network requirements.

- **Design phase**—The initial requirements determined in the Plan phase drive the network design specialists' activities. They design the network according to those initial requirements, incorporating any additional data gathered during network analysis and network audit (when upgrading an existing network) or through discussion with managers and network users. The network design specification that is produced provides the basis for the implementation activities.

- **Implement phase**—Implementation begins after the design has been approved. The network is built according to the design specifications. Implementation also verifies the design.

- **Operate phase**—Operation is the final test of the design's appropriateness. The fault detection and correction and performance monitoring that occur in daily operations provide initial data for the network life cycle's Optimize phase.

- **Optimize phase**—The Optimize phase is based on proactive network management, whose goal is to identify and resolve issues before real problems arise. Reactive fault detection and correction (troubleshooting) is necessary when proactive management cannot predict and mitigate the failures. In the PDIOO process, the Optimize phase has special significance. It can lead to network redesign if too many network problems and errors arise because of design issues, or as network performance degrades over time as actual use and capabilities diverge from their predicted values. Redesign can also be required when requirements change significantly. In this case, the performance data regarding responsiveness, throughput, and resource utilization that is collected for optimization provides baseline information. Examples of problems that could be discovered include feature incompatibilities, insufficient capacity on a link, performance problems on a device when multiple features are enabled, scalability of protocols as the network grows, and so forth.

- **Retirement**—A network can be taken out of production when it, or a part of it, is recognized as being out-of-date. For example, it might be possible to reuse retired backbone equipment toward the edge of the network, where the performance requirements might be less aggressive. (For example, Cisco 7500 routers were common in network backbones a few years ago, but they are now being used as workgroup routers.)

Although Design is one of the five PDIOO phases, all the other phases influence design decisions and the Design phase interacts closely with them, as follows:

- The Plan phase requirements directly influence the design because they are the basis for network design.

- The Implement phase includes the initial verification of the design on the actual network.

- During the Operate and Optimize phases the final decision is made about the appropriateness of the design, based on network analysis and any problems that arise. The network can be redesigned to correct any discovered errors.

Design Methodology

When working in an environment that requires creative production in a tight schedule (for example, when designing an internetwork), using a methodology can be helpful. A *methodology* is a documented, systematic way of doing something. The design methodology presented here is a set of steps that can be followed so that the design process does not have to be redefined for each design project.

Following a design methodology can have many advantages:

- It ensures that no step is missed when the process is followed.
- It provides a framework for the design process deliverables.
- It encourages consistency in the creative process, enabling network designers to set appropriate deadlines and maintain customer and manager satisfaction.
- It allows customers and managers to validate that the designers have indeed thought about how to meet their requirements.

The design methodology consists of multiple steps. Some steps are intrinsic to the PDIOO Design phase, while other steps are related to other PDIOO phases. The design methodology presented here includes seven mandatory steps and one optional step:

Step 1   **Identify customer requirements**—In this step, which is typically completed during the PDIOO Plan phase, the initial requirements are extracted from the information provided by the network owner (the designer's customer).

Step 2   **Characterize the existing network**—Characterization of the existing network includes two substeps: the network audit and network analysis. During the network audit step, the existing network is thoroughly checked for integrity and quality. During the network analysis step, network behavior is analyzed (traffic analysis, congestions, and so forth); this is typically completed within the PDIOO Optimize phase.

NOTE   Step 2 is only present when an existing network is being redesigned.

Step 3   **Design the topology and network solutions**—This step undertakes the actual design of the network. Decisions are made about network infrastructure (hardware, software, physical topology, routing protocols, high availability, and so on), intelligent network services (Quality of Service [QoS], security, network management, and so on), and network solutions (Voice over Internet Protocol [VoIP], content networking, and so on). The data for making these decisions is gathered during the first two steps.

Step 4   Plan the implementation—During this step, the implementation procedures are prepared in advance to expedite and clarify the actual implementation. Cost assessment is also undertaken at this time. This step is performed during the PDIOO Design phase.

Step 5   Build a pilot network—During this optional step, a pilot or prototype network can be constructed to verify the correctness of the design. This is done either late in the PDIOO Design phase or early in the PDIOO Implement phase. The goal of this step is to identify any problems and correct them before implementing the entire network.

Step 6   Document the design—The actual design documents are written during this step. This step is started in the PDIOO Design phase; it might not be completed until the Implement phase has begun (for example, if a pilot is constructed, its results are included in the design documents). (For a more detailed description of design documents, refer to the "Documenting the Design" section later in this chapter.)

NOTE   The design document includes information that has been documented in all other steps.

Step 7   Implement and verify the design—The actual implementation and verification of the design take place during this step by building a network. This step maps directly to the Implement phase of the PDIOO methodology.

NOTE   The pilot or prototype network (in Step 5) verifies the design somewhat; however, the design is not truly verified until it is actually implemented.

Step 8   Monitor and optionally redesign—The network is put into operation after it is built. During operation, the network is constantly monitored and checked for errors. If troubleshooting problems become too frequent or even impossible to manage, a network redesign might be required; hopefully this can be avoided if all previous steps have been completed properly. This step is, in fact, a part of the Operate and Optimize phases of the PDIOO methodology.

NOTE	A pilot or prototype network should be used as often as possible to identify and correct problems that might have lead to a redesign.

The remaining sections in this chapter detail each of the eight design methodology steps.

Identifying Customer Requirements

To design a network that meets customers' needs, the organizational goals, organizational constraints, technical goals, and technical constraints must be identified. This section describes the process of determining what applications and network services already exist and which ones are planned, along with associated organizational and technical goals and constraints. We begin by explaining how to assess the scope of the design project and complete the list of requirements. After gathering all customer requirements, the designer must identify and gather missing information and reassess the scope of the design project to develop a comprehensive understanding of the customer's needs.

Assessing the Scope of the Network Design Project

In assessing the scope of a network design, a network designer must determine whether the design is for a new network or if it is a modification of an existing network. The network designer must establish whether the design is for an entire enterprise network, a subset of the network, or simply a single segment or module; for example, the designer must ascertain whether the design is for a set of Campus local-area networks (LANs), a wide-area network (WAN), or a remote-access network. The network designer must also determine whether the design addresses a single function or the network's entire functionality.

An example of a design that would involve the entire network is one in which all branch office LANs are upgraded to support Fast Ethernet. A project to reduce bottlenecks on a slow WAN is an example that would likely affect only a WAN.

The Open Systems Interconnection (OSI) reference model is important during the design phase. The network designer should review the project scope from the protocol layer perspective and decide whether the design is needed only for the network layer, or if other layers are also involved. For example:

- The network layer includes the routing and addressing design.
- The application layer includes the design of application data transport (such as transporting voice).

- The physical and data link layers include decisions about the connection types and the technologies to be used, such as Gigabit Ethernet, Asynchronous Transfer Mode (ATM), and Frame Relay (FR).

NOTE	Appendix C, "Open System Interconnection (OSI) Reference Model" details the seven layers of the OSI reference model.

The following table presents decision examples. We have also provided blank table templates for use in your designs.

Table 2-1 exhibits sample results of assessing the scope of design for a sample enterprise, Corporation X.

Table 2-1   *Corporation X Network Design Scope Assessment*

Scope of Design	Comments
Entire network	The central office needs a backbone redesign. All branch offices' LANs will be upgraded to Fast Ethernet technology.
Network layer	Introduction of private IP addresses requires a new addressing plan. Certain LANs must also be segmented. Routing must be redesigned to support the new addressing plan and to provide greater reliability and redundancy.
Data link layer	The central office backbone and some branch offices must have built-in redundancy. Redundant equipment and redundant links are needed.

Use Table 2-2 as a template for identifying the scope of the network design.

Table 2-2   *Design Scope Template*

Scope of Design	Comments

Identifying Required Information

Determining requirements includes extracting initial requirements from the customer and then refining these with other data that has been collected from the organization.

Extracting Initial Requirements

Initial design requirements are typically extracted from the *Request for Proposal* (*RFP*) or *Request for Information* (*RFI*) documents the customer issues. An RFP is a formal request to vendors for proposals that meet the requirements the document identifies. An RFI is typically a less-formal document an organization issues to solicit ideas and information from vendors about a specific project.

The first step in the design process should be predocumenting (sifting, processing, reordering, translating, and so forth) the design requirements and reviewing them with the customer for verification and approval (obtaining direct customer input, either in oral or written form). This predocumentation is in the form of a draft document.

Figure 2-11 illustrates an iterative approach to developing the design requirements document.

Figure 2-11 *An Iterative Approach to Identifying Customer Requirements*

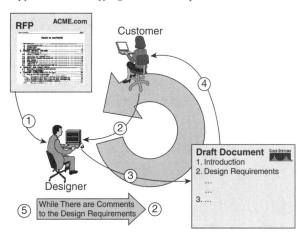

Figure 2-11 illustrates the following steps:

Step 1   Extract the initial customer requirements (from the RFP or RFI).

Step 2   Query the customer for initial requirements (verbal description).

Step 3   Produce a draft document that describes the design requirements.

Step 4   Verify the design requirements with the customer and obtain customer approval.

Step 5   Revise the document as necessary to eliminate errors and omissions.

Steps 2 through 5 are repeated if the customer has additional comments about the draft document.

Identifying Network Requirements

As illustrated in Figure 2-12, the process of gathering requirements can be broken down into five steps. During these steps (which are sometimes called milestones), the designer discusses the project with the customer's staff to determine and gather the necessary data, including appropriate documentation.

Figure 2-12 *Gathering Data for Design*

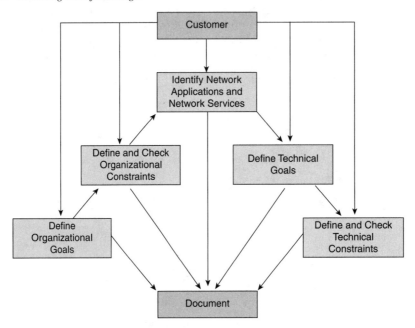

As shown in Figure 2-12, the steps are as follows:

Step 1   Determine the organizational goals.

Step 2   Determine the possible organizational constraints.

Step 3   Identify the planned applications and network services.

Step 4   Determine the technical goals.

Step 5   Determine the technical constraints that must be taken into account.

These steps provide the designer with data that must be carefully interpreted, analyzed, and presented to support the design proposal. Throughout these steps, the designer takes thorough notes, produces documentation, and presents the findings to the customer for further discussion. The process is not unidirectional; the designer might return to a step and make additional inquiries about issues as they arise during the design process.

The next five sections detail these steps.

Organizational Goals

Every design project should begin by determining the organizational goals that are to be achieved. The criteria for success must be determined, and the consequences of a failure understood.

Network designers are often eager to start by analyzing the technical goals before considering the organizational goals and constraints. However, detailed attention to organizational goals and constraints is important for the project's success. In discussions about organizational goals, the designer obtains knowledge about the customer's expectations of the design's positive outcomes for the organization. Both short- and long-term goals should be identified.

Preliminary research of the organization's activities, products, processes, services, market, suppliers, and competitive advantages and the organization's structure enhance the positioning of the technologies and products that are to be used in the network.

The information infrastructure and its communications are central to an organization strategy and its ability to meet its goals. Proper use of information technology reduces expenses and enhances services and competitive advantages. An appropriately-ordered and uniform communication base requires a strategic infrastructure upon which the organization can build its processes for improved flexibility and reliability.

Organizational goals differ from organization to organization. Following are the typical goals that commercial organizations are eager to attain:

- Increase the operation's generated revenue and profitability. A new design should reduce costs in certain segments and propel growth in others. Discuss with the customer expectations about how the new network will influence revenues and profits.

- Shorten development cycles and enhance productivity by improving data availability and interdepartmental communications inside the organization.

- Improve customer support and offer additional customer services that can expedite reaction to customer needs and improve customer satisfaction.

- Open the organization's information infrastructure to all key constituencies (prospects, investors, customers, partners, suppliers, and employees) and build relationships and information accessibility to a new level as a basis for the Network Organizational model.

NOTE   Similar, though not identical, goals are common to governmental, charitable, religious, and educational organizations. Most of these entities focus on using available resources effectively to attain the organization's goals and objectives. In not-for-profit organizations, key measures are typically stated in terms of cost containment, service quality, service expansion, and resource deployment. This section emphasizes the deployment of networks in commercial organizations as an example of the type of research that is required for establishing the network requirements.

To illustrate the importance of considering organizational goals in a network design, consider two manufacturing enterprises that are contemplating network updates. Enterprise A's main reason for change is to improve customer satisfaction. It has received many complaints that customer information is difficult to obtain and understand, and there is a need for online ordering capability. In contrast, Enterprise B is driven by the need to reduce costs—this is a mandate from its CEO. When design decisions are made, these goals will most likely result in different outcomes. For example, Enterprise A might choose to implement an integrated product information database with e-commerce capability, while Enterprise B might not see the value of investing in this technology.

Following are examples of the type of data that can be gathered about some common organizational goals:

- **Increase competitiveness**—List competitive organizations and their advantages and weaknesses. Note possible improvements that might increase competitiveness or effectiveness.

- **Reduce costs**—Reducing operational costs can result in increased profitability (even without a revenue increase) or increased services with the same revenue. List current expenses to help determine where costs could be reduced.

- **Improve customer support**—Customer support services assist with gaining competitive advantage. List current customer support services with comments about possible and desired improvements.

- **Add new customer services**—List current customer services and note future and desired (requested) services.

Table 2-3 present data gathered about the organizational goals of a sample company, Corporation X.

Table 2-3   *Corporation X's Organizational Goals*

Goal	Data	Comments
Increase competitiveness	Corporation Y—well organized purchase department	Use of applications for purchase tracking
	Corporation Z—organized partner network	Use of applications for customer and partner relationship tracking
Reduce cost	Repeating tasks—entering data multiple times, time consuming maintenance	Easier application management and maintenance
		Easier and less time-consuming order tracking
		Easier and less time-consuming network management

Table 2-3   *Corporation X's Organizational Goals (Continued)*

Goal	Data	Comments
Improve customer support	Order tracking Technical support	Introduction of web-based order tracking Introduction of web-based tools for customer technical support
Add new customer services	Current services: Telephone/fax orders Telephone/fax confirmation	Secure web-based ordering Secure web-based confirmations

Table 2-4 is an organizational goals template. Fill in the goals, the data gathered, and comments—especially improvements you desire to achieve with the new design.

Table 2-4   *Organizational Goals Template*

Goal	Data	Comments

Organizational Constraints

When assessing organizational goals, it is important to analyze any organizational constraints that might affect the network design. Typical constraints include the following:

- **Budget**—Reduced budgets or limited resources often force network designers to implement an affordable solution rather than the best technical solution. This usually entails some compromises in availability, manageability, performance, and scalability. The budget must include all equipment purchases, software licenses, maintenance agreements, staff training, and so forth. Budget is often the final decision point for design elements, selected equipment, and so forth. The designer must know how much money is available to invest in a solid design. It also useful to know the areas in which the network can be compromised to meet budget requirements.

- **Personnel**—The availability of trained personnel within the organization might be a design consideration. Organizations might not have trained personnel, or they might not have enough personnel. The designer must know the number and availability of operations personnel, their expertise, and possible training requirements. Additional constraints might be imposed if the organization is outsourcing network management. Familiarity with both the equipment and technologies speeds deployment and reduces cost. Trained technicians must be available to verify that all network elements are working. The designer must consider the network's implementation and maintenance phases, which require adequately trained staff.

- **Policies**—Organizations have different policies about protocols, standards, vendors, and applications. To design the network successfully, the designer must understand these policies. The designer should determine customer policies related to single- or multi-vendor platforms. For example, an end-to-end single vendor solution might be a benefit because compatibility issues do not restrain the network. The designer must recognize and accept the organization's policies to make a solid, sound, acceptable design plan.

- **Schedule**—The organization's executive management must discuss and approve the project time frame to avoid possible disagreements about deadlines. For example, the introduction of new network applications often drives the new network design; the implementation time frames for new applications are often tightly connected and therefore influence the available time for network design.

Table 2-5 shows organizational constraints and accompanying data that has been collected for a sample company, Corporation X.

Table 2-5 *Corporation X's Organizational Constraints*

Constraint	Data	Comments
Budget	$650K	Budget can be extended by a maximum of $78K
Personnel	Two engineers with college degrees and Cisco Certified Network Associate (CCNA) certifications for network maintenance; one has Cisco Certified Network Professional (CCNP) certification Three engineers for various operating systems and applications maintenance	Plans to hire extra engineers for network maintenance

Table 2-5   *Corporation X's Organizational Constraints (Continued)*

Constraint	Data	Comments
Policy	Prefers one vendor and standardized protocols	Current equipment is Cisco, and plans to stay with Cisco The network protocols must be International Organization for Standardization (ISO)-compliant
Schedule	Plans to slowly introduce various new applications in the next nine months	New applications that will be introduced shortly are videoconferencing, Lotus Notes, groupware, and IP telephony Create milestones for the design and implementation process

Use Table 2-6 as a template for documenting organizational constraints. Fill in the constraint, the gathered data, and comments.

Table 2-6   *Organizational Constraints Template*

Constraint	Data	Comments
Budget		
Personnel		
Policy		
Schedule		

Planned Applications and Network Services

In the process of gathering all types of data, the designer must determine what applications are planned for use and their importance. Using a table helps organize and categorize the solutions for the applications and services planned. The table contains the following information:

- **Planned application types**—Include e-mail, groupware (tools that aid group work), voice networking, web browsing, video on demand (VoD), databases, file sharing and transfer, and computer-aided manufacturing.

- **Applications**—Applications that will be used (such as Microsoft Internet Explorer, Lotus Notes).

- **Level of importance**—The importance of the applications is denoted with critical/important/not-important keywords.

- **Comments**—Additional notes that are taken during the data-gathering process.

Table 2-7 shows an example of data gathered about the planned applications for the sample company, Corporation X.

Table 2-7 *Corporation X's Planned Applications*

Application type	Application	Level of Importance (Critical / Important / Not Important)	Comments
E-mail	Lotus Notes	Important	
Groupware	Lotus Notes	Critical	
Voice networking	IP telephony	Critical	The company is introducing IP phones as a replacement for basic telephone service
Web browsing	Internet Explorer, Netscape Navigator, Opera	Not important	
Video on demand	IP/TV	Critical	
Database	Oracle	Critical	All data storage is based on Oracle
Customer support applications	Specific applications	Critical	

NOTE Information on the Opera browser is available at www.opera.com.

Use Table 2-8 as a template for identifying and evaluating planned applications. Fill in the application type, name, level of importance, and comments.

Table 2-8 *Planned Applications Template*

Application Type	Application	Level of Importance (Critical / Important / Not Important)	Comments
E-mail			
Groupware			
Voice networking			
Web browsing			
Video on demand			

Table 2-8   *Planned Applications Template (Continued)*

Application Type	Application	Level of Importance (Critical / Important / Not Important)	Comments
Database			
Customer support applications			

The planned intelligent network services table is similar to the planned application table. It lists intelligent network services that are planned for the network and additional comments about those services.

Intelligent network services include security, QoS, network management, high availability, and IP multicast.

NOTE   Software distribution, backup, directory services, host naming, user authentication and authorization are examples of general services and solutions that are deployed to support a typical organization's many applications.

NOTE   Chapter 3, "Structuring and Modularizing the Network," discusses QoS and IP multicast.

Table 2-9 shows sample data that was gathered about the intelligent network services planned for the sample company, Corporation X.

Table 2-9   *Corporation X's Planned Intelligent Network Services*

Service	Comments
Security	Firewall technology to protect the internal network; virus scanning application to check incoming traffic for viruses; intrusion detection system to detect and inform about possible outside intrusions
QoS	Implementation of QoS to prioritize more important and more delay-sensitive traffic over less important traffic (higher priority for voice and database traffic; lower priority for Hypertext Transfer Protocol [HTTP] traffic)
Network management	Introduction and installation of centralized network management tools (such as HP OpenView with CiscoWorks 2000) for easier and more efficient network management
High availability	Use redundant paths and terminate connections on different network devices
IP multicast	Introduction of IP multicast services (introduction of videoconferencing, e-learning solutions, and IP/TV)

Table 2-10 is a template for identifying and evaluating planned intelligent network services. Fill in the network service and any additional comments.

Table 2-10   *Planned Intelligent Network Services Template*

Service	Comments
Security	
QoS	
Network management	
High availability	
IP multicast	

Technical Goals

As the organization's network grows, so does dependency on the network and the applications that utilize it. Network-accessible organization data and mission-critical applications that are essential to the organization's operations depend on network availability.

The following list describes some common technical goals:

- **Improve network performance**—An increase in the number of users and the introduction of new applications degrades network performance, especially responsiveness and throughput. The first goal of network redesign is to increase performance, by upgrading the speed of the links and/or by partitioning the network into smaller segments.

NOTE   *Performance* is a general term that includes responsiveness, throughput, and resource utilization. The users of networked applications and their managers are usually most sensitive to responsiveness issues; speed is of the essence. The network system's managers often look to throughput as a measure of effectiveness in meeting the organization's needs. Executives who have capital budget responsibility tend to evaluate resource utilization as a measure of economic efficiency. It is important to consider the audience when presenting performance information.

- **Improve security and reliability of mission-critical applications and data**— Increased threats from both inside and outside the enterprise network require the most up-to-date security rules and technologies. Disruptions of network operation due to security breaches or equipment or link failure are highly undesirable in modern networks that have mission-critical applications and data.

- **Decrease expected downtime and related expenses**—When a network failure occurs, downtime must be minimal, and the network must respond quickly to minimize related costs.

- **Modernize outdated technologies**—The emergence of new network technologies and applications demands regular updates to and replacement of outdated equipment and technologies.

- **Improve scalability of the network**—Networks must be designed to provide for upgrades and future growth.

- **Simplify network management**— Network managers understand and use simplified management functions that are easily understood.

Using a table helps the designer identify technical goals. Different goals have different levels of importance; the customer should rate the goals. One way of expressing the level of importance is with percentages. Specific technical goals are rated in importance on a scale from 1 to 100, with the sum totaling 100; this scale provides direction for the designer when choosing equipment, protocols, features, and so forth.

Table 2-11 depicts the desired technical goals that were gathered for the sample company, Corporation X, along with their importance rating and additional comments. In this example, the designer sees that the customer places great importance on availability, scalability, and performance; this suggests that the network design should include redundant equipment, redundant paths, use of high-speed links, and so forth.

Table 2-11 *Corporation X's Technical Goals*

Technical Goals	Importance	Comments
Performance	20	Important on the central site, less important in branch offices
Security	15	The critical data transactions must be secure
Availability	25	Should be 99.9%
Modernize	10	
Scalability	25	The network must be scalable
Manageability	5	
	Total 100	

Use Table 2-12 as a template for identifying and evaluating technical goals. Fill in the goals, their importance rating, and any additional comments.

Table 2-12 *Technical Goals Template*

Technical Goals	Importance	Comments
Performance		
Security		
Availability		
Modernize		
Scalability		
Manageability		

Technical Constraints

Network designers might face various technical constraints during the design process. Good network design addresses constraints by identifying possible tradeoffs, such as the following:

- The network design process is usually progressive; legacy equipment must coexist with new equipment.

- Insufficient bandwidth in parts of the network where the bandwidth cannot be increased because of technical constraints must be resolved by other means.

- If the new network is not being introduced at the same time as new application(s), the design must provide compatibility with old applications.

- Lack of qualified personnel suggests that the designer must consider the need for additional training; otherwise, certain features might have to be dropped. For example, if the network proposal includes the use of IP telephony but the network administrators are not proficient in IP telephony, it might be necessary to propose an alternate solution.

Using a table can facilitate the process of gathering technical constraints. The designer identifies the technical constraints and notes the current situation and the necessary changes that are required to mitigate a certain constraint.

Table 2-13 presents sample technical constraints gathered for Corporation X. Under existing equipment, the designer notes that the coaxial cabling still exists and comments that twisted pair and fiber optics should replace it. The bandwidth availability indicates that the service provider does not have any other available links; the designer should consider changing to another service provider. Application compatibility suggests that the designer should take care when choosing equipment.

Table 2-13   *Technical Constraints for Corporation X*

Technical Constraints	Gathered Data	Comments
Existing equipment	Coaxial cable	The cabling must be replaced with twisted pair and fiber optics in the core
Bandwidth availability	64 kilobits per second (kbps) WAN link	Service provider does not have any other available links to offer
Application compatibility	IPX-based applications	New network equipment must support IPX

Use Table 2-14 as a template for identifying and evaluating technical constraints. Fill in the constraints, the gathered data, and any additional comments.

Table 2-14   *Technical Constraints Template*

Technical Constraints	Gathered Data	Comments
Existing equipment		
Bandwidth availability		
Application compatibility		

Cisco Network Investment Calculator for IP Telephony

If the customer is considering IP telephony (which we discuss in detail in Chapter 8, "Designing Networks for Voice Transport") in its network, the Cisco Network Investment Calculator (CNIC) can be useful for analyzing requirements. The CNIC helps calculate a customer's Return on Investment (ROI) for Cisco IP telephony solutions.

ROI is used to compare investments an enterprise is considering. The return can include profit, cost savings, and other less-tangible items (such as improved customer service, more knowledgeable staff, and so forth).

Compelling ROI data is critical when considering technology solutions in today's business environment. The CNIC facilitates the ROI analysis process by providing a framework for gathering necessary data, analyzing the various costs and benefits, and calculating the ROI. For example, the first step in the ROI process is to determine whether the customer is updating an existing telephony network or implementing a new installation. A new installation can take advantage of savings in areas such as wiring and circuit costs, while a customer replacing an out-of-date telephony system should be able to save in areas such as centralized call processing and network administration.

You can access the CNIC at www.cisco.com/cgi-bin/front.x/roi/cnicHome.pl.

NOTE   You must have a Cisco account to access this CNIC site. You must first complete an IP Telephony ROI online e-learning course and pass the assessment test to gain access to the full CNIC tool.

Characterizing the Existing Network

In many cases, a network already exists and the new design relies on restructuring and upgrading the existing network. The following sections present insights into the process of examining an existing network, describe the tools used to gather the data, and explain how to analyze the obtained data. We conclude with guidelines for creating the summary report that describes the network's health; this report is essential for any successful redesign solution.

Information collected and documented in this step is important because the design might depend on the existing network's hardware, software, and link capacity.

NOTE   This step in the design process is present only when an existing network is being redesigned.

Identifying the Existing Infrastructure and Its Features

The first step in characterizing an existing network is to gather as much information about the network as possible. The characterization of a network is typically based on the following input:

Step 1 **Customer input**—Review existing documentation about the network and use verbal input from the customer to obtain a first impression about the network. Although this step is mandatory, it is usually insufficient, and some results might be incorrect.

Step 2 **Network audit**—Perform a network audit that reveals details of and augments the customer's description of the network.

Step 3 **Traffic analysis**—Use traffic analysis to provide information about the applications and protocols used and possibly to reveal any shortcomings in the network.

The following sections describe each of these steps and the tools used.

Customer Input

Use initial customer data to draft a document that describes the existing network infrastructure. This document should cover the following topics:

- Existing network infrastructure, including
  - **Network topology**—Includes devices, physical and logical links, external connections, bandwidth of connections, frame types (data link encapsulations), and so forth.
  - **Network services**—Includes routing, security, QoS, and so forth.
  - **Network solutions and applications**—Specify those that are in use.
- Information about the expected network functionality and how you expect to use the network.
- Network applications.

After thoroughly examining all this information, you might break the network into modules.

Following are examples of different types of data gathered from a customer, Corporation Y.

Example 1: OSI Network Layer Topology Map

Figure 2-13 presents the network layer (OSI Layer 3 [L3]) topology of the sample network belonging to Corporation Y. The figure illustrates a variety of different Layer 2 (L2) frame types that are being used, including ATM and Frame Relay in the WANs. It also shows the logical connections between the routers on the WANs.

Figure 2-13 *Layer 3 Topology of Corporation Y's Network*

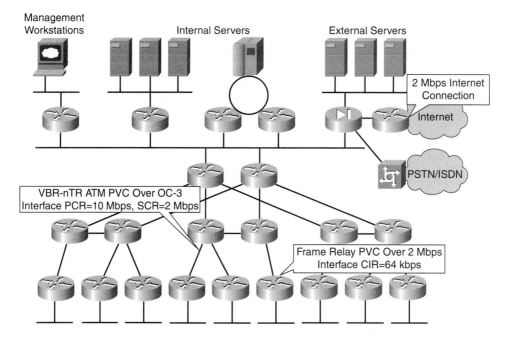

Based on this topology, the relevance of two areas of the network are indicated:

- Routing design:
  - The topology of the entire network is relevant
- Firewall design:
  - The topology around the Internet connection is relevant
  - The internal servers and applications that should be accessible from the Internet are relevant
  - The requirements for outbound connections are relevant

Example 2: Data Link Layer (Layer 2) Topology Map

It is important to include a description of the OSI Layer 2 and Layer 1 topology for some designs. Figure 2-14 illustrates the Layer 2 topology of Corporation Y's network.

Figure 2-14 *Layer 2 Topology of Corporation Y's Network*

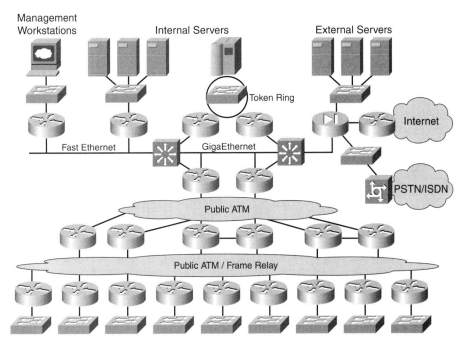

The Layer 2 map in Figure 2-14 reveals more network devices, including LAN devices and interfaces that are connected to a public WAN. However, this map hides the logical (Layer 3) links between the routers on the WAN.

Example 3: Network Services Map

Characterizing an existing network includes identifying the network services used and describing the protocols and major flows through the network. This information provides a necessary foundation for developing a good design.

Figure 2-15 illustrates the network services in Corporation Y's network.

In this sample network, the services include CallManager, Domain Name Service (DNS), address translation, and Simple Network Management Protocol (SNMP).

Example 4: Network Applications Map

Figure 2-16 illustrates the names of the network solutions and the applications in Corporation Y's network. Applications in this example include web (HTTP), e-mail, and File Transfer Protocol (FTP).

Figure 2-15 *Network Services in Corporation Y's Network*

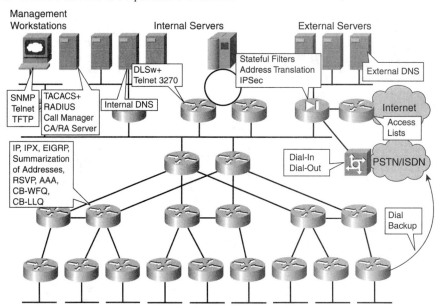

Figure 2-16 *Applications in Corporation Y's Network*

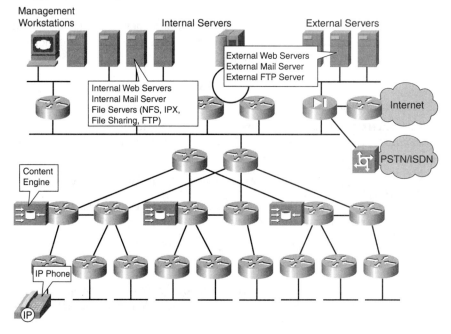

Detailed descriptions of the protocols these applications use should also be added to the network's documentation.

Example 5: Modularizing the Network

Large and complex networks should be divided into smaller logical modules. Figure 2-17 illustrates how Corporation Y's network can be divided into modules by their common characteristics.

Figure 2-17 *Corporation Y's Network Can Be Divided into Logical Modules*

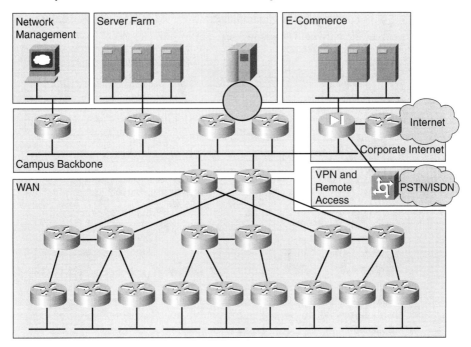

Modularizing the network helps identify similar devices. For example, routers in the WAN module are configured in essentially the same way, while a completely different set of features is used for routers in the corporate Internet module. The design (or redesign) will probably follow similar demarcations.

Chapter 3 discusses more information about modularization and the Enterprise Composite Model.

Auditing the Existing Network

The network audit is the second step in acquiring information about an existing network. The audit provides such details as the following:

- A list of network devices
- Hardware specifications and versions, and software versions of network devices
- Configurations of network devices
- Output of various auditing tools
- Link, central processing unit (CPU), and memory utilization of network devices
- A list of unused ports, modules, and slots in network devices, to be used to understand whether the network is expandable

Figure 2-18 illustrates three different sources of information that can be used in the auditing process: existing documentation, existing tools, and new tools.

Figure 2-18 *Network Audit Information Sources*

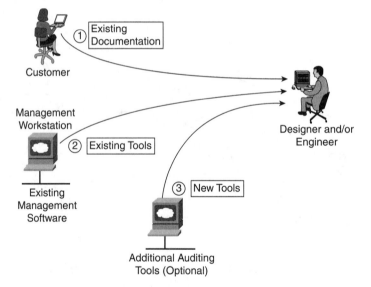

The auditing process starts by consolidating existing information the customer provides. Up-to-date information can be gathered from the existing management software used by the customer. If the customer has insufficient tools, the designer can choose to temporarily introduce additional software tools. If they prove useful, these tools can be used in the network permanently (during the Operate and Optimize phases).

The auditing process might require minor (temporary) network changes. Automated auditing should be used in large networks, for which a manual approach would take too much time.

The auditing process is typically performed from a central location, such as a location in a secure environment that is allowed to access all network devices.

Figure 2-19 illustrates sample information that a manual or automated auditing process collects from the network management workstation. The auditing process should collect all information that is relevant to the redesign. The same process should be used for all network devices that are affected by the design.

Figure 2-19 *Sample Information Collected During a Network Audit*

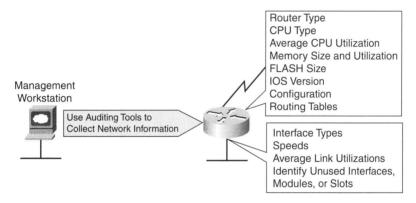

The audit process balances both detail and effort to produce as much information as needed or possible. For example, it should not require that a large set of CPU-heavy auditing tools be purchased and installed in the customer network to collect configurations of network devices.

Tools for Auditing the Network

A small network can be audited without special tools. Monitoring commands can be used for collecting relevant information on a small number of network devices. The approach can be semi-automated by introducing scripting tools to execute the monitoring commands automatically.

In large networks, a manual auditing approach is too time-consuming and less reliable. Following are special tools that can be used to collect the relevant information from the network devices:

- Cisco Works to map a network and collect different types of information (such as network topology, hardware and software versions, configurations, and so on)

- Third-party tools (such as HP OpenView, Visio Enterprise Network Tools, NetZoom, IBM Tivoli, Whatsup Gold, SNMPc, MRTG, Net Inspector Lite, and so on)

- Other vendors' tools to collect relevant information from equipment that is manufactured by those vendors

---

NOTE Cisco Secure Scanner is a now-discontinued product that was used for finding security vulnerabilities. The End of Sales announcement, at www.cisco.com/warp/public/cc/pd/sqsw/nesn/prodlit/1736_pp.htm, identifies potential replacement products.

Key Point: Information on Third-party Tools

Information on the aforementioned third-party tools can be found in the following locations on the World Wide Web:

- — HP OpenView: www.openview.hp.com/

- — Microsoft Visio Enterprise Network Tools: www.microsoft.com/office/visio/evaluation/indepth/network.asp. Note that this product has been discontinued.

- — NetZoom: www.altimatech.com/home/index.php

- — IBM Tivoli: www.tivoli.com

- — Whatsup Gold: www.ipswitch.com/Products/WhatsUp/index.html

- — SNMPc: www.castlerock.com/

- — MRTG: www.mrtg.org/

- — Net Inspector Lite: www.mg-soft.si/netinsp-lite.html

Manual Auditing

The auditing process can be performed manually using various monitoring commands. Use this option with only relatively small networks.

Figure 2-20 illustrates three different types of network devices, information that must be collected, and commands that can be used to obtain auditing information:

- On Cisco routers that run Cisco IOS software, the **show tech-support** command usually displays all information about the router. **show processes cpu** can be used to determine CPU use, and **show processes memory** can be used to determine memory usage.

- On Cisco switches that run CatOS software, the most useful commands vary, depending on the version of the software. Useful commands might include **show version**, **show running-config**, or **show tech-support**, if available.

- On Cisco Secure PIX firewalls, the **show version** and **write terminal** (to see the configuration) commands are useful.

Figure 2-20 *Collecting Audit Information on Cisco Devices*

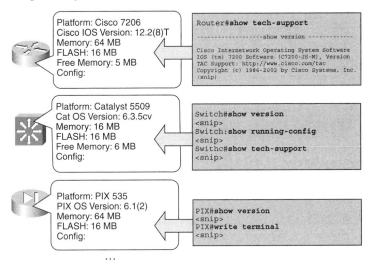

Example 2-1 illustrates the output from the **show processes cpu** command on a Cisco router.

Example 2-1 **show processes cpu** *Command Output*

```
Router#show processes cpu


CPU utilization for five seconds: 24%/20%; one minute: 45%; five minutes: 40%
 PID Runtime(ms)    Invoked     uSecs    5Sec    1Min    5Min TTY  Process
   1       2464     468381         5   0.00%   0.00%   0.00%   0  Load Meter
   2         44         44      1000   0.16%   0.04%   0.01%  66  Virtual Exec
   3          0          2         0   0.00%   0.00%   0.00%   0  IpSecMibTopN
   4    6326689     513354     12324   0.00%   0.25%   0.27%   0  Check heaps
   5          0          1         0   0.00%   0.00%   0.00%   0  Chunk Manager
```

continues

Example 2-1 show processes cpu *Command Output (Continued)*

```
   6        60        58    1034   0.00%   0.00%   0.00%   0  Pool Manager
   7         0         2       0   0.00%   0.00%   0.00%   0  Timers
   8         0        12       0   0.00%   0.00%   0.00%   0  Serial Background
   9      2139    468342       4   0.00%   0.00%   0.00%   0  ALARM_TRIGGER_SC
  10      3851     78081      49   0.00%   0.00%   0.00%   0  Environmental mo
  11      4768     44092     108   0.00%   0.00%   0.00%   0  ARP Input
  12      4408     19865     221   0.00%   0.00%   0.00%   0  DDR Timers
  13         4         2    2000   0.00%   0.00%   0.00%   0  Dialer event
  14        16         2    8000   0.00%   0.00%   0.00%   0  Entity MIB API
  15         0         1       0   0.00%   0.00%   0.00%   0  SERIAL A'detect
  16         0         1       0   0.00%   0.00%   0.00%   0  Critical Bkgnd
  17     57284    377088     151   0.00%   0.00%   0.00%   0  Net Background
  18     15916     59331     268   0.00%   0.00%   0.00%   0  Logger
<more
```

The output in Example 2-1 displays information about the network device CPU utilization, which is important for describing the network's health. Table 2-15 illustrates the **show processes cpu** command output's fields and descriptions.

Table 2-15   show processes cpu *command Output Description*

Field	Description
CPU utilization for five seconds	CPU utilization for the last 5 seconds. The first number indicates the total, and the second number indicates the percentage of CPU time spent at the interrupt level
one minute	CPU utilization for the last minute
five minutes	CPU utilization for the last 5 minutes
PID	The process ID
Runtime (ms)	CPU time, expressed in milliseconds, that the process has used
Invoked	The number of times the process has been invoked
uSecs	Microseconds of CPU time for each process invocation
5Sec	CPU utilization by task in the last 5 seconds
1Min	CPU utilization by task in the last minute
5Min	CPU utilization by task in the last 5 minutes
TTY	Terminal that controls the process
Process	Name of the process

Example 2-2 illustrates the **show processes memory** command's output on a Cisco router.

Example 2-2   **show processes memory** *Command Output*

```
Router#show process memory

Total: 26859400, Used: 8974380, Free: 17885020
 PID TTY  Allocated      Freed    Holding    Getbufs    Retbufs Process
   0   0      88464       1848    6169940          0          0 *Init*
   0   0        428    1987364        428          0          0 *Sched*
   0   0  116119836  105508736     487908     373944      55296 *Dead*
   1   0        284        284       3868          0          0 Load Meter
   2  66       5340       1080      17128          0          0 Virtual Exec
   3   0        668        284       7252          0          0 IpSecMibTopN
   4   0          0          0       6868          0          0 Check heaps
   5   0         96          0       6964          0          0 Chunk Manager
   6   0      17420     231276       6964       5388     254912 Pool Manager
   7   0        284        284       6868          0          0 Timers
   8   0        284        284       6868          0          0 Serial Background
   9   0          0          0       6868          0          0 ALARM_TRIGGER_SC
  10   0        284        284       6868          0          0 Environmental mo
  11   0        316    3799360       7184          0          0 ARP Input
  12   0    2547784    1033916       7372       6804          0 DDR Timers
  13   0        284        284      12868          0          0 Dialer event
  14   0      10744       2284      15328          0          0 Entity MIB API
  15   0         96          0       6964          0          0 SERIAL A'detect
  16   0         96          0       6964          0          0 Critical Bkgnd
  17   0      23412       2632      15404          0          0 Net Background
<more>
```

Table 2-16 illustrates the **show processes memory** command output's fields and descriptions.

Table 2-16   **show processes memory** *Command Output Description*

Field	Description
Total	Total amount of held memory
Used	Total amount of used memory
Free	Total amount of free memory
PID	Process ID
TTY	Terminal that controls the process
Allocated	Bytes of memory allocated by the process
Freed	Bytes of memory freed by the process, regardless of who originally allocated it
Holding	Amount of memory currently allocated to the process

continues

Table 2-16   **show processes memory** *Command Output Description (Continued)*

Field	Description
Getbufs	Number of times the process has requested a packet buffer
Retbufs	Number of times the process has relinquished a packet buffer
Process	Process name
Init	System initialization
Sched	The scheduler
Dead	Processes that are now dead as a group
Total	Total amount of memory held by all processes

Network Health Checklist

Based on the data you have gathered from the customer's network, check off any items that are true in the following Network Health Checklist. On a healthy network, you should be able to check off all the items.

Note that these guidelines are only approximations. Exact thresholds depend on the type of traffic, applications, internetworking devices, topology, and criteria for accepting network performance. As every good engineer knows, the answer to most network performance questions (and most questions in general) is "It depends."

- ☐ No shared Ethernet segments are saturated (no more than 40 percent network utilization).

- ☐ No shared Token Ring segments are saturated (no more than 70 percent network utilization).

- ☐ No WAN links are saturated (no more than 70 percent network utilization).

- ☐ The response time is generally less than 100 milliseconds (1 millisecond = 1/1000 of a second; 100 milliseconds = 1/10 of a second).

- ☐ No segments have more than 20 percent broadcasts/multicasts.

- ☐ No segments have more than one cyclic redundancy check (CRC) error per million bytes of data.

- ☐ On the Ethernet segments, less than 0.1 percent of the packets result in collisions.

- ☐ On the Token Ring segments, less than 0.1 percent of the packets are soft errors that are unrelated to ring insertion.

- ☐ On the Fiber Distributed Data Interface (FDDI) segments, there has been no more than one ring operation per hour that is not related to ring insertion.

☐   The Cisco routers are not over-utilized (5-minute CPU utilization is no more than 75 percent).

☐   The number of output queue drops has not exceeded 100 in an hour on any Cisco router.

☐   The number of input queue drops has not exceeded 50 in an hour on any Cisco router.

☐   The number of buffer misses has not exceeded 25 in an hour on any Cisco router.

☐   The number of ignored packets has not exceeded 10 in an hour on any interface on a Cisco router.

Document any concerns you have about the existing network's health and its ability to support growth.

Analyzing Network Traffic and Applications

Traffic analysis is the third step in characterizing a network.

Traffic analysis verifies the set of applications and protocols that are used in the network and determines the applications' traffic patterns. It might also reveal the additional applications the network is using.

You can perform traffic analysis by using such Cisco router services as NetFlow (which is described in the next section) or by using dedicated hardware- or software-based traffic analyzers that can be moved around the network.

Each discovered application and protocol should be described in the following terms:

- Importance to the customer
- QoS-related requirements
- Security-related requirements
- Its scope—in other words, the network modules in which the application or protocol is used

Use the following interactive approach, illustrated in Figure 2-21, to create a list of applications and protocols used in the network:

Step 1   Use customer input to list expected applications.

Step 2   Use traffic analyzers to verify the customer's list of applications.

Step 3   Present the customer with the new list of applications, and discuss discrepancies.

Step 4   Generate the final list of applications and their requirements (importance, QoS, security), as defined by the customer.

Figure 2-21 *Use an Interactive Traffic Analysis Process*

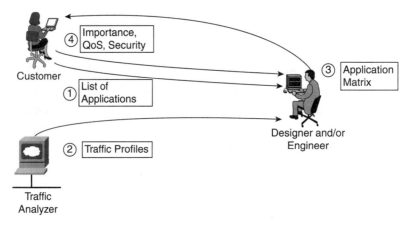

For example, the following information was collected about a fictitious application:

- Name: Application #8
- Description: Accounting software
- Protocol: Transmission Control Protocol (TCP) port 5151
- Servers: 2
- Clients: 50
- Scope: Campus
- Importance: High
- Avg. Rate: 50 kbps with 10-second bursts to 1 megabit per second (Mbps)

Assume that the customer requirement concerns QoS in a classical WAN network module. In this case, the information collected is relevant because it describes the following:

- Application (TCP port 5151) for performing classification
- Importance for evaluating how much bandwidth should be allocated to this application
- Current bandwidth consumption according to the present QoS implementation

However, this information might not be relevant should the customer requirement instead concern a secure and resilient Internet connection. In that case, it might be necessary to gather additional information.

Tools for Analyzing Traffic

Tools used for traffic analysis range from manual identification of applications using Cisco IOS software commands to those in which dedicated software- or hardware-based analyzers capture live packets. Tools include the following:

- **Network-based application recognition (NBAR)**—NBAR can be used to identify the presence of well-known applications and protocols in the network. This information can be gathered during the auditing process.

- **Cisco NetFlow technology**—NetFlow is an integral part of Cisco IOS Software that collects and measures data as it enters specific routers or switch interfaces. NetFlow allows the identification of lesser-known applications as it gathers information about every single flow. This information can be collected manually using the Cisco IOS software **show ip cache flow** command. Cisco FlowCollector and Cisco Network Data Analyzer allow automatic information gathering of each flow in the network segment.

- **Third-party hardware or software-based products**—Can be used to analyze traffic in different subnets of the network. Examples include the following:
  - Sniffer (www.sniffer.com/)
  - Active Network Monitor (www.protect-me.com/anm/)
  - EtherPeek (www.wildpackets.com/)
  - MRTG (www.mrtg.org/)

The next two sections describe NBAR and NetFlow.

NBAR

The purpose of QoS is to provide appropriate network resources (such as bandwidth, delay, jitter, and packet loss) to applications. QoS maximizes the return on network infrastructure investments by ensuring that mission-critical applications receive the required performance and that non-critical applications do not hamper the performance of critical applications.

You can deploy IP QoS by defining application classes or categories. These classes are defined using various classification techniques, which are available in Cisco IOS software. After these classes are defined and configured on an interface, the desired QoS features— such as marking, congestion management, congestion avoidance, link efficiency mechanisms, or policing and shaping—can be applied to the classified traffic to provide the appropriate network resources among the defined classes. Therefore, classification is an important first step in configuring QoS in a network infrastructure.

NBAR is a classification engine that recognizes a wide variety of applications, including web-based and other difficult-to-classify protocols, which utilize dynamic TCP and User Datagram Protocol (UDP) port assignments. When an application is recognized and classified by NBAR, a network can invoke services for that specific application. NBAR ensures that network bandwidth is used efficiently by classifying packets and then applying QoS to the classified traffic.

NOTE   Further details about NBAR can be found at www.cisco.com/en/US/customer/products/sw/iosswrel/ps1839/products_feature_guide09186a0080087cd0.html.

NetFlow

NetFlow switching provides network administrators with access to call detail recording information from their data networks. Exported NetFlow data can be used for a variety of purposes, including network management and planning, enterprise accounting and departmental charge backs, Internet service provider (ISP) billing, data warehousing, and data mining for marketing purposes. NetFlow also provides a highly efficient mechanism with which to process security access lists without paying as much of a performance penalty as other available switching methods incur.

The NetFlow FlowCollector application is used with the NetFlow services data export feature on Cisco routers and Catalyst 5000 series switches. FlowCollector provides fast, scalable, and economical data collection from multiple export devices that export NetFlow data records.

The Network Data Analyzer, formerly called the NetFlow FlowAnalyzer, is a client/server network management application. Together with its companion application—the NetFlow FlowCollector—the Analyzer enables you to collect and analyze traffic data that pertains to any number of communicating end nodes in your network. The Analyzer Display module incorporates a powerful and extensive graphical user interface (GUI).

NOTE   Further details about NetFlow can be found at www.cisco.com/en/US/customer/products/sw/iosswrel/ps1831/products_configuration_guide_chapter09186a00800ca6cb.html.

Further details on FlowCollector can be found at www.cisco.com/en/US/customer/products/sw/netmgtsw/ps1964/products_installation_and_configuration_guide_chapter09186a0080080e4a.html.

Further details on the Network Data Analyzer can be found at www.cisco.com/en/US/customer/products/sw/netmgtsw/ps1974/products_installation_guide_chapter09186a008007fb79.html.

Chapter 10, "Applying Basic Network Management Design Concepts," discusses NetFlow technology in more detail.

Analysis Tools Examples

The following examples illustrate how Cisco tools, Cisco IOS commands, and selected third-party software can be used for traffic analysis.

Example 2-3 is sample output of the IOS NBAR **show ip nbar protocol-discovery** command. This command illustrates the statistics gathered by the NBAR Protocol Discovery feature. Protocol discovery provides an easy way of discovering application protocols that are transiting an interface. The Protocol Discovery feature discovers any protocol traffic supported by NBAR and can be used to monitor both input and output traffic.

This command displays statistics for all interfaces on which protocol discovery is currently enabled. The default output of this command includes an average 30-second bit rate (in bits per second), input byte count, input packet count, and protocol name.

Example 2-3   **show ip nbar protocol-discovery** *Command Output*

```
Router#show ip nbar protocol-discovery


FastEthernet0/0.2
                         Input                  Output
    Protocol             Packet Count           Packet Count
                         Byte Count             Byte Count
                         30 second bit rate (bps) 30 second bit rate(bps)
    ------------------   ----------------------   ----------------------
    http                 46384                  79364
                         5073520                64042528
                         305                    1655

    secure-http          2762                   2886
                         429195                 1486350
                         0                      0
    snmp                 143                    10676
                         17573                  1679322
                         0                      0
    telnet               1272                   12147
                         122284                 988834
                         0                      0
    ntp                  5383                   0
                         624428                 0
                         0                      0
    dns                  305                    235
                         31573                  55690
                         50                     120
```

Example 2-4 is the Cisco IOS **show ip cache flow** command's sample output. This command illustrates the statistics that were gathered by the NetFlow switching feature. By analyzing NetFlow data, a designer can identify the cause of congestion, determine the class of service (CoS) for each user and application, and identify the traffic's source and destination network. NetFlow allows extremely granular and accurate traffic measurements and high-level aggregated traffic collection.

Example 2-4   **show ip cache flow** *Command Output*

```
Router#show ip cache flow

IP packet size distribution (12718M total packets):
   1-32   64   96  128  160  192  224  256  288  320  352  384  416  448  480
   .000 .554 .042 .017 .015 .009 .009 .009 .013 .030 .006 .007 .005 .004 .004

    512  544  576 1024 1536 2048 2560 3072 3584 4096 4608
   .003 .007 .139 .019 .098 .000 .000 .000 .000 .000 .000

IP Flow Switching Cache, 4456448 bytes
  65509 active, 27 inactive, 820628747 added
  955454490 ager polls, 0 flow alloc failures
  Exporting flows to 1.1.15.1 (2057)
  820563238 flows exported in 34485239 udp datagrams, 0 failed
  last clearing of statistics 00:00:03

Protocol         Total  Flows   Packets Bytes  Packets Active(Sec) Idle(Sec)
--------         Flows  /Sec    /Flow  /Pkt     /Sec   /Flow       /Flow
TCP-Telnet      2656855   4.3       86    78    372.3    49.6        27.6
TCP-FTP         5900082   9.5        9    71     86.8    11.4        33.1
TCP-FTPD        3200453   5.1      193   461   1006.3    45.8        33.4
TCP-WWW       546778274 887.3       12   325  11170.8     8.0        32.3
TCP-SMTP       25536863  41.4       21   283    876.5    10.9        31.3
TCP-BGP          24520    0.0       28   216      1.1    26.2        39.0
TCP-other      49148540  79.7       47   338   3752.6    30.7        32.2
UDP-DNS       117240379 190.2        3   112    570.8     7.5        34.7
UDP-NTP         9378269  15.2        1    76     16.2     2.2        38.7
UDP-TFTP          8077    0.0        3    62      0.0     9.7        33.2
UDP-Frag         51161    0.0       14   322      1.2    11.0        39.4
ICMP           14837957  24.0        5   224    125.8    12.1        34.3
IP-other         77406    0.1       47   259      5.9    52.4        27.0
...
Total:        820563238 1331.7      15   304  20633.0     9.8        33.0
```

Table 2-17 provides the **show ip cache flow** command output's fields and descriptions.

Table 2-17   **show ip cache flow** *Command Output Description*

Field	Description
bytes	Number of bytes of memory used by the NetFlow cache
active	Number of active flows in the NetFlow cache at the time this command was entered
inactive	Number of flow buffers that are allocated in the NetFlow cache

Table 2-17   **show ip cache flow** *Command Output Description (Continued)*

Field	Description
added	Number of flows created since the start of the summary period
ager polls	Number of times the NetFlow code looked at the cache to expire entries
flow alloc failures	Number of times the NetFlow code tried to allocate a flow but could not
Exporting flows	IP address and UDP port number of the workstation to which flows are exported
flows exported	Total number of flows exported and the total number of UDP datagrams
failed	Number of flows that the router could not export
last clearing of statistics	Standard time output (hh:mm:ss) since the **clear ip flow stats** command was executed
Activity by protocol display field descriptions are the following:	
Protocol	IP protocol and the well-known port number, as described in RFC 1340
Total Flows	Number of flows for this protocol since the last time statistics were cleared
Flows/Sec	Average number of flows seen for this protocol, per second
Packets/Flow	Average number of packets observed for the flows seen for this protocol
Bytes/Pkt	Average number of bytes observed for the packets seen for this protocol
Packets/Sec	Average number of packets for this protocol per second
Active(Sec)/Flow	Sum of all the seconds from the first packet to the last packet of an expired flow
Idle(Sec)/Flow	Sum of all the seconds from the last packet seen in each non-expired flow

Figure 2-22 is sample output from the MRTG tool; it illustrates the daily throughput on a link to the Internet.

Figure 2-22   *MRTG Tool Can Display Daily Throughput*

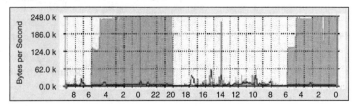

The statistics were last updated **Tuesday, 9 July 2002 at 9:49**,
at which time   had been up for 61 days, 11:17:53.

'Daily' Graph (5 Minute Average)

Max In: 246.0 KB/s (2.0%)   Average In: 113.9 KB/s (0.9%)   Current In: 9565.0 B/s (0.1%)
Max Out: 57.9 KB/s (0.5%)   Average Out: 5801.0 B/s (0.0%)   Current Out: 7370.0 B/s (0.1%)

Summary Report

The result of the network characterization process is a summary report that describes the network's health.

Customer input, network audit, and traffic analysis should provide enough information to identify possible problems in the existing network. The collected information must be converted into a concise summary report that identifies the following:

- Features in the existing network

- Possible drawbacks of and problems in the existing network

- Actions needed to support the new network's requirements and features

With this information, the designer should be able to propose hardware and software upgrades to support the customer requirements.

Example 2-5 presents a sample summary report that identifies different aspects of a network infrastructure.

Example 2-5   *Sample Summary Report*

```
The network uses 895 routers:
-655 routers use Cisco IOS software version 12.2(10)
-221 routers use Cisco IOS software version 12.1(15)
-19 routers use Cisco IOS software version 12.0(25)

Requirement: class-based weighted fair queuing (CBWFQ) in the WAN
Identified problem:
-Cisco IOS software version 12.0 does not support CBWFQ
-15 out of 19 routers with Cisco IOS software 12.0 are in the WAN
-12 out of 15 routers do not have enough memory to upgrade to Cisco IOS
software version 12.2
-5 out of 15 routers do not have enough flash memory to upgrade to Cisco IOS
```

Example 2-5 *Sample Summary Report (Continued)*

```
software version 12.2

Recommended action:
-12 memory upgrades to 64 Megabytes (MB), 5 FLASH upgrades to 16MB
Alternatives:
-Replace hardware as well as software to support CBWFQ
-Find an alternative mechanism for that part of the network
-Find an alternative mechanism and use it instead of CBWFQ
-Evaluate the consequences of not implementing the required feature in that
part of the network
```

The summary report conclusions should identify the existing infrastructure's shortcomings. In Example 2-5, the class-based weighted fair queuing (CBWFQ) feature is required. However, the designer has identified that Cisco IOS software version 12.0 does not support CBWFQ. In addition, some routers do not have enough random-access memory (RAM) and flash memory for an upgrade.

NOTE   CBWFQ is a QoS mechanism for classifying user-defined traffic based on protocols, access control lists (ACLs), and input interfaces. CBWFQ is usually used for classification and queue insertion of time-sensitive data.

Summary report recommendations relate the existing network and the customer requirements. These recommendations can be used to propose upgrading of hardware and software to support the required features, or modifying the customer requirements. In this example, options include evaluating the necessity of the CBWFQ requirement in the WAN.

Creating a Draft Design Document

After thoroughly examining the existing network, the designer creates a draft design document.

Figure 2-23 illustrates a draft design document's (not yet fully developed) index, including the section that describes the existing network. The Design Requirements and Existing Network Infrastructure chapters are closely related—examining the existing network can result in changes to the Design Requirements. Data from both chapters directly influences the network's design.

Figure 2-23 *Draft Design Document Index*

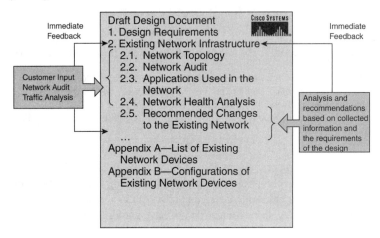

Typical draft documentation for an existing network should include the following items:

- Logical (Layer 3) topology map or maps (divide the topology into network modules if the network is too large to fit into one topology map).

- Physical (Layer 1) topology map or maps.

- The network audit results (types of traffic in the network, traffic congestion points, suboptimal traffic paths, and so on).

- A summary describing the major network services used in the existing network, such as OSPF, Border Gateway Protocol (BGP), and Internet Protocol Security (IPSec). Include a summary description of applications and overlay services used in the network.

- A summary describing issues that might impact the design or the established design requirements.

- A list of existing network devices, with the platform and software versions.

- Configurations of existing network devices. Configurations of all network devices can be attached as either a separate document or an appendix to the design document.

Designing a Topology and Network Solution Using Structured Design Principles

A structured approach to network design is required to achieve the best design result and meet initial design requirements. The goal of the design is to meet the customer's requirements for functionality, capacity, performance, availability, scalability, and flexibility within the budget.

The design's output should be a model of the complete system. To achieve this, the top-down approach is highly recommended. Rather than focusing on the network components, technologies, or protocols, you should focus on a systematic process using the business goals, technical objectives, and existing and future network services and applications. This systematic approach requires structured design practices, such as logical, physical, and functional models.

Top-down Approach to Network Design

Designing a large or even medium-sized network can be a complex project. Procedures have been developed to facilitate the design process by dividing it into smaller, more manageable steps. Identifying the separate steps or tasks ensures a smooth process and reduces potential risks.

A *top-down design* allows the designer to "see the big picture" before getting to the details. Top-down design clarifies the design goals and initiates the design from the perspective of the required applications and network solutions (IP telephony, content networking, and so on). The top-down approach adapts the physical infrastructure to the needs of the network solution. Network devices are chosen only after a thorough requirement analysis. Structured design practices (which we discuss in the next section) should be integrated with the top-down approach, especially in very complex networks.

In contrast to top-down design, the network design approach in which network devices and technologies are selected first is called *bottom-up*, or *connect-the-dots*. This approach often results in an inappropriate network for the required service(s) and is primarily used when a very quick response to the design request is needed. With a bottom-up approach, the risk of having to redesign the network is high.

Guidelines for producing a top-down design include the following:

- Thoroughly analyze the customer's requirements.
- Initiate the design from the top of the OSI model. In other words, define the upper OSI layers (applications and data transport), and then define the lower OSI layers, or the actual infrastructure (routers and media) that is required.
- Gather additional data about the network (protocol behavior, scalability requirements, additional requirements from the customer, and so forth) that might influence the logical and/or physical design. Then adapt the design to the new data, as required.

Structured Design

Structured design focuses on dividing the design task into related, less-complex components:

- First, the applications' logical connectivity requirements are identified, with a focus on the necessary network solutions and the supporting network services.

NOTE Examples of network solutions include voice, content networking, and storage networking. The required network services include availability, management, security, QoS, and IP Multicast.

- The network is then split functionally so the designer can develop the network infrastructure and hierarchy requirements.

NOTE This book uses the Cisco Architecture for Voice, Video, and Integrated Data (AVVID) to provide consistent infrastructure modularization.

- Each of the functional elements is designed separately, yet in relation to other elements. For example, the network infrastructure and intelligent network services designs are tightly connected; they are both bound to the same logical, physical, and functional models. Use the top-down approach during all designs.

After identifying the connectivity requirements, the designer works on each of the functional module's details. The network infrastructure and intelligent network services are composed of logical structures. Each of these structures (such as addressing, routing protocols, QoS, security, and so forth) must be designed separately, but in close relation to other structures. The designer's goal is to create one homogenous network.

Some logical structures are more closely related than others. Network infrastructure elements are more closely related to each other than to intelligent network services; for example, physical topology and addressing design are very closely related, while addressing and QoS are not.

Several approaches to designing a functional element's physical structure exist. The most common approach is a three-layer hierarchical structure: core, distribution, and access. In this approach, three separate, yet related, physical structures are developed instead of a single, large network. A hierarchical approach has many benefits, including the following:

- Cost savings
- Ease of understanding
- Ease of network growth
- Improved fault isolation

NOTE Chapter 3 discusses this core, distribution, and access layer hierarchical model in detail.

Figure 2-24 represents one example of how a network design can be divided into smaller, yet related sections using structured design practices.

Figure 2-24 *Structured Design Example*

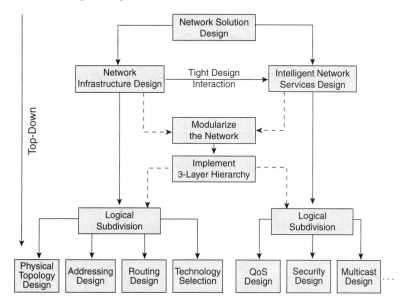

In this example, network infrastructure and intelligent network services design are tightly connected; both are bound to the same logical, physical, and functional models. These elements are subdivided logically. The network infrastructure design is subdivided into physical topology design, addressing design, routing design, and technology selection. The network services design is subdivided into QoS design, security design, and multicast design. All design phases use the top-down approach.

Top-down Design Compared to Bottom-up Approach

There are many benefits of top-down design over a bottom-up approach, including the following:

- Incorporating the customer organization's requirements
- Providing the customer and the designer with the big picture of the desired network
- Providing a design that is appropriate for current requirements and future development

The disadvantage of the top-down approach is that it is more time-consuming than the bottom-up approach; it necessitates a requirement analysis, and the design must be adapted to those identified needs.

A benefit of the bottom-up approach (selecting the devices and technologies and then moving toward services and solutions) is that it allows a quick response to a design request. This design approach should be based on the designer's previous experience.

The major disadvantage of the bottom-up approach is that it can result in an inappropriate design, which leads to costly redesigning.

Top-down Design Example

Consider an example that uses the basics of the top-down approach when designing an IP telephony network solution.

In this example, the customer requires a network that is capable of supporting IP telephony. IP telephony permits the use of same network resources for both data and voice transport, thus reducing costs of having two separate networks. To achieve this, the network must support Voice Over IP (VoIP) technology, as illustrated in Figure 2-25.

Figure 2-25 *A Voice Over IP Network Is Required*

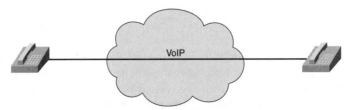

Figure 2-26 illustrates the addition of the required support for the IP telephony technology: an IP-based network. The network includes IP-enabled routers (and other devices, which are not shown in the figure) so that IP routing takes place in the network. To implement IP telephony, the IP network's delay must also be managed; to achieve this, specific QoS mechanisms must also be implemented in the network, as indicated in Figure 2-26.

Figure 2-26 *IP and QoS Are Required for VoIP*

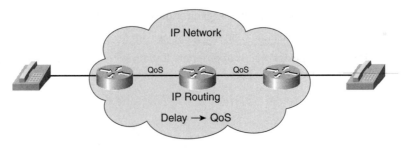

Figure 2-27 illustrates the addition of the call monitoring and management function. This function was previously overlooked; during the top-down design, it became clear that it is necessary. A CallManager is therefore placed inside the network to manage and monitor IP telephone calls.

NOTE   The Cisco CallManager is a server-based application that establishes and maintains signaling and control for IP telephone sessions.

Figure 2-27 *CallManager Is Required for Monitoring and Managing VoIP Calls*

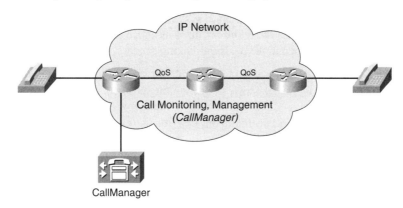

Decision Tables in Network Design

Decision tables are used for making systematic decisions when there are multiple solutions or options to a network issue or problem. Decision tables facilitate the selection of the most appropriate option from many possibilities and can be helpful for justifying why a certain solution was chosen.

Options are usually selected based on the highest level of compliance with given requirements.

In network design, decision tables are used for deciding what network building blocks (routing protocols, type of security, physical topology, and so on) to implement.

Basic guidelines for creating a network design decision table include the following:

Step 1   Determine the network building block about which decisions will be made (the physical topology, routing protocol, security implementation, and so on).

Step 2   Collect possible options for each decision. Be certain to include all (or as many as possible) options to obtain maximum value from the decision table. A thorough survey of the existing state of technology and considerable knowledge are needed to include all options.

Step 3   Create a table of the possible options, including the relevant parameters or properties. Add the requirements that will be tested.

Step 4   Match the given requirements with the specific properties of the given options. (This is where the compliance of a specific option's parameters to the given requirements is determined.)

Step 5   Select the most appropriate option. This is the option with the most matches, if all requirements are treated equally. If some requirements are considered more important than others, a system of weights can be implemented; in this system, each of the requirements is assigned a weight that is proportional to its importance in the decision-making process.

Figure 2-28 is an example of a decision table for selecting a routing protocol based on multiple criteria. In this example, several routing protocols are considered as possible options (OSPF, Intermediate System–Intermediate System [IS-IS], Interior Gateway Routing Protocol [IGRP], Enhanced Interior Gateway Routing Protocol [EIGRP], and Routing Information Protocol version 2 [RIPv2]), with their compliance to five different required parameters. As indicated in the figure, the chosen protocol should include the following properties:

- It should support a large network (up to 100 or more routers). RIPv2 and IGRP protocols do not meet this requirement.

- It must have a high speed of convergence. This precludes RIPv2 and IGRP.

- The use of variable-length subnet mask (VLSM) is required. IGRP does not support VLSM.

- It must be supported on Cisco and other vendors' equipment. Mixed vendor environments do not support EIGRP and IGRP because they do not support Cisco proprietary protocols.

- Network staff should have a good knowledge of the chosen protocol to enable them to troubleshoot the network. Most network administrators have, at best, only a basic knowledge of IS-IS because it is not widely used within enterprises (IS-IS is more commonly deployed in service providers).

NOTE   All requirements in this example have the same level of importance, so no weights are used.

Figure 2-28 *Sample Decision Table for Routing Protocol Selection*

Options Parameters	OSPF	IS-IS	IGRP	EIGRP	RIP v2	Required Network Parameters
Size of Network (Small-Medium-Large-Very Large)	Large	Very Large	Medium	Large	Medium	Large
Speed of Convergence (Very High-High-Low)	High	High	Low	Very High	Medium	High
Use of VLSM (Yes-No)	Yes	Yes	No	Yes	Yes	Yes
Mixed Vendor Devices (Yes-No)	Yes	Yes	No	No	Yes	Yes
Network Support Staff Knowledge (Good-Poor)	Good	Poor	Good	Good	Good	Good

Table 2-18 is a decision table template. It can be used in a similar manner to that of Figure 2-28's routing protocol decision table. To use it, put the parameters as the row headings and the available options as the column headings, and then fill in the appropriate values. Select the option that most closely matches the required parameters.

Table 2-18 *Decision Table Template*

	Options			
Parameter				**Required Network Parameters**

Network Design Tools

Several types of tools can be used to ease the task of designing a complex modern network, including the following:

- **Network modeling tools (NMTs)**—NMTs are helpful when a lot of input design information (such as customer requirements, network audit, analysis results, and so on) exists. NMTs enable modeling of both simple and complex networks. The program processes the information provided and returns a proposed configuration. This configuration can then be modified and reprocessed to add redundant links, support additional sites, and so forth.

- **Strategic analysis tools**—Strategic analysis or what-if tools help designers and other people who are working on the design (engineers, technologists, and business and marketing professionals) rapidly but thoroughly develop network and service plans, including detailed technical and business analysis. These tools attempt to calculate the effects of specific network components through simulated scenarios.

- **Decision tables**—As discussed in the previous section, decision tables are manual tools for choosing specific network characteristics from multiple options, based on required parameters.

- **Simulation and verification tools or services**—These tools or services are used to verify the acquired design, therefore lessening the need for a pilot network implementation.

Figure 2-29 illustrates how the initial requirements information is processed with network design tools to produce a network design.

Figure 2-29 *Using Network Design Tools*

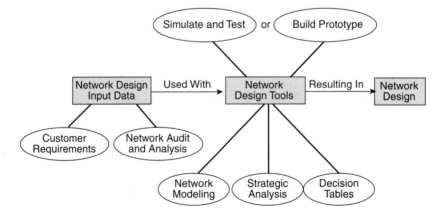

To verify a network design that was produced with the help of network modeling tools, strategic analysis tools, and decision tables, use either simulation and test tools, or build a pilot or prototype network. The pilot or prototype network also serves as a confirmation of appropriateness for the design implementation plan.

Planning a Design Implementation

Planning and documenting the design implementation is the fourth of eight steps in the design methodology presented in this chapter.

The design implementation description should be as detailed as possible. The more detailed the design documentation, the less knowledgeable the network engineer must be in order to implement the design. Very complex implementation steps usually require that the designer carry out the implementation, whereas other staff members (or another company) can perform well-documented, detailed implementation steps.

Implementation must consider the possibility of a failure, even after a successful pilot or prototype network test. The plan should therefore include a test at every step and a procedure to revert to the original setup if there is a problem. List implementation steps and estimated times in a table.

If a design is composed of multiple complex implementation steps, plan to implement each step separately rather than all at once. In case of failure, incremental implementation reduces troubleshooting and reduces the time needed to revert to a previous state.

Implementation of a network design consists of several phases (install hardware, configure systems, launch into production, and so forth). Each phase consists of several steps, and the documentation for each step should contain the following:

- A description of the step
- References to design documents
- Detailed implementation guidelines
- Detailed roll-back guidelines in case of failure
- The estimated time that is necessary for implementation

Figure 2-30 illustrates part of a sample table that lists a design's implementation steps.

Figure 2-30 *Sample Design Implementation Plan*

	Date Time	What	How	Result
Phase 1	22/04/2005	Installing Hardware	Section 6.2.1	√
Step 1		Connecting Switches	Section 6.2.1.1	√
Step 2		Installing Routers	Section 6.2.1.2	
Step 3		Cabling	Section 6.2.1.3	
Step 4		Verifying L2	Section 6.2.1.4	
Phase 2	25/04/2005	Configuring	Section 6.2.2	
Step 1		VLANs	Section 6.2.2.1	
Step 2		IP Addressing	Section 6.2.2.2	
Step 3		Routing	Section 6.2.2.3	
Phase 2	26/04/2005	Launching Into Production	Section 6.2.3	
Step 1		Physical Connection	Section 6.2.3.1	
	. . .	. . .		

Figure 2-30 summarizes the essential steps for completing the design implementation. It describes each step briefly and includes references to help the engineer find further details. The descriptions should refer to the section of the design document that precisely describes what should be accomplished.

Figure 2-31 provides a detailed description of an implementation step. It describes the configuration of EIGRP on 50 routers in the network and lists the two major components of the step (in the per router configuration procedure).

Figure 2-31 *Sample Detailed Design Implementation Step*

Section 7.2.2.3 Configuring routing protocols in the WAN network module:

–Number of routers involved: 50
–Use template from design (see section 5.2.4 "EIGRP design")
–Per router configuration:

- Use passive-interface command on all non-backbone LANs (see section 5.2.4 "EIGRP design")
- Use summarization according to the design (see section 5.2.4 "EIGRP design" and section 5.2.2 "IP addressing and summarization")

– Estimated time: 10 minutes per router
– Roll-back procedure: not required

NOTE The reference to the design document is useful for retrieving the details about the EIGRP implementation.

Building a Prototype or Pilot Network

A design must be verified after it has been completed. It can be tested in an existing, or live, network (pilot) or, preferably, in a prototype network that does not affect the existing network. A successful design implementation in either a pilot or prototype network can be used as a proof of concept in preparation for full implementation. The pilot, or prototype, phase should also be used to verify and update the implementation steps.

Key Point: Pilot Versus Prototype

A pilot network tests and verifies the design before the network is launched, or is a subset of the existing network in which the design is tested.

Before a redesign is applied to the existing network, a prototype network tests and verifies it in an isolated network.

A pilot network is usually used when the design is for a completely new network; pilots can also be used for designs that add to an existing network. A prototype network is usually used to verify designs that must be implemented on an existing network infrastructure.

It is important that the pilot or prototype test the design, including the customer's most important stated requirements. For example, if a key requirement is minimal response time for remote users, ensure that the prototype or pilot verifies that the maximum response time is not exceeded.

A prototype or pilot implementation can have one of two results:

- **Success**—This result is usually enough to prove the concept of the design. Successful implementation of the pilot or prototype network can conclude work on the design.

- **Failure**—This result is usually used to correct the design; the prototype or pilot phase is then repeated. In the case of small deviations, the design can be corrected and tested in the prototype or pilot network immediately.

Documenting the Design

A design's result can be documented in a single document or split into multiple documents. The final design document structure should be similar to the one in Figure 2-32, which includes the following:

- **Introduction**—Should be part of any design document; presents the main reasons leading to the network (re)design.

- **Design requirements**—Also a mandatory part of any design document. It includes customer requirements and design goals that must be fulfilled.

- **Existing network infrastructure**—Required only for a network redesign. The subsections document the results of the existing network characterization steps.

- **Design**—The essential part of the design document. Design details can differ, depending on the type of design project in question (whether it is a completely new network, a network redesign, or simply a new service introduction). Implementation details, such as configuration templates and exact configurations of network devices, can be included to ease the implementation process.

- **Proof of concept**—Can be in the form of pilot or prototype network implementation. Test results are also documented.

- **Implementation plan**—Should be included to enable technical staff to carry out implementation as quickly and smoothly as possible—without requiring the presence of the designer.

- **Appendixes**—Usually include lists and configurations of existing network devices.

Figure 2-32 *Sample Design Document*

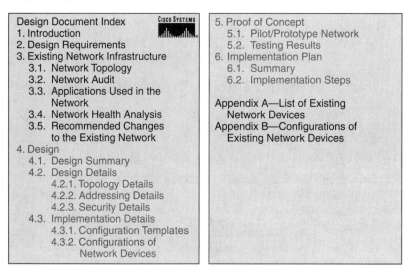

Implementing and Verifying the Design

Successful implementation of the pilot or prototype network might have already concluded work on the design. However, implementation is the designed network's first actual test. Even if a pilot network was used as a proof of concept, only the actual implementation reveals all the design weaknesses. The design's final confirmation is the full, live network implementation.

As part of the implementation phase, the designer assists with the design verification and takes remedial actions, if necessary.

The design document should include a list of checks to be performed both during the pilot or prototype phase and during the implementation, to ensure that the network is functioning as required.

Monitoring and Redesigning the Network

The network is put into operation after it is built. During operation, the network is constantly monitored and checked for errors and problems.

A network redesign might be required if troubleshooting problems become too frequent or even impossible to manage. For example, at least a partial redesign might be necessary if the new network is consistently congested. Solutions might include increasing bandwidth, adding filters, upgrading to devices with more capacity, moving servers that are in high use, and so forth. Hopefully this scenario can be avoided if all previous design steps have been completed properly.

Summary

In this chapter, you learned about the Network Organizational Model and how it opens the corporate information infrastructure to leverage the network advantage.

Every organization uses various policies and procedures to achieve its organizational goals, which can only be accomplished through effective use of the network infrastructure.

You also learned about the PDIOO methodology of network design and the network design process, including how to use structured design principles. The PDIOO methodology reflects a network's life cycle and includes the following phases:

- Plan
- Design
- Implement
- Operate
- Optimize
- Retirement

Although Design is one of the five PDIOO phases, all the other phases influence design decisions, and the Design phase interacts closely with them.

The design methodology presented in this chapter includes seven mandatory steps and one optional step:

Step 1 Identify customer requirements

Step 2 Characterize the existing network

Step 3 Design the topology and network solutions

Step 4 Plan the implementation

Step 5 Build a pilot network (optional)

Step 6 Document the design

Step 7 Implement and verify the design

Step 8 Monitor and optionally redesign

The design document is developed using an iterative and interactive approach and should include the following components:

- Introduction
- Design requirements
- Existing network infrastructure
- Design
- Proof of concept
- Implementation plan
- Appendixes

References

For additional information, refer to the following resource:

- Oppenheimer, P. *Top-Down Network Design—A systems Analysis Approach to Enterprise Network Design*. Cisco Press, 1998.

NOTE Appendix B, "References," lists all websites that are referenced in this chapter.

Case Study and Simulation Exercise

The following case study is on DJMP Industries, a fictitious manufacturer of portable speed bumps. This same case study is used throughout the remainder of the book so you can continue to evaluate your understanding of the concepts presented.

Key Point: Case Study General Instructions

Use the scenarios, information, and parameters provided at each task of the ongoing case study. If you encounter ambiguities, make reasonable assumptions and proceed. For all tasks, use the initial customer scenario and build on the solutions provided thus far.

You can use any and all documentation, books, white papers, and so on.

In each task, you act as a network design consultant. Make creative proposals to accomplish the customer's business needs. Justify your ideas when they differ from the provided solutions.

Use any design strategies and internetworking technologies you feel are appropriate.

The final goal for each case study is a paper solution; you are not required to provide the specific product names.

Appendix G, "Answers to Review Questions, Case Studies, and Simulation Exercises," provides a solution for each task based on assumptions made. There is no claim that the provided solution is the best or only solution. Your solution might be more appropriate for the assumptions you made. The provided solution helps you understand the author's reasoning and offers a way for you to compare and contrast your solution.

DJMP Industries Case Study Scenario

This case study analyzes the network infrastructure of DJMP Industries, a fictitious manufacturer of portable speed bumps. The company has provided a short description of the current situation and its plans. As a network designer, it is your job to identify all the company's requirements and data that will allow you to provide an effective solution.

Company Facts

DJMP Industries is an international company with headquarters in San Jose, California. The company is one of the world's leading suppliers of portable speed bumps. The demand for the company's flagship product is constantly increasing, and the company faces the need for tighter integration of its customers, partners, and suppliers into its information infrastructure.

The company's headquarters site consists of two buildings—the central building and building A. Approximately 200 employees are located at the headquarters. DJMP Industries has three regional offices in the United States (in Boston, Denver, and Houston) with 35,

50, and 50 employees, respectively. The number of workstations is assumed to equal the number of employees. Each regional office has a few smaller remote offices with up to five employees. Currently, eight remote offices are connected (on-demand, using ISDN) to the nearby regional office with the following distribution: Boston has two, and Houston and Denver each have three. Research and Development (R&D) is located in Houston, while Engineering, Production, and Manufacturing, are based in Denver. Production is highly automated.

Current Situation

Because the current situation does not provide for future growth, the company seeks a scalable solution to replace and upgrade the existing infrastructure, especially communications. Solidifying the internal network infrastructure that connects the company offices with the headquarters is the most urgent task. As the company adds new intranet and Internet-based applications to support its expanding business, the requirement for strategic communications infrastructure seems even more urgent.

The applications the company is currently running are custom-developed legacy applications that run on IP and use a proprietary protocol on top of TCP. The routing protocol used is RIPv1, and the IP addressing is flat; in other words, it does not have a hierarchy.

Users frequently experience slow response times. The company performed a monitoring and analysis of the traffic on the links to regional offices and the Internet. The analysis showed the average 24-hour link utilization that is listed in Table 2-19; in this table, the cells indicate the percentage link utilization.

Table 2-19 *DJMP Average 24-hour WAN-link Utilization (%)*

From/To	Headquarters	Boston	Denver	Houston	Internet
Headquarters		32	45	42	10
Boston	25				
Denver	30				
Houston	32				
Internet	25				

Currently, the headquarters' entire campus network is a shared Ethernet LAN, and servers are present in both the central building and building A. There is severe congestion on the LAN, especially at peak hours.

The placement of the servers presents additional problems; although the WAN links are terminated at the central building, regional offices also access building A's servers.

A central firewall that is located in the campus' central building provides Internet connectivity. Figure 2-33 illustrates the core of DJMP's internal network (the smaller offices are not illustrated for clarity reasons).

Figure 2-33 *DJMP's Core Network*

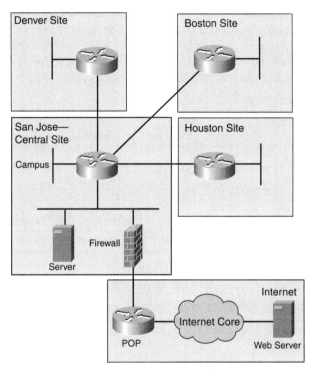

Plans and Requirements

The company is extending its worldwide presence and soon plans to open two international offices—one in Europe (London) and one in Asia (Singapore)— with approximately 10 employees each. The company is considering using the Internet as a connectivity option, with Virtual Private Networks (VPNs) terminated at headquarters. Additionally, the company would like to find a solution that would lower the cost of its international voice calls, and is seriously considering a Voice over IP solution, initially for its international offices only.

The company is seeking a solution for its communications infrastructure. It plans to restructure its campus LAN and is considering switched solutions along with proper server placement. Note that because the effects of introducing the switched LAN are unknown, the company wants some proof of the technology's viability. Because of previous bad experiences with network outages, the LAN solution must be highly redundant.

With the company expansion and modernization of its IT infrastructure, the company plans to introduce several new intranet- and Internet-based applications based on the following Internet protocols: web browsing (HTTP), e-mail, Telnet, and file transfer. The existing legacy applications will remain in use, at least for the next-year-and-a-half, so the company does not expect a decrease in the traffic produced by the legacy applications. The IT department performed a survey of typical application usage patterns, and an external consultant identified five distinct profiles of typical users who will use the new applications: Engineer, Researcher, E-commerce User, Administrator, and Salesperson. Table 2-20 illustrates the estimated applications mix for a typical user in each category, along with the expected usage intensity (light or heavy).

Table 2-20   *DJMP Typical Users and Applications Mix*

User	Web Browsing	E-mail	Telnet	File Transfer
Engineer	Light	Light	Light	Light
Researcher	Heavy	Light		
E-commerce User	Heavy			
Administrator	Light	Heavy	Light	
Salesperson	Light	Light		

Table 2-21 illustrates the distribution of users (by company location) who will initially start using the new applications.

Table 2-21   *DJMP Distribution of New Application Users*

Location	Engineer	Researcher	E-commerce User	Administrator	Salesperson
Headquarters			10	25	
Boston			20		10
Denver	20	5		10	
Houston		25		10	

The introduction of new applications will result in an additional load on the company's links to its regional offices. The tighter integration and growth of remote offices expected in the future will even further increase the traffic load on the WAN links. The company would like to upgrade the WAN infrastructure to provide sufficient bandwidth between the regional offices and headquarters and, at the same time, find a solution for better convergence during the network failures. RIPv1—the current routing protocol—has proven inadequate. The company is aware of the drawbacks of its current IP addressing scheme and is seeking a better solution.

Case Study: Network Upgrade

Complete the following steps:

Step 1   Read the DJMP Industries Case Study Scenario (in the previous section) completely before commencing the exercise.

Step 2   Document any information that you think is missing from the scenario and that you consider necessary for the design. Write down these items and provide a brief comment for each.

Step 3   Outline the major design areas you must address while designing the solution for the given customer scenario; provide a brief comment for each.

Step 4   Assume that you just purchased an extremely powerful network simulation tool. Decide how it can help you in making your design decisions. Write down some possible scenarios in which you could evaluate the effects of the new design by using the simulation tool.

Simulation: New Applications

This exercise is a paper-only version of the simulation that the simulation tool actually performed and includes the results it provided. Review the scenario and simulation results and answer the questions.

Scenario

The customer has provided you with information about its existing network, the planned applications, and the number of users. In addition, you determined that the bandwidths on all of the existing WAN links are 64 kbps. You used a simulation tool to reproduce the existing load on the WAN links. Afterwards, you simulated the additional load imposed by the new applications and graphed the results.

Initial Traffic

Using the data the customer provided about the existing load on the links and the topology of the existing network, the simulation showed that some links were saturated. The simulation focused on a 30-minute interval. Figure 2-34 indicates the loaded links with a dashed line and the links that are not saturated with a solid line. The threshold for considering the link to be loaded is set to 30 percent and is set to 60 percent for the heavily loaded link (there are no heavily loaded links in this case).

Figure 2-34 *Link Utilization on DJMP's WANs*

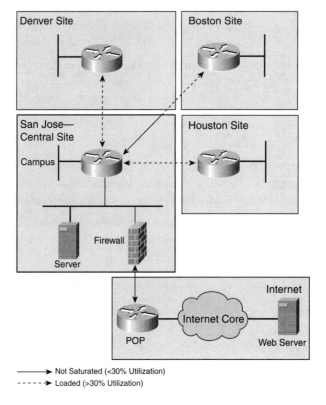

The graphs in Figures 2-35 and 2-36 show the results of simulating 30 minutes of the existing traffic on the WAN links (both directions) and on the link to the Internet.

Figure 2-35 *Simulation Results Between Central, Boston, and Denver with Existing Traffic*

Figure 2-36 *Simulation Results Between Central, Houston, and the Internet with Existing Traffic*

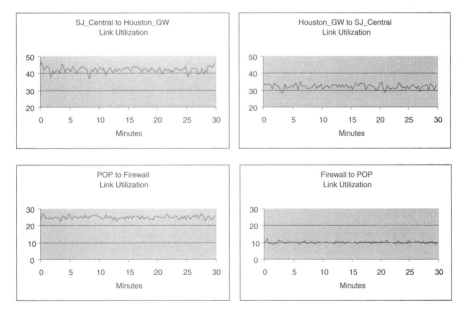

1 Observe the directions in which the load was higher. What can you determine from the results?

New Applications Introduced

You simulated the effect of new applications on the same topology with the same bandwidths of WAN links. The load imposed with new applications and their respective users was determined from the data the customer supplied. You performed the simulation (30-minute intervals. Figures 2-37 and 2-38 display the results. Carefully observe the results for all four simulated links (to all regional offices and the Internet point of presence [POP]).

NOTE   In a real-life situation, the observed interval should be longer and should include the peak-hour traffic that provides the most relevant results. However, the observed interval is set to 30 minutes because of the simulation tool limitations (long calculation times).

Figure 2-37 *Simulation Results Between Central, Boston, and Denver with New Applications*

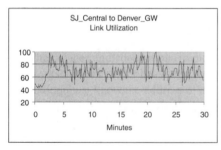
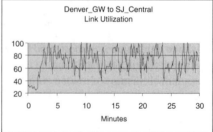
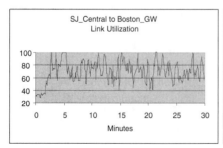
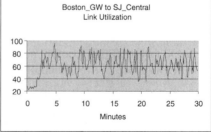

Figure 2-38 *Simulation Results Between Central, Houston, and the Internet with New Applications*

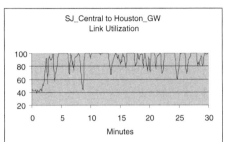

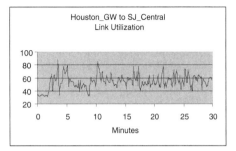

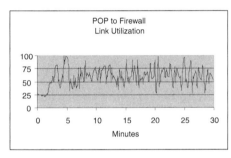

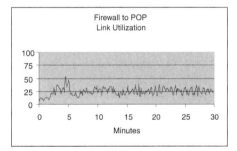

2 What can you determine from the simulation results? Compare the planned number of users and applications for each of the regional offices. In which direction are the links saturated?

3 Comparing the results from the initial traffic simulation with the results from the simulations using the new applications, you observe that the traffic from Denver to the Headquarters is also significant now. Why is this?

HTTP Traffic

You simulated the result of web (HTTP) traffic on the Houston to San Jose link. The average response times per web page were compared for two categories: light HTTP (smaller, less-complex web pages) and heavy HTTP (larger web pages). Figure 2-39 provides the resulting simulation graphs.

Figure 2-39 *Simulation Results for HTTP Traffic*

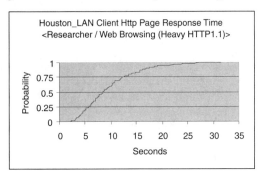 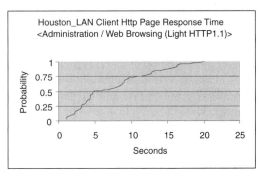

4 What can you determine from the graphs?

Increased Link Speed Between Houston and San Jose

You decided to increase the link speed to 128 kbps on the Houston to San Jose connection. You repeated the simulation and observed the link utilization and the web page response times. The graphs in Figure 2-40 show the results.

Figure 2-40 *Simulation Results When Link Speed Is Increased*

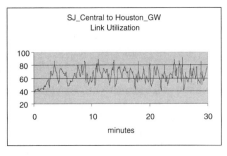 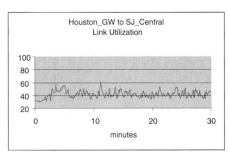

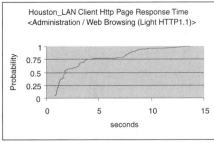 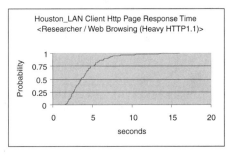

5 What do you observe from the graphs?

Review Questions

Answer the following questions and then refer to Appendix G, "Answers to Review Questions, Case Studies, and Simulation Exercises," for the answers.

1 List three characteristics of a corporation that uses a traditional organizational model.

2 Describe the characteristics of a horizontally integrated organization.

3 What are the four components of the Network Organizational Model architecture?

4 List four guidelines to follow when implementing the Network Organizational Model.

5 What are the two categories of organizational policies?

6 True or false: Organizational structure and procedures influence the organization's network design.

7 Name some network features that must be understood in order to achieve organizational goals.

8 Match the PDIOO network lifecycle phases with their correct descriptions.

Phases:

a   Plan phase

b   Design phase

c   Implement phase

d   Operate phase

e   Optimize phase

f   Retirement

Descriptions:

1   Network is built

2   Produces a network design specification

3   Includes fault detection and correction and performance monitoring

4   Network requirements are identified

5   Network is removed from production

6   Based on proactive management of the network

9 During which PDIOO phase is the initial design verification performed?

10 What are the eight steps of the design methodology?

11 List some determinants of the scope of a design project.

12 What information is required before a network design can begin?

13 What are some typical organizational goals?

14 Corporation X is currently spending $7,000 per month for telephony services provided by its local phone company. The new IP telephony equipment costs $40,000, and the operating costs are $2,000 per month. Determine when the introduction of IP telephony will pay for itself.

   a After eight months

   b After five months

   c After one year

   d It will not pay for itself

15 List some common organizational constraints.

16 Explain why a schedule might be a design constraint.

17 Corporation X is planning to introduce new systems for its employees, including e-learning, videoconferencing, and an alternative telephone service to reduce its operational costs. Which are two planned applications?

   a E-mail

   b IP multicast

   c IP/TV

   d IP Telephony

   e Quality of service (QoS)

18 Users typically think of network performance in terms of what?

   a Throughput

   b Responsiveness

   c Resource utilization

19 Table 2-22 lists Corporation Z's technical constraints.

Table 2-22   *Technical Constraints for Corporation Z*

Technical Constraints	Gathered Data	Comments
Existing cabling	Coaxial cable	New equipment requires fiber optics
Bandwidth availability	64 kbps WAN link	Service provider has no other available links to offer; WAN will be a bottleneck
Application compatibility	AppleTalk-based applications	New network equipment must support AppleTalk

What suggestion do you have for mitigating the bandwidth constraint?

20 What is the Converged Network Investment Calculator?

21 How does traffic analysis help in the characterization of a network?

22 A layer 2 topology map includes which two of the following features?

   a Routers

   b Switches

   c IP addressing scheme

   d Logical WAN links

   e Media type

23 True or false: The auditing process should never require any changes in the network.

24 List some tools that can be used in the network audit process.

25 Which command can be used to determine memory usage on a Cisco router?

   a **show processes memory**

   b **show processes cpu**

   c **show memory utilization**

   d **show version**

26 Which command displays packet size distribution and activity by protocol on a Cisco router?

   a **show ip nbar protocol-discovery**

   b **show ip interface**

   c **show version**

   d **show ip cache flow**

27 What is the difference between a saturated Ethernet segment and a saturated WAN link?

28 Complete this sentence: The network health summary report includes recommendations that _____.

   a relate the existing network and the customer requirements

   b are based on the customer requirements

   c are used to sell more boxes

29 What information is used for understanding an existing network?

30 With a top-down design: (choose 3)

    a The design adapts the physical infrastructure to the requirements.

    b The design adapts the requirements to the physical infrastructure.

    c Network devices are chosen after requirement analysis.

    d Network devices are selected first.

    e The risk of having to redesign the network is high.

    f The risk of having to redesign the network is low.

31 What are the layers in the three-layer hierarchical structure?

    a Core, distribution, and desktop

    b Core, distribution, and access

    c Core, routing, and access

    d Backbone, routing, and access

32 What types of tools can be used during the network design process?

33 What items should be included in the documentation for a network design implementation plan?

34 What is the difference between a pilot and a prototype?

35 What sections are included in a typical final design document?

36 Why is the network designer involved in the implementation phase?

37 What might necessitate a redesign of the network?

This chapter introduces the Enterprise Composite Network Model, which is a modular hierarchical approach to network design. This chapter includes the following sections:

- Network Hierarchy
- Using a Modular Approach in Network Design
- Network Services and Solutions Within Modular Networks
- Summary
- Review Questions

CHAPTER 3

Structuring and Modularizing the Network

This chapter introduces a modular hierarchical approach to network design: the Enterprise Composite Network Model. The Enterprise Composite Network Model is a tool or blueprint that network designers can use to simplify today's networks. To reduce complexity, this blueprint allows you to view the network in terms of its functional, logical, and physical components.

This chapter begins with a discussion of networks' inherent hierarchy. The next section introduces networks' natural functional modularization to complete our discussion of the Enterprise Composite Network Model. The final section contains examples of mapping network services and network solutions to this blueprint.

When you finish this chapter, you will be able to describe the aim and importance of layering in network design models, and describe the Enterprise Composite Network model and its goals and benefits. You will also be able to incorporate network services and solutions into modular networks.

Network Hierarchy

This section explains the hierarchical network structure, which is composed of the access, distribution, and core layers. It discusses the functions that are generally associated with each of these layers and the most common approach to designing a hierarchical network. Historically used in the design of enterprise local-area network (LAN) and wide-area network (WAN) data networks, this model works equally well within the functional modules of the Enterprise Composite Model. These modules are discussed later in this chapter, in the "Using a Modular Approach in Network Design" section.

Hierarchical Network Model

Today's networks are extremely complex, yet critical to meeting an organization's goals. Businesses have increasing requirements for network bandwidth, reliability, and functionality. Network designers are challenged to develop networks that use new protocols and technologies.

The *hierarchical network model* is a tool that network designers can use to help ensure that the network design is scalable, reliable, available, responsive, efficient, adaptable, flexible, and accessible, while also being secure and manageable.

The many benefits of using hierarchical network design models include the following:

- **Cost savings**—After adopting hierarchical design models, many organizations report cost savings because they are no longer trying to do it all in one routing/switching platform. The model's modular nature enables appropriate use of bandwidth within each layer of the hierarchy, thereby reducing wasted capacity.

- **Ease of understanding**—Keeping each design element simple and small facilitates understanding and therefore helps control training and staff costs. Management responsibility and network management systems can be distributed to the different layers of modular network architectures, thereby helping control management costs.

- **Easy network growth**—Hierarchical design facilitates changes. In a network design, modularity allows the creation of design elements that can be replicated as the network grows to facilitate easy network growth. As each network design element requires change, the cost and complexity of making the upgrade are confined to a small subset of the overall network. In large, flat, or meshed network architectures, changes tend to impact a large number of systems.

- **Improved fault isolation**—Structuring the network into small, easy-to-understand elements facilitates improved fault isolation. Because network managers can easily understand the network's transition points, it helps in identifying the failure points.

Hierarchical Network Design Layers

As shown in Figure 3-1, the hierarchical network design model consists of three layers:

- The *access layer* provides local and remote workgroup or user access to the network.
- The *distribution layer* provides policy-based connectivity.
- The *core (or backbone) layer* provides high-speed transport to satisfy the connectivity and transport needs of the distribution layer devices.

Each hierarchical layer focuses on specific functions, thereby allowing the network designer to choose the right systems and features based on their function within the model. This approach helps provide more accurate capacity planning and minimize total costs.

Figure 3-2 illustrates sample network showing the mapping to the hierarchical model's three layers.

Figure 3-1   *The Hierarchical Model's Three Layers*

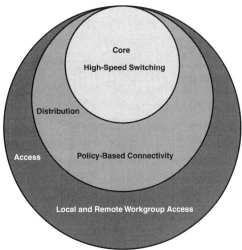

Figure 3-2   *A Sample Network Designed Using the Hierarchical Model*

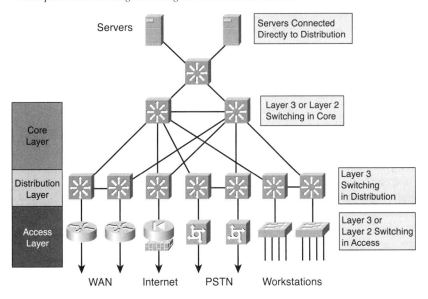

You do not have to implement the layers as distinct physical entities; they are defined to aid successful network design and to represent functionality that must exist within a network. The actual manner in which you implement the layers depends on the needs of the network being designed. Each layer can be implemented in routers or switches, represented by physical media, or combined in a single device. You can omit a particular layer altogether; however, for optimum performance, you should maintain hierarchy.

Hierarchical Model versus Open System Interconnection (OSI) Model

Appendix C, "Open System Interconnection (OSI) Reference Model," reviews the OSI model. The relationship between the hierarchical layer's three layers and the OSI model's seven layers is as follows:

- The devices used to implement all three hierarchical layers must implement the OSI reference model's physical and data link layers to achieve basic connectivity within the network.

- The access layer tends to focus on the protocols of the OSI reference model's application, presentation, session, and transport layers. It is the conceptual "gatekeeper," or the first line of defense. (For example, passwords might be required for a user to access the network from a WAN.)

- The distribution layer evaluates the information provided by the access layer to make policy-based connectivity decisions that are key to the OSI reference model's transport and network layer interaction.

- The concerns of the distribution and core layers overlap somewhat. The distribution layer tends to be traffic-focused (for example, it might look at the type of traffic being sent to decide whether it is allowed), while the core layer is more transport-focused. The core layer's objective is to provide fast transport service with minimal device intervention.

The following sections detail the functionality of the three layers and the devices used to implement them.

Access Layer Functionality

This section describes the access layer functions and the interaction of the access layer with the distribution layer and local or remote users.

The Role of the Access Layer

The *access layer* is the concentration point at which clients access the network. Access layer devices control traffic by localizing service requests to the access media.

The purpose of the access layer is to grant user access to network resources. Following are the access layer's characteristics:

- In the campus environment, the access layer incorporates shared LAN, switched LAN, or subnetted switched LAN (or virtual LAN [VLAN]) access devices with ports that are available for workstations and servers.

- In the WAN environment, the access layer can provide sites with access to the corporate network via some wide-area technology, such as Public Switched Telephone Network (PSTN), Frame Relay (FR), Asynchronous Transfer Mode (ATM), Integrated Services Digital Network (ISDN), leased lines, and Digital Subscriber Line (DSL) over traditional telephone copper lines, or coaxial cable.

- So as not to compromise network integrity, access is only granted to authenticated users or devices (such as those with physical address or logical name authentication). For example, the devices at the access point must be able to detect whether a telecommuter who is dialing in is legitimate, yet they must require minimal authentication steps for the telecommuter.

Layer 2 and Layer 3 Switching in the Access Layer

Access can be provided to end-users as part of the following two different scenarios:

- **Using Layer 2 (L2) switching**—You can implement access to local workstations and servers using shared media LANs or switched media LANs; you can use VLANs to subnet the switched LANs. Each network is a single broadcast domain. One drawback of this is that when any host sends a large number of broadcasts, it effectively blocks the entire network segment. The segment is also a single spanning-tree domain, so any link failure could result in a substantial outage for that part of the network.

NOTE   We discuss spanning tree further in Chapter 4, "Basic Campus Switching Design Considerations."

- **Using Layer 3 (L3) switching**—The most common design for remote users is to use routers. A Layer 3 switch, or router, is the boundary for broadcast domains and is necessary for communicating between broadcast domains (including VLANs). Access routers provide access to remote office environments using various wide-area technologies that are combined with Layer 3 features, such as route propagation, packet filtering, authentication, security, Quality of Service (QoS), and so on. These technologies allow the network to be optimized to satisfy a particular user's needs. In a dialup connection environment, you can implement dial-on-demand routing (DDR) and static routing to control costs.

NOTE   In small networks, the access layer is often collapsed into the distribution layer; in other words, one device might handle all functions of the access and distribution layers.

Figure 3-3 illustrates the use of Layer 2 switching in the access layer with two small VLANs.

Figure 3-3   *Access Layer Implementation Using VLANs*

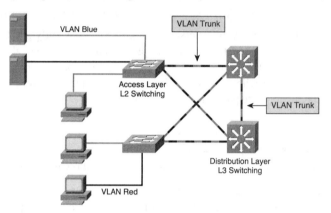

The workstations and servers in Figure 3-3 are attached to Layer 2 switches. The access layer aggregates the end-user switched 10/100 ports and provides uplinks (for example, Fast Ethernet, Fast EtherChannel, or Gigabit Ethernet) to the distribution layer. The network designer configures two small VLANs to satisfy the connectivity requirements and reduce the size of the broadcast domains (each VLAN is a separate Internet Protocol [IP] subnet). The access layer switches are connected to the distribution Layer 3 switches via Layer 2 trunks (Inter-Switch Link [ISL] or 802.1q) so that all switches are aware of the VLAN presence, thereby making it possible for each of them to select a primary path (using per-VLAN spanning tree) and find an alternative one in case of failure. If needed, the distribution routers can route between the VLANs.

Spanning-tree features that are available on switches, such as UplinkFast and PortFast, further improve the network. For example:

- **UplinkFast**—Enables faster failover on an access layer switch when dual uplinks are connected to the distribution layer. These are connected by unblocking the blocked uplink port on a switch immediately after root port failure, thereby transitioning it to the forwarding state immediately, without transitioning the port through the listening and learning states.

- **PortFast**—Enables switch ports that are only connected to a single device (typically a workstation) to immediately enter the spanning-tree forwarding state, thereby bypassing the listening and learning states when they come up. Ports that are only connected to a single device do not have bridging loops, so it is safe to go directly to the forwarding state to significantly reduce the time it takes before the port is usable.

NOTE	Chapter 4 discusses other spanning-tree features.

Distribution Layer Functionality

This section describes distribution layer functions and the interaction of the distribution layer with the core and access layers.

The Role of the Distribution Layer

The *distribution layer* represents both a separation between the access and core layers and a connection point between the diverse access sites and the core layer. The distribution layer determines department or workgroup access.

Following are the characteristics of the distribution layer:

- Distribution layer devices control access to resources that are available at the core layer, and must therefore use bandwidth efficiently. The distribution layer aggregates bandwidth by concentrating multiple low-speed access links into a high-speed core link and using a combination of Layer 2 and Layer 3 switching to segment workgroups and isolate network problems to prevent them from impacting the core layer.

- This layer provides redundant connections for access devices. Redundant connections also provide the opportunity to load balance between devices.

- The distribution layer represents a routing boundary between the access and core layers. Routing and packet manipulation are also performed here.

- The distribution layer allows the core layer to connect diverse sites while maintaining high performance. To maintain good performance in the core, the distribution layer can redistribute between bandwidth-intensive access-layer routing protocols and optimized core routing protocols. Route filtering is also implemented at the distribution layer.

- The distribution layer can summarize routes from the access layer to improve routing protocol performance. For some networks, the distribution layer offers a default route to access-layer routers and only runs dynamic routing protocols when communicating with core routers.

- The distribution layer connects network services to the access layer and implements policies regarding security, traffic loading, and routing. For example, the distribution layer addresses different protocols' QoS needs by implementing policy-based traffic control to isolate backbone and local environments. Policy-based traffic control enables you to prioritize traffic to ensure the best performance for the most time-critical and time-dependent applications.

- The distribution layer is often the layer that delineates broadcast domains; however, this can also be done at the access layer.
- This layer provides any media transitions (for example, between Ethernet and ATM) that need to occur.

Policy-based Decisions

Policy-based decisions for controlling traffic can include the following:

- Filtering by source or destination address
- Filtering on input or output ports
- Hiding internal network numbers by route filtering
- Static routing rather than dynamic routing
- Security (for example, certain packets might not be allowed into a specific part of the network)
- QoS mechanisms (for example, the precedence and type of service [ToS] values in IP packet headers can be set in routers to leverage queuing mechanisms to prioritize traffic)

Distribution Layer Example

Figure 3-4 shows various features of the distribution layer.

Figure 3-4 *Example of Distribution Layer Features*

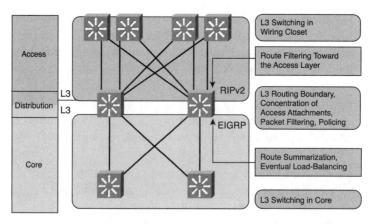

Following are the characteristics of the distribution layer in the routed campus network shown in Figure 3-4:

- Layer 3 switching is used toward the access layer.

- Layer 3 switching is performed in the distribution layer and extended toward the core layer.

- The distribution layer performs two-way route redistribution to exchange the routes between the Routing Information Protocol version 2 (RIPv2) and Enhanced Interior Gateway Routing Protocol (EIGRP) routing processes.

- Route filtering is configured on the interfaces toward the access layer.

- Route summarization is configured on the interfaces toward the core layer.

- The distribution layer contains highly redundant connectivity, both toward the access layer and toward the core layer.

Core Layer Functionality

This section describes core layer functions and the interaction of the core layer with the distribution layer.

The Role of the Core Layer

The function of the core layer is to provide fast and efficient data transport.

Characteristics of the core layer include the following:

- The core layer is a high-speed backbone that should be designed to switch packets as quickly as possible to optimize communication transport within the network.

- Because the core is critical for connectivity, core layer devices are expected to provide maximum availability and reliability. A fault-tolerant network design ensures that failures do not have a major impact on network connectivity. The core must be able to accommodate failures by rerouting traffic and responding quickly to changes in network topology. The core must provide a high level of redundancy. A full mesh is strongly suggested, and at least a well-connected partial mesh with multiple paths from each device is required.

- The core layer should not perform any packet manipulation, such as checking access lists and filtering, which would slow down the switching of packets.

- The core layer must be manageable.

- The core devices must be able to implement scalable protocols and technologies, alternate paths, and load balancing.

Design Consideration: Layer 2 Versus Layer 3 Switching in the Core

Network designers are faced with a decision about whether to implement Layer 2 switching (or bridging) or Layer 3 switching (or routing) in the core layer. Both approaches have substantial benefits and drawbacks.

The example in Figure 3-5 shows Layer 2 switching in the campus core.

Figure 3-5 *Layer 2 Switching in the Campus Core*

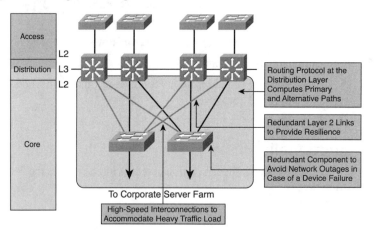

In Figure 3-5, a typical packet between access sites follows these steps:

Step 1 The packet is Layer 2-switched toward a distribution switch.

Step 2 The distribution switch performs Layer 3 switching toward a core interface.

Step 3 The packet is Layer 2-switched across the LAN core.

Step 4 The receiving distribution switch performs Layer 3 switching toward an access LAN.

Step 5 The packet is Layer 2-switched across the access LAN to the destination host.

Figure 3-6 shows Layer 3 switching in the LAN core.

Figure 3-6   *Layer 3 Switching in the Campus Core*

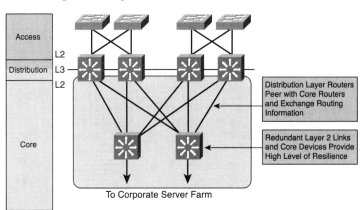

In Figure 3-6, a typical packet between access sites would follow these steps:

Step 1   The packet is Layer 2-switched toward a distribution switch.

Step 2   The distribution switch performs Layer 3 switching toward a core interface.

Step 3   The packet is Layer 3-switched across the LAN core.

Step 4   The receiving distribution switch performs Layer 3 switching toward an access LAN.

Step 5   The packet is Layer 2-switched across access the LAN to the destination host.

Because core devices are responsible for accommodating failures by rerouting traffic and responding quickly to network topology changes, and because performance for routing in the core with a Layer 3 switch incurs no cost, most implementations have Layer 3 switching in the core layer. The core layer can therefore more readily implement scalable protocols and technologies, alternate paths, and load balancing.

Using a Modular Approach to Network Design

This section discusses the Enterprise Composite Network Model and the basic functional areas and modules of an Enterprise network. It focuses on the design considerations both within a network module and between the modules.

NOTE   The access, distribution, and core layers can appear in each functional area of the Enterprise Composite Network Model.

Enterprise Composite Network Model

The Enterprise Composite Network Model is a blueprint, or framework, for designing networks. The modularity that is built into the model allows flexibility in network design and facilitates implementation and troubleshooting. Before introducing the model itself, an overview of the evolution of enterprise networks is provided.

Evolution of Enterprise Networks

We do not have to go far back in history to the time when networks were used primarily for file and print services. These networks were isolated LANs that were built throughout the enterprise organization. As organizations interconnected, these isolated LANs and their functionalities grew from file and print services to include critical applications; the critical nature and complexity of the enterprise networks also grew.

As discussed in the previous section, Cisco introduced the hierarchical model for network designers to divide the enterprise network design (separately for both campus and WAN networks) into access, distribution, and core layers.

This solution has several weaknesses, especially in large networks, that are difficult to implement, manage, and, particularly, troubleshoot. Networks became complex, and it was difficult to evaluate a network solution end-to-end through the network. The hierarchical model does not scale well to these large networks.

An efficient method of solving and scaling a complex task is to break the task into smaller, more specialized tasks. Networks can easily be broken down into smaller tasks because they have natural physical, logical, and functional boundaries. If they are sufficiently large to require additional design or operational separation, these specialized functional modules can then be designed hierarchically with the access, distribution, and core layers.

Enterprise Composite Network Model Overview

A modular model that reduces the enterprise network into further physical, logical, and functional boundaries has been introduced to scale the hierarchical model. Cisco calls this model the *Enterprise Composite Network Model.*

Rather than designing networks using only the hierarchical model, networks can be designed using this Enterprise Composite Network Model, with hierarchy (access, distribution, and core) included in the various modules, as required.

This Enterprise Composite model is not much different from what is already used in practice; the model formalizes current practice. There have always been separate hierarchies for the campus (with access, distribution and core) and for the WAN (the remote office was the access layer, the regional office, provided the distribution layer, and the headquarters was the core). The hierarchies were tied together at the campus backbone.

This model extends the concept of hierarchy from the original two modules—Campus and WAN—to all of the Enterprise Composite Network Model's required modules.

Following are the goals of the Enterprise Composite Network Model:

- A deterministic network with clearly defined boundaries between modules. The model has clear demarcation points. A network designer knows exactly what traffic is allowed into and out of these demarcation points.

- Ease of design and increased network scalability by using a "divide and conquer" method of problem solving, thereby resulting in smaller modules.

- Simplified scalability. Adding a building to the campus, a remote office to a WAN, or servers to the server farm becomes a simpler task.

Following are some of the benefits of the Enterprise Composite Network Model:

- The new model enables network designers to concentrate on each module and the relationships between the modules. There are clear boundaries with well-defined physical and logical entry points that provide clear locations for policy enforcement.

- This model provides additional integrity in network design, allowing the designer to evaluate any network solution (for example, IP telephony, Content Networking [CN], or storage networking) and any intelligent network service (such as security, QoS, or network management) with respect to each network module and in relation to the overall network infrastructure.

Functional Areas of the Enterprise Composite Network Model

Figure 3-7 illustrates the first layer of modularity in the Enterprise Composite Network Model.

Figure 3-7   *The Enterprise Composite Model Functional Areas*

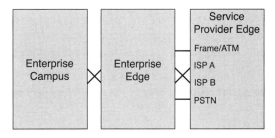

As shown in Figure 3-7, the basic idea in this model is the division of the entire network into functional components—functional areas that contain network modules—while still maintaining the hierarchical concept of the core-distribution-access layers within the network modules, as needed.

NOTE	Access, distribution, and core layers can appear in any functional area or module of the Enterprise Composite Network Model.

The Enterprise Composite Network Model comprises three major functional areas:

- **Enterprise Campus**—This functional area comprises the modules that are required to build a highly robust campus network in terms of reliability, availability, scalability, and flexibility. This area contains all the network elements for independent operation within one campus location. This functional area does not provide any remote connections or Internet access. An enterprise can have more than one campus.

- **Enterprise Edge**—This functional area aggregates the connectivity from the various elements at the edge of the Enterprise network. The Enterprise Edge functional area filters traffic from the edge modules and routes it into the Enterprise Campus. The Enterprise Edge contains all the network elements for efficient and secure communication between the Enterprise Campus and remote locations, business partners, mobile users, and the Internet.

- **Service Provider Edge**—The Service Provider Edge modules are included to enable communication with other networks using different WAN technologies and with Internet service providers (ISPs).

Key Point: Service Provider Edge

The Enterprise does not implement the modules in the Service Provider Edge functional area; they are necessary for enabling communication with other networks.

Figure 3-8 represents a more granular view of the modules within each functional area.

NOTE	Figure 3-8 is reproduced on the inside back cover of this book for your reference.

Each of these modules has specific requirements and performs specific roles in the network; however, their sizes are not meant to reflect their scale in a real network. For example, the Edge Distribution module in the Enterprise Campus represents the aggregation of devices at remote sites to access Enterprise Campus devices.

This model allows network designers to focus only on a selected module and its functions. Designers can describe each network solution and intelligent network service on a per-module basis and validate each as part of the complete enterprise network design.

Modules can be added to achieve scalability if necessary (for example, an organization can add more Enterprise Campus modules if it has more than one campus). The modules can also have submodules.

Figure 3-8   *The Functional Areas of the Enterprise Composite Network Model*

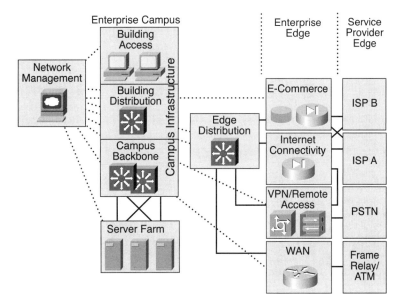

Guidelines for Creating an Enterprise Composite Network

When creating an Enterprise Composite Network, divide the network into Enterprise Campus and Enterprise Edge, where Enterprise Campus includes all devices and connections within one location and Enterprise Edge covers all communications with remote locations and the Internet. Define clear boundaries between the Enterprise Campus and Enterprise Edge networks.

The following sections provide additional details regarding each of the three functional areas and their modules.

Enterprise Campus Modules

This section introduces the Enterprise Campus functional area and describes the purpose of each module therein. It also discusses connections with other modules.

As illustrated in Figure 3-9 and in the following list, the Enterprise Campus functional area comprises four major modules:

- **Campus Infrastructure module**—The Campus Infrastructure module is composed of one or more buildings connected to a backbone. Each layer of the Campus Infrastructure module provides network redundancy and high availability. This module is comprised of three submodules: Building Access, Building Distribution, and Campus Backbone.

- **Network Management module**—The Network Management module supports security, monitoring, logging, troubleshooting, and other common management features from end to end.

- **Server Farm module**—A high-capacity, centralized Server Farm module provides users with internal server resources.

- **Edge Distribution module**—The Edge Distribution module provides connectivity between the Enterprise Campus and the Enterprise Edge.

Figure 3-9   *The Enterprise Campus Functional Area*

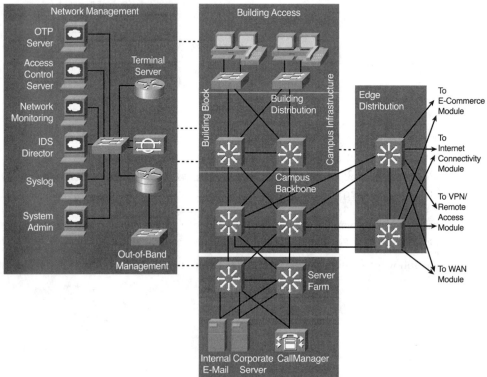

NOTE	The Campus Backbone submodule correlates to the traditional hierarchical model's LAN core layer.

The following sections detail each of the four Enterprise Campus modules.

Campus Infrastructure Module

The *Campus Infrastructure module* interconnects users within a campus with the Server Farm and Edge Distribution modules. This module is composed of one or more buildings connected to the Campus Backbone submodule. Each building contains Building Access and Building Distribution submodules. A Campus Backbone between buildings is added to scale from a building to the campus infrastructure. The Campus backbone also provides the Campus Infrastructure module with connectivity to the Edge Distribution and Server Farm modules.

The Campus Infrastructure module can be logically divided into the Building Block and the Campus Backbone.

Campus Infrastructure Building Block

The Campus Infrastructure design consists of several buildings (building blocks) that are connected across a Campus Backbone submodule.

Each building block contains two submodules:

- **Building Access**—Contains end-user workstations, IP phones, and Layer 2 access switches for connecting devices to the Building Distribution submodule. Building Access performs important services, such as broadcast suppression, protocol filtering, network access, and QoS marking.

- **Building Distribution**—Provides aggregation of the access networks using Layer 3 switching, routing, QoS, and access control. Requests for data flow into these switches, and onward into the Campus Backbone. Responses follow the reverse path. Redundancy and load balancing with the Building Access and Campus Backbone modules are recommended. For example, in Figure 3-9, each Building Distribution submodule has two equal-cost paths into the Campus Backbone. This provides fast failure recovery because each distribution Layer 3 switch maintains two equal-cost paths in its routing table to every destination network. When one connection to the Campus Backbone fails, all routes immediately switch over to the remaining path.

NOTE   In the most general model, the Building Access submodule uses Layer 2 switching, and the Building Distribution submodule uses Layer 3 switching.

Campus Infrastructure Campus Backbone

The Campus Backbone submodule of the Campus Infrastructure module provides redundant and fast-converging connectivity between buildings and with the Server Farm and Edge Distribution modules. It routes and switches traffic as quickly as possible from one module to another. This module usually uses Layer 3 switches for high throughput functions with added routing, QoS, and security features.

Network Management Module

The *Network Management module* performs intrusion detection, system logging, and Terminal Access Controller Access Control System Plus (TACACS+), Remote Authentication Dial-In User Service (RADIUS) and One Time Password (OTP) authentication, as well as network monitoring and general configuration management functions. For management purposes, you should have an out-of-band network (on which no production traffic travels) connection to all network components. For locations where this is impossible (because of geographic or system-related issues), the Network Management module uses the production network. The Network Management module should be designed to provide configuration management for devices in the network using a combination of the following two technologies:

- Cisco IOS routers can act as terminal servers to provide the console ports on the Cisco devices with a reverse-Telnet function throughout the enterprise.

- Devices can also be provided with a dedicated out-of-band connection for network management. This connection should provide more extensive management features (including software changes, content updates, log and alarm aggregation, and Simple Network Management Protocol [SNMP] management).

Server Farm Module

The *Server Farm module* contains internal e-mail and other corporate servers that provide internal users with application, file, print, e-mail, and Domain Name System (DNS) services. As shown in Figure 3-9, because access to these servers is vital, they are typically connected to two different switches to enable full redundancy and/or load sharing. Moreover, the Server Farm module switches are cross connected with the Campus Backbone switches, thereby enabling high reliability and availability of all servers in the Server Farm module.

Edge Distribution Module

The *Edge Distribution module* aggregates the connectivity from the various elements at the enterprise edge and routes the traffic into the Campus Backbone submodule. The Edge Distribution module acts as a boundary between the Enterprise Campus and the Enterprise Edge and is the last line of defense against external attacks. Its structure is similar to that of the Building Distribution submodule. While both modules use access control to filter traffic, the Edge Distribution module can rely on the entire Enterprise Edge functional area devices to perform additional security functions. Both modules use Layer 3 switching to achieve high performance, but the Edge Distribution module can add more security functions because the performance requirements are usually not as great.

NOTE   The Edge Distribution module's performance requirements are also not as high as the Server Farm, in which most of the traffic is concentrated.

Enterprise Campus Example

Figure 3-10 shows how a sample IP Telephony network solution uses all of the Enterprise Campus' modules.

Figure 3-10 *IP Telephony in the Enterprise Campus*

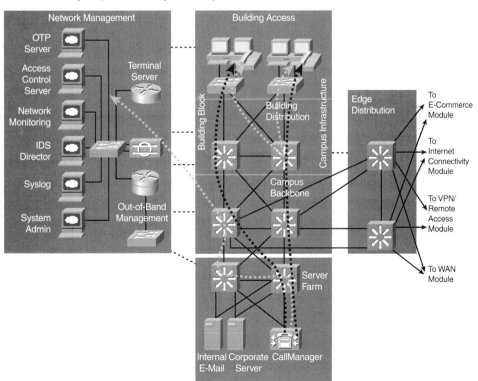

Figure 3-10 illustrates the steps for making a call with an IP phone. The IP phone on the top right of the Building Access submodule is calling the IP phone on the top left:

Step 1 The control session between the calling IP Phone and the CallManager is established. This session involves both the Campus Infrastructure and the Server Farm modules.

Step 2 The CallManager finds the called party (the other IP phone) and informs both parties about the new call.

Step 3 The voice session is established between the IP Phones. Note that this session requires communication only within the Building Distribution and Building Access submodules.

Step 4 A call detail record (CDR) is added in the CallManager or network accounting system (within the Network Management module).

Enterprise Campus Guidelines

Follow these guidelines for creating the modules within an Enterprise Campus functional area:

Step 1 Select modules within the campus that act as buildings with access and distribution layers.

Step 2 Determine the locations and the number of access switches and their uplinks to distribution layer switches.

Step 3 Select the appropriate distribution layer switches, taking into account the number of access layer switches and end-users. Use at least two distribution layer switches for redundancy.

Step 4 Consider two uplink connections from each access layer switch to the two distribution layer switches.

Step 5 Determine where servers are or will be located, and design the Server Farm module with at least two distribution layer switches that connect all servers for full redundancy.

Step 6 Design the Network Management module with out-of-band connections to all critical devices in the campus network.

Step 7 Determine the module within the campus that acts as an interface between the Enterprise Campus and Enterprise Edge functional area—this is the Edge Distribution module. Use distribution layer switches that are appropriate to the network's size, volume, and complexity.

Step 8 Implement the Edge Distribution module in a redundant manner.

Step 9   Design the Campus Infrastructure module's Campus Backbone submodule using at least two switches and accounting for the expected traffic volume between modules.

Step 10   Interconnect all modules of the Enterprise Campus with the Campus Infrastructure module's Campus Backbone submodule in a redundant manner.

Figure 3-11 shows how the Enterprise Campus can be divided into easily manageable building blocks: a Server Farm module, an Edge Distribution module, and a Campus Backbone. Note that the Enterprise Edge is reachable only through the Edge Distribution module.

Figure 3-11   *Enterprise Campus Example*

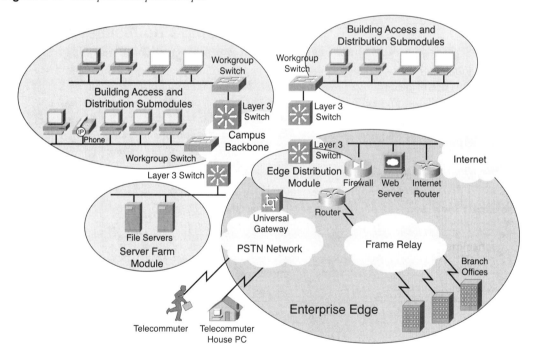

Enterprise Edge Modules

This section describes the components of the Enterprise Edge and explains the importance of each module. As shown in Figure 3-12 and in the following list, the Enterprise Edge functional area is comprised of four modules:

- **E-commerce module**—The E-commerce module includes the devices and services that are necessary for an organization to provide e-commerce applications.

- **Internet Connectivity module**—The Internet Connectivity module provides enterprise users with Internet access.

- **Virtual Private Network (VPN)/ Remote Access module**—The VPN/Remote Access module terminates VPN traffic and dial-in connections from external users.

- **WAN module**—The WAN module provides connectivity between remote sites and the central site over various WAN technologies.

Figure 3-12 *Enterprise Edge Functional Area*

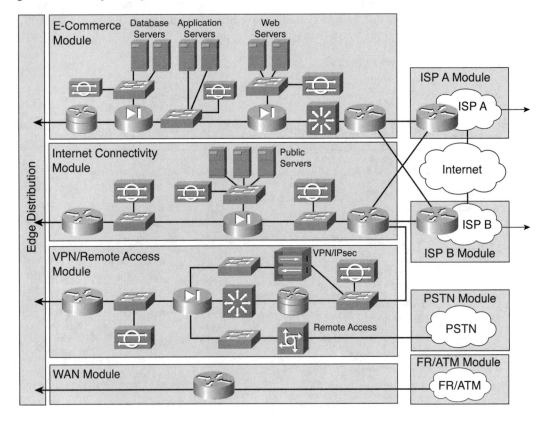

Each module connects to the Edge Distribution module, which provides connectivity between the Enterprise Edge and the Enterprise Campus. Connectivity on the other side of the Edge Distribution module is accomplished through different services and WAN technologies that are typically obtained from service providers.

The following sections detail each of the four modules.

E-commerce Module

The *E-commerce module* enables enterprises to successfully deploy e-commerce applications and take advantage of the opportunities the Internet provides. The majority of traffic is initiated external to the enterprise. All e-commerce transactions pass through a series of intelligent services that provide scalability, security, and high availability within the overall e-commerce network design. To build a successful e-commerce solution, enterprises need the following network devices:

* **Web servers**—Act as the primary user interface for e-commerce navigation.
* **Application servers**—Host the various applications.
* **Database servers**—Contain the application and transaction information that is the heart of the e-commerce business implementation.
* **A firewall or firewall routers**—Govern communication and provide security between the system's various users.
* **Network Intrusion Detection System (NIDS) appliances**—Monitor key network segments in the module to detect and respond to attacks against the network. (Examples of Cisco NIDS appliances include Cisco IDS 4210, 4235, and 4250.)
* **Layer 3 switch with Intrusion Detection System (IDS) modules**—Provide traffic transport and integrated security monitoring.

Internet Connectivity Module

The *Internet Connectivity module* provides internal users with connectivity to Internet services. Internet users can access the information on the public servers (for example, Hypertext Transfer Protocol [HTTP], file transfer protocol [FTP], Simple Mail Transfer Protocol [SMTP], and DNS). Internet session initiation is typically from inside the enterprise toward the Internet. Additionally, this module accepts VPN traffic from remote users and remote sites and forwards it to the VPN/Remote Access module, where VPN termination takes place. The Internet Connectivity module is not designed to serve e-commerce applications. Major components of the Internet Connectivity module include the following:

* **SMTP mail servers**—Act as a relay between the Internet and the intranet mail servers.
* **DNS servers**—Serve as the authoritative external DNS server for the enterprise and relay internal requests to the Internet.
* **Public servers (for example, FTP and HTTP)**—Provide public information about the organization. Each server on the public services segment contains host intrusion detection software to monitor against any rogue activity at the operating system level and in common server applications including HTTP, FTP, and SMTP.
* **Firewalls or firewall routers**—Provide network-level protection of resources, stateful filtering of traffic, and VPN termination for remote sites and users.

- **Layer 2 switches**—Ensure that data from managed devices can cross directly to the IOS firewall only.

- **Edge routers**—Provide basic filtering and Layer 3 connectivity to the Internet.

VPN/Remote Access Module

NOTE   The VPN/Remote Access module is sometimes called the *Remote Access and VPN module*.

The *VPN/Remote* Access module terminates VPN traffic, which the Internet Connectivity Module forwards, from remote users and remote sites. It also uses the Internet Connectivity module to initiate VPN connections to remote sites. Furthermore, the module terminates dial-in connections received through the PSTN and, after successful authentication, grants dial-in users access to the network. Major components of the VPN/ Remote Access module include the following:

- **Dial-in access concentrators**—Terminate dial-in connections and authenticate individual users.

- **VPN concentrators**—Terminate Internet Protocol Security (IPSec) tunnels and authenticate individual remote users.

- **Firewalls**—Provide network-level protection of resources and stateful filtering of traffic, provide differentiated security for remote access users, authenticate trusted remote sites, and provide connectivity using IPSec tunnels.

- **Layer 2 switches**—Provide Layer 2 device connectivity.

- **NIDS appliances**—Provide Layer 4 to Layer 7 monitoring of key network segments in the module.

WAN Module

The *WAN module* uses different WAN technologies for routing traffic between remote sites and the central site. In addition to traditional media (leased lines) and circuit-switched data link technologies (FR and ATM), the WAN module can also use more recent WAN physical layer technologies, including Synchronous Optical Network (SONET)/Synchronous Digital Hierarchy (SDH), cable, DSL, and wireless. This module can use all Cisco devices that support these WAN technologies, in addition to routing, access control, and QoS mechanisms.

Key Point: Enterprise Edge Provides Interfaces to the WAN

The Enterprise Edge does not include WAN connections or links; it only provides the interfaces to the WAN.

Enterprise Edge Guidelines

Follow these guidelines for creating the modules within the Enterprise Edge functional area:

Step 1   Determine which part of the edge is used exclusively for permanent connections to remote locations (branch offices), and assign it to the WAN module. All WAN devices supporting FR, ATM, cable, leased lines, SONET/SDH, and so on are located here.

Step 2   Determine the connections from the corporate network into the Internet and assign them to the Internet Connectivity module. The module should have security implemented to prevent any unauthorized access from the Internet to the internal network. The public web servers reside in this module or the E-commerce module when implemented.

Step 3   Design the VPN/Remote Access module if the enterprise requires VPN connections or dial-in for accessing the internal network from the outside world. Implement a security policy in this module; users should not be able to access the internal network directly without authentication and authorization. The VPN sessions use connectivity from the Internet Connectivity module.

Step 4   Create the E-commerce module (for business-to-business or business-to-customer scenarios) when customers or partners require Internet access to business applications and database servers. Deploy a high-security policy that allows customers to access predefined servers and services yet restricts all other operations.

Service Provider Edge Modules

Figure 3-13 shows the modules within the Service Provider Edge functional area. The enterprise itself does not implement these modules; however, they are necessary to enable communication with other networks and most often use different WAN technologies and ISPs. The modules within the Service Provider Edge functional area are as follows:

- Internet Service Provider module
- PSTN module
- Frame Relay/ATM module

Figure 3-13 *Service Provider Edge Functional Area*

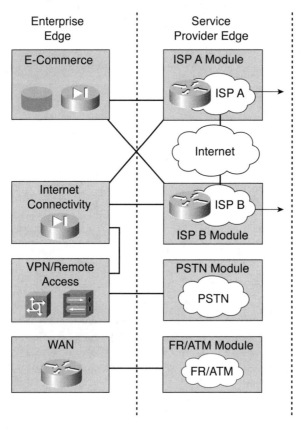

The following sections describe each of these modules.

Internet Service Provider Module

The *Internet Service Provider module* enables enterprise IP connectivity to the Internet. This service is essential for enabling Enterprise Edge services, such as those in the E-commerce, VPN/Remote Access, and Internet Connectivity modules. Enterprises can connect to two or more ISPs to provide redundant connections to the Internet. Physical connection between the ISP and the enterprise can come from any of the WAN technologies.

PSTN Module

The *PSTN module* represents the dialup infrastructure for accessing the Enterprise network using ISDN, analog, and wireless telephony (cellular) technologies. Enterprises can also use this infrastructure for backup of existing WAN links; WAN backup connections are generally established on demand and torn down after an idle timeout.

Frame Relay (FR)/ATM Module

The *Frame Relay/ATM module* covers all WAN technologies for permanent connectivity with remote locations. Traditional FR and ATM are still the most frequently used; however, many modern technologies, including the following, can fit into the same module:

- FR is a connection-oriented, packet-switching technology designed to efficiently transmit data traffic at data rates of up to those used by E3 and T3 connections. Its capability to connect multiple remote sites across a single physical connection reduces the number of point-to-point physical connections required to link sites.

NOTE   E3 is a European standard with a bandwidth of 34.368 megabits per second (Mbps). T3 is a North American standard with a bandwidth of 44.736 Mbps.

- ATM is an alternative to FR and supports higher speeds. It is a high-performance, cell-oriented, switching and multiplexing technology for carrying different types of traffic.
- Leased lines provide the simplest permanent point-to-point connection between two remote locations. The carrier company reserves point-to-point links for the customer's private use. Because the connection does not carry anyone else's communications, the carrier (service provider) can assure a given level of quality. The fee for the connection is a fixed monthly rate.
- SONET/SDH are standards for transmission over optical networks. Europe uses SDH; North America uses SONET, which is its equivalent.
- Cable technology uses existing coaxial cable TV (CATV) cables. Coupled with cable modems, this technology provides much greater bandwidth than telephone lines and can be used to achieve extremely fast access to the Internet or enterprise network.
- DSL is a modern technology that uses existing twisted-pair telephone lines to transport high-bandwidth data, such as voice, data, and video. DSL is sometimes referred to as *last-mile technology* because it is only used for connections from a telephone switching station (service provider) to a home or office, not between

switching stations. DSL is primarily used by telecommuters to access enterprise networks; however, more and more companies are using VPNs to migrate from traditional FR to DSL technology because of their cost-effectiveness.

- Wireless technology is another modern technology for interconnecting remote LANs. The point-to-point signal transmissions take place through the air over a terrestrial radio or microwave platform, rather than through copper or fiber cables. Fixed wireless requires neither satellite feeds nor local phone service. One of the advantages of fixed wireless is its capability to connect with users in remote areas without having to lay down new cables. However, this technology is limited to shorter distances, and weather conditions can degrade it.

- Multiprotocol Label Switching (MPLS) combines the advantages of Layer 3 routing with the benefits of Layer 2 switching. With MPLS, labels are assigned to each packet at the edge of the network. Rather than examining the IP packet header information, MPLS nodes use this label to determine how to process the data. This results in a faster, more scalable, more flexible WAN solution.

Service Provider Edge Guidelines

Follow these guidelines for proper use of Service Provider Edge modules:

- When connecting to the Internet, consider redundant connections to two service providers or two different connections to a single service provider.

- For mobile and remote users who require direct dialup access, choose ISDN, analog modem, or cellular wireless. These technologies provide speeds ranging from 9600 bits per second (bps) to 128 kilobits per second (kbps).

- For higher speeds (greater than or equal to T3/E3 rates), use ATM over SONET or SDH links. ATM might be available at rates as low as T1/E1. It might also be possible to use Packet over SONET when an enterprise can acquire access to dark fiber. (Dark fiber refers to unused fiber-optic cable. For example, a company might have installed more cable than it needed, so it leases the surplus to other companies.)

- When connecting to remote locations via the WAN module with speeds of less than or equal to T3/E3 rates, consider leased line and FR connections. Leased lines are typically cheaper for shorter distances (a few miles or kilometers); however, FR becomes competitive for greater distances. (FR is typically cheaper in the United States, regardless of circuit distance.) Not all service providers offer FR above T1/E1 rates.

- Because DSL brings considerable savings compared to the traditional WAN links, investigate whether it is a possible solution for a concentration of remote locations.

- Use cable connections only for telecommuters, since this technology does not provide any throughput guarantee.

NOTE   Chapter 5, "Designing WANs," discusses WANs in more detail.

Network Services and Solutions Within Modular Networks

Businesses that operate large enterprise networks seek an enterprise-wide infrastructure to serve as a solid foundation for emerging technology solutions such as IP telephony, content delivery, and storage.

This section presents the intelligent network services (such as security and high availability) and network solutions (such as voice transport or CN) within and between modules with respect to the modules that form the Enterprise Composite Network model.

Key Point: The Difference Between Network Solutions and Intelligent Network Services

An intelligent network service is a supporting, but necessary, service. For example, security and QoS are not ultimate services within the network; they are necessary to enable other services and applications. Therefore, security and QoS are not solutions, but intelligent network services. However, voice communication is an ultimate goal of the network and is therefore a network solution.

This section also provides examples of intelligent network services and solutions and illustrates how to map various services to appropriate network modules. Its main focus is to explain the relationship between network modules and describe how concentrating on each module's functions simplifies network design and deployment.

Intelligent Network Services in an Enterprise Composite Network Model

This section describes what the network designer must address when designing support for an intelligent network service in an Enterprise Composite Network Model.

Intelligent Network Services

Since the inception of packet-based communications, networks have always offered a forwarding service. Forwarding is the fundamental activity within an internetwork. In IP, this forwarding service was built on the assumption that end nodes in the network were intelligent, and that the network core did not have intelligence. With advances in networking software and hardware, the network can offer an increasingly rich, intelligent set of mechanisms for forwarding information. Intelligent network services essentially add intelligence to the network infrastructure, beyond simply moving a datagram between two points.

Through intelligent network classification, the network is able to distinguish and identify traffic based on application content and context. The classified traffic can be augmented with advanced network services to regulate performance, ensure security, facilitate delivery, and improve manageability. The intelligent network services allow for application awareness within the network.

Examples of intelligent network services include the following:

- **Network Management**—This service include: LAN management for advanced management of multilayer switches; routed WAN management for monitoring, traffic management, and access control to administer the routed infrastructure of multiservice networks; service management for managing and monitoring service-level agreements; and VPN/security management for optimizing VPN performance and security administration.

- **Security**—Ensures the security of the network through authentication, encryption, and failover. Security features include stateful, application-based filtering, defense against network attacks, per-user authentication and authorization, and real-time alerts.

- **High availability**—Ensures end-to-end availability for services, clients, and sessions. Implementation includes reliable, fault-tolerant network devices to automatically identify and overcome failures, and resilient network technologies.

- **QoS**—Manages the delay, delay variation (jitter), bandwidth availability, and packet loss parameters of a network to meet the diverse needs of voice, video, and data applications. QoS features provide value-added functionality, such as network-based application recognition (NBAR) for classifying traffic on an applications basis, a service assurance agent (SAA) for end-to-end QoS measurements, Resource Reservation Protocol (RSVP) signaling for admission control and reservation of resources, and a variety of configurable queue insertion and servicing functions.

- **IP multicasting**—Provides bandwidth-conserving technology that reduces network traffic by delivering a single stream of information intended for many corporate recipients and homes through the transport network. Multicasting enables distribution of videoconferencing, corporate communications, distance learning, software, and other applications. Multicast packets are replicated only as necessary by Cisco routers that are enabled with Protocol Independent Multicast (PIM) and other supporting multicast protocols that result in the most efficient delivery of data to multiple receivers.

To efficiently support network solutions, deploy the underlying intelligent network services in some or all modules of the enterprise network. Using a modular design, the network designers can create design elements (intelligent network services) on a module basis, as required by a network solution. These design elements can be replicated simply to other enterprise network modules as the network changes. Thus, modularization to small subsets of the overall network simplifies the network design and often reduces the network's cost and complexity.

Intelligent Network Services Example

Figure 3-14 shows a sample network solution that utilizes all modules of the Enterprise Campus and requires different intelligent network services for reliable and secure data transfer.

Figure 3-14 *Intelligent Network Services Example*

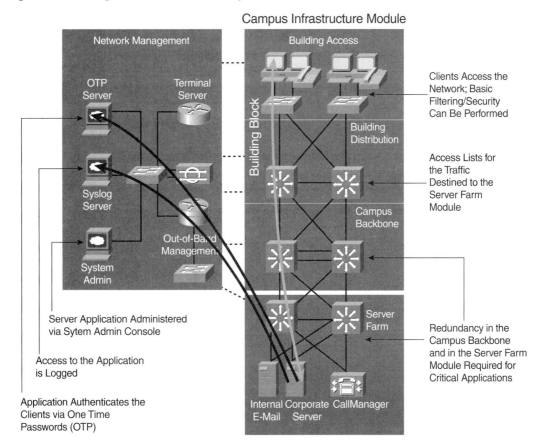

In this example, a client/server application has the following requirements with respect to the Enterprise Campus modules and submodules:

- At the Building Access submodule, the client application is granted controlled access to the network.

- At the Building Distribution submodule, the packet filtering ensures that the application data is forwarded to the Campus Backbone to reach the Server Farm module.

- The Campus Infrastructure module provides duplicate network links with fast convergence.

- In the Server Farm module, the application requires highly redundant connections to file servers.

- The Network Management module is also responsible for granting access to the Server Farm module (using static passwords, or one time passwords, which are described in the following section) and for monitoring and logging successful/ unsuccessful access to the application.

The following sections introduce two examples of intelligent network services—security and high availability—to provide an overview of how you can implement intelligent network services on top of a network infrastructure.

Security in Modular Network Design

Key Point: What is Security?

Security is a mandatory intelligent network service that addresses threats encountered in an enterprise network environment and increases the network's integrity by protecting network resources and users from these internal and external threats.

Understanding the Threats

Without a full understanding of the threats involved, network security deployments tend to be incorrectly configured, too focused on security devices, or lacking appropriate threat response options.

Security functions protect the network resources and users. You should consider security in the following two areas:

- In the Enterprise Campus (internal security)

- At the Enterprise Edge (from external threats)

It is essential to design security solutions in a layered and independent way. You should establish several layers of protection so that security functions at one layer or in one network module should not rely on the security function in other layers or modules.

Several reasons exist for strongly protecting the internal Enterprise Campus functional area by including security functions in each individual element of the Enterprise Campus:

- If the security established at the Enterprise Edge fails, an unprotected Enterprise Campus is vulnerable. Several security layers increase the protection of the Enterprise Campus, where the most strategic assets usually reside.

- A potential attacker could gain physical access to devices in the Enterprise Campus; however, relying on physical security is not enough.

- Often external access does not stop at the Enterprise Edge; some applications require at least an indirect access to the Enterprise Campus resources. Strong security must protect access to these resources.

Figure 3-15 shows how internal security can be designed into the Enterprise Composite Network Model.

Figure 3-15 *Designing Internal Security into the Network*

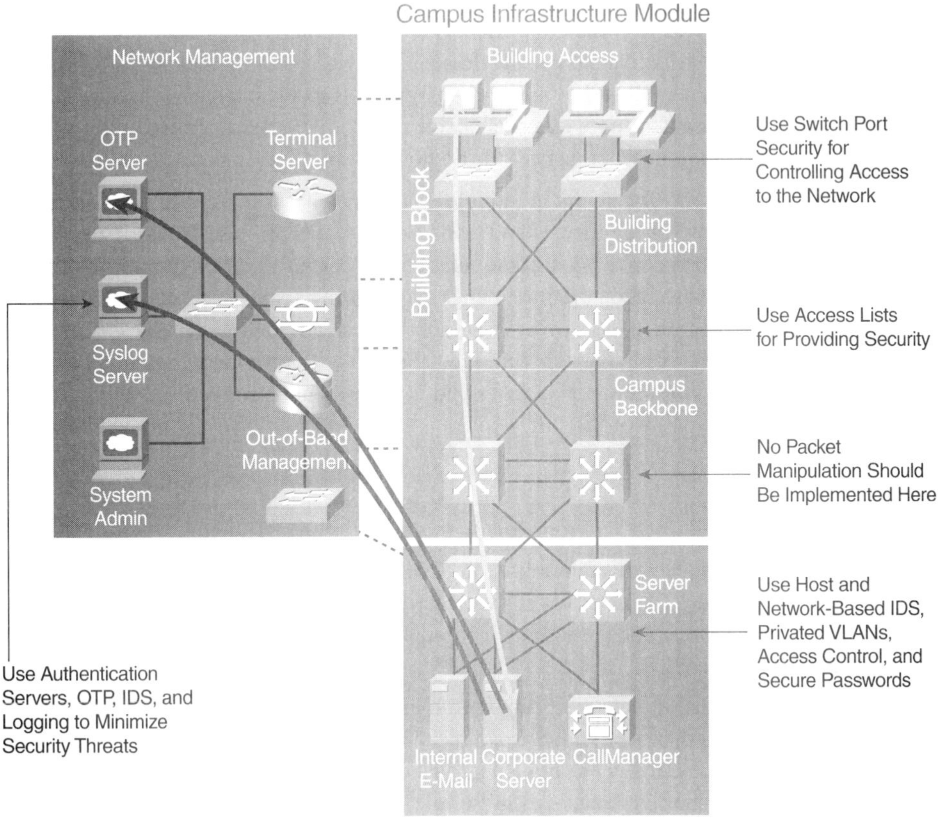

In Figure 3-15, internal security is designed into the Enterprise Campus functional area as follows:

- At the Building Access submodule, access is controlled at the port level using the data link layer information (media access control [MAC] addresses).

- The Building Distribution submodule performs filtering with the intent of keeping unnecessary traffic from the Campus Backbone. This packet filtering at the Building Distribution can be considered a security function in that it actually does prevent some undesired access to other modules. Given that switches in this submodule are Layer 3-aware (multilayer switches), the Building Distribution submodule is the first data path location in which filtering based on network layer information can be performed.

- The Campus Backbone submodule is a high-speed switching backbone and should be designed to switch packets as quickly as possible. This enterprise network module should not perform any security functions because they would slow down the switching of packets.

- The Server Farm module's primary goal is to provide application services to end users and devices. Enterprises often overlook the Server Farm module from a security perspective. Given the high degree of access most employees have to these servers, they can often become the primary goal of internally-originated attacks. Simply relying on effective passwords does not provide a comprehensive attack mitigation strategy. Using host- and network-based IDSs, private VLANs, and access control provides a much more comprehensive attack response. On-board IDS within the Layer 3 switches can inspect traffic flows on the Server Farm module.

- The Network Management module's primary goal is to facilitate the secure management of all devices and hosts within the enterprise architecture. From a security perspective, syslog provides important information regarding security violations and configuration changes by logging security-related events (authentication, and so on). An authentication, authorization, and accounting (AAA) security server also works with the OTP server to provide a high level of security to all local and remote users. AAA and OTP authentication reduces the likelihood of a successful password attack.

Intrusion Detection Systems (IDSs)

IDSs act like an alarm system in the physical world. When an IDS detects something it considers an attack, it can either take corrective action itself or notify a management system so an administrator can take action. Some systems are more or less equipped to respond and prevent such an attack.

Host-based intrusion detection can work by intercepting operating system (OS) and application calls on an individual host. It can also operate via after-the-fact analysis of local log files. While the former approach allows better attack prevention, the latter approach dictates a more passive attack-response role.

Because of their specific role, host-based IDS (HIDS) systems often more effectively prevent specific attacks than network IDS systems, which usually issue only an alert upon discovering an attack. However, this specificity causes loss of perspective to the overall network; this is the area in which NIDS excels.

Cisco recommends combining the two systems, with HIDS on critical hosts and NIDS looking over the whole network, for a complete intrusion detection system.

This information was derived from the SAFE White Paper: A Security Blueprint for Enterprise Networks, available at www.cisco.com/go/safe.

Authentication, Authorization, and Accounting

The three parts of AAA are defined as follows:

- **Authentication**—Authentication determines the users' identity and whether they should be allowed access to the network. Authentication allows network managers to bar intruders from their networks.

- **Authorization**—Authorization allows network managers to limit the network services that are available to each user.

- **Accounting**—System administrators might have to bill departments or customers for connection time or network resources used (such as bytes transferred). Accounting tracks this type of information. You can also use the accounting syslog to track suspicious connection attempts into the network and trace malicious activity.

This information was derived from Cisco Press' *Building Cisco Remote Access Networks (BCRAN)* by Catherine Paquet, 1999.

OTPs

OTPs are a common example of strong authentication. An OTP is a type of two-factor authentication, which involves using something you have combined with something you know. For example, automated teller machines (ATMs) use two-factor authentication—a customer needs both an ATM card and a personal identification number (PIN) to make transactions. With OTP, you need a PIN and your token card to authenticate to a device or software application. A token card is a hardware or software device that generates new, seemingly random passwords at specified intervals (usually 60 seconds). A user combines that random password with a PIN to create a unique password that works for only one instance of authentication. If a hacker learns that password by using a packet sniffer, the information is useless because the password has already expired.

This information was derived from the SAFE White Paper: A Security Blueprint for Enterprise Networks, available at www.cisco.com/go/safe.

External Threats

When designing security in an enterprise network, the Enterprise Edge is the first front where potential outside attacks can be stopped. The Enterprise Edge is like a wall with small doors and strong guards that efficiently control any access.

The following four attack methods are commonly used in attempts to compromise the integrity of the enterprise network from the outside:

- **IP spoofing**—An IP spoofing attack occurs when a hacker uses a trusted computer to launch an attack from inside or outside the network. The hacker can use either an IP address that is in the range of a network's trusted IP addresses, or an authorized external IP address that is trusted and provides access to specified resources on the network. IP spoofing attacks often lead to other types of attacks. For example, a hacker might launch a DoS attack using spoofed source addresses to hide his identity.

- **Password attacks**—Using a packet sniffer to determine usernames and passwords is a simple password attack; however, the term *password attack* usually refers to repeated brute-force attempts to identify username and password information. Trojan horse programs are another method that can be used to determine this information. (A hacker can also use IP spoofing as a first step in a system attack by violating a trust relationship that is based upon source IP addresses; however, first the system would have to be configured to bypass password authentication so that only a username is required.)

- **DoS attacks**—DoS attacks focus on making a service unavailable for normal use and are typically accomplished by exhausting some resource limitation on the network or within an operating system or application.

- **Application layer attacks**—Application layer attacks typically exploit well-known weaknesses in common software programs to gain access to a computer.

DoS

DoS attacks are different from most other attacks because they are not generally targeted at gaining access to your network or its information. These attacks focus on making a service unavailable for normal use and are typically accomplished by exhausting some resource limitation on the network or within an operating system or application.

When involving specific network server applications, such as a web server or an FTP server, these attacks can focus on acquiring and keeping open all the available connections supported by that server, thereby effectively locking out valid users of the server or service. DoS attacks can also be implemented using common Internet protocols, such as Transmission Control Protocol (TCP) and Internet Control Message Protocol (ICMP).

Rather than exploiting a software bug or security hole, most DoS attacks exploit a weakness in the overall architecture of the system being attacked. However, some attacks compromise your network's performance by flooding the network with undesired and often useless network packets, and by providing false information about the status of network resources. This type of attack is often the most difficult to prevent because it requires coordinating with your upstream network provider. If traffic meant to consume your available bandwidth is not stopped there, denying it at the point of entry into your network does little good because your available bandwidth has already been consumed. When this type of attack is launched from many different systems at the same time, it is often referred to as a distributed denial of service attack (DDoS).

This information was derived from the SAFE White Paper: A Security Blueprint for Enterprise Networks, available at www.cisco.com/go/safe.

Application Layer Attacks

A hacker can implement application layer attacks using several different methods. One of the most common methods is exploiting well-known software weaknesses that are commonly found on servers, such as sendmail, HTTP, and FTP. By exploiting these weaknesses, hackers can gain access to a computer with the permissions of the account that runs the application—usually a privileged system-level account. These application layer attacks are often widely publicized in an effort to allow administrators to rectify the problem with a patch. Unfortunately, many hackers also subscribe to these same mailing lists and therefore learn about the attack at the same time (if they have not discovered it already).

The primary problem with application-layer attacks is that they often use ports that are allowed through a firewall. For example, a hacker who executes a known vulnerability against a web server often uses TCP port 80 in the attack. A firewall needs to allow access on that port because the web server serves pages to users using port 80. From a firewall's perspective, it is merely standard port 80 traffic.

This information was derived from the SAFE White Paper: A Security Blueprint for Enterprise Networks, available at www.cisco.com/go/safe.

Figure 3-16 shows these four attack methods and how they relate to the modules of the Enterprise Edge functional area.

Figure 3-16 *Designing Against External Threats*

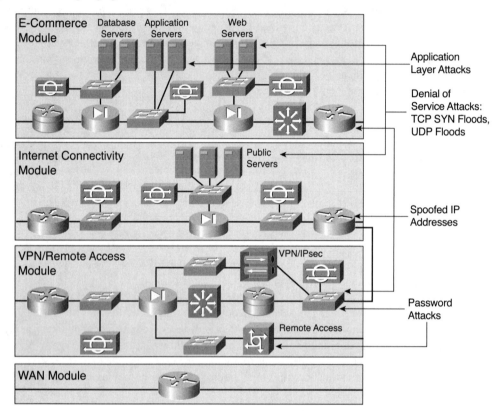

You must balance the ease of use of the network applications and resources against the security measures imposed on the network users.

Because of the complexity of network applications, access control must be extremely granular and flexible, yet still provide strong security. Tight borders between outside and inside cannot be defined because interactions are taking place between the Enterprise Edge and Enterprise Campus. The following are two examples of these interactions:

- Remote users use the WAN or Enterprise Edge's VPN/Remote Access modules to access the Enterprise Campus modules, including the Server Farm module.

- The data that is available to external users at the E-Commerce or Internet Connectivity modules of the Enterprise Edge includes data retrieved from internal servers that reside in the Server Farm module.

NOTE   Chapter 9, "Evaluating Security Solutions for the Network," covers security in the network in more detail.

High Availability in Modular Network Design

Most enterprise networks carry mission-critical information. Organizations that run such networks are usually interested in protecting the integrity of this information. Along with security, these organizations expect the internetworking platforms to offer a sufficient level of resilience.

This section introduces another intelligent network service: high availability. To ensure adequate connectivity for mission-critical applications, high availability is an essential component of an enterprise environment.

Designing High Availability into a Network

Redundant network designs let you meet requirements for high network availability by duplicating network links and devices. Redundancy eliminates the possibility of having a single point of failure on the network. The goal is to duplicate required components whose failure could disable critical applications.

Because redundancy is expensive to deploy and maintain, you should implement redundant topologies with care. Be sure to select a level of redundancy that matches your customer's requirements for availability and affordability. Because of its high cost, most network designers do not implement a completely redundant network often; instead, they implement partially redundancy.

Before you select redundant design solutions, analyze the business and technical goals to establish the required availability. Make sure that you identify critical applications, systems, internetworking devices, and links. Analyze the tolerance for risk and the consequences of not implementing redundancy. Be sure to discuss the tradeoffs of redundancy versus cost and simplicity versus complexity with your customer. Redundancy adds complexity to the network topology and to network addressing and routing.

When addressing the problem of network reliability, network designers must ensure that paths are redundant. It is not enough to simply duplicate all links. Unless all devices are completely fault-tolerant, dual links should terminate at multiple devices; otherwise, devices that are not fault-tolerant become single points of failure. You must take care both in selecting devices and provisioning the links between devices. Duplicate any component whose failure could disable critical applications.

NOTE   The Server Farm and a Campus Backbone are the most critical modules in the Enterprise Campus because all other modules access them. Therefore, they require higher availability than other modules.

The following types of redundancy can exist and be used in different modules of the Enterprise Network:

- Device redundancy, including card and port redundancy
- Redundant physical connections to critical workstations and servers
- Route redundancy
- Link redundancy

The following sections elaborate on each of these types of redundancy.

Key Point: Redundancy

The key requirement in redundancy is to provide alternative paths for mission-critical applications.

High availability is not ensured from end-to-end simply by making the backbone fault-tolerant. If communication on a local segment is disrupted for any reason, that information does not reach the backbone. High availability from end-to-end is only possible when redundancy is deployed throughout the internetwork.

High Availability in the Server Farm

The devices and connections in the Server Farm module require high availability. When a workstation or server has traffic to send to a station that is not local, the server or workstation must know the address of a router on its network segment. If that router fails, the workstation or server needs a mechanism to discover an alternative router. When network designers think about improving the reliability of critical workstations and servers, the solution usually depends on the workstation hardware and operating system software that is in use. Some common ways of connecting include the following:

- **Single attachment**—In this case, the workstation or server needs a Layer 3 mechanism to dynamically find an alternative router. The available mechanisms include address resolution protocol (ARP), Router Discovery Protocol (RDP), routing protocols (such as Routing Information Protocol [RIP]), or Hot Standby Router Protocol (HSRP). The Virtual Router Redundancy Protocol (VRRP) is also used in a VPN environment.

- **Attachment through a redundant transceiver**—Physical redundancy with a redundant transceiver attachment is suitable in environments where the workstation hardware or software does not support redundant attachment options.

- **Attachment through redundant network interface cards (NICs)**—Some environments (for example, most UNIX servers) support a redundant attachment through dual NICs (primary and backup) that the device driver represents as a single interface to the operating system.

- **EtherChannel port bundles**—Fast EtherChannel and Gigabit EtherChannel port bundles group multiple Fast or Gigabit Ethernet ports into a single, logical transmission path between a switch and a router, host, or another switch. The switch distributes frames across the ports in an EtherChannel according to the source and destination MAC addresses. If a port within an EtherChannel fails, traffic previously carried over the failed port switches to the remaining ports within the EtherChannel. The Spanning-Tree Protocol (STP) treats this EtherChannel as one logical link.

Router Discovery

When a workstation has traffic to send to a station that is not local, the workstation has many possible ways of discovering the address of a router on its network segment, including the following:

- **ARP**—Some IP workstations send an ARP frame to find a remote station. A router running proxy ARP can respond with its data link layer address. Cisco routers run proxy ARP by default.

- **Explicit configuration**—Most IP workstations must be configured with a default router's IP address. This is sometimes called the *default gateway*.

  In an IP environment, the most common method for a workstation to find a server is by explicitly configuring a default router. If the workstation's default router becomes unavailable, you must reconfigure the workstation with a different router's address. Some IP stacks enable you to configure multiple default routers, but many IP stacks do not support redundant default routers.

- **RDP**—RFC 1256, *ICMP Router Discovery Messages*, specifies an extension to ICMP that allows an IP workstation and router to run RDP to facilitate the workstation in learning a router's address. With RDP, each router periodically multicasts a Router Advertisement from each of its multicast interfaces, thereby announcing the IP address of that interface. Hosts discover the addresses of their neighboring routers simply by listening for advertisements. When a host that is attached to a multicast link starts up, it can multicast a Router Solicitation to ask for immediate advertisements rather than waiting for the next periodic ones to arrive.

- **Routing protocol**—An IP workstation can run RIP to learn about routers. RIP should be used in passive mode rather than active mode. (*Active mode* means that the station sends RIP packets every 30 seconds; *passive mode* means that the station just listens for RIP packets but does not send any.) The Open Shortest Path First (OSPF) protocol also supports a workstation that runs that routing protocol.

- **HSRP**—Cisco's HSRP provides a way for IP workstations to continue communicating on the internetwork even if their default router becomes unavailable. The HSRP works by creating a phantom router that has its own IP and MAC addresses. The workstations use this phantom router as their default router.

  HSRP routers on a LAN communicate among themselves to designate two routers as active and standby. The active router sends periodic hello messages. The other HSRP routers listen for the hello messages. If the active router fails and the other HSRP routers stop receiving hello messages, the standby router takes over and becomes the active router. Because the new active router assumes the phantom's IP and MAC addresses, end nodes do not see any change at all. They continue to send packets to the phantom router's MAC address, and the new active router delivers those packets.

  HSRP also works for proxy ARP. When an active HSRP router receives an ARP request for a node that is not on the local LAN, the router replies with the phantom router's MAC address rather than its own. If the router that originally sent the ARP reply later loses its connection, the new active router can still deliver the traffic.

- **VRRP**—VRRP operates in a VPN environment where two or more VPN concentrators are connected in parallel. VRRP provides redundancy over the VPN tunnel by dynamically assigning one of the VPN Concentrators on a LAN as the LAN's virtual router, which is called the Master. This Master controls the IP addresses that are associated with the virtual router and forwards packets that are sent to those IP addresses. If the Master becomes unavailable, a backup VPN Concentrator takes its place.

Figure 3-17 shows a server-to-switch connection that is implemented with a redundant transceiver.

Figure 3-17 *Physical Redundancy: Redundant Transceiver*

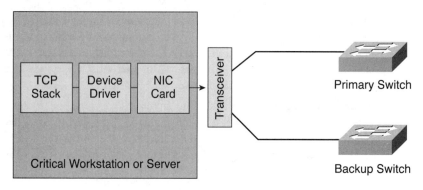

The redundant transceiver has two uplink ports that are usually connected to two access switches. The transceiver activates the backup port after it detects a link failure (carrier loss) on the primary port. The redundant transceiver can only detect physical layer failures; it cannot detect failures inside the switch or failures beyond the first switch. This type of redundancy is most often implemented on servers.

In Figure 3-18, the installation of an additional interface card in the server provides redundancy.

Figure 3-18 *Physical Redundancy: Redundant NICs*

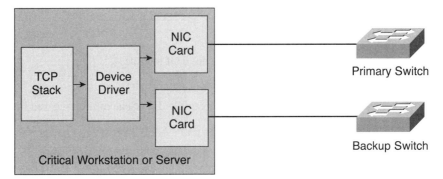

In this case, the device driver presents the configured NIC cards as a single interface (one IP address) to the operating system. If the primary link dies, the backup card is activated. The two NICs might use a common MAC address, or they might use two distinct MAC addresses and send gratuitous ARP messages to provide proper IP-to-MAC address mapping on the switches when the backup interface card is activated.

NOTE   The workstation sends gratuitous ARP messages to update the ARP tables and the forwarding tables on attached neighboring nodes (in this example, the Layer 2 switches).

Designing Route Redundancy

Designing redundant routes has two purposes:

- To minimize the effect of link failures
- To minimize the effect of an internetworking device failure

Redundant routes can also allow load balancing to occur when all routes are up.

Load Balancing

Most IP routing protocols can load balance across up to six parallel links that have equal cost. Use the **maximum-paths** command to change the number of links the router will load balance over for IP; the default is four, and the maximum is six. (Some versions of the IOS can support up to eight paths; however, the IOS documentation still indicates that the maximum is six paths.) To support load balancing, keep the bandwidth consistent within a layer of the hierarchical model so that all paths have the same cost. (Cisco's IGRP and EIGRP are exceptions because they can use a feature called variance to load balance traffic across multiple routes that have different metrics.)

Possible ways to make the connection redundant include

- Parallel physical links between switches and routers
- Backup LAN and WAN links (for example, DDR backup for a leased line)

Following are possible ways to make the network redundant:

- A full mesh to provide complete redundancy and good performance
- A partial mesh, which is less expensive and more scalable

The common approach in designing route redundancy is to implement partial redundancy (using a partial mesh instead of a full mesh, and backup links to the alternative device) by protecting only the most vital points of the network, such as the links between the layers and devices.

A full-mesh design forms any-to-any connectivity and is ideal for connecting a reasonably small number of devices. However, as the network topology grows, the number of links required to maintain a full mesh increases exponentially. (The number of links in a full mesh is $n(n-1)/2$, where n is the number of routers.) As the number of router peers increases, the bandwidth and CPU resources devoted to processing broadcast routing updates and service requests increase.

A partial-mesh network is similar to the full-mesh network with some of its trunks removed. The partial-mesh backbone is appropriate for a campus network, in which the traffic predominantly goes into one centralized Server Farm module.

Figure 3-19 shows route redundancy that is implemented in the Campus Infrastructure.

In this example, the access network is fully meshed with the distribution switches. If a link or distribution switch fails, an access layer switch can still communicate with the distribution layer.

The routers (Layer 3 switches) select the primary and backup paths between the access and distribution layers based on the link's cost as computed by the routing protocol algorithm. The best path is placed in the forwarding table, and, in the case of equal paths, load sharing takes place.

Figure 3-19 *Campus Infrastructure Redundancy Example*

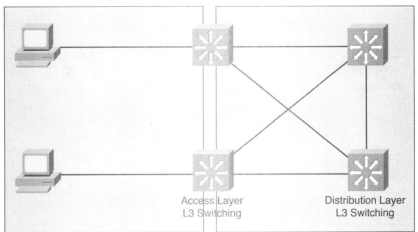

Access Layer
L3 Switching

Distribution Layer
L3 Switching

NOTE   Chapter 7, "Selecting Routing Protocols for a Network," discusses routing protocols in detail.

Designing Link Redundancy

It is often necessary to provision redundant media in mission-critical applications.

In switched networks, switches can have redundant links to each other. This is good because it minimizes downtime, but it can result in broadcasts continuously circling the network in what is called a broadcast storm. Because Cisco switches implement the IEEE 802.1d spanning tree algorithm, this broadcast storm can be avoided (by the Spanning Tree Protocol). The spanning tree algorithm guarantees one, and only one, active path between two network stations. The algorithm permits redundant paths that are automatically activated when the active path experiences problems.

Because WAN links are often critical pieces of the internetwork, redundant media is often deployed in WAN environments.

Figure 3-20 shows link redundancy implemented in the Enterprise Edge.

Figure 3-20 *Enterprise Edge Link Redundancy*

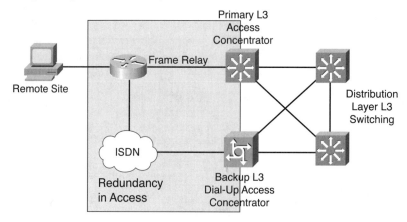

In this example, the remote site establishes a backup connection via the ISDN backup interface.

Network designers can provision backup links so that they are always on, or so that they only become active when a primary link goes down or becomes congested.

As is the case in Figure 3-20, where a Frame Relay circuit is used in parallel with a backup ISDN circuit, the backup links can use different technologies. It is important to provide sufficient capacity to meet the requirements.

Backup Links

Backup links often use a different technology. For example, a leased line can be parallel with a backup dialup line or ISDN circuit. By using what are called *floating static routes*, you can specify that the backup route has a higher administrative distance (used by Cisco routers to select which routing information to use), so it is not normally used unless the primary route goes down.

When provisioning backup links, learn as much as possible about the actual physical circuit routing. Different carriers sometimes use the same facilities, meaning that your backup path is susceptible to the same failures as your primary path. You should do some investigative work to ensure that your backup really is a backup.

You can combine backup links with load balancing and channel aggregation. *Channel aggregation* means that a router can bring up multiple channels (such as ISDN B channels) as bandwidth requirements increase.

Cisco supports the Multilink Point-to-Point Protocol (MPPP) (also referred to as *MLP*), which is an Internet Engineering Task Force (IETF) standard for ISDN B channel (or asynchronous serial interface) aggregation. MPPP does not specify how a router should accomplish the decision-making process to bring up extra channels. Instead, it seeks to ensure that packets arrive in sequence at the receiving router. Then, the data is encapsulated within PPP and the datagram is given a sequence number. At the receiving router, PPP uses this sequence number to recreate the original data stream. Multiple channels appear as one logical link to upper-layer protocols.

Network Solutions in an Enterprise Composite Network Model

This section describes the issues the network designer must address when designing a network solution in an Enterprise Composite Network Model.

Network Solutions

The network infrastructure and the intelligent network services on top of it provide the platform on which network designers implement network solutions (or overlay solutions).

Key Point: What is a Network Solution?

A network solution is a network-based application that runs over the network architecture.

Examples of network solutions include the following:

- Voice transport, including Voice over IP (VoIP) and IP telephony
- IP videoconferencing
- Content networking
- Storage networking

Most network solutions span the entire enterprise network, which is aware of the solutions that are overlaid on top of it. The requirements imposed by the solution vary from network module to module.

The network designer must focus on the specific functions a network solution requires within a specific network module. Such focusing simplifies the design problem. On the other hand, focusing on an individual module and its specific functions means that the designer must specify the required interfaces to other modules.

Using a hierarchical design simplifies the design problem and can facilitate changes. Modularity in network design allows network designers to create design elements that they can replicate as the network grows. Then, as each element in the network design requires change, the cost and complexity of making the upgrade is constrained to a small subset of the overall network.

From the user perspective, the entire enterprise network is an integrated platform on which the network solution is implemented; the users do not see the modularity. The integrity of the deployed solution must also be maintained from the network design perspective.

The following sections introduce two examples of network solutions: IP telephony and Content Networking. They provide an overview of how you can implement a network solution on top of a network infrastructure.

Voice Transport in Modular Network Design

Voice is a typical network solution that runs as an overlay service on the enterprise network. To ensure successful implementation of voice solutions, network designers must consider the enterprise infrastructure. Before adding voice to the network, the data network must be properly configured. After ensuring that the data network is operating properly, you can implement the network design or redesign to enable voice and data to use the common infrastructure.

Two Voice Implementations

Voice transport is a general term that can be divided into the following two implementations:

- **VoIP**—VoIP uses voice-enabled routers to convert analog voice into IP packets or packetized digital voice channels, and route those packets between corresponding locations. Users do not often notice that VoIP is implemented in the network—they use their traditional phones, which are connected to the Private Branch Exchange (PBX). However, the PBX is not connected to the PSTN or to another PBX, but to a voice-enabled router that is an entry point to VoIP. Voice-enabled routers can also terminate IP telephones using Session Initiation Protocol (SIP) for call control and signaling.

- **IP telephony**—For IP telephony, traditional phones are replaced with IP phones. Cisco CallManager, which is a server for call control and signaling, is also used. The IP phone itself performs voice-to-IP conversion, and no voice-enabled routers are required within the enterprise network. It is usually necessary to design and implement QoS services through the transport network. If connection to the PSTN is required, add a voice-enabled router or other gateway in the Enterprise Edge, where calls are forwarded to the PSTN.

Both implementations require properly designed networks that suit these applications. Using a modular approach in a voice network design is especially important because of the voice sensitivity to delay and the complexity of troubleshooting voice networks. All Enterprise Network modules are involved in the voice network solution.

IP Telephony Components

The IP telephony network contains four main voice-specific components:

- **IP phones**—IP phones support the placing of calls in an IP telephony network. They perform voice-to-IP (and vice versa) coding and compression using special hardware. IP phones offer IP phone services such as user directory lookups and Internet access for stock quotes. The phones are active network devices and require power to operate. A network (LAN) connection typically provides the power; however, an option for an external power supply also exists.

- **Switches with inline power**—Switches with inline power enable the modular wiring closet infrastructure to provide centralized power for Cisco IP telephony networks. These switches are similar to traditional switches, with an added option to provide power to LAN ports where IP phones are connected. They also perform some basic QoS mechanisms, such as packet classification, which is a baseline for prioritizing voice through the network.

- **Call-processing manager**—The call-processing manager (CCM) provides central call control and configuration management for IP phones. CCM provides the core functionality to bootstrap IP telephony devices and to perform call setup and call routing throughout the network. CCM supports clustering, which provides a distributed scalable and highly available IP telephony model. (Clustering allows you to add more capacity to the system by simply adding additional servers to the cluster of servers.)

- **Voice gateway**—Voice gateways, which are also called *voice-enabled routers* or *switches*, provide voice services such as voice-to-IP coding and compression, PSTN access, IP packet routing, backup call processing, and voice services. Backup call processing allows voice gateways to take over call processing in case the primary call-processing manager goes offline for any reason. Voice gateways typically support a subset of the call-processing functionality that is supported by CCM.

These components are located in different modules of the Enterprise Network.

Modular Approach in Voice Network Design

Enterprises that want to deploy new network solutions, such as IP telephony, on their networks face new design challenges. They must deploy a delay-sensitive overlay solution from end-to-end in all enterprise network modules.

To simplify design, implementation, and especially troubleshooting, you should use the modular approach. IP telephony implementation requires some modifications to the existing enterprise network infrastructure in terms of performance, capacity, and availability. IP telephony is an end-to-end solution with clients (IP phones) located in the Building Access submodule, and the call-processing manager (CallManager) located in the

Server Farm module. Therefore, all modules in the enterprise network are involved in voice processing and must be adequately considered.

Voice affects the various modules of the network as follows:

- **Building Access submodule**—IP phones and user computers are attached to Layer 2 switches here. Switches provide the IP phones with power. They also provide packet classification, which is essential for proper voice packet manipulation through the network.

- **Building Distribution submodule**—With its Layer 2 or Layer 3 switches, this submodule performs packet reclassifications if the Building Access submodule is unable to perform packet classifications. It concentrates access layer switches (wiring closets) and provides redundant uplinks to the Campus Backbone.

- **Campus Backbone submodule**—The Campus Backbone forms the network's core. All enterprise network modules are attached to it; therefore, virtually all traffic between application servers and clients traverses the Campus Backbone. Fast packet switching is this submodule's focus. With the advent of wire-speed Layer 3-gigabit switching devices, LAN backbones have migrated to switched gigabit architectures, which combine all the benefits of routing with wire-speed packet forwarding.

- **Server Farm module**—This module is composed of Layer 3 switches and CallManagers. Because CallManagers are the heart of IP telephony, redundant links and CallManagers are essential for providing high availability and reliability.

- **Enterprise Edge**—The Enterprise Edge can extend IP telephony from the Enterprise Campus to remote locations via WANs, the PSTN, and the Internet.

Figure 3-21 shows the voice network solution in the Enterprise Composite Network Model. It illustrates how a call is initiated on an IP phone, how the call setup goes through the CallManager, and how the end-to-end session between two IP phones is established. Note that CallManager is only involved in the call setup.

Calls destined for remote locations traverse the Enterprise Edge through the WAN or VPN/Remote Access module. (Calls destined for public phone numbers on the PSTN are routed over the Enterprise Edge through the VPN/Remote Access module.) Calls between IP phones traverse the Building Access, Building Distribution, Campus Backbone, and Server Farm modules. While call setup uses all of these modules, speech employs only Building Access, Building Distribution, and, in some cases, the Campus Backbone.

Figure 3-21 *Voice Network Solution Example*

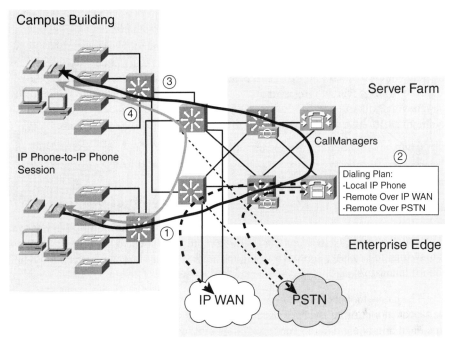

Evaluating the Existing Data Infrastructure for Voice Design

When designing IP telephony, designers must document and evaluate the existing data infrastructure in each enterprise module to help determine upgrade requirements for the IP telephony solution. Items to consider include the following:

- **Performance**—Designers might need to provide infrastructure for additional bandwidth, consistent performance, or higher availability, if required, for the converging environment. The information necessary for evaluating performance includes network maps, device inventory information, and network baseline information. Analyzing this information helps the designer understand the data network upgrade requirements needed to support IP telephony. Links and devices should have sufficient capacity for the additional voice traffic. Links with high peak or busy-hour use might need to be upgraded. Target devices for additional inspection and potential upgrades are those with high CPU use, high backplane use, high memory use, queuing drops, or buffer misses.

- **Availability**—Designers should review the redundancy capabilities in all network modules to ensure that they can meet the availability goals recommended for IP telephony with the current network design (or a new design).

- **Features**—Examine the router and switch characteristics, including the chassis, module, and software version. This evaluation proves useful for determining IP telephony feature capabilities in the existing environment.

- **Capacity**—Evaluate overall network capacity and the impact of IP telephony on a module-by-module basis. This activity ensures that the network meets capacity requirements and that there is not an adverse impact on the existing network and application requirements.

NOTE   Chapter 8, "Designing Networks for Voice Transport," covers voice in detail.

Content Networking in the Modular Network Design

Traditional networks handled static web pages, e-mail, and routine client/server traffic. Today, enterprise networks must handle more sophisticated types of network applications that include voice and video; examples include voice transport, videoconferencing, online training, audio and video broadcasts, and so on.

The large amount of data and its variety requires that the modern network be *content-aware*. In other words, be aware of the content carried across it to optimally handle that content. It is no longer enough to simply add more bandwidth as needs grow. Networks have had to become smarter.

Content Delivery Network (CDN) and Content Networking (CN)

A *Content Delivery Network (CDN)* is a collection of comprehensive architectures and technologies for optimizing website performance and other content delivery. *Content Networking (CN)* adds a layer of intelligence between the fundamental network functions and the applications requested by the users. The goal of CN is to ensure that, transparent to the user, the network serves content with optimal resource usage.

With CN, the network itself manages several functions that the hosts (servers and clients) typically perform. Dedicated network devices store, forward, route, and perform load sharing for the content.

CN is considered a network solution and, as such, it requires proper support by intelligent network services. In addition to security and QoS, CN requires IP multicasting for efficient content delivery.

The types of applications in use affect the choice of CN technology and the required devices. For example, individual online training often uses video on demand (VoD), which is normally done in a unicast manner. On the other hand, corporate announcements are of a broadcast nature and can be efficiently delivered using a multicast technology such as Internet Protocol Television (IP/TV).

Content Delivery Functions

CN offers accelerated content delivery, hosting, and other content-based services. It addresses the need to distribute and receive high-bandwidth, media-rich content across the Internet or an intranet, without performance losses or content delivery delays.

Content Networks typically have three functions:

- **Content caching**—Content caching stores select content from origin servers and delivers specific content to the requesting user. Today, content engines handle static and streaming media content. In the future, dynamic database content and applications will also be cached. Content caching can be present in any network module.

- **Content routing**—Content routing directs a user request to the optimal resource within a global network based on user-defined policies such as rules for specific content, availability of content, network health, current loads for web servers or caches, and various other network conditions. Content routing can be present in any network module.

- **Content switching**—Content switching provides a robust front end for web server farms and cache clusters by performing important functions such as load balancing of user requests across web server farms, policy-based web traffic direction based on full visibility of Uniform Resource Locators (URLs), and so on. Content switching is typically present in the Campus Backbone, Server Farm, E-commerce, and Internet Connectivity modules.

You must manage content delivery in the enterprise network to ensure that it moves to proper places in the network and that the entire network's content is fresh. A management tool is also needed for configuring and monitoring CN devices. The content distribution is managed in the Network Management module.

The following sections expand upon each of these three CN functions.

Content Caching

Content caches (such as the Cisco Content Engine) accelerate content delivery for end users by transparently caching frequently-accessed content and then locally fulfilling content requests rather than traversing the Internet or intranet to a distant server. This solution protects the enterprise network from uncontrollable bottlenecks and accelerates the delivery of content, thereby enabling enterprise employees to be more productive. Caches must store the most needed and most current data.

Figure 3-22 shows how the content caching mechanism works.

Figure 3-22 *Content Caching*

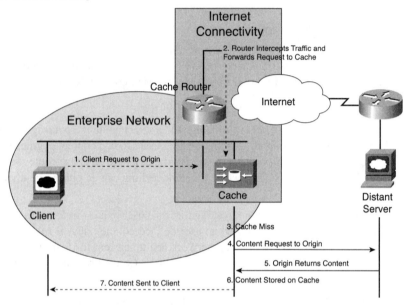

Figure 3-22 illustrates the following steps:

Step 1 A client requests content from an Internet site.

Step 2 The content router intercepts this request and forwards it to the content cache.

Step 3 In this example, the requested content is not in the cache; therefore, causing a cache miss. If the content were in the cache, this process would skip to Step 7.

Step 4 The content cache requests the content from the Internet.

Step 5 The distant server sends the content to the cache.

Step 6 The cache stores the content.

Step 7 The cache sends the content to the client.

Deployment of Content Caches   Content caches can be deployed hierarchically at enterprise branch offices (within an Enterprise Edge) and at the central site (in the Internet Connectivity module) to provide optimal network response times. Caching at the central site reduces Internet access bandwidth consumption. Caching at the branch office reduces bandwidth consumption and improves response time for Internet and intranet connectivity.

NOTE   The placement of network caches is very sensitive. The designer must identify the content to be cached and the major traffic streams and directions before selecting the cache locations.

Benefits of Content Caching   By caching streaming media and web content, you minimize redundant network traffic that traverses WAN links. As a result, WAN bandwidth costs either decrease or grow less quickly. This bandwidth optimization increases network capacity for additional users and traffic and for new services, such as voice. Typical bandwidth savings range from 25 to 60 percent.

Because of content caching, employees can improve their productivity by retrieving content more quickly. The benefits include accelerated content delivery, WAN bandwidth savings, and protection against uncontrollable bottlenecks—all resulting in higher productivity.

Content Routing

As the number of users accessing content on the network grows, it becomes increasingly difficult to provide a high level of availability and rapid response from a single location. Content routing between multiple locations solves this problem.

Content routing ensures the fast delivery of content, regardless of location, and provides high availability and server response.

Figure 3-23 shows how content routing works.

Figure 3-23 *Content Routing*

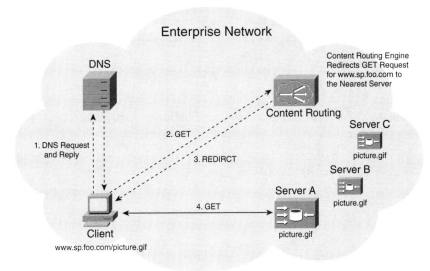

Content routing redirects an end-user's request to the best server based on a set of metrics such as delay, topology, and server load, and a set of policies such as location of content. This network feature enables the accelerated delivery of web content and streaming media. Content routing uses two methods: DNS server lookup and HTTP redirects.

For example, the following steps occur in Figure 3-23:

Step 1 The client requests a picture from a website: www.sp.foo.com/
picture.gif. The client sends a DNS request for this website to the DNS server and receives a DNS reply with the server's IP address.

Step 2 The client sends a request to the server's IP address.

Step 3 The content router intercepts this request and sends a redirect to the client, indicating the IP address of the server the client should contact.

Step 4 The client contacts that server and receives the picture that was requested.

NOTE It is extremely important for the network designer to know the applications used in the network. Proper setting of the content routers and DNS servers requires an extremely good understanding of the applications' behavior.

Content Switching

Content switching is a new generation of networking that is specifically designed to address the unique requirements of web traffic (thus, it is sometimes referred to as *web switching*). Content switching intelligently performs load balancing of traffic across multiple servers or cache devices on the basis of the content's availability and the load on the server or cache device. Content switching occurs at the application layer.

Figure 3-24 shows how content switching works.

Content switches have sophisticated load-balancing capabilities and content-acceleration intelligence. The result is a consistently positive experience for website users.

You can install content switches in front of the servers or cache devices in any Server Farm module, E-commerce module, or Internet Connectivity module.

Figure 3-24 *Content Switching*

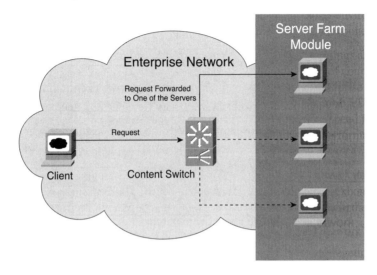

Content Networking Example

Figure 3-25 shows how and where enterprises can implement CN in the Enterprise Composite Network Model.

Figure 3-25 *Content Networking in Modular Network Design*

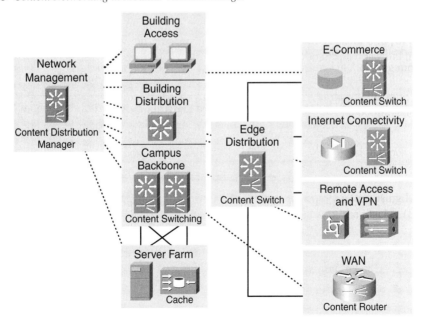

You can deploy content switches inside, or at the edge of, all network modules that contain servers to perform load sharing of requests and forward them to the least-used server. In Figure 3-25, the Server Farm module itself also contains the cache device. With this option, the device servers cache in a more specific way: the so-called reverse-proxy cache relieves the server from serving the external requests by downloading the frequently-accessed pages into the cache.

In the Network Management module, the Cisco Content Distribution Manager performs all the management functions that are necessary for controlling content distribution.

The content router is deployed in the WAN module to ensure that user requests are routed to the nearest servers.

Summary

In this chapter, you learned about the hierarchical network model and the Enterprise Composite Network Model for designing networks.

The hierarchical network model uses the following layers to simplify the tasks required for internetworking:

- The access layer provides access to the network.
- The distribution layer implements policy-based connectivity.
- The core layer provides high-speed data transport.

The Enterprise Composite Network Model comprises three major functional areas:

- Enterprise Campus
- Enterprise Edge
- Service Provider Edge

Service Provider Edge

The Enterprise does not implement the modules in the Service Provider Edge functional area; they are necessary to enable communication with other networks.

The Enterprise Campus functional area is further divided into four major modules:

- Campus Infrastructure module
- Network Management module
- Server Farm module
- Edge Distribution module

The Enterprise Edge functional area comprises four modules:

- E-commerce module
- Internet Connectivity module
- VPN/Remote Access module
- WAN module

The modules within the Service Provider Edge functional area are as follows:

- Internet Service Provider module
- PSTN module
- Frame Relay/ATM module

An intelligent network service is a supporting, but necessary, service. For example, security is an intelligent network service that increases the network's integrity by providing functions that protect the network resources and users from internal and external threats.

The network infrastructure and intelligent network solutions on top of the infrastructure provide a platform on which network solutions are implemented.

Voice is a typical network solution that requires an adequately designed network infrastructure.

A Content Delivery Network is a collection of comprehensive architectures and technologies for optimizing website performance and other content delivery.

References

Refer to the following resources for additional information:

- *Top-Down Network Design: A Systems Analysis Approach to Enterprise Network Design*, Priscilla Oppenheimer. Cisco Press, 1999.
- "Internetworking Design Basics," Cisco Internetwork Design Guide at www.cisco.com/univercd/cc/td/doc/cisintwk/idg4/nd2002.htm.
- SAFE White Paper: A Security Blueprint for Enterprise Networks, www.cisco.com/go/safe.
- SAFE: Extending the Security Blueprint to Small, Midsize and Remote-User Networks, www.cisco.com/go/safe.
- Cisco Architecture for Voice, Video and Integrated Data White Paper, www.cisco.com/warp/public/cc/so/neso/vvda/iptl/avvid_wp.htm.
- Cisco Enterprise Solutions: Cisco Content Delivery Networks, www.cisco.com/en/US/netsol/ns110/ns49/net_solution_home.html.

NOTE   All of the websites referenced in this chapter are also listed in Appendix B, " References."

Review Questions

After answering the following questions, refer to Appendix G, "Answers to Review Questions, Case Studies, and Simulation Exercises," for the answers.

1 Figure 3-26 presents a sample hierarchically-structured network. Some of the devices are marked with letters. How should you map the marked devices to the access, distribution, and core layers in Figure 3-26?

Figure 3-26 *Hierarchical Network*

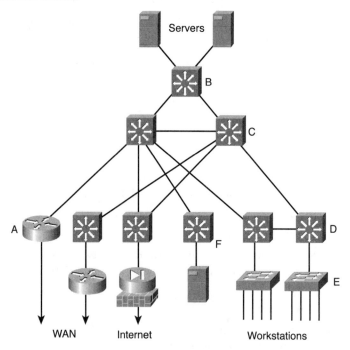

2 Describe the role of each layer in the hierarchical network model.

3 True or false: Each layer in the hierarchical network model must be implemented with distinct physical devices.

4 What features of a Layer 3 switch could be used in the access layer?

5 Which two statements are true?

   a UplinkFast immediately unblocks a blocked port after root port failure.

   b PortFast immediately puts a port into the forwarding state.

   c UplinkFast immediately puts a port into the forwarding state.

   d PortFast immediately unblocks a blocked port after root port failure.

6 Which layer in the hierarchical model provides media translation?

7 What are three roles of the hierarchical model's core layer?

   a Provide fast and efficient data transport

   b Provide maximum availability and reliability

   c Provide access to the corporate network via some wide-area technology

   d Implement policies regarding security

   e Delineate broadcast domains

   f Implement scalable routing protocols

8 Why might the distribution layer need to redistribute between routing protocols?

9 What is a benefit of using Layer 3 switching in the core network layer?

10 What are the functional areas in the Enterprise Composite Network model?

11 What are the modules and submodules within the Enterprise Campus functional area?

12 The Enterprise Edge functional area includes which modules?

13 The Service Provider Edge functional area is composed of which modules?

14 Which module of the Enterprise Composite model would include wireless connectivity to remote locations?

15 What is an advantage of using the Enterprise Composite Network model?

16 What the Campus Backbone submodule's role?

17 Indicate which types of devices would be found in each of these modules (note that some devices are found in more than one module):

— Modules

— E-commerce module

— Internet Connectivity module

— Remote Access and VPN module

Devices

— Web servers

— SMTP mail servers

— Firewall

— Network Intrusion Detection System (NIDS) appliances

— DNS servers

— VPN concentrators

— Public FTP servers

18 What is the role of the Service Provider functional area?

19 Classify each of the following as a network service or a network solution:

— Network management

— Voice over IP

— Storage networking

— Security

— High availability

— QoS

— Content networking

20 Which functions that support security are the responsibility of the Enterprise Composite Network model's Network Management module?

21 High availability from end-to-end is only possible when _____ is deployed throughout the internetwork.

22 What is the purpose of designing route redundancy in a network?

23 A full mesh design is ideal for connecting a _____ number of devices.

a small

b large

24 True or false: Backup links can use different technologies.

25 What components are required in IP telephony?

26 What role does the Building Access submodule play for voice transportation?

27 What should be considered when evaluating the existing data infrastructure for IP telephony?

28 Why is Content Networking important in modern networks?

29 Which content networking function directs a user request to the optimal resource within a global network based on user-defined policies?

30 Which modules can contain content switches?

This chapter introduces general campus switching design considerations and describes modularity in switching designs. It includes the following sections:

- Campus Design Methodology
- Campus Design
- Summary
- Case Study and Simulation Exercise
- Review Questions

Basic Campus Switching Design Considerations

The availability of multigigabit campus switches gives customers the opportunity to build extremely high-performance, high-reliability networks—if they follow correct network design approaches. Unfortunately, some alternative network design approaches can result in a network that has lower performance, reliability, and manageability.

This chapter describes a hierarchical modular design approach called multilayer design. First, it addresses general campus switching design considerations. The differences between Layer 2 (L2) and Layer 3 (L3) switching, and where to use each, are also discussed.

When you finish this chapter, you will be able to understand campus network switch design fundamentals and describe the positioning of switches in campus network modules.

Campus Design Methodology

The multilayer approach to campus network design combines Layer 2 switching with Layer 3 switching to achieve robust, highly-available campus networks. This section discusses the factors you should consider for a Campus local-area network (LAN) design.

Designing an Enterprise Campus

Designing an Enterprise Campus network requires a broad view of the network's overall picture. The network designer must be familiar with both Enterprise Campus design methodologies and Enterprise Campus modules.

Campus design requires an understanding of the organizational network borders (geography) and the existing and planned application traffic flows. Physical characteristics of the network depend on the following criteria:

- Selected transmission media
- The type of technology (switched or shared)
- The type of traffic forwarding (switching) in network devices (Layer 2 or Layer 3)

You should consider the following five factors when deploying the campus network:

- **Network geography**—The distribution of network nodes (for example, host or network devices) and the distances between them significantly affect the campus solution—especially the physical transmission media.

- **Network applications**—In terms of bandwidth and delay, the application requirements place stringent requirements on a campus network solution.

- **Data link layer technology (shared or switched)**—The dedicated bandwidth solution of LAN switching is replacing the traditional approach, in which all devices share the available bandwidth using hubs. The network designer must consider these options, especially when migrating or upgrading existing networks.

- **Layer 2 versus Layer 3 switching**—The network devices and their features determine the network's flexibility, but also contribute to the network's overall delay. Layer 2 switching is based on media access control (MAC) addresses, and Layer 3 switching is based on network layer addresses—usually Internet Protocol (IP) addresses.

- **Transmission media (physical cabling)**—Cabling is one of the biggest long-term investments in network deployment. Therefore, transmission media selection depends not only on the required bandwidth and distances, but also on the emerging technologies that might be deployed over the same infrastructure in the future. The network designer must thoroughly evaluate the cost of the medium (including installation costs) and the available budget in addition to the technical characteristics, such as signal attenuation and electromagnetic interference. Two major cabling options exist: copper-based media (for example, unshielded twisted pair [UTP]) and optical fiber.

The following sections examine these factors.

Network Geography

The location of Enterprise Campus nodes and the distances between them determine the network's geography. When designing the Enterprise Campus network, the network designer's first step is to identify the network's geography. The network designer must determine the following:

- **Location of nodes**—Nodes (end users, workstations, or servers) within an organization can be located in the same room, building, or geographical area.

- **Distances between the nodes**—Based on the location of nodes and the distance between them, the network designer decides which technology should be used, the maximum speeds, and so on. (Media specifications typically include a maximum distance, how often regenerators can be used, and so on.)

The following geographical structures can be identified with respect to the network geography:

- Intra-building
- Inter-building
- Distant remote building
- Distant remote building over 100 km

These geographical structures serve as guides to help determine Enterprise Campus transmission media and the logical modularization of the Enterprise Campus network. The following sections describe these geographical structures.

Intra-Building Structure

An *intra-building campus network structure* provides connectivity for the end nodes, which are all located in the same building, and gives them access to the network resources. (The access and distribution layers are typically located in the same building.)

User workstations are usually attached to the floor-wiring closet with UTP cables. To allow the most flexibility in the use of technologies, the UTP cables are typically Category 5 (CAT 5) or better. Wiring closets usually connect to the building central switch (distribution switch) over optical fiber. This offers better transmission performances and is less sensitive to environmental disturbances.

Inter-Building Structure

As shown in Figure 4-1, an *inter-building network structure* provides the connectivity between the individual campus buildings' central switches (in the distribution and/or core layers). Typically placed only a few hundred meters to a few kilometers apart, these buildings are usually in close proximity.

Figure 4-1   *Inter-Building Network Structure*

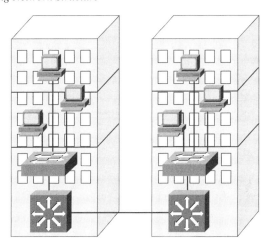

Because the nodes in all campus buildings usually share common devices such as servers, the demand for high-speed connectivity between the buildings is high. To provide high throughput without excessive interference from environmental conditions, optical fiber is the media of choice between the buildings.

Distant Remote Building Structure

When connecting distances that exceed a few kilometers (usually within a metropolitan area), the network designer's most important factor to consider is the physical media. The speed and cost of the network infrastructure depend heavily on the media selection.

Usually, the bandwidth requirements are higher than the physical connectivity options can support. In such cases, the network designer must identify the organization's critical applications and then select the equipment that supports intelligent network services, such as quality of service (QoS) and filtering capabilities that allow optimal use of the bandwidth.

Some companies might own their media, such as fiber or copper lines. However, if the organization does not own physical transmission media to certain remote locations, the Enterprise Network Campus must connect through the Enterprise Edge wide-area network (WAN) module using connectivity options from public service providers (such as metropolitan area network [MAN]).

Network Geography Considerations

Table 4-1 compares the types of connectivity, availability importance, required throughput, and expected cost for each geographical structure.

Table 4-1 *Network Geography Considerations*

Parameter	Intra-building		Inter-building	Distant Remote Building	Distant Over 100 km
Connectivity type	UTP	Fiber	Fiber MM/SM	Fiber SM	Copper/fiber
Availability importance	High	Medium	Medium	Low	Low
Required throughput	Medium	High	High	Medium	Low
Cost	$	$$	$$$	$$$$	$$$$$

MM = Multimode; SM = single-mode

Depending on the distances and environmental conditions that result from the respective geographical scopes, various connectivity options exist—ranging from traditional copper media to fiber-based transmission media.

Typically, availability within a building is very important, and it decreases with distance between buildings. (This is because the physical buildings in the campus often form the core of the campus network; communication to buildings located farther from the core is not as important.)

The throughput requirements increase close to the network's core and close to the sites where the servers reside.

A quick review of Table 4-1 reveals a combination of a high level of availability, medium bandwidth, and a low price for the Enterprise Campus network when all nodes are located in the same building. The cost of transmission media increases with the distance between nodes. A balance between the desired bandwidth and available budget are usually required to keep the cost reasonable; bandwidth is often sacrificed.

Network Application Characterization

Application characterization is the process of determining the characteristics of the network's applications. Network designers should determine which applications are critical to the organization and the network demands of these applications to determine enterprise traffic patterns inside the Enterprise Campus network. This process should result in information about network bandwidth usage and response times for certain applications. These parameters influence the selection of the transmission medium and the desired bandwidth.

Different types of application communication result in varying network demands. The following sections review four types of application communication:

- Client-client
- Client-distributed server
- Client-Server Farm
- Client-Enterprise Edge

Client-Client Applications

From the network designer's perspective, client-client applications include those applications in which the majority of network traffic passes from one network edge device to another through the organization's network, as shown in Figure 4-2. Typical client-client applications include the following:

- **IP telephony**—Two peers establish communication with the help of a telephone manager workstation; however, the conversation occurs directly between the two peers when the connection is established.

- **File sharing**—Some operating systems (or even applications) require direct access to data on other workstations.

- **Videoconference systems**—This application is similar to IP telephony. However, the network requirements for this type of application are usually higher, particularly bandwidth consumption and QoS requirements.

Figure 4-2 *Client-Client Application*

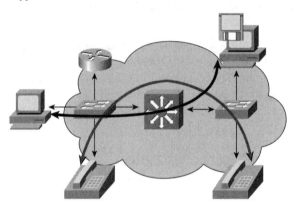

Client-Distributed Server Applications

Historically, clients and servers were attached to a network device on the same LAN segment.

With increased traffic on the corporate network, an organization can decide to split the network into several isolated segments. As shown in Figure 4-3, each of these segments has its own servers, known as *distributed servers*, for its application. In this scenario, servers and users are located in the same virtual LAN (VLAN). Department administrators manage and control the servers. The majority of department traffic occurs in the same segment, but some data exchange (to a different VLAN) can happen over the campus backbone. For traffic passing to another segment, the overall bandwidth requirement might not be crucial. For example, Internet access must go through a common segment that requires less performance than the traffic to the local segment servers.

Figure 4-3   *Client-Distributed Server Application*

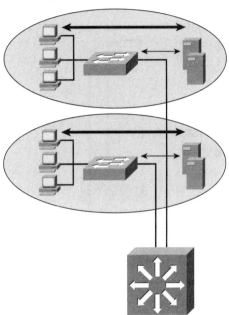

Client-Server Farm Applications

In a large organization, the organizational application traffic passes across more than one wiring closet, or VLAN. Such applications include

- Organizational mail servers (such as Lotus Notes and Microsoft Exchange)

- Common file servers (such as Novell, Microsoft, and Sun)

- Common database servers for organizational applications (such as Sybase, Oracle, and IBM)

A large organization requires its users to have fast, reliable, and controlled access to the critical applications. To fulfill these demands and keep administrative costs down, the solution is to place the servers in a *common Server Farm*, as shown in Figure 4-4. The placement of servers in a Server Farm requires the network designer to select a network infrastructure that is highly resilient (providing security), redundant (providing high availability), and that provides adequate throughput. High-end LAN switches with the fastest LAN technologies, such as Gigabit Ethernet, are typically deployed in such an environment.

Figure 4-4 *Client-Server Farm Application*

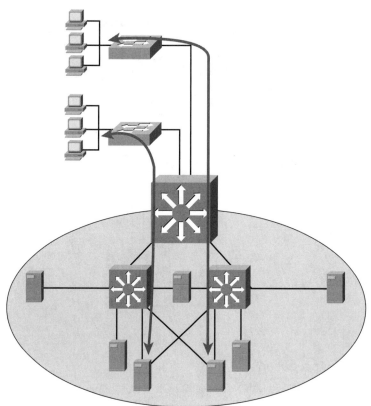

Client-Enterprise Edge Applications

As shown in Figure 4-5, *Client-Enterprise Edge applications* use servers on the Enterprise Edge. These applications exchange data between the organization and its public servers.

The most important communication issue between the Enterprise Campus Network and the Enterprise Edge is not performance, but security. High availability is another important characteristic; data exchange with external entities must be in constant operation. Applications installed on the Enterprise Edge can be crucial to organizational process flow; therefore, any outages can increase costs.

Typical Enterprise Edge applications are based on web technologies. Examples of these application types, such as external mail servers and public web servers, can be found in any organization.

Figure 4-5   *Client-Enterprise Edge Application*

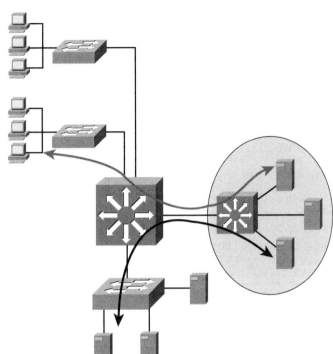

Organizations that support their partnerships through e-commerce applications also place their e-commerce servers into the Enterprise Edge. Communication with these servers is vital because of the two-way replication of data. As a result, high redundancy and resiliency of the network, along with security, are the most important requirements for these applications.

Application Requirements

Table 4-2 compares the types of applications and their requirements for the most important network parameters. The following sections discuss these parameters.

Table 4-2 *Network Application Requirements*

Parameter	Client-Client		Client-Distributed Servers	Client-Server Farm	Client-Enterprise Edge Servers
Connectivity type	Shared	Switched	Switched	Switched	Switched
High availability	Low	Low	Medium	High	High
Total required throughput	Low	Medium	Medium	High	Medium
Total network cost	Low	Low	Medium	High	Medium

Connectivity

The wide use of LAN switching at Layer 2 has revolutionized local-area networking and has resulted in increased performance and more bandwidth for satisfying the requirements of new organizational applications. LAN switches provide this performance benefit by increasing bandwidth and throughput for workgroups and local servers.

NOTE   The shared media for client-client (also termed *peer-to-peer*) communication is suitable only in a limited scope, typically when the number of client workstations is very low (for example, in small home offices).

Throughput

The required throughput varies from application to application. An application that exchanges data between users in the workgroup usually does not require a high throughput network infrastructure. However, organizational-level applications usually require a high-capacity link to the servers, which is usually located in the Server Farm.

NOTE   Client-client communication, especially in the case of frequent file transfers, could be intensive, and the total throughput requirements can be high.

Applications located on servers in the Enterprise Edge are normally not as bandwidth-consuming (compared to the applications in the Server Farm) but may require high-availability and security features.

High Availability

High availability is a function of the application and the entire network between a client workstation and a server that is located in the network. Although network availability is primarily determined by the network design, the individual components' mean time between failures (MTBF) is a factor. It is recommended that you add redundancy to the distribution layer and the campus.

Cost

Depending on the application and the resulting network infrastructure, the cost varies from low in a client-client environment to high in a highly redundant Server Farm. In addition to the cost of duplicate components for redundancy, costs include the cables, routers, switches, software, and so forth.

Data Link Layer Technologies

Traditionally, network designers had a limited number of hardware options when purchasing a technology for their campus networks. Hubs were used for wiring closets, and routers were used to break the network into logical segments. The increasing power of desktop processors and the requirements of client/server and multimedia applications drove the need for greater bandwidth in traditional shared-media environments. These requirements are prompting network designers to replace hubs with LAN switches.

Key Point: Bandwidth Domains and Broadcast Domains

A *bandwidth domain*, which is known as a *collision domain* for Ethernet LANs, includes all devices that share the same bandwidth. For example, when using switches or bridges, everything associated with one port is a bandwidth domain.

A *broadcast domain* includes all devices that see each other's broadcasts (and multicasts). For example, all devices associated with one router port reside in the same broadcast domain.

Devices in the same bandwidth domain also reside in the same broadcast domain; however, devices in the same broadcast domain can reside in different bandwidth domains.

All workstations residing in one bandwidth domain compete for the same LAN bandwidth resource. All traffic from any host in the bandwidth domain is visible to all the other hosts. In the case of an Ethernet collision domain, two stations can cause a collision by transmitting at the same time. The stations must then stop transmitting and try again at a later time, thereby delaying traffic transmittal.

All broadcasts from any host residing in the same broadcast domain are visible to all other hosts in the same broadcast domain. Desktop protocols such as AppleTalk, Internetwork Packet Exchange (IPX), and IP require broadcasts or multicasts for resource discovery and advertisement. Hubs, switches, and bridges forward broadcasts and multicasts to all ports. Routers do not forward these broadcasts or multicasts to any ports. In other words, routers block broadcasts (which are destined for all networks) and multicasts; routers forward only unicast packets (which are destined for a specific device) and *directed broadcasts* (which are destined for all devices on a specific network).

Shared Technology

Shared technology using hubs or repeaters is based on all devices sharing a segment's bandwidth. Initially, the entire Ethernet segment was a single common bus—the cable itself. With the introduction of hubs and new structured wiring, the physical network bus topology changed to a star topology. This topology resulted in fewer errors in the network because of the repeaters receiving an electrical signal and boosting the signal before forwarding it to all other segment participants (on all other repeater ports). All devices on all ports of a hub or repeater are on the same bandwidth (collision) domain.

Switched LAN Technology

Switched LAN technology uses the same physical star topology as hubs but eliminates the sharing of bandwidth. Devices on each port of a switch are in different bandwidth (collision) domains; however, all devices are still in the same broadcast domain. The LAN switches provide an efficient way of transferring network frames over the organizational network. In case of a frame error, the switch does not forward the frame as a hub or repeater would.

Comparing Switched and Shared Technologies

Table 4-3 presents some of the most obvious differences and benefits of switched technology compared to shared technology. It uses Fast Ethernet as an example.

Table 4-3   *Switched Versus Shared Fast Ethernet Technologies*

Parameter	Switched	Shared
Bandwidth	>10 Megabits per second (Mbps)	<100 Mbps
Range	From 1 meter	<500 meters
Intelligent services	Yes	No
High availability	Yes	No
Cost	$$	$

Bandwidth

The major drawback of shared technology is that all network devices must compete for the same bandwidth; only one frame flow is supported at a time. Bandwidth in shared technology is limited to the speed on a network segment (in this case, 100 Mbps for Fast Ethernet). Because of collisions, aggregate network bandwidth is less than this.

LAN switching technology supports speeds from Ethernet (10 Mbps) onward and enables multiple ports to simultaneously forward frames over the switch. Thus, the utilized aggregate network bandwidth could be much greater than with shared technology.

NOTE   A Layer 3 device separates network segments from each other into different broadcast domains. A traditional network's Layer 3 device was a router; in a modern network, the preference is for a Layer 3 switch.

Range

In a shared network, the network's diameter (the largest distance between two network devices) is constrained by the transmission media's physical characteristics because of the collision detection algorithm—the maximum distance between devices is limited to ensure that no collisions occur. In a shared environment, all devices reside in the same collision domain. The hub improves the frame's physical characteristics but does not check for frame errors. Every station on the segment must compete for resources and be able to detect whether two or more network stations are transmitting at the same time. The Ethernet standard for shared technology defines how long the sending device must possess the bus before it actually sends the data, so collisions can be detected. Because of this time limitation, the length or range of the segment is defined and never reaches more than 500 meters in the best-case scenario.

In a switched environment, devices on each port are in different collision domains. Collision detection is only a concern on each physical segment, and the segments themselves are limited in length. Because the switch stores the entire frame or part of it before forwarding it, the segments do not generate any collisions. The media that is used does not constrain the overall network's diameter.

Intelligent Services

The traditional shared technology is not capable of supporting new network features; this became important with the increasing number of organizational client/server and multimedia applications. LAN switches perform several functions at Layer 3, and even at higher Open System Interconnection (OSI) layers. Modern networks are required to support intelligent network services (such as QoS), security, and management; LAN switches have the ability to support these.

High Availability

Many organizational processes that run on the network infrastructure are critical for the organization's success. Consequently, high availability has become increasingly important. While shared networks do not offer the required capability, the LAN switches do.

Switches can be interconnected with multiple links without creating loops in the network (using the Spanning Tree protocol). Hubs cannot be interconnected with redundant links.

Cost

Considering all the benefits LAN switches offer, you might expect the cost per port to be much higher on switches than on hubs. However, with wide deployment and availability, the price per port for LAN switches is almost the same as it is for hubs or repeaters.

NOTE	All of the previously listed factors have mostly eliminated shared technologies; the majority of new networks use only switched technologies. Shared technologies are present in only some parts of existing networks and in smaller home offices.

Layer 2 and Layer 3 Switching Design Considerations

LAN switches have traditionally been only Layer 2 devices. Modern switches provide higher OSI level functionalities and can effectively replace routers in the LAN switched environment. Deploying pure Layer 2 or selecting Layer 3 switches in the enterprise network is not a trivial decision. It requires a full understanding of the network topology and customer demands.

Key Point: Layer 2 Versus Layer 3 Switching

The difference between Layer 2 and Layer 3 switching is the type of information that is used inside the frame to determine the correct output interface. Layer 2 switching forwards frames based on data link layer information (MAC address), while Layer 3 switching forwards frames based on network layer information (such as IP address).

When deciding on the type of LAN switch to use and the features to be deployed into a network, consider the following factors:

- **Network service capabilities**—The network services the organization requires (QoS, and so on).

- **Size of the network segments**—How the network is segmented, based on traffic characteristics.

- **Convergence times**—The maximum amount of time the network can be unavailable in the event of network outages.

Spanning-Tree Domain Considerations

Layer 2 switches use the Spanning Tree Protocol (STP) to ensure that only one active path exists between two switches. If a physical loop exists (for redundancy), STP puts ports on the switch in *blocking state* (thereby effectively disabling the ports, from a data perspective) to ensure a loop-free network. In the event of a failure, the blocked port is re-enabled (put into a *forwarding state*). An *STP domain* is a set of switches that communicates via STP. STP is illustrated in Figure 4-6.

Figure 4-6   *STP*

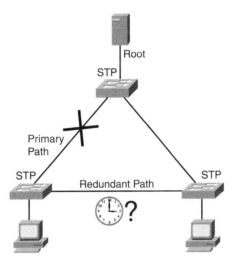

STP selects a root switch (or root bridge, according to IEEE 802.1d standard terminology) and determines whether any redundant paths exist. After the switch comes online, it takes up to 50 seconds before the root switch and redundant links are detected. At this time, the switch ports go through the listening and learning states; from there they progress to either the forwarding or blocking state. No ordinary traffic can travel through the network at this time.

NOTE   The default STP Forward Delay timer is 15 seconds; it determines how long the port stays in both the listening and learning states (for a total of 30 seconds). The Maximum Age timer defaults to 20 seconds; this is the time during which a switch stores a BPDU before discarding it, and therefore determines when the switch recognizes that a topology change has occurred. The addition of 30 seconds and 20 seconds composes the 50 seconds referred to previously.

When the primary link goes down and the redundant link must be activated, a similar event occurs. The time it takes for a redundant path to be activated depends on whether the failure is direct (a port on the same switch) or indirect (a port on another switch). Direct failures take 30 seconds because the switch bypasses the 20-second Maximum Age timer (and associated Blocking State for the port); from there it moves straight to the listening state (for 15 seconds), and then to the learning state (for 15 seconds). For indirect failures, the switch port must first wait 20 seconds (Maximum Age Timer) before it can transition to the listening state and then the learning state, for a total of 50 seconds. Thus, when a link fails, up to 50 seconds might pass before another link becomes available.

Cisco has implemented several features that have improved STP convergence. Recent standardization efforts have also proposed some new enhancements to the STP. Following is a brief description of the STP enhancements that result in faster convergence; this convergence is comparable to Layer 3 convergence and, in some instances, even exceeds it.

- **PortFast**—Used for ports in which end-user stations and/or servers are directly connected. When PortFast is enabled, there is no delay in passing traffic because the switch immediately puts the port in the forwarding state (skipping the listening and learning states). Two additional measures that prevent potential STP loops are associated with the PortFast feature:

  — **Bridge Protocol Data Unit (BPDU) Guard**—PortFast transitions the port into STP forwarding mode immediately upon linkup. Since the port still participates in STP, the potential of STP loop exists (if some device attached to that port also runs STP). The BPDU guard feature enforces the STP domain borders and keeps the active topology predictable. If the port receives a BPDU, the port is transitioned into *errdisable state* (meaning that it was disabled due to an error) and an error message is reported.

NOTE   Additional information regarding the errdisable state is available in *Recovering From errDisable Port State on the CatOS Platforms*, at www.cisco.com/en/US/tech/tk389/tk214/technologies_tech_note09186a0080093dcb.shtml.

  — **BPDU Filtering**—This feature allows the user to block PortFast-enabled nontrunk ports from transmitting BPDUs. Spanning tree does not run on these ports.

- **UplinkFast**—If the link to the root switch goes down and the link is directly connected to the switch, UplinkFast enables the switch to put a redundant path (port) into active state within a second.

- **BackboneFast**—If a link on the way to the root switch fails but is not directly connected to the switch, BackboneFast reduces the convergence time from 50 seconds to between 20 and 30 seconds. When this feature is used, it must be enabled on all switches in the STP domain.

In addition to features that enable faster convergence of the STP, features exist that prevent errors from resulting in unpredictable STP topology changes that could lead to STP loops. These features include the following:

- **STP Loop Guard**—When one of the blocking ports in a physically redundant topology stops receiving BPDUs, usually STP creates a potential loop by moving the port to forwarding state. With the STP Loop Guard feature enabled and if a blocking port no longer receives BPDUs, that port is moved into the STP loop-inconsistent blocking state instead of the listening/learning/forwarding state. This feature avoids loops in the network that result from unidirectional or other software failures.

- **BPDU Skew Detection**—This feature allows the switch to keep track of late-arriving BPDUs (by default, BPDUs are sent every 2 seconds) and notify the administrator via syslog messages. Skew detection generates a report for every port on which BPDU has ever arrived late (this is known as *skewed*). Report messages are rate-limited (one message every 60 seconds) to protect the CPU.

- **Unidirectional Link Detection (UDLD)**—If the STP process that runs on the switch with a blocking port stops receiving BPDUs from its upstream (designated) switch on that port, STP creates a forwarding loop or STP loop by eventually aging out the STP information for this port and moving it to the forwarding state. The UDLD is a Layer 2 protocol that works with the Layer 1 mechanisms to determine a link's physical status. If the port does not see its own device/port ID in the incoming UDLD packets for a specific duration of time, the link is considered unidirectional from the Layer 2 perspective. Once UDLD detects the unidirectional link, the respective port is disabled and the error message is generated.

Although spanning tree was previously considered to have very slow convergence (up to 50 seconds), the latest standard enhancements render its convergence comparable to (or even exceeding) that of routing protocols. The following enhancements are useful in environments that contain several VLANs:

- **Rapid STP (RSTP, defined in IEEE 802.1W)**—RSTP provides rapid convergence of the spanning tree by assigning port roles and determining the active topology. The RSTP builds upon the IEEE 802.1d STP to select the switch with the highest switch priority as the root switch and then assigns the port roles (root, designated, alternate, backup, and disabled) to individual ports. These roles assist in rapid STP convergence, which can be extremely fast (within a second) because of the topology knowledge.

- **Multiple STP (MSTP, sometimes referred to as MISTP [Multiple Instances of STP], defined in IEEE 802.1S)**—MSTP uses RSTP for rapid convergence by enabling several (topologically identical) VLANs to be grouped into a single spanning tree instance, with each instance including a spanning tree topology that is independent of other spanning tree instances. This architecture provides multiple forwarding paths for data traffic, enables load balancing, and reduces the number of spanning tree instances that are required to support a large number of VLANs.

Load Sharing Guidelines

Layer 2 and Layer 3 switches handle load sharing differently, as described in the following sections.

Layer 2 Load Sharing

Because Layer 2 switches are aware of only MAC addresses, they cannot perform any intelligent load sharing. In an environment characterized by multiple VLANs per access switch and more than one connection to the uplink switch, the solution is to put all uplink connections into trunks (Inter-switch link [ISL] or 802.1q). Each trunk carries all VLANs; however, without additional configuration, the STP protocol disables all nonprimary uplink ports. This configuration can result in a bandwidth shortage because the traffic for all the VLANs passes through the same link. To overcome this problem, the STP parameters must be configured to carry some VLANs across one uplink and the rest of the VLANs across the other uplink. For example, one uplink could be configured to carry the VLANs with odd numbers, while the other uplink is configured to carry the VLANs with even numbers. The top of Figure 4-7 illustrates this situation.

Figure 4-7 *Layer 2 Versus Layer 3 Load Sharing*

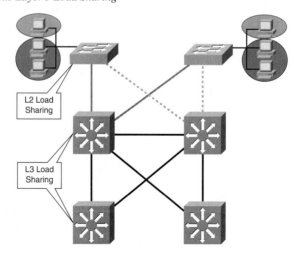

Layer 3 Load Sharing

Layer 3-capable switches can perform load sharing based on IP addresses. As illustrated in the lower portion of Figure 4-7, most modern Layer 3 devices with load sharing capability can balance the load per packet or per destination-source IP pair.

The advantage of Layer 3 IP load sharing is that links are used more proportionately than with Layer 2 load sharing, which is based on VLANs only. For example, the traffic in one VLAN can be very heavy while the traffic in another VLAN is very low; in this case, per-VLAN load sharing by using even and odd VLANs is not appropriate. Due to the dynamic nature of organizational applications, Layer 3 load sharing is more appropriate. Layer 3 allows for dynamic adaptation to link utilization and depends on the routing protocol design. Layer 3 switches also support Layer 2 load sharing, so they can still apply per-VLAN load sharing while connected to other Layer 2 switches.

Layer 2 Versus Layer 3 Switching

Table 4-4 compares Layer 2 and Layer 3 switching with respect to various campus network features. Considerations for deployment include

- Pure Layer 2 switching throughout the network
- Various combinations of Layer 2 and Layer 3 switching, including
    - Layer 3 switching in the distribution layer only
    - Layer 3 switching in the distribution and core layers
- Layer 3 switching throughout the network

Table 4-4   *Layer 2 Versus Layer 3 Switching*

Parameter	Layer 2 Everywhere	Layer 3 in Distribution Only	Layer 3 in Core and Distribution	Layer 3 Everywhere
Policy domain	Layer 2 Access Control List (ACL) and QoS	Layer 2 and Layer 3 ACL and QoS	Layer 2 and Layer 3 ACL and QoS	Layer 2 and Layer 3 ACL and QoS
Load sharing	Per VLAN	Per VLAN Per destination	Per VLAN Per destination	Per VLAN Per destination
Failure domain	VLAN	Access, core	Access	Segment
Convergence	STP	Distribution: Routing protocol hold-timer (quick) Other: STP	Core and distribution: Routing protocol hold-timer (quick) Access: STP	Routing protocol hold-timer (quick)
Cost	$→	$$→	$$$→	$$$$

The following sections elaborate on the features in Table 4-4.

Policy Domain

The *policy domain* is the scope of the network that is affected by a certain policy. A *network policy* is a formal set of statements that define how network resources are allocated among devices. In addition to selected hosts or applications, the policies can be applied to individual users, groups, or entire departments. For example, policies can be based on the time of day or client authorization priorities. Network managers implement policies and policy statements and store them in a policy repository or on the device itself. The devices then apply the configured policies to network resources.

The size of the policy domain depends on the switching layer and on the mechanisms for policy implementation. In pure Layer 2 switching, the policy domain overlaps with the switching domain's boundaries; Layer 3 switching offers much more flexibility. In Layer 2 switching, the access control lists (ACLs) and various QoS mechanisms can only be applied to switched ports and MAC addresses; in the Layer 3 switching, the ACL and QoS mechanisms are extended to IP addresses, or even applications (for example, using Transmission Control Protocol [TCP] and User Datagram Protocol [UDP] ports).

Load Sharing

When multiple links exist, they can be used for redundancy and/or traffic load sharing. As discussed in the "Load Sharing Guidelines" section of this chapter, Layer 2 switches only offer load sharing by distributing VLANs across different uplink ports. Layer 3 switches, however, can perform load sharing between ports based on IP destinations.

Failure Domain

A *failure domain* defines the scope of the network that is affected by network failures. In a Layer 2-switched domain, a misconfigured or malfunctioning workstation can introduce errors that impact or disable the entire domain. Problems of this nature are often difficult to localize.

A failure domain is

- Bounded by Layer 3 switching
- Bounded by the VLAN when Layer 2 switching is deployed in an entire campus

Convergence

As discussed in the "Spanning-Tree Domain Considerations" section of this chapter, loop prevention mechanisms in a Layer 2 topology cause the STP to take between 30 and 50 seconds to converge. To eliminate STP convergence issues in the campus backbone, all the links connecting backbone switches must be routed links, not VLAN trunks. This also limits the broadcast and failure domains.

In the case where the Layer 3 switching is deployed everywhere, convergence is within seconds (depending on the routing protocol implemented) because all the devices detect their connected link failure immediately and act upon it promptly (sending respective routing updates).

In a mixed Layer 2 and Layer 3 environment, the convergence time not only depends on the Layer 3 factors (including routing protocol timers such as hold-time and neighbor loss detection), but also on the STP convergence.

Using Layer 3 switching in a structured design reduces the scope of spanning tree domains. It is common to use a routing protocol, such as Enhanced Interior Gateway Protocol (EIGRP) or Open Shortest Path First (OSPF), to handle load balancing, redundancy, and recovery in the backbone.

Cost

The cost of deploying Layer 3 switching in comparison to Layer 2 switching increases with the scope of Layer 3 switching deployment. Layer 3 switches are more expensive than their Layer 2 counterparts; for example, Layer 3 functionality can be obtained by adding cards and software to a modular Layer 2 switch.

Transmission Media

An Enterprise Campus can use various physical media to interconnect devices.

Selecting the type of cable is an important consideration when deploying a new network or upgrading an existing one. Cabling infrastructure represents a long-term investment—it is usually installed to last for ten years or more. In addition, even the best network equipment does not operate as expected with poorly chosen cabling.

A network designer must be aware of physical media characteristics because they influence the maximum distance between devices and the network's maximum transmission speed.

Twisted-pair cables (copper) and optical cables (fiber) are the most common physical transmission media used in modern networks.

Unshielded Twisted-Pair (UTP) Cables

UTP consists of four pairs of isolated wires that are wrapped together in plastic cable. No additional foil or wire is wrapped around the core wires (thus, they are *unshielded*). This makes these wires less expensive, but also less immune to external electromagnetic influences than shielded cables. UTP is widely used to interconnect workstations, servers, or other devices from their network interface card (NIC) to the network connector at a wall outlet.

The characteristics of twisted-pair cable depend on the quality of their material. As a result, twisted-pair cables are sorted into categories. Category 5 or greater is recommended for speeds of 100 megabits per second (Mbps) or higher. Because of the possibility of signal attenuation in the wires and carrier detection, the maximum cable length is usually limited to 100 meters . For example, if one PC starts to transmit and another PC is more than 100 meters away, the second PC might not detect the signal on the wire and therefore start to transmit, causing a collision on the wire.

One of the frequent considerations in the cabling design is electromagnetic interference. Due to high susceptibility to interference, UTP is not suitable for use in environments with electromagnetic influences. Similarly, UTP is not appropriate for environments that can be affected by the UTP's own interference.

NOTE   Some security issues are also associated with electromagnetic emissions—it is easy to eavesdrop on the traffic carried across UTP because these cables emit electromagnetic signals that can easily be detected.

Optical Cables

Typical requirements that lead to the selection of optical cable as a transmission media include distances longer than 100 meters, and immunity to electromagnetic interference. There are different types of optical cable; the two main types are multimode (MM) and single-mode (SM).

Both MM and SM optical cable have lower signal losses than a twisted pair cable; therefore, optical cables automatically enable longer distances between devices. However, fiber cable has precise production and installation requirements, resulting in a higher cost than twisted pair cable.

Multimode fiber is optical fiber that carries multiple light waves or modes concurrently, each at a slightly different reflection angle within the optical fiber core. Because modes tend to disperse over longer lengths (modal dispersion), MM fiber transmission is used for relatively short distances. Typically, light emitting diodes (LEDs) are used with MM fiber. The typical diameter of an MM fiber is 50 or 62.5 micrometers.

Single-mode (also known as *monomode*) *fiber* is optical fiber that carries a single wave (or laser) of light. Lasers are typically used with SM fiber. The typical diameter of an SM fiber core is between 2 and 10 micrometers.

Copper Versus Fiber

Table 4-5 presents some of the critical parameters that influence the network transmission medium selection.

Table 4-5   *Copper Versus Fiber Media*

Parameter	Copper	Fiber
Bandwidth	Ethernet: <1 gigabits per second (Gbps) LRE: <15 Mbps	<10 Gbps
Range	Ethernet: <100 m LRE: <1.5km	MM: 550 m* SM: <100 km*
Deployment area	Wiring closet	Inter-node and inter-building
Other considerations	Interference, grounding	Coupling loss
Installation cost	$	$$$

* When using Gigabit Ethernet

NOTE   Table 4-5 lists Ethernet as a technology; this includes Ethernet, Fast Ethernet, and Gigabit Ethernet. Long Reach Ethernet (LRE) is also listed. This latter technology is Cisco proprietary and runs on voice-grade copper wires; it allows higher distances than traditional Ethernet and is used as an access technology in WANs. Chapter 5, "Designing WANs," further describes LRE.

The following sections elaborate on the parameters in Table 4-5.

Bandwidth

The *bandwidth parameter* indicates the required bandwidth in a particular segment of the network, or the connection speed between the nodes inside or outside the building.

Range

The *range parameter* is the maximum distance between network devices (such as workstations, servers, printers, and IP phones) and network nodes, and between network nodes.

Table 4-6 summarizes the bandwidth and range characteristics of the transmission media types.

Table 4-6   *Transmission Media Types Bandwidth and Range Characteristics*

Parameter	Twisted-Pair	MM Fiber	SM Fiber
Distance (range)	Up to 100 meters	Up to 2 kilometers (km) (Fast Ethernet) Up to 550 m (Gigabit Ethernet)	Up to 40 km Up to 100 km (Gigabit Ethernet)
Speed (bandwidth)	Up to 1 Gpbs	Up to 1 Gbps	10 Gbps
Cost	Cheap to install	Moderate	High price

Copper cables are typically used for connectivity of network devices to the wiring closet where

- Distances are less than 100 meters
- Speeds of 100 Mbps are satisfactory
- Cost must be kept within reasonable limits

NOTE   Fast EtherChannel (FEC) and Gigabit EtherChannel solutions group several parallel links between LAN switches into a channel that is seen as a single link from the Layer 2 perspective. Two protocols have been introduced for automatic EtherChannel formation: the Port Aggregation Control Protocol (PagP), which is Cisco proprietary, and the Link Aggregation Control Protocol (LACP), which is standardized and defined in IEEE 802.3ad.

Deployment Area

Deployment area indicates whether wiring is required for wiring closet only (where users access the network), for inter-node, or even for inter-building connections.

Connection from the wiring closet to the building central node can use UTP. As for most inter-node and especially inter-building connections, MM, or even SM, fiber is probably needed if there are high-speed requirements.

Other Considerations

When deploying UTP in an area with high electrical or magnetic interference—for example, in an industrial environment—you must pay special attention to media selection. In such environments, the disturbances might interfere with data transfer and therefore result in an increased number of frame errors. Electrical grounding can isolate some external disturbance, but the wiring increases the costs. Fiber optic installation is the only reasonable solution for such networks.

Optical fiber requires a precise technique for cable coupling. Even a small deviation from the ideal position of optical connectors can result in either a loss of signal or a large number of frame losses. Careful attention during optical fiber installation is imperative because of the traffic's high sensitivity to coupling misalignment. In environments where the cable does not consist of a single fiber from point to point, coupling is required and loss of signal can easily occur.

Installation Cost

Along with the cost of the medium, you must also seriously consider installation cost. Installation costs are significantly higher than UTP installation costs because of strict requirements for optical cable coupling.

Cabling Example

Figure 4-8 illustrates a typical campus network structure. End devices such as workstations, IP phones, and printers are no more than 100 m away from the LAN switch. UTP wiring can easily handle the required distance and speed; it is also easy to set up, and the price/performance ratio is reasonable.

Figure 4-8   *A Campus Network Uses Many Different Types of Cables*

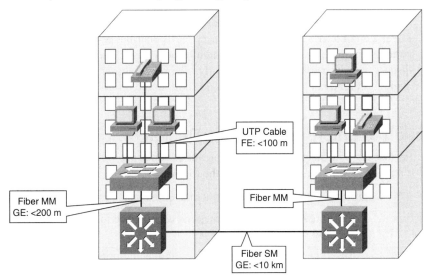

Optical fiber cables handle higher speeds and distances that can be required among switch devices. MM optical cable is usually satisfactory inside the building. Depending on distance, organizations use MM or SM optical for inter-building communication cable. If the distances are short (up to 500 m), MM fiber is a more reasonable solution for speeds up to 1 Gbps.

However, an organization can install SM fiber if its requirements are for longer distances, or if they are planning for future higher speeds (for example, 10 Gbps). The current specification provides Gigabit Ethernet connectivity on SM fiber up to 5 km; however, Cisco has already provided modules that support connectivity up to 10 km, and even up to 100 km.

NOTE	Selecting the less expensive type of fiber might satisfy a customer's current need, but this fiber might not meet the needs of future upgrades or equipment replacement. Replacing cable can be very expensive. Planning with future requirements in mind might result in higher initial costs, but ultimately lower costs.

Campus Design

Campus building blocks are comprised of multilayer devices that connect to the campus backbone. A building design is appropriate for a building-sized network that contains several thousand networked devices; a campus design is appropriate for a large campus that consists of many buildings. To scale from a building model to a campus model, network designers must add a campus backbone between buildings.

This section discusses advanced network traffic considerations and building design using Layer 2 and Layer 3 switching in the access and distribution layers. It describes traffic patterns, multicast traffic, and QoS, and uses both Layer 2 and Layer 3 technologies to discuss campus backbone design. Finally, we investigate server placement within the campus and present guidelines for connectivity to the rest of the enterprise network.

Introduction to Enterprise Campus Design

As discussed in Chapter 3, "Structuring and Modularizing the Network," the Enterprise Campus network can be divided into the following modules:

- **Campus Infrastructure**—This module contains the following submodules:
    - **Building Access**—Aggregates end user connections and provides access to the network.
    - **Building Distribution**—Provides aggregation of access devices and connects them to the campus backbone.
    - **Campus Backbone**—Interconnects the building distribution submodules with the Edge Distribution module and provides high-speed transport.

- **Server Farm**—Connects the servers to the enterprise network and manages the campus server availability and traffic load balancing.

- **Edge Distribution**—Connects the Enterprise Edge applications to the network campus. Security is the main consideration in this module.

- **Network Management**—The Network Management module requirements are similar to those for the Server Farm module, with the exception of the bandwidth requirement. The Network Management module typically does not require high bandwidth.

This section identifies major requirements for designing campus networks within these modules.

Enterprise Campus Module Requirements

As shown in Table 4-7, each Enterprise Campus module has different requirements. For example, this table illustrates how modules that are located closer to the users require a higher degree of scalability. This means that the network designer must consider an option for expanding the Campus network easily in the future, without redesigning the complete network. For example, adding new workstations to a network should result in neither high investment cost nor performance degradations.

Table 4-7   *Enterprise Campus Design Requirements*

Requirement	Building Access		Building Distribution	Campus Backbone	Server Farm	Edge Distribution
Technology	Shared	Layer 2 switched	Layer 2 and 3 switched	Layer 2 and 3 switched	Layer 3 switched	Layer 3 switched
Scalability	High	High	Medium	Low	Medium	Low
High availability	Low	Medium	Medium	High	High	Medium
Performance	Low	Low	Medium	High	High	Medium
Cost per port	Low	Low	Medium	High	High	Medium

The end user usually does not require high performance and high availability, but they are crucial to the campus backbone—especially the Server Farm module.

The price per port increases with increased performance and availability. The campus backbone and Server Farm require a guarantee of higher throughput so they can handle all traffic flows and not introduce additional delays or drops to the network traffic.

The Edge Distribution module does not require the same performance as in the campus backbone. However, it can require other features and functionalities that increase the overall cost.

Enterprise Campus Design Considerations

Designing an Enterprise Campus means not only dividing the network into modules, but also optimizing performance and the cost of each module while providing scalability and high availability. Before designing a campus network, you must take the following considerations relating to network traffic into account:

- **Application traffic patterns**—Identify the organizational traffic flows. This includes the type of traffic and its bandwidth requirements and traffic patterns.

- **Multicast traffic**—Identify the features that constrain multicast streams to the relevant ports. If present in the Enterprise Campus network and incorrectly designed, multicast traffic can use a great amount of bandwidth.

- **Delay sensitive traffic**—Identify and incorporate the appropriate QoS mechanisms to manage the diverse requirements for delay and delay variations.

As Table 4-8 shows, the Enterprise Campus can be built on either a shared or switched (Layer 2 or Layer 3) foundation technology. In the building access layer, workstations with low demand can be connected via shared technology; however, this option is only suitable for some small (home) offices that have a few devices without any special bandwidth requirements. Where higher speeds are required, shared technology is not appropriate, and LAN switching is the only option. The remaining consideration is whether to use Layer 2 or Layer 3 switching technology.

Table 4-8   *Enterprise Campus Design Decisions*

Requirement	Building Access		Building Distribution	Campus Backbone	Server Farm	Edge Distribution
Technology	Shared	Layer 2 switched	Layer 2 and 3 Switched	Layer 2 and 3 switched	Layer 3 switched	Layer 3 switched
Application traffic	Distant	Local/ distant	Distant	Distant	Local/ distant	Distant
Multicast traffic aware	No	Layer 2 limited	Yes	Yes	Yes	Yes
QoS (delay sensitive) traffic support	No	Queuing/marking per port Marking per application				

Consideration of the applications and traffic is required to ensure that the appropriate equipment for the individual modules is selected. Application traffic patterns, multicast traffic, and QoS are important network design issues.

Layer 2 switches usually support multicast and QoS features, but with limited capability. A Layer 3 switch, or in the case of IP multicast, at least a so-called *Layer 3-aware switch*, might be required.

A Layer 2 multicast-aware switch that works closely with the Layer 3 device (router) can distinguish which hosts belong to the multicast stream and which do not. Thus, the Layer 2 switch can forward the multicast stream to only selected hosts.

Layer 2 QoS support is usually limited to port marking capability and queuing on only uplink trunk ports, especially on low-end switches. Layer 2 switches are usually incapable of marking or queuing based on the Layer 3 parameters of packets. However, several recent platforms have added support for Layer 2, Layer 3, and Layer 4 class of service (CoS) and type of service (ToS) packet marking and policing.

The following sections examine network traffic patterns, multicast traffic, and QoS considerations in the Enterprise Campus modules.

Network Traffic Patterns

Campus traffic patterns are generally categorized as local (within a segment or submodule) or distant (passing several segments and crossing the module boundaries).

Network traffic patterns have changed through the years. The characteristic of traditional campus networks was 80 percent local traffic and 20 percent distant traffic; this is known as the *80/20 rule*. In modern campus networks, the ratio is closer to 20/80 because the servers are no longer present in the workgroup, but are instead placed separately in the Server Farm. The 20/80 ratio results in a much higher load on the backbone because the majority of the traffic from client workstations to the servers passes through the backbone.

80/20 Rule in the Campus

When designing a switched campus, network designers ensure that each switched segment corresponds to a workgroup. By placing the workgroup server in the same segment as its clients, most of the traffic can be contained. The 80/20 rule refers to the goal of containing at least 80 percent of the traffic within the local segment.

The campus-wide VLAN model is highly dependent upon the 80/20 rule. If 80 percent of the traffic is within a workgroup (VLAN), 80 percent of the packets flowing from the client to the server are switched locally.

The conventional 80/20 rule underlies traditional network design models. With the campus-wide VLAN model, the logical workgroup is dispersed across the campus, but is still organized so that 80 percent of traffic is contained within the VLAN. The remaining 20 percent of traffic leaves the network through a router.

20/80 Rule in the Campus

Many new and existing applications currently use distributed data storage and retrieval. The traffic pattern is moving toward what is now referred to as the *20/80 rule*. With the 20/80 rule, only 20 percent of traffic is local to the workgroup LAN, and 80 percent of the traffic leaves the workgroup.

In a traditional network design, only a small amount of traffic passes through the Layer 3 devices. Because performance was not an issue, these devices have traditionally been routers. Modern enterprise networks utilize servers that are located in Server Farms or in the enterprise edge. With an increasing amount of traffic from clients to distant servers, performance requirements are higher in the building distribution and campus backbone. Therefore, devices that have a very high speed of Layer 3 processing are necessary; these devices are Layer 3 switches.

Network Traffic Pattern Example

Figure 4-9 illustrates examples of the 80/20 and 20/80 rules in a campus network.

Figure 4-9 *Traffic Patterns in Traditional and Modern Networks*

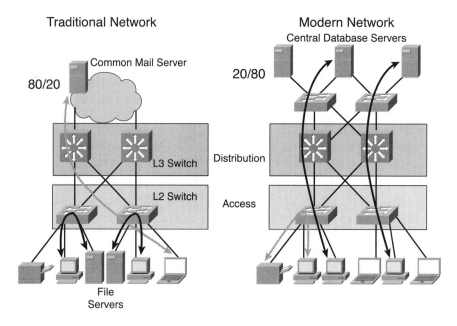

Company A, shown on the left side of Figure 4-9, has several independent departments. Each department has its own VLAN, in which the servers and printers are located. File transfers from other department servers or workstations are necessary only occasionally. This traffic must pass the distribution layer, which is represented by the Layer 3 switch. The only common resource the departments use is the mail server, which is located in the corporate network's core.

Company B, shown on the right side of Figure 4-9, also has several departments; however, they use common resources. Not only do they use file servers from their own department, but they also use services from common data storage, such as an Oracle database. This type of configuration requires a higher-performance Layer 3 switch on the distribution layer. The access layer switch (Layer 2) concentrates users into their VLANs. The servers on the other side of the network are also organized into groups and are connected to Layer 2 switches. Distribution layer switches in the middle enable fast, reliable, and redundant communication among the groups on both sides of the network. Figure 4-9 illustrates that the majority of the communication takes place between servers and users, and only a small amount of traffic is switched inside the group.

Multicast Traffic Considerations

IP multicast is a bandwidth-conserving technology that reduces traffic by simultaneously delivering a single stream of information to potentially thousands of corporate recipients.

Videoconferencing, corporate communications, distance learning, distribution of software, stock quotes, and news are some applications that take advantage of the multicast traffic stream. IP multicast delivers source traffic to multiple receivers.

IP multicast is based on the concept of a multicast group. Any group of receivers can express an interest in receiving a particular data stream. This group does not require any physical or departmental boundaries; rather, the hosts can be located anywhere on the corporate network. Hosts that are interested in receiving data that flows to a particular group must join the group using the Internet Group Management Protocol (IGMP).

Figure 4-10 illustrates a typical situation with IP multicast. Multicast-enabled routers ensure that traffic is delivered properly by using one of the multicast routing protocols, such as Protocol Independent Multicast (PIM). The router forwards the incoming multicast stream to the switch port.

Figure 4-10 *Multicast Traffic Handled by Router*

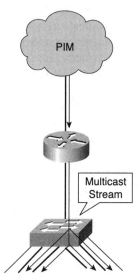

However, the default behavior for a Layer 2 switch is to forward all multicast traffic to every port that belongs to the same VLAN on the switch (a behavior known as *flooding*). This behavior defeats the purpose of the switch, which is to limit the traffic to only the ports that must receive the data.

NOTE   Support for broadcast and multicast suppression is available on several switched platforms. The suppression is done with respect to the incoming traffic rate and is either bandwidth-based or measured in packets per second. The threshold can be set to any value between 0 and 100 percent (or as a number of packets when packet-based suppression is turned on). When the data on the port exceeds the threshold, the switch suppresses further activity on the port for the remainder of the 1-second period.

Static entries can sometimes be set to specify which ports should receive the multicast traffic. Dynamic configuration of these entries simplifies the switch administration.

Several methods exist for Cisco switches to deal efficiently with multicast in a Layer 2 switching environment. Following are the most common methods:

- **Cisco Group Management Protocol (CGMP)**—CGMP allows switches to communicate with a router to determine whether any of the users attached to them are part of a multicast group. The multicast receiver registration is accepted by the router (using the IGMP) and communicated via CGMP to the switch; the switch adjusts its forwarding table accordingly. CGMP is a Cisco proprietary solution that is implemented on all Cisco LAN switches.

- **IGMP snooping**—With IGMP snooping, the switch intercepts multicast receiver registrations and adjusts its forwarding table accordingly. IGMP snooping requires the switch to be Layer 3-aware because IGMP is a network layer protocol. Typically, the IGMP packet recognition is hardware-assisted.

NOTE   Additional methods for addressing the problem of multicast frames in a switched environment include the Generic Multicast Registration Protocol (GMRP) and the Router-Port Group Management Protocol (RGMP). GMRP, which is used between the switch and the host, is not yet widely available. RGMP is a Cisco solution for router-only multicast interconnects in a switched environment. (More information on RGMP is available in *Configuring RGMP*, at www.cisco.com/en/US/products/hw/switches/ps708/products_configuration_guide_chapter09186a008007e6f8.html.)

QoS Considerations for Delay-sensitive Traffic

A Campus Network transports many types of applications and data, including high-quality video and delay-sensitive data (such as real-time voice). Bandwidth-intensive applications stretch network capabilities and resources, but they can also enhance many business processes. Networks must provide secure, predictable, measurable, and sometimes guaranteed services. Achieving the required QoS by managing delay, delay variation (jitter), bandwidth, and packet loss parameters on a network can be the key to a successful end-to-end business solution. QoS mechanisms are techniques that are used to manage network resources.

The assumption that a high-capacity, nonblocking switch with multigigabit backplanes never needs QoS is incorrect. Most networks or individual network elements are oversubscribed. In fact, it is easy to create scenarios in which congestion potentially occurs and that therefore require some form of QoS. Uplinks from the access layer to the distribution layer, or from the distribution layer to the core, most often require QoS. The sum of the bandwidths on all ports on a switch where end devices are connected is usually greater than that of the uplink port. When the access ports are fully used, congestion on the uplink port is unavoidable.

Depending on traffic flow and uplink oversubscription, bandwidth is managed with QoS mechanisms on the access, distribution, or even core switches.

QoS Categories

Layer 2 QoS is similar to Layer 3 QoS, which Cisco IOS software implements. You can configure the following four QoS categories on LAN switches:

- **Classification and marking**—Packet classification features allow the partitioning of traffic into multiple priority levels, or classes of service. These features inspect the information in the frame header (Layer 2, Layer 3, and Layer 4) and determine the frame's priority. *Marking* is the process of changing a frame's CoS setting (or priority).

- **Scheduling**—Scheduling is the process that determines the order in which queues are serviced. CoS is used on Layer 2 switches to assist in the queuing process. Layer 3 switches can also provide QoS scheduling; Layer 3 IP QoS queue selection uses the IP DiffServ Code Point (DSCP) or the IP packet's IP precedence field.

NOTE   For more information on DSCP and IP precedence, refer to the Cisco *Implementing Quality of Service Policies with DSCP* document at www.cisco.com/en/US/tech/tk543/tk757/ technologies_tech_note09186a00800949f2.shtml.

- **Congestion management**—A network interface is often congested (even at high speeds, transient congestion is observed), and queuing techniques are necessary to ensure that traffic from the critical applications is forwarded appropriately. For example, real-time applications such as VoIP and stock trading might have to be forwarded with the least latency and jitter.

- **Policing and shaping**—Policing and shaping is the process of reducing a stream of data to a predetermined rate or level. Unlike traffic shaping, in which the frames can be stored in small buffers for a short period of time, policing simply drops or lowers the priority of the frame that is out of profile.

QoS in LAN Switches

When configuring QoS features, select the specific network traffic, prioritize it according to its relative importance, and use congestion-management techniques to provide preferential treatment. Implementing QoS in the network makes network performance more predictable and bandwidth use more effective.

Figure 4-11 illustrates where the various categories of QoS are implemented in LAN switches.

Figure 4-11 *QoS in LAN Switches*

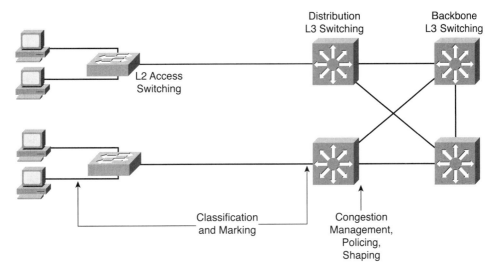

Because they do not have knowledge of Layer 3 or higher information, access switches provide QoS based only on the switch's input port. For example, traffic from a particular host can be defined as high-priority traffic on the uplink port. The scheduling mechanism of an access switch's output port ensures that traffic from such ports is served first. The proper marking of input traffic ensures the expected service when traffic passes through the distribution and core layer switches.

Distribution and core layer switches are typically Layer 3-aware and can provide QoS selectively—not only on a port basis, but also according to higher-layer parameters, such as IP addresses, port numbers, or even QoS bits in the IP packet. These switches make QoS classification more selective by differentiating the traffic based on the application. QoS in distribution and core switches must be provided in both directions of traffic flow. The policing for certain traffic is usually implemented on the distribution layer switches.

QoS Example with Voice Traffic Across a Switch

QoS for voice over IP (VoIP) consists of keeping packet loss and delay within certain tolerable levels that do not affect the voice quality. Voice requires low jitter and low packet loss. One solution would be to simply provide sufficient bandwidth at all points in the network. A better alternative is to apply a QoS mechanism at the network's oversubscribed points.

A reasonable design goal for VoIP end-to-end network delay is 150 milliseconds, a level at which the speakers do not notice the delay. A separate outbound queue for real-time voice traffic can be provided to achieve guaranteed low delay for voice at campus speeds. Bursty data traffic, such as a file transfer, should be placed in a different queue. Packet loss is not an issue if low delay is guaranteed by providing a separate queue for voice. Figure 4-12 illustrates this situation.

Figure 4-12 *QoS for VoIP Example*

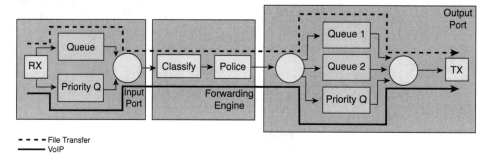

QoS maps well to the multilayer campus design. Packet classification is a multilayer service that is applied at the wiring-closet switch (access switch), which is the network's ingress point. VoIP traffic flows are recognized and then classified by their port number—the IP ToS is set to low delay voice for VoIP packets. Wherever the VoIP packets encounter congestion in the network, the local switch or router applies the appropriate congestion management based on this ToS value.

Building Access and Distribution Layers Design

In a conventional campus-wide VLAN design, network designers apply Layer 2 switching to the access layer, while the distribution layer switches support Layer 3 capabilities. In small networks, both access and distribution layers can be merged into a single switch.

Building Access Layer Considerations

The access layer aggregates the workstations or hosts on a Layer 2 device (a switch or hub). The Layer 2 node represents one logical segment and is one broadcast domain. VLAN support might be required where multiple departments coexist in the same wiring closet.

The policies implemented on the access switch are based on Layer 2 information. These policies focus on and include the following features:

- Port security
- Access speeds
- Traffic classification priorities that are defined on uplink ports

When implementing the campus infrastructure's building access submodule, consider the following questions:

- How many users or host ports are currently required in the wiring closet, and how many will it require in the future? Should the switches support fixed or modular configuration?

- What cabling is currently available in the wiring closet, and what cabling options exist for uplink connectivity?

- What Layer 2 performance does the node need?

- What level of redundancy is needed?

- What is the required link capacity to the distribution layer switches?

- How will the VLANs and STP deployed? Will there be a single VLAN, or several VLANs per access switch? Will the VLANs on the switch be unique or spread across multiple switches? The latter design was common a few years ago, but today campus-wide (or access layer-wide) VLANs are not desirable.

- Are additional features, such as port security, multicast traffic management, and QoS (traffic classification based on ports), required?

Based on the answers to these questions, the network designer can select the devices that satisfy the access layer's customer requirements. The access layer should maintain the simplicity of traditional LAN switching, with the support of basic network intelligent services and business applications.

Redundant paths can be used for failover and load balancing. Layer 2 switches can support features that are able to accelerate STP timers and provide for faster convergence and switchover of traffic to the redundant link, including BackboneFast, UplinkFast, and RSTP.

Disabling STP on a device is not encouraged because of possible loops. STP should only be disabled on carefully selected ports, and typically only on those in which the hosts are connected. Several other methods enable loop-resistant deployment of the STP, including BPDU Filtering and the BPDU guard feature on the access links where PortFast is configured. On the uplinks, BPDU skew detection, STP loop guard, and UDLD are additional measures against STP loops.

The "Layer 2 and Layer 3 Switching Design Considerations" section of this chapter discusses these STP features.

Building Access Design Examples

Figure 4-13 illustrates examples of a small and a medium-sized campus network design.

Figure 4-13 *Small and Medium Campus Access Layer Designs*

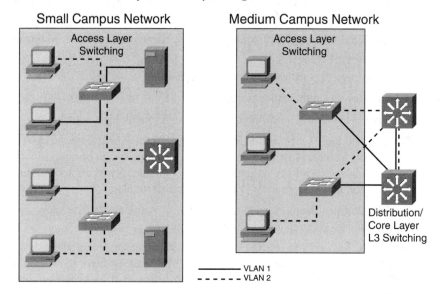

Following are some characteristics of a small campus network design:

- Network servers and workstations in small campus networks connect to the same wiring closet.

- Switches in small campus networks do not usually require high-end performance.

- The network designer does not have to physically divide the network into a modular structure (building access and building distribution modules).

- Low-end multilayer switches could provide the Layer 3 services closer to the end user when there are multiple VLANs at the access layer.

- Small networks often merge the distribution and access layers.

Because of their performance requirements, medium-size campus networks are built on Layer 2 access switches and are connected by uplinks to the distribution Layer 3 switches. This forms a clear structure of building access and building distribution modules. If redundancy is required, an additional Layer 3 switch can be attached to the network's aggregation point with full link redundancy.

Building Distribution Layer Considerations

The building distribution layer aggregates the access layer and uses a combination of Layer 2 and Layer 3 switching to segment workgroups and isolate segments from failures and broadcast storms. This layer implements many policies based on access lists and QoS settings. The distribution layer can protect the core network segment from any impact of access layer problems by implementing all the policies.

One most frequently asked question regarding implementation of a building's distribution layer is whether a Layer 2 switch is sufficient, or a Layer 3 switch must be deployed. To make this decision, answer the following questions:

- How many users will the distribution switch handle?

- What type and level of redundancy are required?

- As intelligent network services are introduced, can the network continue to deliver high performance for all its applications, such as Video On Demand, IP multicast, or IP telephony?

The network designer must pay special attention to the following network characteristics:

- **Performance**—Distribution switches should provide wire-speed performance on all ports. This feature is important because of access layer aggregation on one side and high-speed connectivity of the core module on the other side. Future expansions with additional ports or modules can result in an overloaded switch if it is not selected properly.

- **Intelligent network services**—Distribution switches should not only support fast Layer 2 and/or Layer 3 switching, but should also incorporate intelligent network services such as high availability, QoS, security, and policy enforcement.

- **Manageability and scalability**—Expanding and/or reconfiguring distribution layer devices must be easy and efficient. These devices must support the required management features.

With the correct selection of distribution layer switches, the network designer can easily add new building access modules.

NOTE   Layer 3 switches are usually preferred for the distribution layer switches because this layer must support intelligent network services, such as QoS and traffic filtering.

The network designer must also decide where redundancy should be implemented and which mechanisms should be used: Layer 2 and STP, or Layer 3 (routing protocol) redundant paths. If advanced STP features such as RSTP, UplinkFast, or BackboneFast are not implemented, Layer 2 redundancy and STP configuration can take up to 50 seconds. If the aforementioned features are supported and enabled on the switch, the switchover time could be from 1 second (in the case of RSTP deployment) to 30 seconds. Routing protocols usually switch over in a few seconds (EIGRP in a redundant configuration is usually faster than OSPF because of the default 5-second shortest path first [SPF] algorithm delay recalculation).

Building Distribution Layer Example

Figure 4-14 illustrates a sample network. In this figure, each access layer module has two equal-cost paths to the distribution module switches. The distribution layer switch also has two equal-cost paths to the backbone to ensure fast failure recovery and possibly load sharing.

Figure 4-14 *Redundancy in the Building Distribution Layer*

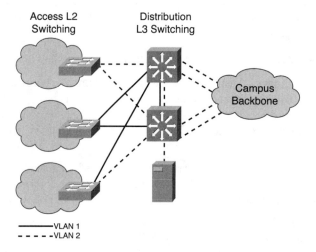

Because of the redundancy in this example, the network designer must also address STP on the distribution layer, particularly when the possibility of Layer 2 loops exists. Figure 4-14 illustrates the access layer that is connected to both distribution switches, which are also directly interconnected. If the same VLAN spreads across all links, STP must be implemented on the access and distribution switches. If the link to the access layer fails, STP recovery time might also be a concern. STP features such as UplinkFast, BackboneFast, or RSTP can reduce the time taken to switch from one active link to another. If the connectivity to the campus backbone is based on Layer 3, STP on those ports is not necessary.

Campus Backbone Design

Low price per port and high-port density can govern wiring closet environments, but high-performance wire-rate multilayer switching drives the campus backbone design.

A campus backbone should be deployed where three or more buildings are to be connected in the enterprise campus. Backbone switches reduce the number of connections between the distribution layer switches and simplify the integration of enterprise campus modules (such as the Server Farm and Edge Distribution modules). Campus backbone switches are Layer 2 and Layer 3 switches that are primarily focused on wire-speed forwarding on all interfaces. Backbone switches are differentiated by the level of performance achieved per port rather than by high port densities.

When implementing the campus backbone, the first issue the network designer must solve is the switching mechanism—and consequently, the entire campus backbone design (Layer 2, Layer 3, or mixed Layer 2/Layer 3). Other issues to consider include the following:

- The Layer 2/Layer 3 performances needed in the campus network's backbone.

- The number of high-capacity ports for distribution layer aggregation and connection to other campus modules, such as the Server Farm or Edge Distribution.

- Redundancy requirements. To provide adequate redundancy, at least two separate switches (ideally located in different buildings) must be deployed.

The following sections discuss different campus backbone designs.

Layer 2 Campus Backbone Design

The simplest Layer 2-based backbone consists of a single Layer 2 switch that represents a single VLAN, with a star topology toward distribution layer switches. A single IP subnet is used in the backbone, and each distribution switch routes traffic across the backbone subnet. In this case, no loops exist, STP does not put any links in blocking mode, and STP convergence does not affect the backbone.

Figure 4-15 illustrates another Layer 2 campus backbone that has two switches for backbone redundancy and a single VLAN configured per switch.

Figure 4-15 *Single VLAN Layer 2 Campus Backbone Design*

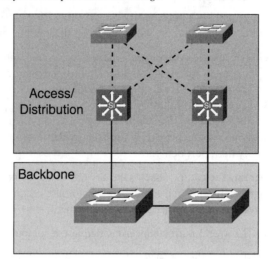

To prevent STP loops in the design in Figure 4-15, the distribution switch links to the backbone must be defined as routed interfaces (this is possible because the distribution switches are Layer 3 switches), not as VLAN trunks. This solution can lead to problems resulting from numerous Layer 3 connections between the routers that are attached to the Layer 2 backbone—especially if this includes a large number of routers.

NOTE   One of the additional drawbacks of a Layer 2-switched backbone is the lack of mechanisms to efficiently handle broadcast and multicast frames—an entire backbone is a single broadcast domain. Although the broadcast/multicast suppression feature can prevent the flood of such packets, this traffic increases CPU utilization on network devices and consumes available bandwidth in the backbone network.

Split Layer 2 Campus Backbone Design

You can implement an alternative solution that uses Layer 2 in a backbone with two VLAN domains, each on one switch but without a connection between the switches. Figure 4-16 illustrates this solution, which is known as a *split Layer 2 backbone*.

Figure 4-16 *Split Layer 2 Campus Backbone Design*

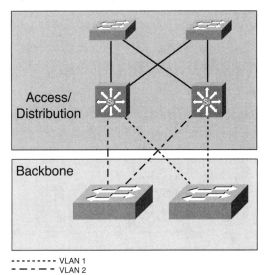

The advantage of this design is the two equal-cost paths across the backbone, which provide for fast convergence and possible load sharing.

Although the design increases high availability, it still suffers from the usual Layer 2 problems with inefficient handling of broadcast and multicast frames. In the particular case shown in Figure 4-16, the broadcast domain is limited to a single switch (that has one VLAN).

Layer 3 Campus Backbone Design

For large enterprise networks, a single or two-broadcast domain backbone is not the recommended solution. As illustrated in Figure 4-17, the most flexible and scalable campus backbone consists of Layer 3 switches.

Figure 4-17 *Layer 3 Campus Backbone Design*

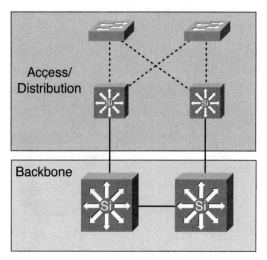

Layer 3-switched campus backbones provide several improvements over the Layer 2 backbone, including the following:

- A reduced number of connections between Layer 3 switches. Each Layer 3 distribution switch (router) connects to only one Layer 3 campus backbone switch (router). This implementation simplifies any-to-any connectivity between distribution and backbone switches.

- Flexible topology without any spanning-tree loops. There is no Layer 2 switching in the backbone or on the distribution links to the backbone because all links are routed links. Arbitrary topologies are supported because of the routing protocol used in the backbone.

- Multicast and broadcast control in the backbone.

- Scalable to an arbitrarily large size.

- Better support for intelligent network services due to Layer 3 support in the backbone switches.

One of the main considerations when using Layer 3 backbone switches is Layer 3 switching performance. Layer 3 switching requires more sophisticated devices for high-speed packet routing. Modern Layer 3 switches support routing in the hardware, even though the hardware might not support all the features. If the hardware does not support a selected feature, it must be performed in software; this can dramatically reduce the data transfer. For example, QoS and access list tables might not be processed in the hardware if they have too many entries, thereby resulting in switch performance degradation.

Dual-path Layer 3 Campus Backbone Design

As illustrated in Figure 4-18, dual links to the backbone are usually deployed from each distribution layer switch to provide redundancy and load sharing in the Layer 3-switched campus backbone.

Figure 4-18 *Dual-path Layer 3 Campus Backbone Design*

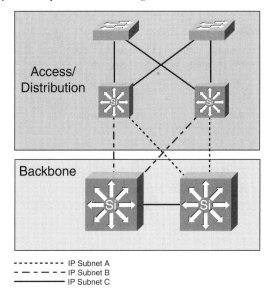

This design's main advantage is that each distribution layer switch maintains two equal-cost paths to every destination network. Thus, recovery from any link failure is fast and higher throughput in the backbone results because load sharing is possible.

The core switches should deliver high-performance, multilayer switching solutions for an enterprise campus. They should also address requirements for the following:

- Gigabit speeds
- Data and voice integration
- LAN/WAN/MAN convergence
- Scalability
- High availability
- Intelligent multilayer switching in backbone/distribution and server aggregation environments

NOTE   In some situations, the campus backbone can be implemented as a mixture of Layer 2 and Layer 3 designs. Special requirements, such as the need for auxiliary VLANs for VoIP traffic and private VLANs for Server Farms, can influence the design decision.

The auxiliary VLAN feature allows IP phones to be placed into their own VLAN without any end-user intervention.

On the other hand, the private VLAN feature simplifies Server Farm designs in which the servers are separated and have no need to communicate between themselves (such as in hosting services implementation). These servers can be placed in a private VLAN with proper port assignments on the switches to ensure that servers do not communicate between themselves, while at the same time maintaining communication with external world. (More information on private VLANs is available in *Securing Networks with Private VLANs and VLAN Access Control Lists*, at www.cisco.com/en/US/products/hw/switches/ps700/products_tech_note09186a008013565f.shtml.)

Network Management Module Integration

Another consideration associated with the campus backbone is the question of network management module integration. Although a campus-wide management VLAN was used in the past, this approach has been replaced by the Layer 3 switching approach, in which the Network Management module is on its own subnet and its traffic is routed across the network.

Server Placement

Within a campus network, servers may be placed locally in a building access module, a building distribution module, or a separate Server Farm module. Servers also have numerous physical connectivity options. This section discusses these topics.

Local Server in a Building Access Module

If a server is local to a certain workgroup that corresponds to one VLAN and all workgroup members and the server are attached to an access layer switch, most of the traffic to the server is local to the workgroup. This scenario follows the conventional 80/20 rule for campus traffic distribution. If required, an access list at the distribution module switch could hide these servers from the enterprise.

Server in a Building Distribution Module

In some mid-size networks, a network designer can also attach servers to distribution switches. The designer can define these servers as building-level servers that communicate with clients in different VLANs but that are still within the same physical building. A network designer can create a direct Layer 2-switched path between a server and clients in a VLAN in two ways:

- With multiple network interface cards (NICs), making a direct attachment to each VLAN.

- With a trunk connection or a separate VLAN on the distribution switch for the common servers.

If required, the network designer can selectively hide servers from the rest of the enterprise by using an access list on the distribution layer switch.

Server Farm

Centralizing servers in an enterprise campus is a common practice. In some cases, the enterprise consolidates services into a single server. In other cases, servers are grouped at a data center for physical security and easier administration. These centralized servers are grouped into a Server Farm module.

Server Directly Attached to Backbone

The campus backbone generally transports traffic quickly, without any limitations. Servers in medium-sized networks can be connected directly to backbone switches, making the servers only one hop away from the users. However, the need for additional traffic control in the backbone arises out of the need for controlled server access. Policy-based (QoS and ACL) control for accessing the Server Farm is implemented in the Building Distribution or Edge Distribution modules.

Switches in the Server Farm Module

Larger enterprises place common servers in a Server Farm module and connect them to the backbone via multilayer distribution switches. Because of high traffic load, the servers are usually Fast Ethernet-attached, Fast EtherChannel-attached, or even Gigabit Ethernet-attached. Access lists at the Server Farm module's Layer 3 distribution switches implement the controlled access to these servers. Redundant distribution switches in a Server Farm module and solutions such as the Hot Standby Router Protocol (HSRP) provide fast failover. (Chapter 3 discusses HSRP.) The Server Farm module distribution switches also keep all server-to-server traffic off the backbone.

Rather than being installed on only one server, modern applications are distributed among several servers. This approach improves application availability and responsiveness. Therefore, placing servers in a common group (in the Server Farm module) and using intelligent Layer 3 switches provides the applications and servers with the required scalability, availability, responsiveness, throughput, and security.

Server Farm Design Guidelines

As shown in Figure 4-19, you can implement the Server Farm as a high-capacity building block attached to the campus backbone by using a modular design approach. One of the main concerns regarding the Server Farm is that it receives the majority of the traffic from the entire campus. Random frame drops can result because the uplink ports on switches are frequently oversubscribed. To guarantee that no random frame drops exist for business-critical applications, the network designer must apply QoS mechanisms to the server links.

NOTE   Switch oversubscription occurs when some switches allow more ports (bandwidth) in the chassis than the switch's hardware is capable of transferring through its internal structure.

Figure 4-19   *Server Farm Design*

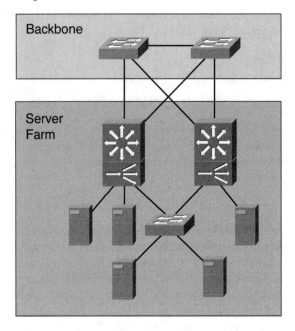

You must design the Server Farm switches with less oversubscription than switches that reside in the building access or distribution modules have. For example, if the campus consists of a few distribution modules that are connected to the backbone with Fast Ethernet, you should attach the Server Farm module to the backbone with either Gigabit Ethernet or multiple Fast Ethernet links.

The switch performance and the bandwidth of the link from the Server Farm to the backbone are not the only considerations. You must also evaluate the server's capabilities. Although server manufacturers support a variety of NIC connection rates (such as Gigabit Ethernet), the underlying network operating system might not be able to transmit at maximum capacity. As such, oversubscription ratios can be raised, thereby reducing the Server Farm's overall cost.

Server Connectivity Options

Servers can be connected in several different ways. For example, a server can attach by one or two Fast Ethernet connections. If the server is dual-attached, one interface can be active while the other is in hot standby. Installing multiple single-port or multiport NICs in the servers allows dual-homing using various modes, resulting in higher server availability.

Within the Server Farm, multiple VLANs can be used to create multiple policy domains as required. If one particular server has a unique access policy, a network designer can create a unique VLAN and subnet for that server. If a group of servers has a common access policy, the entire group can be placed in a common VLAN and subnet. Access control lists can be applied on the interfaces of the Layer 3 switches.

NOTE   Several other solutions improve server responsiveness and evenly distribute the load to them. Content switches provide a robust front end for Server Farms by performing functions such as load balancing of user requests across Server Farms to achieve optimal performance, scalability, and content availability. See Chapter 3 for more information on content switching.

The Effect of Applications on Switch Performance

Server Farm design requires that you consider the average frequency at which packets are generated and the packets' average size. These parameters are based on the enterprise applications' traffic patterns and number of users of the applications.

Interactive applications, such as conferencing, tend to generate high packet rates with small packet sizes. In terms of application bandwidth, the packets-per-second (pps) limitation of the Layer 3 switches might be more critical than the throughput. Applications that involve large movements of data, such as file repositories, transmit a high percentage of full-length packets. For these applications, uplink bandwidth and oversubscription ratios become key factors in the overall design. Actual switching capacities and bandwidths vary based on the mix of applications.

Designing Connectivity to the Remainder of the Enterprise Network

The Enterprise Campus functional area's Edge Distribution module connects the Enterprise Campus with the Enterprise Edge functional area.

Recall that the Enterprise Edge functional area is comprised of the following four modules:

- **E-commerce module**—Enables enterprises to successfully deploy e-commerce applications.

- **Internet Connectivity module**—Provides internal users with connectivity to Internet services.

- **Virtual Private Network (VPN)/Remote Access module**—Terminates VPN traffic that is forwarded by the Internet Connectivity module, remote users, and remote sites. This module also terminates dial-in connections that are received through the Public Switched Telephone Network (PSTN).

- **WAN module**—Uses different WAN technologies for routing the traffic between remote sites and the central site.

The Edge Distribution module filters and routes traffic into the core (the campus backbone). Layer 3 switches are the key devices that aggregate edge connectivity and provide advanced services. The switching speed is not as important as security in the Edge Distribution module, which isolates and controls access to servers that are located in the Enterprise Edge modules (for example, servers in an E-commerce module or public servers in an Internet Connectivity module). These servers are closer to the external users and therefore introduce a higher risk to the internal campus. To protect the core from threats, the switches in the Edge Distribution module must protect the campus against the following attacks:

- **Unauthorized access**—All connections from the Edge Distribution module that pass through the campus backbone must be verified against the user and the user's rights. Filtering mechanisms must provide granular control over specific edge subnets and their ability to reach areas within the campus.

- **IP spoofing**—IP spoofing is a hacker technique for impersonating another user's identity by using their IP address. Denial of Service (DoS) attacks use the IP spoofing technique to generate server requests using the stolen IP address as a source. The server does not respond to the original source, but it does respond to the stolen IP address. DoS attacks are a problem because they are difficult to detect and defend against; attackers can use a valid internal IP address for the source address of IP packets that produce the attack. A significant amount of this type of traffic renders the attacked server unavailable and interrupts business.

- **Network reconnaissance**—Network reconnaissance (or discovery) sends packets into the network and collects responses from the network devices. These responses provide basic information about the internal network topology. Network intruders use this approach to find out about network devices and the services that run on them.

Therefore, filtering traffic from network reconnaissance mechanisms before it enters the enterprise network can be crucial. Traffic that is not essential must be limited to prevent a hacker from performing network reconnaissance.

- **Packet sniffers**—Packet sniffers, or devices that monitor and capture the traffic in the network, represent another threat. Packets belonging to the same broadcast domain are vulnerable to capture by packet sniffers, especially if the packets are broadcast or multicast. Because most of the traffic to and from the Edge Distribution module is business critical, corporations cannot afford this type of security lapse. Layer 3 switches can prevent such an occurrence.

NOTE   Chapter 3 and Chapter 9, "Evaluating Security Solutions for the Network," further discuss security threats.

With the correct selection of network edge switches, all connectivity and security requirements can be met. The basic request, such as the need for ACLs, requires a switch that is Layer 3-aware. Only switches that provide such advanced features as intrusion detection can satisfy the requirements for tighter restrictions.

Design Guidelines for the Edge Distribution Module

Figure 4-20 illustrates an example of Edge Distribution design. In terms of overall functionality, the campus Edge Distribution module is similar to the Campus Building Distribution submodule in some respects. Although both modules use access control to filter traffic, the Edge Distribution module can rely on Enterprise Edge modules to perform additional security functions to some degree. Both modules use Layer 3 switching to achieve high performance, but the Edge Distribution module can offer additional security functions because its performance requirements are not as high. The Edge Distribution module provides the last line of defense for all traffic that is destined for the Campus Infrastructure module. This line of defense includes mitigation of spoofed packets, mitigation of erroneous routing updates, and provisions for network layer access control.

Alternatively, the Edge Distribution module can be combined with the Campus Backbone submodule if performance requirements are not as stringent; this is similar to combining the Server Farm module and Campus Building Distribution submodule.

Security can be implemented in this scenario by using intrusion detection line cards in the Layer 3 switches. (Network Intrusion Detection Systems [NIDSs] reduce the need for external appliances at the points where the critical edge modules connect to the campus; performance reasons can dictate that dedicated intrusion detection is implemented in the various edge modules, as opposed to simply the Edge Distribution module.)

Figure 4-20 *Edge Distribution Design Example*

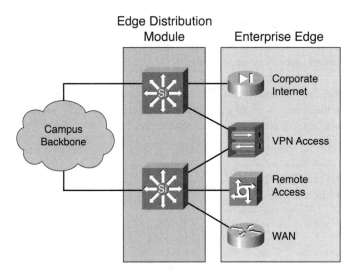

Summary

This chapter discussed campus network design fundamentals using a multilayer design and the positioning of switches in campus modules.

Geography, application requirements, data link layer technology, cabling, and type of traffic forwarding are the factors you must consider when designing a campus network.

Location of nodes and the distance between them determine a campus network's geography. Intra-building, inter-building, and distance remote building are geographical structures that serve as guides to determine Enterprise campus requirements.

Characterization of applications that are used on a network can determine enterprise traffic patterns. Four types of application communication are client-client, client-distributed server, client-Server Farm, and client-Enterprise Edge.

Switched technology has many benefits over shared technology, including higher bandwidth support, larger network diameter, additional Layer 2 and Layer 3 services, and high availability.

Deciding whether to use Layer 2 or Layer 3 switching involves the consideration of network service capabilities, the size of the network segments, and maximum network failure convergence time that can be tolerated.

The most common physical transmission media used in modern networks are twisted-pair cables (copper) and optical cables (fiber). The choice of physical media depends on bandwidth and the distance between devices.

Network traffic affects the campus design. Considerations include application traffic patterns, the presence of multicast traffic, and the presence of delay-sensitive traffic. Multicast design considerations can prevent flooding of the traffic to all switched ports.

The Building Access module aggregates the workstations or hosts on a Layer 2 device. The distribution layer aggregates the access layer and uses a combination of Layer 2 and Layer 3 switching to segment workgroups and isolate segments from failures and broadcast storms.

The Campus Backbone and Server Farm modules require fast and resilient connectivity. Campus backbone switches are Layer 2 and Layer 3 switches that are primarily focused on wire-speed forwarding on all interfaces.

In the Edge Distribution model, the speed of switching is not as important.

References

For additional information, refer to the following resources:

- Introduction to Gigabit Ethernet, www.cisco.com/warp/public/cc/techno/media/lan/gig/tech/gigbt_tc.htm

- Gigabit Campus Network Design—Principles and Architecture, www.cisco.com/warp/public/cc/so/neso/lnso/cpso/gcnd_wp.htm

- Gigabit Networking Gigabit Ethernet Solutions, www.cisco.com/warp/partner/synchronicd/cc/techno/lnty/etty/ggetty/tech/gesol_wp.htm

NOTE   You must be a registered user to access this document.

- SAFE: A Security Blueprint for Enterprise Networks, www.cisco.com/go/safe
- LAN Design Guide for the Midmarket, www.cisco.com/warp/public/cc/pd/si/casi/ca3500xl/prodlit/lan_dg.htm

NOTE   Appendix B, "References," lists all the Web sites referenced in this chapter.

Case Study and Simulation Exercise

This case study is a continuation of the DJMP Industries case study we introduced in Chapter 2, "Applying Design Principles in Network Deployment."

Key Point: Case Study General Instructions

Use the scenarios, information, and parameters provided at each task of the ongoing case study. If you encounter ambiguities, make reasonable assumptions and proceed. For all tasks, use the initial customer scenario and build on the solutions provided thus far.

You can use any and all documentation, books, white papers, and so on.

In each task, you act as a network design consultant. Make creative proposals to accomplish the customer's business needs. Justify your ideas when they differ from the provided solutions.

Use any design strategies and internetworking technologies you feel are appropriate.

The final goal for each case study is a paper solution; you are not required to provide the specific product names.

Appendix G, "Answers to Review Questions, Case Studies, and Simulation Exercises," provides a solution for each task based on assumptions made. There is no claim that the provided solution is the best or only solution. Your solution might be more appropriate for the assumptions you made. The provided solution helps you understand the author's reasoning and offers a way for you to compare and contrast your solution.

Case Study: Enterprise Campus Design

Complete these steps:

Step 1   You might want to review the DJMP Industries Case Study Scenario in Chapter 2.

Step 2   Propose the optimal campus design that addresses the scenario requirements (switched solution, redundancy, servers in a separate segment, and so on).

Simulation 1: Shared Versus Switched LAN

This exercise is a paper-only version of the simulation that the simulation tool actually performed and includes the results it provided. Review the scenario and simulation results and answer the questions.

Scenario

The customer (DJMP Industries) plans to restructure its flat campus network, which consists of workstations and servers that are located in the central building and building A. The company is considering Ethernet switching technology as a replacement for the 10BaseT Ethernet hubs. You have been asked to determine what effect the introduction of the switches might have on the load of the links and to estimate the network's responsiveness and utilization with respect to the existing applications.

To provide some proof of future network efficiency, you will model FTP and HTTP performance on the network using shared and then switched Ethernet platforms.

Client Accessing Server in Unloaded Shared Ethernet

The customer has provided the information about its existing network and the number of users. As illustrated in Figure 4-21, you began the initial network behavior evaluation by simulating the load on the LAN links, which was posed by a single client accessing the web server.

Figure 4-21 *Single Client Accessing Web Server on Unloaded Shared Ethernet*

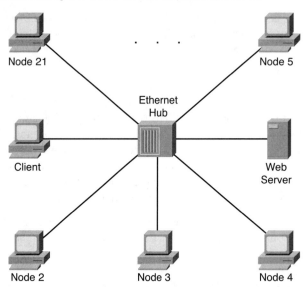

You performed the simulation (using 10-minute intervals), observed the effect of traffic growth, and compared the results among different scenarios.

The relevant statistics of interest for this case are the link (Ethernet) utilization and the HTTP response times.

The graph in Figure 4-22 shows the network load's simulation results that resulted from the HTTP session between the client and the server. The low Ethernet utilization number indicates that the HTTP traffic exchanged between the client and the server does not represent a significant load in the network.

Figure 4-22 *Ethernet Utilization on Unloaded Shared Ethernet*

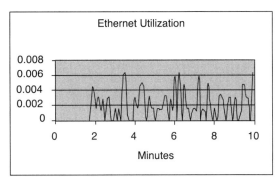

The graphs in Figure 4-23 show the simulation results of the HTTP response times. On average, the HTTP page response times are within the range of 0.01 and 0.015 seconds, whereas the HTTP object response times vary from approximately 0.004 to 0.01 seconds (every HTTP page consists of several objects).

Figure 4-23 *HTTP Response Times on Unloaded Shared Ethernet*

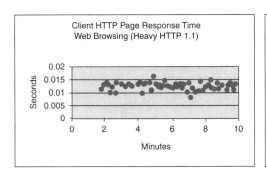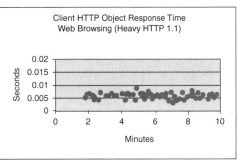

The graphs in Figure 4-24 show the simulation results of the probability that the HTTP response time is equal to a particular value.

Figure 4-24 *Probability of HTTP Response Times on Unloaded Shared Ethernett*

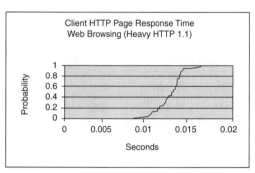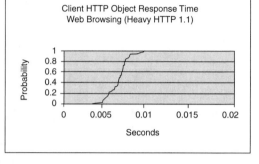

1 What can you observe from the graphs in Figures 4-23 and 4-24?

Client Accessing Server in Loaded Shared Ethernet

Your task now is to create a scenario in which the background traffic is simulated to provide a more realistic picture of the ongoing traffic in the network. The client continues to access the web server while all the other clients concurrently initiate FTP sessions to an FTP server; as illustrated in Figure 4-25, a separate FTP server is introduced to eliminate the effect of the server utilization. Therefore, the HTTP session is tested in a heavily-loaded, shared Ethernet network.

Figure 4-25 *Single Client Accessing the Web Server on Loaded Shared Ethernet*

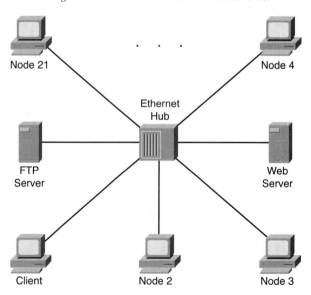

You performed the simulation and compared the results with those from the previous simulation. The graph in Figure 4-26 describes the increased network utilization as a result of the concurrent FTP and HTTP conversations.

Figure 4-26 *Ethernet Utilization on a Loaded Shared Network*

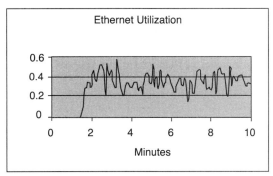

The next step is to observe the HTTP response times again. When examining the graphs in Figure 4-27, you notice that, in general, the results match those that were obtained in the unloaded network. There are some deviations, presumably because of the retransmissions that lower the probability of an immediate response. The delayed responses seem evenly distributed throughout the observed interval.

Figure 4-27 *HTTP Response Times on Loaded Shared Ethernet*

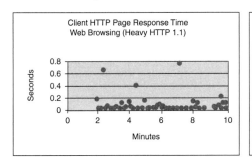
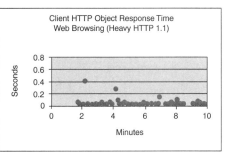
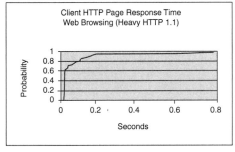
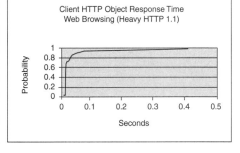

2 What can you determine from the results? What is the reason for the delayed HTTP responses?

Introducing Switched Ethernet

In the third simulation scenario, the shared Ethernet is replaced with switched Ethernet, which Figure 4-28 shows being implemented with a single LAN switch. The traffic pattern remains the same as in the previous scenario—the client is accessing a web server while all other clients are accessing an FTP server.

Figure 4-28 *Single Client Accessing the Web Server on Switched Loaded Ethernet*

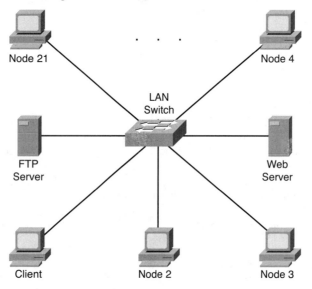

Figure 4-29 shows the results of this simulation. By examining the HTTP response time carefully, it seems that the background FTP traffic does not significantly affect the web communication. Everything is back to normal, the HTTP response times are constantly low, and there is no sign of individual deviations that could compromise the overall statistic numbers.

Figure 4-29 *HTTP Response Times on Loaded Switched Ethernet*

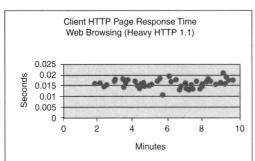
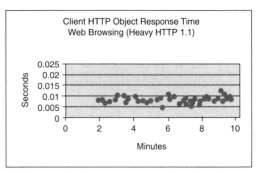

The graph in Figure 4-30 illustrates the probability of receiving a prompt HTTP response. The possibility is almost as high as when a stand-alone HTTP session was simulated (with no background traffic). This leads you to the conclusion that switching technology might be the obvious solution.

Figure 4-30 *HTTP Response Probabilities on Loaded Switched Ethernet*

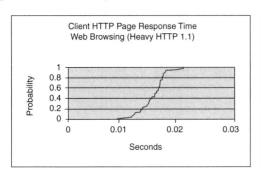
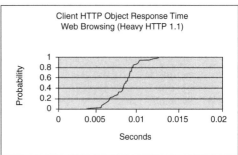

3 You concluded that the introduction of the Layer 2 switch represents a significant improvement in this case. How did you determine this from the previous graphs?

Simulation 2: Layer 2 Versus Layer 3 Switching

This exercise is a paper-only version of the simulation that the simulation tool actually performed, including the results the tool provided. Review the scenario and the simulation results and answer the questions.

Scenario

This simulation inspects the impact of Layer 2 versus Layer 3 switching on the load in various parts of the structured campus network.

After successfully deploying the switching technology, the company is considering further improvements to its campus network design. It has already finished some baseline wiring work in the central building and in Building A and is facing some Layer 2 and Layer 3 design issues.

You decided to model the company's network to match the existing situation using the following architecture:

- Each building contains distribution-layer switches, to which the access-layer (wiring closet or data center concentrator) switches are connected.
- The distribution layer devices are connected via two central core switches (the campus backbone).
- The whole campus is fully redundant.

To provide comparable results, you need a reference traffic flow. Therefore, you decided to focus solely on the communication between the two workstations—WS_A and WS_B— that are located in different floors of building A, and the server in the central building.

Initial Traffic

In the simulation, Workstations A and B communicate with the server using various loads, as illustrated by the graph in Figure 4-31.

Figure 4-31 *Simulation Load*

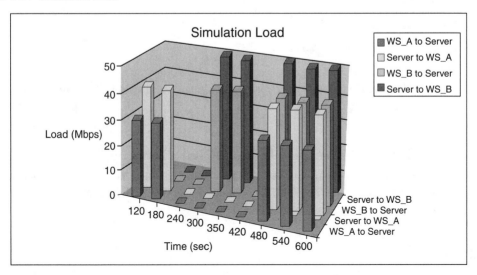

Layer 2 Only Design

As shown in Figure 4-32, you began the simulation by turning on the Layer 2 functionality on all switches in the campus network. Soon you realized that, even in the highly redundant Layer 2 network, the number of possible paths reduces to only one, as determined by STP. STP computes loop-free networks, and any redundant links belonging to the same LAN or VLAN are placed in the blocking state and cannot be used.

Figure 4-32 *Layer 2 Only Design*

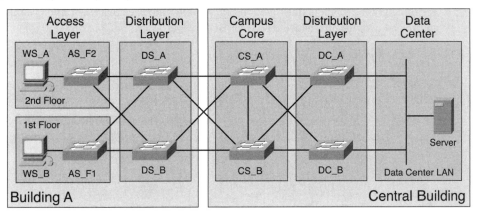

Loaded Network

Figure 4-33 depicts the result of simulating 10 minutes of traffic originated by both workstations toward the server, and vice versa. The average-loaded links (30 percent) appear as solid lines, and the heavily-loaded links (60 percent) appear as dotted lines. The resulting dashed and dotted arrows indicate that the load is not balanced; specifically, all traffic moves over a single path: DS_B → CS_A → DC_B.

Figure 4-33 *Layer 2 Only Loaded Network*

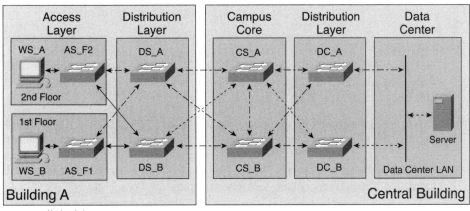

Link Failure

Use of redundant links terminating at separate devices helps increase the network's reliability. This is especially true for the observed case, in which you expect that the link or node failure would neither impact the network (at least not for a longer period) nor result in a load imbalance.

To prove this, you studied the effect of the link and node failure on the network performance by tearing down the DS_B → CS_A link and afterwards disabling the DC_B node. The resulting graph, which is illustrated in Figure 4-34, indicates that the traffic is simply redirected over the alternative path, DS_B → CS_B → DC_A.

Figure 4-34 *Link Failure on the Layer 2 Only Loaded Network*

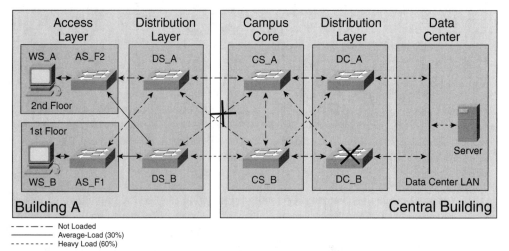

4 Does the traffic immediately start using the original path once the link or node has fully recovered?

Layer 3 Switching in Distribution

Next, you decided to replace distribution-layer Layer 2 switches with Layer 3 switches, thereby eliminating the STP path selection restrictions. This was expected to improve the efficiency of the distribution to core link usage.

Figure 4-35 presents the results of the simulation. The traffic is perfectly balanced from the ingress Layer 3 switch all the way to the destination. The sharing is proportional on pairs of source-destination distribution switches, so all the distribution switches are equally loaded (see the arrows representing the load: dotted for average load and solid for heavy load). The access layer contains the only remaining sub-optimal paths.

Figure 4-35 *Balanced Traffic with Layer 3 Switching in the Distribution Layer*

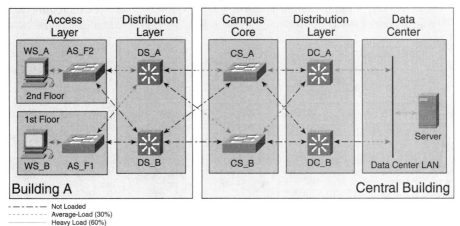

5 Examining the results in Figure 4-36, you might notice that no load sharing occurs in building A's access layer. Is this a result of the default routing on the workstations using distribution switch DS_A for the primary exit point, or a result of the attached Layer 2 switch placing the secondary port in the blocking mode?

Traffic Flow

The graph in Figure 4-36 shows the path (using thick lines) taken by the packet that is originated by workstation WS_A and destined for the server in the central building. It is obvious that the network resources are used more fairly.

Figure 4-36 *Traffic Flow from WS_A to the Server*

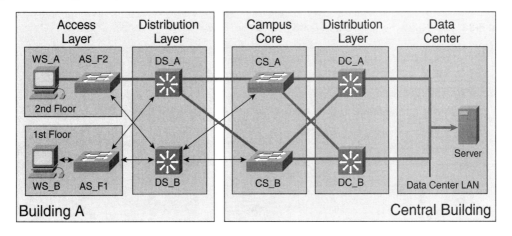

Figure 4-37 shows the path (using thick lines) the packets take in the opposite direction, from the server toward the workstation WS_A. The server uses default routing to send the packets out of the local LAN and therefore does not utilize the redundant path at all.

Figure 4-37 *Traffic Flow from Server to the WS_A*

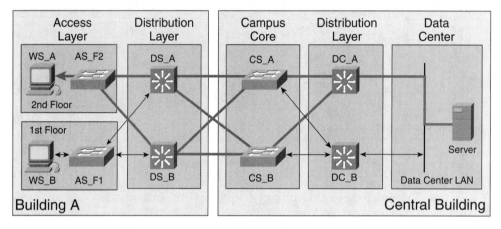

Failure Resilience

The network is now tested against severe failure events, such as link loss, by simulating a failure of the CS_A → DC_A link. Figure 4-38 shows the result; the traffic from WS_A to the server is represented by a thick line. As expected, the network does not change its behavior under link failure. The load balancing from the ingress Layer 3 switch to the destination is still perfect, but on a reduced topology. The load distribution ratio on DS_A → CS_A versus DS_A → CS_B is 1:2 because the load is shared between distribution-layer next hops.

Figure 4-38 *Link Failure Scenario Showing WS_A to Server Traffic*

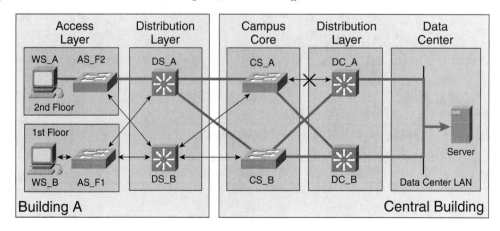

Figure 4-39 illustrates the return path from the server to WS_A (shown as thick lines).

Figure 4-39 *Link Failure Scenario Showing Server to WS_A Traffic*

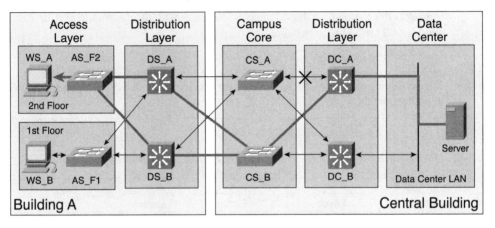

> **6** In Figure 4-39, why is the return path completely bypassing the CS_A switch?

Layer 3 Switching in Core and Distribution

At this point, you change the core so that the core and distribution layer switches are all Layer 3 switches. As illustrated in Figure 4-40, the simulated load is perfectly shared from the distribution layer across the core on a hop-by-hop basis.

Figure 4-40 *Layer 3 Switching Results in a Balanced Load*

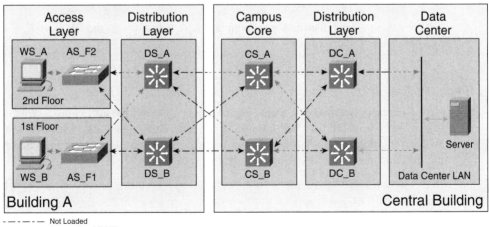

Load Sharing Under Failure

Next you simulated failure of the link CS_B to DC_B. Figure 4-41 illustrates the resulting path (shown as thick lines) taken by the WS_A traffic to the server. The way the load sharing is done is comparable to the previous case, with the distribution Layer 3 switches and Layer 2 switching in the core.

NOTE   The actual impact of Layer 3 switches in the core can only be seen if the convergence after the failure is taken into account.

Figure 4-41 *Link Failure Is Accommodated by WS_A to Server Traffic with the Layer 3 Core*

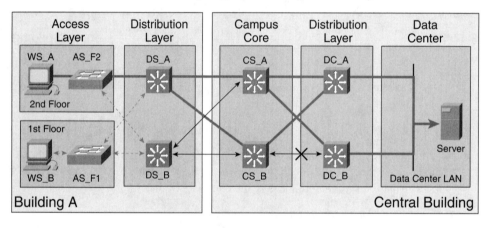

7   What is the load distribution ratio on DS_A → CS_A versus the DS_A → CS_B link in Figure 4-41? Explain.

Layer 3 Access Switch

No load sharing occurs in the access-layer LAN or VLAN if the access-layer switch is a Layer 2 switch and all the workstations use the same default gateway (distribution-layer switch). To achieve load sharing in the access layer, the workstations must be configured to use different next hops (DS_A and DS_B, in this case) for their default routes.

In this scenario, the AS_F1 access-layer switch is upgraded to a Layer 3 switch to achieve more optimal load sharing in the access layer.

Figure 4-42 illustrates the result of the simulation (shown as thick lines): load sharing from AS_F1 toward DS_A and DS_B is perfect.

Figure 4-42 *Load Sharing in Access the Layer with a Layer 3 Switch*

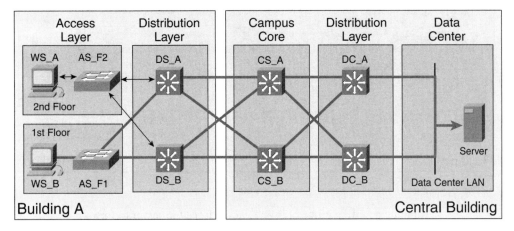

   8 The workstation WS_B is not running any routing protocol; rather, it depends on the default routing. What is a proper next-hop address?

IP Routing Process on the Server

In the last scenario, OSPF is configured on the server. The server starts participating in the campus routing and can rely on OSPF to load-share its traffic toward the workstations.

Figure 4-43 shows the result of the server to WS_A path simulation (shown as thick lines): the load distribution is achieved from the access layer to the destination.

Figure 4-43 *Load Sharing with the Server Running OSPF*

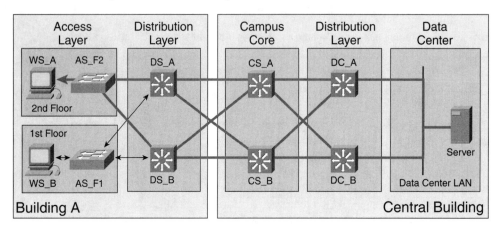

9 Running a routing protocol is one way to force the server to forward packets to both distribution-layer switches. Can you think of any other option?

Review Questions

Answer the following questions and then refer to Appendix G, "Answers to Review Questions, Case Studies, and Simulation Exercises," for the answers.

1 What factors must be considered when designing a campus network?

2 A company keeps all its servers and workstations within one building. What geographical design structure should be chosen?

3 What are some of the differences between inter-building and distant remote network geographical structures?

4 The Engineering department has requirements to use a bandwidth- and processor-intensive research application. What type of application communication should it use?

5 What are some of the benefits of using LAN switches over hubs?

6 Some users in a department use an application that generates many broadcast frames, which results in up to 10 Mbps bandwidth utilization. Which of the following solutions is the most optimal in this case?

   a Provide 100 Mbps or higher connections to all users in a domain

   b Limit the number of broadcast frames in a domain for all department users

   c Optimize the application

   d Put the application users into a separate broadcast domain

7 What type of cable would you recommend for connecting two switches that are 115 m apart?

8 What is the intended result of the application characterization process?

9 With default Spanning Tree Protocol parameters, how long could it take before the redundant link is available when the currently active link fails?

10 Compare the range and bandwidth specifications of UTP, MM fiber, and SM fiber.

11 What are the benefits of using Layer 3 switches over Layer 2 switches?

12 The users in an organization are divided along their workgroup lines into VLANs. Workgroup servers are located within these workgroup VLANs. The organization has also placed mail and web servers, to which all corporate users have access, in a separate VLAN. What is the expected traffic flow in this organization?

13 A company is using video on demand, which utilizes IP multicast as part of its distance-learning program. The routers are configured for IP multicast. Taking into account that the majority of the LAN switches are Layer 2 switches, which protocol should be enabled on the LAN switches to reduce flooding?

14 Which Enterprise Campus modules typically have both high availability and high performance requirements?

15 What is the difference between the 80/20 rule and the 20/80 rule?

16 A link between the building distribution and campus backbone is oversubscribed, yet carries mission-critical data along with Internet traffic. How would you ensure that the mission-critical applications are not adversely affected by the bandwidth limitations?

17 What are two uses of redundant paths?

18 A corporate network is spread over four floors. There is a Layer 2 switch on each floor, each with more than one VLAN. One connection from each floor leads to the basement, where all WAN connections are terminated and all servers are located. Traffic between VLANs is essential. What type of device should be used in the basement?

19 What applications might require the network to handle multicast traffic?

20 What functions does the Building Distribution submodule provide?

21 What is the main focus of the campus backbone?

22 An organization requires a highly available core network and uses IP telephony for all of its voice communication, both internal and external. Which devices and topology would you recommend for the campus backbone design?

23 A company has mission-critical applications hosted on common servers that are accessible to selected employees throughout the company's multiple buildings. Where and how would you recommend that these servers be placed within the network?

24 What is the function of the Edge Distribution module?

This chapter discusses the wide-area network technologies in the Enterprise Edge functional area of the Enterprise Composite Network Model. This chapter includes the following sections:

- Enterprise Edge WAN Design Methodology
- Selecting WAN Technologies
- Summary
- Case Study
- Review Questions

CHAPTER 5

Designing WANs

This chapter addresses the external component of the Enterprise Edge functional area of the Enterprise Composite Network Model—that is, the wide-area network (WAN) function that provides access to remote sites and the outside world. This chapter presents the methodology that is used for selecting WAN technologies and explains WAN transport media options. It also discusses general WAN considerations, such as ownership, reliability, and backup. It details WAN choices, including the latest technologies such as wireless, cable, Digital Subscriber Line (DSL), and Multiprotocol Label Switching (MPLS). It also explores Virtual Private Networks (VPNs) and the use of the Internet as a backup WAN.

NOTE   Chapter 9, "Evaluating Security Solutions for the Network," discusses WAN interconnection security.

After completing this chapter, you will be able to explain the functions of the WAN and its role in the Enterprise Edge network, describe the methodology of designing and implementing WAN networks, identify application requirements, and select the appropriate WAN transport for a given application.

Enterprise Edge WAN Design Methodology

This section introduces the concept of the WAN, beginning with the definition of a WAN and the ownership of the WAN medium (leased media versus public networks). It discusses Integrated Services Digital Network (ISDN), Frame Relay (FR), and Asynchronous Transfer Mode (ATM) in this context. This section also addresses the steps you should follow when designing a WAN. Finally, it concludes with a general discussion of how design influences the process of selecting hardware components and software features.

Introduction to WANs

First, you should understand what a WAN is and its primary design objectives.

Key Point: A WAN

A *WAN* is a data communications network that covers a relatively broad geographic area. It uses the transmission facilities provided by service providers (carriers), such as telephone companies.

Switches, or concentrators, which connect the WAN links, relay information through the WAN and enable the services it provides. A network provider often charges users a fee, called a *tariff*, for the services provided by the WAN. Therefore, WAN communication is often known as a *service*.

WAN technologies, such as ISDN, Frame Relay, and ATM, generally function at the lower three layers (physical layer, data link layer, and network layer) of the Open System Interconnection (OSI) reference model. MPLS is a Layer 3 technology.

NOTE   Please see Appendix C, "Open System Interconnection (OSI) Reference Model," for OSI reference model details.

Designing a WAN is a challenging task. A well designed WAN must reflect an organization's goals, characteristics, and policies. Therefore, the first design step is to understand the networking requirements. WAN networking is driven by two primary objectives:

- **Application availability**—The selected technology should be sufficient for current and future (to some extent) application requirements. Networks carry application information between computers. If the applications are not available to network users, the network fails to achieve its design objectives.

- **Cost of investment and usage**—The associated costs of investment and usage should stay within budget limits. WAN designs are always subject to budget limitations. Selecting the right type of WAN technology is critical to providing reliable services for end-user applications in a cost-effective and efficient manner.

WAN Technologies in the Enterprise Edge

The purpose of the Enterprise Composite Network Model is to modularize the enterprise network; the model concentrates all WAN connections in a single functional area: the

Enterprise Edge. This section discusses the considerations surrounding the use of different WAN technologies in the Enterprise Edge functional area and its modules (E-commerce, Internet, VPN/Remote Access, and WAN).

A WAN provides the Enterprise Edge network with access to remote sites and the outside world. Using various Layer 2 (L2) and Layer 3 (L3) technologies, WAN technologies operate between the Enterprise Edge and the Service Provider Edge.

One of the main issues in WAN connections is selecting the appropriate physical WAN technology. The three categories of switching techniques, each with some advantages and disadvantages, are as follows:

- Traditional WAN technologies
- Emerging WAN technologies
- Internet service provider (ISP) networks

NOTE   The term *emerging WAN technologies* is used to differentiate them from the *traditional WAN technologies.*

The following sections discuss these technologies.

Traditional WAN Technologies

Leased lines and circuit-switched networks (such as ISDN) offer users dedicated bandwidth that cannot be taken by other users. In contrast, packet-switched networks have traditionally offered more flexibility and used network bandwidth more efficiently than circuit-switched networks. However, cell switching combines some aspects of circuit and packet switching to produce networks with low latency and high throughput.

Traditional WAN technologies include the following:

- **Leased lines**—Point-to-point connections that are indefinitely reserved for transmissions, rather than being used only when transmission is required. The carrier establishes the connection by either dedicating a physical wire or by delegating a channel usingfrequency division multiplexing (FDM) or time-division multiplexing (TDM).
- **Circuit-switched networks**—A type of network that, for the duration of the connection, obtains and dedicates a physical path to a single connection between two network endpoints. Ordinary voice phone service over the Public Switched Telephone Network (PSTN) is circuit-switched; the telephone company reserves a specific physical path to the number being called for the call's duration. During that time, no one else can use the physical lines that are involved. Other circuit-switched examples include asynchronous serial and ISDN.

- **Packet and cell-switched networks**—A carrier creates permanent virtual circuits (PVCs) or switched virtual circuits (SVCs), which deliver packets of data among customer sites. Users share common carrier resources and can use different paths through the WAN (for example, when congestion or delay is encountered with SVCs). This allows the carrier to use its infrastructure more efficiently than it can with leased point-to-point links. Examples of packet-switching networks include X.25, FR, and Switched Multimegabit Data Services (SMDS).

- **ATM**—A dedicated-connection cell switching technology. It organizes digital data into cell units of a fixed size (53 bytes) and transmits them over a physical medium using digital signal technology. Each ATM cell can be processed asynchronously (relative to other related cells), queued, and multiplexed over the transmission path. ATM provides support for multiple Quality of Service (QoS) classes to meet delay and loss requirements.

Emerging WAN Technologies

DSL, Long Reach Ethernet (LRE), cable, wireless, and MPLS represent an emerging group of modern technologies that either offer a new means of transport or convert an existing medium into a data-enabled system.

These technologies are described as follows:

- **Digital Subscriber Line**—A technology that delivers high bandwidth over traditional copper telephone lines. Following are the four most common DSL varieties:

  - Asymmetric DSL (ADSL) is the most common. Because ADSL operates at frequencies (from 100 kilohertz [kHz] to 1.1 megahertz [MHz]) that are above the voice channel (300 to 3400 hertz [Hz]), plain old telephone (POTS) technology and ADSL can share the same line.

  - Symmetric DSL (SDSL), also known as Single-Pair DSL and Symmetric DSL, delivers 1.544 Mbps both downstream and upstream over a single copper twisted pair. The use of a single twisted pair limits the operating range of SDSL to 10,000 feet (3048.8 meters).

  - High-data-rate DSL (HDSL) delivers 1.544 megabits per second (Mbps) of bandwidth each way over two copper twisted pairs. Because HDSL provides T1 speed, telephone companies have been using HDSL to provision local access to T1 services whenever possible. Because the operating range of HDSL is limited to 12,000 feet (3658.5 meters), signal repeaters are installed to extend the service. HDSL requires two twisted pairs, so it is deployed primarily for PBX network connections, digital loop carrier systems, interexchange points of presence (POPs), Internet servers, and private data networks.

  - Very-high-data-rate DSL (VDSL) delivers 13 to 52 Mbps downstream and 1.5 to 2.3 Mbps upstream over a single twisted copper pair. The operating range of VDSL is limited to 1,000 to 4,500 feet (304.8 to 1,372 meters).

NOTE   Cisco's DSL frequently asked questions (FAQs) and their answers can be found at www.cisco.com/en/US/partner/netsol/ns110/ns10/ns11/ns55/ netqa09186a00800a3764.html.

You must be a registered user to access this document.

- **Long Reach Ethernet**—Enables the use of Ethernet over existing telephone-grade wire using DSL coding and digital modulation techniques. LRE offers a maximum of 15 Mbps on a short distance symmetric channel. The channel's speed decreases with distance.

- **Cable**—A technology for data transport that uses a coaxial cable medium. The cable network is a high-speed copper platform that supports analog and digital video services such as Interactive TV (iTV) and video on demand (VoD) over coaxial cables. This is a good option for environments where cable television is widely deployed.

- **Wireless**—A term used to describe telecommunications in which electromagnetic waves, rather than a form of wire, carry the signal over the communication path. Some common examples of wireless equipment used today include cellular phones and pagers, Global Positioning System (GPS), cordless computer peripherals, satellite television, and wireless local-area networks (WLANs).

- **MPLS**—A technology that combines the advantages of Layer 3 routing with the benefits of Layer 2 switching. With MPLS, labels are assigned to each packet at the edge of the network. Rather than examining the IP packet header information, MPLS nodes use this label to determine how to process the data. This results in a faster, more scalable and flexible WAN solution.

NOTE   The "Selecting WAN Technologies" section of this chapter further describes these emerging WAN technologies.

Internet Service Provider Networks

An ISP's Internet Protocol (IP) network that spans an Enterprise network's remote sites is an alternative to WAN connections. This type of connection requires full cooperation at the IP layer, between the Enterprise Edge and service provider (SP) network. However, this type of network service does not guarantee the quality of sessions and is considered a best effort connection.

Types of WAN Interconnections

Figure 5-1 illustrates the three connection types for a WAN connecting the Enterprise Edge modules with the outside world, which is represented by the service provider network. Typically, the intent is to provide the following connections:

- Connectivity between the Enterprise Edge and the Internet Service Provider Edge modules

- Layer 3 connectivity between Enterprise sites across the ISP network, using VPN or remote access

- Connectivity between Enterprise sites across the SP carrier network

Figure 5-1   *Different Types of WAN Connections Are Appropriate for Different Uses*

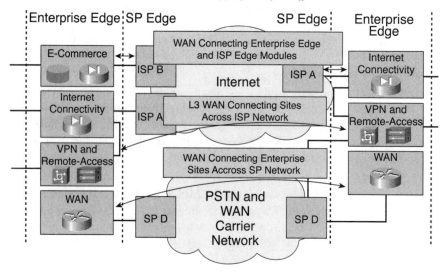

NOTE   The available service provider offerings often limit designers and thus directly affect the WAN selection process.

WAN Design Methodology: Planning and Designing

This section describes the planning and designing aspects of the WAN design methodology. The methodology espoused here follows the guidelines of the PDIOO (Plan-Design-Implement-Operate-Optimize) methodology introduced in Chapter 2, "Applying Design

Principles in Network Deployment." The network designer should follow these steps when planning and designing the Enterprise Edge based on the PDIOO methodology:

Step 1   **Analyzing customer requirements**—The initial step in the design methodology is to analyze the requirements of the network and its users. User needs constantly change in response to changing business conditions and changing technology. For example, as more voice and video-based network applications become available, there is pressure to increase network bandwidth.

Step 2   **Characterizing the existing network**—The second step is to analyze the existing networking infrastructure and its capacity for migration toward a more sophisticated design. Together with the network's physical description, the analysis should evaluate the possibility of extending the network to support new sites, new features, or the reallocation of existing nodes. For example, the future integration of data and telephone systems requires considerable changes in the network's configuration. In this case, a detailed evaluation of current options is important.

Step 3   **Designing the topology and network solutions**—The final step in the design methodology is to develop the overall network topology and its appropriate services. This must take into account the projected traffic pattern, technology performance constraints, and network reliability. The design document must describe a set of discrete functions performed by the Enterprise Edge modules and the expected level of service provided by each selected technology, as dictated by the SP.

The network is a strategic element in the overall information system design. As such, it requires the implementation of many protocols and features to permit scalability and manageability without constant manual intervention.

Planning and designing WAN networks involves a number of trade-offs, including the following:

- Application aspects of the requirements driven by the performance analysis
- Technical aspects of the requirements dealing with the geographic regulations and the effectiveness of the selected technology
- Cost of the equipment combined with the cost of the owned or leased media or communication channel

The network's design should also be adaptable for the inclusion of future technologies and should not include any design elements that limit the adoption of new technologies as they become available. There might be trade-offs between these considerations and cost throughout the network design and implementation. For example, many new internetworks are rapidly adopting voice over IP (VoIP) technology. Network designs should be able to support this technology without requiring a substantial upgrade by provisioning hardware and software that has future-proofed options for expansion and upgradability.

Application Requirements of WAN Design

Just as application requirements drive the Enterprise Campus design (as illustrated in Chapter 4, "Basic Campus Switching Design Considerations"), they also affect the Enterprise Edge WAN design. Application availability is a key user requirement; the chief components of application availability are response time, throughput, packet loss, and reliability. Table 5-1 analyzes these components, which are discussed in the following sections.

Table 5-1 *Application Requirements on the WAN*

Requirement	Data File Transfer	Data Interactive Application	Real-time Voice	Real-time Video
Response time	Reasonable	Within a second	150 ms of delay with low jitter	Minimum delay and jitter
Throughput	High	Low	Low	High
Packet loss	Medium	Low	Low	Minimum
Downtime (reliability)	Reasonable	Low	Low	Minimum
	← Zero downtime for mission-critical applications →			

Response Time

Response time is the time between the entry of a command or keystroke and the host system's command execution or response delivery.

Users accept response times up to some limit, at which point user satisfaction falls to nearly zero. Applications for which fast response time is considered critical include interactive online services, such as point-of-sale machines.

NOTE Voice and video applications use the terms *delay* and *jitter*, respectively, to express the responsiveness of the line and the deviation of the delays.

Throughput

In data transmission, *throughput* is the amount of data that is moved successfully from one place to another in a given time period.

Applications that put high-volume traffic onto the network have more effect on throughput than interactive end-to-end connections. Throughput-intensive applications typically involve file-transfer activities that usually have low response-time requirements and can often be scheduled at times when response-time sensitive traffic is low (such as after normal work hours). This could be accomplished via time-based access lists, for example.

Packet Loss

In telecommunication transmission, packet loss is expressed as a *bit error rate (BER)*, which is the percentage of bits that have errors relative to the total number of bits received in a transmission. BER is usually expressed as 10 to a negative power. For example, a transmission might have a BER of 10 to the minus 6 (10^{-6}), meaning that 1 bit out of 1,000,000 bits transmitted was in error. The BER indicates how frequently a packet or other data unit must be retransmitted because of an error. A BER that is too high might indicate that a slower data rate can improve the overall transmission time for a given amount of transmitted data; in other words, a slower data rate can reduce the BER, thereby lowering the number of packets that must be resent.

Reliability

Although reliability is always important, some applications have requirements that exceed typical needs. Financial services, securities exchanges, and emergency, police, or military operations are examples of organizations that require nearly 100 percent uptime for critical applications. These situations imply a requirement for a high level of hardware and topological redundancy. Determining the cost of any downtime is essential for determining the relative importance of the network's reliability.

Technical Requirements: Maximum Offered Traffic

The goal of every WAN design is to optimize link performance in terms of offered traffic, link utilization, and response time. To optimize link performance, the designer must balance between end-user and network manager requirements, which are usually diametrically opposed. End users usually require minimum application response times over a WAN link, while the network manager's goal is to utilize the existing WAN link. WAN resources have finite capacity.

Response time problems really only affect users. For example, it probably does not matter to the network manager if query results are returned 120 ms sooner rather than later. Response time is a thermometer of usability for users. Users perceive the data processing experience in terms of how quickly they can get their screen to update. They view the data processing world in terms of response time and do not usually care about link utilization.

The graphs in Figure 5-2 illustrate the response time and link utilization that are relative to the offered traffic. The response time increases with the offered traffic to an unacceptable point for the end user. Similarly, the link utilization increases with the offered traffic to the point that the link becomes saturated. The designer's goal is to determine the maximum offered traffic that is acceptable for both the end user and the network manager.

Figure 5-2   *Determining the Maximum Offered Traffic*

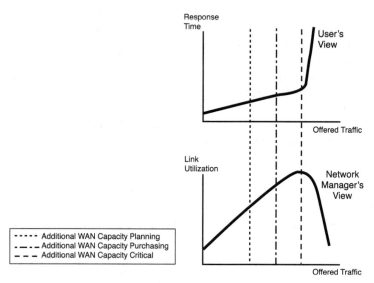

However, planning for additional WAN capacity should occur much earlier than the critical point—usually at about 50% link utilization. Additional bandwidth purchasing should start at about 60% utilization; if the link utilization reaches 75%, increasing the capacity is critical.

Technical Requirements: Bandwidth

Bandwidth is the amount of data transmitted or received per unit time, such as 10 megabits per second.

In a qualitative sense, the required bandwidth is proportional to the data's complexity for a given level of system performance. For example, it require more bandwidth to download a photograph in 1 second than it takes to download a page of text in 1 second. Large sound files, computer programs, and animated videos require even more bandwidth for acceptable system performance. One of the main issues involved in WAN connections is the selection of appropriate technologies that provide sufficient bandwidth. Table 5-2 illustrates the ranges of bandwidths that are commonly supported by the given technologies.

Table 5-2   *WAN Physical Media Bandwidths*

WAN Media Type	<= 1.5/2 Mbps	From 1.5/2 Mbps to 45/34 Mbps	From 45/34 Mbps to 100 Mbps	From 100 Mbps to 1 Gbps
Bandwidth	Low	Medium	High	Higher
Copper	Serial or async serial, ISDN, TDM (DS0, E1/ T1), X25, FR, ADSL	LRE (up to 15 Mbps), ADSL (8 Mbps downstream)		
Fiber		Ethernet, TDM (T3/E3)	Fast Ethernet, ATM over SONET/SDH, POS	Gigabit Ethernet, ATM over SONET/ SDH, POS
Coaxial		Shared bandwidth; 27 Mbps downstream, 2.5 Mbps upstream		
WAN Wireless		P2M: Up to 22 Mbps downstream, 18 Mbps upstream-shared. P2P: Up to 44 Mbps		

P2M = point-to-multipoint; P2P = point-to-point; POS = Packet over SONET/SDH

Bandwidth is free in the local-area network (LAN), where connectivity is limited only by hardware and implementation costs. In the WAN, bandwidth has typically been the overriding cost, and delay-sensitive traffic such as voice has remained separate from data. However, new applications and the economics of supporting them are forcing these conventions to change.

Evaluating Cost-effectiveness of WAN Ownership

In the WAN environment, the following usually represent fixed costs:

- Equipment purchases, such as modems, channel service unit/data service units (CSU/ DSUs), and router interfaces
- Circuit-provisioning
- Network-management tools and platforms

Recurring costs include the monthly circuit fees from the SP and the WAN's support and maintenance, including any network management center personnel.

NOTE   Because the WAN infrastructure is often leased from an SP, WAN designs must optimize the bandwidth's cost and efficiency.

From the ownership prospective, lines can be divided into the following three broad categories:

- **Private**—A private WAN uses private transmission systems to connect distant LANs. The owner of a private WAN must buy, configure, and maintain the physical layer connectivity (copper, fiber, wireless, coaxial) and the terminal equipment that is required to connect locations. This makes private WANs expensive to build, labor-intensive to maintain, and difficult to reconfigure for constantly changing business needs. The advantages of using a private WAN include higher levels of security and transmission quality.

- **Leased**—A leased WAN leases dedicated bandwidth from a carrier company, with either private or leased terminal equipment. However, the company pays for the allocated bandwidth whether it is used or not, and operating costs tend to be high.

NOTE   When the WAN medium and devices are privately owned, transmission quality is not necessarily improved, nor is it reliability higher.

- **Shared**—A shared WAN shares the physical resources with many users. Carriers offer a variety of circuit or packet-switching transport networks for user traffic. Linking LANs and private WANs into shared network services is a trade-off between cost, performance, and security. An ideal design optimizes shared network services cost advantages with a company's performance and security requirements.

NOTE   Circuits often span regional or national boundaries, meaning that several ISPs handle a connection in the toll network. In these cases, devices the subscriber owns (private) and devices the carrier leases to or shares with the subscriber determine the path.

Comparing WAN Technologies

Table 5-3 evaluates various WAN technologies against the main aspects that influence technology selection. This table provides the network designer with baseline information for comparing the performances of different technologies. The final decision is always left to the network designer's judgment and is often constrained by the service provider offerings, limited by the availability of the technologies, or limited by cost.

Table 5-3   *WAN Characteristics*

WAN Type	BW	Latency	Jitter	Connection Time	Cost per Time	Investment	Reliability	Availability
Analog modem	L	H	H	H	H	L	L	H
ISDN	L	M/H	H	M	H	L	M	H
P2P protocols over sync or async serial	L	M	M	L	M	M	M	H
X.25, FR	L	L	L	L	M	M	M	H
TDM	M	L	L	L	M	M	M	H
Ethernet over fiber	M/H	L	L	L	M	M	M	M
Leased lines	M/H	L	L	L	M/H	H	H	L
POS and ATM over SONET/ SDH	H	L	L	L	M	M	H	M
ADSL, LRE	L/M	M/H	M/H	L	L	M	M	M
Cable modem	L/M	M/H	M/H	L	L	M	L	M
Wireless	L/M	M/H	M/H	L	L	M	L	L
MPLS	H	L	L	L	M	M	H	L

BW = bandwidth; L = low; M = medium; H = high

WAN Design Methodology: Implementation

This section describes the next step in the WAN design methodology—using the design document and vendor documentation to select the WAN hardware components and software features.

When selecting hardware, you should use vendor documentation to evaluate the WAN hardware components. The selection process typically considers the Layer 2 function and features of the particular devices, including their port densities, packet throughput, expandability capabilities, and readiness to provide redundant connections.

The next step is to deploy the appropriate software features; when using Cisco equipment, this software is Cisco IOS. Software features typically focus on Layer 3 performance. While some of these features, such as Layer 3 forwarding mechanisms, support the forwarding of traffic, other features provide support for throughput, bandwidth optimization, and security (using access lists), for example. Subsequent sections discuss the following features:

- Redundant links in an Enterprise Edge network
- Optimizing bandwidth in a WAN
- Data compression
- Window size
- Queuing to improve link utilization
- Traffic shaping and policing to rate-limit traffic classes

Redundant Links in an Enterprise Edge Network

WAN links, which are often critical to corporate operations, are capable of connecting geographically-dispersed sites. However, in addition to being relatively unreliable, these links are often much slower than the LANs they connect. Therefore, the combination of uncertain reliability, lack of speed, and high importance makes the WAN link a good candidate for redundancy. Figure 5-3 presents an example of redundant WAN links.

Backup links must be provisioned to become active when a primary link fails or becomes congested. Backup links often use different technologies; for example, DSL is used in parallel with a backup ISDN circuit.

Optimizing Bandwidth in a WAN

It is expensive to transmit data over a WAN. Therefore, you can use one of many different techniques—such as data compression, tuning window size, queuing, policing (limiting) access rate, or traffic shaping—to optimize bandwidth usage and improve overall performance. The following sections describe these techniques.

Figure 5-3   *Redundant WAN Links*

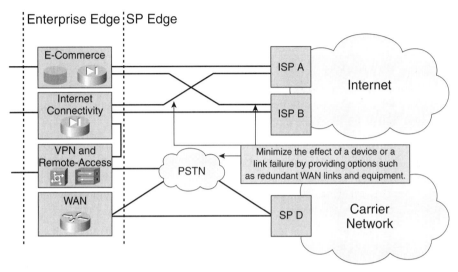

Data Compression

Compression is the reduction of data size to save transmission time. Compression enables more efficient use of the available WAN bandwidth, which is often limited and is generally a bottleneck.

Compression allows higher throughput because it squeezes packet size and therefore increases the amount of data that can be sent through a transmission resource in a given time period. Compression can take place on an entire-packet, header-only, or payload-only basis. Payload compression is performed on a Layer 2 frame's payload and therefore compresses the entire Layer 3 packet.

You can easily measure the success of these solutions using compression ratio and platform latency. While compression might seem a viable WAN bandwidth optimization feature, it might not always be appropriate.

Cisco IOS software supports the following data software compression types:

- FRF.9 Frame Relay Payload Compression
- Link Access Procedure Balanced (LAPB) payload compression using Lempel-Ziv Stack (LZS) algorithm, which is commonly referred to as the Stacker (STAC) or Predictor algorithm
- High-level data link control (HDLC) using LZS
- X.25 payload compression of encapsulated traffic
- Point-to-Point Protocol (PPP) using Predictor

- Van Jacobson header compression for TCP/IP (conforms to RFC 1144)
- Microsoft Point-to-Point Compression (MPCC)

Compression Techniques

The basic function of data compression is to reduce the size of a frame of data that is to be transmitted over a network link. Data compression algorithms use two types of encoding techniques, statistical and dictionary.

- *Statistical compression*, which uses a fixed, usually nonadaptive encoding method, is best applied to a single application where the data is relatively consistent and predictable. Because the traffic on internetworks is neither consistent nor predictable, statistical algorithms are usually not suitable for data compression implementations on routers.

- An example of *dictionary compression* is the Lempel-Ziv algorithm, which is based on a dynamically-encoded dictionary that replaces a continuous stream of characters with codes. The symbols represented by the codes are stored in memory in a dictionary-style list. This approach is more responsive to variations in data than statistical compression.

Cisco internetworking devices use the Stacker (abbreviated as STAC) and Predictor data compression algorithms. Developed by STAC Electronics, STAC is based on the Lempel-Ziv algorithm. The Cisco IOS software uses an optimized version of STAC that provides good compression ratios but requires many central processing unit (CPU) cycles to perform compression.

The Predictor compression algorithm tries to predict the next sequence of characters in the data stream by using an index to look up a sequence in the compression dictionary. It then examines the next sequence in the data stream to see whether it matches. If so, that sequence replaces the looked-up sequence in the dictionary. If not, the algorithm locates the next character sequence in the index, and the process begins again. The index updates itself by hashing a few of the most recent character sequences from the input stream.

The Predictor data compression algorithm was obtained from the public domain and optimized by Cisco engineers. It uses CPU cycles more efficiently than STAC does, but it also requires more memory.

Real-time Transport Protocol and Compression

Real-time Transport Protocol (RTP) is used for carrying packetized audio and video traffic over an IP network. RTP is not intended for data traffic, which uses TCP or User Datagram Protocol (UDP). RTP provides end-to-end network transport functions intended for applications that have real-time transmission requirements such as audio, video, or simulation data over multicast or unicast network services. Because RTP header compression (cRTP) compresses the voice headers from 40 bytes to 2 or 4 bytes, it offers significant bandwidth savings. cRTP is also referred to as *Compressed Real-time Transfer Protocol*.

Software Versus Hardware Compression

Hardware-assisted data compression achieves the same goal as software-based data compression, except that it accelerates compression rates by offloading the task from the main CPU to specialized compression circuits. Compression is implemented in the compression hardware that is installed in a system slot.

Impact of Compression and Encryption on Router Performance

System performance can be affected when compression or encryption is performed in software rather than hardware. Perform the following operations to determine whether these services are stressing a router's CPU:

— Use the **show processes** Cisco IOS software command to obtain a baseline reading before enabling encryption or compression.

— Enable the service and use the **show processes** command again to assess the difference.

Cisco recommends that you disable compression or encryption if the router CPU load exceeds 40 percent, and that you disable compression if encryption is enabled. Also, do not enable compression on your routers if the files being sent across the network are already compressed.

Window Size

Window size is the number of frames the sender can send before it must wait for an acknowledgment. The *current window* is defined as the number of frames that can be sent at the current time; this is always less than or equal to the window size.

Window size is an important tuning factor for achieving high throughput on a WAN link. The acknowledgment procedure confirms the correct delivery of the data to the recipient. Acknowledgment procedures can be implemented at any protocol layer but are particularly important in a protocol layer that provides reliability, such as hop-by-hop acknowledgment in a reliable link protocol or end-to-end acknowledgment in a transport protocol (for example, TCP). This form of data acknowledgment provides a means of self-clocking the network, such that a steady state flow of data between the connection's two endpoints is possible.

For example, if the window size is set to 8, the sender must stop after sending eight frames in the event that the receiver does not send an acknowledgment. This might be unacceptable for long (high latency) WAN links or very fast links, in which the transmitter would waste the majority of its time waiting. The more acknowledgments (smaller window size) and the longer the distance, the lower the throughput. Therefore, on highly reliable WAN links that do not require many acknowledgments, the window size should be adjusted to a higher value to enable maximum throughput. However, the risk is frequent retransmissions in the case of poor links, which can dramatically reduce the throughput. Adjustable windows and equipment that can adapt to line conditions are strongly recommended.

Selective ACK

The TCP *selective acknowledgment* mechanism, which is defined in RFC 2018, *TCP Selective Acknowledgment Options,* helps overcome the limitations of the TCP acknowledgments.

TCP performance can be affected if multiple packets are lost from one window of data; a TCP sender can learn about only one lost packet per round-trip. With selective acknowledgment enabled (using the **ip tcp selective-ack** global configuration command in Cisco IOS), the receiver returns selective acknowledgment packets to the sender, informing the sender about data that has been received. The sender can then resend only the missing data segments.

This feature is used only when a multiple number of packets drop from a TCP window; performance is not impacted when the feature is enabled but not used.

Queuing to Improve Link Utilization

To improve link utilization, Cisco has developed QoS techniques to avoid temporary congestion and to provide preferential treatment for critical applications. QoS mechanisms such as queuing, policing (limiting) the access rate, and traffic shaping enable network operators to deploy and operate large-scale networks that efficiently handle both bandwidth-hungry (such as multimedia and web traffic) and mission-critical applications (such as Systems Network Architecture [SNA] sessions).

Key Point: QoS and Bandwidth

QoS does not create bandwidth; rather, QoS optimizes the use of existing resources, including bandwidth. If WAN links are constantly congested, the network either requires greater bandwidth, or it should use compression. QoS queuing strategies are unnecessary if WAN links are never congested.

Queuing is configured on outbound interfaces and is appropriate for cases in which WAN links are congested from time to time.

Queuing allows network administrators to manage the varying demands of applications on networks and routers. When positioning the role of queuing in networks, the primary issue is the duration of congestion.

Following are the two types of queues:

- **Hardware queue**—Uses a first-in, first-out (FIFO) strategy, which is necessary for the interface drivers to transmit packets one by one. The hardware queue is sometimes referred to as the transmit queue, or TxQ.

- **Software queue**—Schedules packets into the hardware queue based on the QoS requirements. The following sections discuss the three main types of queuing: weighted fair queuing (WFQ), priority queuing (PQ), and custom queuing (CQ).

NOTE   Chapter 8, "Designing Networks for Voice Transport," describes other types of software queuing.

WFQ

WFQ handles problems that are inherent in queuing schemes on a FIFO basis. WFQ assesses the size of each message and ensures that high-volume senders do not force low-volume senders out of the queue. WFQ ensures that the different traffic flows are sorted into separate streams, or conversation sessions, and alternately dispatched. The algorithm also solves the problem of round-trip delay variability. When high-volume conversations are active, their transfer rates and inter-arrival periods are quite predictable.

WFQ is enabled by default on most low-speed serial interfaces on Cisco routers. This makes it very easy to configure (there are few adjustable parameters), but does not allow much control over which traffic takes priority. Priority or custom queuing should be used if control is necessary.

PQ

PQ is useful for time-sensitive, mission-critical protocols such as IBM SNA. PQ works by establishing four interface output queues (high, medium, normal, and low), each serving a different level of priority; queues are configurable for queue type, traffic assignment, and size. The dispatching algorithm begins servicing a queue only when all higher-priority queues are empty. This way, PQ ensures that the most important traffic that is placed in the higher-level queues gets through first, at the expense of all other traffic types. As shown in Figure 5-4, the high-priority queue is always emptied before the lower-priority queues are serviced. Traffic can be assigned to the various queues based on protocol, port number, or other criteria. Because priority queuing requires extra processing, you should not recommend it unless it is necessary.

Figure 5-4 *Priority Queuing Has Four Queues; the High-Priority Queue Is Always Emptied First*

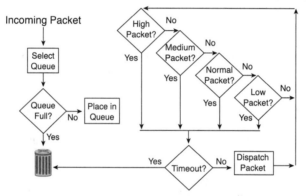

CQ

CQ is a different approach for prioritizing traffic. Like priority queuing, traffic can be assigned to various queues based on protocol, port number, or other criteria. However, custom queuing handles the queues in a round-robin fashion.

CQ works by establishing up to 16 interface output queues that are configurable in terms of type, traffic assignment, and size. CQ specifies the transmission window size of each queue in bytes. When the appropriate number of frames is transmitted from a queue, the transmission window size is reached and the next queue is checked. CQ is a less drastic solution for mission-critical applications than PQ because it guarantees some level of service to all traffic.

Custom queuing is fairer than priority queuing, but priority queuing is more powerful for prioritizing a mission-critical protocol. For example, with CQ, you can prioritize a particular protocol by assigning it more queue space; however, it will never monopolize the bandwidth.

Figure 5-5 illustrates the custom queuing process.

Figure 5-5   *Custom Queuing Services Each Queue in a Round-Robin Fashion*

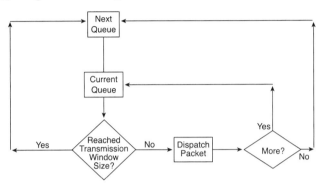

Like priority queuing, custom queuing causes the router to perform extra processing. Do not recommend custom queuing unless you have determined that one or more protocols need special processing.

Traffic Shaping and Policing to Rate-limit Traffic Classes

Traffic shaping and traffic policing, also referred to as *Committed Access Rate (CAR)*, are similar mechanisms in that they both inspect traffic and take action based on the various characteristics of that traffic. These characteristics can be based on whether the traffic is over or under a given rate, or based on some bits in the headers, such as the Differentiated Services Code Point (DSCP) or IP Precedence.

Policing either discards the packet or modifies some aspect of it, such as its IP Precedence, when the policing agent determines that the packet meets a given criteria. For example, an enterprise's policy management scheme could deem the traffic generated by a particular resource (such as the first 100 kbps) as first-class traffic, so it receives a top priority marking. Traffic above the first 100 kbps generated by that same resource could drop to a lower priority class or be discarded altogether. Similarly, all incoming streaming MP3 traffic could be limited to, for example, 10 percent of all available bandwidth so that it does not starve other applications.

By comparison, *traffic shaping* attempts to adjust the transmission rate of packets that match a certain criteria. Topologies that have high-speed links (such as a central site) feeding into lower-speed links (such as a remote or branch site) often experience bottlenecks at the remote end because of the speed mismatch. Traffic shaping helps eliminate the bottleneck situation by throttling back traffic volume at the source end. It reduces the flow of outbound traffic from a router interface into a backbone transport network when it detects congestion in the downstream portions of the backbone transport network or in a downstream router. Traffic shaping accomplishes this by holding packets in a buffer and releasing them at a pre-configured rate. Routers can be configured to transmit at a lower bit rate than the interface bit rate. For example, service providers or large enterprises can use the feature to partition T1 or T3 links into smaller channels to match services ordered by customers. Packet loss in the service provider's network can be limited by throttling the traffic back at the source, thereby improving service predictability.

NOTE   This generic traffic shaping works on a variety of Layer 2 data link technologies, including Frame Relay, SMDS, and Ethernet.

Frame Relay Traffic Shaping

Although generic traffic shaping works with Frame Relay, the Frame Relay traffic-shaping feature (introduced in Cisco IOS Release 11.2) offers the following capabilities:

— **Rate enforcement on a per-virtual circuit (VC) basis**—A peak rate can be configured to limit outbound traffic to either the Committed Information Rate (CIR) or some other defined value.

— **Generalized backward explicit congestion notification (BECN) support on a per-VC basis**—The router can monitor BECNs and throttle traffic based on BECN marked packet feedback.

— **Priority/custom queuing support at the VC level**—This allows for finer granularity in traffic queuing, based on an individual VC.

Cisco IOS Release 11.3 added the Frame Relay Router ForeSight feature, which allows Cisco Frame Relay routers to process and react to StrataCom switch ForeSight messages and adjust virtual circuit level traffic shaping in a timely manner.

Selecting WAN Technologies

Numerous WAN technologies exist today, and new technologies are constantly emerging. The most appropriate WAN selection usually results in high efficiency and leads to customer satisfaction. The network designer must be aware of all possible WAN design choices while taking into account customer requirements.

This section analyzes various scenarios to in describing the characteristics of the most commonly deployed WAN technologies. The scenarios considered include the following:

- Remote access
- Backup WAN
- Dispersed sites

- IP connectivity
- Virtual private networks (VPNs)
- The Internet as a backup WAN

Technologies for Remote Access

This section discusses remote access connections using the following scenario:

- **Objective**—An Enterprise is considering a unified solution for remote access. The connection should be seamless to users, as if they were in company headquarters.

- **Application requirements are as follows**:
  - Low volume data file transfer and interactive traffic
  - No specifics regarding the quality of the connection are stated

- **Connectivity requirements are as follows**:
  - Layer 2 WAN technologies from remote sites to the Enterprise Edge network. Investment and operating costs are issues
  - Options—Permanent connections for remote branch offices and on-demand connections for remote users

When designing remote access networks, technology selection is primarily driven by the initial customer description of the type of connection—for example, Layer 2 or IP connection. Further analysis of the application requirements and service provider offerings determines the most suitable of a wide range of remote access technologies.

Figure 5-6 illustrates the connections between the remote sites and the Enterprise Edge network for this scenario. The network designer must provide a solution that is the most appropriate of the numerous options provided by the service provider.

Figure 5-6   *Remote Access Connection Requirements*

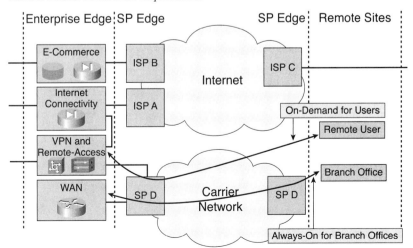

As mentioned in the scenario, the initial design options are as follows:

- On-demand connections for remote users
- Permanent connections for remote branch offices

Evaluating Detailed Networking Requirements

The network designer begins by evaluating the network parameters to help select a suitable technology. In this case, the designer considers always-on and on-demand connections for both central and remote sites because the expected performance is slightly different. Table 5-4 shows the evaluation results.

Table 5-4 *Remote Access Scenario Detailed Network Requirements*

WAN Type	BW	Latency	Jitter	Connection Time	Cost per Time	Investment	Reliability	Availability
Remote user (on-demand connection)	L	M	M	M	H	L	M	H
Central site (on-demand connection)	L/M	M	M	M	H	L	M	H
Remote branch office (always-on connection)	L	M	M	L	L	L	M	H
Central site (always on connection)	L/M	M	M	L	L	L	M	H

BW = bandwidth; L = low; M = medium; H = high

Table 5-5 compares the characteristics of candidate technologies based on the requirements in Table 5-4. (Table 5-5 is a duplicate of Table 5-3, with the viable alternatives highlighted.) Based on the requirements, analog modem or ISDN appears to be the choice for on-demand connections, with X.25, FR, and TDM for permanent connections.

Table 5-5 *Candidate WAN Technologies*

WAN Type	BW	Latency	Jitter	Connection Time	Cost per Time	Investment	Reliability	Availability
Analog modem	L	H	H	H	H	L	L	H
ISDN	L	M/H	H	M	H	L	M	H

Table 5-5   *Candidate WAN Technologies (Continued)*

WAN Type	BW	Latency	Jitter	Connection Time	Cost per Time	Investment	Reliability	Availability
P2P protocols over sync or async Serial	L	M	M	L	M	M	M	H
X.25, FR	L	L	L	L	M	M	M	H
TDM	M	L	L	L	M	M	M	H
Ethernet over fiber	M/H	L	L	L	M	M	M	M
Leased lines	M/H	L	L	L	M/H	H	H	L
POS and ATM over SONET/ SDH	H	L	L	L	M	M	H	M
ADSL, LRE	L/M	M/H	M/H	L	L	M	M	M
Cable modem	L/M	M/H	M/H	L	L	M	L	M
Wireless	L/M	M/H	M/H	L	L	M	L	L
MPLS	H	L	L	L	M	M	H	L

BW = bandwidth; L = low; M = medium; H = high

NOTE   X.25, FR, TDM, and ISDN provide the capability to connect multiple remote sites over a single physical connection at the central site. This reduces the number of point-to-point (p2p) physical connections required to link sites.

When faced with multiple choices, the network designer must provide a broad analysis comparing the benefits and drawbacks of a particular technology. As shown in the following three sections, in this case a comparison is made between analog modem and ISDN on-demand connections, and between X.25 or FR and TDM for permanent connection.

On-Demand Connections: ISDN Versus Analog Modem

Prior to ISDN availability, POTS provided data connectivity over the PSTN using analog modems. This dialup service offers a cost-effective method for providing connectivity across the WAN. This is especially true when combined with applications such as dial-on-demand routing (DDR).

DDR

DDR is a technique whereby a router can dynamically initiate and close a circuit-switched session when transmitting end-station demands. A router is configured to consider certain traffic interesting (such as traffic from a particular protocol) and other traffic uninteresting. When the router receives interesting traffic that is destined for a remote network, a circuit is established, and the traffic is transmitted normally. If the router receives uninteresting traffic and a circuit is already established, that traffic is also transmitted normally. The router maintains an idle timer that is only reset when it receives interesting traffic. If the router does not receive any interesting traffic before the idle timer expires, the circuit is terminated. Likewise, if the router receives uninteresting traffic and no circuit exists, the router drops the traffic.

Connectivity over ISDN provides the network designer with increased bandwidth, reduced call setup time, reduced latency, and lower signal/noise ratios. For these reasons, ISDN selection makes sense for this scenario.

Always-on Connections: TDM Versus Packet Switching

Rather than only using connections as required, TDM indefinitely reserves point-to-point connections for transmissions. The carrier establishes the TDM connection by delegating a channel within the circuit.

In contrast, packet-switched networks traditionally offer more flexibility and use network bandwidth more efficiently than TDM networks because the network resources are shared dynamically and subscribers are charged on the basis of their network usage.

NOTE   Some applications, such as interactive voice, are notoriously unforgiving. The design of the packet networks that carry voice should use QoS features to prioritize voice traffic and manage congestion in nondisruptive ways.

Always-on Connections: Frame Relay Versus X.25

Frame Relay is often described as a streamlined version of X.25, which offers fewer robust capabilities, such as windowing and retransmission of lost data. FR typically operates over WAN facilities that offer more reliable connection services and a higher degree of reliability than the media for which X.25 was designed. FR is a Layer 2 protocol, while X.25 also provides services at Layer 3 (the network layer). This enables FR to offer higher performance and greater transmission efficiency than X.25 and makes FR suitable for current WAN applications, such as LAN interconnection.

NOTE   X.25 is a legacy technology that is still used in some environments but is being replaced by faster and more efficient technologies, such as FR.

Packet-Switched Network Topologies

There are three basic design approaches for packet-switched networks: star, full mesh, and partial mesh topologies. Figure 5-7 shows these three approaches, which are described in the following sections.

Figure 5-7   *Three Topologies for Packet-Switched Networks*

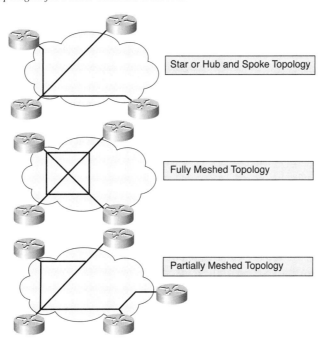

Star or Hub and Spoke Topology

Fully Meshed Topology

Partially Meshed Topology

Star Topology

A *star topology* (also called a *hub and spoke topology*) features a single internetworking hub that provides access from leaf networks into the core router. Communication between leaf networks is only possible through the core router. The advantages of a star approach are simplified management and minimized tariff costs, which result from the low number of circuits. However, the disadvantages are significant, including the following:

- The central router (hub) represents a single point of failure.

- The central router limits overall performance for access to centralized resources because it is a single pipe that handles all traffic that is intended for the centralized resources or for the other regional routers.

- The topology is not scalable.

- Traffic flow between regional routers is suboptimal.

Fully Meshed Topology

In a *fully meshed topology*, each routing node on the periphery of a given packet-switching network has a direct path to every other node on the cloud (providing any-to-any connectivity). The key rationale for creating a fully meshed environment is to provide a high level of redundancy. Although a fully meshed topology facilitates support of all network protocols, it is not tenable in large packet switched internetworks. Key issues include the following:

- The large number of virtual circuits that are required (one for every connection between routers). The number of circuits required in a full mesh topology is $n(n-1)/2$, where n is the number of routers.

- Problems associated with the requirement for large numbers of packet and broadcast replications.

- The configuration complexity for routers in the absence of multicast support in non-broadcast environments.

Partially Meshed Topology

A *partially meshed topology* reduces the number of routers within a region that have direct connections to all other nodes within that region. All nodes are not connected to all other nodes. For a non-meshed node to communicate with another non-meshed node, it must send traffic through one of the collection point routers. There are many forms of partially meshed topologies.

In general, partially meshed approaches provide the best balance for regional topologies in terms of the number of virtual circuits, redundancy, and performance.

Design as a Never-ending Process

The remote access design is an integral part of the total network solution and must scale to meet growing demand. It is up to the designer to analyze and estimate further requests for improved performance and additional services. These demands might have several solutions. The final goal is an infrastructure that has efficient, reliable, and secure connections. Table 5-6 illustrates some sample demands for remote access and possible solutions.

Table 5-6   *Growing Demands for Remote Access*

Additional Demands	Solutions
Growing number of users Peak hours of use New applications	Increased traffic requires additional capacities at the concentration site
Minimum down-time	Adding new access server and link capacities (load-sharing, redundancy)
Time sensitive traffic Securing access and data	Dedicated bandwidth or QoS Firewalls for access control, encryption, intrusion detection
Management	Management systems

For example, planning for peak usage is crucial. Small groups can use Basic Rate Interfaces (BRI) for ISDN connections, but larger operations could require one or multiple channelized T1/E1 or even T3/E3 circuits. For example, 200 modem users calling in the peak time between 1 p.m. and 3:30 p.m. would require 200 DS0 channels, which equals nine Primary Rate Interface (PRI) circuits (each PRI has 23 DS0 channels that can be used for data and one that is used for signaling).

WAN Backup Technologies

This section describes various backup options for providing alternative paths for remote access, using the following scenario:

- **Objectives**—A designer is seeking a WAN backup solution for providing high availability between the headquarters and branch offices. Branch offices should experience minimum downtime in case of primary link failure. A backup connection can be established, either via dialup or by using permanent connections.

- **The connectivity options for this scenario are as follows**:
  - Dial backup routing
  - Permanent secondary WAN link
  - Shadow PVC

The following sections describe these options.

Dial Backup Routing

Dial backup routing is a way of using a dialup service for backup purposes. In this scenario, the switched circuit provides the backup service for another type of circuit, such as point-to-point or packet switching. The router is configured to initiate the dial backup line when it detects a failure on the primary circuit. The dial backup line then supports the WAN connection until the primary circuit is restored, at which time the dial backup connection terminates.

Figure 5-8 shows a typical scenario for providing ISDN backup for an FR connection to remote locations. This includes the following:

Step 1   The link between Routers D and A fails. (Note that sometimes interfaces remain in the "up" state even if the link fails, and the only way to detect that something went wrong is to detect the loss of a neighbor.)

Step 2   The backup interface feature on Router D detects a data-link connection identifier (DLCI) loss.

Step 3   Router D immediately selects an alternate ISDN dial backup interface to establish a connection to Router B.

Step 4   A routing protocol recalculates the paths toward the remote sites; when this is complete, the network is converged.

Step 5   When the primary connection is reestablished, the ISDN connection becomes obsolete and is torn down.

Figure 5-8   *ISDN Dial Backup Routing Example*

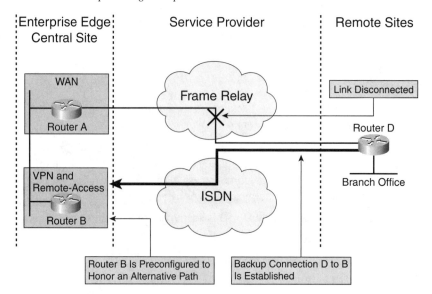

| NOTE | Using point-to-point subinterfaces on Router D with ISDN as a backup is the preferred solution when providing dial backup in the FR environment. |

| NOTE | The number of remote offices determines the number of ISDN connections Router B requires to support the dial backup application. |

Permanent Secondary WAN Links

Deploying an additional permanent WAN link between each remote office and the central office makes the network more fault-tolerant. This solution offers the following two advantages:

- **Provides a backup link**—The backup link is used if a primary link that connects any remote office with the central office fails. Routers can automatically route around failed WAN links using floating static routes and routing protocols, such as the Internet Gateway Routing Protocol (IGRP), Open Shortest Path First (OSPF), and Intermediate System-to-Intermediate System (IS-IS). If one link fails, the routing protocol recalculates and sends all traffic through another link. This allows applications to proceed if a WAN link fails, thereby improving application availability.

- **Increased bandwidth**—Both the primary and secondary links can be used because they are permanent. This results in increased bandwidth if the routers support load balancing between two parallel links (with equal or unequal costs). The routing protocol performs load balancing automatically. This increased bandwidth decreases response times.

Cost is the primary disadvantage of duplicating WAN links to each remote office. For example, in addition to new equipment, including new WAN router interfaces, a large star network with 20 remote sites might need 20 new virtual circuits.

In the example in Figure 5-9, the connections between the Enterprise Edge and remote sites use permanent primary and secondary WAN links for redundancy. A routing protocol, such as the Enhanced Interior Gateway Routing Protocol (EIGRP), that supports load balancing over unequal paths on either a per-packet or a per-destination basis, is used to increase the utilization of the backup link.

If the WAN connections are relatively slow (less than 56 kbps), per-packet load balancing is used. Load balancing occurs on a per-destination basis when fast switching is enabled. If WAN connections are faster than 56 kbps, fast switching on the routers is more appropriate.

Figure 5-9 *Example of Permanent Secondary WAN Link*

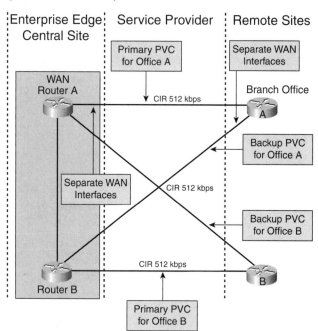

Switching Modes: Process, Fast, and Other Modes

With process switching, the router examines the incoming packet and looks up the Layer 3 address in the routing table, which is located in main memory, to associate this address with a destination network or subnet. Process switching is a scheduled process performed by the system processor. Process switching is slow compared to other switching modes because of the latency caused by scheduling and the latency within the process itself.

An inbound access list can be process-switched because each packet must usually be examined individually and compared to an access list; however, later versions of the Cisco IOS now allow access lists to be fast switched. Compression and encryption of packets also use process switching. Anything that requires router processor cycles is process switched. Process switching slows down the network and increases the CPU utilization values.

With fast switching, an incoming packet matches an entry in the fast-switching cache (also called the *route cache*), which is located in main memory. This cache is populated when the first packet to the destination is process switched. Fast switching is done via asynchronous interrupts, which are handled in real time.

Fast switching results in higher throughput because

— It uses the cache created by previous packets.

— It runs at the interrupt level.

— The route cache is usually much shorter than a routing table, so the searching takes less time.

Other switching modes are available on some routers (including Autonomous Switching, Silicon Switching, Optimum Switching, Distributed Switching, and NetFlow Switching). Cisco Express Forwarding (CEF) technology is the latest advance in Cisco IOS switching capabilities for IP. It is a scalable, distributed Layer 3 switching solution that is designed to accommodate the changing network dynamics and traffic characteristics that result from increasing numbers of short duration flows, which are typically associated with web-based applications and interactive-type sessions. Rather than using a route-cache model, which results in continuous cache changes because of the different destinations and dynamic network changes, CEF uses a Forwarding Information Base (FIB). The FIB mirrors the IP routing table's entire contents; there is a one-to-one correspondence between FIB table entries and routing table prefixes. This offers significant benefits in terms of performance, scalability, network resilience, and functionality, particularly in large, complex networks that have dynamic traffic patterns.

Shadow PVC

With shadow PVCs, as long as the maximum load on the shadow PVC does not exceed a certain rate (such as 1/4 of the primary speed) while the primary PVC is available, the SP provides a secondary PVC without any additional charge. If the traffic limit on the shadow PVC is exceeded while the primary PVC is up, the SP can charge for the excess load on the shadow PVC.

Figure 5-10 illustrates redundant connections between remotes sites and the Enterprise Edge using the shadow PVCs that are offered by the SP. Because of the potential for additional costs, the routers must avoid sending any unnecessary data, except routing traffic, over the shadow PVC.

Figure 5-10 *Shadow PVC Example*

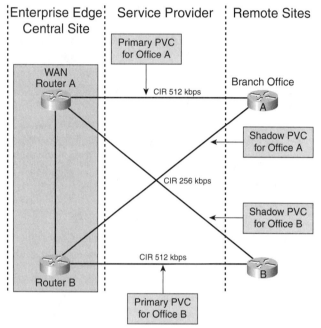

Connecting Dispersed Enterprise Sites

This section examines how to establish a WAN communication between dispersed Enterprise Edge networks, using the following scenario:

- **Objective**—Use a Layer 2 WAN to connect two distant Enterprise Edge networks in one unified network. The connection should be granted similarly to that of the remote branch offices.

- **Application requirements**:

    — High volume data file transfer and interactive traffic

    — Time-sensitive voice and video data are expected and require good-quality transmission

The following sections discuss some connectivity options.

Point-to-Point Connection

A *point-to-point link* provides a pre-established WAN communication path from a customer's premises, through a carrier network (such as a telephone network), to a customer's remote network. For a point-to-point line, the carrier allocates a physical medium to the subscriber and provides end-to-end connectivity. This is done by either spanning physical links or by sharing common infrastructure, using FDM or TDM for example. The bandwidth requirements and the distance between the two connected points are usually the basis for the circuits' costs.

Synchronous Optical Network (SONET) and Synchronous Digital Hierarchy (SDH) as a Point-to-Point Alternative

SONET/SDH is a bandwidth-efficient alternative. SONET/SDH establishes high-speed circuits using TDM frames in ring topologies over an optical infrastructure. It results in guaranteed bandwidth, regardless of actual usage (for example, common bit rates are 155 Mbps and 622 Mbps, with a current maximum of 10 Gigabits per second [Gbps]; higher speeds are expected in the future).

NOTE   SONET is an American National Institute Standard (ANSI) specification. SDH is the SONET-equivalent specification proposed by the International Telecommunications Union (ITU). While European carriers use SDH widely, North American and Asia/Pacific Rim carriers use SONET more frequently.

SONET/SDH rings support two IP encapsulations for user interfaces, ATM and Packet over SONET/SDH (POS), which sends native IP packets directly over SONET/SDH frames.

SONET/SDH rings provide major innovations for transport and have important capabilities, such as proactive performance monitoring and automatic recovery (*self-healing*) via an automatic protection switching (APS) mechanism. These capabilities increase their reliability to cope with system faults. Failure of a link or a network element does not lead to failure of the entire network.

Dense Wavelength Division Multiplexing

Dense Wavelength Division Multiplexing (DWDM) increases bandwidth on the optical medium. DWDM, which improves the use of multi-channel signaling on a single strand of fiber by increasing its bandwidth, is a crucial component of optical networks. It maximizes the use of installed fiber cable and allows new services to be provisioned efficiently over existing infrastructure. Flexible add and drop modules allow individual channels to be dropped and inserted along a route. An open architecture system allows the connection of a variety of devices, including SONET terminals, ATM switches, and IP routers. DWDM is also used inside the SONET/SDH ring.

Dark Fiber

Dark fiber can be leased from an SP and connected to a company's own infrastructure. Thus, the dark fiber connection eliminates the need for SONET/SDH multiplexers, which are required in SONET/SDH rings. The edge devices connect directly over the site-to-site dark fiber using a Layer 2 encapsulation, such as Gigabit Ethernet. When such connectivity is used to transmit data over significantly long distances, regenerators or DWDM concentrators are inserted into the link to maintain signal integrity and provide appropriate jitter control.

Figure 5-11 illustrates a SONET/SDH ring, DWDM, and dark fiber, which are all widely-deployed architectures in an SP environment.

Figure 5-11 *High-end Enterprise Connections*

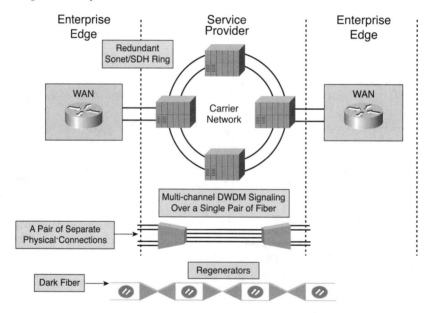

IP Connectivity and Emerging WAN Technologies

This section uses the following scenario to describe some of the various IP connectivity options that are available for IP users in geographically dispersed locations:

- **Objective**—Provide IP connectivity for remote users and branch offices to the E-commerce and Internet connectivity modules.

- **Application requirements**—Low volume traffic from remote sites; expects best-effort quality.

- **Connectivity options**—IP access through an ISP.

The intent is to provide IP connectivity between two distant sites of the enterprise network. The majority of ISPs support at least some of the numerous traditional WAN technologies, such as Analog Modem, ISDN, Point-to-Point protocols over Synchronous or Asynchronous serial links, X.25, FR, TDM, and Ethernet over fiber technologies. In some cases, ISPs support emerging technologies such as DSL, LRE, cable, wireless, and MPLS.

NOTE   Usually the ISPs do not own WAN resources; rather, they lease them from WAN SPs (carriers).

The following sections introduce these emerging technologies.

DSL Technologies

The advantage of DSL is its capability to transform PSTN copper lines into fast conduits for voice, video, and data. DSL works by way of two modems at either end of the wire.

Like dial-up, cable, wireless, and T1, DSL is a transmission technology that enables SPs to deliver a wide variety of services to their customers. These can include premium, high-speed Internet and intranet access, voice, VPNs, videoconferencing, and video on demand.

Basic DSL Implementations

DSL can be separated into two basic categories: *ADSL* and *SDSL*.

With ADSL, traffic can move upstream and downstream at different speeds. A maximum upstream rate of 2 Mbps and downstream rate of 8 Mbps are attainable. For example, data that travels from the Internet to the end-user computer (*downstream*) could be moving at 1.5 Mbps, while data traveling from the end-user computer to the Internet (*upstream*) could be traveling at 384 kbps. ADSL can also be provisioned for symmetric speeds of up to 640 kbps, thereby making it a viable residential and home office solution. ADSL also allows PSTN telephony services concurrently on the same line.

Key Point: Downstream versus Upstream

Downstream refers to data that travels from the Internet to the end-user computer.

Upstream refers to data that travels from the end-user computer to the Internet.

With symmetric DSL, traffic in either direction travels at the same speed: up to 1.54 Mbps. However, unlike ADSL, SDSL does not allow PSTN telephony services concurrently on the same line. SDSL is a viable business solution and an excellent choice for running applications such as web and e-mail servers.

NOTE   SDSL is sometimes referred to as *single-pair DSL*.

Other Implementations of DSL

The term *xDSL* covers a number of similar, yet competing forms of DSL, including the following latest implementations:

- ISDN DSL (IDSL) is similar to ISDN. The primary difference is that IDSL is always on, can reach speeds of 144 kbps, and is very capable (through compression) of reaching speeds of 512 kbps.

- HDSL is a mature T1 technology that provides symmetric communications up to 1.54 Mbps. Data travels over two pairs of wires, instead of one, and does not support PSTN.

- HDSL-2 is a full-rate-only symmetric service; however, it is different from HDSL because it exists over a single twisted pair wire. HDSL-2 was conceived specifically to provide spectral compatibility with ADSL. This coexistence with ADSL is crucial and, in this regard, the technology is superior to SDSL.

- G.SHDSL combines the best of SDSL and HDSL-2. The standard defines multi-rates, as SDSL does today, but it provides the spectral compatibility of HDSL-2.

- VDSL is an extremely fast asymmetric DSL technology that provides data and PSTN service on a single, twisted pair of wires. VDSL is reserved for users who reside in close proximity to a central office and are utilized by LRE technology.

The next sections walk you through an ADSL architecture and design example.

ADSL Architecture

Figure 5-12 illustrates a typical ADSL service architecture. The network consists of Customer Premises Equipment (CPE), the Network Access Provider (NAP), and the Network Service Provider (NSP), as follows:

- CPE refers to an end-user workstation, such as a PC, together with an ADSL modem or an ADSL terminating unit router (ATU-R).

- The NAP provides ADSL line termination by using DSL access multiplexers (DSLAMs).

- The DSLAM forwards traffic to the local access concentrator, the NSP, which is used for Layer 3 termination.

Figure 5-12 *Sample ADSL Architecture*

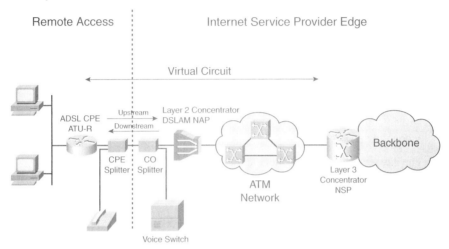

An ADSL circuit connects an ADSL modem on each end of a twisted-pair telephone line. This creates three information channels:

- Medium-speed downstream channel
- Low-speed upstream channel
- Basic telephone service channel

Filters, or splitters, split off the basic telephone service channel from the digital modem. This guarantees uninterrupted basic telephone service, even if ADSL fails.

Designing ADSL Point-to-Point Protocol Networks

Figure 5-13 illustrates a typical DSL network, including (from left to right) customer workstations and PCs on a LAN, CPE (DSL routers), a DSL access concentrator on an ATM transport network, an NSP concentrator, and both packet and ATM core networks.

Figure 5-13 *ADSL Point-to-Point Protocol Implementations*

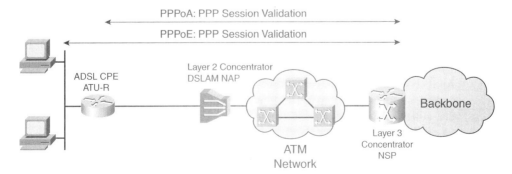

Two very popular PPP implementations exist in ADSL designs: PPP over ATM (PPPoA) and PPP over Ethernet (PPPoE).

PPPoA Implementation

In the PPPoA architecture, the CPE acts as an Ethernet-to-WAN router, and the PPP session is established between the CPE and the Layer 3 access concentrator (the NSP). A PPPoA implementation involves configuring the CPE with PPP authentication information (login and password). This is the architecture's main advantage over pure bridging implementations because it provides per-session authentication, authorization, and accounting (AAA).

The advantages of PPPoA include the following:

- The NAP usually has an existing provisioning system that connects PVCs from one end of the ATM network to the other.

- ATM end-to-end is the basis of the infrastructure. Therefore, it might be easier to put a subscriber into a specific traffic class.

- Any protocol can ride transparently on top of the ATM virtual circuit. Therefore, addressing these protocols is fully transparent to the network.

- The CPE requires little, if any, configuration.

PPPoE Implementation

In the PPPoE architecture, the CPE acts as an Ethernet-to-WAN bridge, and the PPP session is established between the end user's PC or PPPoE router and the Layer 3 access concentrator (the NSP).

The client initiates a PPP session by encapsulating PPP frames into an Ethernet frame and then bridging the frame (over ATM/DSL) to the gateway router (the NSP). From this point, the PPP sessions can be established, authenticated, and addressed. The client receives its IP address using PPP negotiation from the termination point (the NSP).

LRE Technology

LRE is an innovative technology that enables the use of Ethernet over existing, unconditioned, telephone-grade wire (copper twisted pair). The technology allows Ethernet LAN transmissions to coexist with either POTs, ISDN, or advanced Private Branch Exchange (PBX) signaling services over the same pair of ordinary copper wires. LRE technology uses the newest coding and digital modulation techniques from the DSL world in conjunction with Ethernet, the most popular LAN protocol.

An LRE system provides a point-to-point transmission that can deliver a symmetrical, full duplex, raw data rate of up to 15 Mbps over distances of up to 1 mile (1.6 km). Products that utilize LRE technology are simple to install and interface easily with any existing Ethernet solution.

Cable Technology

Cable service providers can support both residential and commercial customers with the following features:

- Digital video services that allow cable operators to customize digital program lineups and support a smooth migration path to new digital services, such as iTV and VoD.

- Data-over-cable services for Internet or intranet access.

- Managed access that allows multiple service operators (MSOs) to give subscribers their choice of ISPs.

- Cable VoIP services.

Cable Components

Figure 5-14 illustrates some of the components that are used to transmit data and voice on a cable network. The *Universal Broadband Router (uBR)*, also referred to as the *Cable Modem Termination System (CMTS)*, provides the high-speed data connectivity and is deployed at the cable company's headend. The uBR forwards data upstream to connect with either the PSTN or the Internet. The *cable modem (CM)*, also referred to as the *cable access router*, at the customer location offers support for transmission of voice, modem, and fax calls over the TCP/IP cable network.

Figure 5-14 *Data and Voice over IP over Cable*

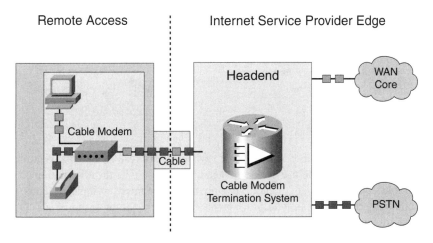

Cable operators usually install CMs at the customer premises to support small businesses, branch offices, and corporate telecommuters.

The uBR is designed to be installed at a cable operator's headend facility or distribution hub and to function as the CMTS for subscriber-end devices.

The Data over Cable Service Interface Specification (DOCSIS) is the protocol that describes the data-over-cable procedures that the equipment must support.

Cable System Topology

Figure 5-15 illustrates the Hybrid Fiber Coaxial (HFC) topology, which uses a high-speed fiber backbone and coaxial cables to connect end users. The cable backbone network is usually a SONET ring that runs on optical fiber. The SONET ring (or dark fiber) directly supports analog and digital video. The video signal is transmitted over fiber to the node, converted to an electrical signal, and forwarded to the subscriber over the coaxial cable. IP packets running over the SONET infrastructure are implemented into the data and packet telephony portion of the network.

Figure 5-15 *Cable System Topology*

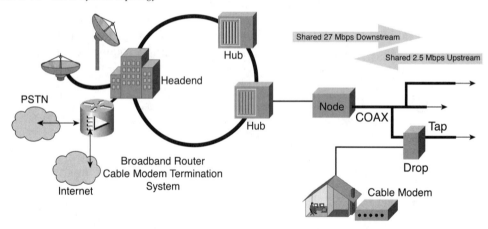

The deployment of fiber technology into the network resulted in what is now referred to as an *HFC network*. The use of fiber instead of coax permits the elimination of numerous amplifiers in the cascade in order to support the customer serving area. Thus, the operating company can significantly improve signal quality and eliminate numerous components that are susceptible to failure, while significantly reducing operating and maintenance costs.

Upstream and Downstream Data Flow

A data service is delivered to a subscriber through channels in a coaxial or optical fiber cable, to a cable modem that is installed externally or internally to a subscriber's computer or television set. One television channel is used for upstream signals from the cable modem to the CMTS, and another channel is used for downstream signals from the CMTS to the cable modem.

When a CMTS receives signals from a cable modem, it converts these signals into IP packets that are then sent to an IP router for transmission across the Internet. When a CMTS sends signals to a cable modem, it modulates the downstream signals for transmission across the cable, or across the optical fiber and cable, to the cable modem. All cable modems can receive signals from and send signals to the CMTS, but not to other cable modems on the line.

The actual bandwidth for Internet service over a cable TV line is shared 27 Mbps on the download path to the subscriber, with about 2.5 Mbps of shared bandwidth for interactive responses in the other direction. Upstream and downstream transmissions employ TDM access sharing by using either the QuadraPhase Shift Keying (QPSK) or the Quadrature Amplitude Modulation (QAM) technique.

CM-to-CMTS Interface

DOCSIS Radio Frequency (RF) Interface Specification (available at www.cablemodem.com/downloads/specs/SP-RFIv2.0-I03-021218.pdf) defines the interface between the cable modem and the CMTS. This interface's upstream Physical Media Dependent (PMD) sublayer uses a frequency division multiple access/time division multiple access (FDMA/TDMA) (called TDMA mode) or FDMA/TDMA/synchronous code division multiple access (S-CDMA) (called S-CDMA mode) burst-type format.

FDMA means that multiple RF channels are assigned; a CM transmits on a single RF channel. TDMA means that upstream transmissions have a burst nature; multiple CMs share a given RF channel via the dynamic assignment of time slots. S-CDMA means that multiple CMs can transmit simultaneously on the same RF channel and during the same TDMA time slot using different codes.

Modulation is done via either QPSK or QAM. QPSK is a method of modulating digital signals onto a radio-frequency carrier signal using four phase states to code 2 digital bits. QAM is a method of modulating digital signals onto a radio-frequency carrier signal; it involves both amplitude and phase coding.

The downstream PMD sublayer conforms to ITU-T Recommendations J.83, Annex B for Low-Delay Video Applications. The downstream also uses QAM modulation techniques.

CATV Transmission

Before converting to their respective channel assignments in the downstream frequency domain, signals from broadcasters and satellite services are descrambled.

The hub distributes the video signals to the Optical Node, which converts the optical signal to an electrical signal and amplifies and forwards it downstream over coaxial cable for distribution to the cable operator's customers.

Wireless Technologies

With wireless technologies, networks that do not have the limitations of wires or cables are becoming available. Wireless implementations include the following:

- **Broadband fixed wireless**—Designed to connect two or more networks, typically located in different buildings, at high data rates for data-intensive, line-of-sight applications. A series of wireless bridges or routers can connect discrete, distant sites into a single LAN, thereby interconnecting hard-to-wire sites, noncontiguous floors, satellite offices, school or corporate campus settings, temporary networks, and warehouses.

- **Mobile wireless**—Includes cellular voice and data applications. Wireless technology usage increased with the introduction of digital services on wireless. Second and third generation mobile phones offer better connectivity and higher speeds, as follows:

  - **Global System for Mobile (GSM)**—GSM is a digital mobile radio standard that uses TDMA technology in three different bands: 900, 1800, and 1900 MHz. The transfer data rate is 9.6 kbps. One of the unique benefits of the GSM service is its international roaming ability, a result of roaming agreements established among the various operators.

  - **General Packet Radio Service (GPRS)**—GPRS extends the capability of GSM speed and mainly supports intermittent and bursty data transfer. Speeds offered to the client are in the range of ISDN speeds (64 kbps to 128 kbps).

  - **Universal Mobile Telephone Service (UMTS)**—UTMS is a so-called *third-generation (3G) broadband*, packet-based transmission of text, digitized voice, video, and multimedia at data rates up to 2 Mbps. UMTS offers a consistent set of services to mobile computer and phone users, regardless of their location in the world.

- **Wireless LAN**—Developed because of demand for LAN connections over the air and often used for intra-building communication. Wireless LAN technology can replace a traditional wired network, or at least extend its reach and capabilities. Similar to their wired counterparts, in-building wireless LAN equipment consists of PC client adapters and access points, which perform similar functions to wired networking hubs. To add functionality and range, access points can be incorporated to act as the center of a star topology and function as a bridge to an Ethernet network. To support widespread access, Cisco has teamed with industry-leading SPs and other partners to enable secure, Ethernet-speed connections. The current standard IEEE 802.11b discusses speeds of 1 to 11 Mbps in the 2.4 Gigahertz (GHz) band. The IEEE 802.11a standard even surpasses these limits by enabling speeds up to 54 Mbps over wireless in the 5 GHz band.

NOTE   The latest standard, IEEE 802.11g, provides over 20 Mbps in the 2.4 GHz band.

Broadband Fixed Wireless Example

Figure 5-16 illustrates a situation in which an ISP offers connectivity through the use of access points that use wireless technology. The routers can be configured for point-to-point or point-to-multipoint applications and allow multiple line-of-site sites to share a single, high-speed connection.

Figure 5-16 *Broadband Fixed Wireless Network*

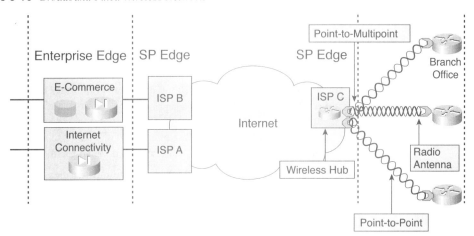

The *system* consists of a hub (or headend, or base station) that communicates with one or many customers through a radio transmission system. The headend is an outdoor unit, or transformer, that connects to a wireless modem card inside a Cisco uBR. The other transformer at the remote premises connects to a wireless network module in a router.

Point-to-Point or Point-to-Multipoint Wireless Connections

Point-to-Multipoint hub sites communicate with many sites by allocating separate sectors in channel, with up to 22 Mbps downstream and 18 Mbps upstream, shared-bandwidth. Some customers require a data rate that is higher than the SP can supply within the multipoint system's traffic capacity. However, the SP can satisfy those customers by installing point-to-point links from the same hub as the point-to-multipoint system. A point-to-point link utilizes the channel for a single connection (with a maximum 44 Mbps).

Thus, the hub can be a mixture of point-to-multipoint and point-to-point systems. In both cases, integrating the wireless card directly into the router brings with it all the Cisco IOS features and network management.

The headends, or hubs, utilize a Cisco uBR with a multipoint line card that delivers up to 22 Mbps downstream and 18 Mbps upstream shared bandwidth per 6-MHz channel pair. (This is several times faster than E1/T1 lines for a fraction of the cost, thus eliminating the need for expensive leased lines or fiber-optic cable.) Also necessary for deployment on the hub end is an outdoor, point-to-multipoint transceiver that converts intermediate frequency (IF) to radio frequency (RF) for transmitting or receiving voice or data with less chance of signal loss. At the user's site, an antenna sends and receives communications from other external locations. A cable connection to the wiring closet links a Cisco 2600 or 3600 series router equipped with a multipoint subscriber network module, which also delivers up to 22 Mbps downstream and 18 Mbps upstream bandwidth per 6-MHz channel pair.

Benefits of Using Wireless Solutions

The following list summarizes the main benefits of using wireless technology:

- **Completes the access technology portfolio**—Customers commonly use more than one access technology for servicing various parts of their network and during their networks' migration phase, at which time upgrading occurs on a scheduled basis. Point-to-point or point-to-multipoint wireless enables a fully comprehensive access technology portfolio to work with existing dial, cable, and DSL technologies.

- **Goes where cable and fiber cannot**—The inherent nature of wireless is that it does not require wires or lines to accommodate the data/voice/video pipeline. As such, the system carries information across geographical areas that are prohibitive in terms of distance, cost, access, or time. It also sidesteps the numerous issues of incumbent local exchange carrier (ILEC) co-location.

- **Involves reduced time to revenue**—Companies can generate revenue in less time by deploying wireless solutions than with comparable access technologies because a wireless system can be assembled and brought online in as little as two to three hours.

- **Comparable (or reduced) costs compared to copper**—Although paying fees for access to elevated areas such as masts, towers, and building tops is not unusual, these fees, the associated logistics, and contractual agreements are often minimal compared to the costs of trenching cable.

NOTE   Chapter 9 discusses wireless network security.

MPLS

MPLS is an Internet Engineering Task Force (IETF) standard architecture that combines the advantages of Layer 3 routing with the benefits of Layer 2 switching. With MPLS, short fixed-length labels are assigned to each packet at the edge of the network; rather than examining the IP packet header information, MPLS nodes use this label to determine how to process the data. The MPLS standards evolved from the efforts of many companies, including Cisco's Tag Switching technology.

MPLS enables scalable VPNs, end-to-end QoS, and other IP services that allow efficient utilization of existing networks with simpler configuration, management, and quicker fault correction.

MPLS Operation

MPLS is a connection-oriented technology whose operation is based on a label, which is attached to each packet as it enters the MPLS network. A label identifies a *flow* of packets (for example, voice traffic between two nodes), also called a *Forwarding Equivalence Class (FEC)*. An FEC is a grouping of packets; packets belonging to the same FEC receive the same treatment in the network. The FEC can be determined by various parameters, including source or destination IP address or port numbers, IP protocol, or IP precedence. Therefore, the FEC can define the flow's QoS requirements. In addition, appropriate queuing and discard policies can be applied for FECs.

The MPLS network nodes, called *Label Switched Routers (LSRs)*, use the label to determine the next-hop for the packet. The LSRs do not need to examine the packet's IP header; rather, they forward it based on the label.

A *Label Switched Path (LSP)* must be defined for each FEC before packets can be sent. It is important to note that labels are locally significant to each MPLS node only; therefore, the nodes must communicate what label to use for each FEC. The protocols used for this communication are the *Label Distribution Protocol (LDP)*, or an enhanced version of the Resource Reservation Protocol (RSVP). An interior routing protocol (such as OSPF or EIGRP) is also used within the MPLS network to exchange routing information.

A unique feature of MPLS is its capability to perform label stacking, in which multiple labels can be carried in a packet. The top label, which is the last one in, is always processed first. Label stacking enables multiple LSPs to be aggregated, thereby creating tunnels through multiple levels of an MPLS network.

An MPLS label is a 32-bit field that is placed between a packet's data link layer header and its IP header. Following are the components of an MPLS label:

- **Label value**—A 20-bit value. A label of 0 indicates that the label stack must be popped (removed), and that the forwarding of the packet must then be based on the IP header. Label values 1 through 15 are reserved for other purposes.

- **Exp**—A 3-bit experimental field.

- **S**—A 1-bit field. When the S bit is set to 1, it indicates that this label is the bottom of the label stack.

- **Time to Live (TTL)**—An 8-bit field. Since LSRs do not examine IP headers, the TTL field is included in the label field so its functionality can be supported.

Figure 5-17 illustrates the flow of two packets through an MPLS network.

Figure 5-17 *Labels Are Used to Assign a Path for a Packet Flow Through an MPLS Network*

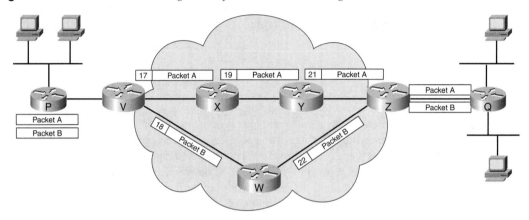

<table>
<tr><td>**NOTE**</td><td>The links shown in Figure 5-17 are meant to be generic; thus, they do not represent any particular type of interface.</td></tr>
</table>

In Figure 5-17, each of the MPLS nodes has previously communicated the labels it uses for each of the defined FECs to its neighboring nodes. Packet A and Packet B represent different flows; for example, Packet A might be from an FTP session, while Packet B is from a voice conversation. Without MPLS, these packets would take the same route through the network.

For Packets A and B, Router V is the *ingress edge LSR*: the point at which the packets enter the network. Router V examines each packet and determines the appropriate FEC. Packet A is assigned label 17 and is sent to Router X; Packet B is assigned label 18 and is sent to Router W. As each LSR receives a labeled packet, it removes the label, locates the label in its table, applies the appropriate outgoing label, and forwards the packet to the next LSR in the LSP. When the packets reach Router Z (the *egress edge LSR*, or the point at which the packets leave the MPLS network), Router Z removes the label and forwards the packets appropriately, based on its IP routing table.

<table>
<tr><td>**NOTE**</td><td>Packets sent between the same endpoints might belong to different FECs, and therefore might flow through different paths in the network.</td></tr>
</table>

MPLS Services

The following are some of the most common services provided by MPLS:

- **Traffic engineering**—MPLS allows traffic to be directed through a specific path, which might be different from the least-cost path determined by the IP routing protocol. This ability to define routes and resource utilization is known as traffic engineering. MPLS is, aware of packets' flows, so it can route packets on a flow-by-flow basis, according to the flow's requirements.

- **QoS support**—MPLS creates a connection-oriented network for IP traffic, thereby providing the foundation for QoS traffic controls. For example, it might provide guaranteed bandwidth to specific traffic between two locations.

- **Fast reroute (FRR)**—Because FRR allows extremely quick recovery from node or link failure, it prevents applications from timing out and losing data.

- **MPLS VPNs**—MPLS VPNs are much easier to deploy than traditional VPNs. They scale easily with increasing numbers of routes and customers, and provide the same level of privacy as Layer 2 technologies. MPLS VPNs can also support non-unique IP addresses in various locations; for example, two organizations that both use the 10.0.0.0 private address space can be supported.

- **Multiprotocol support**—MPLS can be used in an ATM network, a Frame Relay network, or a pure IP-based Internet.

Virtual Private Networks

A *VPN* is connectivity deployed on a shared infrastructure; it has the same policies and performance as a private network, but with lower total cost of ownership. The infrastructure used can be the Internet, an IP infrastructure, or any WAN infrastructure, such as an FR network or an ATM WAN. The following sections discuss these topics:

- VPN applications
- VPN connectivity options including Overlay VPNs, VPDNs (Virtual Private Dialup Networks), and peer-to-peer VPNs
- The benefits of VPNs

VPN Applications

VPNs can be grouped according to their applications:

- **Access VPN**—Access VPNs provide access to a corporate intranet (or extranet) over a shared infrastructure and have the same policies as a private network. Remote-access connectivity is through dialup, ISDN, DSL, wireless, and/or cable technologies. Access VPNs enable businesses to outsource their dial or other broadband remote access connections without compromising their security policy.

They encompass two architectural options: client-initiated or Network Access Server (NAS)-initiated connections. With client-initiated VPNs, users establish an encrypted IP tunnel from their PCs across an SP's shared network to their corporate network. With NAS-initiated VPNs, the tunnel is initiated from the NAS. In this scenario, remote users dial into the local SP POP, and the SP initiates a secure, encrypted tunnel to the corporate network.

- **Intranet VPN**—Intranet VPNs link remote offices by extending the corporate network across a shared infrastructure. The intranet VPN services are typically based on extending the basic remote access VPN to other corporate offices across the Internet or across the SP's IP backbone. Note that there are no performance guarantees with VPNs across the Internet—no one is responsible for the Internet. The main benefits of intranet VPNs are reduced WAN infrastructure needs, which result in lower ongoing leased-line or FR charges and operational savings.

- **Extranet VPN**—Extranet VPNs extend the connectivity to business partners, suppliers, and customers across the Internet or an SP's network. The security policy becomes very important at this point; for example, the company does not want a hacker to spoof any orders from a business partner.

VPN Connectivity Options

The following connectivity options can provide IP access through VPNs:

- Overlay VPNs
- Virtual private dialup networks (VPDNs)
- Peer-to-peer VPNs

The following sections describe these options.

Overlay VPNs

With overlay VPNs, the provider's infrastructure provides virtual point-to-point links between customer sites. Overlay VPNs are implemented with a number of technologies, ranging from traditional Layer 1 and Layer 2 technologies (such as ISDN, SONET/SDH, FR, and ATM) to modern Layer 3 IP-based solutions (such as Generic Routing Encapsulation [GRE] and IPsec).

From the Layer 3 perspective, the provider network is invisible: the customer routers are linked with emulated point-to-point links. The routing protocol runs directly between routers that establish routing adjacencies and exchange routing information. The provider is not aware of customer routing and does not have any information about customer routes. The provider's only responsibility is the point-to-point data transport between customer sites.

Although they are well known and easy to implement, the overlay VPNs are more difficult to operate and have higher maintenance costs for the following reasons:

- Every individual virtual circuit must be provisioned.

- Optimum routing between customer sites requires a full mesh of virtual circuits between sites.

- Bandwidth must be provisioned on a site-to-site basis.

The concept of VPNs was introduced early in the emergence of data communications with technologies such as X.25 and FR. These technologies use virtual circuits to establish the end-to-end connection over a shared SP infrastructure. In the case of overlay VPNs, emulated point-to-point links replace the dedicated links and cause statistical sharing of the provider infrastructure. This enables the provider to offer the connectivity for a lower price and results in lower operational costs.

Figure 5-18 illustrates an overlay VPN. The router on the left (in the Enterprise Edge module) has one physical connection to the SP, with two virtual circuits provisioned. Virtual Circuit 1 (VC #1) provides connectivity to the router on the top right. Virtual Circuit 2 (VC #2) provides connectivity to the branch office router on the bottom right.

Figure 5-18 *Overlay VPNs Extend the Enterprise Network*

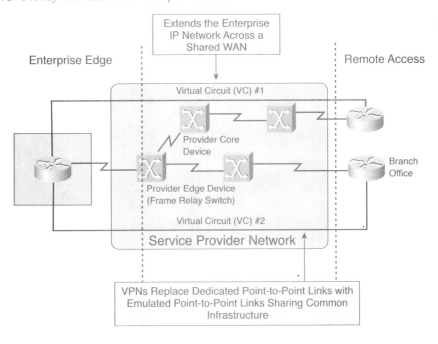

VPDNs

VPDNs enable an enterprise to configure secure networks that rely upon an ISP. With VPDNs, the customers use a provider's dial-in infrastructure for their private dialup connections. Analog, dial-in, ISDN, DSL, or cable technologies are used to connect to the local SP edge.

The ISP agrees to forward the company's traffic from the ISP's point of presence (POP) to a company-run home gateway. Network configuration and security remain in the client's control. The SP supplies a virtual tunnel between the company's sites using Cisco's Layer 2 Forwarding (L2F), Point-to-Point Tunneling (PPTP), or IETF Layer 2 Tunneling Protocol (L2TP) tunnels.

Figure 5-19 illustrates an example of a VPDN. In this figure, the ISP terminates the dialup connections at the L2TP Access Concentrator (LAC) and forwards traffic through dynamically established tunnels to a remote access server called the L2TP Network Server (LNS). A VPDN can be used with any available access, and ubiquity is important. (This means that VPDNs should work with a modem, ISDN, xDSL, or cable connections.) A VPDN provides potential operations and infrastructure cost savings because a company can outsource its dial equipment, thereby avoiding the costs of being in the remote access server business.

Figure 5-19 *A VPDN for Remote Access*

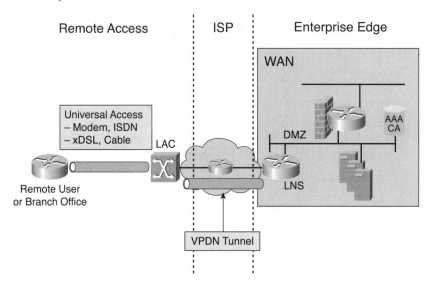

VPDN Tunnels

Access VPN connectivity involves the configuration of VPDN tunnels. Following are the two types of tunnels:

— The client PC initiates *voluntary tunnels*. The client dials into the SP network, a PPP session is established, and the user logs on to the SP network. The client then runs the VPN software to establish a tunnel to the network server.

— *Compulsory tunnels* require SP participation and awareness, leaving the client no influence over tunnels selection. The client still dials in and establishes a PPP session. The SP (not the client) then establishes the tunnel to the network server.

Peer-to-Peer VPNs

In a new paradigm called peer-to-peer VPN, the provider actively participates in customer routing.

Traditional peer-to-peer VPNs are implemented with packet filters on shared provider edge (PE) routers, or with dedicated per-customer PE-routers. In addition to high maintenance costs for the packet filter approach or equipment costs for the dedicated per-customer PE-router approach, both methods require the customer to accept the provider-assigned address space or to use public IP addresses in the private customer network.

Modern MPLS VPNs provide all the benefits of peer-to-peer VPNs, but alleviate most of the peer-to-peer VPN drawbacks such as the need for common customer addresses. Overlapping addresses, which are usually the result of companies using private addressing, are one of the major obstacles to successful peer-to-peer VPN implementations. MPLS VPNs solve this problem by giving each VPN its own routing and forwarding table in the router, thus effectively creating virtual routers for each customer.

NOTE   RFC 2547, *BGP/MPLS VPNs*, defines MPLS VPNs.

Benefits of VPNs

The benefits of using VPNs include the following:

- **Flexibility**—VPNs offer flexibility because site-to-site and remote-access connections can be set up quickly and over existing infrastructure to extend the network to remote users. Extranet connectivity for business partners is also a possibility. A variety of security policies can be provisioned in a VPN, thereby enabling flexible interconnection of different security domains.

- **Scalability**—VPNs allow an organization to leverage and extend the classic WAN to more remote and external users. VPNs offer scalability over large areas because IP transport is universally available. This arrangement reduces the number of physical connections and simplifies the underlying structure of a customer's WAN.

- **Lower network communication cost**—Lower cost is a primary reason for migrating from traditional connectivity options to a VPN connection. Reduced dialup and dedicated bandwidth infrastructure and service provider costs make VPNs attractive. Customers can reuse existing links and take advantage of the statistical packet multiplexing features.

Internet as a WAN Backup Technology

This section describes the Internet as an alternate option for a failed WAN connection. This type of connection is considered *best effort* and guarantees a 0 kbps committed bandwidth rate.

Common methods for connecting noncontiguous private networks over a public IP network include the following:

- IP routing without constraints
- Generic Routing Encapsulation tunnels
- IPSec tunnels

The following sections describe these methods.

IP Routing without Constraints

When relying on the Internet to provide a backup for branch offices, a company must fully cooperate with the ISP, including gaining connectivity by announcing its networks. The backup network—the Internet—therefore becomes aware of the company's networks. The data is sent unencrypted.

Layer 3 Tunneling with GRE and IPSec

Layer 3 tunneling uses a Layer 3 protocol to transport over another Layer 3 network. Usually, Layer 3 tunneling is used either to connect two noncontiguous parts of a non-IP network over an IP network, or to connect two IP networks over a backbone IP network. This can possibly hide the IP addressing details of the two networks from the backbone IP network.

Following are the two Layer 3 tunneling methods for connecting noncontiguous private networks over a public IP network:

- **GRE**—A standardized Layer 3 carrier encapsulation that is designed for generic tunneling of protocols. In the Cisco IOS, GRE tunnels IP over IP; this process is useful when building a small-scale IP VPN network that does not require substantial security.

  GRE enables simple and flexible deployment of basic IP VPNs. Deployment is easy, and there is no change to the intermediate systems (ISP backbones). However, tunnel provisioning is not very scalable in a full-mesh network because every point-to-point association must be defined separately. Packet payload is not protected against sniffing and unauthorized changes, and there is no authentication of sender.

  Using GRE tunnels as a mechanism for backup links has several drawbacks, including administrative overhead, scaling to large numbers of tunnels, and processing overhead of the GRE encapsulation.

- **IPSec**—Provides security for the transmission of sensitive information over unprotected networks (such as the Internet) by encrypting the tunnel's data. IPSec acts as the network layer, in tunneling or transport mode, and protects and authenticates IP packets between participating IPSec devices. Following are some features of IPSec:
  — Data confidentiality—An IPSec sender can encrypt packets before transmitting them across a network.
  — Data integrity—An IPSec receiver can authenticate packets sent by an IPSec sender to ensure that the data has not been altered during transmission.
  — Data origin Authentication—An IPSec receiver can authenticate the source of the sent IPsec packets. This service depends on the data integrity service.
  — Anti-replay—An IPSec receiver can detect and reject replay.
  — Easy deployment, with no change to the intermediate systems (ISP backbones).
  — No change to existing applications (transparent).
  — Uses the Internet Key Exchange (IKE) for automated key management.
  — Has interoperability with Public Key Infrastructure (PKI).

NOTE   IPsec can be combined with GRE tunnels to provide security in the generic tunnels. This would encrypt the GRE payload if the payload is IP.

IPSec

IPSec is standards-based and provides a robust security solution. In addition to data confidentiality services, it provides data authentication services (including authenticating the origin of the data) and anti-replay services (so that the receiver can reject old or duplicate packets). Because it is standards-based, IPSec allows Cisco devices to interoperate with other non-Cisco IPSec-compliant networking devices, including PCs and servers.

IPSec also allows the use of digital certificates using the IKE protocol and Certification Authorities (CAs). A *digital certificate* contains information to identify a user or device, such as the name, serial number, company, or IP address. It also contains a copy of the device's public key. CA, which is a third party whom the receiver explicitly trusts to validate identities and create digital certificates, signs the certificate. When using digital certificates, each device is enrolled with a CA. When two devices want to communicate, they exchange certificates and digitally sign data to authenticate each other. Manual exchange and verification of keys are not required.

When adding a new device to the network, you must simply enroll it with a CA; none of the other devices need modification. When the new device attempts an IPSec connection, certificates are automatically exchanged, and the device can be authenticated.

Figure 5-20 illustrates two noncontiguous networks that are connected over a point-to-point logical link with a backup implemented over an IP network using a GRE IP tunnel. Such tunnels are configured between a source (ingress) router and a destination (egress) router, and are visible as interfaces on each router.

Figure 5-20 *Backup GRE Tunnel over a Public IP Network*

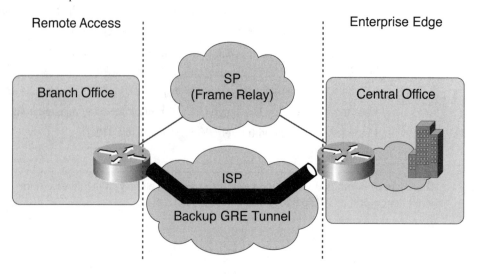

A packet that is to be forwarded across the tunnel is already formatted in a packet, with the data encapsulated in the standard IP packet header. This packet is further encapsulated with a new GRE header and placed into the tunnel with the destination IP address set to the tunnel endpoint, the new next hop. When the GRE packet reaches the tunnel endpoint, the GRE header is stripped away, and the packet continues to be forwarded to the destination with the original IP packet header.

Summary

This chapter discussed the WAN functions in the Enterprise Edge. The role of the WAN is to connect distant sites in a reliable and efficient manner over transmission facilities provided by SPs.

Traditional WAN technologies include

- Leased lines
- Circuit-switched networks
- Packet- and cell-switched networks
- ATM

Emerging WAN technologies include

- DSL
- LRE
- Cable
- Wireless
- MPLS

Planning and designing WAN networks involves making trade-offs between application requirements, technical requirements, and cost.

WAN implementation entails selecting appropriate hardware components and software features. Some of these features include compression, queuing, traffic shaping, and policing.

Dialup services are cost-effective for connectivity across WANs. ISDN provides increased bandwidth, reduced call setup time, and reduced latency.

Because the network resources are shared dynamically, packet-switched networks traditionally offer more flexibility and use network bandwidth more efficiently than TDM networks.

You can implement a WAN backup with dial backup routing, a permanent secondary WAN link, or a shadow PVC.

DSL technology allows the use of PSTN copper lines as high-speed data links. LRE enables the use of Ethernet LAN tansmissions over PSTN lines.

CATV operators can use the extra available bandwidth for data, VoIP, and managed access services.

Wireless technologies allow networks to be available without the constraints of cables.

MPLS provides a scalable, flexible WAN with the benefits of both Layer 3 routing and Layer 2 switching.

VPNs that are deployed on a shared infrastructure guarantee the same policies and performance as a private network. The following connectivity options can provide IP access through VPNs:

- Overlay VPNs
- VPDNs
- Peer-to-peer VPNs

References

For additional information, refer to the following resources:

- Cisco Product Documentation: www.cisco.com/univercd
- IT-related definitions and acronyms: www.whatis.com/
- VPNs: www.cisco.com/warp/public/779/largeent/learn/technologies/VPNs.html
- Managed VPN services: www.cisco.com/warp/public/779/servpro/services/vpn/

Case Study

This case study is a continuation of the DJMP Industries case study first introduced in Chapter 2.

Case Study General Instructions

Use the scenarios, information, and parameters provided at each task of the ongoing case study. If you encounter ambiguities, make reasonable assumptions and proceed. For all tasks, use the initial customer scenario and build on the solutions provided thus far.

You can use any and all documentation, books, white papers, and so on.

In each task, you act as a network design consultant. Make creative proposals to accomplish the customer's business needs. Justify your ideas when they differ from the provided solutions.

Use any design strategies and internetworking technologies you feel are appropriate.

The final goal for each case study is a paper solution; you are not required to provide the specific product names.

Appendix G, "Answers to Review Questions, Case Studies, and Simulation Exercises," provides a solution for each task based on assumptions made. There is no claim that the provided solution is the best or only solution. Your solution might be more appropriate for the assumptions you made. The provided solution helps you understand the author's reasoning and offers a way for you to compare and contrast your solution.

Case Study: WAN Upgrade and Backup

Complete the following steps:

Step 1   You might want to review the DJMP Industries Case Study Scenario in Chapter 2. Focus on the WAN issues and the new international offices integration. Also, review the New Applications Simulation (presented at the end of Chapter 2) for the results of WAN link simulation under the new expected load.

Recall that the current WAN bandwidths are 64 kbps, and that all the links are leased lines. The existing equipment supports upgrades to higher speeds (no changes to router interfaces and cables are needed; they are all synchronous serial interfaces up to 2 Mbps). Regional office routers are already equipped with ISDN BRI interfaces. The central router at the headquarters still has one free WAN slot.

Step 2   Propose the optimal WAN upgrade and WAN backup scenario, including for the international offices.

Review Questions

Answer the following questions and then refer to Appendix G, "Answers to Review Questions, Case Studies, and Simulation Exercises," for the answers.

1 What type of cable is used for each of the following?

— ADSL

— VDSL

— Cable

— LRE

2 What is the definition of a WAN?

3 What advantages do the emerging WAN technologies bring to a network?

4 What is a WAN's objective in the Enterprise Edge?

5 Compare the response time and throughput requirements of a file transfer and an interactive application.

6 Which technologies are suitable for WAN connections over 50 Mbps?

7 What can be done if WAN links are constantly congested?

8 Match the terms with their definitions:

Terms:

— Compression

— Bandwidth

— Response time

— Window size

— Throughput

Definitions:

— The amount of data transmitted or received per unit time

— The number of frames that can be sent before the sender must wait for an acknowledgment

— Percentage of bits that contain errors relative to the total number of bits received in a transmission

— The amount of data successfully moved from one place to another in a given time period

— Reduction of data size for the purpose of saving transmission time

— The time between a command or keystroke entry and the host system's command execution or response delivery

9 Why is ISDN better than POTS for data connections?

10 How do X.25 and Frame Relay technologies compare?

11 Why are fully meshed networks not always appropriate?

12 What is the difference between dial backup and dial-on-demand routing?

13 What is the difference between SONET and SDH?

14 What is Packet over SONET/SDH (POS)?

15 Identify the key ADSL devices shown in Figure 5-21.

Layer 3 concentrator

Layer 2 concentrator—DSLAM

Splitter

ADSL CPE

Figure 5-21 *ADSL Devices*

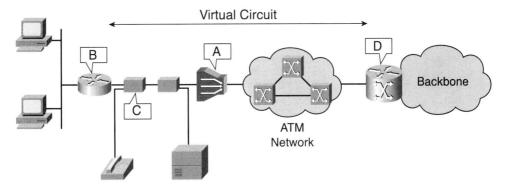

16 What different roles does the ADSL CPE have for PPPoA and PPPoE?

17 Which of the following two statements do not describe the operation of cable networks?

   a The cable modem termination system (CMTS) enables the coax users to connect with either the PSTN or the Internet.

   b The actual bandwidth for Internet service over a cable TV line is shared 2.5 Mbps on the download path to the subscriber, with about 27 Mbps of shared bandwidth for interactive responses in the other direction.

   c All cable modems can receive from and send signals to the CMTS and other cable modems on the line.

   d The cable backbone network is usually a SONET ring that runs on optical fiber.

18 For what purpose is broadband fixed wireless used?

19 What are some of the benefits of using a wireless network?

20 What is an MPLS Forwarding Equivalence Class?

21 How many bits are in the MPLS label field?

22 True or false: Packets sent from Device A to Device B through an MPLS network always take the same path through the network.

23 What is the difference between an overlay VPN and VPDN?

24 What is the most appropriate method for an Internet connection to be a secure backup solution for an Enterprise WAN link?

25 Define downstream and upstream.

26 What is the difference between ADSL and SDSL?

27 Is the goal of the wireless network to broaden the connectivity options or to increase the access speed?

This chapter discusses IP addressing design and includes the following sections:

- Designing IP Addressing
- Introduction to IPv6
- Summary
- Case Study
- Review Questions

CHAPTER 6

Designing IP Addressing in the Network

This chapter discusses the design of Internet Protocol (IP) addressing and provides guidelines for building an efficient IP addressing solution.

The chapter begins with an overview of IP addressing and general considerations for planning a network addressing scheme. It continues with a discussion of the specific considerations for IP version 4 (IPv4), followed by an introduction to IP version 6 (IPv6) and a discussion of migration strategies.

NOTE   In this chapter, the term *IP* refers to IPv4.

After completing this chapter, you will be able to explain IP address structures and various IP address types and their impact on an address plan. You will also be able to explain IPv6-specific design considerations.

Designing IP Addressing

This section explains the IPv4 address structure, private and public address types, and how to determine the size of the network in relation to the addressing plan. Finally, we discuss the following considerations: routing protocol choice, various IP address assignment strategies, and name resolution.

IPv4 Addresses

First, we look at IPv4 addresses in detail. The following sections explain IPv4 address structure, format, subnets and address classes.

IPv4 Address Structures

NOTE   See Appendix A, "IPv4 Addressing Job Aids," for introductory information about IPv4 addressing.

In general, addresses can be structured as either hierarchical or flat.

A *hierarchical address* consists of related parts that denote a hierarchy and provide more flexibility when locating a destination address. Examples of hierarchical addresses include the following:

- **The telephone system**—The telephone system has a hierarchy of 1) the country code; 2) the area code; 3) the first three digits of the telephone number (the local exchange); and 4) the last four digits of the telephone number (the individual telephone number). When a long distance (remote) call is placed to another country, the country prefix is dialed, followed by an area code and the telephone number.

- **A postal address**—A postal address describes a person's location by country, state or province, ZIP or postal code, city, street address, and name.

A *flat address* consists of only one part, and only the complete address has meaning. Examples of flat addresses include the following:

- **Media Access Control (MAC) layer addresses**—Each device on a LAN has a MAC-layer address, which is used to communicate at the data link layer.

- **Various personal identification numbers (IDs)**—For example, each person might have a social security number and a library identification number.

Flat addresses are typically assigned on a first-come-first-serve basis. For example, if you were the first person to request a social security number, you would receive number 0001; if you were the 25th person, you would receive 0025.

IP addresses are hierarchical addresses. They define networks and devices (nodes and hosts) that are associated with each network. An IP address consists of the following two parts:

- The *network* portion, which identifies a specific network. Routers use this portion to decide to which network to send the packet (datagram), and therefore the interface from which to send it. IP networks can also be subdivided into subnetworks.

- The *host* (or *device* or *node*) portion, which identifies a specific device in a network.

Each network device is known by its assigned unique IP address.

As illustrated in Figure 6-1, a router uses a network layer address to route a packet. When a router receives a packet, the routing decision is made based upon the network part of the destination address. The router looks up the destination address in its routing table, and, if the destination address resides within a known network, the router forwards the packet to the next hop or interface that its routing table specifies.

Figure 6-1   *A Router Uses the Network Part of the Destination Address*

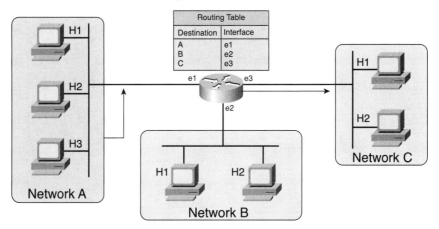

Once a packet leaves the router, the next-hop gateway is responsible for forwarding the packet to its final destination. If the router does not have a destination network in its routing table, the packet is forwarded to a predetermined default gateway, if configured; otherwise, the packet is discarded, and the sending host is informed that the network is unreachable.

The routing table lists the known networks, which can be learned in the following ways:

- Dynamic routing protocols (such as Routing Information Protocol [RIP], Open Shortest Path First [OSPF], Intermediate System–Intermediate System [IS-IS], Interior Gateway Routing Protocol [IGRP], Enhanced Interior Gateway Routing Protocol [EIGRP], and Border Gateway Protocol [BGP]).

- Static routes, which are manually entered by a network administrator.

- Networks that are directly connected to a router interface.

IPv4 Address Format

The IPv4 protocol has been used in internetworking for many years, and most modern IP networks are based on IPv4.

Recall that IP addresses are 32 bits, as shown in Figure 6-2. The 32 bits are grouped into four sets of 8 bits (octets), separated by dots, and represented in decimal format; this is known as *dotted decimal notation*. Each bit in an octet has a binary weight (128, 64, 32, 16,

8, 4, 2, 1), so that the octet's minimum value is 0 (all bits set to 0) and its maximum value is 255 (all bits set to 1).

Figure 6-2 *IPv4 Address Structure*

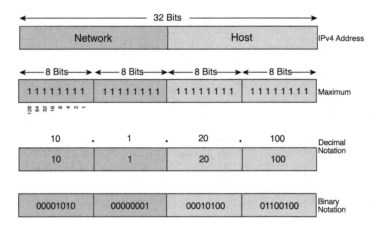

Subnet Mask

The *network mask*, which is also called the *subnet mask*, is used to interpret an IP address, and it provides the distinction between the network and the host parts of the IP address. A subnet mask is 32 bits long and, like the IPv4 address, is divided into 4 octets. As with the IPv4 address, each bit in an octet has a binary weight (128, 64, 32, 16, 8, 4, 2, 1). The mask consists of a specified number of consecutive 1s, with the remaining bits set to 0. In the mask, the point at which 1s stop and 0s begin is the boundary between the network and host parts in the address.

A network mask is typically written in either decimal notation (for example, 255.255.0.0) or prefix notation (for example, /16). In the latter case, the number after the "/" indicates the number of consecutive 1s in the mask. Network masks can also be written in hexadecimal format (for example, FF.FF.0.0).

Number of Host Addresses

To determine the number of available host addresses, use the formula 2^n-2, where n is the number of bits set to 0 in the subnet mask. (2 is subtracted because a host cannot be represented with a host part of either all 0s or all 1s.) You can determine the host part of the first IPv4 address that is available for hosts in a particular network by setting the last bit (reading from right to left) to 1 and all others to 0. You can determine the last available IPv4 address by setting the last bit in the host part to 0 and all other bits to 1.

IPv4 Address Classes

IPv4 address space is divided into address classes.

IP addressing defines five address classes: A, B, C, D, and E. Only Classes A, B, and C are available for addressing devices; Class D is used for multicast groups, and Class E is reserved for experimental use.

As illustrated in Table 6-1 for Class A, B, and C addresses (this is sometimes called the *first octet rule*), an address's first octet defines its class. The bits that represent network and subnet information in an IP address are known as the *prefix*; the number of such bits is known as the *prefix length*. The Prefix Length column in Table 6-1 indicates the default prefix lengths for the three address classes.

Table 6-1   *IP Address Classes A, B, and C Are Available for Addressing Devices*

Class	Format (N = network number, H = host number)	Prefix Length	Higher-order Bit(s)	Address Range	Number of Hosts
Class A	N.H.H.H	8 bits	0	1.0.0.0 to 126.0.0.0	16,777,214
Class B	N.N.H.H	16 bits	10	128.0.0.0 to 191.255.0.0	65,534
Class C	N.N.N.H	24 bits	110	192.0.0.0 to 223.255.255.0	254

NOTE   Class D addresses have higher-order bits 1110 and are in the range 224.0.0.0 to 239.255.255.255. Class E addresses have higher-order bits 1111 and are in the range 240.0.0.0.0 to 255.255.255.255.

Following is a description of the address classes:

- **Class A**—These addresses have a first octet that begins with binary 0, resulting in a range of 1 to 126 for the first octet (0 and 127 are reserved). The network mask is set at 255.0.0.0 or /8. An individual Class A network has 16,777,214 available host addresses if no subnetting is done.

- **Class B**—These addresses have a first octet that begins with binary 10, resulting in a range of 128 to 191 for the first octet. The network mask is set at 255.255.0.0 or /16. An individual Class B network has 6,5534 available host addresses if no subnetting is done.

- **Class C**—These addresses have a first octet that begins with binary 110, resulting in a range of 192 to 223 for the first octet. The network mask is set at 255.255.255.0 or /24. An individual Class C network has 254 available host addresses if no subnetting is done.

- **Class D**—Class D is reserved for multicast addresses and cannot be used to address hosts. Multicast addresses are used with the OSPF routing protocol (224.0.0.5, 224.0.0.6) and the EIGRP routing protocol (224.0.0.9), for example.

- **Class E**—Class E is reserved for research.

Internet service providers (ISPs) assign the Class A, B, and C addresses to users. ISPs obtain address allocations from a local Internet registry (LIR), a national Internet registry (NIR), or their appropriate Regional Internet Registry (RIR). The Internet Assigned Numbers Authority (IANA) is responsible for allocating addresses to the RIRs, according to their needs.

NOTE   The Internet Assigned Numbers Authority can be found at www.iana.org/.

Some examples of IPv4 addresses follow:

- Address 170.1.20.100 is Class B and consists of network part 170.1 and host part 20.100. Written in binary notation, the address is 10101010.00000001.00010100.01100100.

- Address 192.168.1.1 is Class C and consists of network part 192.168.1 and host part 1. Written in binary notation, the address is 11000000.10101000.00000001.00000001.

- Address 193.18.9.45 is a Class C address because the 193 falls into the 192–223 range.

- Address 172.31.1.2 is a Class B address because the 172 falls into the 128–191 range.

Prior to applying for the addresses from the public number authority, the designer should know the number of networks and IPv4 addresses for which to apply. The required IPv4 address class for the planned network is obtained from the information about the network size, the number of locations, and the size of the individual locations.

The number of required networks is equal to the number of locations. The address class for a location corresponds to the number of required IPv4 addresses for that particular location. For example, a network consists of three locations and requires 490 IP addresses (300 for the first location, 100 for the second location, and 90 for the third location). If using Class C addresses, at least two Class C addresses are required, partitioned into smaller networks (subnets). In another example, a network with one location requires 180 IP addresses. The required IPv4 address class is Class C, which offers 254 host addresses.

Since IPv4 address space is almost exhausted, the public number authority and ISPs most likely assign one C class or a subnet of a C class only to the applicant. When more IPv4 addresses are required than have been assigned, the designer must overcome the restriction by using private IPv4 addresses. The "Private Versus Public Addresses" section of this chapter explains private IPv4 addresses.

Subnets

Subnetting uses a subnet mask that is longer than an address class's default mask. When subnetting, some bits from the host part are used for the subnetwork part. Subnetting provides network administrators with extra flexibility, makes more efficient use of network address utilization, and constrains broadcast traffic because a broadcast does not cross a subnet's boundaries (a router interface).

A given network address can be divided into many subnetworks. For example, 172.16.1.0, 172.16.2.0, 172.16.3.0, and 172.16.4.0 are all subnets of the Class B network 171.16.0.0.

Following are some examples of IP addresses and masks:

- IPv4 address 172.1.20.5, with a mask of 255.255.255.192 or a prefix of /26.
  - The binary representation of the address is 10101100.00000001.00010100.00000101.
  - The binary representation of the mask is 11111111.11111111.11111111.11000000.
  - The address is Class B, with 10 bits of subnetting.
  - The network is 172.1.20.0, using 26 bits to denote the network part.
  - The host part is .5, using 6 bits to denote the host part.
  - The number of available host addresses is $2^6 - 2 = 62$.
  - The first host address is 172.1.20.1, and the last one is 172.1.20.62.
- IPv4 address 10.200.200.25, with a mask of 255.255.128.0 or a prefix of /17.
  - The binary representation of the address is 00001010.11001000.11001000.00011001.
  - The binary representation of the mask is 11111111.11111111.10000000.00000000.
  - The address is Class A, with 9 bits of subnetting.
  - The network is 10.200.128, using 17 bits to denote the network part.
  - The host part is 72.25, using 15 bits to denote the host part. Note that when the boundary is not on the octet, the host's decimal notation is nonsensical.
  - The number of available host addresses is $2^{15} - 2 = 32,766$.
  - The first host address is 10.200.128.1, and the last one is 10.200.255.254.

Determining the Size of the Network

The first step in IP addressing plan designing is determining the size of the network to establish how many IP addresses are needed. To gather the required information, the following questions need to be answered:

- **How many locations does the network consist of?** — The designer must determine the number of locations and their type.

- **How big is the network?** — A network designer must determine the number of devices that need to be addressed for example — end-systems, router interfaces, switches, firewall interfaces, and so forth.

- **What are the IP addressing requirements for individual locations?** — The designer must collect information about which systems will use dynamic addressing, which will use static addresses, and which systems can use private instead of public addresses.

- **What class of addresses and how many networks can be obtained from the public number authority?** — The designer should make decisions based on the collected information about the network size to apply for the required number of addresses. As noted earlier, these public addresses are obtained from ISPs; ISPs obtain address blocks from the IANA.

The following subsections cover the first two points, while the remainder of the chapter focuses on the IP addressing requirements noted in the last two points.

Determining the Network Topology

Initially, the designer should acquire a general picture of the network topology to correctly gather the information about network size and its relation to the IP addressing plan.

With the general network topology information, the designer acquires data about the number of locations, location types, and their correlations. For example, the detailed information topology shown in Figure 6-3 can be presented in a table, as shown in Table 6-2.

Figure 6-3   *Sample Network Topology*

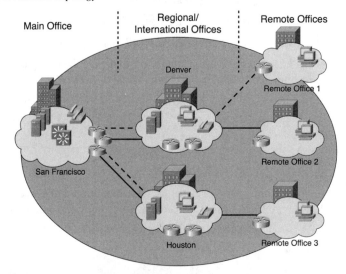

Table 6-2   *Network Location Information for the Topology in Figure 6-3*

Location	Type	Comments
San Francisco	Main Office	The central location where the majority of users are located
Denver	Regional Office	Connects to the San Francisco main office
Houston	Regional Office	Connects to the San Francisco main office
Remote Office 1	Remote Office	Connects to the Denver regional office
Remote Office 2	Remote Office	Connects to the Denver regional office
Remote Office 3	Remote Office	Connects to the Houston regional office

Use Table 6-3 as a worksheet or template for network location information.

Table 6-3   *Network Location Information Template*

Location	Type	Comments

Size of Individual Locations

The information about the size of the individual locations is closely related to the overall network size; it is vital for determining the IP address range size so that IP addresses can be assigned to all network devices. Workstations, servers, IP phones, router interfaces, switches, firewall interfaces, and so forth are counted. As shown in Table 6-4 for the topology in Figure 6-3, this information can be presented in a table.

Table 6-4   *Network Locations Size for the Topology in Figure 6-3*

Location	Office Type	Work-stations	Servers	IP Phones	Router Inter-faces	Switches	Firewall Inter-faces	Reserve	SUM
San Francisco	Main	600	35	600	17	26	12	20%	1290
Denver	Region al	210	7	210	10	4	0	20%	441
Houston	Region al	155	5	155	10	4	0	20%	329

Table 6-4   *Network Locations Size for the Topology in Figure 6-3 (Continued)*

Location	Office Type	Work- stations	Servers	IP Phones	Router Inter- faces	Switches	Firewall Inter- faces	Reserve	SUM
Remote Office 1	Remote	12	1	12	2	1	0	10%	28
Remote Office 2	Remote	15	1	15	3	1	0	10%	35
Remote Office 3	Remote	8	1	8	3	1	0	10%	21
SUM		1000	50	1000	45	37	12		2144

Some additional addresses should be reserved to allow for seamless potential network growth. The commonly suggested reserve is 20% for the main and regional offices, and 10% for the remote offices; however, this can vary from case to case. To ensure that you obtain a more precise estimate of the required resources, carefully discuss future network growth with the customer.

Use Table 6-5 as a worksheet or template for determining the size of network locations.

Table 6-5   *Network Locations Size Template*

Location	Office Type	Work- stations	Servers	IP Phones	Router Inter- faces	Switches	Firewall Inter- faces	Reserve	SUM
SUM									

Network Size for IP Addressing

The network size, in terms of the IP addressing plan, is the number of devices and interfaces that need an IP address.

A summary of the individual locations is documented to establish the overall network size. This summary provides the minimum overall number of IP addresses that are required for addressing the network. As previously mentioned, because all networks tend to grow, some reserve (usually up to 20%) should be made for potential network expansion. (Depending on the circumstances, more reserve might be required.) This summary size information can be presented in a table, as Table 6-6 shows for the topology in Figure 6-3. (Note that Table 6-6 is just a summary of the information in Table 6-4.)

Table 6-6   *Overall Network Size for the Topology in Figure 6-3*

Device Type	Number	Comments
Workstation	1000	All types of workstations (mobile, fixed)
Servers	50	Internal and public servers
IP phones	1000	IP telephony will replace basic telephone
Router interfaces	45	Physical and virtual interfaces
Switches (management interfaces)	37	
Firewall interfaces	12	
SUM	**2144**	**Add 20% for potential future growth**

Use Table 6-7 as a worksheet or template for determining network size.

Table 6-7   *Overall Network Size Template*

Device Type	Number	Comments
SUM		

Private Versus Public Addresses

The IPv4 address space is divided into public and private sections. Private addresses are reserved IPv4 addresses that are to be used only internally within a company's network. These private addresses should not be used on the Internet and must therefore be mapped to a company's external registered address when sending anything on the Internet. Public IPv4 addresses are provided for external communication.

The following sections describe private and public address use.

Private IPv4 Addresses

RFC 1918, *Address Allocation for Private Internets* (available at www.cis.ohio-state.edu/cgi-bin/rfc/rfc1918.html), defines the private IPv4 addresses, which are

- 10.0.0.0/8 (10.0.0.0 to 10.255.255.255)
- 172.16.0.0/12 (172.16.0.0 to 172.31.255.255)
- 192.168.0.0/16 (192.168.0.0 to 192.168.255.255)

NOTE   The "How Private Address and Public Address Network Parts Interconnect" section of this chapter discusses mapping private addresses to public addresses.

Public IPv4 Addresses

Public addresses are those that are assigned by an ISP; they are allocated to the ISP from the IANA (as previously discussed in the "IPv4 Address Classes" section). Public addresses can be any Class A, B, or C address that is not in the private address space.

When to Use Private or Public IPv4 Addresses

As illustrated in Figure 6-4, public IPv4 addresses are provided for external communication, and private IP addresses are used for internal communication.

Figure 6-4   *Private and Public Addresses Can Be Used in a Network*

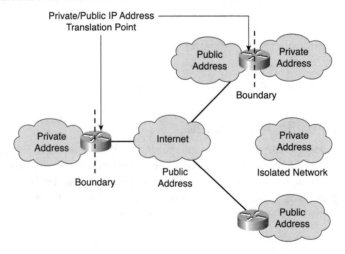

A network connected to the Internet uses the public IPv4 address space so it can share resources and exchange data with other networks. A network that requires no connection to the Internet uses the private IPv4 address space; such addresses are prohibited for use in public networks.

A private IPv4 address can be used more than once in different networks.

A network can use either private IPv4 addresses only, public IPv4 addresses only, or both.

NOTE   Public (legal) addresses should be saved for Internet devices (such as outside Domain Name System [DNS] servers, web servers, or File Transfer Protocol [FTP] servers), and private addresses should be used in the internal network.

Private Versus Public Address Selection Criteria

Very few public IPv4 addresses are currently available, so the public number authority and ISPs can only assign a subset of Class C addresses to their customers. Therefore, in most cases, the assigned number of public IPv4 addresses is inadequate for addressing the entire network.

The solution to the problem is the use of private IPv4 addresses within a network, and the translation of these private addresses to public addresses when Internet connectivity is required.

When selecting addresses, the designer should consider the following questions:

- Are private, public, or both IPv4 address types required?
- How many end systems need access to only the public network? This is the number of end systems that need a limited set of external services (such as e-mail, file transfer, or web browsing) but do not need unrestricted external access. These end systems do not have to be visible to the public network.
- How many end systems must have access and be visible to the public network? This is the number of Internet connections and various servers that must be visible to the public (such as public servers and servers used for e-commerce, like web servers, database servers, and application servers). It defines the number of required public IPv4 addresses. These end systems require globally unambiguous IPv4 addresses.
- How and where will the boundaries between the private and public IPv4 addresses cross?

The following sections consider these questions.

Requirements for Private and Public IPv4 Address Types

The decision about when to use private, public, or both address types depends on the Internet connection present, the number of publicly visible servers, and the size of the network, as follows:

- **No Internet connectivity**—In this case, the network is isolated and there is no need to acquire public IPv4 addresses. The entire network can be addressed with private IPv4 addresses. Access to the public network is not required.

- **Internet connectivity, no publicly accessible servers**—Public IPv4 addresses are required because the network is connected to the Internet. Because there are not any publicly accessible servers, one public IPv4 address and a translation mechanism can be used to allow Internet access. The private IPv4 addresses are used to address the internal network.

- **Internet connectivity, publicly accessible servers**—Public IPv4 addresses must be acquired to address the connection to the Internet and to address all publicly accessible servers. The number of public addresses corresponds to the number of Internet connections and publicly accessible servers. Private IPv4 addresses are used to address the internal network.

- **All end-systems are to be publicly accessible**—In this case, only public IPv4 addresses are required; they are used to address the entire network.

How Private Address and Public Address Network Parts Interconnect

According to its needs, a network can use both public and private addresses. A router acts as the interface between the network's private and public sections.

When private addresses are used for addressing in a network and this network must be connected to the Internet, a translation mechanism (such as Network Address Translation [NAT]) must be used to translate from private to public addresses, and vice versa. NAT is required if accessibility to the public Internet or public visibility are required.

As shown in Figure 6-5, NAT can be used to translate the following:

- **One private address to one public address**—Used in cases when servers from the internal network with private IPv4 addresses must be visible from the public network. The translation is defined statically to translate from the server's private IPv4 address to the public IPv4 address.

- **Many private addresses to one public address**—Used for end-systems that require access to the public network and do not have to be visible to the outside world.

- **Combination**—It is not uncommon to see a combination of the previous techniques be deployed throughout modern networks.

Figure 6-5   *Private/Public Address Translation*

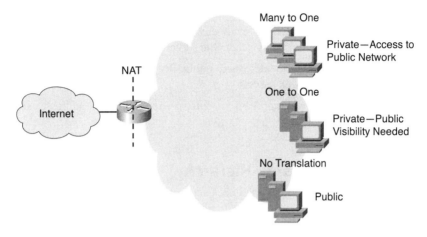

For additional details about NAT, see Appendix F, "Network Address Translation."

Guidelines for the Use of Private and Public Addresses in an Enterprise Network

As shown in Figure 6-6, the typical Enterprise network uses both private and public IPv4 addresses.

Figure 6-6   *Private and Public IPv4 Addresses Are Used in the Enterprise Network*

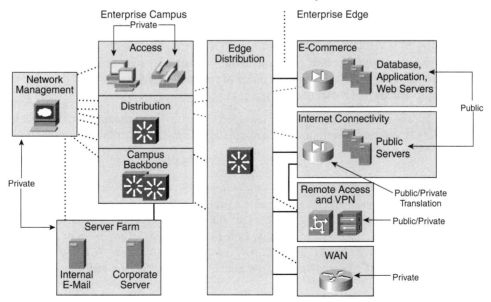

Private IPv4 addresses are used throughout the Enterprise network, excluding the following modules:

* The Internet Connectivity module, where public IPv4 addresses are used for Internet connections and publicly accessible servers.

* The E-commerce module, where public IPv4 addresses are used for the database, application, and web servers.

* The Remote Access and VPN module, where public IPv4 addresses are used for certain connections.

Implementing IP Addressing Hierarchy

The IP addressing hierarchy influences network routing. The following sections provide general instructions on how to plan IP addressing to reduce routing overhead and explain the issues (summarization, fixed length subnet masking, variable length subnet masking, and classful and classless routing protocols) that influence the IP addressing plan and the routing protocol choice.

NOTE   Chapter 7, "Selecting Routing Protocols for a Network," discusses routing protocols in detail.

Route Summarization

It is important to design route summarization, also referred to as *route aggregation* or *supernetting*, when designing IP addressing.

With route summarization, one route in the routing table represents many other routes. Summarizing routes reduces the number of routes in the routing table, the routing update traffic, and overall router overhead.

Reducing routing update traffic on low-speed lines can be important. If the Internet had not adapted route summarization by standardizing on classless interdomain routing (CIDR), it would not have survived.

NOTE   CIDR is a mechanism that was developed to help alleviate the problem of IP address exhaustion. The idea behind CIDR is that multiple Class C addresses can be combined, or aggregated, to create a larger (that is, more hosts allowed), classless set of IP addresses. CIDR is described in RFC 1519, *Classless Inter-Domain Routing (CIDR): an Address Assignment and Aggregation Strategy*, available at www.cis.ohio-state.edu/cgi-bin/rfc/rfc1519.html.

The telephone architecture has handled *prefix routing*, or routing that is based only on the prefix part of the address, for many years. For example, a telephone switch in Detroit, Michigan does not have to know how to reach a specific line in Portland, Oregon. It must simply recognize that the call is not local. A long-distance carrier must recognize that 503 is for Oregon, but does not have to know the details of how to reach the specific line in Oregon.

Prefix routing is not new in the IP environment, either. A router only has to know how to reach the next hop; it does not have to know the details of how to reach an end node that is not local. As in the telephone example, IP routers make hierarchical decisions. Recall that an IP address is comprised of a prefix part and a host part. Routers use the prefix to determine the path for a destination address that is not local. The host part is used to reach local hosts.

For summarization to work correctly, the following requirements must be met:

- Multiple IP addresses must share the same leftmost bits.
- Routers must base their routing decisions on a 32-bit IP address and a prefix length of up to 32 bits.
- Routing protocols must carry the prefix length with the 32-bit IP address.

For example, assume that a router has the following networks behind it:

192.108.168.0

192.108.169.0

192.108.170.0

192.108.171.0

192.108.172.0

192.108.173.0

192.108.174.0

192.108.175.0

Each of these networks could be advertised separately; however, this would mean advertising eight routes. Instead, this router can summarize the eight routes into one route and advertise 192.108.168.0/21. By advertising this one route, the router is saying, "Route packets to me if the destination has the first 21 bits the same as the first 21 bits of 192.108.168.0."

Figure 6-7 illustrates how this summary route is determined. The addresses all have the first 21 bits in common and include all the combinations of the other 3 bits in the network portion of the address; therefore, only the first 21 bits are needed to determine whether the router can route to one of these specific addresses.

Figure 6-7 *Find the Common Bits to Summarize Routes*

192.108.168.0 =	11000000 01101100 10101	000	00000000
192.108.169.0 =	11000000 01101100 10101	001	00000000
192.108.170.0 =	11000000 01101100 10101	010	00000000
192.108.171.0 =	11000000 01101100 10101	011	00000000
192.108.172.0 =	11000000 01101100 10101	100	00000000
192.108.173.0 =	11000000 01101100 10101	101	00000000
192.108.174.0 =	11000000 01101100 10101	110	00000000
192.108.175.0 =	11000000 01101100 10101	111	00000000

Number of Common Bits = 21
Number of Non-Common Network Bits = 3
Number of Host Bits = 8

IP Addressing Hierarchy Criteria

IP addressing hierarchy has an important impact on the routing protocol choice, and vice versa.

The decision about how to implement the IP addressing hierarchy is usually an administrative decision that is based on the following questions:

- Is hierarchy needed within an IP addressing plan?
- What are the criteria for dividing a network into route summarization groups?
- How is route summarization performed, and what is the correlation with routing?
- Is a hierarchy of route summarization groups required?
- How many end systems does each route summarization group or subgroup contain?

The following sections consider these questions.

Determining the Summarization Groups

The network designer decides how to implement the IP addressing hierarchy based on the network's size, geography, and topology. In large networks, hierarchy within the IP addressing plan is mandatory for a stable network (including stable routing tables). Consider the following factors when deciding whether to implement hierarchy:

- **Influence of IP addressing on routing**—An IP addressing plan influences the network's overall routing. Before allocating blocks of IP addresses to different parts of the network and assigning IP addresses to devices, consider the criteria for an appropriate and effective IP addressing scheme. Routing stability, service availability, network scalability, and modularity are some of the crucial and preferred network characteristics, and are directly affected by IP address allocation and deployment.

- **Modular design and scalable solutions**—Whether building a new network or adding a new service on top of an existing infrastructure, a modular design delivers a long-term, scalable solution. Modularity in terms of IP addressing allows the aggregation of routing information on a hierarchical basis.

- **Route aggregation**—Route aggregation can be used to reduce routing overhead and improve routing stability and scalability. However, to implement route aggregation, a designer must be able to divide a network into contiguous IP address areas and have a solid understanding of IP address assignment, route aggregation, and hierarchical routing.

The network is usually divided into route summarization groups based on its size, geography, and topology. In this case, the size of the network means the number of prefixes that must be advertised. To reduce the routing overhead in a large network, a multilevel hierarchy might be required. The depth of hierarchy depends on the network size and the size of the upper level summarization group. Figure 6-8 shows an example of a network hierarchy.

Figure 6-8   *Network Aggregation*

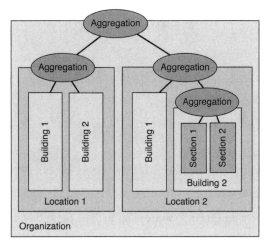

Network locations typically represent the first level of hierarchy in enterprise networks; each location is typically a summarization group.

A second level of hierarchy can be done within first level summarization groups. For example, a large location can be divided into smaller summarization groups that represent the buildings at a location. Not all first level summarization groups require a second level of hierarchy.

To further minimize the potential routing overhead and instability, a third level of hierarchy can be performed within the second level summarization group. The sections within individual buildings can represent the third level summarization group.

Impact of Poorly Designed IP Addressing

Poorly designed IP addressing usually results in IP addresses that are randomly assigned on an as-needed basis. In this case, the IP addresses are most likely dispersed through the network. A poor design provides no option for dividing the network into contiguous address areas, and therefore no means of implementing route summarization.

Figure 6-9 shows an example network with poorly designed IP addressing; it uses a dynamic routing protocol. Suppose a certain link in the network is *flapping* (changing its state from UP to DOWN, and vice versa) ten times per minute. Because dynamic routing is used, the routers that detect the change send routing updates to their neighbors, those neighbors to their neighbors, and so on. Because no aggregation is possible, the routing update is propagated throughout the entire network, even if there is no need for a distant router to have knowledge of that link.

Figure 6-9   *A Flat IP Addressing Scheme Results in Excess Routing Traffic*

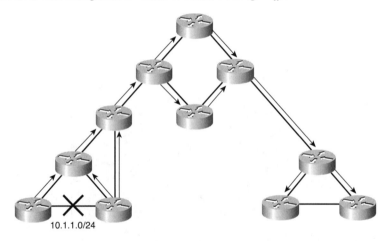

10.1.1.0/24

Impacts of poorly designed IP addressing include the following:

- **Excess routing traffic consumes bandwidth**—When any route changes, routers must send routing updates. Without summarization, more updates are reported and the routing traffic thus consumes more bandwidth.

- **Constant routing table recalculation**—Routing updates require routing table recalculation, which affects the router's performance and ability to forward traffic.

- **Routing loops and black-hole routing**—When too many changes in the routing information databases prevent a router from synchronizing its view on the routing tables with its neighbors, routing loops and black-hole routing can occur. Results of a local routing loop can have global consequences for a major service's availability.

NOTE	Well-designed IP addressing enables efficient aggregation of routing advertisements, thereby narrowing the effect of routes that might flap (the scope of flapping propagation).

Impact of Route Aggregation

Implementing route aggregation on border routers between contiguously addressed areas improves control over routing table growth.

Figure 6-10 implements route summarization (aggregation) on the area borders in a sample network. In case of a link failure, routing updates are not propagated to the rest of the network; rather, they stay in the area. This reduces bandwidth consumption related to routing overhead and relieves routers from unnecessary routing table recalculation.

Figure 6-10 *Hierarchical IP Addressing Plan Results in Reduced Routing Traffic*

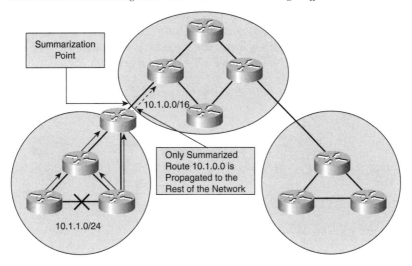

NOTE	Efficient aggregation of routing advertisements narrows the scope of routing update propagation and significantly decreases the cumulative frequency of routing updates.

When to Use Fixed or Variable Subnet Masking

When performing subnetting, subnet masks can be the same or different for the entire major network. This, in turn, influences the choice of routing protocol.

Key Point: FLSM and VLSM

A major network is a Class A, B, or C network.

Fixed Length Subnet Masking (FLSM) is when all subnet masks in a major network must be the same size.

Variable Length Subnet Masking (VLSM) is when subnet masks within a major network can be different sizes. In modern networks, VLSM should be used to conserve the IP addresses.

Some routing protocols require FLSM. FSLM requires that all subnets of a major network have the same subnet mask and therefore results in less efficient address space allocation.

For example, in the top network shown in Figure 6-11, network 172.16.0.0/16 is subnetted using FLSM. Each subnet is given a /24 mask. The network is comprised of multiple LANs that are connected by point-to-point WAN links. Because FLSM is used, all subnets have the same subnet mask. This is inefficient, because even though only two addresses are needed, the point-to-point links have a /24 subnet mask with 254 available addresses.

Figure 6-11 *Fixed Versus Variable Length Subnet Mask*

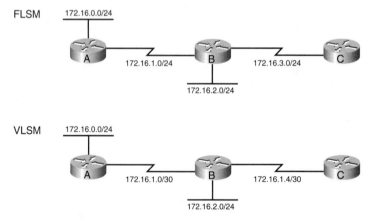

VLSM makes it possible to subnet with different subnet masks and therefore results in more efficient address space allocation. VLSM provides greater capability to perform route summarization because it allows more hierarchical levels within an addressing plan.

VLSM relies on providing prefix length information explicitly with each address use. The length of the prefix is evaluated independently at each place where it is used. The ability to have a different prefix length at different points supports more efficient use of the IP address space and reduces routing traffic. Efficient addressing of large subnets (such as an Ethernet with many hosts) and small subnets (such as a point-to-point serial line with only two hosts) is permitted. If the small subnets are grouped, routing information can be summarized (aggregated) into fewer routing table entries.

For example, in the bottom network shown in Figure 6-11, network 172.16.0.0/16 is subnetted using VLSM. The network is comprised of multiple LANs that are connected by point-to-point WAN links. The point-to-point links have a subnet mask of /30, thus providing only two available addresses. The WAN network requires less address space, thereby leaving valuable addresses free for other applications.

IP Addressing Plan and Routing Protocol Considerations

Decisions about IPv4 addressing and routing protocols are interdependent.

Routing protocols can be classified as either *classful* or *classless*.

Key Point: Classful Versus Classless Routing

With classful routing, routing updates do not carry the subnet mask.

With classless routing, routing updates do carry the subnet mask.

Classful Routing

As illustrated at the top of Figure 6-12, the following rules apply when classful routing protocols are used:

- The routing updates do not include subnet masks.
- FLSM is required when subnetting is performed.
- When a routing update is received and the routing information is about:
  - Routes within the same major network as configured on the receiving interface, then the subnet mask configured on the receiving interface is assumed to also apply to the received routes. Therefore, subnetting must be done with FLSM.
  - Routes in a different major network as configured on the receiving interface, then the default major network mask assumed to apply to the received routes. Therefore, subnetted networks must be contiguous.
- All subnets of the same major network (Class A, B, or C) must use the same subnet mask and be contiguous.
- Automatic route summarization is performed across major network (Class A, B, or C) boundaries.

Because of these constraints, classful routing is no longer used often in modern networks.

Figure 6-12 *Classful Versus Classless Routing Protocols*

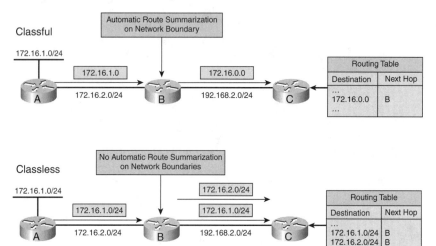

Examples of classful routing protocols include RIP version 1 (RIPv1) and IGRP.

Classless Routing

As illustrated at the bottom of Figure 6-12, the following rules apply when classless routing protocols are used:

- Routing updates include subnet masks.
- VLSM is supported.
- Route summarization can be manually configured.

All currently deployed modern networks should use classless routing. Examples of classless routing protocols include RIP version 2 (RIPv2), EIGRP, OSPF, IS-IS, and BGP.

Classful and Classless Routing Protocol Examples

Figure 6-13 illustrates an example network with a discontiguous 172.16.0.0 network that runs a classful routing protocol. Routers A and C automatically summarize across the major network boundary, so both send routing information about 172.16.0.0 rather than the individual subnets (172.16.1.0/24 and 172.16.2.0/24). Because Router B now has two entries for the major network 172.16.0.0, it puts both entries into its routing table; routing problems occur.

Figure 6-13 *Classful Routing Protocols Do Not Send the Subnet Mask in the Routing Update*

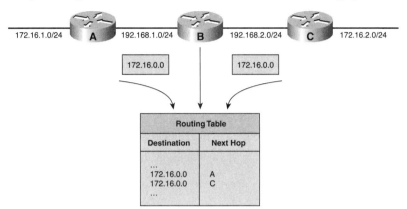

Figure 6-14 is the same network as in Figure 6-13, but it is now running a classless routing protocol. In this example, Router B learns about both subnetworks 172.16.1.0/24 and 172.16.2.0/24, one from each interface; routing is performed correctly.

Figure 6-14 *Classless Routing Protocols Send the Subnet Mask in the Routing Update*

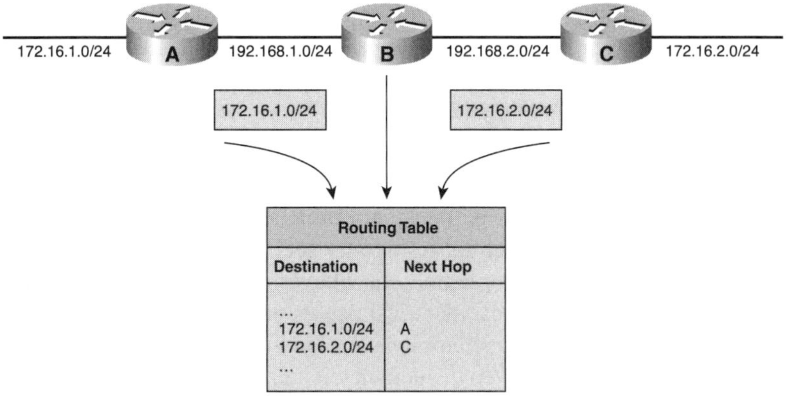

Methods of Assigning IP Addresses

Next, we discuss methods of assigning IP addresses to end systems and explain their influence on administrative overhead.

A host, workstation, server, and so forth must have a valid IP address to communicate on the network. From an end user's standpoint, it does not matter how the end system received the address; what matters is that it works. However, the selected IP address assignment strategy can create a large administrative overhead and attendant burdens for the network administrator.

Address assignment includes assigning an IP address, a default gateway, servers that resolve names to IP addresses, time servers, and so forth.

Before selecting the desired IP address assignment method, you should answer the following questions:

- How many devices need an IP address?
- Which devices require static IP address assignment?
- Is IP address renumbering expected?
- Is the administrator required to track devices and their IP addresses?
- Do additional parameters (default gateway, name server, and so forth) have to be configured?
- Are there any availability issues?
- Are there any security issues?

Static Versus Dynamic IP Address Assignment Methods

Following are the two basic IP address assignment strategies:

- **Static**—Statically assigns an IP address to a system. The network administrator configures the IP address, default gateway, and name servers manually by entering them into a special file or files on the end system with either a graphical or text interface. Static address assignment presents an extra burden for the administrator, who must configure the address on every end system on the network; this is especially true for large-scale networks.

- **Dynamic**—Dynamically assigns addresses to the end systems. Dynamic address assignment relieves the administrator of manually assigning an address to every network device. The administrator must set up a server to assign the address. On that server, the administrator defines the address pools and additional parameters that should be sent to the host (default gateway, name servers, time servers, and so forth). On the host, the administrator must enable the host to acquire the address dynamically; this is often the default choice. When IP address reconfiguration is needed, the administrator reconfigures data on the server, which then performs the host-renumbering task. Examples of available address assignment protocols include Reverse Address Resolution Protocol (RARP), Boot Protocol (BOOTP), and Dynamic Host Configuration Protocol (DHCP). DHCP provides the most features.

When to Use Static and Dynamic Address Assignment

When selecting either a static or dynamic end-system IP address assignment method, consider the following:

- **The number of end systems**—If the number of end systems is very high (more than 30), dynamic address assignment is preferred.

- **Renumbering**—If renumbering is likely to happen and there are numerous end systems, the dynamic address assignment method is the correct choice. With DHCP, only DHCP server reconfiguration is needed; with static assignment, all hosts must be reconfigured.

- **Address tracking**—If the network policy requires address tracking, the static address assignment method might be easier to implement than the dynamic address assignment method. However, address tracking is also possible with dynamic address assignment with additional DHCP server configuration.

- **Additional parameters**—DHCP server is the easiest solution if additional parameters must be configured. The parameters only have to be entered on the server, which then sends those parameters to the clients with the address.

- **High availability**—Statically assigned IP addresses are available at any time. Dynamically assigned IP addresses must be acquired from the server; if the server fails, the address cannot be acquired. To overcome such situations, a redundant DHCP server is required.

- **Security**—In most cases, anyone who connects to the network can acquire a valid IP address with the dynamic IP address assignment method. This imposes some security risk. Static addresses pose only a minor security risk.

The use of one address assignment method does not exclude the use of another.

Guidelines for Assigning IP Addresses in the Enterprise Network

The typical Enterprise network uses both static and dynamic address assignment methods.

As shown in Figure 6-15, the static IP address assignment method is typically used in the Network Management and Server Farm modules of the Enterprise Campus functional area, and in all modules of the Enterprise Edge functional area (the E-commerce, Internet Connectivity, Remote Access and VPN, and WAN modules). Static addresses are required for systems such as servers or network devices, in which the IP address must be known at all times for connectivity, general access, or management.

Figure 6-15 *IP Address Assignment in Enterprise Network*

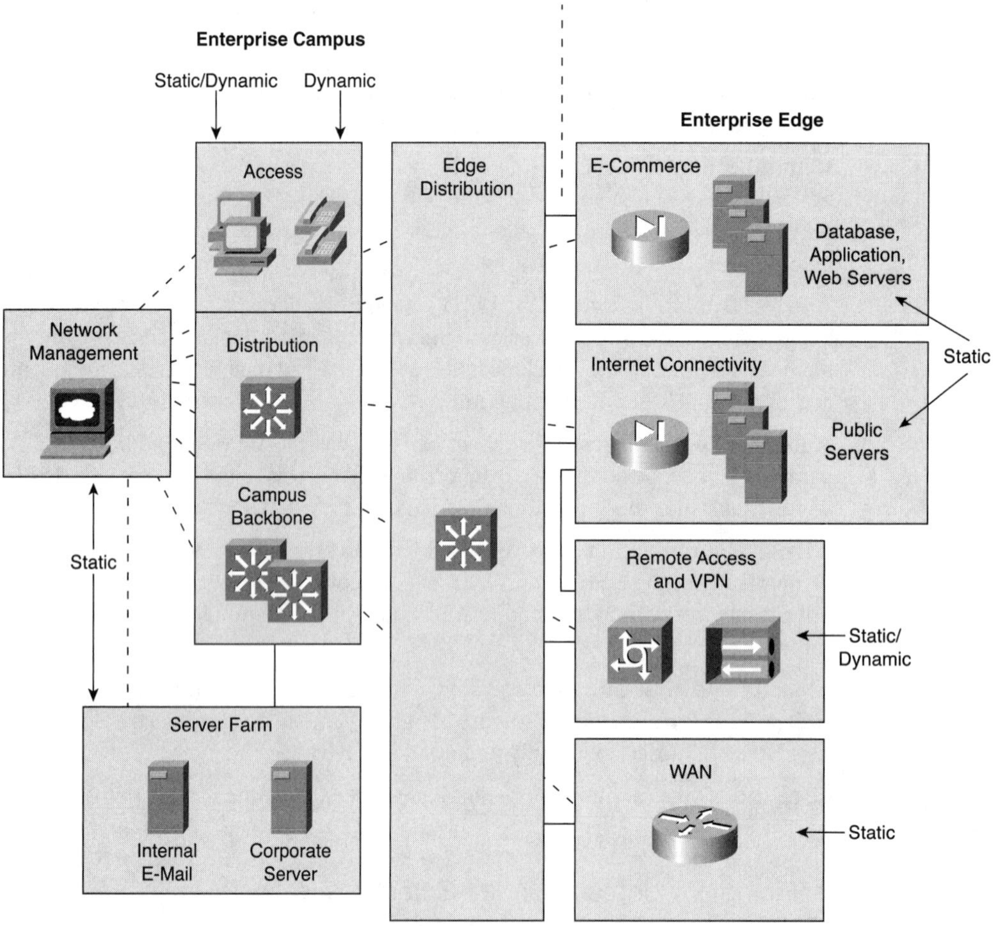

The dynamic IP address assignment method is used for assigning IP addresses to various workstations and IP phones.

Using DHCP to Assign IP Addresses

An administrator can use a DHCP server for assigning dynamic addresses. DHCP server software can coexist on a single server with many other applications. In addition to the IPv4 address and the subnet mask, DHCP can send additional parameters (default gateway, DNS server, and so forth).

As shown in Figure 6-16, when a host is started, its address-acquire process sends an IPv4 address request (usually a broadcast request), including its physical hardware address (MAC address), to the network. The DHCP server intercepts the request and responds with the host IPv4 address, subnet mask, and additional IPv4 parameters.

Figure 6-16 *IPv4 Address Assignment with DHCP*

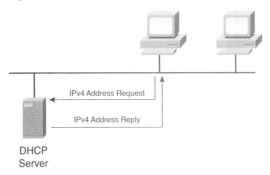

DHCP offers the following three address allocation mechanisms:

- **Manual**—The network administrator assigns the IPv4 address to a specific MAC address. DHCP is simply used to dispatch the assigned address to the host.

- **Automatic**—DHCP assigns a permanent IPv4 address to a host.

- **Dynamic**—DHCP assigns an IPv4 address to a host for a limited time (called a *lease*), or until the host explicitly releases the address. This mechanism allows automatic address reuse when the host to which it has been assigned no longer needs the address.

NOTE   DHCP is defined in RFC 2131, *Dynamic Host Configuration Protocol*, available at www.cis.ohio-state.edu/cgi-bin/rfc/rfc2131.html.

Name Resolution

The following discussion covers the purpose of name resolution, provides information about different available name resolution strategies, and discusses DNS name resolution.

Names are used to identify different hosts and resources on the network and to provide user-friendly interaction with computers; a name is much easier to remember than an IP address.

Hosts (computers, servers, printers, and so forth) identify themselves to each other using various naming schemes. Each computer on the network can have an assigned name to provide easier communication between devices and among users. Because the IP network layer protocol uses IP addresses to transport datagrams, a name that is used to identify a host must be mapped or resolved into an IP address; this is known as *name resolution*. To select the desired name resolution method, you should answer the following questions:

- How many hosts require name resolution?
- Are applications that depend on name resolution present?
- Is the network isolated, or is it connected to the Internet?
- If the network is isolated, how frequently are new hosts added and how frequently do names change?

Static Versus Dynamic Name Resolution

The process of resolving a host name to an IP address can be either static or dynamic. Following are the differences between the two name resolution methods:

- **Static**—With static name-to-IP-address resolution, both the administrative overhead and the configuration are very similar to a static address assignment strategy. The network administrator must manually define name-to-IP-address resolutions in a special file by entering the name and IP address pairs into the file using either a graphical or text interface. Manual entries create additional work for the administrator; they must be entered on every host and are prone to errors and omissions.

- **Dynamic**—The dynamic name-to-IP-address resolution is similar to the dynamic address assignment strategy. The administrator only has to enter the name-to-IP-address resolutions on a special server rather than on every host. The server then performs the job of name-to-IP-address resolution. The dynamic name-to-IP-address resolution method facilitates renumbering and renaming.

When to Use Static or Dynamic Name Resolution

The selection of either a static or dynamic end system name resolution method depends on the following criteria:

- **The number of hosts**—Dynamic name resolution is preferred if the number of end systems is high (more than 30).

- **Isolated network**—If the network is isolated (no connections to the Internet) and the number of hosts is small, static name resolution might be appropriate. The dynamic method is also possible; the choice is an administrative decision.

- **Internet connectivity**—When the network is connected to the Internet, static name resolution is not an option, and dynamic name resolution using DNS is mandatory.

- **Frequent changes and adding of names**—When dealing with frequent changes and adding names to a network, dynamic name resolution is recommended.

- **Applications depending on name resolution**—If applications that depend on name resolution are used, dynamic name resolution is recommended.

Using DNS for Name Resolution

For hosts to resolve symbolic names to actual network addresses, they must know the DNS server address. Queries on the name server are performed through resolver or name resolver programs, which are usually part of the host operating system. An application sends a query to a name resolver, which resolves the request with either the local database (HOSTS file) or the DNS server.

When numerous host or Fully Qualified Domain Name (FQDN) names must be resolved to IP addresses, statically defined resolutions in HOSTS files are unwieldy to maintain. To ease this process, a DNS server can be used for name resolution.

NOTE   FQDN is a complete domain name for a specific host on the Internet that has enough information to be converted into a specific IP address. The FQDN consists of a host name and a domain name. For example, www.cisco.com is the FQDN on the web for the cisco web server. The host is www, the domain is cisco, and the top-level domain name is com.

To enable DNS name resolution, the network administrator must set up the DNS server, enter information about host names and corresponding IP addresses, and configure the hosts to use the DNS server for name resolution.

A DNS server is special software that usually resides on dedicated hardware. DNS servers are organized in a hierarchical structure. A DNS server can query other DNS servers to retrieve partial resolutions for a certain name; for example, one DNS server could resolve cisco.com and another could resolve www.

In the example shown in Figure 6-17, the following transactions occur:

Step 1   A user wants to browse www.cisco.com. Because the host does not know that site's IP address, it queries the DNS server.

Step 2   The DNS server responds with the appropriate IP address for www.cisco.com.

Step 3   The host establishes a connection to the appropriate IP address (site).

NOTE   RFC 2136, *Dynamic Updates in the Domain Name System (DNS UPDATE)*, available at www.cis.ohio-state.edu/cgi-bin/rfc/rfc2136.html, specifies a technology that helps to reduce the administrative overhead of maintaining address-to-name mappings.

Figure 6-17 *Name Resolution with DNS*

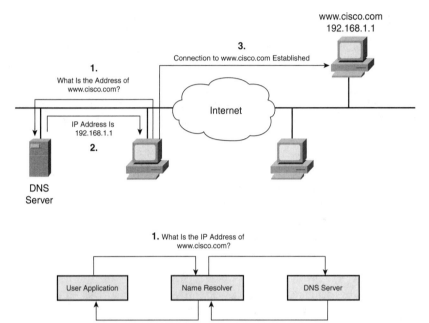

NOTE   The IP addresses shown in the examples are private addresses. In practice, public addresses would be used on the Internet.

Introduction to IPv6

This section on IPv6-specific design considerations provides an overview of IPv6 addressing, explains the impact of the IPv6 address structure and various address types on an addressing plan, and briefly describes the IPv6 routing protocols. It explains new address assignment and name resolution strategies for IPv6. Because the migration from IPv4 to IPv6 does not happen automatically, this section also covers possible transition strategies.

NOTE   RFC 2460, *Internet Protocol, Version 6 (IPv6)*, defines the IPv6 standard. This RFC is available at www.cis.ohio-state.edu/cs/Services/rfc/rfc-text/rfc2460.txt.

Information on IPv6 features supported in specific Cisco IOS releases can be found in *Cisco IOS Software Release Specifics for IPv6 Features*, at www.cisco.com/univercd/cc/td/doc/product/software/ios123/123cgcr/ipv6_c/ftipv6s.htm.

IPv6 Address Structure

First, we focus on the IPv6 address structure and features and discuss the advantages of IPv6 over IPv4.

IPv6 Features

IPv6, a successor to IPv4, has been designed to overcome IPv4's limitations.

The main benefits of IPv6 include the following:

- **Larger address space**—IPv6 increases the IP address size from 32 bits to 128 bits. This allows more support for addressing hierarchy levels, a much greater number of addressable nodes, and simpler auto-configuration of addresses.

- **Global unique IP addresses**—Every node can have a unique global IP address, which eliminates the need for NAT.

- **Site multi-homing**—IPv6 allows hosts to have multiple IPv6 addresses, and networks to have multiple IPv6 prefixes. This facilitates connection to multiple ISPs without breaking the global routing table.

- **Header format efficiency**—A fixed header size makes processing more efficient.

- **Improved privacy and security**—IPv6 introduces optional security headers.

- **Flow labeling capability**—A new capability enables the labeling of packets belonging to particular traffic "flows" for which the sender requests special handling, such as non-default quality of service (QoS) or "real-time" service.

- Increased mobility, QoS, and multicast capabilities.

IPv6 Address Format

An IPv6 address is 128 bits long and provides a much larger address space than IPv4. IPv6 can provide approximately $3.4*10^{38}$ addresses (340,282,366,920,938,463,374,607,432,768,211,456), or approximately $5*10^{28}$ addresses for every person on the planet.

IPv6 addresses are represented as a series of 16-bit hexadecimal fields separated by colons (:), in the format x:x:x:x:x:x:x:x. Techniques are available to shorten written IPv6 addresses, including the following:

- The leading 0s within a field are optional.

- IPv6 addresses often contain successive hexadecimal fields of 0s. To shorten IPv6 addresses, two colons (::) can be used to compress successive hexadecimal fields of 0s (the colons represent successive hexadecimal fields of 0s). This can be done at the beginning, middle, or end of an IPv6 address, *but is allowed only once in an address.* To determine the number of missing 0s in an IPv6 address, write the two parts of the address separately and fill in between with 0s until there are 128 bits.

For example, the IPv6 address 2031:**0000**:130F:**0000**:**0000**:**0**9C0:876A:130B can be written as 2031:**0**:130F::9C0:876A:130B. An *incorrect* way to write this address is 2031::130F::9C0:876A:130B; two colons are only allowed once within an address.

As another example, the address 0:0:0:0:0:0:0:0 can be written as :: because it contains all 0s.

NOTE   IPv6 addressing architecture is described in RFC 2373, *IP Version 6 Addressing Architecture,* which is available at www.cis.ohio-state.edu/cgi-bin/rfc/rfc2373.html.

Like the IPv4 prefix, the IPv6 prefix represents the *network* portion of the address. The IPv6 prefix is written in a *prefix/prefix-length* format; the prefix-length is a decimal value that indicates the number of higher-order bits in the address that are included in the prefix. For example, 1080:5E40::/32 indicates that the higher-order 32 bits represent the network portion of the address.

A single interface can have multiple IPv6 addresses of different types.

IPv6 Datagram Structure

To provide more efficient processing, IPv6 introduces a new packet header structure with a fixed header size.

As shown in Figure 6-18, the IPv6 packet header has the following eight fields:

- **Version**—A 4-bit field that indicates the IP version–in this case, IPv6.

- **Traffic Class**—An 8-bit field that tags packets with a traffic class that is used in differentiated services.

- **Flow Label**—A 20-bit field that can be used by a source to label sequences of packets for which the source requests special handling by the IPv6 routers (for example, non-default QoS or real-time service). If a host or router does not support the functions of the Flow Label field, the field is set to 0 for the packets originated by the device, left unchanged for the packets that are forwarded, and ignored for the received packets.

NOTE   At the moment, the use of the Flow Label field is still experimental and is subject to change as the requirements for flow support in the Internet are clarrified.

- **Payload Length**—A 16-bit field that is similar to the Total Length field in the IPv4 packet header. The Payload Length field indicates the total length of the packet's data.

- **Next Header**—An 8-bit field that is similar to the Protocol field in the IPv4 packet header. The value of the Next Header field defines the type of information that follows the basic IPv6 header (for example, a Transmission Control Protocol [TCP] or User Datagram Protocol [UDP] packet).

- **Hop Limit**—This 8-bit field specifies the maximum number of hops the IPv6 packet can traverse and is similar to the IPv4 packet header's Time to Live (TTL) field.

- **Source IPv6 Address**—This field is 16 octets or 128 bits, and contains the packet's source address.

- **Destination IPv6 Address**—This field is 16 octets or 128 bits, and contains the destination address of the packet.

Figure 6-18 *IPv6 Datagram Structure Includes a 40-Octet Header*

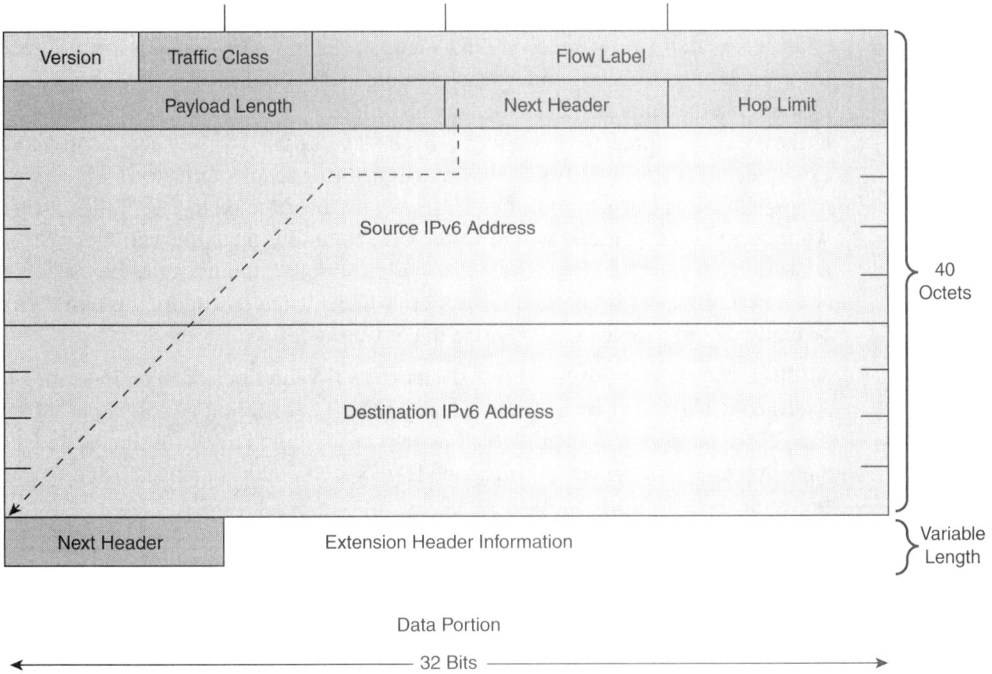

The header has a total length of 40 octets (320 bits). All fields are aligned to 64 bits to enable more efficient processing. Extension headers, if any, follow the eight fields, which are followed by the data portion of the packet.

IPv6 Address Types and Scopes

In this section, we cover the various IPv6 address types and their scopes.

IPv6 Address Scope Types

Similar to IPv4, a single source can address datagrams to either one or many destinations at the same time in IPv6.

Following are the types of IPv6 addresses:

- **Unicast (one-to-one)**—This is the same as IPv4 unicast: a single source sends data to a single destination. A packet sent to a unicast IPv6 address is delivered to the interface identified by that address. The next section discusses the different types of IPv6 unicast addresses.

- **Anycast (one-to-nearest)**—An identifier for a set of interfaces that typically belong to different nodes. A packet sent to an anycast address is delivered to the closest interface (as defined by the routing protocols in use) that is identified by the anycast address. In other words, receivers that share the same characteristics are assigned the same anycast address. A sender who is interested in contacting a receiver with those characteristics sends packets to the anycast address, and the routers deliver the packet to the receiver nearest to the sender. Anycast can be used for service location. For example, an anycast address could be assigned to a set of replicated FTP servers. A user in China who wants to retrieve a file would be directed to the Chinese server, while a user in the Europe would be directed to the European server. Anycast addresses are allocated from the unicast address space and must not be used as the source address of an IPv6 packet. Nodes to which the anycast address is assigned must be explicitly configured to recognize the anycast address.

- **Multicast (one-to-many)**—This is the same as IPv4 multicast: an address for a set of interfaces (in a given scope) that typically belong to different nodes. A packet sent to a multicast address is delivered to all interfaces identified by the multicast address (in a given scope). (IPv6 uses a 4-bit scope ID to specify address ranges that are reserved for multicast addresses for each scope.)

NOTE   IPv6 has no concept of broadcast addresses; multicast addresses are used instead.

IPv6 Unicast Addresses

Following are the different unicast addresses that IPv6 supports:

- Global aggregatable address (also called global unicast address)
- Site-local address
- Link-local address
- IPv4-compatible IPv6 address

Global Aggregatable Unicast Address

Key Point: IPv6 Global Aggregatable Unicast Address

The IPv6 global aggregatable unicast address is equivalent to the IPv4 unicast address.

The structure of aggregatable global unicast addresses enables summarization (aggregation) of routing prefixes to limit the number of routing table entries in the global routing table. Aggregatable global addresses that are used on links are aggregated upward, through organizations, then to intermediate-level ISPs, and eventually to top-level ISPs. The structure, which is shown in Figure 6-19, is described as follows:

- A fixed prefix of binary 001 (2000::/3) indicates an aggregatable global IPv6 address.

- At the top of the hierarchy, several International Registries assign blocks of addresses (13 bits) to top-level aggregators (TLAs). These TLAs are the public transit points (exchanges) where long-haul providers establish peer connections.

- A reserved field of 8 bits allows growth of the TLA and Next-Level Aggregator (NLA) fields. The field must equal 0.

- TLAs allocate blocks of addresses (24 bits) to NLAs, which represent large providers and global corporate networks.

- When an NLA is a provider, it further allocates its addresses to its subscribers using a 16-bit Site Level Aggregator (SLA). If the NLA is a global corporate network, the SLA can be used for identifying individual sites or subnetworks.

- Individual organizations use the 64-bit Interface ID field to identify interfaces on a link. The field must be unique to the link.

Figure 6-19 *IPv6 Global Aggregatable Unicast Address Structure*

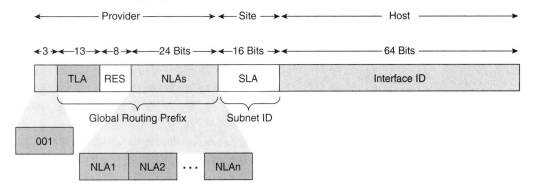

Site-Local Unicast Address

Key Point: Site-Local Unicast Addresses

Site-local unicast addresses are similar to private addresses in IPv4.

Site-local addresses can number a site without having a global prefix. These addresses are IPv6 unicast addresses that use the prefix FEC0::/10 (1111 1110 11) and concatenate the subnet identifier (the 16-bit field) with the interface identifier (a 64-bit field), as shown in Figure 6-20. Site-local addresses can be considered private addresses and can be used to restrict communication to a limited domain. For example, they can be used to assign numbers to a device, such as a printer, that will never communicate with the IPv6 Internet.

Figure 6-20 *IPv6 Site-Local Unicast Address Structure*

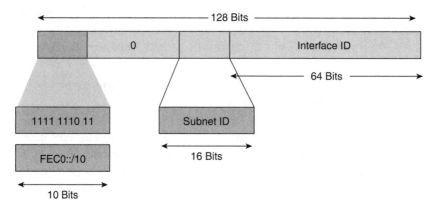

IPv6 routers must not advertise routes or forward packets that have site-local source or destination addresses outside the site.

Link-Local Unicast Address

A link-local address is only useful in the context of the local link network.

As shown in Figure 6-21, a link-local address is an IPv6 unicast address that can be automatically configured on any interface by using the link-local prefix FE80::/10 (1111 111010) and the interface identifier. Link-local addresses are used in the neighbor discovery protocol and the stateless autoconfiguration process, which we discuss in more detail in the "IPv6 Address Assignment Strategies" section.

Key Point: Link-Local Unicast Addresses

A link-local unicast address can serve as a method for connecting devices on the same local network without requiring either site-local or globally unique addresses.

Many routing protocols also use link-local addresses. An IPv6 router must not forward packets that have either link-local source or destination addresses to other links.

Figure 6-21 *IPv6 Link-Local Unicast Address Structure*

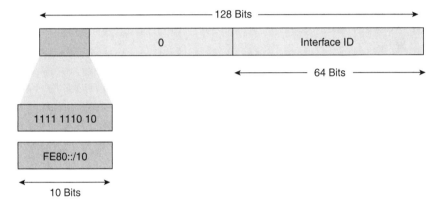

IPv4-compatible IPv6 Address

The IPv4-compatible IPv6 address is used in IPv6 transition mechanisms (discussed in the "IPv4 to IPv6 Transition" section) to dynamically tunnel IPv6 packets over IPv4 infrastructures. The IPv4-compatible IPv6 address is an IPv6 unicast address that embeds an IPv4 address in the low-order 32 bits and 0s in the high-order 96 bits of the IPv6 address.

The format of an IPv4-compatible IPv6 address is 0:0:0:0:0:0:A.B.C.D, or ::A.B.C.D. The entire 128-bit IPv4-compatible IPv6 address is used as a node's IPv6 address, and the IPv4 address that is embedded in the low-order 32 bits is used as the node's IPv4 address. IPv4-compatible IPv6 addresses are assigned to nodes that support both the IPv4 and IPv6 protocol stacks and are used in automatic tunnels (discussed in the "IPv4 to IPv6 Transition" section).

For example, the IPv4 address 192.168.30.1 would convert to the IPv4-compatible IPv6 address 0:0:0:0:0:0:192.168.30.1. Other acceptable representations for this address are ::192.168.30.1 and ::C0A8:1E01.

IPv6 Address Assignment Strategies

As with IPv4, IPv6 allows two address assignment strategies: static and dynamic (also called *autoconfiguration*).

Static IPv6 Address Assignment

Static address assignment in IPv6 is the same as in IPv4—the administrator must enter the IPv6 address configuration manually on every device in the network.

Dynamic IPv6 Address Assignment

IPv6 dynamic address assignment strategies allow dynamic assignment of IPv6 addresses, as follows:

- **Link local address**—The host configures its own link-local address autonomously, using the link-local prefix FE80::0/10 and an identifier for the interface.

- **Stateless autoconfiguration**—A router on the link advertises—either periodically or upon the host's request—its site-local and global prefixes and its willingness to function as a default router for the link. Hosts can automatically generate site-local and global IPv6 addresses without either manual configuration or a server (such as a DHCP server) by using the prefixes in these router messages. For example, Figure 6-22 shows an Ethernet interface on which the host uses the prefix advertised by the router as the top 64 address bits; the remaining 64 bits contain the 48-bit MAC address in an extended universal identifier 64-bit (EUI-64) format.

- **Stateful using DHCPv6**—DHCPv6 is an updated version of DHCP for IPv4. DHCPv6 enables more control than stateless autoconfiguration and can be used for renumbering nodes without any routers. It can also be used for automatic domain name registration of hosts using a DNS server. DHCPv6 uses multicast addresses.

EUI-64 Format

The EUI-64 format interface ID is derived from the 48-bit link-layer MAC address by inserting the hex number FFFE between the upper 3 bytes (the Organizational Unique Identifier [OUI] field) and the lower 3 bytes (the serial number) of the link-layer address. To make sure that the chosen address is from a unique MAC address, the seventh bit in the high-order byte is set to 1 (equivalent to the IEEE G/L bit) to indicate the uniqueness of the 48-bit address.

The information in this sidebar is derived from "The ABCs of IP Version 6," available at www.cisco.com/warp/public/732/abc/docs/abcipv6.pdf.

Figure 6-22 *IPv6 Stateless Autoconfiguration Allows a Host to Automatically Configure Its IPv6 Address*

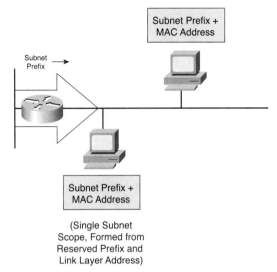

Dynamic IPv6 Renumbering

With the IPv6 stateless autoconfiguration feature, network renumbering is much easier. For example, in Figure 6-23, the administrator wants to renumber the network (use a new prefix). The administrator takes the following steps:

Step 1 The new prefix is configured on the router, so it is added to the router advertisement messages that are sent on the link; the advertisements contain both the old and new prefixes.

Step 2 The nodes use the address created from the new prefix and the address created from the old prefix. The old prefix has lifetime parameters configured to determine the transition period, after which the old prefix is removed from the router advertisement messages.

Step 3 When the old prefix is removed from the router advertisements, only addresses that contain the new prefix are used on that link.

Figure 6-23 *Dynamic IPv6 Address Assignment*

IPv6 Name Resolution

The following sections discuss available name resolution strategies and name resolution on a dual-stack (IPv4 and IPv6) host.

Static and Dynamic IPv6 Name Resolution

IPv6 and IPv4 name resolutions are very similar.

The following two name resolutions are available with IPv6:

- **Static name resolution**—Accomplished by manual entries in the host's local configuration files.

- **Dynamic name resolution**—Accomplished using a DNS server, which has built-in support for IPv6 server usually along with IPv4 support. As shown in Figure 6-24, an IPv6-aware application requests the destination host name's IPv6 address from the DNS server with a request for an A6 record (an address record for the IPv6 host; a new DNS feature). The task of querying for the address is done with the name resolver, which is usually part of the operating system. The network administrator must set up the appropriate DNS server with IPv6 support and connect it to the IPv6 network with a valid IPv6 address. The hosts must also have IPv6 addresses.

Figure 6-24 *IPv6 Name Resolution*

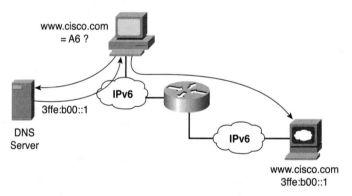

IPv4- and IPv6-Aware Applications and Name Resolution

A dual-stack host is aware of both IPv4 and IPv6 protocol stacks and has a new Application Program Interface (API) that is defined to support both IPv4 and IPv6 addresses and DNS requests.

An application can use both IPv4 and IPv6. An application can be converted to the new API while still using only IPv4.

As shown in Figure 6-25, an IPv6- and IPv4-enabled application chooses which stack is used (the typical default is IPv6) and asks the DNS server for the destination host's address. After receiving the response from the DNS server, the application then requests the source host to connect to the destination host using IPv6.

Figure 6-25 *Dual-stack Name Resolution*

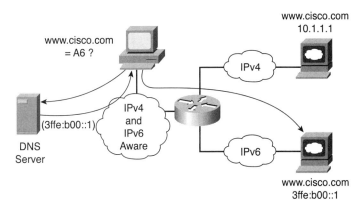

IPv4 to IPv6 Transition Strategies and Deployments

IPv4 to IPv6 migration does not happen automatically. The following sections present the differences between IPv4 and IPv6 and discuss possible transition strategies and deployments.

Differences Between IPv4 and IPv6

Regardless of which protocol is used, the communication between IPv4 and IPv6 domains must be transparent to end users. The major differences to consider between IPv4 and IPv6 include the following:

- IPv4 addresses are 32 bits long, while IPv6 addresses are 128 bits long.

- An IPv6 packet header is different from an IPv4 packet header. The IPv6 header is longer and simpler (new fields were added to the IPv6 header and some old fields were removed).

- IPv6 has no concept of broadcast address; instead, it uses multicast addresses.

- Routing protocols must be changed to support native IPv6 routing.

IPv4 to IPv6 Transition

The transition from IPv4 to IPv6 will be a slow process; it will take several years because of the high cost of upgrading equipment. In the meantime, IPv4 and IPv6 must coexist.

To enable smooth end user-transparent communication between the IPv4 and IPv6 parts of a network, different solutions are available to the network administrator.

Three primary mechanisms help with the transition from IPv4 to IPv6:

- **Dual-stack**—Both the IPv4 and the IPv6 stacks run on a system that can communicate with both IPv6 and IPv4 devices.

- **Tunneling**—Uses encapsulation of IPv6 packets to traverse IPv4 networks, and vice versa.

- **Translation**—Mechanism that translates one protocol to the other to facilitate communication between the two networks.

The following sections describe these mechanisms.

NOTE   Cisco has designed the IPv6 on the Multiprotocol Label Switching (MPLS) Provider Edge (PE) routers (6PE) feature, which allows smooth integration of IPv6 into MPLS networks. Because the MPLS routers switch packets based on labels rather than address lookups, customers with an MPLS backbone can scale IPv6 traffic easily and do not need to make costly hardware upgrades.

Dual-Stack Transition Mechanism

As shown in Figure 6-26, a dual-stack node enables both IPv4 and IPv6 stacks.

Applications can communicate with both IPv4 and IPv6 stacks; the IP version choice is based on name lookup and application preference. This is the most appropriate method for the campus and access networks during the transition period, and it is the preferred technique for transition to IPv6. Operating systems use a dual-stack approach to support the maximum number of applications.

Operating systems that support IPv6 stack include FreeBSD, Linux, Sun Solaris, NT 4, and Windows 2000/XP.

NOTE   Procedures are available for hosts with the installation of a specific module (a new API defined to support both IPv4 and IPv6 addresses and DNS requests) in the host's TCP/IP stack. This must be done on every host. The module intercepts IP traffic through the API and converts it on the fly for the IPv6 counterpart.

Figure 6-26 *A Dual-stack Node Has Both IPv4 and IPv6 Stacks*

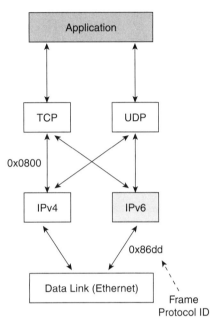

Tunneling Transition Mechanism

The purpose of tunneling is to encapsulate packets of one type in packets of another type. When transitioning to IPv6, tunneling encapsulates IPv6 packets in IPv4 packets, as shown in Figure 6-27.

Figure 6-27 *Tunneling IPv6 Packets Within IPv4 Packets*

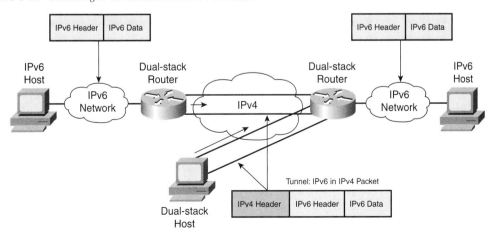

By using overlay tunnels, isolated IPv6 networks can communicate without having to upgrade the IPv4 infrastructure between them. Both routers and hosts can use tunneling.

The following different techniques are available for establishing a tunnel:

- **Manually configured**—Tunnel source and tunnel destination are manually configured with IPv4 and IPv6 addresses. Tunnels can be configured between border routers or between a border router and a host.

- **Semi-automated**—A tunnel broker that uses a Web-based service to create a tunnel achieves semi-automation. A tunnel broker is a server on the IPv4 network that receives tunnel requests from dual-stack clients, configures the tunnel on the tunnel server or router, and associates the tunnel from the client to one of the tunnel servers or routers. A simpler model combines the tunnel broker and server onto one device.

- **Automatic**—Various automatic mechanisms to achieve tunneling exist, including the following:

  - **IPv4-compatible**—The tunnel is constructed on the fly using an IPv4-compatible IPv6 address (an IPv6 address that consists of 0s in the upper bits and an embedded IPv4 address in the lower 32 bits). Because it does not scale, this mechanism is only appropriate for testing.

  - **6to4**—The 6to4 tunnel treats the IPv4 network as a virtual link. Each 6to4 edge router has an IPv6 address with a /48 prefix, which is the concatenation of 2002::/16 and the IPv4 address of the edge router; 2002::/16 is a specially assigned address range for the purpose of 6to4. The edge routers automatically build the tunnel using the IPv4 addresses that are embedded in the IPv6 addresses.

    When the edge router receives an IPv6 packet with a destination address in the range of 2002::/16, it determines from its routing table that the packet must traverse the tunnel. The router extracts the IPv4 address embedded (in the third to sixth octets, inclusive) in the IPv6 next-hop address, the address of the router at the other end of the tunnel, and encapsulates the IPv6 packet in an IPv4 packet with the destination edge router's extracted IPv4 address. This IPv4 address is the IPv4 address of the 6to4 router at the destination site. The packet then passes through the IPv4 network. The destination edge router de-capsulates the IPv6 packet from the received IPv4 packet and forwards the IPv6 packet to its final destination. (A 6to4 relay router, which offers traffic forwarding to the IPv6 Internet, is required for reaching a native IPv6 Internet.)

— **6over4**—A router connected to a native IPv6 network and with a 6over4-enabled interface can be used to forward IPv6 traffic between 6over4 hosts and native IPv6. IPv6 multicast addresses are mapped into the IPv4 multicast addresses. The IPv4 becomes a virtual Ethernet for IPv6; to achieve this, an IPv4 multicast-enabled network is required.

Translation Transition Mechanism

Dual-stack and tunneling techniques manage the interconnection of IPv6 domains. For legacy equipment that will not be upgraded to IPv6 and for some deployment scenarios, techniques are available for connecting IPv4-only nodes to IPv6-only nodes. Translation is basically an extension of NAT techniques.

As shown in Figure 6-28, an IPv6 node behind a translation device has full connectivity to other IPv6 nodes and NAT functionality for communicating with IPv4 devices.

Figure 6-28 *Translation Mechanism*

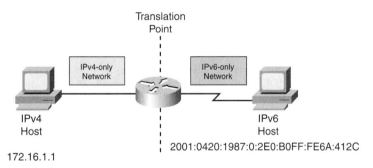

Translation techniques are available for translating IPv4 addresses to IPv6 addresses, and vice versa. Like current NAT devices, they can be translated at either the transport layer or the network layer. The two main network translation solutions are NAT-Protocol Translation (NAT-PT) and Dual-Stack Transition Mechanism (DSTM).

NAT-PT and DSTM

The NAT-PT translation mechanism translates at the network layer between IPv4 and IPv6 addresses and allows native IPv6 hosts and applications to communicate with native IPv4 hosts and applications. An Application Level Gateway (ALG) translates between the IPv4 and IPv6 DNS requests and responses. (NAT-PT is defined in RFC 2766, *Network Address Translation-Protocol Translation (NAT-PT),* which is available at www.cis.ohio-state.edu/cgi-bin/rfc/rfc2766.html.)

The DSTM translation mechanism is used for dual-stack hosts in an IPv6 domain that have not yet had an IPv4 address assigned to the IPv4 side, but that must communicate with IPv4 systems or allow IPv4 applications to run on top of their IPv6 protocol stack. The mechanism requires a dedicated server that dynamically provides a temporary global IPv4 address for the duration of the communication (using DHCPv6) and uses dynamic tunnels to carry the IPv4 traffic within an IPv6 packet through the IPv6 domain.

The information in this sidebar is derived from "The ABCs of IP Version 6," which is available at www.cisco.com/warp/public/732/abc/docs/abcipv6.pdf.

NOTE   ALGs use a dual-stack approach and enable a host in one domain to send data to another host in the other domain. This method requires that all application servers are converted to IPv6.

IPv6 Routing Protocols

The routing protocols available in IPv6 include interior gateway protocols (IGPs) within an autonomous system and exterior gateway protocols (EGPs) between autonomous systems.

As with IPv4 CIDR, IPv6 uses the same *longest-prefix match* routing. Updates to the existing IPv4 routing protocols were necessary for handling longer IPv6 addresses and different header structures. Currently, the following updated routing protocols or draft proposals are available:

- **IGPs**
    - RIP new generation (RIPng)
    - OSPF version 3 (OSPFv3)
    - Integrated IS-IS version 6 (IS-ISv6)
- **EGP** — BGP4+

RIP New Generation

RIP new generation (RIPng) is a distance-vector protocol with a limit of 15 hops that uses split-horizon and poison reverse to prevent routing loops. IPv6 features include the following:

- RIPng is based on the IPv4 RIPv2 and is similar to RIPv2
- RIPng uses an IPv6 prefix and a next-hop IPv6 address
- A multicast group, FF02::9, is the all-RIP-routers multicast group and is used as the destination address for RIP updates
- RIPng uses IPv6 for transport

NOTE   RIPng is defined in RFC 2080, *RIPng for IPv6,* available at www.cis.ohio-state.edu/cgi-bin/rfc/rfc2080.html.

Open Shortest Path First Version 3

OSPFv3 is a new protocol implementation for IPv6 that has the following features:

- OSPFv3 is similar to OSPF's IPv4 version
- OSPFv3 carries IPv6 addresses
- OSPFv3 uses link-local unicast addresses as source addresses
- OSPFv3 uses IPv6 for transport

NOTE   OSPFv3 is defined in RFC 2740, *OSPF for IPv6,* available at www.cis.ohio-state.edu/cgi-bin/rfc/rfc2740.html.

Integrated IS-IS Version 6

The large address support in Integrated IS-ISv6 facilitates the IPv6 address family. IS-ISv6 is the same as IS-IS for IPv4, with the following extensions added for IPv6:

- Two new type length, values (TLVs)
  - IPv6 Reachability
  - IPv6 Interface Address
- A new protocol identifier

BGP4+

Multiprotocol extensions for BGP4 enable other protocols to be routed besides IPv4, including IPv6. Additional IPv6-specific extensions are also incorporated into BGP4+, including the definition of a new identifier for the IPv6 address family.

NOTE   RFC 2283, *Multiprotocol Extensions for BGP-4,* available at www.cis.ohio-state.edu/cgi-bin/rfc/rfc2283.html, defines multiprotocol extensions to BGP. RFC 2545, *Multiprotocol Extensions for BGP-4,* available at www.cis.ohio-state.edu/cgi-bin/rfc/rfc2545.html, defines BGP4+ for IPv6.

NOTE   Cisco routers support RIPng, IS-ISv6, and BGP4+ routing protocols. Some platforms also support OSPFv3.

Summary

In this chapter, you learned about IPv4 and IPv6 addressing.

An IPv4 address is 32 bits long. A subnet mask indicates how to interpret an IPv4 address. When subnetting, some bits from the host part are used for the subnetwork part.

The IP addressing plan depends on the network size, which includes the number and type of locations and the number and type of devices at each location.

A network designer should decide when and how to use private and public IPv4 addresses. The private IPv4 addresses are as follows:

- 10.0.0.0/8 (10.0.0.0 to 10.255.255.255)
- 172.16.0.0/12 (172.16.0.0 to 172.31.255.255)
- 192.168.0.0/16 (192.168.0.0 to 192.168.255.255)

A hierarchical addressing plan reduces routing overhead by allowing route summarization, or aggregation. With route summarization, one route in the routing table represents many other routes. Summarizing routes reduces the number of routes in the routing table, the routing update traffic, and overall router overhead.

Dynamic address assignment using DHCP reduces administrative overhead.

Dynamic name resolution using DNS introduces more flexibility into the network.

Using 128-bit addresses, IPv6 has a larger address space. IPv6 addresses are represented as a series of 16-bit hexadecimal fields separated by colons (:) in the format x:x:x:x:x:x:x:x.

The IPv6 header has a total length of 40 octets (320 bits).

The types of IPv6 addresses are unicast (one-to-one), anycast (one-to-nearest), and multicast (one-to-many). The types of unicast addresses are global aggregatable, site-local, link-local, and IPv4-compatible IPv6 addresses.

Stateless autoconfiguration of IPv6 addresses allows hosts to automatically generate site-local and global addresses. Stateful dynamic address assignment using DHCPv6 provides more control.

IPv6 dynamic name resolution requires DNS servers that have IPv6 protocol stack support.

IPv4 to IPv6 transition strategies are used in the IPv4 to IPv6 migration process and include dual-stack use, tunneling mechanisms, and translation mechanisms.

RIPng, IS-ISv6, and BGP4+ are the IPv6 routing protocols that are currently available. OSPFv3 is also available on some platforms.

References

For additional information, refer to the following resources:

- "The ABCs of IP Version 6," www.cisco.com/warp/public/732/abc/docs/abcipv6.pdf.

- Bradner, Scott O. and Allison Mankin. *IPng Internet Protocol Next Generation*. Reading, Massachusetts: Addison-Wesley, 1995.

- Cisco IOS IPv6, www.cisco.com/warp/public/732/Tech/ipv6.

- Cisco IP Version 6 Solutions, www.cisco.com/univercd/cc/td/doc/cisintwk/intsolns/ipv6_sol/index.htm.

- Comer, Douglas E. and David L Stevens. *Internetworking with TCP/IP*. Englewood Cliffs, New Jersey: Prentice-Hall, 1991.

- Designing Large-Scale IP Internetworks, www.cisco.com/univercd/cc/td/doc/cisintwk/idg4/nd2003.htm.

- Subnetting an IP Address Space, www.cisco.com/univercd/cc/td/doc/cisintwk/idg4/nd20a.htm.

Case Study

This case study is a continuation of the DJMP Industries case study we first introduced in Chapter 2, "Applying Design Principles in Network Deployment."

Case Study General Instructions

Use the scenarios, information, and parameters provided at each task of the ongoing case study. If you encounter ambiguities, make reasonable assumptions and proceed. For all tasks, use the initial customer scenario and build on the solutions provided thus far.

You can use any and all documentation, books, white papers, and so on.

In each task, you act as a network design consultant. Make creative proposals to accomplish the customer's business needs. Justify your ideas when they differ from the provided solutions.

Use any design strategies and internetworking technologies you feel are appropriate.

The final goal for each case study is a paper solution; you are not required to provide the specific product names.

Appendix G, "Answers to Review Questions, Case Studies, and Simulation Exercises," provides a solution for each task based on assumptions made. There is no claim that the provided solution is the best or only solution. Your solution might be more appropriate for the assumptions you made. The provided solution helps you understand the author's reasoning and offers a way for you to compare and contrast your solution.

Case Study: Network Addressing Plan

Complete the following steps:

Step 1   You might want to review the DJMP Industries Case Study Scenario in Chapter 2.

Step 2   Propose the optimal IP addressing plan for the given network scenario. Take into account that you must also use a new routing protocol and ensure some WAN backup. The future campus will be completely restructured and more granular.

Step 3   Propose possible methods of IP address assignment.

Review Questions

Answer the following questions and refer to Appendix G, "Answers to Review Questions, Case Studies, and Simulation Exercises," for the answers.

1 For the address 172.17.7.245/28:

— What is the mask?

— What class is the address?

— What is the host part?

— What is the network part?

— How many hosts can reside on this subnet?

2 What information must be collected to determine the size of the network?

3 Approximately how much reserve in the number of network devices should be included for future growth purposes?

4 Which of the following IPv4 addresses cannot be used in public networks?

a 172.167.20.1/24

b 192.168.1.200/28

c 172.30.100.33/24

d 172.32.1.1/16

5 In what situation would both private and public IPv4 addresses be required?

6 What type of routing protocol can support VLSM?

7 What are some disadvantages of a flat IP addressing scheme?

8 What are some advantages of a hierarchical IP addressing scheme?

9 What is the difference between classless and classful routing protocols?

10 What are the advantages of using DHCP versus static address assignment?

11 What are the three DHCP address allocation mechanisms?

12 What is the advantage of using dynamic name resolution versus static name resolution?

13 Describe the process that is used when DNS resolves a URL, such as www.cisco.com.

14 How many bits are in an IPv6 address?

15 How long is the IPv6 packet header?

16 What field of the IPv6 packet header is analogous to the IPv4 TTL field?

17 Which IPv6 packet header field is used to label sequences of packets?

18 One-to-many IPv6 addresses are called _____.

19 What types of IPv6 unicast addresses must not be forwarded to the Internet by a router?

20 How many bits are used for interface ID in an IPv6 unicast address?

21 What IPv6 prefix would be used to connect devices on the same network?

22 What are the three address assignment strategies that are available in IPv6?

23 How does the IPv6 stateless autoconfiguration work?

24 What feature allows DNS to support IPv6?

25 Can a host support IPv4 and IPv6 simultaneously?

26 What are three mechanisms for transitioning from IPv4 to IPv6?

27 Which operating systems support both IPv4 and IPv6?

28 Describe how 6to4 tunneling works.

29 Which IPv6 routing protocols do Cisco routers currently support?

30 What is the multicast address that is used for RIPng?

This chapter discusses IP routing protocols and contains the following sections:

- Routing Protocol Selection Criteria
- Routing Protocol Features
- Routing Protocol Deployment
- Summary
- Case Study
- Review Questions

CHAPTER 7

Selecting Routing Protocols for a Network

This chapter describes considerations for selecting the most appropriate network routing protocol. First, we present general routing protocol features that should be evaluated during the selection process. Then we describe existing routing protocols in terms of their benefits and drawbacks when deployed in corporate networks.

The chapter concludes with a discussion of routing protocol deployment scenarios, in which we cover convergence and redundancy, multiple routing protocols in the network, redistribution, summarization, and so forth.

After completing this chapter, you will be able to determine the major criteria for selecting the appropriate routing protocol, explain the main features of major routing protocols, and deploy routing protocols in a hierarchical enterprise network.

NOTE   Chapter 1, "Internetworking Technology Review," contains introductory information on routing protocols.

For more details about Internet Protocol (IP) routing protocols, see *CCNP Self-Study: Building Scalable Cisco Internetworks (BSCI)*, by Catherine Paquet and Diane Teare, Cisco Press, 2004.

NOTE   In this chapter, the term *IP* refers to IP version 4 (IPv4).

Routing Protocol Selection Criteria

There are many ways to characterize routing protocols, including the following methods:

- Static versus dynamic routing
- Distance vector versus link-state versus hybrid protocols
- Interior versus exterior routing protocols
- Routing protocol metrics

- Routing protocol convergence
- Hierarchical versus flat routing protocols

The following sections discuss these methods in more detail.

Static Versus Dynamic Routing

While static routes are configured manually, routing protocols generate dynamic routes. Each method has advantages and disadvantages in specific network scenarios, as discussed in the following sections.

Static Routing

The term *static routing* means the use of manually configured or injected static routes for traffic forwarding purposes. (The injected static routes are generated by the authentication, authorization, and accounting [AAA] process.)

NOTE   The Configuring Large-Scale Dial-Out document, available at www.cisco.com/en/US/ partner/products/sw/iosswrel/ps1835/ products_configuration_guide_chapter09186a00800ca6ef.html, discusses dynamic static routes generated by AAA.

You must be a registered user to access this document.

Static routing is primarily used for the following purposes:

- Routing to and from stub networks. A stub network only carries traffic for local hosts. It typically has only one entry/exit point; even if it contains paths to more than one other network, it does not carry traffic for other networks. (Therefore, a stub network cannot be a transit network.)
- Smaller networks that are not expected to grow significantly.
- Special features such as dial-on-demand routing (DDR).
- To specify routes toward dialing peers in dial-in environments.

Configuration and maintenance of static routes is time-consuming. To be implemented properly, it requires complete knowledge of the entire network.

Figure 7-1 illustrates a stub network scenario, in which the use of static routes is favored over a dynamic routing protocol. On the right side, Figure 7-1 shows a stub network with a single entry/exit point over the S0 interface of Router A. On the stub network router (Router A), a static default route is configured so that the S0 link forwards all traffic toward destinations outside the stub network. On Router B, a static route is installed toward the stub network and then redistributed into the routing protocol so that reachability information for the stub network is available throughout the rest of the network.

Figure 7-1   *Use Static Routes with a Stub Network*

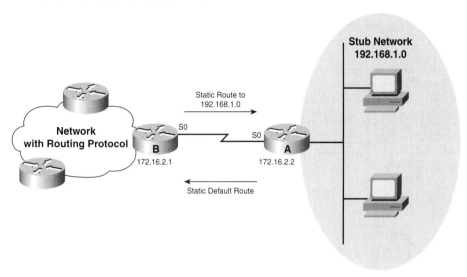

By using static and default static routes in this scenario, no traffic from the dynamic routing protocol is present on the serial link or in the stub network. In addition, the processor and memory requirements for both routers are lower; in the stub network, a low-end router would suffice.

Dynamic Routing

The term *dynamic routing* means that a dynamic routing protocol is used to spread routing information across the network to select the best routes toward destinations. Dynamic routing protocols have two major advantages over static routes:

- Dynamic adaptation to changes in the network
- Easier configuration and much less work for an administrator, even in small networks

The use of dynamic routing protocols is favored in almost all network scenarios; exceptions include DDR, stub networks, and dial-in scenarios.

Dynamic routing protocols must do the following:

- Find sources from which routing information can be received (usually neighboring routers)
- Select the best paths toward all reachable destinations, based on received information
- Maintain this routing information
- Have a means of verifying routing information (periodic updates or refreshes)

Figure 7-2 shows an example of network routers that run two dynamic IP routing protocols; some routers run the Enhanced Interior Gateway Routing Protocol (EIGRP) and some run the Routing Information Protocol version 2 (RIPv2). IP reachability information is thereby propagated throughout the network via RIPv2 and EIGRP.

Figure 7-2   *Two Dynamic Routing Protocols Running in a Network*

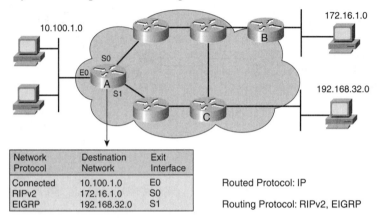

Network Protocol	Destination Network	Exit Interface
Connected	10.100.1.0	E0
RIPv2	172.16.1.0	S0
EIGRP	192.168.32.0	S1

Routed Protocol: IP

Routing Protocol: RIPv2, EIGRP

NOTE   Sometimes it is necessary to run two or more routing protocols in the same network. In this case, information from one routing protocol is usually redistributed to another protocol.

In Figure 7-2, Router A has all the required information to reach the existing destinations. It selected the best paths for all three specified networks and inserted them into its IP routing table. The network is therefore converged; the exchange of routing information is complete, and the network is in a stable state.

The path toward the 10.100.1.0 network is chosen via the only possible method: the connected E0 interface. Following the information received from the RIPv2 routing process, the path toward network 172.16.1.0 is chosen via the S0 interface. According to the information received from the EIGRP process, the path toward the 192.168.32.0 network is chosen via the S1 interface.

Distance Vector Versus Link-State Versus Hybrid Protocols

There are two main types of routing protocols:

- **Distance vector protocols**—In a distance vector protocol, routing decisions are made on a hop-by-hop basis. Each router relies on its neighbor routers to make the correct routing decisions. The router passes only the results of this decision (its routing table) to its neighbors. Distance vector protocols are typically slower to converge and do not scale well; however, they are easy to implement and maintain. Examples of distance vector protocols include RIP (also called RIP version 1 [RIPv1]), RIPv2 (sometimes called next-generation RIP), and the Interior Gateway Routing Protocol (IGRP).

NOTE   The Border Gateway Protocol (BGP) is also a distance vector protocol; however, as an exterior protocol, it has some different features and behaviors from the others. Exterior protocols and BGP are discussed later in this chapter.

- **Link-state protocols**—Each router floods information about itself (its link states) either to all other routers in the network, or to a part of the network (area). Each router makes its own routing decision based on all received information and using the shortest path first (SPF) algorithm (also called the *Dijkstra algorithm*), which calculates the shortest path to any destination. Link-state protocols are fast to converge, have less routing traffic overhead, and scale well. However, because of their complexity, they are more difficult to implement and maintain. The IP link-state protocols are Open Shortest Path First (OSPF) and Integrated Intermediate System-to-Intermediate System (IS-IS).

A third type of protocol also exists: the *hybrid interior gateway protocol*, which is Cisco's EIGRP. EIGRP has characteristics of both distance vector and link-state protocols; it supplements IGRP distance vector behavior with some link-state characteristics and some proprietary features. EIGRP is a fast converging and scalable routing protocol.

Key Point: Distance Vector Versus Link-State Versus Hybrid Routing Protocols

Recall that link-state routing protocols flood routing information to all nodes in the internetwork (depending on how the protocol is configured, this can be constrained to an area). However, each router sends only the portion of the routing table that describes the state of its own links.

Distance vector protocols call for each router to send all or some portion of its routing table, but only to its neighbors.

Essentially, link-state protocols send small updates everywhere, while distance vector protocols send larger updates only to neighboring routers. Hybrid, or advanced, routing protocols send small updates only to neighboring routers.

Table 7-1 summarizes the categorization of IP routing protocols.

Table 7-1 *Categorizing IP Routing Protocols*

Category	Routing Protocol
Distance vector	RIP, RIPv2, IGRP, BGP
Link-state	OSPF, IS-IS
Hybrid	EIGRP

Distance Vector Example

A distance vector router's understanding of the network is based on its neighbor's perspective of the topology; thus, the distance vector approach is sometimes referred to as *routing by rumor*. Distance vector protocols periodically send complete routing tables to all connected neighbors, and convergence might be slow because triggered updates are not typically used (RIPv2 is an exception).

NOTE *Triggered updates*, or *flash updates*, are sent only when a change happens (the link goes down or comes up, or link parameters that affect routing are changed—for example, a bandwidth change).

Most traditional distance vector protocols do not send triggered updates. However, Cisco's implementations of all IP distance vector protocols (RIP, RIPv2, and IGRP) do send triggered updates.

Figure 7-3 shows an example network that runs a distance vector protocol. In this network, the routing updates are periodic and include the entire routing table.

Figure 7-3 *Distance Vector Routing Sends the Entire Routing Table Periodically*

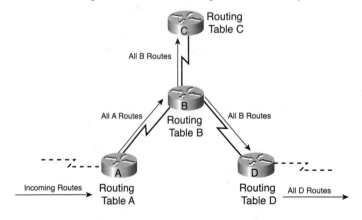

In large networks, the routing tables become enormous and cause a lot of traffic on the links.

RIPv2, which is a standardized protocol developed from the RIPv1 protocol, is an example of a distance vector protocol. The characteristics of RIPv2 include the following:

- Hop count is used as the metric for path selection
- The maximum allowable hop count is 15
- By default, routing updates are sent every 30 seconds (RIPv2 uses multicast not broadcast)
- RIPv2 permits variable-length subnet masks on the network

RIPv2 might be a good solution if a distance vector protocol seems adequate for implementation in a network, and the network includes equipment from multiple vendors.

Link-State Example

Both link-state protocols that support IP (OSPF and Integrated IS-IS) use the Hello protocol for establishing neighbor relationships. Each router understands a complete network topology from information shared through the neighbor relationships. Because each router has the complete network topology, the SPF algorithm creates the shortest path tree for all reachable destinations and therefore selects the best routes.

Figure 7-4 shows a network that uses a link-state protocol. Triggered updates, which include only data on the state of links that have changed, are sent in this network.

Figure 7-4 *Link-State Routing Only Sends Changed Data When There Is a Change*

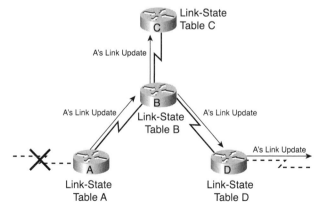

In link-state protocols, the information about connected links (including the subnets on those links) on all routers is flooded throughout the network or to a specific area of the network. Therefore, all network routers have detailed knowledge of the entire network, unlike with the distance vector routing protocols, where routers only receive knowledge of the best routes from neighboring devices.

After the initial exchange of all link states and upon reaching the full (converged) state of operation, almost no periodic updates are sent through the network. (In OSPF, periodic updates are sent every 30 minutes for each specific route, but not at the same time for all routes; this lessens the routing traffic volume.) Updates are only flooded through the network when a change in a link state occurs (either the link goes down, comes up, or link parameters that affect routing—such as bandwidth—are changed). These updates are called *triggered updates*.

Most of the control packets used in link-state operations are sent via multicast. This can cause problems when deploying link-state protocols in nonbroadcast multiaccess (NBMA) networks, such as Frame Relay and Asynchronous Transfer Mode (ATM).

Choosing Between Distance Vector and Link-State Protocols

The following guidelines help you ascertain which type of routing protocol you should deploy:

- Choose distance vector protocols when:

  — The network is a simple, flat network that does not require a special hierarchical design

  — The administrators do not have enough knowledge to operate and troubleshoot link-state protocols

  — Specific types of networks, such as hub and spoke networks, are being implemented

  — Worst-case convergence times in a network are not a concern

- Choose link-state protocols when:

  — The network design is hierarchical; this is usually the case for large networks

  — The administrators have good knowledge of the implemented link-state protocol

  — Fast convergence of the network is crucial

Interior Versus Exterior Routing Protocols

An *Autonomous System* (*AS*), otherwise known as a *domain*, is a collection of routers that are under a common administration, such as a company's internal network or an Internet service provider's (ISP's) network. Because the Internet is based on the AS concept, two types of routing protocols are required:

- **Intra-AS (inside an AS) routing protocols**—Are *interior gateway protocols (IGPs)*. Examples of IGPs include RIP, RIPv2, OSPF, IGRP, IS-IS, and EIGRP.

- **Inter-AS (between autonomous systems) routing protocols** —Are *exterior gateway protocols (EGPs)*. BGP is the only widely-used EGP protocol.

Different types of protocols are required for the following reasons:

- Inter-AS connections require more options for manual selection of routing characteristics. EGPs should be able to implement various policies.

- The speed of convergence (distribution of routing information) and finding the shortest (or fastest) path to the destination are crucial for intra-AS routing protocols.

Therefore, the routing metrics of EGP protocols include more parameters to allow the administrator to influence the selection of certain routing paths. EGPs have slower convergence and more complex configurations. Alternatively, IGPs tend to use less complicated metrics to ease and speed up the decisions about best routing paths. This results in easier configuration and faster convergence.

IGP and EGP Example

Figure 7-5 shows three autonomous systems (domains) that are interconnected with inter-domain links. IGPs are implemented for intra-AS (intra-domain) routing.

Figure 7-5   *Interior Protocols Are Used Inside and Exterior Protocols Are Used Between Autonomous Systems*

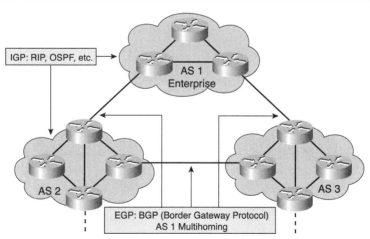

If the autonomous systems must communicate with each other, they require some form of inter-domain routing among the networks. Static routes are used in simple cases; typically, an EGP is used.

BGP is the most dominant EGP that is currently in use. BGP is particularly useful when an AS connects to the Internet via multiple ISPs, as illustrated in Figure 7-5. *Multi-homing* is the implementation of redundant connectivity for inter-AS connections. To comply with the contractual requirements from specific ISPs, an administrator can apply specific policies (such as traffic exit points, return traffic path, and levels of quality of service [QoS]) when using BGP.

Routing Protocol Metrics

This section presents the impact of routing metrics on routing decisions and describes the different types of metric parameters. It provides a comparison between the types of metrics that are used for different routing protocols.

What Is a Routing Metric?

Routing protocols are used to select the best paths through which to forward user data traffic across networks. They adapt dynamically to changes in the networks and constantly try to maintain the best possible forwarding paths in all directions.

To choose the most appropriate path through the network, routing protocols must be able to evaluate all available paths. The *routing protocol metric* is the value that is used in best path determination.

Different routing protocols use different parameters for routing metric calculation. The most popular are *hop count* (how many hops or routers away is the destination network), *bandwidth* (using the highest bandwidth path), and *delay* (using the lowest latency path).

Figure 7-6 shows network 172.16.1.0, which is connected to Router A. The parameters for route metric calculation are forwarded in routing protocol updates.

Figure 7-6   *Routing Protocol Metrics Are Passed in Updates*

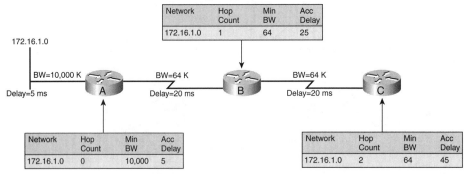

In this case, the EIGRP method of route metric parameters is used, and the minimum bandwidth and cumulative delay influence best path selection (the path with the highest minimum bandwidth and lowest delay is preferred). Figure 7-6 shows the following steps:

Step 1   Router A, which is the originator for the route 172.16.1.0, sends out the initial metric values to Router B.

Step 2 Router B takes into account the parameters of its link toward Router A, adjusts the parameters (bandwidth, delay, hop count) appropriately, calculates its metric toward the 172.16.1.0 network, and sends the routing update to Router C.

Step 3 Router C adjusts the parameters again and calculates its metric toward the destination network 172.16.1.0 from those parameters.

Metrics Used by Routing Protocols

Different routing protocols calculate their routing metrics from different parameters and with different formulas. Some use simple metrics (such as RIP), and some use complex metrics (such as IGRP and EIGRP).

For RIP, only hop count is used to determine the best path (the path with the smallest hop count is preferred). In the case of link-state protocols (OSPF and IS-IS), a cumulative cost or metric is used (the lowest cost or metric path is selected). The cost or metric usually reflects the bandwidth.

NOTE On Cisco routers, the bandwidth and delay metrics can be manually configured and do not necessarily reflect the link's true speed.

These bandwidth and delay metrics should only be changed if the consequences are well understood. For example, a bandwidth change might affect the QoS that is provided to data. As another example, EIGRP limits the amount of routing protocol traffic that it sends to a percentage of the bandwidth value; changing the value could result in either too much bandwidth being used for routing protocol updates, or updates not being sent in a timely manner.

Because bandwidth is not taken into account, routing protocols that use only hop count for routing decisions (such as RIP and RIPv2) are not suitable for networks that have significantly different transmission speeds on redundant paths. For networks that use diverse media on redundant paths, routing protocols must account for bandwidth and possibly the delay of the links.

IGRP and EIGRP use almost the same method of metric calculation, with bandwidth, delay, reliability, loading, and maximum transmission unit (MTU) as the formula's metric criteria. By default, only minimum bandwidth and accumulated delay of the path toward the destination network are taken into account. You should only use the other parameters if you fully understand the consequences because, if misconfigured, they can affect convergence and cause routing loops.

IGRP and EIGRP Metric Calculation

IGRP calculates the metric by adding together weighted values of different link characteristics to a destination network. The formula used is as follows:

Metric = (K1 * bandwidth) + (K2 * bandwidth) / (256–load) + (K3 * delay)

If K5 does not equal 0, an additional operation is performed:

Metric = Metric * [K5 / (reliability + K4)]

The K values in the previous formulas are constants that can be defined using the **metric weights** router configuration command. The default constant values are K1 = K3 = 1 and K2 = K4 = K5 = 0, so by default, the formula is:

Metric = bandwidth + delay

To determine the bandwidth used in this calculation, find the smallest of all bandwidths from the outgoing interfaces along the path to the destination, in kilobits per second (kbps), and divide 10,000,000 by that number. Note that the bandwidth given in the Cisco IOS **show interface** command is in kilobits per second.

To determine the delay used in this calculation, add all the delays from the outgoing interfaces along the path to the destination, in microseconds, and divide this number by 10. Note that the delay given in the Cisco IOS **show interface** command is in microseconds.

Figure 7-7 presents a sample network to illustrate the IGRP metric calculation.

Figure 7-7   *Network for IGRP Metric Calculation Example*

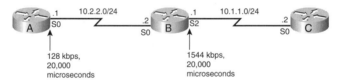

In Figure 7-7, Router B advertises network 10.1.1.0 to Router A. The metric that Router B advertises for 10.1.1.0 is calculated as follows:

Bandwidth = 10,000,000/1,544 = 6476

Delay = 20000/10 = 2000

Metric = Bandwidth + Delay = 8476

Router A calculates the metric it puts in its routing table for 10.1.1.0 as follows:

Bandwidth = 10,000,000/128 = 78125 (using the minimum bandwidth in the path—in this case, 128 kbps)

Delay = (20000 + 20000)/10 = 4000

Metric = Bandwidth + Delay = 82125

The EIGRP metric is the IGRP metric multiplied by 256 because the metric for EIGRP is a 32-bit number; this provides additional granularity for route selection.

This information was adapted from the information at www.cisco.com/warp/public/103/3.html.

OSPF and IS-IS use cost or metric for path calculation, respectively, usually reflecting the link's bandwidth. As a result, the highest accumulated bandwidth (lowest cost or metric) is used to select the best path.

BGP uses the AS-path attribute as part of its metric. The length of this attribute, or the number of autonomous systems that must be traversed to reach a destination, is usually a factor that influences the path selection, and it can be compared to hop count. BGP incorporates additional path attributes, which can influence routing decisions and be manually configured.

Routing Protocol Convergence

Whenever a change occurs in a network's topology, all the routers in that network must learn the new topology. This process is both collaborative and independent; the routers share information with each other, but they must calculate the impact of the topology change independently. Because they must mutually develop an independent agreement of the new topology, they are said to converge on this consensus.

Convergence properties include the speed of propagation of routing information and the calculation of optimal paths. The quicker the convergence, the more optimal the routing protocol is said to be.

Key Point: Convergence Time

The network is converged when all routing tables are synchronized and each contains a usable route to each destination network.

Convergence time is the time it takes for all routers in a network to agree on the current topology. The size of the network, the routing protocol in use, and numerous configurable timers can affect convergence time.

Network convergence must occur whenever a new routing protocol is started and whenever a change takes place in the network. It occurs in both new networks and those that are already operational. Convergence is even more important when changes to the network take place.

A network is not completely operable until it has converged. Therefore, short convergence times are required for routing protocols.

RIPv2 Convergence Example

RIPv2 is a distance vector protocol that periodically propagates its routing information. Distance vector protocols use the principle of hold-down to prevent routing loops. Putting a route in hold-down after the route has failed (perhaps due to a link failure) means that, if a routing update arrives with the same or a worse metric, the new route is not installed until the hold-down timer expires. Even though the destination might no longer be reachable, a route in hold-down is still used for forwarding traffic for the entire hold-down period.

In Figure 7-8, the Ethernet link (Network N) between Routers A and C has failed. The network runs RIPv2 as a routing protocol. Following are the RIPv2 convergence steps:

Step 1   Router C detects the link failure and sends a *triggered update* to Routers D and B. (A triggered update is also called a *flash update*. It is sent because something happened, as compared to a *periodic update*, which is sent periodically—every 30 seconds, in the case of RIP and RIPv2.)

The route is *poisoned* (sent with infinite distance to announce unreachability) to B and D and removed from Router C's routing table.

Step 2   Router C sends a request to its neighbors for an alternate path to network N. (A broadcast request is used for RIPv1, and a multicast request is used for RIPv2.)

Step 3   Router D does not report an alternate path; Router B reports a route with a weaker metric.

The route via B is immediately placed in Router C's routing table. Note that Router C does not put Network N in hold-down because the entry was already removed from its routing table.

Step 4   Router C advertises the route via B in a periodic update to D.

There is no change to Router D's table because the route is in hold-down in Router D.

Step 5   When Router D's hold-down timer expires, the route is added to the table and propagated to Router E in a periodic update.

Figure 7-8   *RIPv2 Convergence Example*

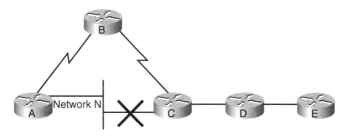

Therefore, the convergence time at Router E consists of the hold-down time plus one or two update intervals.

Comparison of Routing Protocol Convergence

As shown in Figure 7-9, different routing protocols need different amounts of time to converge in a given network. Although the convergence might depend on the network's topology and structure, it has been proven that pure distance vector protocols are slower to converge than link-state protocols—the use of periodic updates and the hold-down mechanism are the main reasons for slow convergence. So, the fast converging protocols should be used when the network's convergence is crucial.

Figure 7-9   *Routing Protocol Convergence Comparison*

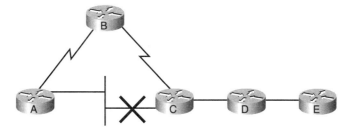

Protocol	Convergence Time to Router E
RIP	Hold-down + 1 or 2 Update Intervals
IGRP	Hold-down +1 or 2 Update Intervals
EIGRP	Matter of Seconds
OSPF	Matter of Seconds

Link-state protocols usually converge much more quickly because of instant propagation of routing updates. Therefore, whenever a change occurs in a link state, a link-state update floods through the entire network and results in fast convergence. There is no need to wait for the hold-down timer to expire and for the next periodic update, as in distance vector protocols.

| NOTE | The default hold-down time is 180 seconds for RIP and 280 seconds for IGRP. These values can be adjusted manually. If adjustments are made, they should be done in the entire autonomous system to keep everything consistent. |

EIGRP is a special case because it incorporates the distance vector principle of metric propagation (only the best routes are sent to the neighbors); however, it does not have periodic updates, nor does it implement the principle of hold-downs. The most distinct feature of EIGRP is the fact that it stores all available backup routes in its topology table. When those backup routes exist for a lost destination, the switchover to the best backup route is almost immediate and involves no action from other network devices. Very fast convergence can be achieved with proper EIGRP deployment.

Flat Versus Hierarchical Routing Protocols

The "Implementing IP Addressing Hierarchy" section of Chapter 6, "Designing IP Addressing in the Network," discusses hierarchical versus flat networks, classful versus classless routing protocols, and Variable Length Subnet Masking (VLSM). The following sections discuss routing protocols that support hierarchical and flat designs.

Flat Routing Protocols

Flat routing protocols have no means of limiting route propagation in a major network (within a Class A, B, or C network) environment. These protocols are typically *classful distance vector protocols*.

Recall that being *classful* means that routing updates do not include subnet masks, and that the protocol performs automatic route summarization on major class network boundaries. These protocols require fixed-length subnets (because they do not support VLSM).

Being *distance vector* means that entire routing tables are sent to neighbors periodically.

Flat protocols do not scale well because, in a large network, they produce significant volumes of routing information that consume too many network resources; the routed traffic (application data and user traffic) should use these resources instead.

Examples of flat routing protocols include RIPv1, IGRP, and RIPv2. (However, note that RIPv2 is a classless protocol.)

Hierarchical Routing Protocols

To solve the problems associated with flat routing protocols, additional features are implemented into hierarchical routing protocols to support large networks—for example, some support an area-based design.

Hierarchical routing protocols are typically *classless link-state protocols*.

Recall that being *classless* means that routing updates include subnet masks (therefore, VLSM is supported).

Hierarchy is part of the implementation of *link-state protocols* with the concept of backbone and non-backbone areas. When using link-state protocols such as OSPF and IS-IS, large networks are divided into multiple areas.

Route summarization can be performed manually in hierarchical protocols and is required in most cases. With the help of route summarization, smaller routing updates are propagated among areas; this results in higher scalability and a better fit for large networks. The impact of instabilities in one part of the network can also be isolated successfully, and convergence is greatly improved. The summarization can be performed on an arbitrary bit boundary within an IP address. (However, note that OSPF only supports summarization on area border routers and autonomous system border routers.)

NOTE Although it is a classless hybrid protocol, EIGRP is considered a flat routing protocol because it is not area-based. Because EIGRP also supports manual summarization, EIGRP can emulate a hierarchical network design (dividing the network into areas). A hierarchical design is not necessary in EIGRP, but it is recommended for large networks.

Although it too is classless and supports manual summarization, RIPv2 is also considered a flat protocol. RIPv2 is not recommended for large networks because it is a distance vector protocol.

Deciding Which Routing Protocol Is Best for Which Network

Considering the factors we discussed in the previous sections of this chapter, this section provides guidelines for choosing the most appropriate routing protocol for different networks.

Comparison of Routing Protocols

There is no best or worst routing protocol. The decision about which routing protocol to implement (or, if multiple routing protocols should indeed be implemented in a network) can only be made after you have carefully considered the design goals and examined the network's physical topology in detail.

Table 7-2 summarizes some characteristics of IP routing protocols. The following sections briefly discuss each protocol and provide some general guidelines for implementing the routing protocols in different network environments.

Table 7-2 *IP Routing Protocol Comparison*

Feature	RIPv1	RIPv2	IGRP	EIGRP	OSPF	IS-IS
Hierarchical				X	X	X
Flat	X	X	X	X		
Distance Vector	X	X	X	X		
Link-State				X	X	X
Classless		X		X	X	X
Classful	X		X			
Multi-access (LAN) support	X	X	X	X	X	X
Point-to-Point support	X	X	X	X	X	X
NBMA Point-to-Multipoint (Frame Relay) support				X	X	

When to Choose RIPv1 or RIPv2

RIPv1 is the oldest routing protocol and its operation is simple. It is a classful distance vector protocol, its metric is based only on hop count, and it does not support VLSM or manual route summarization. RIPv1 is not very common in modern networks.

NOTE   Cisco's implementation of RIPv1 also supports flash updates.

RIPv2 is an enhanced version of RIPv1 that supports VLSM and flash updates. RIPv2 is primarily implemented in small networks, especially small hub and spoke networks that use point-to-point links. RIPv2 is also used in dialup networks because it can freeze its routing table and wait for the dialup link to connect to begin exchanging routing information (this is sometimes called a *snapshot routing feature*). RIPv2 is seldom used in local-area network (LAN) environments because it has no notion of its neighbors, and it cannot detect a failure in neighboring routers quickly to provide fast convergence.

The main issue with RIPv2 in NBMA environments is associated with the split-horizon rule, which prevents the propagation of routing updates to all connected routers that are reachable through the same physical interface on which the routing update was received (even though they are over different virtual circuits). The use of RIPv1 and RIPv2 in NBMA networks is not appropriate. The workaround for the NBMA split horizon problem is using logical point-to-point subinterfaces to change the NBMA network into a logical collection of point-to-point links.

When to Choose IGRP

IGRP is the original Cisco routing protocol. It is a classful distance vector protocol with a more complex metric calculation than RIP; it takes into account minimum bandwidth and accumulated delay. IGRP is suitable for small to medium networks; however, like RIP, it also has problems with NBMA networks' split-horizon feature. Another of IGRP's problems is its slow convergence, which is caused by its pure distance vector operation. In most networks, EIGRP has replaced IGRP.

When to Choose EIGRP

Based on IGRP, EIGRP is a powerful routing protocol. It is a hybrid protocol that incorporates the best aspects of distance vector and link-state features. For example, it has a topology table, it does not perform periodic route propagation, and it does perform triggered updates. It is well suited to almost all environments, including LAN, point-to-point, and NBMA. In NBMA, the split-horizon functionality can be disabled for EIGRP.

EIGRP is not suitable for dialup environments because it must maintain the neighbor relationship, and because it uses periodic hello packets to keep the dialup connections up all the time.

NOTE   EIGRP is a Cisco proprietary protocol that is licensed to a few other vendors.

When to Choose OSPF

OSPF is a standards-based, link-state protocol that is based on the SPF algorithm (also known as the *Dijkstra algorithm*) for best path calculation. It was initially designed for networks that consist of point-to-point links, but was later successfully adapted for operation in LAN and NBMA environments. Suppressing the Hello protocol over OSPF dialup lines (this is known as the *OSPF Demand Circuit operation*) tunes OSPF for dialup operation. Because of the hierarchical requirement, there are design considerations when you use OSPF in larger networks. One backbone area is required, and all nonbackbone areas must be directly attached to that backbone area. Expansion of the backbone area can cause design issues because the backbone area must remain contiguous.

When to Choose Integrated IS-IS

Integrated IS-IS is a standards-based, link-state protocol that is similar in operation to OSPF; it also uses the SPF algorithm for best path calculation. An IS-IS network consists of two types of areas: a backbone (using level 2 routers) and a connected nonbackbone (using level 1 routers). In contrast to OSPF, the IS-IS backbone can be expanded easily to accommodate new level 1 areas. Integrated IS-IS is a proven protocol for very large networks. Integrated IS-IS does not adapt to NBMA point-to-multipoint networks. Integrated IS-IS is not suited for dialup networks because, unlike OSPF, it does not include a Hello protocol suppression capability.

The deployment of Integrated IS-IS in networks requires more knowledge than for other IGPs. Integrated IS-IS is based on the Open System Interconnection (OSI) IS-IS protocol, and the numbering of IS-IS areas is done in an OSI-based environment rather than in IP. IS-IS is deployed in many service provider networks.

Routing Protocol Features

Routing protocols vary in their support for many features, including VLSM, summarization, scalability, and fast convergence. As mentioned previously, there is no global best protocol—the choice depends on many factors. The following sections discuss the most common routing protocols and evaluate their suitability for given network requirements.

First, we discuss On-Demand Routing (ODR); ODR is not technically a routing protocol, but it allows IP routing for stub networks without the overhead of static routes. The focus then turns to interior routing protocols, including RIPv2, EIGRP, OSPF, and Integrated IS-IS. We also describe BGP, which is an exterior routing protocol.

On-Demand Routing (ODR)

ODR is a Cisco proprietary feature that provides IP routing with minimum overhead for stub networks. It avoids the overhead of a general, dynamic routing protocol without incurring the configuration and management overhead of static routing.

A stub router resembles a spoke router in a hub and spoke network topology, where the hub router is the only router to which the spoke router is adjacent. In such a network topology, the IP routing information that is required to represent this topology is fairly simple. The stub routers have a common connection (typically a WAN) to the hub router, and a small number of LAN segments (stub networks) are directly connected to the stub router. These stub networks can consist of only end systems and the stub router, and they do not require the stub router to learn any dynamic IP routing information.

ODR allows easy installation of IP stub networks in the hub router so it can dynamically maintain routes to the stub networks. Installation is accomplished without requiring IP routing protocol configuration on the stub routers.

ODR uses the Cisco Discovery Protocol (CDP) to carry minimal routing information between the hub and the stub routers.

CAUTION   Using the **no cdp run** global configuration command disables the propagation of ODR stub routing information entirely. Using the **no cdp enable** interface configuration command disables the propagation of ODR information on a particular interface.

Example: ODR Usage in Hub and Spoke Topology

As illustrated in Figure 7-10, the hub router eliminates the need to configure a default route on each stub router by providing default route information to the stub routers. On stub routers that support the ODR feature, the stub router advertises IP prefixes that correspond to the IP networks that are configured on all interfaces that are connected directly. (If an interface has multiple logical IP networks configured, only the primary IP network is advertised through ODR.) Because ODR advertises IP prefixes, it is able to carry VLSM information.

Figure 7-10 *ODR in a Hub and Spoke Topology*

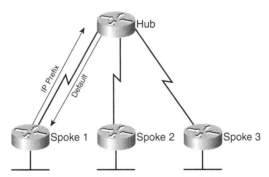

Once ODR is enabled on a hub router (with the **router odr** global configuration command), the hub router begins installing stub network routes in the IP forwarding table. The hub router can also be configured to filter the learned routes and redistribute them into any configured dynamic IP routing protocols.

No IP routing protocol must be configured on the stub router. From the standpoint of ODR, a router is automatically considered a stub when no IP routing protocols have been configured.

NOTE   ODR is a Cisco proprietary feature and can therefore only be implemented on connections between Cisco devices.

RIPv2 to RIPv1 Comparison

RIPv2 was introduced to address the need for a simple distance vector protocol that supports VLSM, manual summarization, and authentication of routing data.

RIPv2 includes many enhancements to RIPv1, including the following:

- RIPv2 supports VLSM because it carries subnet prefixes in routing updates (it is a classless routing protocol).

- RIPv2 uses multicast for routing traffic propagation (versus the broadcast that RIPv1 uses) to reduce routing traffic overhead in multiaccess networks.

- In RIPv2, manual summarization of routes is available, therefore introducing a degree of hierarchy in RIPv2 networks. (RIPv1 and RIPv2 automatically summarize at the major network boundary only; this feature cannot be turned off in RIPv1, but it can be disabled in RIPv2.)

NOTE   Cisco IOS 12.0 introduced RIPv2's manual summarization feature with the **ip summary-address rip** command. This command provides limited summarization support; RIP advertises a summarized local IP address pool on the specified interface to dialup clients. More information on this feature is available in *IP Summary Address for RIPv2*, at www.cisco.com/en/US/products/sw/iosswrel/ps1830/products_feature_guide09186a 0080087ad1.html.

- Authentication of routing packets was introduced to lessen the possibility of malicious attacks on the RIPv2 routing process. It can be used in either plain text mode, in which passwords are sent in a nonencrypted form over the line (allowing replay attacks), or in Message Digest 5 (MD5) mode, in which passwords are never sent, but are used in the one-way packet information encryption process. MD5 encryption process creates a "fingerprint" of a packet, which is verified by the receiving router.

- RIPv2 supports flash or triggered updates, which result in faster convergence than traditional RIPv1 implementations. (Recall, however, that Cisco's implementation of RIPv1 also supports triggered updates.)

RIPv2 retains two major weaknesses from RIPv1:

- A RIPv2 network can have a network diameter with a maximum of 15 hops. If implemented correctly, RIPv2 can be used in only small to medium networks, at best.

NOTE   The network diameter is the distance (in hops) between the most distant edge routers in the network.

- A more serious problem is the use of hop count as the only metric parameter. This does not pose a problem in networks that have similar media characteristics (bandwidth and delay of links) on all links. In networks that have diverse physical media speeds on redundant links, suboptimal paths for routed data traffic are more likely to be chosen. Figure 7-11 illustrates how RIPv2 chooses the path for data traffic from one end system to another across a slower 64 kbps serial link, rather than across the three faster T1 (1.544 Mbps) links.

Figure 7-11 *RIPv2 Might Choose a Slow Path*

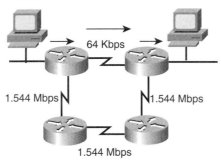

CAUTION   Care must be taken when combining RIPv2 routers and RIPv1 compatible hosts. Because it cannot apply the supplied subnet mask, a RIPv1 host can misinterpret route information.

NOTE   A Cisco router can be configured to send only RIPv1 routes, only RIPv2 routes, or both:

EIGRP

EIGRP is a Cisco proprietary protocol for routing IPv4, Internetwork Packet Exchange (IPX), and AppleTalk traffic. EIGRP was developed from IGRP, which is a pure distance vector protocol. EIGRP is a hybrid routing protocol; it is a distance vector protocol with additional link-state protocol features.

EIGRP features include the following:

- Uses triggered updates (EIGRP has no periodic updates).
- Uses a topology table to maintain all routes received from its neighbors, not simply the best routes.
- Establishes adjacencies with neighboring routers using the Hello protocol.
- Supports VLSM.
- Supports manual route summarization.
- Can be used to create hierarchically structured, large networks.

Routes are propagated in EIGRP in a distance vector manner, from neighbor to neighbor, and only the best routes are sent onward. A router that runs EIGRP does not have a complete view of a network because it only sees the routes it receives from its neighbors. In a pure link-state operation (OSPF and IS-IS), all routers in the same area have identical information and, therefore, have a complete view of the area and its link states.

EIGRP uses the same metric formula as IGRP, multiplied by 256 to add granularity. Like IGRP, EIGRP uses minimum bandwidth and cumulative delay of the path in its metric calculation, by default. Other parameters can also be used in this calculation, including worst reliability between source and destination, worst loading on a link between source and destination, and the smallest MTU.

EIGRP Terminology

Some EIGRP-related terms include the following:

- **Neighbor table**—Each EIGRP router maintains a neighbor table, which lists adjacent routers. (This table is comparable to OSPF's neighborship (adjacency) database; it serves the same purpose, which is to ensure bidirectional communication between each of the directly connected neighbors.) EIGRP keeps a neighbor table for each supported network protocol, such as an IP neighbor table, an IPX neighbor table, and an AppleTalk neighbor table.

- **Topology table**—An EIGRP router maintains a topology table for each configured network protocol: IP, IPX, and AppleTalk. All learned routes to a destination are maintained in the topology table.

- **Routing table**—EIGRP chooses the best routes to a destination from the topology table and places these routes in the routing table. The router maintains one routing table for each network protocol.

- **Successor**—A route that is selected as the primary route to a destination. Successors are the entries that are kept in the routing table.

- **Feasible successor**—A neighbor that is downstream with respect to the destination, but is not the least cost path and is therefore not used for forwarding data. In other words, it is a backup route to the destination. These routes are selected at the same time the successors are identified, but they are kept in a topology table. Multiple feasible successors for a destination can be retained.

EIGRP Characteristics

The characteristics that make EIGRP suitable for deployment in a network's core include the following:

- **Fast convergence**—One advantage of EIGRP is its fast converging Diffusing Update Algorithm (DUAL) route calculation mechanism. This mechanism allows the insertion of backup routes (the feasible successors), which are used in case of primary route failure, into the EIGRP topology table. Because it is a local procedure, the switchover to the backup route is immediate and does not involve action in any other routers.

- **Improved scalability**—Along with fast convergence, manual summarization also improves scalability. EIGRP summarizes routes on the classful network boundaries by default. This auto summarization can be turned off, and manual summarization can be incorporated at any point. Manual summarization of subnet routes improves scalability and network performance because the routing protocol uses fewer resources.

- **Use of VLSM**—Because EIGRP is a classless routing protocol, it sends subnet mask information in its routing updates and therefore supports VLSM.

- **Reduced bandwidth usage**—Because EIGRP does not use periodic routing table updates like other distance vector protocols do, it uses less bandwidth—particularly in large networks where the number of routes becomes large. On the other hand, EIGRP uses the Hello protocol to establish and maintain adjacencies with its neighbors. If many neighbors are reachable over the same physical link, as is the case in NBMA networks, the Hello protocol might create significant routing traffic overhead. Therefore, the network must be designed appropriately to make use of all EIGRP advantages.

- **Multiple network layer protocol support**—EIGRP supports multiple network layer protocols through Protocol Dependent Modules (PDMs). PDMs include support for IPv4, IPX, and AppleTalk.

NOTE   EIGRP is a Cisco proprietary protocol that can only pass protocol information with licensed devices.

OSPF

OSPF is a standardized protocol for routing IPv4. In 1988, the Internet Engineering Task Force (IETF) developed it to replace RIP in larger, more diverse media networks.

OSPF was developed for use in large, scalable networks where RIP's inherent limitations failed to satisfy requirements. OSPF is superior to RIP in all aspects. It has much faster convergence; supports VLSM, manual summarization; and hierarchical structure; provides better calculation of the metric for best path selection, and does not have hop count limitations. At its inception, OSPF supported the largest networks.

In 1998, minor changes in OSPF version 2 addressed some of version 1's problems while maintaining full backward compatibility.

NOTE   OSPF version 2 is described in RFC 2328, *OSPF Version 2,* which is available at www.cis.ohio-state.edu/cgi-bin/rfc/rfc2328.html.

OSPF Hierarchical Design

Although OSPF was developed for large networks, its implementation requires proper design and planning; this is especially important for networks with 50 or more routers.

The concept of multiple separate areas inside one domain (or AS) was implemented in OSPF to reduce the amount of routing traffic and make networks more scalable.

In OSPF, there must always be one backbone area—Area 0—to which all other nonbackbone areas must be directly attached.

A router is a member of an OSPF area when at least one of its interfaces operates in that area. Routers that reside on boundaries between the backbone and a nonbackbone area are called *Area Border Routers (ABRs)* and have at least one interface in each area. The boundary between the areas is created in the ABR itself.

If external routes are propagated into the OSPF AS, the router that redistributes those routes is called the *Autonomous System Boundary Router (ASBR)*.

Careful design and correct mapping of areas to the network topology are important because manual summarization of routes can only be performed on ABRs and ASBRs.

When traffic is sent from one nonbackbone area to another, it always crosses the backbone area. For example, in Figure 7-12, the Area 1 ABR must forward traffic from Area 1 to Area 2 and into the backbone. The Area 2 ABR receives it from the backbone and forwards it to the appropriate destination inside Area 2.

Figure 7-12 *Traffic from OSPF Area 1 to Area 2 Must Go Through the Backbone, Area 0*

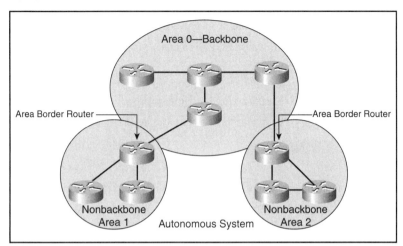

OSPF Characteristics

OSPF is a link-state protocol that has the following characteristics for deployment in the core of networks:

- **Fast convergence**—OSPF achieves fast convergence times using triggered link-state updates, which include one or more link-state advertisements (LSAs). LSAs describe the state of links on specific routers and are propagated unchanged over one area. Therefore, all routers in the same area have identical topology tables; each router has a complete view of all links and devices in the area. Depending on the type, LSAs are usually changed by the ABRs when they cross into another area.

  When the OSPF topology table is fully populated, the SPF algorithm is applied to calculate the shortest paths to the destination networks. Triggered updates and metric calculation based on the cost of a specific link ensure quick selection of the shortest path toward the destination. The OSPF link cost value is inversely proportional to the link's bandwidth.

- **Very good scalability**—OSPF's multiple area structure guarantees good scalability characteristics. However, strict area implementation rules require proper design to allow implementation of other scalability features, such as manual summarization of routes on ABRs and ASBRs, stub areas, totally stubby areas, and not-so-stubby areas (NSSAs). The stub, totally stubby, and NSSA features for nonbackbone areas decrease the amount of LSA traffic from the backbone Area 0 into nonbackbone areas. This allows low-end routers to run in the network's peripheral areas (because fewer LSAs mean smaller OSPF topology tables, less OSPF memory usage, and lower central processing unit [CPU] usage in stub area routers).

- **Reduced bandwidth usage**—Along with the area structure, the use of triggered (not periodic) updates and manual summarization uses less bandwidth by limiting the volume of link-state update propagation.

- **VLSM support**—Because OSPF is a classless routing protocol, it supports VLSM to achieve better use of IP address space.

- **Use over dialup**—OSPF (unlike Integrated IS-IS) can be adjusted for usage over dial-up connections by suppressing the Hello protocol. This mode of OSPF operation is called OSPF Demand Circuit (DC).

Integrated IS-IS

IS-IS is the dynamic link-state routing protocol for the OSI protocol suite. It distributes routing information for routing Connectionless Network Protocol (CLNP) data. CLNP is the OSI network layer; it is the OSI equivalent of IP.

IS-IS was adapted to the IP environment because IP is recognized as the main network layer protocol worldwide. Integrated IS-IS is an extended version of IS-IS for mixed OSI and IPv4 environments. Integrated IS-IS tags CLNP routes with information regarding IP networks and subnets.

Even if Integrated IS-IS is only used for routing IP (and not CLNP), OSI protocols are used to form the neighbor relationships between the routers; therefore, for Integrated IS-IS to work, OSI addresses must still be assigned to areas. This proves to be a major disadvantage when implementing Integrated IS-IS because OSI knowledge is not widespread in the networking community.

IS-IS Terminology

Four significant architectural entities exist in an OSI network: hosts, areas, a backbone, and a domain. The following list describes these entities and how routers fit into an OSI network:

- A *domain* is any portion of an OSI network that is under a common administrative authority; this is the equivalent of an AS in OSPF.

- One or more areas within any OSI domain can be defined. An *area* is a logical entity that is formed by a set of contiguous routers and the data links that connect them. All routers in the same area exchange information about all the hosts that they can reach.

- The areas are connected to form a *backbone*. All routers on the backbone know how to reach all areas.

- An *end system* (*ES*) is any nonrouting host or node. An *intermediate system* (*IS*) is a router. These terms are the basis for the OSI ES-IS and IS-IS protocols.

To simplify router design and operation, OSI distinguishes between Level 1, Level 2, and Level 3 routing. Level-1 ISs communicate with other Level-1 ISs in the same area. Level-2 ISs route between Level-1 areas and form an intradomain routing backbone. Level-3 routing occurs between separate domains. Hierarchical routing simplifies backbone design because Level-1 ISs only need to know how to reach the nearest Level-2 IS. Level-1 ISs are responsible for routing to ESs inside an area. This is similar to OSPF internal nonbackbone routers in a completely stubby area. Level-1 routers are also referred to as station routers because they enable stations (ESs) to communicate with each other and the remainder of the network.

Like internal backbone routers in OSPF, Level-2 ISs only route between areas.

An Integrated IS-IS Network

Network designers using Integrated IS-IS must fully understand the principles behind OSI addressing.

In Integrated IS-IS (shown in Figure 7-13), the backbone Level-2 and Level-1-2 routers are not a part of a special backbone area, as they are in OSPF. Level-2 routers belong to Level-1 areas and only form adjacencies with other Level-2 (and Level-1-2) routers. An IS-IS Level-2 backbone resembles a chain of Level-2 (and Level-1-2) routers that winds its way through Level 1 areas.

Unlike in OSPF, the Integrated IS-IS backbone area can be expanded easily.

Figure 7-13 *An Integrated IS-IS Network*

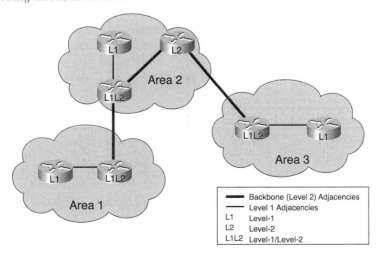

Level-1-2 routers are used to establish adjacencies with both the Level-2 backbone routers and the Level-1 internal routers. Like OSPF ABRs, Level-1-2 routers pass internal area information into the Level-2 backbone. Because the Level 2 backbone must remain contiguous at all times, backbone link redundancy should be considered.

In Figure 7-13, the Level-1-2 routers (also called Level-1/Level-2 routers) form Level-1 adjacencies with Level-1 routers, and Level-2 (or backbone) adjacencies with Level-2 and other Level-1/Level-2 routers. When a backbone router does not have Level-1 neighbors, it can be configured as a Level-2-only router.

Changing Level-1 routers into Level-1/Level-2 or Level-2 routers can easily expand the Integrated IS-IS backbone. In OSPF, entire areas must be renumbered to achieve this.

Integrated IS-IS Characteristics

Integrated IS-IS is a proven protocol for very large networks. Live Integrated IS-IS networks with thousands of routers exist because they have excellent scalability and convergence characteristics, including the following:

- **VLSM support**—Like all link-state protocols, Integrated IS-IS includes support for VLSM.

- **Fast convergence**—Similar to OSPF, Integrated IS-IS owes its fast convergence characteristics to its link-state operation (including flooding of triggered link-state updates). Another feature that guarantees fast convergence and less CPU usage is the Partial Route Calculation (PRC). Although Integrated IS-IS uses the same algorithm for best path calculation as does OSPF, the full SPF calculation is initially performed on network startup only. When IP subnet information changes, only a PRC for the subnet in question is run on routers. This saves router resources and enables faster calculation. A full SPF calculation must be run for each OSPF change.

NOTE   Introduced in Cisco IOS Release 12.0(24)S, the OSPF incremental SPF feature is more efficient than the full SPF algorithm. Therefore, it allows OSPF to converge on a new routing topology more quickly in reaction to a network event. Information on this feature is available in *OSPF Incremental SPF,* at www.cisco.com/univercd/cc/td/doc/product/software/ios120/120newft/120limit/120s/120s24/ospfispf.htm.

- **Excellent scalability**—Routing protocol scalability is an important characteristic for large networks. Because of its hierarchical area-based network topology, Integrated IS-IS delivers excellent scalability. Integrated IS-IS networks are more scalable and flexible than OSPF networks; their backbone area design is not as strict as OSPF, thereby allowing for easy backbone extension.

- **Reduced bandwidth usage**—Triggered updates and the absence of periodic updates ensure that less bandwidth is used for routing information.

The disadvantage of Integrated IS-IS is its close association with the OSI world. Because few network administrators have an adequate knowledge of OSI addressing and operation, implementation of Integrated IS-IS might be difficult. Integrated IS-IS offers inherent support for LAN and point-to-point environments only, while NBMA point-to-multipoint environment support is not included. In NBMA environments, point-to-point links (subinterfaces) must be established for correct Integrated IS-IS operation.

Choosing the Appropriate Interior Routing Protocol

Figure 7-14 displays an example of a decision table for selecting a routing protocol based on multiple criteria. Several routing protocols are considered as possible options (OSPF, IS-IS, IGRP, EIGRP, and RIPv2), and their compliance with five different required parameters is tested. The chosen protocol should have the following properties:

- It should support a large network (up to 100 or more routers). RIPv2 and IGRP protocols do not meet this requirement.

- It must have a high speed of convergence. This precludes RIPv2 and IGRP.

- VLSM use is required. IGRP does not support VLSM.

- It must support Cisco and other vendors' equipment. EIGRP and IGRP are Cisco proprietary protocols, so they do not support mixed vendor environments.

- Network staff should have a good knowledge of the chosen protocol so they can troubleshoot the network. Most network administrators have only a basic knowledge of IS-IS because it is not a widely used protocol.

Figure 7-14 *Example Decision Table for Selecting a Routing Protocol*

Parameters \ Options	OSPF	IS-IS	IGRP	EIGRP	RIP v2	Required Network Parameters
Size of Network (Small-Medium-Large-Very Large)	Large ✔	Very Large ✔	Medium ✘	Large ✔	Medium ✘	Large
Speed of Convergence (Very High-High-Low)	High ✔	High ✔	Low ✘	Very High ✔	Medium ✘	High
Use of VLSM (Yes-No)	Yes ✔	Yes ✔	No ✘	Yes ✔	Yes ✔	Yes
Mixed Vendor Devices (Yes-No)	Yes ✔	Yes ✔	No ✘	No ✘	Yes ✔	Yes
Network Support Staff Knowledge (Good-Poor)	Good ✔	Poor ✘	Good ✔	Good ✔	Good ✔	Good
	✔	✘	✘	✘	✘	

In this example, OSPF was the most suitable option because it satisfied all the given requirements. IS-IS and EIGRP are the next closest matches, failing on only one item; RIPv2 and IGRP follow.

When choosing routing protocols, you can use Table 7-3 as a decision table template. Two additional rows have been added to allow you to specify some additional parameters (such as physical topology type) that might be important in your network.

Table 7-3 *Routing Protocol Selection Decision Table Template*

Parameters	OSPF	IS-IS	IGRP	EIGRP	RIP v2	Required Network Parameters
Size of Network (Small-Medium-Large-Very Large)	Large	Very Large	Medium	Large	Medium	
Speed of Convergence (Very High-High-Medium-Low)	High	High	Low	Very High	Medium	
Use of VLSM (Yes-No)	Yes	Yes	No	Yes	Yes	
Mixed Vendor Devices (Yes-No)	Yes	Yes	No	No	Yes	
Network Support Staff Knowledge (Good-Poor)						

Border Gateway Protocol

BGP is an EGP that is primarily used to interconnect Autonomous Systems. BGP is a successor to EGP, the Exterior Gateway Protocol (note the dual use of the EGP acronym). Because EGP is obsolete, BGP is currently the only EGP in use.

RFC 1771, *A Border Gateway Protocol 4 (BGP-4),* available at www.cis.ohio-state.edu/cgi-bin/rfc/rfc1771.html, defines a BGPv4 Autonomous System as "a set of routers under a single technical administration, using an IGP and common metrics to route packets within the AS, and using an EGP to route packets to other" autonomous systems.

In its core, BGP is a distance vector protocol that uses AS path metrics as a basis for routing decisions. BGP enhancements include numerous additional metric parameters, or *path attributes* as they are called in BGP, which allow administrators to influence routing decisions in BGP. Inter-AS routing involves a lot of strategic routing policy decisions, with which ISPs must comply.

BGP Implementation Example

In Figure 7-15, BGP is used to interconnect multiple autonomous systems. Because of multiple connections between autonomous systems and the need for path manipulation, the use of static routing is excluded. The redundant connectivity of one AS to multiple ISP autonomous systems is called *multi-homing*. Figure 7-15 shows AS 65000 redundantly connected to three ISPs (65500, 65250, and 64500).

NOTE   Private AS numbers are in the range of 64512 to 65535. ISPs use public AS numbers; private AS numbers are only used for non-ISPs (customers), or in special cases; however, the examples in this book use private AS numbers.

Figure 7-15 *BGP Is Used to Interconnect Autonomous Systems*

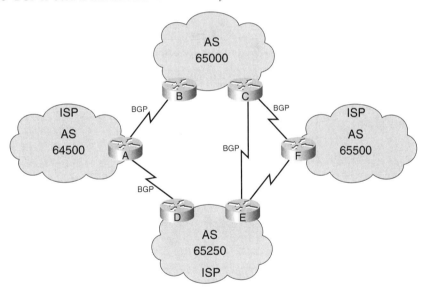

BGP use in an AS is most appropriate when the effects of BGP are well understood and at least one of the following conditions exists:

- The AS has multiple connections to other autonomous systems.
- The AS is a transit AS, meaning that it allows packets to transit through it to reach other autonomous systems (for example, it is an ISP).
- The flow of traffic entering or leaving the AS must be manipulated.

The use of static routes is recommended for inter-AS routing if none of these requirements exists.

NOTE BGP implementation requires considerable knowledge. Improper implementations can cause immense damage, especially when neighbors exchange complete BGP Internet tables (which can have more than 100,000 routes).

External and Internal BGP

BGP uses TCP to communicate. Any two routers that have formed a TCP connection to exchange BGP routing information—in other words, a BGP connection—are called *peers*, or *neighbors*. BGP peers can be either internal or external to the AS.

When BGP is running between routers within one AS, it is called *internal BGP* (*IBGP*). IBGP is run within an AS to exchange BGP information within the AS so it can be passed to other autonomous systems. As long as they can reach each other, routers that run IBGP do not have to be directly connected to each other (for example, when an IGP is running within the AS).

When BGP runs between routers in different autonomous systems, it is called *external BGP* (*EBGP*). Routers that run EBGP are usually connected directly to each other.

Figure 7-16 illustrates IBGP and EBGP neighbors.

Figure 7-16 *Routers That Have Formed a BGP Connection Are BGP Peers or Neighbors, Either External or Internal*

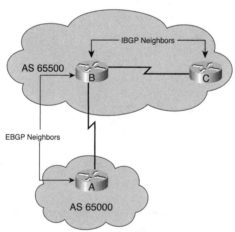

IBGP can be run on all routers, or on specific routers inside the AS. Neighbor reachability information can be acquired via the IGP running in the AS or via configured static routes.

IBGP is usually not the only protocol that runs in the AS; it is merely used to avoid redistributing an entire Internet routing table into an IGP. An ISP (a transit AS) typically has all routers in the AS (or at least all routers in the transit path within the AS) running

BGP; IBGP is used to carry the EBGP routes across the AS. In this way, redistribution into IGP (which could throttle IGP routing because of the amount of routing data) is successfully avoided.

The primary use for IBGP is to carry EBGP (inter-AS) routes through the AS. This is necessary because, in most cases, the EBGP tables are too large for an IGP to handle. Even if EBGP has a small table, the loss of external routes triggering extensive computations in the AS IGP should be prevented.

Other useful implementations of IBGP include the following:

- Applying policy-based routing in an AS with the help of BGP path attributes.

- QoS Policy Propagation on BGP (QPPB), which uses IBGP to spread common QoS parameters (such as Type of Service) from one router to other routers in the network and results in a synchronized QoS policy.

- In Multiprotocol Label Switching (MPLS) Virtual Private Networks (VPNs), where the multiprotocol version of BGP is used to carry MPLS VPN information.

Routing Protocol Deployment

The following sections present deployment examples of routing protocols and discuss the following advanced routing features: redistribution, filtering, and summarization. These allow for coexistence of multiple routing protocols and greater scalability.

Hierarchical Network Structure and Routing Protocols

Recall from Chapter 3, "Structuring and Modularizing the Network," that the hierarchical layered network model provides a framework for a designer to choose the most appropriate systems and features for a specific network. A network can be divided into layers and modules with specific functions that are required in each individual network module. The three-layer hierarchical network architecture divides the network into the following three basic layers (which are not necessarily implemented as distinct physical entities):

- **Core layer**—Also called the *backbone*, this layer provides high-speed data transport between sites and buildings, achieved with either Layer 2 or Layer 3 devices. It incorporates load sharing with parallel links and fast convergence.

- **Distribution layer**—Provides diverse packet manipulation and policing. It acts as an intermediate point between the access and core layers.

- **Access layer**—Provides network access to local and remote workgroups and users. The campus environment primarily uses switches with ports that are available to the users; the WAN environment provides access to remote sites via wide-area technology; the Internet and Remote Access environments provide connectivity to remote users.

The choice of routing protocols depends on the network design goals; therefore, the decision is made only after the goals and network topology are determined. Multiple routing protocols are possible in large enterprise networks. (For example, when a network upgrade is performed, the old routing protocol usually coexists with the new one during the transition period.)

As discussed in previous sections of this chapter, routing protocols differ in many ways. For example, how routing information is exchanged, how convergence timers are set, the metrics used for optimal route determination, the required amount of processing power and memory, and the availability of a routing protocol on different platforms can determine whether a routing protocol is more or less suitable for a network or parts of a network.

The following sections explain why certain protocols are suitable for different hierarchical network layers, and the advantages and disadvantages of individual protocols.

Routing in the Core Layer (Backbone)

The function of the core layer is to provide high-speed transmission of data between sites. The core is critical for connectivity and, therefore, incorporates a high level of redundancy using redundant links and load sharing between equal-cost paths. In the event of a link failure, it must immediately converge, and adapt quickly to change to provide a seamless transport service.

EIGRP, OSPF, and IS-IS all adapt to changes quickly and have short convergence times; therefore, they are suitable for use in the core layer, as shown in Figure 7-17. The decision to use EIGRP, OSPF, or IS-IS should be based on the underlying physical topology, IP addressing, equipment used, and possible issues related to the routing protocol in a particular situation.

Figure 7-17 *Core, Distribution, and Access Layer Routing Protocols*

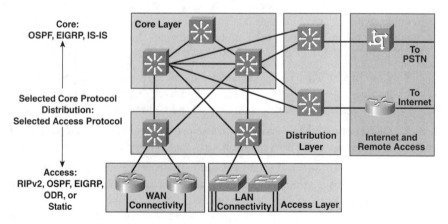

Following are considerations for routing protocol use in the core:

- OSPF imposes a strict hierarchical design. OSPF areas must map to the IP addressing plan; this task cannot always be achieved.

- EIGRP restricts vendor selection. EIGRP is a Cisco proprietary protocol that is licensed to select vendors. Multiple routing protocols with redistribution can be used to overcome this restriction.

- Even if only routing IP, IS-IS requires detailed knowledge of the OSI protocol suite for proper configuration.

- RIP is not recommended as a core routing protocol. Its convergence is slow and can result in disrupted connectivity, thus denying the basic core function. In addition, because the RIP metric is based on hop count, it is unsuitable when diverse media are used. The number of hops is limited to 15.

- Using static routing in the core is not an option because static routing requires administrative intervention for changes and link failures.

Routing in the Distribution Layer

The distribution layer is the intermediate point between the core and access layers. Besides other issues (such as IP addressing), the choice of routing protocol depends on the routing protocols that are used in the core and access layers.

For example, if EIGRP is the core routing protocol and RIP is the access layer routing protocol, both routing protocols are used on the distribution devices; therefore, redistribution with filtering must be applied to provide connectivity, as illustrated in Figure 7-17. Routing protocols used in the distribution layer vary among EIGRP, OSPF, IS-IS, RIP, ODR, and so forth.

Routing in the Access Layer

The access layer provides local and remote users with access to network resources. As with the core, the underlying physical topology, IP addressing, and the equipment used drive the choice of routing protocol. The available processing power and memory in the access layer equipment also influence the routing protocol choice. The routing protocols that should be used in the access layer are RIPv2, OSPF, EIGRP, and ODR.

NOTE	Routing protocols that run in the access layer are also called *edge routing protocols*.

As illustrated in Figure 7-17, using static routing in the access layer is also a possibility.

Considerations for routing protocol use in the access layer include the following:

- IS-IS is generally not suitable for the access layer because it requires extensive knowledge for configuration; also, it is not suitable for dialup networks.

- RIPv2 is simple in its operation and is suitable for small hub and spoke networks with point-to-point and dialup links. RIPv2 does not have a high demand for memory and processing power.

- EIGRP provides the administrator with more routing control and is also suitable for NBMA environments, where there is a split-horizon issue (for example, Frame Relay or ATM multipoint interfaces). The use of EIGRP is restricted when equipment from multiple vendors is part of the overall design. EIGRP is also not suitable for dialup environments.

- The limitations of using OSPF as an access layer routing protocol include its high memory and processing power requirements and its strict hierarchical design requirement. The high memory and processing power requirements can be reduced using summarization and careful area planning. OSPF can be used in various environments, such as LAN, NBMA, and dialup. More knowledge is required to configure OSPF properly than is required for RIPv2 and EIGRP.

Remote Access and Internet Connectivity

As shown in Figure 7-18, remote access is used to provide connectivity to corporate networks for remote users via dialup connections. In a dialup environment, AAA can be used for static routing when dynamic routing is not needed. If dynamic routing is required, a snapshot-capable protocol (such as RIP) can be used to achieve dynamic routing and minimize the costs related to the routing protocol.

Figure 7-18 *Internet and Remote Access Connectivity*

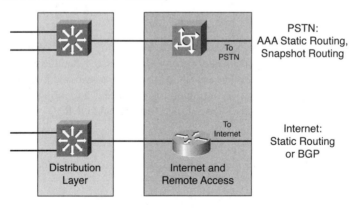

Snapshot routing allows you to remove the constraints of building and maintaining static routes/services when using a hub and spoke topology in a DDR environment. Dynamic routing protocols update the routing tables during the active time, and a snapshot of the routing table is kept in between for a configurable period of time (the quiet period). The snapshot prevents the routes from aging.

Depending on whether multiple exit points exist and on redundancy requirements, use either static routes or BGP for Internet connectivity. Static routes use less overhead than BGP routing and are used when only one exit point exists. Use BGP with multiple exit points and when multi-homing is desired.

Route Redistribution

This section explains the need and prerequisites for route redistribution and discusses possible redistribution points.

In a network that uses multiple routing protocols, Cisco routers allow the exchange of routing information through a feature called *route redistribution*.

The following are possible reasons why you might need multiple protocols:

- When you are migrating from an older IGP to a new IGP, multiple redistribution boundaries might exist until the new protocol has completely displaced the old protocol. Dual existence of protocols is effectively the same as a long-term coexistence design.

- When you want to use another protocol, but you need to keep the old protocol because of the host systems' needs.

- Different departments might not want to upgrade their routers, or they might not implement a sufficiently strict filtering policy. In these cases, you can protect yourself by terminating the other routing protocol on one of your routers.

- If you have a mixed router vendor environment, you can use a Cisco-specific protocol in the Cisco portion of the network, and then use a common protocol to communicate with non-Cisco devices.

Redistribution of routes is required when:

- Multiple routing protocols are used in the network; for example, RIPv2, EIGRP, and OSPF.

- Multiple routing domains are used in the network; for example, two EIGRP routing processes.

Redistribution occurs on the boundaries between routing protocols and between domains. As shown in Figure 7-19, redistribution occurs on a router with interfaces that participate in multiple routing protocols and/or routing domains.

Figure 7-19 *Redistribution Occurs on the Boundaries Between Protocols or Domains*

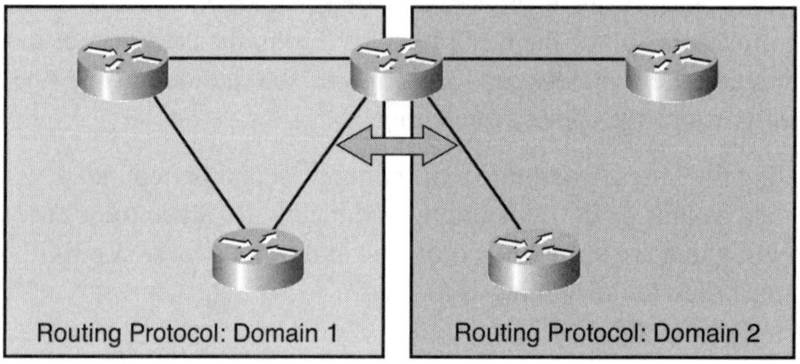

Routing Protocol: Domain 1   Routing Protocol: Domain 2

Route Redistribution Possibilities

Redistribution is usually applied between the core and edge protocols. As shown in Figure 7-20, redistribution is possible in two ways:

- **One-way route redistribution**—Routing information is redistributed from one routing protocol or domain to another, but not vice versa. When this occurs, static or default routes are required in the opposite direction to provide connectivity.

- **Two-way route redistribution**—Routing information is redistributed from one routing protocol or domain to another, and vice versa. Static or default routes are not required because all routing information is passed between two entities.

Specific routes can be filtered and the administrative distance of redistributed routes can be changed in either of these cases. These methods of manipulating redistributed routes help reduce the possibility of routing loops and ensure that traffic is routed optimally.

Figure 7-20 *Route Redistribution Can Be One-way or Two-way*

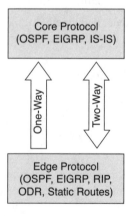

Core Protocol
(OSPF, EIGRP, IS-IS)

One-Way   Two-Way

Edge Protocol
(OSPF, EIGRP, RIP,
ODR, Static Routes)

Route Redistribution Planning

When deciding where and how to use route redistribution, determine the following:

- The routing protocols and domains that will be used in the network
- The routing protocol and domain boundaries (boundary routers)
- The direction of route redistribution (one-way or two-way redistribution)

If route redistribution is not carefully designed, suboptimal routing and routing loops can be introduced into the network. This occurs when routes are redistributed in a network that has redundant paths between dissimilar routing protocols or domains. Route filtering (described in the "Route Filtering" section of this chapter) solves this problem.

Core and Access Layer Route Redistribution

Redistribution occurs on routing protocol and domain boundaries. Therefore, redistribution is usually needed in the distribution layer because multiple routing protocols and domains collide here.

Figure 7-21 shows an example network with redistribution points throughout the enterprise network. In this case, the enterprise core uses OSPF as a routing protocol; RIP and EIGRP provide dynamic routing toward remote sites.

Figure 7-21 *Route Redistribution in an Enterprise Network*

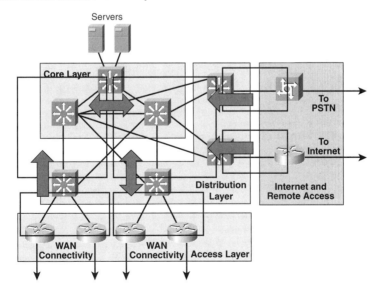

In this example, some remote sites only require connectivity to the server farm; therefore, one-way redistribution is performed to inject routes from these remote sites into the enterprise core. RIP is then configured to propagate only the default route down to the access router. The access router only advertises its own LAN to the distribution router, thereby greatly reducing the RIP update volume.

Some remote sites require connectivity to the entire network. Two-way redistribution is required to provide this connectivity.

Redistribution in the core is only necessary when multiple routing protocols or multiple routing domains are used there. In this example, two OSPF processes are run in the core; redistribution between those processes is necessary to provide connectivity.

For example, if part of the core were running EIGRP, and the other part were running OSPF because not all of its equipment supported EIGRP, two-way redistribution would be required to provide connectivity.

Remote-access and Internet Route Redistribution

Redistribution is typically necessary when remote access or Internet connectivity is required.

For remote access with AAA static routing, AAA static routes can be redistributed into the core routing protocol. In the opposite direction, default routing provides connectivity for remote users.

For Internet connectivity with only one exit point, that exit point is the Internet traffic's default route and is therefore propagated through the core routing protocol. When multiple exit points exist toward multiple ISPs, BGP is used to provide Internet connectivity, and redistribution can be used.

CAUTION Redistribution with BGP requires careful planning. For more details, see *CCNP Self-Study: Building Scalable Cisco Internetworks (BSCI)*, Catherine Paquet and Diane Teare, Cisco Press, 2004.

Route Filtering

As mentioned, route filtering can be required when redistributing routes. Route filtering allows the network administrator to prevent the advertisement of certain routes through the routing domain.

Filtering can occur either on the routing domain boundary where redistribution occurs, or within the routing domain to isolate some parts of the network from other parts.

Filtering is used with route redistribution, primarily to prevent suboptimal routing and routing loops that might occur when routes are redistributed at multiple redistribution points. Route filtering is also used to prevent routes about certain networks, such as a private IP address space, to be sent to or received from remote sites.

IGP Filtering

In an enterprise network, route filtering is likely to occur at redistribution points, as illustrated in Figure 7-22. Routes that are redistributed between the access layer and the distribution layer can be filtered. For example, routes learned by the distribution layer via redistribution from the access layer are filtered prior to being redistributed back into the access layer. Route filtering toward the access layer might, for example, block all routes except the default route, which is injected into the access layer. This filtering relieves the access layer routers from receiving too many updates and storing a large number of routes.

Figure 7-22 *Route Filtering Can Be Used at Redistribution Points*

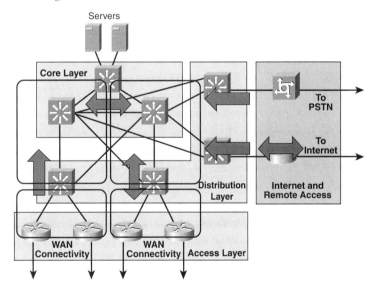

Following are the conditions under which route filtering can be configured at redistribution points:

- Between the access layer (for example, WAN and Internet connectivity, and remote access) and the distribution layer
- Between different routing protocols in the core
- In the core, between multiple routing domains that use the same routing protocol

Integrating Interior Routing Protocols with BGP

As shown in Figure 7-23, BGP on border routers typically announces only the major network (the prefix that was assigned to the enterprise network) to the external domains, excluding any details about subnets. This is done using the BGP **network** router configuration command, which allows BGP to advertise a network that is already part of its IP routing table.

Figure 7-23 *Integrating IGPs with BGP*

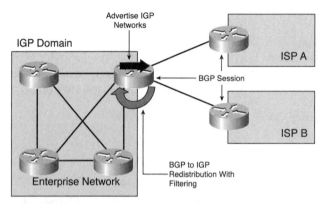

Internal networks can be redistributed into BGP, summarized into one major subnet (that covers the assigned public address space), and advertised to the external domains.

However, redistributing from an IGP into BGP is not recommended because any change in the IGP routes—for example, if a link goes down—can cause a BGP update. This method could result in unstable BGP tables.

If redistribution is used, make sure that only local routes are redistributed. For example, routes learned from other autonomous systems (that were learned by redistributing BGP into the IGP) must not be sent out from the IGP again because routing loops could result. Private addresses must also be filtered out of the redistributed routes. Configuring this filtering can be complex.

Conditional advertisement of a default candidate route is usually done in the opposite direction—from BGP into the IGP. One of the major networks received via BGP is redistributed into IGP and marked as the default candidate, thus achieving effective conditional default advertising. If multiple connections exist on the border routers, BGP selects the best path to external networks. To select between the primary and backup links, a higher cost must be assigned to the redistributed route on the secondary router when two exit points exist.

The redistribution of all BGP routes into IGP is not advised because non-BGP participating routers do not require full Internet routing, and IGP protocols are unable to process large numbers of advertised routes.

IBGP

As illustrated in Figure 7-24, it is important that the IGP in the enterprise network announce the next-hop address advertised by EBGP (in other words, that it be known within the network via the IGP) when using IBGP in the enterprise network.

Figure 7-24 *The EBGP Next-Hop Address Must Be Known Inside the Network*

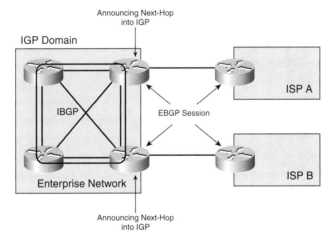

In Figure 7-24, the IGP is only used, from the BGP perspective, to propagate the IP subnets of the BGP next-hop address. (The IGP also propagates the enterprise networks, including access layer networks. All necessary routes are advertised into BGP at the domain borders.)

Next-Hop Attribute

The BGP next-hop attribute indicates the next-hop IP address that is to be used to reach a destination.

For EBGP, the next hop is the IP address of the neighbor that sent the update. In Figure 7-25, Router A advertises 172.16.0.0 to Router B, with a next hop of 10.10.10.3, and Router B advertises 172.20.0.0 to Router A, with a next hop of 10.10.10.1. Therefore, Router A uses 10.10.10.1 as the next-hop attribute to reach 172.20.0.0, and Router B uses 10.10.10.3 as the next-hop attribute to reach 172.16.0.0.

Figure 7-25 *The BGP Next-Hop Attribute*

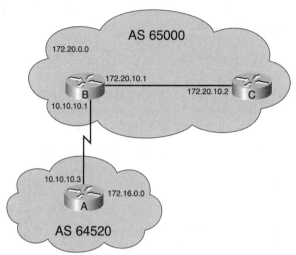

For IBGP, the protocol states that the next hop advertised by EBGP should be carried into IBGP. Because of that rule, Router B advertises 172.16.0.0 to its IBGP peer Router C, with a next hop of 10.10.10.3 (Router A's address). Therefore, Router C knows the next hop to reach 172.16.0.0 is 10.10.10.3, not 172.20.10.1, as you might expect.

Therefore, Router C must know how to reach the 10.10.10.0 subnet, either via an IGP or a static route; otherwise, it drops packets that are destined for 172.16.0.0 because it will not be able to reach the next-hop address for that network.

When running BGP over a multiaccess network, such as Ethernet, a BGP router uses the appropriate address as the next-hop address (by changing the next-hop attribute) to avoid inserting additional hops into the network. This feature is sometimes called a *third-party next hop.*

BGP is often used to offload the IGP in networks with large core and small distribution sites. BGP runs in the core, and the core IGP only propagates IP subnets that are used in the core itself to provide BGP next-hop address reachability. Other IGP domains (noncore) propagate their subnets, including access layer networks. All routes are advertised into BGP at the domain borders (on core routers).

Route Summarization

Chapter 6, "Designing IP Addressing in the Network," explains route summarization (which is also called *route aggregation* or *supernetting*). Because it is a method of representing a series of network numbers in a single summary address, summarization can reduce the number of routes a router must maintain.

This section explains when and where route summarization should be applied, and the prerequisites for its use.

The Value of Route Summarization

A large, flat network is not scalable because routing traffic consumes considerable network resources that are better used by the application data and user traffic. When a network change occurs, it is propagated throughout the network. This requires processing time for route recomputation and bandwidth to propagate routing updates.

A network hierarchy can reduce both routing traffic and unnecessary route recomputation. To accomplish this, the network must be divided into areas that enable route summarization. With summarization in place, a *route flap* (a route that goes down and up continuously) that occurs in one network area does not influence routing in other areas. Instabilities are isolated and convergence is improved, thereby reducing the amount of routing traffic, the size of the routing tables, and the required memory and processing power for routing.

Summarization can be achieved manually or automatically with routing protocols that provide such options.

NOTE   To permit the implementation of summarization, the underlying IP addressing plan must be well planned and modular.

Route Summarization Example

Summarization can be implemented at multiple levels and should therefore be modeled on the hierarchical (recursive) tree-like model. This allows multilayer partitioning of a network into variable-size areas in a very scalable and flexible manner.

For example, in Figure 7-26, the network consists of a central office, two regional offices, and some remote offices that connect to the regional offices. The addressing plan uses 10.0.0.0/8 to address the network. The central office and regional offices are assigned /16 address blocks (for example, 10.1.0.0/16 and 10.2.0.0/16). Each address block is further divided into smaller address blocks according to its needs (for example, 10.2.0.0/16 could be divided into 10.2.1.0/24, 10.2.2.0/24, and 10.2.3.0/24 for LAN networks, and

10.2.4.0/30, 10.2.4.4/30, and 10.2.4.8/30 for WAN connections). The summarization should follow the addressing plan and summarize networks from an individual location into a larger address block (for example, 10.2.1.0/24, 10.2.2.0/24, 10.2.3.0/24, 10.2.4.0/30, 10.2.4.4/30, and 10.2.4.8/30 could summarize to 10.2.0.0/16).

Figure 7-26 *Route Summarization Should Follow the IP Addressing Plan*

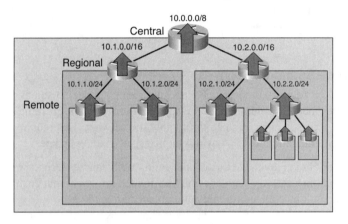

Summarization in the Enterprise Composite Network Model

Smaller routing updates are propagated between areas with the help of route summarization; this results in higher scalability and a better fit for large networks. As shown in Figure 7-27, summarization in a large network can be configured at multiple levels, as follows:

- The first level of summarization can be achieved at WAN connectivity and remote-access points. Remote networks can be summarized into major networks, and only those major networks are advertised to the distribution routers. Special care should be taken not to advertise overlapping summary routes because this would disrupt connectivity.

- The second level of summarization can be achieved at the distribution layer, in the same manner as the first level. All distribution layer routers should summarize access networks on all interfaces toward the core.

Summarization can take place on core routers toward the distribution layer if the addressing in the core allows summarization of core networks. When all distribution routers are connected to the core in a redundant way (primary or secondary link), summarization from the core toward the distribution layer must be performed carefully. To achieve this, the routing protocol must allow summarization on each interface, enabling different subnet masks to be used for the summaries on the primary and backup link. When the distribution layer routers receive two summary routes, the more specific route is installed in the routing table. Summaries on the primary links must use a longer subnet mask.

Figure 7-27 *Route Summarization Can Be Configured at Multiple Levels*

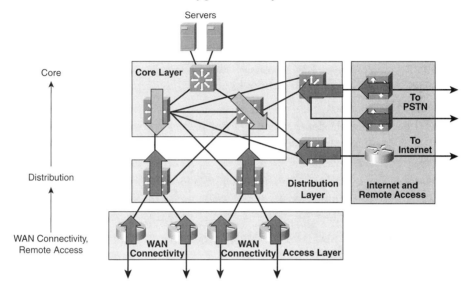

Summary

In this chapter, you learned about selecting routing protocols for your network.

Static routes are only used in very small networks or for specific scenarios (for example, DDR, stub networks, and so on). Dynamic routing protocols adapt to changes in the network and are much easier to configure than static routes.

Distance vector protocols are easier to implement, but in general, have limited scalability and slow convergence compared to link-state protocols.

Exterior gateway protocols are used for inter-AS connectivity, whereas interior gateway protocols enable intra-AS connectivity.

Routing protocols use different methods for metric calculation, thus resulting in more or less optimal routing paths. RIPv1 and RIPv2 use hop count; OSPF uses a cost (related to bandwidth); Integrated IS-IS uses a metric (also related to bandwidth); IGRP and EIGRP use a formula that takes into account minimum bandwidth and accumulated delay by default. BGP uses the AS-path attribute as part of its metric.

Link-state protocols generally have faster convergence times than distance vector protocols.

Routing protocols that enable a hierarchical design are adapted for deployment in large networks.

On-Demand Routing (ODR) is an alternative to static routes or dynamic routing protocols in hub and spoke networks.

Because of its limitations of using hop count as its metric and allowing a maximum of only 15 hops, RIPv2 is suitable for deployment in small networks.

EIGRP is a powerful Cisco proprietary routing protocol that includes a topology table for maintaining all routes received from its neighbors; the best of these routes are put in the routing table.

OSPF is a powerful, open-standard protocol that was developed to overcome the limitations of RIP. OSPF includes multiple areas inside an AS to reduce the amount of routing traffic and result in more scalable networks.

Derived from OSI IS-IS standards and suitable for very large networks, Integrated IS-IS is a complex routing protocol.

BGP is an EGP that is primarily used for inter-AS routing. BGP that runs between routers within one AS is called IBGP; BGP that runs between routers in different autonomous systems is called EBGP.

In a network that uses multiple routing protocols, Cisco routers allow the exchange of routing information through a feature called route redistribution.

Route filtering allows the network administrator to prevent the advertisement of certain routes through the routing domain. Filtering can occur either on the routing domain boundary where redistribution occurs, or within the routing domain to isolate some parts of the network from other parts.

Route summarization can reduce the number of routes a router must maintain because it is a method of representing a series of network numbers in a single summary address.

References

For additional information, refer to these resources:

- Configuring Large-Scale Dial-Out, www.cisco.com/en/US/partner/products/sw/iosswrel/ps1835/products_configuration_guide_chapter09186a00800ca6ef.html.

- Designing Large Scale IP Internetworks, www.cisco.com/univercd/cc/td/doc/cisintwk/idg4/nd2003.htm.

- Doyle, Jeff. *CCIE Professional Development: Routing TCP/IP Volume I*. Cisco Press, 1998.

NOTE   You must be a registered user to access this document.

- McQuerry, Steve. *CCNA Self-Study: Interconnecting Cisco Network Devices.* Cisco Press, 2000.

- Paquet, Catherine and Diane Teare. *CCNP Self-Study: Building Scalable Cisco Internetworks (BSCI).* Cisco Press, 2004.

Case Study

This case study is a continuation of the DJMP Industries case study introduced in Chapter 2.

Case Study General Instructions

Use the scenarios, information, and parameters provided at each task of the ongoing case study. If you encounter ambiguities, make reasonable assumptions and proceed. For all tasks, use the initial customer scenario and build on the solutions provided thus far.

You can use any and all documentation, books, white papers, and so on.

In each task, you act as a network design consultant. Make creative proposals to accomplish the customer's business needs. Justify your ideas when they differ from the provided solutions.

Use any design strategies and internetworking technologies you feel are appropriate.

The final goal for each case study is a paper solution; you are not required to provide the specific product names.

Appendix G, "Answers to Review Questions, Case Studies, and Simulation Exercises," provides a solution for each task based on assumptions made. There is no claim that the provided solution is the best or only solution. Your solution might be more appropriate for the assumptions you made. The provided solution helps you understand the author's reasoning and offers a way for you to compare and contrast your solution.

Case Study: Routing Protocol Selection

Complete these steps:

Step 1 You might want to review the DJMP Industries Case Study Scenario in Chapter 2.

Step 2 Propose the most suitable routing protocol and explain major deployment issues.

Simulation: Network Convergence

This exercise is a paper-only version of the simulation that the simulation tool actually performed and includes the results it provided. Review the scenario and simulation results and answer the questions.

Network Convergence Scenario

This simulation addresses the campus network's network convergence issues. Its focus is on Layer 2 versus Layer 3 convergence details.

Although the time the network needs to recover depends on the combination of the routing protocol and the structure of the network, designers usually stand by the following two rules:

- Layer 3 networks improve convergence times after various failures occur.

- Compared to link-state protocols, pure distance vector protocols are slower to converge.

You decide to prove the previous statements in the company's campus network by testing the network adaptability after some typical network failures.

Initial Traffic

For testing purposes, you configure bidirectional traffic at the rate of 5000 packets per second (pps) between workstation WS_A in building A and the server in the central building. This serves as a point of reference for the traffic flow in the simulation tests.

Layer 2 (Bridged) Network Convergence

The first simulation tests the convergence in a pure Layer 2 network. The results are used later, in comparison with other models.

As illustrated in Figure 7-28, the reference (WS_A to server) traffic was sent over the path determined by the Spanning Tree Protocol (STP): AS_F2 → DS_B → CS_A → DC_B.

Figure 7-28 *Layer 2 Network: Initial Path Taken from WS_A to Server*

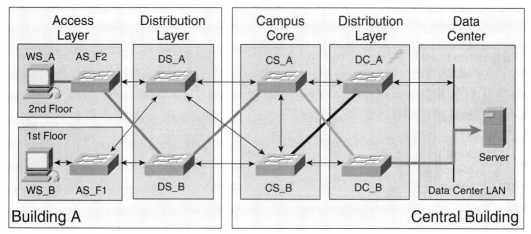

You begin studying the effect of the link and node failure on the network performance by tearing down and then restoring the CS_A → DC_B link, between the 200th and the 300th second. The second test involves disabling the CS_A node at the 400th second. At the 500th second, CS_A is restored.

Test #1—Convergence Around Link Failure

At 200 seconds, the CS_A → DC_B link fails.

The simulation tool generates a route report (in the log file) that keeps track of the traffic from the WS_A to the server. The last packet that reached the destination is seen at the 199th second.

1 second later, the CS_A switch starts recalculating the STP tree by entering the listening mode first. Because the CS_A switch cannot yet provide an alternative path, subsequent packets are dropped on the troubled port, as shown by the thick lines in Figure 7-29.

Figure 7-29 *Layer 2 Network: CS_A to DC_B Link Failure*

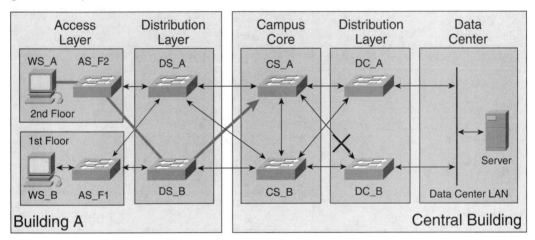

The first packet after the link failure is seen at its destination at the 248th second, after the STP has found an alternative path. Figure 7-30 illustrates how the packet flows across the alternate route, AS_F2 → DS_B → CS_B → DC_B.

Figure 7-30 *Layer 2 Network: STP Recalculates After Link Failure*

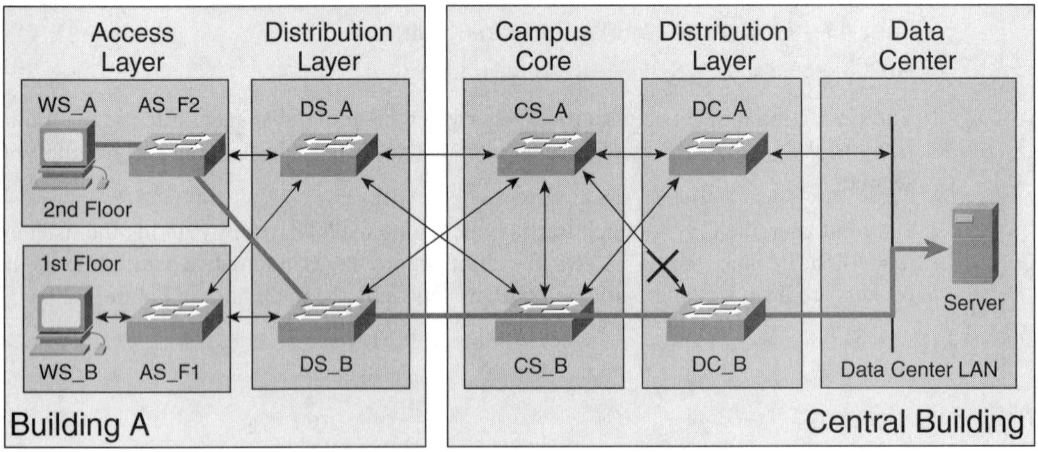

Packet flow is interrupted again after the CS_A → DC_B link is reestablished. The last packet is seen at the 299th second, and the first packet after link reestablishment is seen only at the 315th second. After the link reestablishment, the packets again flow over the previous path selected by the STP, AS_F2 → DS_B → CS_A → DC_B.

Conclusions

Because of the STP, the Layer 2 (bridged) network is disrupted after a link failure for almost 50 seconds, and there is another (approximately 15 seconds) disruption after link reestablishment.

1 The outage that occurred because of the primary link loss can be explained as the consequence of the STP recalculation. What is the reason for the second delay, after the primary path has physically recovered?

Test #2—Convergence Around Node Failure

The CS_A node fails at 400 seconds. As illustrated by the thick lines in Figure 7-31, the last packet is seen at the 399th second, and it takes the best STP route.

Figure 7-31 *Layer 2 Network: Last Packet Path Before CS_A Failure*

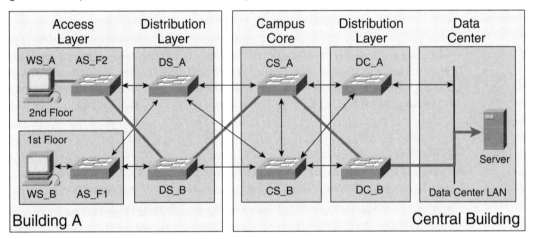

The first packet after link failure is seen at its destination at the 448th second; again, the convergence time is almost 50 seconds. As illustrated by the thick lines in Figure 7-32, the packet flows across an alternate route.

Figure 7-32 *Layer 2 Network: STP Recalculates After CS_A Failure*

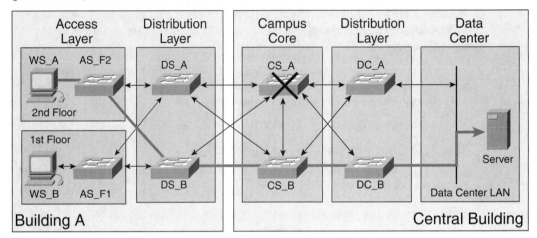

After the node CS_A recovers (at the 500th second), the packet flow is interrupted again. The last packet is seen at the 499th second, and the first packet after the node recovery is seen only at the 515th second. After the node recovery, the packets flow over the previous path, selected by the STP (AS_F2 → DS_B → CS_A → DC_B), yet again.

Conclusions

Because of the STP, the Layer 2 (bridged) network is disrupted after a node failure for almost 50 seconds; another 15-second disruption occurs after node recovery.

  2 Why do the link and node incidents impose the same disruption times before network recovery?

Convergence in Mixed Layer 2/Layer 3 Network

In this simulation, the distribution switches in the campus have been upgraded to Layer 3 switches that run OSPF.

NOTE   To avoid load sharing and thus simplifying the failure analysis, the OSPF cost has been lowered on one path across the network.

As illustrated by thick lines in Figure 7-33, the traffic between the WS_A and the server flows over only one path: AS_F2 → DS_A → CS_A → DC_A.

Figure 7-33 *Layer 2/3 Network: Initial Path Taken from WS_A to Server*

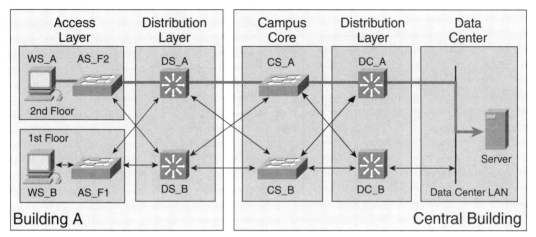

This failure scenario incorporates the following subsequent events: the 100 second flap of the DC_A → CS_A link triggered at the 200th second, followed by the complete outage of the DC_A node operation between the 400th and 500th second.

Test #1—Convergence Around Link Failure

The CS_A → DC_A link fails at 200 seconds. The link loss event immediately triggers the DC_A router to generate and distribute a new OSPF Link State Packet, which notifies other routers (Layer 3 switches) about a recent change. The convergence time is 6 seconds— approximately 1 second for the change in the link status to be propagated from DC_A to other routers, and a 5-second delay (the default) before the SPF algorithm is run in all routers.

With the failure of the CS_A → DC_A link, the first successful packet transmission is seen in the log at the 205th second. As illustrated by the thick lines in Figure 7-34, there are now two alternate equal-cost paths across the network, across which the packets are load-shared.

Figure 7-34 *Layer 2/3 Network: Path Taken After CS_A to DC_A Link Failure*

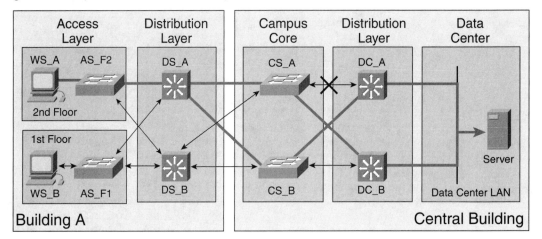

After the CS_A → DC_A link is reestablished at 300 seconds, the packet flow is not interrupted as it was with the Layer 2 solution. However, the convergence to the recovered path takes approximately 30 seconds—the total time it takes for an OSPF adjacency to be established across the recovered link, the adjacency databases to be exchanged, the changes propagated across the network, and the SPF algorithm to run on all routers. The packet traversing the network at the 330th second follows the primary path (as configured initially by tuning the OSPF cost parameter) again.

Conclusions

Using OSPF, the network is disrupted for approximately 6 seconds following a link failure—the time it takes the SPF algorithm to be run on all routers. Traffic flow is not disrupted following the link recovery, but the traffic returns to the primary path approximately 30 seconds after link recovery.

Test #2—Convergence Around Node Failure

At 400 seconds, the DC_A node fails. As shown by the thick lines in Figure 7-35, the last successful packet is seen at the 399th second, and the next packet is dropped.

Figure 7-35 *Layer 2/3 Network: Packets Are Initially Dropped When DC_A Fails*

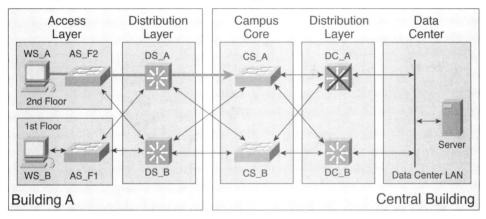

None of the other OSPF routers are directly connected to the DC_A node; therefore, they cannot detect the loss of a link and propagate a new update. However, the change is learned through a lost adjacency (missing Hello packets).

The OSPF convergence time is between 35 and 45 seconds. This is the time that it takes OSPF, through the OSPF dead timer, to discover that the neighbor is down (between 30 and 40 seconds with default timers on LAN interfaces), the time that it takes for the change to be propagated across the network (less than 1 second), and the time for the SPF run (up to 5-seconds delay).

After 35 seconds, the router DS_A appears to be propagating the traffic across an alternate route (DS_A → CS_A → DC_B) and, at the same time, sending some traffic to CS_B. The latter action is a result of the OSPF Hold time that has not yet expired. The DS_A router is under the impression that the failed DC_A can still be reached through the CS_B switch and it is therefore used as an alternate path, as shown by the thick lines in Figure 7-36.

Figure 7-36 *Layer 2/3 Network: DS_A Is Rerouting Around the DC_A Failure*

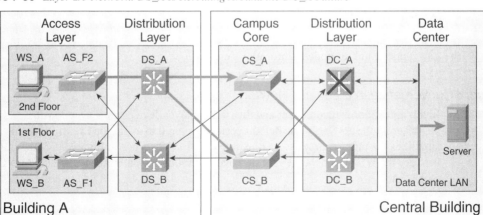

After 45 seconds, the convergence is complete. As illustrated by the thick lines in Figure 7-37, the packet only flows across an alternate route.

Figure 7-37 *Layer 2/3 Network: OSPF Convergence After DC_A Failure*

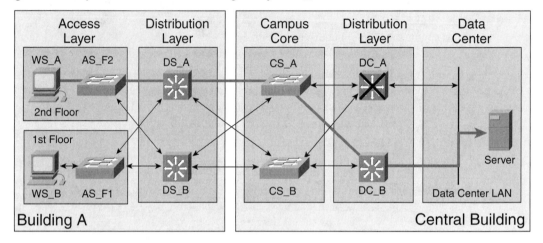

After DC_A recovers at 500 seconds, traffic flow is not interrupted; however, the path recovery takes longer—the packet traversing the network at the 519th second still follows the backup path. The path recovery takes approximately 20 seconds and does not interrupt the packet flow.

Conclusions

When using OSPF in a mixed Layer 2/Layer 3 network, the network is disrupted for approximately 35 to 45 seconds after a Layer 3 switch failure (the exact time depends on OSPF timer settings). Traffic flow is not disrupted after node recovery, and the traffic is rerouted to the primary path only after the OSPF re-establishment is complete (after approximately 20 seconds).

3 If you chose RIP instead of OSPF, the convergence time would change significantly under a link or node failure. Why does this occur?

Network Convergence in a Layer 3 Network

In this simulation, all core layer and distribution layer devices are Layer 3 switches; OSPF is run across the network. The default costs are altered to avoid load sharing, so this simplifies the failure analysis. As illustrated by the thick lines in Figure 7-38, the traffic between the WS_A and the server flows over the following path: AS_F2 → DS_A → CS_A → DC_A.

Figure 7-38 *Layer 3 Network: Initial Path from WS_A to Server*

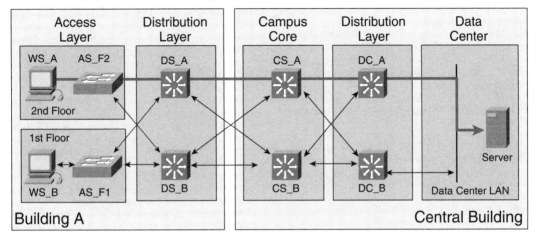

The failure scenario used in the previous simulation remains in place: the 100-second flap of the DC_A → CS_A link triggered at the 200th second, followed by the DC_A node outage between the 400th and 500th second.

Test #1—Convergence Times Around Link Failure

At 200 seconds, the CS_A → DC_A link fails. The packet flow is not interrupted because both involved routers (CS_A and DC_A) immediately propagate the loss of an attached link by using a new OSPF Link State Advertisement. The CS_A router reroutes the traffic across the DC_B node. The first packet after the link failure takes the paths illustrated by the thick lines in Figure 7-39.

Figure 7-39 *Layer 3 Network: Immediate Rerouting After Link Failure*

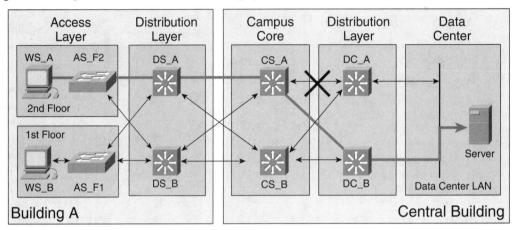

The other routers need some time to receive an update. Additionally, the SPF recalculation is delayed for 5 seconds because of OSPF behavior. Therefore, it takes approximately 5 to 6 seconds for the other routers to recalculate the possible paths after the link failure. As a result of the recalculation, there are two alternate equal-cost paths across the network, and the packets are load-shared across them. The thick lines in Figure 7-40 illustrate this.

Figure 7-40 *Layer 3 Network: Packets Are Load-shared After Link Failure*

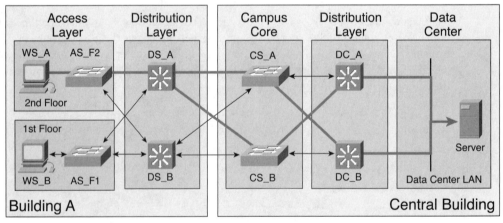

After the link CS_A → DC_A is reestablished at 300 seconds, the packets continue to flow over the backup paths until the primary link's OSPF is fully reestablished

   4 From the simulation log, it appears that the switchover to the primary path takes a long time—approximately 50 seconds. Why?

Conclusions

When using OSPF in the entire campus network, no disruption follows a link failure. The router that is attached to the lost link immediately reroutes traffic over the alternative link, while the other routers need some time to be notified about the change and complete the SPF recalculation. Upon recovering the link, traffic flow is not disrupted; however, the traffic is only rerouted on the primary path approximately 50 seconds after link recovery.

Test #2—Convergence Times Around Node Failure

At 400 seconds, the DC_A node fails. The OSPF convergence time is again immediate, and packet loss results. The rerouted path is illustrated by the thick lines in Figure 7-41.

Figure 7-41 *Layer 3 Network: Immediate Rerouting After DC_A Router Failure*

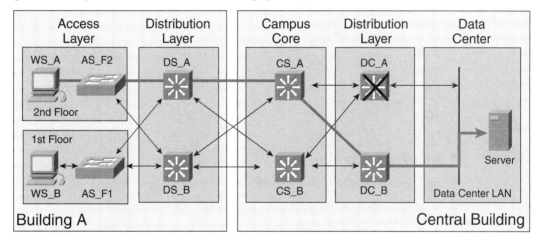

After the node DC_A recovers at 500 seconds, the path recovery again takes longer than expected; the packet traversing the network at the 550th second is finally switched back to the primary path.

Conclusions

Traffic flow is not disrupted after node failure and recovery, but the traffic is rerouted to the primary path only after the OSPF establishment is complete—after approximately 50 seconds.

Review Questions

Answer the following questions and then refer to Appendix G, "Answers to Review Questions, Case Studies, and Simulation Exercises," for the answers.

1 In what situations is static routing preferred over dynamic routing?

2 What must dynamic routing protocols do in order to be effective?

3 How do distance vector and link-state routing protocols differ?

4 What are triggered updates?

5 Which type of routing protocol is used for interconnecting autonomous systems?

6 Do IGPs or EGPs typically have faster convergence?

7 What parameters do the following routing protocols use in their metric calculation?

RIP

EIGRP

OSPF

IGRP

BGP

IS-IS

8 What is convergence?

9 How does the speed of convergence affect the network?

10 What is an advantage of a hierarchical network versus a flat network?

11 A large organization has decided to connect all of its regional offices to their appropriate branch offices. Each regional office has a minimum of two and a maximum of five branch offices to connect. The branch offices use low-end routers that are directly connected to the regional office router via Frame Relay permanent virtual circuit (PVC) links, which effectively creates a hub and spoke topology (star network). No physical connections exist between the branch office routers. The protocol that runs between the regional and branch offices does not need to be the same as in the rest of the network where OSPF is run. What are the two best options for establishing IP connectivity?

a Deploy EIGRP both ways.

b Deploy IS-IS both ways.

c Deploy RIPv2 with a default route for branch office connectivity to the rest of the network.

d Use static routing both ways with a default static route from each branch to the regional office, and static routes on each regional router toward the branch networks.

12 On-demand routing (ODR) is best suited for what network topology?

13 What Cisco protocol does ODR use?

14 What are the advantages of RIPv2 over RIPv1?

15 A network consists of links with varying bandwidths. Would RIPv2 be a good routing protocol choice in this network? Why or why not?

16 What are some features of EIGRP that make it an appropriate choice for a core routing protocol?

17 What is a feasible successor?

18 Does OSPF support manual route summarization on all routers?

19 What is an OSPF link-state advertisement (LSA)?

20 What is the OSPF metric?

21 For what network layer protocols does Integrated IS-IS provided support?

22 What is the difference between an IS-IS backbone and an OSPF backbone?

23 Why might Integrated IS-IS be better than OSPF in a very large network?

24 What is BGP multi-homing?

25 Why is BGP used for inter-AS routing?

26 Which routing protocols are likely to be used in the core layer?

27 Is IS-IS typically a good choice of routing protocol for the access layer?

28 What is route redistribution?

29 Which parts of the Enterprise Composite Network model are likely to implement redistribution?

30 What is route filtering?

31 When is route filtering required?

32 Why does the EBGP next-hop address have to be announced by the IGP into a network that runs IBGP?

33 What is route summarization, and why would a network need it?

34 What is the best summary route for the following networks?

- 172.16.168.0/24
- 172.16.169.0/24
- 172.16.170.0/24
- 172.16.171.0/24
- 172.16.172.0/24
- 172.16.173.0/24
- 172.16.174.0/24
- 172.16.175.0/24

This chapter discusses voice design principles and contains the following sections:

- Traditional Voice Architectures and Features
- Integrating Voice Architectures
- Capacity Planning Using Voice Traffic Engineering Concepts
- Summary
- Case Study Simulation
- Review Questions

CHAPTER 8

Designing Networks for Voice Transport

This chapter introduces voice design principles and provides guidelines for a successful integrated network deployment. It begins with an overview of traditional voice architectures and features, continues with the benefits of integrated voice architectures, and explains the reasons for migrating voice from a traditional architecture to integrated architectures.

This chapter describes how converged voice networks can run the same applications as a telephony network, but in a more cost-effective and scalable manner. It describes voice and data networking concepts and the signaling protocols used with modern telephony systems, and introduces three technologies for voice transmission across data networks: Voice over Internet Protocol (VoIP), Voice over Frame Relay (VoFR), and Voice over Asynchronous Transfer Mode (VoATM). Internet Protocol (IP) telephony is also introduced.

This chapter also discusses voice traffic engineering concepts on both the public switched telephone network (PSTN) and the VoIP network. Finally, it discusses various recommendations for ensuring acceptable voice quality and class of service (CoS).

NOTE   Chapter 9, "Evaluating Security Solutions for the Network," discusses IP telephony security.

After completing this chapter, you will be able to describe the architecture, features, and signaling of traditional telephony, and identify the packet telephony network drivers, goals, and design guidelines. You will also be able to describe possible issues in packet telephony, identify the quality of service (QoS) solutions, and plan resource capacities for quality packet telephony.

Traditional Voice Architectures and Features

This section introduces the traditional telephony infrastructure and explains its major components. It describes how voice is routed and transmitted across a digital network, introduces basic circuit switching concepts, and presents various signaling applications. The section concludes with a description of the services that are found in traditional public switched telephone networks.

Analog and Digital Signaling

Although people are well equipped for analog communications, analog transmission is not particularly efficient. Analog signals must be amplified when they become weak from transmission loss. However, amplification of analog signals also amplifies noise. To obtain clear voice connections, analog speech must be converted to a digital format and sent over a digital network. At the other end of the connection, the digital signal is converted back to the analog format (the normal sound waves that the ear can pick up). Digital signals are more immune to noise, and the digital network does not induce any additional noise when amplifying signals.

Pulse code modulation (PCM) is the process of digitizing analog voice signals. Several steps are involved in converting an analog signal into PCM digital format, as shown in Figure 8-1 and described here:

- **Filtering**—Filters out the signal's non-speech frequency components. Most of the energy of spoken language ranges from 300 Hz to (approximately) 3400 Hz; this is the 3100 Hz bandwidth (or range) for standard speech. Analog waveforms are put through a voice frequency filter to filter out anything greater than 4000 Hz.

- **Sampling**—Samples the filtered input signal at a constant sampling frequency. This is accomplished by using a process called pulse amplitude modulation (PAM). This step uses the original analog signal to modulate the amplitude of a pulse train that has a constant amplitude and frequency. The filtered analog signal is sampled at a rate of 8000 times per second.

- **Digitizing**—Digitizes the samples in preparation for transmission over a telephony network; this is the PCM process. PCM takes the PAM process one step further by encoding each analog sample using binary code words. An analog-to-digital converter is required on the source side, and a digital-to-analog converter is required on the destination side.

Figure 8-1 *Analog to Digital Conversion Process*

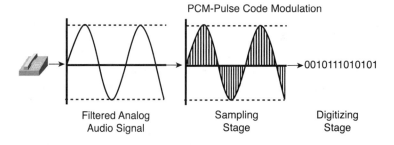

PCM-Pulse Code Modulation

0010111010101

Filtered Analog Audio Signal

Sampling Stage

Digitizing Stage

The digitizing process is further divided into the following steps:

- **Quantization and coding**—A digitizing process that converts each analog sample value into a discrete value to which a unique digital code word can be assigned. As the input signal sample enters the quantization phase, it is assigned to a *quantization interval*. All quantization intervals are equally spaced throughout the dynamic range of the input analog signal. Each quantization interval is assigned a discrete value in the form of a binary code word. The standard word size used is 8 bits and enables 256 possible quantization intervals.

Key Point: PCM Maximum Transmission Rate

Since the input analog signal is sampled 8000 times per second and each sample is given an 8-bit-long code word, the maximum transmission bit rate for telephony systems using PCM is 64,000 bits per second.

- **Companding**—Refers to the process of first compressing an analog signal at the source and then expanding this signal back to its original size when it reaches its destination. (Combining the terms *compressing* and *expanding* into one word created the term companding.) During the companding process, input analog signal samples are compressed into logarithmic segments and each segment is quantified and coded using uniform quantization. The compression process is logarithmic, meaning that the compression increases as the sample signals increase. In other words, the larger sample signals are compressed more than the smaller sample signals, thereby causing the quantization noise to increase as the sample signal increases. This results in a more accurate value for smaller amplitude signals, and a uniform signal-to-noise ratio (SNR) across the input range. Two basic variations of logarithmic companding are commonly used: the A-law companding standard is used in Europe, and u-law is used in North America and Japan. The methods are similar; they both use logarithmic compression to achieve linear approximations in 8-bit words, but they are not compatible.

A-law and u-law Companding

Following are the similarities between A-law and u-law companding:

- Both are linear approximations of logarithmic input/output relationship.
- Both are implemented using 8-bit code words (256 levels, one for each quantization interval). 8-bit code words allow for a bit rate of 64 kilobits per second (kbps), calculated by multiplying the sampling rate (twice the input frequency) by the size of the code word (2 * 4 kilohertz [KHz] * 8 bits = 64 kbps).

- Both break a dynamic range into a total of 16 segments: eight positive and eight negative segments. Each segment is twice the length of the preceding one, and uniform quantization is used within each segment.

- Both use a similar approach to coding the 8-bit word. The first bit (the most significant bit [MSB]) identifies polarity; bits 2, 3, and 4 identify the segment, and the final 4 bits quantize the segment.

The differences between A-law and u-law include the following:

- Different linear approximations lead to different lengths and slopes.

- The numerical assignment of the bit positions in the 8-bit code word to segments and quantization levels within segments are different.

- A-law provides a greater dynamic range than u-law.

- u-law provides better signal/distortion performance for low level signals than A-law.

- A-law requires 13 bits for a uniform PCM equivalent. u-law requires 14 bits for a uniform PCM equivalent.

- An international connection should use A-law; u to A conversion is the responsibility of the u-law country.

This information was adapted from Cisco's "Waveform Coding Techniques" document, available at www.cisco.com/warp/public/788/signalling/waveform_coding.html#subfirstsix.

Private Branch Exchanges (PBXs) and the PSTN

This section introduces the private branch exchange and the public switched telephone network. It describes where they are both used and their major features.

Differences Between a PBX and a Public Telephone Switch

As shown in Table 8-1, PBXs and public telephone switches share many similarities, but they also have many differences.

Table 8-1   *PBX and PSTN Comparison*

PBX	PSTN Switch
Used in the private sector	Used in the public sector
Scales to thousands of phones	Scales to hundred of thousands of phones
Mostly digital	Mostly digital
Uses 64 kbps circuits	Uses 64 kbps circuits

Table 8-1   *PBX and PSTN Comparison (Continued)*

PBX	PSTN Switch
Uses proprietary protocols to control phones	Uses open standard protocols between switches and phones
Interconnects remote branch subsystems	Interconnects with other PSTN switches, PBXs, and telephones

A *PBX* is a business telephone system that provides business features such as call hold, call transfer, call forward, follow-me, call-park, conference calling, music on hold, call history, and voice mail. Most of these features are not found in public systems.

Both the PBX and PSTN switch systems use 64 kbps circuits; however, the scale is very different. The PSTN switch can support hundreds of thousands of telephones, while a PBX can only support several thousand.

Key Point: PSTN and PBX

The PSTN switch's primary task is to provide residential telephony. However, a PBX supports user telephones within a company.

PBX vendors often create proprietary protocols to enable their PBXs to intercommunicate and carry additional features through their voice network transparently. In addition, only the vendor's telephones can be connected to its PBX. This forces enterprise networks to consolidate to one brand of PBX, and the enterprise business customer is restricted to one vendor.

NOTE   Many vendors are beginning to implement standards-based signaling protocols that enable interoperability between different vendors' PBXs. The two standards are Q Signaling (QSIG) and Digital Private Network Signaling System (DPNSS).

Figure 8-2 illustrates the location of and communication between the PSTN and PBXs.

PSTN switches connect residential and business users, while PBXs are mainly used for business purposes. PBXs are typically located at corporate locations, whereas PSTN switches build the PSTN network and are located in central offices (COs).

Figure 8-2   *PBXs and the PSTN Interconnect to Facilitate Communication*

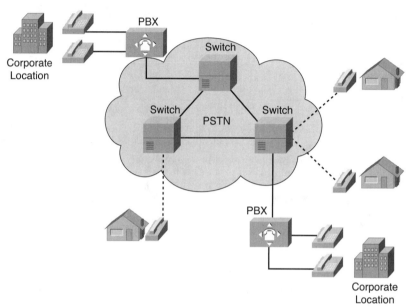

PBX Features

As mentioned, a PBX is a small version of a telephone switch that is used for business purposes. A PBX provides many call features, such as call hold, transfer, forward and park, conferencing, music on hold, call history, and voice mail, which business customers require. This switch often connects to the PSTN through a T1 or E1 digital circuit. A PBX supports end-to-end digital transmission, employs PCM switching technology, and supports both analog and digital proprietary telephones.

NOTE   The trunk that is used to carry a digital transmission in North America is called *T1*. A T1 trunk can carry 24 fixed channels (each channel can be for either voice or data), digitized at 64 kbps for an aggregate carrying capacity of 1.544 megabits per second (Mbps). Outside North America, the trunk that is used to carry a digital transmission is called an E1. An E1 line can carry 30 fixed channels, digitized at 64 kbps, for an aggregate carrying capacity of 2.048 Mbps.

A local PBX provides several advantages:

- Local calls between telephones within the PBX or group of PBXs are free of charge.
- Most PBX telephone system users are not calling externally through T1 or E1 circuits at the same time; therefore, cost savings on PSTN trunks are realized.

- When adding a new user, changing a voice feature, or moving a user to a different location, there is no need to contact the PSTN carrier; the local administrator can reconfigure the PBX.

However, the PBX adds another level of complexity: the enterprise customer must configure and maintain the PBX.

Figure 8-3 illustrates a typical enterprise telephone network that has proprietary telephones connected to the PBX and a trunk between the PBX and the PSTN network.

Figure 8-3 *A PBX Can Save on the Number of Trunks to the PSTN*

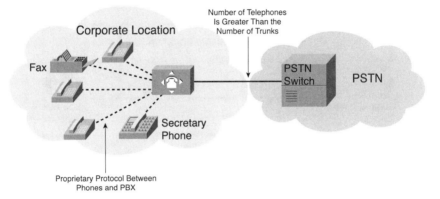

Enterprises install PBXs because the number of telephones is usually greater than the number of simultaneous calls to the PSTN network. Only a small percentage of telephones are active at one time. Companies with a PBX only need the number of external lines (to the PSTN) to equal the maximum possible number of simultaneous calls.

PSTN Switch Features

The PSTN resembles a single large network with telephone lines connected. In reality, the PSTN is composed of circuits, switches, signaling devices, and telephones. Many different companies can own and operate different systems within the PSTN.

The PSTN switch's primary role is to connect the calling and called parties. If the two parties are physically connected to the same PSTN switch, the call remains local; otherwise, the call is forwarded to the destination switch that owns the called party. A PSTN switch connects business PBXs, and public and private telephones and interconnect with other PSTN switches. Large PSTN switches are located at COs, which, combined with cable and other transmission media, provide circuits throughout the telephony network.

PSTN switches are deployed in hierarchies. CO switches interconnect with tandem switches, which perform CO interswitch communication; they do not connect PBXs or end-user telephones.

Local Loops, Trunks, and Interswitch Communications

Figure 8-4 illustrates a typical telephone infrastructure and connections between telephony devices.

Figure 8-4   *Local Loops, Trunks, and Interswitch Communication*

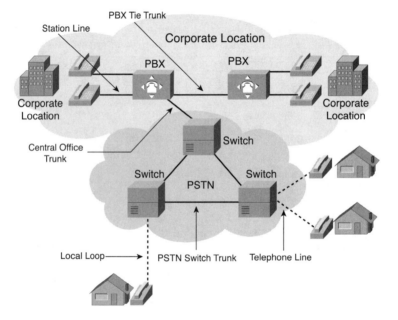

The telephone infrastructure starts with a simple pair of copper wires running to the end user's home. This physical cabling is known as a *local loop;* the local loop physically connects the home telephone to the CO PSTN switch. The communication between the CO switch and the end-user home is known as the *telephone line*, and it usually runs over the local loop. Similarly, the connection between an enterprise PBX and its telephones is called the *station line*.

A trunk is a communication path between two telephony systems. The following three trunk types are available:

- **Tie**—Connects enterprise PBXs without connecting to the PSTN (in other words, not connecting to a CO).

- **Central office**—Connects CO switches to enterprise PBXs. The telephone service provider is responsible for running trunks between its CO and enterprise PBXs.

- **PSTN switch**—Interconnects CO switches.

As shown in Figure 8-5, foreign exchange (FX) trunks are analog interfaces that are used to interconnect telephones and PBXs.

Figure 8-5   *Foreign Exchange Trunks*

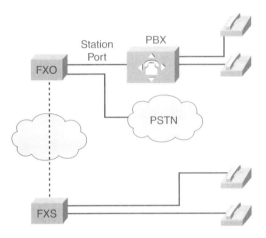

Two types of foreign exchange trunks exist:

- **Foreign Exchange Office (FXO)**—Interface allows an analog connection on a PSTN central office, or on a station interface on a PBX. The FXO interface sits on the connection's PBX end. It plugs directly into the line side of the PBX so the PBX thinks the FXO interface is a telephone. The PBX notifies the FXO of an incoming call by sending ringing voltage to the FXO. Likewise, the FXO answers a call by closing the loop to allow current flow. Once current is flowing, the FXO interface transports the signal to the FXS.

- **Foreign Exchange Station (FXS)**—Interface emulates a PBX. It connects directly to a standard telephone, fax machine, or similar device and supplies ring, voltage, and dial tone to the end device.

Basic Telephony Signaling

In a telephony system, a signaling mechanism is required for establishing and disconnecting telephone communications. You must understand the signaling mechanisms used to know how the telephony system works.

Telephony Signaling

A signaling mechanism is required to establish and disconnect telephone communications in a telephony system.

The following signaling forms are used when a telephone call is placed across the country:

- Between the telephone and PBX
- Between the PBX and PSTN switch
- Between the PSTN switches
- Between two PBXs

In the broadest sense, there are two signaling realms, as shown in Figure 8-6:

- **Subscriber signaling**—Between a PSTN or PBX switch and subscriber (telephone)
- **Trunk signaling**—Between PSTN switches, a PSTN switch and PBX, or PBX switches

Figure 8-6 *Telephony Signaling Includes Subscriber and Trunk Signaling*

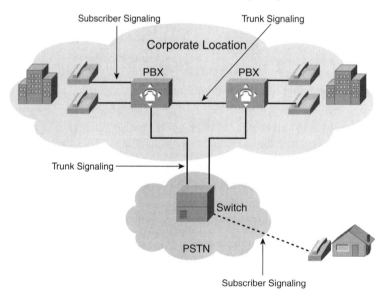

Simple signaling examples include the ringing of the telephone, a dial tone, and a ring-back tone. Following are the four basic categories of signals that are commonly used in telephone networks:

- **Supervision signaling**—Used to initiate a telephone call request on a line or trunk, hold or release an established connection, initiate or terminate charging, and recall an operator on an established connection.

- **Address signaling**—Involves the passing of dialed digits (pulse or tone) to a PBX or PSTN switch. These dialed digits provide the switch with a connection path to another telephone or customer premises equipment (CPE).

- **Call progress signals**—Used to indicate certain conditions, such as an incoming telephone call or a busy telephone, by audible tones or recorded announcements.

- **Network management signals**—Used to control the bulk assignment of circuits or to modify the operating characteristics of switching systems in a network in response to overload conditions.

For a telephone call to take place, all four types of signaling occur.

Analog Telephony Signaling

The most common methods of analog subscriber signaling are loop start and ground start. The most common analog trunk signaling method is E&M (derived from a combination of recEive and transMit, and sometimes also known as *Ear and Mouth*). These methods are as follows:

- **Loop start**—Loop start is the simplest and least intelligent signaling protocol, and the most common form of subscriber loop signaling. It provides a way to indicate *on-hook* and *off-hook* conditions in a voice network. The creation of the electrical loop initiates a call (off-hook), and loop closure terminates the call (on-hook). This type of signaling is not common for PBX signaling, and it has a significant drawback in which *glare* can occur. Glare occurs when two endpoints try to seize the line at the same time, which unknowingly connects two people. Because business callers use telephones regularly and the possibility for glare is high, loop start signaling is only acceptable for residential use.

- **Ground start**—A modification of loop start, ground start provides positive recognition of connects and disconnects (off-hook and on-hook). It uses current detection mechanisms at each end of the trunk, thereby enabling PBXs to agree which end will seize the trunk before it is actually seized. This form of signaling minimizes the effect of glare. Ground start is preferred when there is a high volume of calls; therefore, PBXs typically use this type of signaling.

- **E&M**—E&M is a common trunk signaling technique that is used between PBXs. In E&M, voice is transmitted over either two- or four-wire circuits, with five types of E&M signaling (Type I, II, III, IV, and V). E&M uses separate paths (or leads) for voice and signaling. The M (Mouth) lead sends the signal and the E (Ear) lead receives the signal.

NOTE   Digital loop-start and ground-start signaling are used between FXO and FXS devices.

Analog and Digital Trunk Signaling

There are two trunk signaling implementation methods. Analog signaling is usually provided through channel associated signaling (CAS), while digital signaling is provided through common channel signaling (CCS).

CAS exists in many varieties that operate over various analog and digital facilities. The analog facilities are either two- or four-wire, and the digital facilities are either North American T1 or European E1. CAS sends its signal for call setup in the same channel as a voice call. Examples of CAS signaling include the following:

- **R1 signaling (on T1 facilities)**—This type of signaling is used in North America.
- **R2 signaling (on E1 facilities)**—This type of signaling is used in Europe, Latin America, Australia, and Asia.

Modern telecommunication networks require more efficient means of signaling, so they are moving toward CCS systems. CCS uses a common link to carry signaling information for several trunks. It differs from CAS signaling because it uses a separate channel for call setup. This form of signaling has faster connect times and offers the possibility of a number of practically unlimited services.

Examples of CCS signaling include

- E1 signaling
- DPNSS
- Integrated Services Digital Network (ISDN)
- QSIG
- Signaling System 7 (SS7)

The following sections further describe the latter three types.

ISDN Digital Signaling

ISDN provides digital telephony and data-transport services that are offered by regional telephone carriers. ISDN involves the digitalization of the telephone network, permitting voice, data, text, graphics, music, video, and other source material to be transmitted on the same facility.

ISDN enables PBXs to connect over the PSTN and create voice Virtual Private Networks (VPNs). This is accomplished by delivering PBX signaling over the network to distant PBXs.

Following are the two ISDN access methods:

- **ISDN Basic Rate Interface (BRI)**—Offers two B channels and one D channel (2B+D). The BRI B-channel service operates at 64 kbps and carries user data and voice. The BRI D-channel service operates at 16 kbps and carries both control and signaling information. BRI is typically used for residential and small office, home office (SOHO) applications.

- **ISDN Primary Rate Interface (PRI)**—Designed to use T1 or E1 circuits, it offers 23 B channels and one D channel (23B+D) in North America and 30 B channels and one D channel (30B+D) in Europe. The PRI B-channel service operates at 64 kbps and carries user data and voice. The PRI D-channel service also operates at 64 kbps and carries both control and signaling information. PRI is typically used for enterprise (business) applications.

QSIG Digital Signaling

QSIG is a peer-to-peer signaling system that is used in corporate voice networking to provide standardized inter-PBX communications. It has an important mechanism that provides a standard method for the transparent transportation of PBX features across a network.

QSIG features include the following:

- Standards-based protocol that enables interconnection of multivendor equipment
- Enables inter-PBX basic services and generic feature transparency between PBXs, and supplementary services
- Interoperability with public and private ISDN
- Operability in any network configuration and is compatible with many PBX-type interfaces
- No restrictions on private numbering plans

SS7 Digital Signaling

SS7 is a CCS international standard for the common channel signaling system. SS7 defines the architecture, network elements, interfaces, protocols, and management procedures for a network that transports control information between PSTN switches. SS7 is used between PSTN switches and replaces per-trunk in-band signaling.

As shown in Figure 8-7, SS7 is implemented on a separate data network within the PSTN; it provides call setup and teardown, network management, fault resolution, and traffic management services. The SS7 network is used solely for network control. Out-of-band signaling via SS7 provides numerous benefits for internetworking design, including reduced call setup time, bearer capability, and other progress indicators.

Figure 8-7   *SS7 Signaling Is Used Between PSTN Switches*

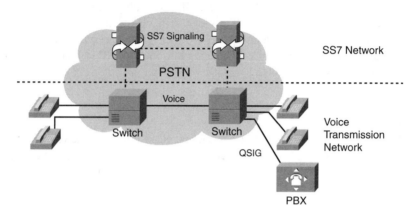

Key Point: SS7 Signaling Is on a Separate Network

When using SS7, all trunk channels are used for voice and data, and the associated
signaling is carried separately over the SS7 network.

PSTN Numbering Plans

PSTN numbering plans are the foundation for routing voice calls through the PSTN network.

Numbering Plans

For any telephone network to function, each telephone must be identified by a unique
address. Voice addressing relies on a combination of international and national standards,
local telephone company practices, and internal customer-specific codes. The International
Telecommunications Union Telecommunication Standardization Sector (ITU-T)
recommendation E.164 defines the international numbering plan. Each country's national
numbering plan must conform to the E.164 recommendation and work in conjunction with
the international numbering plan in a hierarchical fashion. Public switched telephone
service providers must ensure that their numbering plan aligns with the E.164
recommendation, and that their customers' networks conform.

Voice Routing

Voice routing is closely related to the numbering plan and signaling. Basic routing allows
a call to be established from the source telephone to the destination telephone. However,
most routing is more sophisticated and enables subscribers to select services or divert calls

from one subscriber to another. Routing results from establishing a set of tables or rules within each switch. As each call arrives, the path to the desired destination and the type of services available are derived from these tables or rules.

North American Numbering Plan

As illustrated in Figure 8-8, the North American Numbering Plan (NANP) is an example of a PSTN numbering plan. It conforms to the ITU-T recommendation E.164. NANP numbers are 10 digits in length and occur in the following format: NXX-NXX-XXXX, where N is any digit 2–9 and X is any digit 0–9. The first three digits are called the area code, the second three digits are called the central office code, or prefix, and the final four digits are called the line number. NANP is also referred to as *1+10*. When a 1 is the first number dialed, a 10-digit number follows. This enables the end-office switch to determine whether it should expect a 7- or 10-digit telephone number (although many local calls now require 10-digit rather than 7-digit dialing).

Figure 8-8   *North American Numbering Plan Has 10-Digit Numbers*

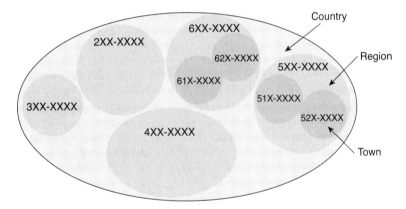

Figure 8-9 illustrates how the NANP routes telephone calls. In this example, the lower telephone is dialing 212-4321, which is the telephone number of the top-right phone. A PSTN switch forwards the signal as soon as it receives enough digits to send the call to the next switch. The last switch in the series receives all the digits and rings the destination telephone (in this case, the telephone on the top right).

NOTE   If CCS is used, the SS7 first determines through the out-of-band signaling that there is a path to the destination and that the end station can accept the call, and then it allocates the trunks.

Figure 8-9 *Routing Calls Based on the NANP*

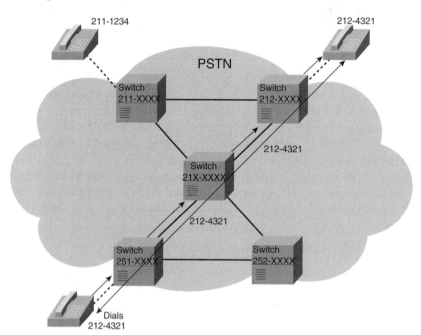

PSTN Services

This section introduces PSTN services and explains how they are offered to business customers. It discusses how corporations use different applications to drive their business, the main features of these applications, and how enterprise and PSTN networks work together.

The modern PSTN offers many different services, each with a desirable suite of features and functionality. Service providers offer competitive services to differentiate themselves and generate additional revenue from these offerings.

The following PSTN services are described in subsequent sections:

- Centrex
- Virtual private voice networks
- Voice mail
- Call center
- Interactive voice response

Centrex

Key Point: Centrex

Centrex is a set of specialized business solutions (primarily, but not exclusively, for voice service) in which the service provider owns and operates the equipment that provides both call control and service logic functions; therefore, it is located on the service provider's premises.

Centrex can be a useful outsourcing solution because it frees the customer from the costs and responsibilities of major equipment ownership. The Centrex customer pays a monthly fee to the service provider.

Centrex enables the PSTN to offer features in a Closed User Group (CUG) where, regardless of geographical location, a telephone call can be placed to all telephones within the group using only four to five digits. The telephones within the group can be located at many distant locations; however, within the system, they appear as though they reside at a single location.

The benefits of Centrex technology include the following:

- **Lower capital investment cost**—Because the service provider owns the infrastructure, the startup costs for a Centrex service are much lower than for purchasing a traditional PBX.

- **Scalability**—The customer can buy the exact number of lines that are needed and add or remove lines easily. In contrast, when a station is removed from a PBX, there are no cost savings because the equipment has already been purchased. When adding stations to a PBX, there are costs for the line cards and periodic costs for new common equipment, such as shelves to accommodate the line cards.

- **Simplicity**—The service provider is responsible for installing and configuring the service. With a PBX, the customer assumes this responsibility.

- **Operations and maintenance**—The service provider is responsible for the day-to-day operations and maintenance of Centrex. This includes adding new lines and changing faulty components. With a PBX, the customer is responsible for these functions and for keeping an inventory of spare parts.

- **Upgrades**—Centrex service providers continue to upgrade the service. This includes major evolutionary upgrades, such as analog to IP, and more mundane upgrades, such as installing a new switch that offers more features.

- **Reliability**—The Centrex service provider monitors the network 24/7 and provides staff for immediate response to alarms and equipment failures.

- **Standardized telephones**—Centrex station equipment uses standardized protocols and conforms to an open interface. This allows multiple equipment suppliers to manufacture Centrex telephones, and the customer can purchase any brand of telephone.

- **Space savings**—The Centrex infrastructure is located at the service provider premises. In contrast, PBX solutions are located at the customer premises; the customer must provide floor space for the equipment and ensure that the storage rooms meet certain environmental requirements, such as air conditioning, humidity, and fire protection.

Virtual Private Voice Networks

Key Point: Virtual Private Voice Networks

Virtual private voice networks interconnect corporate voice traffic among multiple locations over the PSTN.

Virtual private voice networks are alternatives to tie lines among locations. Service providers offer competitively priced virtual private voice network services by maximizing the private use of the public infrastructure. PSTN facilities are thus balanced by corporate use during weekdays and residential use during nights and weekends.

Because the same PSTN switch does not typically serve multiple locations and because tie trunks between locations are fairly expensive, virtual private voice networks are economical solutions in situations where multiple distant PBXs need to communicate. With virtual private voice networks, PBXs are connected to the PSTN, not directly over tie trunks. The PSTN service provider provides call routing among locations, and all PBX features are carried transparently across the PSTN.

Deployment of a voice-capable network eases the process of adding new and multiple sites to an existing virtual private voice network. Adding a new location and provisioning the appropriate translation and dialing plans is much easier in a virtual private voice network than with traditional tie trunks, where end-to-end connections are required between the new location and each existing location.

The major benefit of virtual private voice networks is the lower interconnection costs. The drawback is that the corporation owns the PBXs, which the corporation must therefore purchase and maintain.

Voice Mail

Voice messaging is an optional service for PSTN customers. It provides customers with the facility to divert their incoming PSTN calls to a voice mailbox when they are unable to answer their telephones, such as when the line is busy, when they are not available, or for all calls.

The voice messaging capability offers voice messaging service subscribers (residential and business) notification and access to their wire line or wireless mailbox for message retrieval via various message waiting indicator (MWI) services (such as a flashing light, message display, special dial tone, or announcement).

The benefits of voice mail systems include the following:

- Improved communication because it allows people to communicate verbally in nonreal time.
- Elimination of time zone and business hour issues.
- Reduced labor for operators.
- Fewer callbacks.
- 24-hour availability.

Call Center

A *call center* is a place of doing business by telephone, combined with a centralized database that uses an automatic call distribution (ACD) system.

Key Point: Call Centers

Call centers require live agents to accept and handle calls.

Using ACD, callers are greeted by a customized announcement and queued until the call can be answered. While queued, customers can hear music or customized announcements. The ACD system generally offers inbound call routing. Inbound calls can be routed to a group and then routed to a specific agent within that group. The ACD software sends each call to an available agent according to instructions contained in the database.

Following are the steps in an ACD system:

Step 1 The ACD software accepts an incoming call.

Step 2 The call is queued.

Step 3 The caller is welcomed via a recorded message.

Step 4 The ACD sends the call to the next available agent.

Step 5 If no agent is available, the caller is notified to wait on the line for the next available agent.

ACD supports the following features:

- Calls are queued until an available agent is assigned.

- Agents are divided into smaller thematic groups, and each agent within a group can answer the call for that group.

- Call routing is configurable, enabling easy adjustments for business needs.

- Statistics are available that provide information regarding the level of customer service and the agents' productivity.

Interactive Voice Response

Key Point: Interactive Voice Response

Interactive voice response (IVR) systems allow callers to exchange information over the telephone without an intermediary live agent.

The caller and the IVR system interact using a combination of spoken messages and dual tone multifrequency (DTMF) touch-tone telephone pad buttons. The IVR system plays a voice message that prompts a caller to enter information through the touch-tone telephone handset. The touch-tone buttons are used to enter numbers, make menu selections, and answer yes or no questions. Each response takes the customer to another question. This sequence repeats until the caller receives the required information or completes the task.

Integrating Voice Architectures

This section discusses integrated voice architecture concepts, components, mechanisms, and issues. The reasons for migrating from traditional networks to integrated architectures using voice over IP are introduced, and the main drivers of the new IP packet telephony network are discussed. The components that are required for successful deployment of voice on an existing data network are introduced, and various issues concerning voice quality are discussed. QoS mechanisms are introduced, along with their impact on voice quality. The section concludes with the introduction of Voice over Frame Relay and Voice over Asynchronous Transfer Mode, which are still of interest for some environments.

One means of creating an integrated network is to replace the PBX tie lines with IP connections. Voice traffic is converted to IP packets and directed over IP data networks through voice-enabled routers; this implementation is VoIP.

IP telephony is another implementation solution. IP phones *themselves* convert voice into IP packets. The PBX becomes a dedicated network server that runs specialized software. Such implementations do not use telephone cabling. Instead, they send all signals over standard network cabling (Ethernet). (For details, see the "IP Telephony Introduction" section later in this chapter.)

Both these designs are cost-effective because of the reduced number of tie lines and higher link efficiency. In addition, both voice and data networks use the same wide-area network (WAN) infrastructure. It is much easier to manage a single network than two separate networks because they have fewer administrators, a simplified management infrastructure, and lower administrator training costs.

Voice over IP Introduction

VoIP involves digitizing voice traffic and putting it in IP packets to send over an IP network, including the Internet.

Drivers for Integrating Voice and Data Networks

Although a PSTN is effective for carrying voice signals, many business drivers are forcing the need for a new type of network for the following reasons:

- Data has overtaken voice as the primary traffic on many voice networks
- Companies want to reduce WAN costs by migrating to integrated networks that can carry any type of data
- The PSTN cannot create and deploy features quickly enough
- Data, voice, and video cannot converge on the current PSTN structure
- The architecture that is built for voice is not flexible enough to carry data optimally

Time-division Multiplexing in PSTN

Time-division multiplexing (TDM) is used in networks that are commonly deployed by telephone companies, including the PSTN.

As illustrated in Figure 8-10, TDM is a digital transmission technique for carrying multiple signals simultaneously over a single trunk line by interleaving bits of each signal into different time slots.

Figure 8-10 *Circuit-switched Networks Use Time-Division Multiplexing*

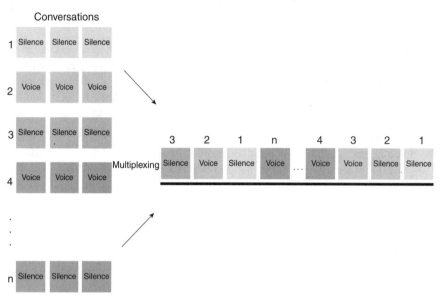

TDM converts all signals to a digital format. An analog signal is converted to a 64,000 bits per second digital channel. 24 or 30 such channels are then multiplexed together at great speed and comprise a T1 or E1 trunk, respectively. In effect, information from up to 24 (or 30) different sources is placed on a single trunk, like train cars on a track.

Though TDM cannot allocate bandwidth on demand like packet switching, TDM's fixed allocation of bandwidth ensures that a channel is never blocked because of competition for bandwidth resources, and performance is not degraded because of network congestion. Because TDM ensures time synchronization between sender and receiver, it is often used for delay-sensitive applications such as voice and video.

Figure 8-11 illustrates a typical enterprise WAN network with separate data and voice tie lines.

With time slot allocation, the number of simultaneous calls cannot exceed the number of TDM slots in the trunk. One call always allocates one TDM slot, regardless of whether silence or speech is transmitted. Time slot allocation ensures that connections always have access to a trunk, thereby resulting in a low delay. However, because of the allocation method, the overall trunk utilization, also known as *trunk efficiency,* becomes relatively low.

The low trunk efficiency that is found in circuit-switched networks is a major driver for converged packet-switched networks, in which bandwidth is only consumed when there is traffic.

Figure 8-11 *Traditional Separate Voice and Data Networks*

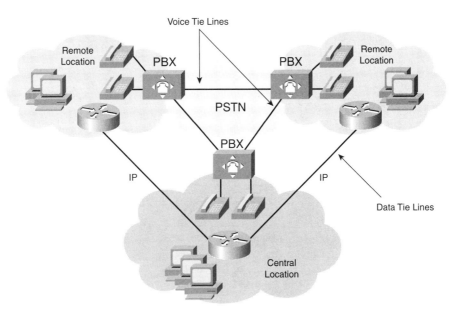

Open Standards Are Drivers for Converged Networks

Integrating data, voice, and video in a network not only changes the infrastructure; a converged network also enables more rapid development of new features and opens up application development to different software vendors.

Multiple vendors can develop applications for converged networks, thereby resulting in more software options and increased flexibility. The customer is no longer limited to a voice solution wherein a single vendor provides all the applications for its equipment.

Figure 8-12 illustrates how the traditional circuit-switching model changes into the new packet-switching model.

Key Point: Packet-Versus Circuit-Switched Networks

Whether or not either caller is talking, circuit-switched (classical voice) calls require a permanent duplex 64 kbps dedicated circuit between the two telephones. During the call, no other party can use the 64 kbps connection, and the company cannot use it for any other purpose.

Packet-switched networking only uses bandwidth when it is required. This difference is an important benefit of packet-based voice networking.

Figure 8-12 *Converged Networks Use a Packet-Switching Model*

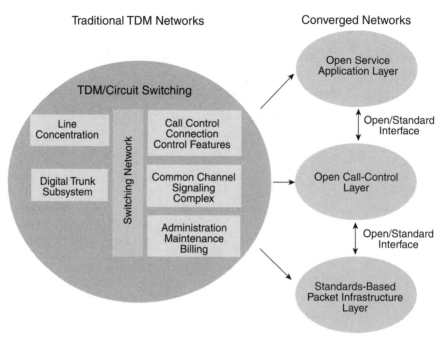

The packet-switching model is comprised of the following three independent layers, with the open standard interfaces between them:

- **Packet infrastructure layer**—Replaces the circuit-switching infrastructure in this new model. The transport of upper layer applications is based on IP because of its broad applicability. Any underlying technology can be used, including leased circuits, Asynchronous Transfer Mode (ATM) virtual circuits, wireless, cable modems, Synchronous Optical Network (SONET), Ethernet, and so on. Routers, which replace traditional circuit switching, switch IP packets that carry voice.

  Unless bandwidth is substantially over-provisioned, the packet infrastructure layer requires some QoS functionality to minimize latency and jitter. This same packet infrastructure layer transports voice control packets and the voice packets themselves.

- **Open call control layer**—This layer directs voice calls to the appropriate destinations. It maps telephone numbers or user names into IP source and destination addresses, which are understood by the packet infrastructure layer. The main call control protocols in an IP network are ITU-T H.323 (described in the next section), Simple Gateway Control Protocol (SGCP), Media Gateway Control Protocol (MGCP), and session initiation protocol (SIP). Functions of these protocols are analogous to systems running SS7 in the circuit-switched world.

- **Open service application layer**—This layer, which is provided by application servers, includes voice mail, directory services, call distribution, accounting and billing, service provisioning, network management, and so on. Some of the applications are used to keep the voice infrastructure up and running, while others provide value-added calling features.

This layer approach enables new features to be developed quickly and efficiently. When building a network that has open interfaces from the packet layer to the call control layer and from the call control layer to the application layer, telephony vendors no longer need to develop applications. They can write standard application programming interfaces (APIs) and allow other vendors to build the applications. The only limitations are that the applications must run on IP, and that they conform to APIs.

An advantage of the packet-switching three-layer model is that call routing, control, and application functions can be widely distributed and based on industry standards. Enterprises can mix and match equipment from multiple vendors and geographically deploy these systems wherever they are needed.

On an IP network, voice servers and application servers can be located virtually anywhere. As with data application servers, the rationale for enterprises to maintain voice servers diminishes over time. As voice moves to IP networks (using the public Internet for inter-enterprise traffic, and private intranets for intra-enterprise traffic), service providers supply the functionality of call and voice application servers.

Figure 8-13 presents an integrated network with IP WAN that carries voice and data at the same time.

Figure 8-13 *Integrated Voice and Data Traffic in a Converged Network*

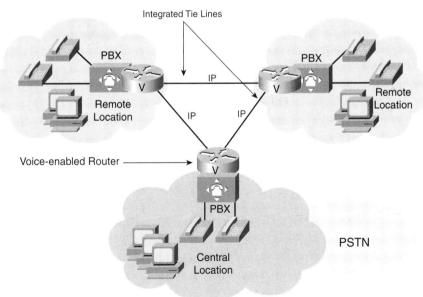

H.323

H.323 is an umbrella protocol for packet-based audio, video, and data communications across IP-based networks.

An Introduction to H.323

The ITU-T H.323 standard is a foundation for audio, video, and data communications across IP-based networks, including the Internet. By complying with the H.323 standard, multimedia products and applications from multiple vendors can interoperate, thereby allowing users to communicate without concern for compatibility.

The H.323 standard is broad in scope and includes standalone devices (such as IP telephones and voice gateways), embedded personal computer technology (such as PCs with Microsoft's NetMeeting), and point-to-point and multipoint conferences. H.323 addresses call control (including session setup, monitoring, and termination), multimedia management, and bandwidth management.

Communications under H.323 are a mix of audio, video, data, and control signals. To establish a voice call, H.323 refers to other standards: the Q.931 call setup in the H.225 standard, and H.245 signaling. The H.225 call signaling channel uses the Q.931 protocol to establish a connection between two H.323 devices. The H.245 control channel is a reliable channel that carries the control messages that govern the H.323 device's operation. These include codec capabilities exchange, the opening and closing of logical channels, preference requests, flow control messages, and general commands and indications.

NOTE   The term *codec* can have the following two meanings:

1   An integrated circuit device that typically uses pulse code modulation to transform analog signals into a digital bit stream, and digital signals back into analog signals (coder-decoder).

2   In Voice over IP, Frame Relay, and ATM, codec is a software algorithm that is used to compress and decompress speech or audio signals.

Key Benefits of the H.323 Protocol

Following are the key benefits of using the H.323 standard for voice, video, and data communications:

- **Codec standards**—H.323 establishes standards for compressing and decompressing audio and video data streams to ensure that equipment from different vendors shares some areas of common support.

- **Interoperability**—H.323 allows users to conference without worrying about compatibility at the receiving point. In addition to ensuring that the receiver can decompress information, H.323 establishes methods for receiving clients to negotiate their capabilities with senders. The standard also establishes common call setup and control protocols.

- **Network independence**—H.323 is designed to run on top of a common network infrastructure.

- **Platform and application independence**—H.323 is not tied to any hardware or operating system. H.323-compliant platforms are available on many different devices, including personal computers, IP-enabled telephone handsets, and voice-enabled gateways.

- **Bandwidth management**—Video and audio traffic is bandwidth-intensive and can clog a corporate network. H.323 addresses this issue by providing bandwidth management; network managers can limit the number of simultaneous H.323 connections within their network, or the amount of bandwidth available to H.323 applications. These limits ensure that critical traffic is not disrupted.

- **Multicast support**—H.323 supports multicast transport in multipoint conferences. Multicast sends a single packet to a subset of destinations on the network, without replication. In contrast, unicast sends multiple point-to-point transmissions, while broadcast sends to all destinations. In unicast or broadcast, the network is used inefficiently because packets are replicated throughout the network. Multicast transmission uses bandwidth more efficiently because all the stations in the multicast group receive from a single data stream.

- **Flexibility**—An H.323 conference can include endpoints with different capabilities. For example, a terminal with audio-only capabilities can participate in a conference with terminals that have video and data capabilities. An H.323 multimedia terminal can share the data portion of a videoconference with a data-only terminal while sharing voice, video, and data with other H.323 terminals.

H.323 Components

H.323 defines four major components for a network-based communications system: terminals, gateways, gatekeepers, and multipoint control units (MCUs).

Terminals

Terminals are client endpoints on the LAN that provide real-time, two-way H.323 communications. All terminals must support voice communications; video and data are optional. Examples of H.323 terminals are PCs with NetMeeting software, and IP telephones.

Gateways

A *gateway* is an optional element in the voice network and can be a voice-enabled router or switch. Gateways provide many services, such as translation between H.323 endpoints and other non-H.323 devices, which allows H.323 endpoints and non-H.323 endpoints to communicate. In addition, the gateway also translates between audio and video codecs and performs call setup and clearing on both the LAN side and the circuit-switched network side.

Gateways are not required between two terminals' connections because endpoints can communicate with each other directly. Terminals use the H.245 and Q.931 protocols to communicate with H.323 gateways.

Gatekeepers

A *gatekeeper* manages H.323 endpoints, allowing them to register with the gatekeeper, locate another H.323 endpoint or gatekeeper, and thus establish a call. A gatekeeper is usually used in larger, more complex networks. The gatekeeper function can be performed by Cisco IOS routers or by third-party software.

The terminals, gateways, and MCUs that are managed by a single gatekeeper are known as an H.323 zone. The gatekeeper serves as the central point for all calls within its zone and provides call control services to registered H.323 endpoints. All H.323 devices (gateways and terminals) in the zone register with the gatekeeper so the gatekeeper can perform its basic functions, such as H.323 address translation, admission control, bandwidth control, and zone management. Optionally it can provide call authorization and directory services.

The gatekeeper can balance calls among multiple gateways, either by integrating their addressing into the Domain Name System (DNS), or via Cisco IOS configuration options. For instance, if a call is routed through a gatekeeper, that gatekeeper can forward the call to the corresponding gateway based on some routing logic. In many ways, the H.323 gatekeeper functions as a virtual voice switch.

The Importance of a Gatekeeper

Figure 8-14 illustrates different voice design options and emphasizes the importance of a gatekeeper, especially in large voice network designs.

Figure 8-14 *The Importance of a Gatekeeper in Voice Networks*

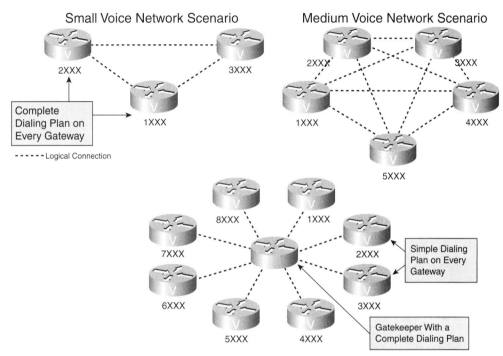

Voice network design depends primarily on the number of voice gateways and, consequentially, the number of logical connections between them. The maximum number of logical connections between voice gateways, and thus the network's complexity, can be represented by the formula $(N * (N-1))/2$, where N is the number of voice gateways in the system. For example, the maximum number of logical connections between three voice gateways is three, between five voice gateways is 10, and between eight voice gateways is 28. The complexity of the network grows quickly, and adding one voice gateway to the existing network means reconfiguring all other voice gateways; therefore, network maintenance becomes quite difficult. A solution for this issue is the use of a gatekeeper that stores the dialing plan of the entire zone. Gateways only have to register with the gatekeeper, and the gatekeeper provides all call control services to them. Thus, the configuration of a voice gateway becomes simpler and does not require any modifications when adding a new voice gateway to the system.

Multipoint Control Units

An *MCU* is an endpoint on the LAN that enables three or more terminals and gateways to participate in a multipoint H.323 conference. An MCU can be located on the terminal, gateway, or gatekeeper.

H.323 Example

Figure 8-15 illustrates the components that are typically involved in an H.323 call and the interactions between them.

Figure 8-15 *Interactions of H.323 Components*

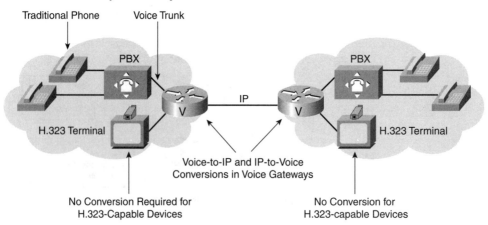

If traditional telephones are used and the calls must be transported across the IP network, a voice gateway is required on both sides. In this example, the gateway is a voice-enabled router that performs voice-to-IP and IP-to-voice conversions in special hardware called a *digital signal processor (DSP)*. After voice is converted into IP packets, the packets are transmitted across the IP network. The receiving router performs the same function in the reverse order—it converts IP packets back to voice signals and forwards them through the PBX to the destination telephone.

A voice gateway is not required when using H.323-capable devices (terminals) that communicate over IP. In this case, the router forwards IP packets it received from the H.323 device to the appropriate outgoing interface.

IP Telephony Introduction

IP telephony refers to cost-effective communication services, including voice, facsimile, and voice-messaging applications, that are transported via the IP network (packet-switched) rather than the PSTN (circuit-switched). IP telephony also provides IP-based PBX functionality.

Key Point: VoIP Versus IP Telephony

VoIP uses voice-enabled routers to convert analog voice from traditional telephones into IP packets and route those packets between corresponding locations. Users do not often notice that VoIP is implemented in the network; they use their traditional phones, connected to a PBX. However, the PBX is not connected to the PSTN or to another PBX, but to a voice-enabled router that is an entry point to VoIP.

IP telephony replaces traditional phones with IP phones and uses Cisco CallManager, which is a server for call control and signaling. The IP phone itself performs voice-to-IP conversion, and voice-enabled routers are not required within the enterprise network. If connection to the PSTN is required, a voice-enabled router or other gateway must be added where calls are forwarded to the PSTN.

The basic steps for originating an IP telephone call include converting the analog voice signal into a digital format and compressing and translating the digital signal into IP packets for transmission across the IP network. The process is reversed at the receiving end.

The IP telephony architecture includes four distinct components: infrastructure, call processing, applications, and clients. These components are described as follows:

- **Infrastructure**—The infrastructure is based on Layer 2 and Layer 3 switches and voice-enabled routers that interconnect endpoints with the IP and PSTN network. Endpoints are attached to the network using switched 10/100 Ethernet ports. Voice-enabled routers perform conversions between circuit-switched (PSTN) and IP networks.

- **Call processing**—*Cisco CallManager* is the software-based call-processing component of the Cisco enterprise IP telephony solution. CallManager provides a scalable, distributable, and highly available enterprise IP telephony call processing solution. CallManager performs much like the PBX in a traditional telephone network, including call setup and processing functions.

NOTE   For additional CallManager features, please refer to www.cisco.com/warp/public/cc/pd/nemnsw/callmn/prodlit/index.shtml.

- **Applications**—Applications use the IP telephony infrastructure and add additional features to the system. Voice mail, interactive voice response, Contact Center, and Automated Attendant are among the applications that are available in IP telephony. The open service application layer allows third-party companies to develop software that interoperates with Cisco CallManager.

- **Client devices**—Client devices are IP telephones and software applications that allow communications across the IP network. The Cisco CallManager centrally manages the IP telephones and powers them through Ethernet connections. They are usually located in the access layer and are connected to access switches.

IP Telephony Design Goals

An IP telephony network's overall design goals are as follows:

- **End-to-end IP telephony**—Using end-to-end IP telephony between sites where IP connectivity is already established. IP telephony could be simply deployed as an overlayed service that runs on the existing infrastructure.

- **Toll quality voice**—To make IP telephony widely employable, voice quality should be on the same level as in the traditional telephony; this is known as *toll quality voice*.

- **Reduced long distance costs**—Long distance costs should be lower than with traditional telephony. This can be accomplished by utilizing the public Internet or private IP networks for routing telephone calls.

- **More efficient WAN usage**—To make the IP telephony cost effective, the existing WAN capacity must be used more efficiently.

- **High availability**—For providing high availability of IP telephony, the primary voice path between sites (the Intranet or Internet) should be backed up with the PSTN as the secondary voice path.

- **Lower cost of ownership**—IP telephony should offer lower total ownership cost and greater flexibility than traditional telephony.

- **Enabling new applications**—New applications should be simply built around IP telephony by third-party software.

- **Improved productivity**—IP telephony should improve productivity of remote workers, agents, and stay-at-home staff.

- **Reduced operational and equipment costs**—Data and telephony network consolidation should lead to savings in operational and equipment costs.

The following sections illustrate some example IP telephony designs.

Single Site IP Telephony Design

Figure 8-16 illustrates a design model for an IP telephony network within a single campus or site.

Figure 8-16 *Single Site IP Telephony Design*

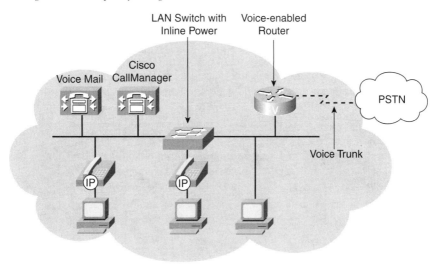

Single site IP telephony design consists of a Cisco CallManager, IP telephones, switches with inline power, applications such as voice mail, and a voice-enabled router at the same physical location. IP telephones are powered through the Ethernet interface of a LAN switch. For users to make external calls, gateway trunks are connected to the PSTN.

Single-site deployment allows each site to be completely self-contained. All calls to the outside world and remote locations are placed across the PSTN. Service is not lost if an IP WAN failure occurs or if there is insufficient bandwidth. There is no loss of the call processing service or functionality. The only external requirements are a PSTN carrier and route diversity within the PSTN network.

Centralized IP Telephony Design

Figure 8-17 presents the centralized call processing design model with a Cisco CallManager at the central site that connects to a remote location through the IP WAN.

Remote IP telephones rely on the centralized Cisco CallManager to handle their call processing. Applications such as voice mail and IVR systems are also centralized, thus reducing the overall cost of ownership and centralized administration and maintenance.

The remote location requires IP connectivity with the Enterprise Campus. IP telephones, powered by a local LAN switch, convert voice into IP packets and send them to the local LAN. The local router forwards the packets to the appropriate destination based on its routing table. Because the IP phones convert voice to IP, no voice capabilities are necessary on the router.

Figure 8-17 *Centralized IP Telephony Design*

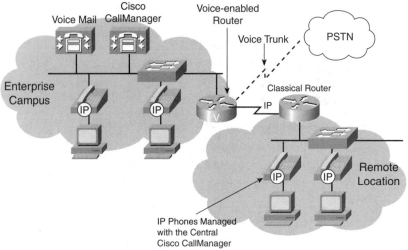

The Cisco CallManager and IP telephones on the remote location do not detect the WAN link between them. They communicate as if they were on the same LAN.

NOTE   The router in the Enterprise Campus network is voice-capable to enable voice communication with the outside world through the PSTN.

Internet IP Telephony Design

Figure 8-18 depicts the Internet IP telephony design, where the Internet is used for communicating between distant locations.

The Internet Service Provider (ISP) supplies Internet connectivity for enterprise locations. The ISP is not aware of IP telephony packets on its infrastructure. However, if high-quality voice communication over the Internet is required, the service provider must implement QoS mechanisms. Enterprises and ISPs usually sign a service-level agreement (SLA) that guarantees bandwidth and latency levels that are suitable for voice transport.

Internet IP telephony requires every location to have IP telephones and a call processing engine (such as the Cisco CallManager). Because Cisco routers that connect locations to the Internet see only data packets (some of which contain voice), no additional hardware is generally required.

Figure 8-18 *Internet IP Telephony Design*

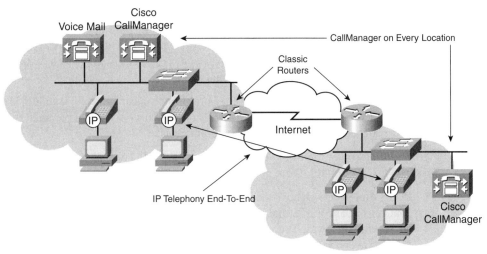

Voice Routing

Voice-enabled routers (voice gateways) are used for enabling voice to be carried to the PSTN, PBX, or analog phone from IP networks.

Voice Ports

When an interface on a voice gateway carries voice data, it is referred to as a *voice port*. A *voice port* is a physical port that comes with a voice module; this is what makes a router voice-enabled. A voice port carries one or more calls to the PSTN network, an Enterprise PBX, or an analog phone.

The voice module enables connectivity with other traditional circuit-switched voice devices and networks and converts voice into IP packets (and vice versa). Specialized processors, which are called digital signal processors and are located on the voice module, perform coding and compression of voice. The following interface types (voice ports) support voice processing (via VoIP) on Cisco voice gateways:

- ISDN PRI on an E1 or T1 voice module
- E1-R2 signaling on an E1 voice module
- T1-CAS signaling on a T1 voice module
- FXS on a low-capacity voice module
- FXO on a low-capacity voice module
- ISDN BRI on a low-capacity voice module

Dial Peers

When using a voice-enabled router (voice gateway) to facilitate communication between H.323 devices and traditional telephony, you should configure the applicable PSTN and VoIP dial peers on the voice gateway to enable voice routing between them. *Dial peers* are logical peers that are associated with physical voice ports. The voice gateway establishes a connection based on the configuration of dial peers.

Dial peers associate destination phone numbers with physical voice ports and IP, Frame Relay, and ATM addresses. They describe the connection's operational parameters. Dial peers are associated with incoming and outgoing calls.

Figure 8-19 illustrates the configuration of two types of dial peers, Plain Old Telephone System (POTS) and VoIP. There are four types of dial peers in total, as follows:

- **POTS dial peer**—Defines the characteristics of a traditional telephony network connection. The POTS dial peer maps a telephone dial string to a specific voice port on the voice gateway. The voice port connects the voice gateway to the local PSTN, PBX, or telephone.

- **VoIP dial peer**—Defines how to direct VoIP calls that originate locally on the router to their destination in the IP cloud. The VoIP dial peer contains the address of the remote voice gateway or other VoIP device where the call is terminated. There are several different ways to define the destination VoIP address:

  - Statically configuring the gateway's IP address.

  - Defining the name of the gateway, which can be resolved through the DNS name resolution.

  - Using the Registration, Admission, and Status protocol (RAS). When using RAS, the gateway determines the destination target by querying the H.323 gatekeeper.

- **VoFR dial peer**—Mapped to the Frame Relay data-link connection identifier (DLCI) of the interface from which the call exits the router. The destination telephone number is also mapped to the peer.

- **VoATM dial peer**—Mapped to the ATM virtual circuit of the interface, from which the call exits the router. The destination telephone number is also mapped to the peer.

Figure 8-19 *Dial Peers Associate Destinations with Voice Ports*

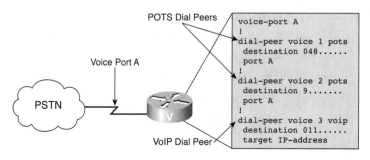

Relationship Between Dial Peers and Call Legs

Dial peers are used to apply attributes to call legs and to identify the call origin and destination.

A voice call over a packet network is segmented into discrete call legs that are associated with dial peers. A *call leg* is a logical connection between two voice gateways, or between a voice gateway and an IP telephony device.

Attributes that are applied to a call leg include QoS, codec, voice activity detection (VAD), and fax rate. There are two types of call legs: inbound and outbound. As illustrated in Figure 8-20, these call legs are defined from the voice gateway's (router's) perspective. An *inbound call leg* originates outside the voice gateway. An *outbound call leg* originates from the voice gateway. For inbound call legs, a dial peer might be associated with the calling number or the port designation. Outbound call legs always have a dial peer associated with them, and the destination pattern is used to identify the outbound dial peer. The call is associated with the outbound dial peer at setup time.

Figure 8-20 *Call Legs Are Defined from the Router's Perspective*

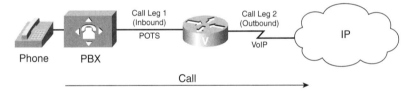

Unless otherwise configured, when a call arrives on the voice gateway, the gateway presents a dial tone to the caller and collects digits until it can identify the destination dial peer. After the dial peer has been identified, the call is forwarded through the next call leg, to the destination.

Voice Issues

Overall voice quality is a function of many factors, including delay, jitter, packet loss, and echo. This section discusses these factors and ways to minimize them.

Packet Delays

Voice quality in an IP network is directly affected by two main factors: packet loss and packet delay. Packet loss causes voice clipping and skips, while packet delay can cause voice quality degradation. When designing networks that transport voice over packet, frame, or cell infrastructures, you should understand and account for the network's delay components. Correctly accounting for all potential delays ensures that overall network performance is acceptable.

The generally accepted limit for good-quality voice connection delay is 150 milliseconds (ms) one-way. (There is a negligible difference in voice quality measurements that use networks built with a 200 ms delay budget.) As delays rise, the communication between two people falls out of synch (for example, they speak at the same time or both wait for the other to speak). This condition can be called *talker overlap*. The International Telecommunication Union (ITU) describes network delay for voice applications in recommendation G.114. As shown in Table 8-2, this recommendation defines three bands of one-way delay.

Table 8-2   *Recommended Delays for One-way Voice Traffic*

Delay	Effect on Voice Quality
0 to 150 ms	Acceptable for most user applications.
150 to 400 ms	Acceptable provided that administrators are aware of the transmission time and its impact on the transmission quality of user applications. (This is the expected range for a satellite link.)
Above 400 ms	Unacceptable for general network planning purposes; however, this limit is exceeded in some exceptional cases.

Voice packets are delayed if the network is congested because of poor network quality, underpowered equipment, congested traffic, or insufficient bandwidth. Packet loss and delay potential should be assessed during the initial design of voice on an IP network. Understanding the causes of packet loss and delay and their impact on business guides the design for QoS in all areas of an enterprise network. Different QoS mechanisms can be used to enable a high-quality voice network.

Delay can be classified into two types: fixed network delay and variable network delay.

Fixed Network Delay Considerations

Fixed network delays result from delays in network devices and contribute directly to the overall connection delay. As shown in Figure 8-21, fixed delays have three components: propagation delay, serialization delay, and processing delay.

Propagation delay is the length of time it takes to travel the distance between the sending and receiving endpoints. This form of delay, which is limited by the speed of light, can be ignored for most designs because it is relatively small compared to other types of delay. A popular estimate of 10 microseconds/mile or 6 microseconds/kilometer is used for estimating propagation delay.

Figure 8-21 *Fixed Delays Result from Delays in Network Devices*

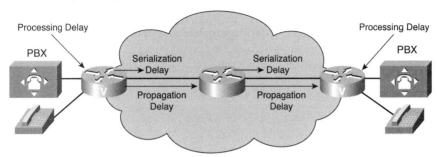

NOTE Propagation delay has a noticeable impact on the overall delay on satellite links only.

Serialization delay is the fixed delay you encounter when sending a voice or data frame onto the network interface (the result of placing bits on the circuit) and is directly related to the link speed. The higher the circuit speed, the less time it takes to place the bits on the circuit, and the less serialization delay. Serialization delay is a constant function of link speed and packet size. It is calculated by the formula (packet length)/(bit rate), which shows how large serialization delay occurs because of slow links or large packets. Serialization delay is always predictable; for example, when using a 64 kbps link and 80-byte frame, the delay is exactly 10 ms.

NOTE The previous example is calculated as follows:

- 64 kbps = 64000bits/sec * 1 byte/8bits = 8000 bytes/sec = 8000 bytes/1000 ms = 8 bytes/ms
- Serialization delay = packet length/bit rate = 80 bytes/8 bytes/ms = 10 ms

NOTE Serialization delay is only a factor for slow speed links up to 1 Mbps.

Processing delay, which is also known as *coder delay*, is the time the DSP takes to compress a block of PCM samples. Because different coders work in different ways, this delay varies depending on the voice coder that is used and the processor speed. Processing delays can be placed into the following categories:

- **Coding, compression, decompression, and decoding delays**—Depends on the algorithm that is employed. These functions can be performed in either hardware or software. Using specialized hardware such as a DSP dramatically improves the quality and reduces the delay that is associated with different voice compression schemes.

- **Packetization delay**—Results from the process of holding the digital voice samples for placement into the payload until enough samples are collected to fill the packet or cell payload. Partial packets can be sent to reduce excessive packetization delay, which is associated with some compression schemes.

Variable Network Delay Considerations

Variable network delay is more unpredictable and difficult to calculate than fixed network delay. Variable delays arise from queuing delays in the egress trunk buffers on the serial port that is connected to the WAN.

As shown in Figure 8-22 and described in the following sections, the following three factors contribute to a variable network delay: queuing delay, dejitter buffers, and variable packet sizes.

Figure 8-22 *Variable Delays Can Be Unpredictable*

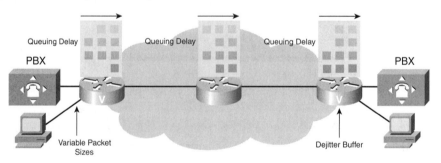

Queuing Delay

Key Point: Queuing Delay

Congested output queues on network interfaces are the most common sources of variable delay. Queuing delays are dependent on the link speed and the state of the queue.

Queuing delay occurs when a voice packet is waiting on the outgoing interface for others to be serviced first. This waiting time is statistically based on the arrival of traffic; the more inputs, the more likely that contention is encountered for the trunk. It is also based on the size of the packet that is currently being serviced.

Because voice should have absolute priority in the voice gateway queue, a voice frame should only wait for either a data frame that is already being sent, or for other voice frames ahead of it. For example, assume that a 1500-byte data packet is queued before the voice packet. The voice packet must wait until the entire data packet is transmitted, which produces a delay in the voice path. If the link is slow (for example, 64 kbps), the queuing delay might be more than 150 ms, which results in an unacceptable voice delay.

Link Fragmentation and Interleaving (LFI) is a solution for queuing delay situations. With LFI, large packets are fragmented into smaller frames and interleaved with small voice packets. Therefore, a voice packet does not have to wait until the entire data packet is sent. LFI reduces and ensures a more predictable voice delay.

Dejitter Buffers

Because network congestion can occur at any point in a network, interface queues can be filled instantaneously. This leads to a difference in delay times between packets that reside in the same voice stream.

Key Point: Dejitter Buffers

The variable delay between packets is called *jitter*.

Dejitter buffers are used at the receiving end to smooth delay variability and allow time for decoding and decompression.

Dejitter buffers help on the first talk spurt to provide smooth playback of voice traffic. Setting these buffers too low causes overflows and data loss, while setting them too high causes excessive delay.

In effect, dejitter buffers reduce or eliminate delay variation by converting it to fixed delay. However, depending on the variance of the delay, dejitter buffers always add delay to the total budget.

Dejitter buffers work most efficiently when packets arrive with a fairly uniform delay. Constant delay can be accomplished by avoiding network congestions, for which various QoS congestion avoidance mechanisms exist. If there is no variance in delay, dejitter buffers can simply be disabled, and the constant delay thus reduced.

NOTE   When using dejitter buffers, constant delay is always added to the total delay budget. Therefore, do not use dejitter buffers unless it is absolutely necessary.

Variable Packet Sizes

Variable delay is based on the size of the packet that is currently being serviced; larger packets take longer to transmit than do smaller packets. Therefore, a queue that combines large and small packets experiences varying lengths of delay.

LFI provides a solution for variable packet size delay by fragmenting packets into equal size frames. Configuring LFI fragmentation on a link provides a fixed delay; however, set the fragment size so that only data packets, not voice packets, become fragmented.

Jitter

Jitter is a variation in the delay of received packets.

At the sending side, the packets are sent in a continuous stream and are spaced evenly. Because of network congestion, improper queuing, or configuration errors, this steady stream can become lumpy; in other words, as shown in Figure 8-23, the delay between each packet can vary instead of remaining constant. This can be annoying to listeners.

Figure 8-23 *Jitter Is the Variation in the Delay of Received Voice Packets*

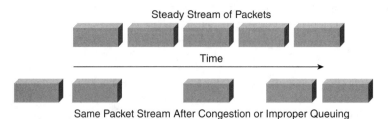

When a voice gateway receives an audio stream for VoIP, it must compensate for the jitter it encounters. The mechanism that handles this function is the dejitter buffer (as mentioned previously in the "Dejitter Buffers" section), which must buffer the packets and then play them out in a steady stream to the DSPs, which will convert them back to an analog audio stream. Because the dejitter buffer adds some additional delay to the delay budget, avoid it if it is not needed. The dejitter buffer is also referred to as the *playout delay buffer*.

Packet Loss

Packet loss causes voice clipping and skips. Packet loss can occur because of congested links, improper network QoS configuration, poor packet buffer management on the routers, routing problems, and so forth.

The industry standard codec algorithms that are used in the Cisco DSP can use interpolation to correct for up to 30 ms of lost voice. The Cisco VoIP technology uses 20-ms samples of voice payload per VoIP packet. Therefore, only a single packet can be lost during any given time for the codec correction algorithms to be effective.

Key Point: Small Packet Losses Are Not Audible

For packet losses as small as one packet, the DSP interpolates the conversation with what it thinks the audio should be, and the packet loss is not audible.

NOTE Losses also occur if the packets are received out of range of the dejitter buffer, in which case the packets are discarded.

Echo

In a voice telephone call, an echo occurs when callers hear their own words repeated. An *echo* is the audible leak of the caller's voice into the receive (return) path.

Echo is a function of delay and magnitude. The echo problem grows with the delay (the later the echo is heard) and the loudness (higher amplitude). When timed properly, an echo can be reassuring to the speaker. But if the echo exceeds approximately 25 milliseconds, it can be distracting and cause breaks in the conversation.

Key Point: An Echo Indicates a Problem at the Other End

Perceived echo most likely indicates a problem at the other end of the call. For example, if a person in Toronto hears an echo when talking to a person in Vancouver, the problem is likely to be at the Vancouver end.

The following VoIP network elements can affect echo:

- **Hybrid transformers**—A typical telephone is a two-wire device, while trunk connections are four-wire; a hybrid transformer is used to interface between these connections. Hybrid transformers are often prime culprits for signal leakage between analog transmit and receive paths. Echo is usually caused by a mismatch in impedance from the four-wire network switch conversion to the two-wire local loop.

- **Telephones**—The analog telephone terminal itself presents a load to the PBX. This load should be matched to the output impedance of the source device (the FXS port). Some (typically inexpensive) telephones are not matched to the FXS port's output impedance and are sources of echo. Headsets are particularly notorious for poor echo performance.

  When digital telephones are used, the point of digital-to-analog conversion occurs inside the telephone. Extending the digital transmission segments closer to the actual telephone decreases the potential for echo.

NOTE   The belief that adding voice gateways (routers) to a voice network creates echo is a common misconception. Digital segments of the network do not cause leaks; so, technically, voice gateways cannot be the source of echo. However, adding routers does add delay, which can make a previously imperceptible echo perceptible.

An echo canceller must be placed in the network to improve the quality of telephone conversation. An *echo canceller* is a component of a voice gateway that reduces the level of echo that has leaked from the receive path into the transmit path.

Echo cancellers are built into low bit-rate codecs and operate on each DSP. By design, echo cancellers are limited by the total amount of time they wait for the reflected speech to be received. This is known as an *echo trail* or *echo cancellation time* and is usually between 16 and 32 milliseconds.

To understand how echo cancellers work, assume that a person in Toronto is talking to a person in Vancouver. When the person in Toronto's speech hits an impedance mismatch or other echo-causing environment, it bounces back to that person, who can hear the echo several milliseconds after speaking.

Recall that the problem is at the *other* end of the call (called the *tail circuit*)—in this case, in Vancouver. To remove the echo from the line, the router in Vancouver must keep an inverse image of the Toronto person's speech for a certain amount of time. This is called *inverse speech*. The echo canceller in the router listens for sound coming from the person in Vancouver and subtracts the inverse speech of the person in Toronto to remove any echo.

The ITU-T defines an irritation zone of echo loudness and echo delay. A short echo (around 15 ms) does not have to be suppressed, while longer echo delays require strong echo suppression. Therefore, all networks that produce one-way time delays greater than 16 ms require echo cancellation. It is important to configure the appropriate echo cancellation time. If the echo cancellation time is set too low, callers still hear echo during the phone call. If the configured echo cancellation time is set too high, it takes longer for the echo canceller to converge and eliminate the echo.

Attenuating the signal below the noise level can also eliminate echo.

Voice Coding and Compression

In traditional telephony applications, PCM is used on synchronous digital channels with a constant stream of bits generated at 64 kbps, whether or not there is conversation. The average call has hundreds of brief silent periods, each of which wastes bandwidth and money. There is no alternative to this waste on standard telephone connections.

Packet voice transport can be used to avoid this bandwidth waste. In packet voice applications, speech is transported as data packets, which are only generated when there is actual speech to transport. Packet voice transport can reduce the effective bandwidth that is required for speech transport by approximately one third. Other strategies, including compression, can further reduce bandwidth requirements.

The following sections introduce coding and compression algorithms and standards.

Coding and Compression Algorithms

Advances in technology have greatly improved the quality of compressed voice and have resulted in a variety of coding and compression algorithms:

- **PCM**—The toll quality voice that is expected from the PSTN. PCM runs at 64 kbps and provides no compression, and therefore no opportunity for bandwidth savings.

- **Adaptive Differential Pulse Code Modulation (ADPCM)**—Provides three different levels of compression. The quality change is virtually imperceptible when compared to 64 kbps PCM. Some fidelity is lost as compression increases. Depending on the traffic mix, cost savings generally run at 25 percent for 32 kbps ADPCM, 30 percent for 24 kbps ADPCM, and 35 percent for 16-kbps ADPCM.

- **Low-Delay-Code Excited Linear Prediction Compression (LD-CELP)**—This algorithm models the human voice. Depending on the traffic mix, cost savings can be up to 35 percent for 16-kbps LD-CELP.

- **Conjugate Structure-Algebraic Code Excited Linear Prediction Compression (CS-ACELP)**—Provides 8 times the bandwidth savings over PCM. CS-ACELP is a more recently-developed algorithm that is modeled after the human voice and delivers quality that is comparable to LD-CELP and 24 kbps ADPCM. Cost savings are approximately 40 percent for 8-kbps CS-ACELP.

- **Code Excited Linear Prediction Compression (CELP)**—Provides huge bandwidth savings over PCM. Cost savings can be up to 50 percent for 5.3-kbps CELP.

The following section details voice coding standards based on these algorithms.

Voice Coding Standards (Codecs)

The ITU has defined a series of standards for voice coding and compression:

- **G.711**—Uses the 64 kbps PCM voice coding technique. G.711-encoded voice is already in the correct format for digital voice delivery in the public telephone network or through PBXs.

- **G.726**—Uses the ADPCM coding at 40, 32, 24, and 16 kbps. ADPCM voice can also be interchanged between packet voice and public telephone or PBX networks, provided that the latter has ADPCM capability.

- **G.728**—Uses the LD-CELP voice compression, which requires only 16 kbps of bandwidth. CELP voice coding must be transcoded to a public telephony format for delivery to or through telephone networks.

- **G.729**—Uses the CS-CELP compression that enables voice to be coded into 8 kbps streams. There are four forms of this standard, all of which provide speech quality similar to that of 32 kbps ADPCM.

- **G.723**—Uses the CELP compression for compressing speech at a very low bit rate. This codec has two associated bit rates: 5.3 and 6.3 kbps.

Codec Mean Opinion Score

Each codec provides a certain quality of speech. The quality of transmitted speech is a listener's subjective response. The *mean opinion score (MOS)* is a common benchmark used to determine the quality of sound that is produced by specific codecs.

With MOS, a wide range of listeners judge the quality of a voice sample (corresponding to a particular codec) on a scale of 1 (bad) to 5 (excellent). The scores are averaged to provide the MOS for that sample. Table 8-3 shows the relationship between codecs and MOS scores. It is evident that MOS decreases with increased codec complexity.

Table 8-3   *Voice Coding and Compression Results*

Algorithm	ITU Standard	Data Rate	MOS Score
PCM	G.711	64 kbps	4.1
ADPCM	G.726	16/24/32 kbps	3.85
LD-CELP	G.728	16 kbps	3.61
CS-ACELP	G.729	8 kbps	3.92
CELP	G.723	6.3/5.3 kbps	3.9/3.65

Codec Design Considerations

Although it might seem logical from a bandwidth consumption standpoint to convert all calls to low bit rate codecs to save bandwidth and consequently decrease infrastructure costs, the designer should consider both the expected voice quality and the bandwidth consumption when choosing the optimum codec. The designer should also consider the disadvantages of strong voice compression, including signal distortion resulting from multiple encodings. For example, when a G.729 voice signal is tandem-encoded three times, the MOS score drops from 3.92 (very good) to 2.68 (unacceptable). Another drawback is the codec-induced delay with low bit rate codecs.

Key Point: G.729 Is Usually Recommended

G.729 is a recommended voice codec for most WAN networks because of its relatively low bandwidth requirements and high MOS.

VoIP Control and Transport Protocols

Voice communication over IP can be considered a mix of control signals and voice conversations that are coded and compressed into IP packets.

Both reliable and unreliable transmissions are required for voice communication. These types of communications are described as follows:

- **Reliable transmission**—Reliable transmission guarantees sequenced, error-free, flow-controlled transmission of packets; however, it can delay transmission and reduce throughput. A connection-oriented mode is used for data transmission. In the IP stack, this type of transmission is accomplished with Transmission Control Protocol (TCP). Reliable transport (TCP) is used for all voice call control functions.

- **Unreliable transmission**—Unreliable transmission uses a connectionless mode for data transmission. The User Datagram Protocol (UDP), which provides best-effort delivery, provides this type of transmission in the IP stack. UDP is used for voice conversation transport between two endpoints.

Key Point: Voice Uses UDP

Control signals and data require reliable transport (using TCP) because the signals must be received in the order in which they were sent, and they cannot be lost. However, voice loses its value with time; if a voice packet is delayed, it might lose its relevance to the end user. Therefore, voice conversation uses the more efficient, unreliable transport (using UDP).

The following sections detail the protocols that are used for voice conversation traffic and call control functions.

Voice Conversation

As shown in Figure 8-24, the *Real-Time Transport Protocol (RTP)*, which runs on top of UDP, provides voice conversation between two IP endpoints. Because of the time-sensitive nature of voice transport, UDP is the logical choice for carrying voice.

Figure 8-24 *VoIP Control and Transport Protocols Use TCP and UDP*

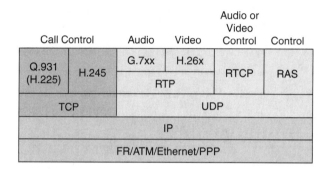

With voice conversation, more information is needed on a packet-by-packet basis than UDP offers, so RTP has been added for voice transport. RTP carries packet sequence and time-stamping information. RTP uses sequence information to determine whether the packets are arriving in order, and it uses the time-stamping information to determine the inter-arrival packet time (to determine the jitter). This information is essential for high-quality Voice over IP conversations.

Using RTP is important for real-time traffic; however, a few drawbacks exist. The IP/UDP/RTP packet headers are 20, 8, and 12 bytes, respectively. These add up to a 40-byte header, which is twice as big as the payload (compressed voice) when using G.729 codec. This large header adds considerable overhead to the voice traffic and reduces voice efficiency.

NOTE   Large IP/UDP/RTP headers can be compressed by using RTP header compression (using Compressed RTP [cRTP]). The "Bandwidth Considerations" section of this chapter further describes cRTP.

NOTE   Cisco IOS 12.0(7)T introduced the Express RTP Header Compression feature. Before this feature was available, if compression of cRTP was enabled, compression was performed in the process-switching path and slowed down packet transmission. With Express RTP header compression, compression occurs by default in the fast-switched path or the Cisco Express Forwarding-switched (CEF-switched) path, depending on which switching method is enabled on the interface.

Call Control Functions

Call control functions are the heart of voice communication. These functions include signaling for call setup, capability exchange, signaling of commands and indications, and messages to open and describe the content of logical channels. The following separate signaling functions provide overall system control:

- **H.225 call signaling channel**—Uses Q.931 to establish a connection between two terminals.

- **H.245 control channel**—A reliable channel that carries control messages that govern voice operation, including capabilities exchange, opening and closing of logical channels, preference requests, flow control messages, and general commands and indications. Capabilities exchange is one of the fundamental capabilities in the ITU recommendation.

- **Registration, Admission, and Status signaling**—Performs registration, admission, bandwidth changes, status, and disengage procedures between gateways and gatekeepers. The RAS protocol runs on UDP/IP. RAS is only used if a gatekeeper is present.

- **Real-time Transport Control Protocol (RTCP)**—Provides a mechanism for hosts that are involved in an RTP session to exchange information about monitoring and controlling the session. RTCP monitors quality for such elements as packet counts, packet loss, and inter-arrival jitter.

Figure 8-24 also shows these functions.

Bandwidth Considerations

This section introduces bandwidth considerations that must be addressed when designing voice on IP networks.

Bandwidth availability is the first and biggest issue when designing voice on IP networks. The amount of bandwidth per call increases or decreases greatly, depending on which codec is used and how many voice samples are required per packet. However, the best coding mechanism does not necessarily result in the best voice quality; for example, the better the compression, the worse the voice quality. The designer must decide which is more important, better voice quality or more efficient bandwidth consumption.

NOTE   The G.729 (8 kbps) codec is recommended on all WAN links. This is the default codec on the VoIP dial peers.

Reducing the Amount of Voice Traffic

Two techniques reduce the amount of traffic per voice call and therefore use available bandwidth more efficiently: the compressed Real-time Transport Protocol and voice activity detection (VAD).

Compressed Real-time Transport Protocol

All voice packets that are encapsulated into IP consist of two components: voice samples and IP/UDP/RTP headers. Although voice samples are compressed by the DSP and can vary in size based on the codec that is used, the headers are a constant 40 bytes. When compared to the 20 bytes of voice samples in a default G.729 call, the headers make up a considerable amount of overhead. cRTP compresses the headers to 2 or 4 bytes, thereby offering significant bandwidth savings. cRTP is sometimes referred to as *RTP header compression*.

Enabling compression on a low-bandwidth serial link can greatly reduce the network overhead and conserve WAN bandwidth if there is a significant volume of RTP traffic. In general, enable cRTP on slow links up to 2 Mbps. However, cRTP is not recommended for higher speed links because of its high central processing unit (CPU) requirements.

NOTE   Because cRTP compresses VoIP calls on a link-by-link basis, all links on the path must be configured for cRTP.

Voice Activity Detection

On average, about 35 percent of calls are silence. In traditional voice networks, all voice calls use a fixed bandwidth of 64 kbps regardless of how much of the conversation is speech and how much is silence. All conversation and silence is packetized with VoIP networks. VAD suppresses packets of silence. Rather than sending VoIP packets of silence, VoIP gateways can interleave data traffic with VoIP actual conversations; this results in more effective use of the network bandwidth.

Voice Bandwidth Requirements

When building voice networks, one of the most important factors to consider is correct bandwidth capacity planning. One of the most critical concepts to understand within capacity planning is how much bandwidth is used for each VoIP call.

Table 8-4 presents a selection of codec payload sizes and the required bandwidth, without compression and with cRTP. The last column shows the number of uncompressed and compressed calls that can be made on a 512 kbps link.

Table 8-4   *Voice Bandwidth Requirements*

Codec	Payload Size (Bytes)	Bandwidth (kbps)	Bandwidth with cRTP (kbps)	Number of Calls on a 512 kbps Link (No Compression/with cRTP)
G.711 (64 kbps)	160	83	68	6/7
G.726 (32 kbps)	60	57	36	8/14
G.726 (24 kbps)	40	52	29	9/17
G.728 (16 kbps)	40	35	19	14/26
G.729 (8 kbps)	20	26.4	11.2	19/46
G.723 (6.3 kbps)	24	18.4	8.4	28/64
G.723 (5.3 kbps)	20	17.5	7.4	30/73

The following assumptions are made in Table 8-4's bandwidth calculations:

- IP/UDP/RTP headers are 40 bytes
- RTP header compression can reduce the IP/UDP/RTP headers to 2 or 4 bytes (Table 8-4 uses 2 bytes)
- A Layer 2 header adds 6 bytes

Table 8-4 uses the following calculations:

- Voice packet size = (Layer 2 header) + (IP/UDP/RTP header) + (voice payload)
- Voice packets per second (pps) = codec bit rate/voice payload size
- Bandwidth per call = voice packet size * voice packets per second (pps)

For example, perform the following steps to calculate the bandwidth that is required for a G.729 call (8 kbps codec bit rate) with cRTP and default 20 bytes of voice payload:

- Voice packet size (bytes) = (Layer 2 header of 6 bytes) + (compressed IP/UDP/RTP header of 2 bytes) + (voice payload of 20 bytes) = 28 bytes
- Voice packet size (bits) = (28 bytes) * 8 bits per byte = 224 bits
- Voice packets per second = (8 kbps codec bit rate)/(8 bits/byte * 20 bytes) = (8 kbps codec bit rate)/(160 bits) = 50 pps
- Bandwidth per call = voice packet size (224 bits) * 50 pps = 11.2 kbps

Result: The G.729 call with cRTP requires 11.2 kbps of bandwidth.

QoS Mechanisms and Their Impact on Voice Quality

QoS mechanisms are important for networks that carry delay-sensitive traffic.

Modern integrated networks include protocols that are used by a variety of applications. This creates the demand for traffic prioritization to satisfy the requirements of time-critical applications (including voice). At the same time, the needs of less-time-dependent applications, such as file transfer, must be addressed.

If the network is designed to support a variety of traffic types on a single data path between routers, different QoS techniques must be considered to ensure that each data type is treated fairly.

Use the following guidelines to determine whether you require congestion management QoS:

- Traffic prioritization is important for delay-sensitive, interactive transaction-based applications. Always grant strict priority to delay-sensitive traffic at the expense of less-critical traffic.

- Prioritization is most effective on WAN links in which the combination of bursty traffic and relatively lower data rates can cause temporary congestion.

- Depending on the average packet size, prioritization is most effective when it is applied to links at T1/E1 bandwidth speeds or lower.

- If users of network applications notice poor response time, congestion management features must be considered.

- If there is no congestion on the WAN link, there is no reason to implement traffic prioritization.

Designing Voice QoS

The following steps summarize the aspects a designer should consider when determining whether to implement QoS in the network:

Step 1 Determine whether the WAN is congested—that is, whether application users perceive performance degradation.

Step 2 Determine the network goals and objectives based on the mix of network traffic. Following are some possible objectives:

- — To establish fair distribution of bandwidth allocation across all traffic types

- — To grant strict priority to voice traffic at the expense of less-critical traffic

- — To customize bandwidth allocation so that network resources are shared among all applications, each having specific bandwidth requirements

Step 3 Analyze the traffic types and determine how to distinguish them.

Step 4 Review the available QoS mechanisms and determine which approach best addresses the requirements and goals.

Step 5 Configure the routers for the chosen QoS strategy and observe the results.

The following section introduces some QoS mechanisms that can be used in voice networks.

QoS Mechanisms

As detailed in the following sections, these QoS mechanisms are available for voice:

- Bandwidth reduction
- Bandwidth reservation
- QoS classification
- Congestion avoidance
- Congestion management

Bandwidth Reduction

While many mechanisms exist to optimize throughput and reduce delay in network traffic within the QoS portfolio, QoS does not create additional bandwidth. As compression squeezes packets, it both increases the perceived throughput and decreases perceived latency because packets take less time to transmit. The bandwidth reduction mechanisms are payload compression, IP RTP compression, IP TCP header compression, and VAD.

Bandwidth Reservation

The Resource Reservation Protocol (RSVP) provides the network's capability of reserving bandwidth along the routing path and ensures a certain level of quality for delay-sensitive traffic.

QoS Classification

Because most QoS mechanisms support multiple classes, some classification is required to provide certain flows with priority. Classification is usually performed with access control lists or route maps. Setting the IP precedence bits in packets reflects the result of QoS classification. Voice is usually marked as an IP precedence of critical (5).

IP Precedence

IP precedence utilizes the 3 precedence bits in the IPv4 header's type of service (ToS) field to specify each packet's class of service. The IP precedence value ranges from 0 to 7, with 7 being the highest precedence and 0 being the lowest precedence. The IP precedence values are as follows:

— 0: routine

— 1: priority

— 2: immediate

— 3: flash

— 4: flashOverride

— 5: critical

— 6: internet

— 7: network

Congestion Avoidance

Congestion avoidance shapes and polices excess traffic from different flows, thereby causing applications to reduce the amount of traffic they send. *Shaping* is used to create a traffic flow that limits the flow's full bandwidth potential. *Policing* is similar to shaping, but it discards traffic that exceeds the configured rate. Cisco supports the Generic Traffic Shaping (GTS) method. Following are the supported policing methods:

- **Committed access rate (CAR)**—CAR can be used to rate-limit traffic based on certain matching criteria, such as incoming interface, IP precedence, or IP access list. Actions such as transmit, drop, or set precedence can be taken when traffic matches the criteria and conforms to or exceeds the rate limit.

- **Random early detection (RED)**—RED is a congestion avoidance mechanism that takes advantage of TCP's congestion control mechanism. By randomly dropping packets before periods of high congestion, RED tells the packet source to decrease its transmission rate.

- **Weighted random early detection (WRED)**—WRED selectively drops packets that are based on IP precedence: packets with a higher IP precedence are less likely to be dropped than packets with a lower precedence. Therefore, higher priority traffic is delivered with a higher probability than lower priority traffic.

Congestion Management

A queuing algorithm is used to sort an abundance of incoming traffic and to determine a method of prioritizing it onto an output link. The goal of congestion management is to classify traffic into QoS classes and prioritize it according to importance. Delay-sensitive traffic should have enough bandwidth and prioritized forwarding, while the least important traffic should have the remaining bandwidth. Cisco IOS software includes the following queuing mechanisms:

- **Priority Queuing (PQ)**—Defines how traffic is prioritized in the network. Four traffic queues can be configured. A series of filters based on packet characteristics (such as source IP address and port) is configured to cause the router to place some traffic, such as voice traffic, in the highest queue, and other traffic in the lower three queues. The highest priority queue is serviced first until the queue is empty; next, the lower queues are serviced in sequence.

- **IP RTP Priority**—Provides a strict priority queuing scheme for delay-sensitive traffic, such as voice. Voice traffic can be identified by its RTP port numbers and classified into a priority queue. The result is that delay-sensitive voice is serviced as strict priority over other non-voice traffic.

- **Custom Queuing (CQ)**—Allocates bandwidth proportionally for each class of traffic. CQ specifies the number of bytes or packets that are drawn from the queue, which is useful on slow interfaces. It services queues by cycling through them in a round robin fashion, sending the portion of allocated bandwidth for each queue before moving to the next queue. If one queue is empty, the router sends packets from the next queue that contains packets that are ready to send.

- **Weighted Fair Queuing (WFQ)**—Offers dynamic, fair queuing that divides bandwidth across queues of traffic based on weights. WFQ recognizes IP precedence. It applies priority, or weights, to identified traffic to classify it into conversations and determine how much bandwidth each conversation is allowed relative to other conversations. WFQ is a flow-based algorithm that simultaneously schedules voice traffic to the front of a queue to reduce response time, and shares the remaining bandwidth fairly among high-bandwidth flows.

- **Class-Based Weighted Fair Queuing (CBWFQ)**—Provides WFQ based on defined classes, but with no strict priority queue available for real-time traffic. All packets are serviced fairly based on weight; no class of packets can be granted strict priority. This scheme poses problems for voice traffic that is largely intolerant of delay, especially variation in delay. For voice traffic, variations in delay introduce irregularities of transmission that manifest as jitter in the conversation.

- **Low Latency Queuing (LLQ)**—Adds strict priority queuing to CBWFQ. LLQ is a combination of CBWFQ and PQ. Strict priority queuing allows delay-sensitive data, such as voice data, to be dequeued and sent first (before packets in other queues are dequeued), thereby giving delay-sensitive data preferential treatment over other traffic.

Key Point: LLQ for Voice

LLQ is the preferred queuing mechanism for designing voice on IP networks.

NOTE   Chapter 5, "Designing WANs," also covers queuing.

The following documents contain additional information about QoS and queuing:

— *Cisco IOS Quality of Service Solutions Configuration Guide,* available at www.cisco.com/univercd/cc/td/doc/product/software/ios122/122cgcr/ fqos_c/index.htm.

— *QoS Features for Voice,* available at www.cisco.com/univercd/cc/td/doc/ product/software/ios122/122cgcr/fqos_c/fqcprt7/qcfvoice.htm.

Use the most recent version of Cisco IOS software to obtain the best queuing features. If possible, use LLQ and classify voice in a priority queue. Set the voice class's bandwidth to the aggregate voice bandwidth on the link and allow for a little overhead. Use IP RTP Priority if LLQ is not available.

Figure 8-25 illustrates why LLQ is the preferred queuing mechanism for voice transport on integrated networks.

Figure 8-25 *With LLQ Voice, Traffic Achieves High Priority*

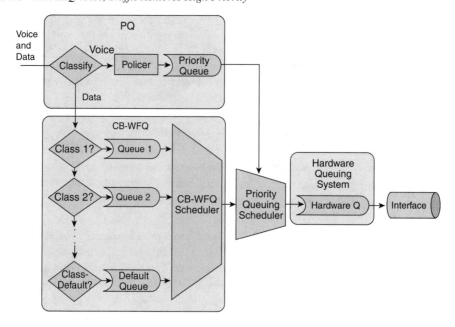

The advantage of LLQ is that it guarantees bandwidth for voice through the policing mechanism and gives it a priority. LLQ reduces jitter in voice conversations. The remaining traffic is classified using CBWFQ.

AutoQoS for Voice over IP

Cisco AutoQoS is an innovative technology that simplifies network administration challenges, thereby reducing QoS complexity, deployment time, and cost in Enterprise networks. AutoQoS incorporates intelligence in Cisco IOS software and Cisco Catalyst Operating System software to provision and manage large-scale QoS deployments.

The first phase of AutoQoS provides capabilities for automating VoIP deployments for enterprises that want to deploy IP telephony but that lack the expertise and/or staffing to plan and deploy IP QoS and IP services. AutoQoS simplifies deployment and speeds provisioning of QoS technology over a Cisco network infrastructure. Successful QoS deployments can be provisioned and managed using Cisco AutoQoS together with CiscoWorks QoS Policy Manager (QPM).

As described in Figure 8-26, AutoQoS addresses five key elements of QoS deployment.

Figure 8-26 *Cisco AutoQoS Simplifies QoS Deployment*

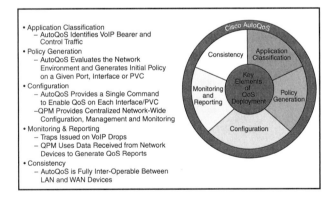

AutoQoS provides QoS provisioning for individual routers and switches, thereby simplifying deployment and reducing human error. It addresses the major elements of end-to-end QoS deployments, leveraging decades of networking experience, extensive lab performance testing, and input from a broad base of customer installations to determine the optimal QoS configuration for typical VoIP deployments. Only one command is required to enable QoS for VoIP on each Cisco router and switch. An AutoQoS-generated policy can be modified to meet your specific requirements.

QPM provides centralized QoS design, administration, and traffic monitoring that scales to large QoS deployments. While AutoQoS allows a user to configure QoS at the device level, enterprises use QPM to cost-effectively manage QoS in their IP network. QPM wizards intelligently guide users through Campus-to-WAN QoS policy configuration, while Cisco- and customer-defined policy libraries streamline global QoS configuration for voice, video, and data. QPM also enables the user to measure traffic throughput for service classes and top applications, including IP Telephony; users can also troubleshoot problems with real-time and historical QoS feedback.

Table 8-5 details platform support for the initial release of AutoQoS.

Table 8-5   *Cisco AutoQoS Platform Support*

Device	Platforms	Software
Switches	Cisco Catalyst 2950EI Cisco Catalyst 3550	Cisco IOS Software Release 12.1(12c)EA1
	Cisco Catalyst 4500	Cisco IOS Software Release 12.1(19)E
	Cisco Catalyst 6500	Cisco Catalyst Operating System 7.5.1
Routers	Cisco 2600 Series Cisco 2600XM Series Cisco 3600 Series Cisco 3700 Series Cisco 7200 Series	Cisco IOS Software Release 12.2(15)T

NOTE   You can find additional details about AutoQos in *Quality of Service Deployments: Cisco AutoQos*, available at www.cisco.com/warp/public/732/Tech/qos/docs/ autoqos_datasheet.pdf.

NOTE   Additional information about CiscoWorks QoS Policy Manager 3.0 is available at www.cisco.com/en/US/products/sw/cscowork/ps2064/ps4622/index.html.

Voice over Frame Relay

Frame Relay is commonly used in corporate data networks for its flexible bandwidth, widespread accessibility, support of a diverse traffic mix, and technological maturity. VoFR was introduced to enable companies to utilize the same infrastructure for voice transport.

Key Point: VoFR Versus VoIP over Frame Relay

Designers often confuse VoFR with VoIP that runs over Frame Relay. When carrying the voice from source to destination, no IP is involved in any stage of VoFR. In VoFR implementations, a voice-enabled router encodes the voice that was received from the PBX directly into Frame Relay frames and forwards those frames onto the Frame Relay network.

Frame Relay is not a LAN solution and therefore cannot be used from end to end, like Voice over IP. VoFR connects distant PBXs and keeps the existing telephone equipment in place. VoFR is a logical progression for corporations that already run data over Frame Relay.

Frame Relay is usually deployed at low speeds (from about 64 kbps to 512 kbps), which brings its own challenges in terms of preserving voice quality over these links. Frame Relay's key component is the contracted data rate, which is called the *committed information rate (CIR)* that is purchased for the link.

To ensure proper voice quality, you must strictly adhere to traffic shaping to CIR. Traffic shaping shapes the total permanent virtual circuit (PVC) traffic to conform to CIR, committed burst (Bc), and excess burst (Be). Data traffic should be marked as discard eligible (DE) to ensure that if the traffic exceeds the traffic contract, the carrier drops the data packets and the voice traffic is not affected.

VoFR Implementations

VoFR supports two main voice implementations:

- **Static FRF.11 trunks**—Like permanent switched trunks, these are used to create fixed point-to-point connections, which are typically used to connect two PBXs. This functionality is sometimes referred to as *tie-line emulation*. In this case, the VoFR system provides transportation of the voice connection channels, but does not provide telephone call switching based on dial plan information. PBXs perform all telephone call switching.

- **Dynamic switched VoFR calls**—The VoFR system includes dial plan information that is used to process and route calls based on the telephone numbers the callers dial. Every VoFR router in the path contains the dial plan information within dial-peer entries.

Figure 8-27 illustrates the two possible implementations of VoFR: static FRF.11 trunk and dynamic switched VoFR calls.

Figure 8-27 *Static Versus Dynamic VoFR Implementation*

Static FRF.11 Trunk Implementation

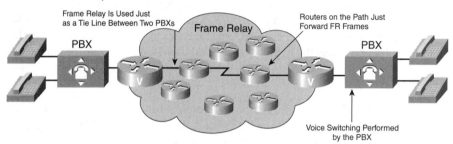

Dynamic Switched VoFR Implementation

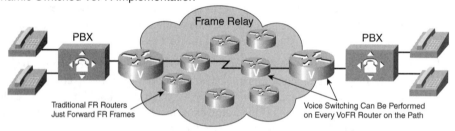

VoFR Design Guidelines

Implementing VoFR requires users to shift how they conceive and build their networks.

The two extremes for designing a VoFR network include a fully meshed topology and a hub and spoke topology.

Fully Meshed Topology

Figure 8-28 illustrates a fully meshed topology. This is feasible in a private Frame Relay network because the user can theoretically define one PVC for each telephone number and establish any-to-any connectivity without paying surcharges. Implementing this type of interconnectivity in the public Frame Relay network is similar to building a leased-line meshed network, which can be prohibitively expensive. A fully meshed topology minimizes the number of network transit hops and maximizes the ability to establish different qualities of service; a fully virtual meshed topology network minimizes delay and improves voice quality, but results in the highest network cost.

NOTE   A DLCI identifies a PVC in a Frame Relay network.

Figure 8-28 *A Fully Meshed Frame Relay Topology Can Be Costly*

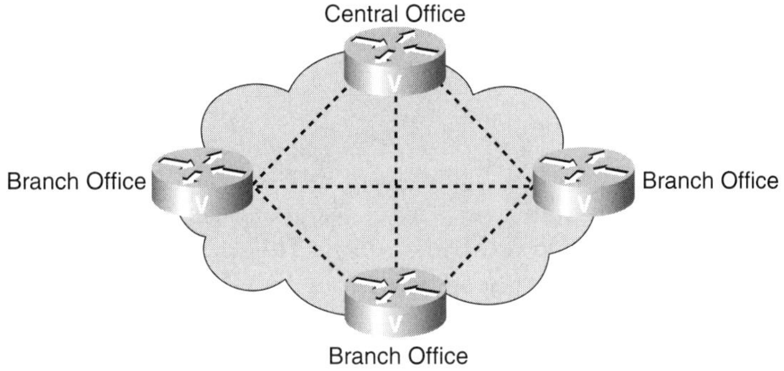

Hub and Spoke Topology

Figure 8-29 illustrates a hub and spoke topology, which is the optimal network topology for VoFR. This paradigm presumes that the majority of voice and data traffic occurs between a branch office and the central headquarters. It is more economical to designate single PVCs between individual branches and the central office than to construct a network that maps PVCs from branch to branch. Most Frame Relay providers charge on the basis of the number of PVCs used. To reduce costs, both data and voice segments can be configured to use the same PVC, thereby reducing the number of PVCs required. In this design, the central site switch reroutes voice calls. This design has the potential to create a transit hop when voice must travel from one remote office to another remote office, thereby adding some extra delay and reducing voice quality.

Figure 8-29 *Hub and Spoke Frame Relay Topology Is Optimal for VoFR*

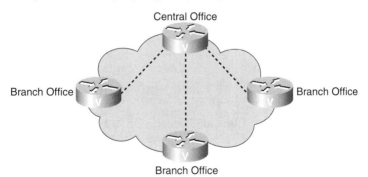

Key Point: Hub and Spoke Topology for VoFR

A hub and spoke is the optimal topology for VoFR.

Voice over ATM

VoATM enables voice traffic (such as telephone calls and faxes) to be transported over an ATM network. This section describes which ATM classes of services and adaptation types should be used for voice transport when using VoATM.

ATM Introduction

ATM is a multiservice, high speed, scalable technology. It is a dominant switching fabric in carrier backbones that supports services with different transfer characteristics.

ATM transports voice, data, graphics, and video simultaneously at very high speeds. It transmits information in fixed-length (53-byte) cells based on application demand and priority. 5 bytes are used for the ATM cell header, leaving 48 bytes for voice or data.

The basic characteristics of ATM are as follows:

- Uses small, fixed-sized cells (53 bytes)
- Connection-oriented protocol
- Supports multiple service types
- Applies to LAN and WAN traffic
- ATM virtual circuits emulate PSTN circuits
- Minimizes delay and delay variation (jitter)

ATM Classes of Services

The ATM Forum and the ITU have specified the following different classes of service to represent different possible traffic types for VoATM:

- **Real-time services: Constant bit rate (CBR) and variable bit rate (VBR) classes**—These classes of service are designed primarily for voice communications because they have provisions for transporting real-time traffic and are suitable for guaranteeing a certain level of service. In particular, CBR allows the amount of bandwidth, end-to-end delay, and delay variation to be specified during the call setup.

- **Non-real-time services: Unspecified bit rate (UBR) and available bit rate (ABR) classes**—These classes of service are designed principally for bursty traffic and are therefore more suitable for data applications. UBR, in particular, makes no guarantees about the delivery of the data traffic.

ATM networks typically have low overall jitter, and VBR real-time service from the network ensures that voice packets are transported efficiently within the backbone to minimize delay and jitter.

Key Point: ATM Class of Service for VoATM

VBR is the preferred ATM class of service for VoATM transport.

ATM Adaptation Types

The method of transporting information through an ATM network depends on the nature of the traffic. Different ATM adaptation types have been developed for different traffic types, each with its benefits and downsides.

ATM adaptation L1 (AAL1) is the most common adaptation layer that is used with CBR services, while ATM adaptation L2 and L5 (AAL2 and AAL5) are widely used for voice over packet transports.

AAL5 Adaptation Type

AAL5 uses separate voice and data virtual circuits or mixed voice and data traffic on the same virtual circuit. This method of VoATM is most often used for toll bypass enterprise networks.

AAL2 Adaptation Type

The ATM Forum standardized VoATM with the use of AAL2-based cells. These solutions are standards-based and are deployed for PSTN access where voice and data use separate virtual circuits because data traffic does not use AAL2 cells. AAL2 enables a variable payload within cells. This functionality improves bandwidth efficiency over structured or unstructured circuit emulation that uses AAL1. In addition, AAL2 supports voice compression and silence suppression. It allows multiple voice channels with varying bandwidth on a single ATM connection.

Key Point: AAL2 for VoATM

AAL2 is the preferred solution for VoATM.

AAL1 Adaptation Type

AAL1 is also called *circuit emulation service (CES)*. It uses ATM to provide trunking between two points and typically uses AAL1 cells with CBR service. CBR, the highest ATM service quality class, provides CES, which transmits a continuous bit stream of information. This allocates a constant amount of bandwidth to a connection for the duration of a transmission. Although it guarantees high quality voice, CES monopolizes bandwidth that could be used for other applications. In addition, in the interest of reducing delay, CES might send the fixed-size ATM cells half empty rather than waiting 6 milliseconds for 47 bytes of voice to fill the cell. This wastes more than 20 bytes of bandwidth per ATM cell. Using AAL1 for VoATM increases the overhead of voice transmissions and wastes bandwidth; therefore, it is not recommended.

VoATM Design Guidelines

Figure 8-30 illustrates a VoATM implementation. As voice traffic is sent over ATM, the signal is encapsulated using a special AAL2 encapsulation for multiplexed voice. The ATM PVC must be configured to support real-time voice traffic, and the AAL2 voice encapsulation must be assigned to the PVC. For traffic shaping between voice and data PVCs, the PVC must also be configured to support VBR for real-time networks.

Figure 8-30 *VoATM Implementation Using AAL2 and PVCs with VBR*

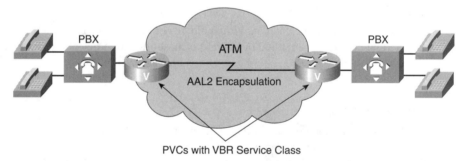

Traffic shaping is necessary for ensuring that the carrier does not discard the incoming calls. To configure voice and data traffic shaping with VBR, the peak, average, and burst options for voice traffic must be configured. The burst value is mandatory if the PVC carries bursty traffic. Based on these values, the PVC can effectively handle the bandwidth for the number of voice calls.

To send VoATM, a voice gateway is necessary for coding voice into cells for transport, and for decoding those cells at the destination. A voice gateway must also handle the telephone signaling that is used by both the voice source and destination to receive the called party's number and deliver call progress signals. A voice gateway must understand the signaling or addressing the ATM network cloud needs to reach the various destination voice gateways. This capability is important when translating between a traditional voice network and an ATM network.

Capacity Planning Using Voice Traffic Engineering Concepts

The section presents capacity planning design guidelines for minimizing degraded voice service in integrated networks. From trunks and DSPs to WAN and campus components, detailed capacity planning of all network resources is required. Calls must be rerouted via the next available route in extreme situations, when a shortage of these resources occurs. This section focuses on resource planning with regard to Grade of Service (GoS), voice quality, and costs.

On-net and Off-net Calling

Many companies oversubscribe their inter-location tie lines, assuming that not all callers use telephones and data connections over those tie lines at the same time. When these tie lines become congested and additional voice calls cannot be established over the tie lines, a feature called on-net/off-net calling can be used:

- **On-net calling**—Refers to voice calls that are transmitted over private inter-location tie lines; the call originates and terminates on the private network. Use on-net calling whenever possible because it utilizes the existing private infrastructure.

- **Off-net calling**—If the private tie line is congested, voice gateways select an alternative path, which is usually the PSTN. This type of calling is referred to as off-net calling because the calls go off the private network. These calls are usually more expensive, but the quality of the voice conversation is sustained. Off-net calling is also used when the called party cannot be reached over the private network; however, a long distance call should stay on-net for as long as possible and go off-net as close to its destination as possible. This feature is referred to as *automatic route selection*, or *least-cost routing*.

The following two combinations of on-net and off-net calling exist:

- **On-net to off-net calling**—A call originates in the private network and is carried over private tie lines close to the call's destination and then connected to the PTSN. This is sometimes referred to as *Tail End Hop Off (TEHO)*.

- **Off-net to on-net calling**—A call originates at sites that are connected via the PTSN and terminates in the private network. This is sometimes referred to as *Head End Hop On (HEHO)*.

NOTE   Cisco CallManager and voice gateways allow on-net and off-net automatic route selection and manual route selection. Manual route selection enables callers to dial an access number, such as 9, to access an outbound (PSTN) trunk, or 8 to reach other locations on the corporate network. With this feature, a caller selects the path manually.

Figure 8-31 shows how on-net and off-net calling are performed.

Figure 8-31 *On-net and Off-net Calling*

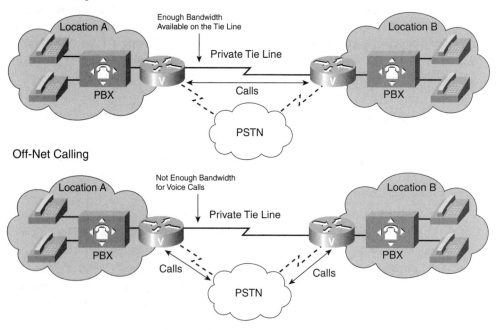

The top network in Figure 8-31 shows on-net calling—the user places a call from Location A to Location B across the data network using a private tie line.

In off-net calling (shown in the lower network in Figure 8-31), either the user dials an access code or the voice gateway automatically selects the path by which to access the PSTN. A second dial tone can usually be heard when the call reaches the PSTN. At this point, the user dials the destination number.

When on-net resources are unavailable to complete the call, the voice gateway responds in the following ways:

- If the far-end voice gateway has no available circuit to the PBX to which it is connected, the router sends the *busy-back signal* (which indicates a busy, or congested, state along the route) and the near-end router reroutes the call off-net.

- If the near-end voice gateway that uses QoS features detects that there is not enough bandwidth to complete the call, it reroutes the call off-net.

Figure 8-32 shows an example of least-cost routing using private tie lines on the long-distance portion of the call, and then using the PSTN locally to the destination number.

Figure 8-32 *Least-cost Routing Example*

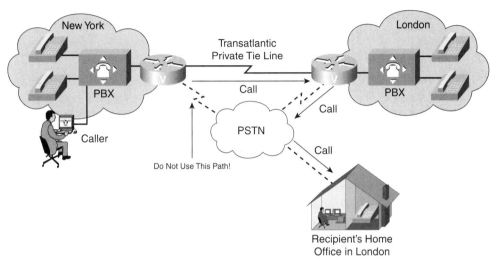

In Figure 8-32, a caller in a branch office in New York places a call to a recipient in a home office in London, England. On New York's voice gateway, the voice is coded and compressed into the VoIP call and transported over the private tie line to the London office, where the signal is decoded, decompressed, and transported over the PSTN to the home office.

Considerations When Migrating to an Integrated Network

When migrating from separate data and voice networks to an integrated network, you must consider several factors about the dialing plan and on-net and off-net calls to ensure a smooth migration and a manageable network. These factors include the following:

- Does the dialing plan remain unchanged from the user's perspective, or will a new access code be introduced to allow users to choose the IP network or the PSTN?

- Will the IP network only carry on-net calls, or will it also provide gateways to the PSTN? If it only accommodates on-net calls, only the company's private dialing plan must be implemented.

- If off-net calls are also to be accommodated, the gateway might have to translate an internally dialed number to a publicly accessible PSTN number; this includes adding and deleting country and regional area or city codes.

- How will users select between off-net and on-net calls?

- How will least-cost routing be accommodated?

GoS

GoS, the probability of a voice call being blocked, is a key component of resource and capacity planning.

Grade of Service Introduction

Key Point: GoS

GoS is the probability that a call will be blocked while attempting to seize circuits during the busiest hour.

The GoS is written as a blocking factor, Pxx, where xx is the percentage of calls that are blocked for a traffic system. For example, traffic facilities that require P01 GoS define a 1 percent probability of callers being blocked.

The number of simultaneous conversations affects the voice traffic. Users vary widely in the number of calls they attempt per hour and the length of time they hold a circuit. Any user's attempts and holding times are independent of the other users' activities. To determine traffic capacity, a common method is to use a call logger and plot the number of simultaneous calls on the network to determine the probability that exactly x simultaneous calls will occur. Voice systems can be provisioned to allow the maximum number of simultaneous conversations that are expected at the busiest time of the day.

Common methods of measuring voice traffic are Erlang and centum call seconds (CCS), which we discuss in the following sections.

Erlang

The *Erlang* is one of the most common measurements of voice traffic—one Erlang equals one full hour, or 3600 seconds, of telephone conversation. For example, if a trunk carries 12.35 Erlangs during an hour, an average of a little more than 12 lines (connections) are busy. Erlang tables show the amount of traffic potential for specified numbers of circuits for given probabilities of receiving a busy signal. The calculation results are usually stated in centum (hundreds) call seconds.

Key Point: Erlang

One Erlang equals one full hour, or 3600 seconds, of telephone conversation.

The traffic potential shown in the Erlang tables is the *busy hour traffic* (*BHT*), or the number of hours of call traffic during the busiest hour of the telephone system's operation.

Centum Call Second

Key Point: Centum Call Second

A CCS represents 1/36th of an Erlang.

To calculate a centum call second, multiply the number of calls per hour by their average duration in seconds and divide the result by 100.

A system port that can handle a continuous one-hour call has a traffic rating of 36 centum call seconds. Station traffic varies greatly among users, but the typical range is approximately 6 to 12 centum call seconds per port. If no exact statistical data exists, we can assume that the average typical trunk traffic is 30 centum call seconds per port.

For example, one hour of conversation, or one Erlang, might be 10 6-minute calls or 15 4-minute calls. Receiving 100 calls, with an average length of 6 minutes, in one hour is equivalent to 10 Erlangs, or 360 centum call seconds.

Erlang Tables

Erlang tables combine offered traffic, number of circuits, and grade of service in the following traffic models:

- **Erlang B**—This is the most common traffic model, which is used to calculate how many lines are required if the traffic (in Erlangs) during the busiest hour is known. The model assumes that all blocked calls are cleared immediately.

- **Extended Erlang B**—This model is similar to Erlang B, but it takes into account the additional traffic load caused by blocked callers who are immediately trying to call again. The retry percentage can be specified.

- **Erlang C**—This model assumes that all blocked calls stay in the system until they can be handled. This model can be applied to the design of call center staffing arrangements in which calls that cannot be answered immediately enter a queue.

NOTE   Erlang tables can be found at www.erlang.com/.

Figure 8-33 shows part of an Erlang B table. The column headings show the GoS, the row headings show the number of circuits (simultaneous connections), and the table cells provide the amount of BHT for the specified number of circuits with the specified GoS.

Figure 8-33 *An Erlang B Table Is Used to Determine Required Trunk Capacity*

	No. of Erlangs Increases with the Increased Blocking Probability			No. of Erlangs Increases with the No. of Simultaneous Connections		
GOS= Blocking Probability	.003	.005	.01	.02	.03	.05
No. of Circuits						
1	.003	.006	.011	.021	.031	.053
2	.081	.106	.153	.224	.282	.382
3	.289	.349	.456	.603	.716	.900
4	.602	.702	.870	1.093	1.259	1.525
5	.996	1.132	1.361	1.658	1.876	2.219
6	1.447	1.822	1.900	2.278	2.543	2.961
7	1.947	2.158	2.501	2.936	3.250	3.738
8	2.484	2.730	3.128	3.627	3.987	4.543
9	3.053	3.333	3.783	4.345	4.748	5.371
10	3.648	3.961	4.462	5.084	5.530	6.216

Busy Hour Traffic (BHT) in Erlangs

The required trunk capacity, which equals the number of circuits that are required for the known amount of traffic, can be estimated by using the Erlang B traffic model; the busy hour traffic and blocking probability are required as inputs. (After determining the number of required circuits, some organizations move circuits from the current network to the integrated network, while other organizations take this opportunity to update traffic engineering information and conduct a traffic study.)

Busy Hour Traffic

The BHT value represents the quantity of traffic expressed in Erlangs; one Erlang can be considered equivalent to one hour of calls. You must provide an estimate for this figure, which represents the number of hours of traffic that is transported across a trunk group in its busiest hour. For example, if you know from your call logger that 350 calls are made on a trunk group in an hour and that the average call duration is 180 seconds, you can calculate the busy hour traffic as follows:

- BHT = Average call duration (seconds) * calls per hour/3600
- BHT = 180 * 350/3600
- BHT = 17.5 Erlangs

Blocking Probability

The *blocking probability value (GoS)* describes the calls that cannot be completed because insufficient lines have been provided. A value of 0.01 means that 1 percent of calls would be blocked. Usually, a blocking factor of 5 percent (0.05) is used in traffic engineering.

Erlang Examples

Having established the BHT and blocking probability, the required number of circuits can be estimated using the Erlang B traffic model. For example, given a BHT = 3.128 Erlangs, a blocking = 0.01, and looking at the Erlang table in Figure 8-33, the number of required circuits is eight.

NOTE   An Erlang table calculator can be found at www.erlang.com/calculator/erlb/.

NOTE   Most telecommunication organizations currently use a blocking factor of 5 percent; this means that 5 percent of the time during the busy hour, users are expected to wait or busy out because of trunk unavailability. Degrading the service by 1 percentage point results in large trunk savings because circuit numbers (and therefore cost) decrease exponentially with increasing GOS.

As another example, look at Figure 8-33; 4.462 Erlangs of traffic is offered for 10 circuits (simultaneous connections) with a GoS P01 (1 percent block probability). 4.462 Erlangs equals approximately 160 centum call seconds (4.462 * 36). Assuming that there are 20 users in the company, perform the following steps to calculate how long each user can talk:

- BHT = Average call duration (seconds) * calls per hour/3600
- 4.462 = Average call duration (seconds) * 20/3600
- Average call duration = 800 seconds = 13.3 minutes

In another example, six circuits at P05 GoS handle 2.961 Erlangs. 2.961 Erlangs equals approximately 107 centum call seconds (2.961 * 36). Assuming that there are 10 users in the company, to calculate how long every user can talk, do the following:

- BHT = Average call duration (seconds) * calls per hour/3600
- 2.961 = Average call duration (seconds) * 10/3600
- Average call duration = 1066 seconds = 17 minutes

Trunk Capacity Calculation Example

The objective of this example is to determine the number of circuits, or the trunk capacity, that is required between each branch office and an enterprise's headquarters office.

The following assumptions apply to this example network:

- The network design is based on a star topology that connects each branch office directly to the main office.

- There are approximately 15 people per branch office.

- The bidirectional voice and fax call volume totals about two-and-a-half (2.5) hours per person per day (in each branch office).

- Approximately 20 percent of the total call volume is between the headquarters and each branch office.

- The busy-hour loading factor is 17 percent (in other words, the busy-hour traffic is 17% of the total traffic).

- One 64 kbps circuit supports one call.

- The acceptable GoS is P05.

Following are the voice and fax traffic calculations for this example:

- 2.5 hours call volume per user per day * 15 users = 37.5 hours daily call volume per office

- 37.5 hours * 17 percent (busy hour load) = 6.375 hours of traffic in the busy hour

- 6.375 hours * 60 minutes per hour = 382.5 minutes of traffic per busy hour

- 382.5 minutes per busy hour * 1 Erlang/60 minutes per busy hour = 6.375 Erlangs

- 6.375 Erlangs * 20 percent of traffic to headquarters = 1.275 Erlangs volume proposed

To determine the appropriate number of trunks that are required to transport the traffic, the next step is to consult Erlang table, given the desired GoS; this organization chose a P05 GoS. Using the 1.275 Erlangs and GoS = P05, as well as the Erlang B table (in Figure 8-33), four circuits are required for communication between each branch office and the headquarters office.

Off-net Calls Cost Calculation Example

It is important to design a network so that voice calls that oversubscribe the allocated network bandwidth are kept off the network and rerouted via an alternate path, such as the PSTN. A voice QoS category called *Call Admission Control (CAC)* is a base for handling oversubscribed calls off-net. For example, if the WAN access link from a branch office is provisioned to carry no more than five simultaneous calls, the sixth call must not be allowed onto the network because it will impair voice quality. This is also known as *protecting voice from voice*.

The following example calculates the off-net cost of calls between two locations, New York and London, as shown in Figure 8-34. The PSTN path is used when the transatlantic tie line cannot accept additional on-net calls.

Figure 8-34 *Off-net Calls Are Sometimes Required*

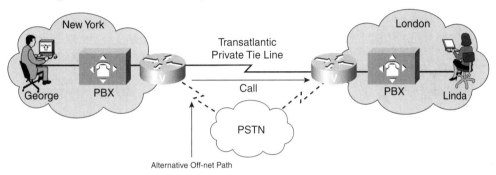

Assume that all calls between these two sites use 64 kbps of bandwidth, which corresponds to one circuit, and that a GoS of .03 is acceptable. How many minutes per month of calls use off-net calling because of the service block on the transatlantic tie line? The transatlantic tie line can simultaneously carry a maximum of 10 calls. In the calculation, we assume that a 1-minute call between New York and London costs $1.

NOTE   The $1 per minute rate is used here for ease of calculation.

The calculation is as follows:

- According to the Erlang B table in Figure 8-33, 5.53 Erlangs can be offered at P03 and 10 circuits.

- At P03, 3 percent of the 5.53 Erlangs of calls are overflowed and sent off-net.

- Therefore, in the peak hour, .03 * 5.53 Erlangs * 60 minutes = 10 overflow minutes.

- Assume that there are two peak hours per day and 21 business days per month. Thus, 21 days * 2 peak hours per day *10 overflow minutes = 420 overflow minutes per month.

- 420 overflow minutes per month * $1 per overflow minute = $420.

The calculation shows that 420 minutes per month of off-net calling between New York and London is used, costing $420. Compare this cost to that of adding circuits between New York and London to see whether it is worth adding bandwidth.

DSP Resources for Voice Coding

A *DSP* is a hardware component that allows the voice gateway module to convert voice signal information to packet-based protocols so that voice traffic is transmitted in IP packets. To support VoIP, a DSP converts signal information from telephony-based protocols (such as DS0) to packet-based protocols (IP).

NOTE   The number of voice channels purchased with a new voice gateway does not correspond to the number of DSPs.

A codec is a technology for compressing and decompressing data that is implemented in DSPs. Some codec compression techniques require more processing power than others. Codec complexity is divided into medium and high complexity. The difference between a medium and high complexity codec is the amount of CPU utilization that is necessary to process the codec algorithm, and the number of voice channels that a single DSP can support. For this reason, medium complexity codecs can also be run in high complexity mode, but with fewer (usually half) channels available per DSP.

The relationship between coding mechanism, DSPs, and voice channels is as follows:

- Medium complexity codecs allow the DSPs to process up to four voice calls per DSP. Medium complexity codecs include G.711, G.726, G.729a, and G.729ab.

- High complexity codecs allow the DSPs to process up to two voice calls per DSP. High complexity codecs include G.728, G.723, G.729, and G.729b.

NOTE   G.729 is a high complexity algorithm, and G.729a (also known as *G.729 Annex-A*) is a medium complexity variant of G.729 with slightly lower voice quality. G.729b is a high complexity algorithm, and G.729ab is a medium complexity variant of G.729b with slightly lower voice quality. The G.729b codec provides built-in IETF voice activity detection and comfort noise generation (CNG), while the G.729 codec does not.

For example, assume that a VoIP network is implemented between two locations that use two voice gateways with 30 DSP resources. Because of the resulting high bandwidth savings, the G.729a codec was used. The G.729a is a medium complexity codec that allows up to four voice calls per DSP. Therefore, up to 4 * 30 = 120 voice channels can be established between the two locations.

WAN Capacity Planning

This section shows how to calculate the required WAN capacity for voice to prevent blockage of service or degraded service by tying together the calculations that were performed in previous sections.

WAN capacity planning for voice and data transport depends on several parameters, including the number of simultaneous voice calls, sampling rate, codec, link type, header compression techniques, and use of VAD.

NOTE Any conversation requires two streams: one in each direction.

The most important issue in the WAN capacity planning process is the number of simultaneous calls that are permitted across a WAN link. You can limit the number of calls across a WAN link using GoS and CAC.

The next step is to understand the amount of bandwidth that is required for one voice call. Depending on the situation, bandwidth requirements for a voice call can vary. It is important to understand a VoIP packet's components and the variables that affect overall utilization.

Recall that every voice packet includes payload (the voice traffic), RTP header, UDP header, IP header, and a link header. All media types include RTP, UDP, and IP headers at 40 bytes per packet; they only differ in link header size.

The sampling rate does not significantly impact bandwidth for the payload. However, when overhead (the headers) is added, the required bandwidth increases significantly for 50 packets per second versus 33 packets per second.

NOTE Recall that the voice packets per second is calculated as follows: codec bit rate (bps)/voice payload size (bits per packet).

Use RTP header compression and VAD to improve bandwidth allocations. Recall that RTP header compression reduces the size of the IP/UDP/RTP header from 40 bytes to 2 bytes, and reduces bandwidth requirements. VAD uses the theory that, in any given voice call, only one party talks at a time, so periods of non-activity are not transmitted across the link. VAD is expected to save overall bandwidth by as much as 50 percent. However, planners must be careful, because 100 percent of the expected bandwidth can be required for one voice stream at any given time.

WAN Capacity Calculation

Figure 8-35 provides a table of per-call bandwidth requirements for various codecs and frame types. Using the information in Figure 8-35 and the number of simultaneous calls, network planners can estimate the required bandwidth for each WAN site.

Figure 8-35 *Per-call Bandwidth Requirements*

Codec	Ethernet 14 Bytes of Header	PPP 6 Bytes of Header	ATM 53- Byte Cells with 48- Byte Payload	Frame Relay 4 Bytes of Header
G.711 at 50 pps	85.6 kbps	82.4 kbps	106 kbps	81.6 kbps
With cRTP	70.4 kbps	67.2 kbps	84.8 kbps	66.4 kbps
With cRTP & VAD	35.2 kbps	33.6 kbps	51 kbps	33.2 kbps
G.711 at 33 pps	78.4 kbps	76.3 kbps	84.8 kbps	75.7 kbps
With cRTP	67.7 kbps	64.5 kbps	84.8 kbps	65.6 kbps
With cRTP & VAD	33.9 kbps	32.3 kbps	42.4 kbps	32.8 kbps
G.729 at 50 pps	29.6 kbps	26.4 kbps	42.4 kbps	25.6 kbps
With cRTP	14.4 kbps	11.2 kbps	21.2 kbps	10.4 kbps
With cRTP & VAD	7.2 kbps	5.6 kbps	10.7 kbps	5.2 kbps
G.729 at 33 pps	22.4 kbps	20.3 kbps	28.3 kbps	19.7 kbps
With cRTP	12.3 kbps	10.1 kbps	14.1 kbps	9.6 kbps
With cRTP & VAD	6.1 kbps	5.1 kbps	7.1 kbps	4.8 kbps

Remember that WAN links are generally full duplex; therefore, an equal amount of bandwidth should be allocated in each direction for one voice call. Be careful when using VAD to estimate bandwidth because the values in the table do not represent the actual required bandwidth in any one direction at any particular time.

Example Calculation

In this example, an organization has a remote office that has 20 permanent employees. The remote office has three analog lines, so users cannot always place calls because an outside line is not always available. The network planner determines that this occurs approximately ten times a day, which is an unacceptable level. Therefore, the network planner deploys VoIP using the existing Frame Relay link between the main office and the remote office, thereby providing enough bandwidth for four simultaneous voice calls.

The network planner tests compression techniques and decides to use G.729 encoding with cRTP over Frame Relay at 50 pps. Using the information in Figure 8-35, the network planner determines that each call uses approximately 10.4 kbps per stream. However, the planner is uncomfortable with only (10.4 *4 =) 41.6 kbps in each direction and decides that, to guarantee voice quality, 64 kbps should be allocated across Frame Relay for voice calls.

Because the remote office currently has 64 kbps committed information rate (CIR) over Frame Relay for transporting data, the planner intends to double CIR to 128 kbps and configure the appropriate QoS, traffic shaping, and link fragmentation and interleaving to provide acceptable voice quality.

Combining GoS with WAN Capacity Calculation

GoS and Erlangs are used to estimate the number of circuits that are required in a network. By determining the per-call bandwidth requirements and the number of circuits (simultaneous calls), planners can calculate the amount of bandwidth that is required to meet a certain GoS.

This WAN capacity calculation can be used to estimate the bandwidth that must be provided through an IP-based network to satisfactorily transport a given BHT level. The calculation is based on the Erlang B traffic model.

Key Point: BHT, Blocking Probability, and Per-call Bandwidth

The three variables involved in these calculations are BHT, blocking probability, and per-call bandwidth. Here is a review of these terms:

— BHT (in Erlangs) is the number of hours of call traffic during the telephone system's busiest hour of operation.

— Blocking probability (the GoS) is the call failure rate because an insufficient number of lines are available. For example, 0.03 means that three calls were blocked per 100 calls attempted.

— Per-call bandwidth is the amount of bandwidth, in kbps, that is required through an IP-based network to carry one voice call.

We discussed each of these variables previously; now we combine them to estimate the total required bandwidth.

To determine the required WAN capacity, you should first determine the appropriate number of required connections. Using the desired blocking probability, the BHT, and the traffic engineering Erlang tables, the number of required connections (circuits) can be determined. You can calculate the required per-call bandwidth using the selected voice coding, header compression, sampling, and link type.

Key Point: Determining the Required WAN Capacity

To determine the required WAN capacity, multiply the number of circuits by the required per-call bandwidth.

For example, assume that, based on the Erlang table, 10 circuits are required between two locations to satisfy user demands. The designer decides to use a PPP link between the two locations to transport VoIP. Voice is coded with the G.729 codec using 50 samples per second, and the header is compressed with the cRTP.

As shown in Figure 8-35, the per-call bandwidth table shows that one voice call requires 11.2 kbps of bandwidth. Therefore, 10 * 11.2 = 112 kbps of bandwidth is required between the two locations, in each direction, to carry ten simultaneous voice calls.

Call Admission Control

CAC mechanisms extend QoS's ability to protect voice traffic from being negatively affected by other voice traffic, and to keep excess voice traffic off the network.

If the WAN access link between two PBXs has the bandwidth to carry only two VoIP calls, admitting a third call impairs the voice quality of all three calls. The queuing mechanisms that provide policing—not CAC—cause this problem. If packets that exceed the configured or allowable rate are received, they are tail-dropped from the queue. The queuing mechanism cannot distinguish which IP packet belongs to which voice call; any packets that exceed the given arrival rate within a certain period of time are dropped. Thus, all three calls experience packet loss, which the end users perceive as clips.

NOTE   This problem is easier for the Layer 2 voice transport mechanisms (VoFR and VoATM) to solve, but is particularly challenging for the predominant VoIP applications.

Call Rerouting Alternatives

When CAC is implemented, the outgoing gateway detects that insufficient network resources are available for a call to proceed. The call is rejected and the originating gateway must find another means of handling the call; there are several possibilities, most of which depend on the gateway's configuration. In the absence of any specific configuration, the outgoing gateway provides the calling party with a reorder tone. PSTN switches or PBXs often intercept this tone with an announcement such as "All circuits are busy; please try your call again later."

The outgoing gateway can be configured for the following rerouting scenarios:

- The call can be rerouted via an alternate packet network path, if such a path exists.
- The call can be rerouted via the PSTN network path.
- The call can be returned to the originating TDM switch with the reject cause code.

Figure 8-36 shows examples of a VoIP network with and without CAC.

Figure 8-36 *Call Admission Control Keeps the Quality of Existing Calls*

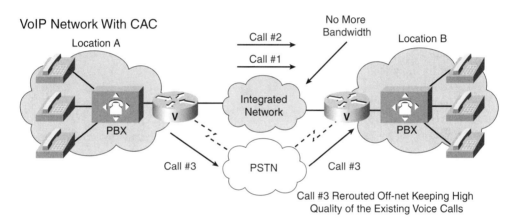

The upper diagram in Figure 8-36 illustrates what happens when the WAN access link between two PBXs has the bandwidth to carry only two VoIP calls without CAC. In this example, admitting the third call impairs the voice quality of all three calls.

The lower example in Figure 8-36 illustrates how the outgoing gateway detects that insufficient network resources are available to allow a call to proceed. The third call is automatically rerouted off-net, thereby maintaining the voice quality of the two existing calls.

Campus IP Telephony Capacity Planning

Capacity planning is a critical process for enterprise IP telephony migration and overall success. In traditional data environments, capacity planning focuses on link utilization and control plane resources for network devices, including CPU and memory. However, IP telephony networks require three distinct capacity planning processes: Cisco CallManager processing requirements planning, network capacity and performance planning, and trunking capacity planning. The following sections describe these processes.

Planning Cisco CallManager Processing Requirements

Cisco CallManager processing requirements planning helps to ensure that the Cisco CallManager servers have sufficient resources for normal call processing, voice conferencing, and other IP telephony services. This planning process typically leads to an improved network design that can better support the organization's requirements.

Cisco CallManager processing planning involves investigating CPU and memory requirements and supported configurations. Cisco CallManager servers are configured in clusters for larger applications. Clustering guidelines include using a dedicated server for database replication or publishing and backup Cisco CallManager capabilities for the desired number of IP telephones. Cisco CallManager services are assigned weights for their impact on CPU and memory requirements within each Cisco CallManager configuration.

Planners must investigate the number of desired IP telephones in the configuration and the desired service weight to design a configuration that includes the server model and the number of servers configured in the cluster. Each Cisco CallManager server should not control more than 2500 IP telephones.

Planning for Network Capacity and Performance

Network performance and capacity planning helps to ensure that the network consistently has bandwidth available for data and IP telephony traffic, and that voice packets consistently meet delay and jitter requirements. This process can also lead to an improved overall design that better supports IP telephony requirements.

Following is the recommended process for network capacity and performance planning:

Step 1   Determine the current traffic load and data traffic requirements for a combined IP telephony and data architecture.

Baselining network utilization helps determine the current traffic load and data traffic requirements for a combined IP telephony and data architecture. Perform this step for major distribution, backbone, and required WAN links. A relatively homogenous environment can require only a sample baseline calculation from representative links, rather than data from the entire network. Two types of utilization statistics are used to describe link utilization: peak utilization and average utilization.

Step 2   Determine IP telephony traffic overhead in required network sections based on busy hour estimates, gateway capacities, and Cisco CallManager capacities.

Determine the IP telephony overhead per building or per WAN site. In the LAN environment, however, network planners are not typically concerned with the amount of IP telephony overhead. Differentiate buildings or sites that require more or less voice traffic. For example, there might be an organization with one building that houses engineers who do not typically spend much time on the telephone, and another building with Support Center personnel who use the telephone constantly. Estimate busy hour call volume and use an Erlang calculator to determine busy hour call requirements. Use the busy hour call requirements and the voice encoding method to determine busy hour bandwidth requirements.

Step 3   Determine minimum bandwidth requirements by combining the busy hour data traffic and busy hour voice traffic.

To determine the minimum bandwidth requirements over WAN links, add the busy hour data traffic to the busy hour voice traffic at the same time to determine link bandwidth requirements. When both data and voice are implemented, the designer must also determine the growth requirements over time and perform link trending to determine overall bandwidth requirements. Baselining and trending link utilization over time ensures that the network consistently meets both data and voice requirements.

Step 4   Determine the required design changes and QoS requirements based on IP telephony design recommendations and voice bandwidth requirements.

Step 5   Before implementation, validate baseline IP telephony performance with a performance baseline to determine voice readiness. The audit should investigate potential network issues across major network paths. Issues can include queuing delay, CPU utilization, link utilization, buffer utilization, and error rates. Also, conduct an audit after full IP telephony implementation to baseline the working solution and help determine potential issues with the additional traffic load and performance requirements.

Planning Trunking Capacity

Trunking capacity planning involves investigating the number of circuits that are required for PBX interconnectivity, voice mail connectivity, PSTN connectivity, and site-to-site connectivity for off-net trunking or off-net overflow. In addition, circuit capacity planning should define the existing blocking factor (GoS) for potential capacity issues. The recommended GoS is P01, or 1 percent.

Capacity planning for voice trunking is already an established capacity planning process in the voice world, and the same process applies to trunking capacity for IP telephony.

Summary

In this chapter, you learned about designing networks to transport voice.

To obtain clear voice connections, analog speech must be converted to a digital format and sent over a digital network. PCM is the process of digitizing analog voice signals; it involves filtering, sampling, and digitizing.

The PSTN switch's primary task is to provide residential telephony. In contrast, a PBX supports user telephones within an enterprise because it provides business features such as call hold, call transfer, call forward, and so on. Enterprises install PBXs because the number of telephones is usually greater than the number of simultaneous calls to the PSTN network; therefore, the enterprise only needs the number of external lines (to the PSTN) to equal the maximum possible number of simultaneous calls.

The telephone infrastructure includes telephone and station lines and various trunks. Some form of analog or digital signaling mechanism is required to set up and tear down calls; signaling methods include loop start, ground start, E&M, CAS, and CCS. CCS signaling includes ISDN and SS7.

A PSTN numbering plan governs the routing of voice calls within the PSTN. The NANP is an example of a PSTN numbering plan for North America.

The PSTN offers the following services:

- Centrex
- Virtual private voice networks
- Voice mail
- Call center
- Interactive voice response

Although the PSTN is effective, many business drivers strive to change to an integrated voice and data network. In VoIP, voice traffic is converted to IP packets and directed over IP data networks through voice-enabled routers.

Circuit-switched calls require a permanent duplex 64 kbps dedicated circuit between two telephones for the duration of a call, whether either caller is talking or not. No other party can use the connection during the call. Packet-switched networking only uses bandwidth when it is required; this difference is an important benefit of packet-based voice networking.

The H.323 standard provides a foundation for audio, video, and data communications across IP-based networks. H.323 defines four major components for a network-based communications system: terminals, gateways, gatekeepers, and MCUs.

The IP telephony architecture includes four distinct components: infrastructure, call processing, applications, and clients. Cisco CallManager is the software-based call processing component of the Cisco enterprise IP telephony solution. It performs like the

PBX in a traditional telephone network, including call setup and processing functions. With IP telephony, IP phones themselves convert voice into IP packets. They do not use telephone cabling; instead, they send all signals over standard network cabling.

An interface on a voice gateway that carries voice data is referred to as a voice port. A voice port is a physical port that comes with a voice module; this is what makes a router voice-enabled. Dial peers are logical peers that are associated with physical voice ports; the voice gateway establishes a connection based on the configuration of dial peers.

Overall voice quality is a function of many factors, including delay, jitter, packet loss, and echo. Delay can be classified into two types: fixed network delay and variable network delay.

Compression is the method of reducing the amount of digital information below the traditional 64 kbps. G.729 is a recommended voice codec for most WAN networks because of its relatively low bandwidth requirements (8 kbps) and high MOS (3.92).

Voice communications over IP can be considered a mix of control signals and voice conversation. Control signals and data require reliable transport (using TCP) because the signals must be received in the order in which they were sent and they cannot be lost. However, voice loses its value with time. If a voice packet is delayed, it might lose its relevance to the end user; therefore, voice conversation uses the more efficient, unreliable transport (using UDP).

The following QoS mechanisms are available for voice:

- Bandwidth reduction
- Bandwidth reservation
- QoS classification
- Congestion avoidance
- Congestion management

If the WAN links are not congested, there is no reason to implement QoS mechanisms. LLQ is the preferred queuing mechanism for designing voice on IP networks.

AutoQoS simplifies deployment and reduces human error by providing QoS provisioning for individual routers and switches. QoS deployments can be provisioned and managed using Cisco AutoQoS along with CiscoWorks QPM.

VoFR is intended for connecting existing PBXs; a voice-enabled router encodes the voice that is received from the PBX directly into Frame Relay frames and forwards those frames onto the Frame Relay network.

VBR with AAL2-based cells is the recommended implementation for VoATM.

On-net calling refers to voice calls transmitted over private interlocation tie lines. If the private tie line is congested, voice gateways select an alternative path, usually the PSTN; this is referred to as off-net calling.

When building voice networks, one of the most important factors to consider is proper bandwidth capacity planning. WAN capacity planning depends on the sampling rate, codec, link type, header compression techniques, and the number of simultaneous voice calls.

The following three variables are involved in WAN capacity calculations:

- Busy hour traffic (in Erlangs) is the number of hours of call traffic during the busiest hour of a telephone system's operation.

- Blocking probability (the GoS) is the call failure because an insufficient number of lines are available. The GoS is written as a blocking factor, Pxx, where xx is the percentage of calls that are blocked for a traffic system.

- Per-call bandwidth is the amount of bandwidth in kbps that is required through an IP-based network to carry one voice call.

You can determine the number of required connections (circuits) using the desired blocking probability, the BHT, and the traffic engineering Erlang tables. You can use the selected voice coding, header compression, sampling, and link type to calculate the required per-call bandwidth. To determine the required WAN capacity, multiply the number of circuits by the required per-call bandwidth.

The number of voice channels within one DSP can vary based on the codec complexity; medium complexity codecs allow the DSPs to process up to four voice calls per DSP, while high complexity codecs allow the DSPs to process up to two voice calls per DSP.

IP telephony networks require three distinct capacity planning processes: Cisco CallManager processing requirements, network capacity and performance, and trunking capacity.

References

For additional information, refer to these resources:

- Architecture for Voice, Video and Integrated Data white paper, available at www.cisco.com/warp/public/cc/so/neso/vvda/iptl/avvid_wp.htm.

- Configuring Quality of Service for Voice, www.cisco.com/univercd/cc/td/doc/product/software/ios122/122cgcr/fvvfax_c/vvfqos.htm.

- Davidson, Jonathon, Brian Gracely, and James Peters. *Voice over IP Fundamentals*. Cisco Press, 2000.

- Echo Analysis for Voice over IP, www.cisco.com/en/US/partner/tech/tk652/tk701/technologies_white_paper09186a00800d6b68.shtml.

NOTE   You must be a registered user to access these documents.

- QoS Features for Voice, www.cisco.com/univercd/cc/td/doc/product/software/ ios121/121cgcr/qos_c/qcprt7/qcdvoice.htm.

- Telephony Signaling documents, available at www.cisco.com/pcgi-bin/Support/ browse/index.pl?i=Technologies&f=775.

- Traffic Analysis for Voice over IP, www.cisco.com/univercd/cc/td/doc/cisintwk/ intsolns/voipsol/ta_isd.htm.

- Understanding Codecs: Complexity, Support, MOS, and Negotiation www.cisco.com/warp/public/788/voip/codec_complexity.html.

- Understanding Delay in Packet Voice Networks, www.cisco.com/warp/public/788/ voip/delay-details.html.

- Voice Network Signaling and Control, available at www.cisco.com/warp/public/788/ signalling/net_signal_control.html.

- Voice—Understanding How Inbound and Outbound Dial Peers are Matched on Cisco IOS Platforms, available at www.cisco.com/warp/public/788/voip/ in_dial_peer_match.html.

- Voice over IP (VoIP) and Frame Relay (VoFR) and ATM (VoATM), available at www.cisco.com/pcgi-bin/Support/browse/index.pl?i=Technologies&f=775.

- Waveform Coding Techniques, available at www.cisco.com/warp/public/788/ signalling/waveform_coding.html#subfirstsix.

- Westbay Engineers Limited Home Page, www.erlang.com.

Case Study Simulation

This case study is a continuation of the DJMP Industries case study introduced in Chapter 2, "Applying Design Principles in Network Deployment."

Case Study: General Instructions

Use the scenarios, information, and parameters provided at each task of the ongoing case study. If you encounter ambiguities, make reasonable assumptions and proceed. For all tasks, use the initial customer scenario and build on the solutions provided thus far.

You can use any and all documentation, books, white papers, and so on.

In each task, you act as a network design consultant. Make creative proposals to accomplish the customer's business needs. Justify your ideas when they differ from the provided solutions.

Use any design strategies and internetworking technologies you feel are appropriate.

The final goal for each case study is a paper solution; you are not required to provide the specific product names.

Appendix G, "Answers to Review Questions, Case Studies, and Simulation Exercises," provides a solution for each task based on assumptions made. There is no claim that the provided solution is the best or only solution. Your solution might be more appropriate for the assumptions you made. The provided solution helps you understand the author's reasoning and offers a way for you to compare and contrast your solution.

Simulation: Voice Transport over IP Network

This exercise is a paper-only version of the simulation that was actually performed by the simulation tool, and it includes the results the simulation tool provided. Review the scenario and the simulation results, and answer the questions.

Voice Transport over IP Network Scenario

The focus of this simulation is on the transport of voice over an IP network, or VoIP.

DJMP Industries is considering setting up new international remote offices in Singapore and London. An Internet-based VPN network is to link both international offices with the San Jose headquarters.

Warned about the sensitive nature of voice traffic, the company established and tested a pilot VoIP network in San Jose. They were satisfied with the quality of the voice session, but still have doubts about deploying voice in a real production network. Their major concern is how the data traffic will interfere with voice over the Internet.

To prove the company's expectation, you have been asked to analyze the reference model, which simulates voice over IP. This also provides a foundation for their future decision.

Figure 8-37 illustrates the network's architecture.

Initially, you decided to simulate the responsiveness and utilization of the WAN network without any voice traffic by initiating an application that represents a reference traffic flow. Because clients in London and Singapore are accessing servers in all three locations, you tested with the file transfer application (using the file transfer protocol [FTP]) from both of these sites.

Figure 8-37 *DJMP Network Architecture*

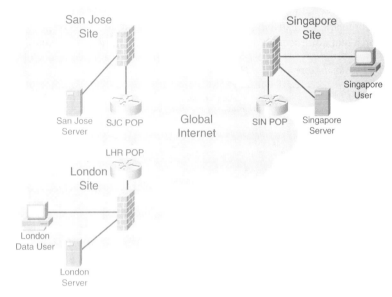

Testing the Data Load

The graphs in Figure 8-38 show the transfer rates that result from the FTP sessions initiated by the clients. The amount of traffic sent and received is measured in bytes per second.

Figure 8-38 *FTP Transfer Rates from London and Singapore*

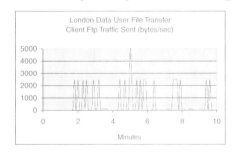

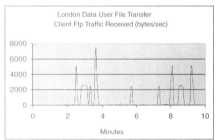

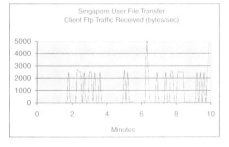

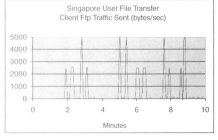

The graphs in Figure 8-39 present the probability density of the FTP download response times over a certain period of time. As indicated by the graph's peak values, the response times are variably distributed within the 7 seconds; most of the responses are received within a tenth of a second, with the rest between the third and the sixth second.

Figure 8-39 *FTP Download Response Time Distribution*

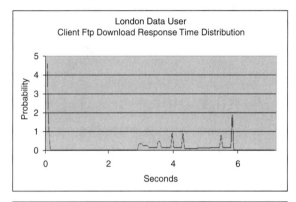

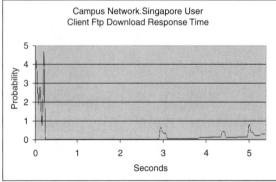

The graphs in Figures 8-40, 8-41 and 8-42 show the utilization of the links as a result of heavy FTP traffic. The load that is placed on the links does not represent a significant burden for the links; however, the effect the data traffic might have on the future voice sessions is worrisome.

Figure 8-40   *Utilization of London Links with FTP Traffic*

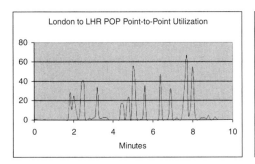

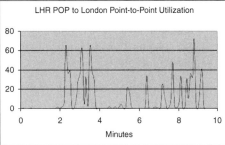

Figure 8-41   *Utilization of Singapore Links with FTP Traffic*

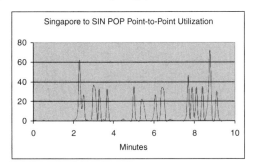

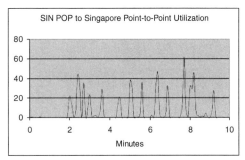

Figure 8-42   *Utilization of San Jose Links with FTP Traffic*

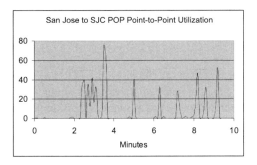

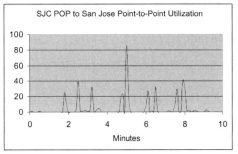

VoIP Pilot

The company was quite satisfied with the results of its pilot VoIP network in San Jose, especially with the quality of sessions that were established over the weekend in the unloaded network. Therefore, you decided to obtain comparable results by simulating the VoIP application and analyzing the results in a more realistic scenario, this time between distant locations.

You decided to simulate the VoIP behavior by initiating an application that represents a reference voice traffic flow. As shown in Figure 8-43, the tested application is a VoIP session between a user in Singapore and a PBX switch in San Jose.

Figure 8-43   *DJMP VoIP Pilot Simulation Architecture*

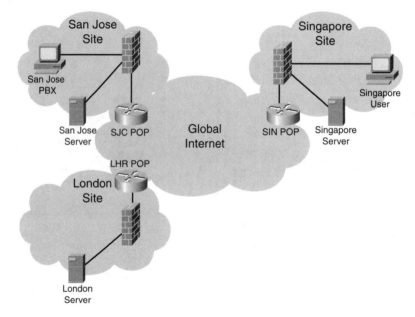

Voice Load on the Network

The graph in Figure 8-44 shows the quality the company might expect in an unloaded network. The end-to-end delay of voice packets, measured in seconds, appears to be constant at slightly below 20 milliseconds.

Figure 8-44 *End-to-End Packet Delay in an Unloaded Network for a Singapore User*

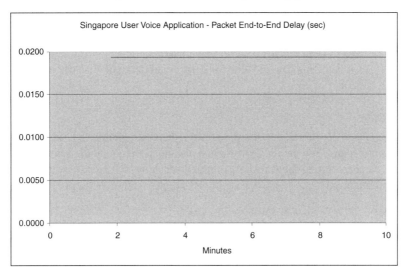

The graphs in Figure 8-45 present the link utilization that resulted from the initial VoIP traffic. The voice traffic presents a constant utilization of approximately 40 percent.

Figure 8-45 *Utilization of Links with Initial VoIP Traffic*

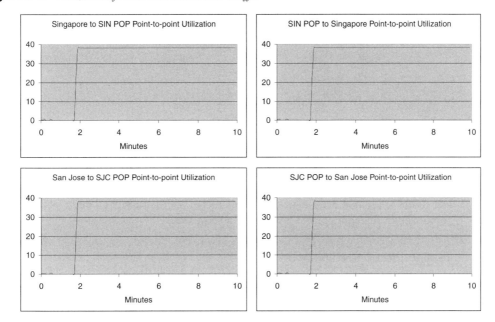

Conclusions

The voice transport over an unloaded network resulted in excellent VoIP quality, no jitter, and a delay that was well within acceptable limits. Also, the load on the links was not too heavy (40 percent utilization, but constant and predictable).

1 What is the maximum value for end-to-end delay that is still acceptable in a voice session?

VoIP in Production

When the VoIP pilot is put into production, the voice quality degrades dramatically during business hours. You decided to simulate the situation by placing a considerable load on the links and collecting the statistics. Figure 8-46 shows the network diagram that is used for this simulation.

Figure 8-46   *DJMP VoIP in Production Simulation Architecture*

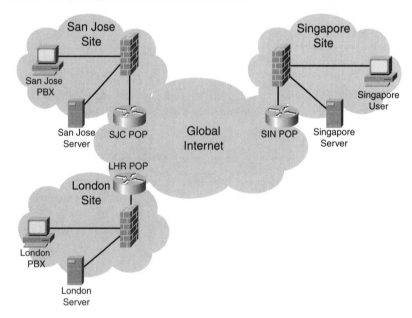

In this case, the reference traffic flow incorporates a combination of data and voice traffic. Data users in London and Singapore communicate with servers at all three locations. A voice user in Singapore places a voice call to San Jose.

Testing the Loaded Network

You performed the simulation and the graphs shown in Figure 8-47, which illustrates the links' utilization, were produced. You compare the data response times with the results from the previous simulation on the unloaded network; the load on the links increased substantially because of the concurrent use of data and voice applications.

Figure 8-47 *Utilization of Links with Production VoIP and Data Traffic*

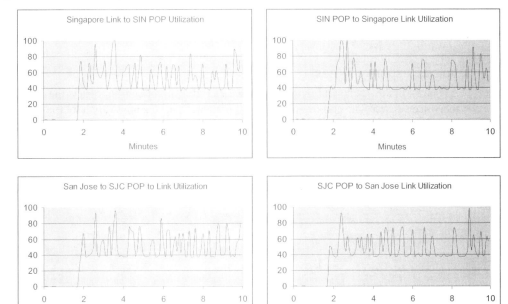

Data Response Times

The graph in Figure 8-48 compares the distribution of FTP download response times under different conditions. The graph's darker line describes the responsiveness of the data network alone, while the lighter line represents the distribution of response times in the combined data and voice network.

Figure 8-48 *Distribution of FTP Download Response Times*

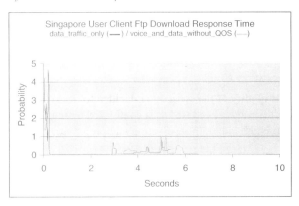

The download response time graph shows a better response time distribution on the data-only network, where the response time increases to 6 seconds. On the data and voice network, the response time distribution increases to 10 seconds.

Voice Response Times

As shown in the graphs in Figure 8-49, the data traffic significantly impacts the quality of the voice session. The end-to-end delays of the voice packets now vary a lot (up to 1.4 seconds); this results in considerable jitter (delay variation) in the voice session.

Figure 8-49 *Voice Packet Delay and Delay Variation (Jitter)*

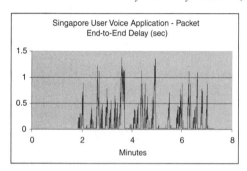
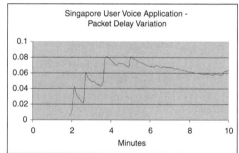

Conclusions

The voice load that is placed on the international links increases the data application response times. When designing networks with both voice and data traffic, consider the effects of an increased load on your existing applications.

The data traffic significantly impacts voice quality and renders it unusable because of long delays and high jitter. When deploying a voice and data network, you must deploy QoS mechanisms to ensure smooth propagation of voice packets.

   2 Why does the jitter disturb the voice session?

Voice and Data Network with QoS

To improve the quality of the voice, you decided to deploy QoS features. WFQ is configured on the routers, and RSVP is configured on the routers and voice stations to support end-to-end bandwidth reservation and preferential forwarding of voice traffic.

The data flow remains as it was in the previous case: data users in London and Singapore communicate with servers at all three locations, and a voice user in Singapore places a voice call to San Jose.

Data Response Times

The graphs in Figure 8-50 compare the download response times with QoS (the dark line in the graphs) or without QoS (the shaded line in the graphs). From these graphs, it is obvious that QoS significantly reduces the distribution of download response times.

Figure 8-50 *Distribution of FTP Download Response Times with and Without QoS*

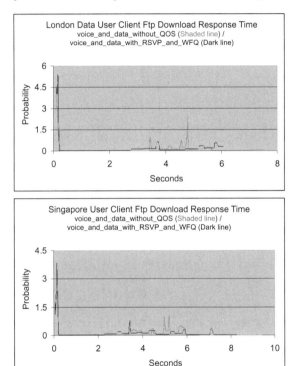

Voice Response Times

As seen in the graphs in Figure 8-51, there is still some delay variation in the voice traffic. This is mainly attributed to individual voice packets that are waiting in a queue behind a data packet.

Figure 8-51   *Voice Packet Delay and Delay Variation (Jitter) with QoS*

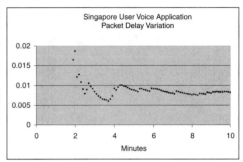

The graph in Figure 8-52 compares the end-to-end delays without QoS (the dark line) and with QoS (the shaded pixels). Deploying QoS causes voice to perform almost as if no data traffic exists.

Figure 8-52   *End-to-End Voice Delay with and Without QoS*

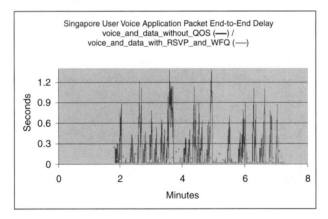

Conclusions

When properly deployed, QoS can significantly increase the voice quality in mixed voice and data networks. When designing voice and data networks over low-speed links or on congested networks, always plan to deploy QoS.

   3   How can QoS mechanisms improve the data propagation in congested networks?

Review Questions

Answer the following questions and then refer to Appendix G, "Answers to Review Questions, Case Studies, and Simulation Exercises," for the answers.

1 What steps are involved in converting analog signals to digital signals?

2 What is pulse amplitude modulation?

3 What is pulse code modulation?

4 Match the following terms with their definitions:

Terms:

— Filtering

— Quantization

— Companding

— Logarithmic compression

Definitions:

— Converting analog sample to a digital code word

— Compression increases as sample signal increases

— Removing nonspeech components

— Compressing and coding signals

5 What are some of the call features provided by PBXs?

6 What are some differences between a PBX and a PSTN switch?

7 How does having a PBX save on communication costs?

8 Match the following terms with their definitions:

Terms:

— Local loop

— Telephone line

— Station line

— Trunk

— Tie trunk

— CO trunk

— PSTN trunk

Definitions:

- — Communication between CO switch and home telephone

- — Connects CO switches to PBXs

- — Physical cabling

- — Communication between two telephony systems

- — Connects PBXs

- — Interconnects CO switches

- — Communication between PBX and business telephone

9 Which signaling method is used between PSTN switches?

10 Which signaling method allows standardized communication between PBXs?

11 What is the difference between CAS and CCS?

12 What is the difference between subscriber and trunk signaling?

13 Describe how a telephone call is routed from location A to location B through the PSTN using NANP.

14 Match the following terms with their definitions:

Terms:

- — Centrex

- — Virtual private voice networks

- — Voice mail

- — Call center

- — Interactive voice response

Definitions:

- — Interconnect corporate voice traffic among multiple locations over the PSTN

- — Does not require live agents

- — Provides customers with the facility to divert their incoming PSTN calls

- — A set of specialized business solutions in which the service provider owns and operates the equipment that provides both call control and service logic functions

- — Requires live agents

15 What is automatic call distribution?

16 What is TDM?

17 What are the advantages of using packet-switched networks for voice traffic?

18 What is the difference between VoIP and IP telephony?

19 What is the difference between an H.323 gateway and an H.323 gatekeeper?

20 What role does an H.323 terminal play in voice networks?

21 What does Cisco CallManager do?

22 What are the four components of IP telephony architecture?

23 How does IP telephony lower costs?

24 What is a voice port?

25 What is a dial peer?

26 Describe how a voice call is processed in a voice gateway.

27 Complete the following sentence:

Dejitter buffers are used on _____ side(s) of the network to smooth out delay variability.

   a   the originating

   b   the receiving

   c   all

28 What is Link Fragmentation and Interleaving (LFI)?

29 What is the acceptable one-way delay limit for good-quality voice?

30 Match the following terms with their definitions:

Terms:

   — Processing delay

   — Propagation delay

   — Jitter

   — Echo

Definitions:

   — Variation in the delay of received packets

   — Audible leak of the caller's voice into the receive (return) path

   — Length of time it takes to travel the distance between the sending and receiving endpoints

   — Time the DSP takes to compress a block of PCM samples

31 Match the following coding standards with their bandwidth requirements.

Coding standards:
— G.711
— G.729
— G.726
— G.723
— G.728

Bandwidth requirements:
— Required bandwidth 5.3 kbps
— Required bandwidth 64 kbps
— Required bandwidth 24 kbps
— Required bandwidth 8 kbps
— Required bandwidth 16 kbps

32 Which ITU voice coding standard results in the highest mean opinion score (MOS)?

33 What protocols are used to transport voice conversation traffic?

34 Will a voice packet loss always be audible?

35 Match the following terms with their definitions:

Terms:
— H.225 channel
— H.245 channel
— RAS
— RTCP

Definitions:
— Used only if a gatekeeper is present
— Uses Q.931 to establish a connection between two terminals
— Monitors quality for hosts that communicate with voice traffic
— Carries control messages that govern voice operation

36 What does voice activity detection do?

37 What does compressed RTP do?

38 Which of these codecs have relatively more IP header overhead compared to the payload? Arrange them in descending order.

G.729

G.711

G.728

39 Which queuing mechanism is recommended for most VoIP designs?

40 What QoS mechanisms are available for voice?

41 What is the difference between AutoQoS and QPM?

42 Why would a hub and spoke topology be beneficial compared to a fully meshed topology for VoFR?

43 What is the difference between static and dynamic VoFR?

44 What is the preferred ATM class of service for VoATM transport?

45 Which is the preferred ATM adaptation type for VoATM?

46 Match the following terms with their definitions:

Terms:

— On-net calling

— Off-net calling

— Least-cost routing

Definitions:

— Voice calls that are transmitted over the PSTN

— Voice calls that are transmitted over private interlocation tie lines

— Calls going to the PSTN at a point that is closest to the destination

47 How does a user know that he has reached the PSTN during a manually selected off-net call?

48 How many centum call seconds (CCS) equals five Erlangs?

49 What does a GoS of P05 mean?

50 Which two parameters are mandatory for trunk capacity calculation?

51 If your call logger says that 290 calls are made on a trunk group in an hour and the average call duration is 180 seconds, what is the busy hour traffic (in Erlangs)?

52 What is the difference between medium and high complexity codecs?

53 Which codecs are high complexity?

54 Which parameters are required for WAN capacity planning to support IP telephony?

55 What is the purpose of the Call Admission Control mechanism?

56 What steps are involved in planning for network capacity and performance in an IP telephony implementation?

57 Why is Cisco CallManager processing requirements planning necessary?

This chapter discusses network security solutions and contains the following sections:

- Identifying Attacks and Selecting Countermeasures
- Identifying Security Mechanisms for a Defined Security Policy
- Selecting Security Solutions within Network Modules
- Summary
- Review Questions

Evaluating Security Solutions for the Network

Network security is one of the essential network services that span the entire network, and it must be addressed within each modular block. Modularity ensures that the network designer can focus on a security problem within a particular network module and integrate a particular solution into a global security solution. A modular approach simplifies the design and ensures that a security breach in one of the network modules remains isolated so it does not affect the entire network.

This chapter introduces Cisco's Security Architecture for Enterprise (SAFE) Blueprint, which employs a modular approach to network security design. We discuss the security threats for each network module, the solutions that mitigate the threats, and their relationship to other modules. Security is evaluated from the physical perspective all the way up to the individual application. Logging and monitoring are described as integral parts of any security solution and as preventive mechanisms that allow attack detection before serious consequences result.

After completing this chapter, you will be able to describe the risks and threats to which an enterprise network is exposed, and select the appropriate security mechanisms in each design module to counter specific threats and comply with an enterprise security policy.

Identifying Attacks and Selecting Countermeasures

This section discusses security threats in an Internet Protocol (IP) network and provides basic descriptions of security solutions for defense against the majority of these threats.

Security as a Network Service in Modular Network Design

Providing security network services becomes more important as networks become increasingly interconnected and data flows more freely. Connectivity is no longer optional in the commercial world, and the possible risks do not outweigh the benefits. Therefore, security services must provide adequate protection to conduct business in a relatively open environment.

Basic Security Assumptions

The following two assumptions must be made about computer networks as compared to classic computer security:

- Modern networks are very large, very interconnected, and run both ubiquitous (such as IP) and proprietary (such as Cisco's Enhanced Interior Gateway Protocol [EIGRP]) protocols. As such, they are often open to access, and a potential attacker can often easily attach to or access such networks remotely. In particular, widespread IP internetworking increases the probability that more attacks will be carried out over large, heavily interconnected networks such as the Internet.

- Computer systems and applications that are attached to those networks are becoming increasingly complex. In terms of security, they become more difficult to analyze, secure, and test. When such systems and their applications are attached to large networks, the risk to computing increases dramatically.

As noted in the following section, some basic security requirements can be established based on these assumptions.

Basic Security Requirements

To adequately protect network resources, the procedures and technologies that are deployed must guarantee the following security-related points:

- Confidentiality of data, guaranteeing that only authorized subjects (such as users, servers, and applications) can *view* sensitive information.

- Integrity of data, guaranteeing that only authorized subjects can change sensitive information. This might also guarantee the data's authenticity.

- System and data availability, which should provide uninterrupted access to important computing resources.

When designing for security, a designer must be aware of the threats (or possible attacks) that could compromise security and their associated risks—that is, how relevant those threats are for a particular system.

Integrity and Confidentiality Threats

The key security threats are integrity violations and confidentiality breaches.

Key Point: Integrity Violations

Integrity violations can occur when an attacker attempts to change sensitive data without proper authorization.

An example of an integrity violation is an attacker obtaining permission to write to sensitive data but then changing or deleting it. The owner might not detect such a change until it is too late, perhaps when the change has already resulted in tangible loss. Because of the difficulty in detecting changes and the possible cascading consequences of late detection, many businesses treat integrity violations as the most serious threat to their business.

Key Point: Confidentiality Breaches

Confidentiality breaches can occur when an attacker attempts to obtain access to read sensitive data.

Confidentiality attacks can be extremely difficult to detect because the attacker can copy sensitive data without the owner's knowledge and without leaving a trace.

The risks of both integrity violations and confidentiality breaches are usually managed by enforcing access control in various ways, including the following:

- Limiting access to network resources using network access control, such as physical separation of networks, restrictive firewalls, and virtual local-area networks (VLANs).

- Limiting access to files and objects using operating system-based access controls, such as UNIX host security and NT domain security.

- Limiting users' access to data by application level controls, such as different user profiles for different roles.

- Using cryptography, such as encryption to provide confidentiality and secure fingerprints or digital signatures to provide data authenticity and integrity, to protect data outside the application.

Figure 9-1 illustrates potential confidentiality and integrity threats to network resources that an outside attacker might exploit. In this example network, an attacker might do the following if adequate protection is not in place:

- Access an internal server and copy confidential data (a confidentiality breach)

- Deface (change) the corporate web page (an integrity breach)

- Intercept data that is sent over the Internet between a branch office and the central site and change or read it in transit (a confidentiality or integrity breach)

Figure 9-1 *Integrity and Confidentiality Threats*

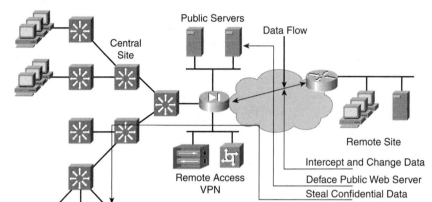

Availability Threats

Figure 9-2 depicts potential availability threats to network resources that an attacker might exploit. In this network, an attacker might do the following if adequate protection is not in place:

- Flood a network connection with random traffic in an attempt to consume as much bandwidth as possible. This can deny service to legitimate users of that connection.

- Flood a public server with an enormous number of connection requests, thereby rendering the server unresponsive to legitimate users.

These are known as a *denial of service* (*DoS*) attacks.

Figure 9-2 *Availability Threats Can Deny Service to Network Users*

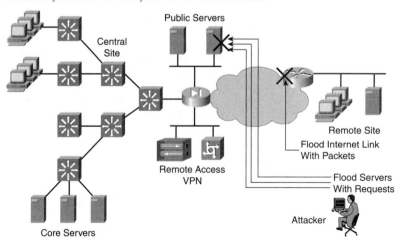

DoS Attacks

Key Point: DoS Attacks

DoS attacks aim to compromise the availability of a network, host, or application.

DoS attacks are considered a major risk because they can easily interrupt a business process and cause significant loss. These attacks are relatively simple to conduct, even by an unskilled attacker, and are usually the consequence of either of the following:

- A host or application's failure to handle an unexpected condition, such as maliciously formatted input data, an unexpected interaction of system components, or simple resource exhaustion.

- A network, host, or application's inability to handle an enormous quantity of data, which crashes the system or brings it to a halt. The difficulty of defending against such an attack depends on the complexity of distinguishing legitimate data from attacker data.

The Need for Network Security

Network security employs risk management to reduce risk to acceptable levels. The organization defines an acceptable level of risk based on such factors as

- The value of the organization's data
- The expectation of loss in the event of compromise
- The severity and probability of risks

The weighting of these factors is called *risk assessment*, which is a continuously recurring procedure of knowing the following factors:

- What assets to protect
- The value of the assets
- The cost of expected loss that would result from a compromise
- The severity and probability of attacks directed against the assets

Risk assessment results in the development of a *network security policy*, which documents the level of risk and suggests the methods of managing the risk to an acceptable level.

The network security policy describes risk management measures as they relate to potential threats. It does not usually consider security implementation details; rather, it provides a more general security philosophy that directs the implementation of security mechanisms.

Key Point: Risk Assessment and Network Security

Risk assessment defines threats, their probability, and their severity.

A *network security policy* enumerates risks that are relevant to the network and how those risks will be managed.

A *network security design* implements the security policy.

Because the severity and probability of risks change daily, risk management and the consequent building of the security policy must be a continuous process. A good example is the use of cryptography to provide confidentiality through encryption. A company's encryption algorithm and the length of the encryption key might have to be reconsidered if a relatively inexpensive and exceptionally fast code-cracking computer, which allows decryption of high-value secrets, becomes available. In this case, the organization must choose a stronger algorithm to provide protection against the new threat.

Evaluating potential damage is possible, to some degree, for most scenarios, and care should be taken so that the cost of security does not exceed the cost of potential security incidents. In the commercial world, it is common practice to build systems that have just enough security to bring potential losses down to the desired level. Alternatively, organizations that have higher security requirements might want to implement stronger measures to mitigate potential unforeseen risks.

A security designer must evaluate the severity of a particular risk, including the damage a successful attack could cause. However, it is often difficult to associate a value with an asset. For example, consider the following:

- A large hospital system's medical database, in which disastrous consequences result if confidentiality is breached.

- A corporation's public web page, which, if defaced (an integrity violation), can become a public relations nightmare even though it might not result in any serious confidentiality breach.

Network Devices as Targets

The classic guideline for developing trusted systems specifies that a trusted system must enforce an organization's security policy, and the system itself must be secure against attacks. The same principles can be applied to network security: in a secured network, network devices provide security services to network users, and the devices themselves must be resistant to attacks.

If an attacker can subvert a network device, many potential attacks can be conducted from the compromised device, including the following:

- Intercepting data flowing through the network and analyzing and/or altering it (compromising confidentiality and integrity)

- Attacking related security services that rely on trust among network devices (for example, injecting malicious routing information or subverting authentication protocols that are used by the compromised device)

- DoS by making the device unavailable or by changing its settings to deny connectivity

Depending on the device's location and importance, the scope of a security breach can be enormous and the results devastating. Consider the following sample attacks on network devices:

- A core enterprise switch is compromised, resulting in an attacker's ability to analyze and alter all mission-critical data that switches through it.

- An enterprise remote-access server is compromised, thereby allowing an attacker to gather and use user passwords for further intrusions and perhaps to dial out and attack other networks.

- A firewall is compromised, thereby allowing an attacker to reconfigure it and open arbitrary connections into the protected network.

- A border router is compromised, thereby allowing an attacker to intercept the company's Internet traffic and perhaps deny connectivity.

- A core Internet Service Provider (ISP) router is compromised, thereby allowing an attacker to influence routing in the entire ISP network, intercept traffic of countless customers, and impersonate secure servers.

- An attacker breaks into an ISP core router and configures the router to intercept all Domain Name System (DNS) traffic and send it to another system. The attacker now has the means to change the data in any DNS reply and can redirect any client to any Internet server.

These examples illustrate the importance of protecting Internet core devices to prevent large-scale attacks, and protecting enterprise devices to prevent smaller-scale, yet devastating, problems. The following section presents some guidelines for device security.

Network Device Security Guidelines

Securing network infrastructure involves several technical and nontechnical steps; as illustrated in Figure 9-3, the following are the most important steps:

- Teaching the network administrators to use clearly-defined, secure management procedures to avoid accidental human error.

- Treating each network device as a high-value host and hardening (strengthening) it against possible intrusions. This involves common practices such as running only the minimal necessary services and only establishing trust with authentic partners (for example, configuring authenticated routing protocols).

- Providing secure device management channels using strong authentication, session encryption, and change control—for example, using One Time Passwords (OTPs), configuration command authorization, and administrator auditing.

- Patching the device software so security recommendations and identified security issues remain up-to-date.

Figure 9-3 *Securing Network Devices Involves Technical and NonTechnical Means*

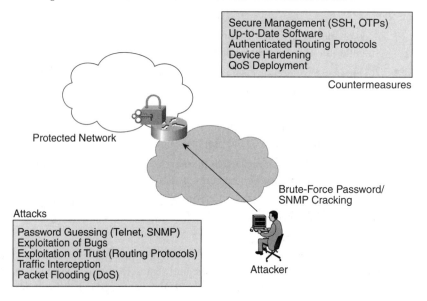

NOTE   *Secure shell (SSH)*, which is mentioned in Figure 9-3, is a UNIX command interface that is used for gaining secure access to a remote computer.

Some Cisco routers now support it; see the following document for details: www.cisco.com/univercd/cc/td/doc/product/software/ios120/120newft/120limit/120s/ 120s5/sshv1.htm.

Securing devices by using these techniques is important to overall security. As the following section details, the networks themselves can also be targets of attacks.

Networks as Targets

Certain types of threats are directed at networks as a whole. Such attacks can include

- **Reconnaissance attacks**—In which the network is being searched for possible targets; examples include network mapping and network-wide probing.

- **DoS attacks**—In which connectivity to an entire network is compromised.

- **Traffic attacks**—In which data flowing over a network is compromised—for example, the reading and changing of data in transit on a network.

The following sections discuss reconnaissance and DoS attacks. Traffic attacks are covered later in this chapter, in the "Transmission Confidentiality" and "Maintaining Data Integrity" sections.

Reconnaissance Attacks Against Networks

Reconnaissance is usually the prelude to a more focused attack against a particular target. Following are some well-known reconnaissance methods that are used against networks to determine what subnets, hosts, and services are available as potential targets:

- Gathering information about a network from registries, such as the DNS or the Internet registrars' databases.

- Discovering access possibilities using network mapping tools (for example, using the **traceroute** command), *war dialing* (attempting to discover and connect to dialup access points), and *war driving* (attempting to discover and connect to misconfigured wireless access points).

- Network mapping attempts using tools that range from primitive (for example, using the **ping** command or Simple Network Management Protocol [SNMP] queries) to very sophisticated (for example, sending seemingly legitimate packets to map a network). Attackers use tools to discover the reachability of hosts, subnets (host scans), or services (port scans), and to look for specific applications.

For an attacker, a reconnaissance attack provides a list of potential targets and weaknesses that were already discovered in the reconnaissance phase. The attacker can now prioritize the targets, determine how difficult the attack would be, and choose further actions.

As shown in Figure 9-4, it is possible to stop most reconnaissance attacks using perimeter defenses, such as firewalls that perform network access control to limit connectivity. In addition, information provided by devices should be limited to the information that is necessary to support business needs (this is known as *device hardening*).

Figure 9-4 *Reconnaissance Attacks Against Networks Can Be Mitigated Using Perimeter Defenses*

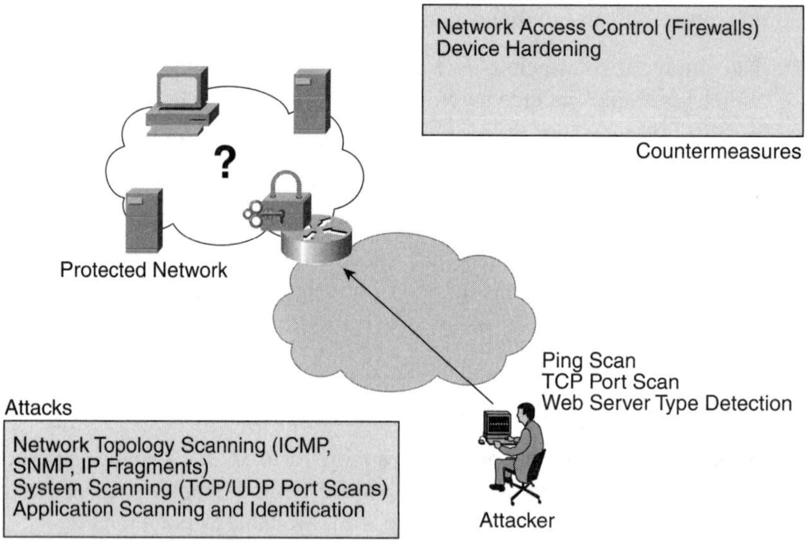

DoS Attacks Against Networks

DoS attacks on a network can compromise connectivity to or from that network, effectively disconnecting it from its neighbors and therefore compromising its availability. The two methods of causing a DoS attack on a device—sending malformed data and sending a large quantity of data—also apply to networks as a whole. Following are two examples of DoS attacks against a network:

- An attacker sends a poisonous packet (an improperly formatted packet, or a packet that is improperly processed by the receiving device) to a device, causing it to crash or halt upon receipt. This can disrupt all communications over the device.

- An attacker sends a continuous stream of packets, thereby overwhelming the available bandwidth of some network links; in most cases, it is impossible to differentiate between an attacker and legitimate traffic, and it is impossible to trace an attack to its source quickly.

If an attacker compromises many systems in the Internet core, the attacker might be able to take advantage of the Internet's virtually unlimited bandwidth to unleash packet storms at various targets. This has already happened on the Internet and is called a *distributed DoS (DDOS)* attack.

Most DoS attacks are extremely difficult to trace and defend against. They can cause significant downtime and are considered among the most serious risks to networked businesses.

DoS Protection Guidelines

DoS attacks that use poisonous data to disable network devices are mitigated by limiting access to devices and using up-to-date (in terms of security patches) software. A critical vulnerability can be discovered in some of the software packages (such as web server software) that many businesses use on their servers. When vulnerabilities become known, many attackers scan networks to locate vulnerable hosts. Scans can quickly discover hundreds, and perhaps thousands, of vulnerable systems in an organization. A restrictive firewall at the network boundary can manage this risk by exposing only a few public servers.

In contrast, DoS attacks that take advantage of resource exhaustion are difficult to trace and expensive (or even impossible) to mitigate. The attacker's goal is to make it difficult or impossible for the network to distinguish between the attacker's data and the legitimate users' data. Defending against these attacks requires a mixture of the following techniques:

- Heuristic-based defense mechanisms, which try to identify the malicious data and discard it before it overwhelms a service. A good example of this is the Transmission Control Protocol (TCP) Intercept feature of Cisco IOS software and Cisco Secure PIX Firewall systems. (For a description of this feature, refer to the TCP Intercept sidebar later in this section).

- Buying more resources than necessary, such as having multiple high bandwidth links to support an e-commerce site even though the normal traffic pattern does not warrant such bandwidth. This could render many DoS attacks useless, but at a higher cost to the defender. If this solution eliminates the threat and makes sense financially, it will mitigate the problem.

- Having plenty of backup options, such as redundant servers and redundant connections, which are not all vulnerable to the same type of DoS attacks.

Figure 9-5 illustrates these DoS defense solutions.

Figure 9-5 *Mitigating DoS Attacks Against Networks*

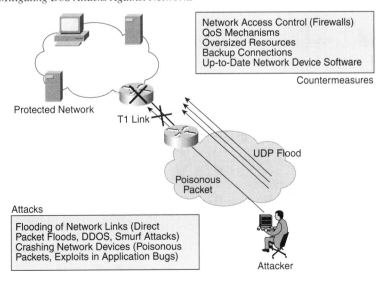

NOTE   A *smurf attack*, noted in Figure 9-5, occurs when an attacker sends ping packets that appear to originate from another device (call it Device A) to the broadcast address. The replies to this ping, from all devices in the network, can overload the device (Device A).

TCP Intercept

The TCP intercept feature of Cisco IOS software and Cisco Secure PIX Firewall systems implements software to protect TCP servers from TCP SYN-flooding attacks, which are a type of DoS attack. A *SYN-flooding attack* occurs when a hacker floods a server with a barrage of connection requests. The connections cannot be established because these messages have unreachable return addresses. The resulting volume of unresolved open connections eventually overwhelms the server and can cause it to deny service to valid requests; this prevents legitimate users from connecting to a website, accessing e-mail, using File Transfer Protocol (FTP) service, and so on.

The TCP intercept feature helps prevent SYN-flooding attacks by intercepting and validating TCP connection requests before they reach the server. In intercept mode, the TCP intercept software intercepts TCP synchronization (SYN) packets from clients to servers that match an extended access list. The software establishes a connection with the client on behalf of the destination server; if successful, it establishes the connection with the server on behalf of the client and knits the two half-connections together transparently. Thus, connection attempts from unreachable hosts never reach the server. The software continues to intercept and forward packets throughout the duration of the connection.

In the case of illegitimate requests, the software's aggressive timeouts on half-open connections and its thresholds on TCP connection requests protect destination servers while still allowing valid requests.

This information was adapted from the information at www.cisco.com/en/US/partner/products/sw/iosswrel/ps1831/products_configuration_guide_chapter09186a00800d9818.html.

DDoS Attacks

The worst attack is the unstoppable one. When performed properly, DDoS is this type of attack. DDoS works by causing tens or hundreds of machines to simultaneously send spurious data to an IP address. The goal of such an attack is generally not to shut down a particular host, but to make the entire network unresponsive. For example, consider an organization with a 1.5-Mbps connection to the Internet that provides e-commerce services to its website users. The organization has intrusion detection, firewalls, logging, and active monitoring in place; unfortunately, none of these security devices help when a hacker launches a successful DDoS attack. Consider a scenario with 100 devices around the world, each with a 500 kbps Internet connection. If these systems are told to flood the serial interface of the e-commerce organization's Internet router, they can easily flood the 1.5-Mbps link with erroneous data. Even if each host can generate only 100 kbps of traffic, that amount is still almost ten times the amount of traffic that the e-commerce site can handle. As a result, legitimate web requests are lost, and the site appears down to most users. The local firewall drops all erroneous data, but by then the damage is done. The traffic has crossed the WAN connection and filled up the link.

Only by cooperating with its ISP can this e-commerce company hope to thwart such an attack. The ISP can configure rate limiting on the outbound interface to the company's site, which would drop most undesired traffic when it exceeds a prespecified amount of the available bandwidth. However, the key to this solution is to correctly flag traffic as undesired traffic.

Common forms of DDoS attacks are Internet Control Message Protocol (ICMP) floods, TCP SYN floods, or User Datagram Protocol (UDP) floods. In an e-commerce environment, this type of traffic is fairly easy to categorize; only when limiting a TCP SYN attack on port 80 (Hypertext Transfer Protocol [HTTP]) does an administrator run the risk of locking out legitimate users during an attack.

Hosts and Applications as Targets

An attacker's ultimate target is often a host, or an application that runs on a host, that processes sensitive data to which the attacker wishes to obtain access. The host and application must be suitably protected against this potential threat. Attackers seek permissions to read or write to sensitive data, thereby compromising confidentiality and integrity; they might also want to cause a DoS attack in a specific application.

Applications can be attacked directly; for example, an attacker might find a flaw in an application and bypass its access controls to obtain read or write access to sensitive data. The complexity of current applications makes such flaws common. In addition, secure development is too costly or not feasible for many businesses.

In another scenario, an attacker might gain access to sensitive data by compromising other system components. For example, an attacker first obtains basic user-level access to the system on which the sensitive data resides. Then, by exploiting a flaw in any local application, the attacker attains system administration privileges (this is known as *privilege escalation*). Using those privileges, the attacker might be able to read or write to most objects on the system, including the target application's sensitive data.

Host and Application Protection Guidelines

To manage host and application risks, multiple protection methods are used together to form a multilayered security system. A multilayered security system does not rely on a single security mechanism to perform a function because that mechanism might be compromised. Instead, different security mechanisms provide a similar protection function and back each other up; this is considered good practice in security system designs.

As shown in Figure 9-6, host and application protection methods include the following defenses:

- Network access control methods (such as firewalls), which only allow access to minimal services and select users.

- Strong host security policies, which protect the operating system and its services from compromise. Such a system resists an attacker when alternate paths to sensitive data are attempted.

- Cryptography, which can provide confidentiality, integrity, and authenticity guarantees for data if it is used properly. Cryptographic methods often protect data when it is outside of the application's control. For example, data on a disk drive is encrypted and can only be read by a specific application. More commonly, all data between the client and the server is encrypted, thereby providing confidentiality over an unsafe network.

- Application access controls, which, coupled with secure programming, are the most significant cornerstones of application security. Secure development is typically expensive and slow. With the creation of safer high-level languages and developers' awareness of security in programming issues, many current systems can provide high levels of application security. Most stock software, which many businesses still use, is vulnerable to simple security attacks.

Military computer networks contain good examples of managing risks to applications. Data in military systems is often labeled with its level of sensitivity (such as secret, top secret, and so forth), and each application executes with a certain level of access (secret, top secret, and so forth). If an attacker subverts an application, the operating system prevents the application from accessing data that is more sensitive than its level of access. This enforcement is simple to implement and does not allow users to change security labels. It works well in military practice because it adheres to the organizational structure. However, in commercial environments, such systems break down because people and data are less hierarchically organized, and access control management is more complex and more difficult to implement securely.

Figure 9-6 *Hosts and Applications Can Be Targets*

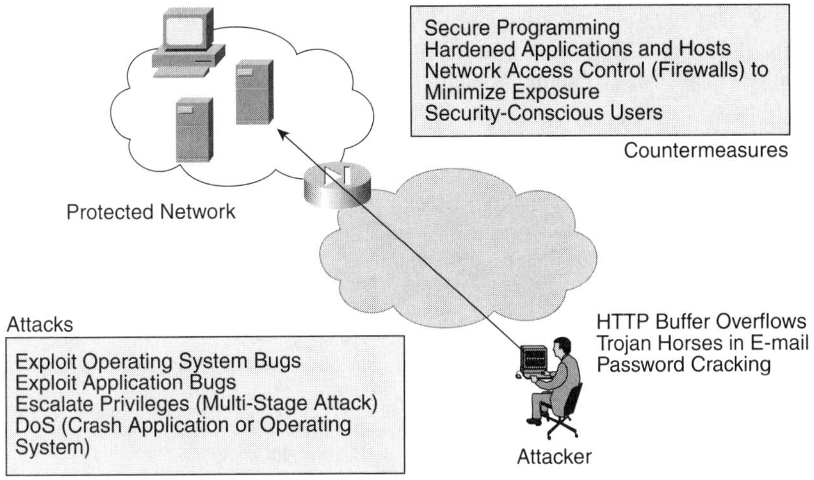

Secure Programming
Hardened Applications and Hosts
Network Access Control (Firewalls) to
Minimize Exposure
Security-Conscious Users

Countermeasures

Protected Network

Attacks

Exploit Operating System Bugs
Exploit Application Bugs
Escalate Privileges (Multi-Stage Attack)
DoS (Crash Application or Operating
System)

HTTP Buffer Overflows
Trojan Horses in E-mail
Password Cracking

Attacker

Identifying Security Mechanisms for a Defined Security Policy

This section discusses the various aspects of a well-documented security policy, which must be defined by the customer or cooperatively by the customer and the network designer, during the initial gathering of customer requirements. We describe possible security mechanisms and explain their impact on network design, operation, and performance.

Security Policy

Network security employs risk management to lower risks to an acceptable level. Risk assessment is the key aspect in identifying and managing the risks that are relevant to a network. Risk assessment results in the development of a network security policy, which documents the level of risk and suggests methods of managing the risk to an acceptable level.

The following sections discuss a process for developing a security policy and documenting it.

The Security Wheel

Risks change over time, and so should the security policy. The *security wheel* is the complete process of initial risk assessment, developing the initial security policy, implementing network security, monitoring and testing of the security, and reassessing the risks. It includes the major tasks of securing networks: reevaluating what is already secured and identifying new risks. The security policy often changes to accommodate current risks, and new measures are deployed to manage them. As described in the next section the security policy includes multiple elements to simplify this task and to address different areas of risk management.

Documenting the Security Policy

Figure 9-7 illustrates a sample security policy and how it can be divided into multiple documents that are applicable to the network segments. A general document describes the overall risk management policy, identifies the corporation's assets, and identifies where protection must be applied. It also documents how risk management responsibility is distributed throughout the enterprise.

Figure 9-7   *Network Security Policy Documents*

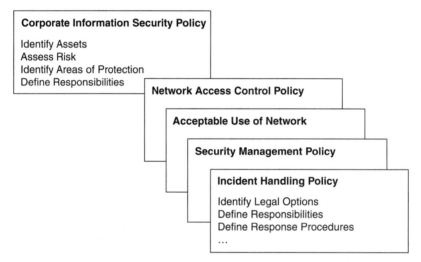

Other documents like the following might address more specific areas of risk management:

- A general Network Access Control Policy can document how data is categorized (such as confidential, internal, and top secret) and what general access control principles are implemented in the networks.

- An Acceptable Use of Network document is usually clearly written and distributed to end users. This document informs users about their risk management roles and responsibilities.

- A Security Management Policy can define how to perform secure computer infrastructure management.

- An Incident Handling Policy can, for example, document the procedures to be used to ensure the reliable and acceptable handling of emergency situations.

Numerous other areas can be covered in separate documents, depending on the organization's requirements.

Security Policy Example

Consider an organization that wants to develop specific guidelines for Internet access as a part of an overall security policy. The organization's overall Information Technology (IT) security policy states that access should be limited only to necessary services, that no user should install or run unauthorized applications, and that all transactions that cross security perimeters should be audited. As a result, the organization deploys the following Internet access restrictions:

- The firewalls only allow access using HTTP and e-mail.

- Internet access to websites should only be business-related.

- The protected network does not allow executable code to be downloaded from external sources.

- The network devices must log all connections to the Internet.

These restrictions are enforced on network devices, documented (in an Acceptable Internet Use document), and distributed to all employees.

Physical Security

Physical security is critical to the successful implementation of network security and can significantly influence the strength of the total security design. This section documents aspects of physical security and provides guidelines for its successful inclusion in the overall security policy.

Physical Threats

Physical security is an aspect of network security design that is often overlooked. In a network, where most of the protection is implemented inside network devices, physical access to the device or the communications media can compromise security. Consider the following potential physical threats:

- A network device does not always enforce all of its security settings when an attacker accesses the hardware directly (for example, it can allow console access, memory probing, and installation of unreliable software).

- Access to the physical communication medium (such as unrestricted access to a switch port, unrestricted wireless network access, or access to the telecommunications infrastructure) can allow an attacker to impersonate trusted systems and view, intercept, and change data that is flowing in a network.

- An attacker might use physically destructive attacks against devices and networks (such as physical force, attacks on the power network, and electromagnetic surveillance and attacks).

A good security policy must anticipate possible physical attacks and assess their relevance in terms of possible loss, probability, and simplicity of attack.

Figure 9-8 illustrates possible physical breaches of network security. In this sample network, an attacker might do the following:

- Break into the computing center and obtain physical access to a firewall and then compromise its physical connections to bypass it or access the console of routers and switches and alter their security settings.

- Obtain physical access to the copper media of the corporate wide-area network (WAN) or the public switched telephone network (PSTN) and easily intercept all communications over the wires. An attacker can read and change sensitive data that is not protected by cryptography.

- Steal a device, such as a home office router or laptop computer, and use it to obtain access to the corporate network.

Figure 9-8 *Physical Security Is Often Overlooked*

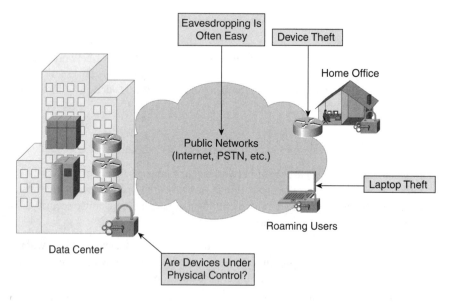

Physical Security Guidelines

The traditional method of managing the risk of physical compromise is to deploy physical access controls using techniques such as locks or alarms. In addition, it is important to identify how a physical security breach might interact with network security mechanisms. For example, there could be a significant risk if an attacker obtained physical access to a switch port that is located in a corporate building and acquired unrestricted access to the corporate network. If, during the policy's development, it were incorrectly assumed that only legitimate users could obtain such access, the attacker would be able to connect to the network without authentication and thus bypass network access control.

A security designer must identify the consequences of device theft on network security. For example, if a laptop computer is stolen from a roaming user, does it contain cryptographic keys that enable the attacker to connect to the enterprise network while impersonating a legitimate user? Moreover, does the network administrator have some scalable means of revoking such credentials that the attacker could obtain through physical theft?

Sometimes a significant portion of the network infrastructure is beyond the enterprise's physical control, and physical controls cannot be enforced at the media access level. For example, many enterprises rely on the fact that the physical infrastructure of the service provider's Frame Relay network is well protected, despite the fact that access to its wire conduits can be obtained easily. Cryptography provides confidentiality, protects the integrity of communication over unsafe networks, and is fully under the enterprise's control. An example is an enterprise that simultaneously transmits sensitive and non-sensitive data over an asynchronous transfer mode (ATM) or Frame Relay link public circuit. Using IP security (IPSec) protection, the sensitive traffic is protected when it is routed over the untrusted WAN, while other traffic is sent unencrypted.

Another example is a government intelligence agency that is concerned about the theft of laptops that might contain extremely sensitive data. To manage this risk, the agency deploys robust file encryption software on the laptops; this software only decrypts sensitive files upon special request. Sensitive information is therefore hidden from a potential thief, who could otherwise read raw data from the laptop's disk.

Authentication

This section introduces the principles of network authentication and presents guidelines for integrating network authentication into a network security design.

Access Control Mechanisms

Modern network security revolves around access control, which is the ability to enforce a policy that states which subjects (such as users, servers, and applications) can access which network resources. With this policy enforced, access control aims to provide the desired confidentiality and integrity of sensitive data. Depending on the granularity of security mechanisms, access rights can be categorized further—for example, into rights that allow a subject to read or write data (to modify it).

Key Point: Authentication and Authorization

Network access control mechanisms are usually classified as either of the following:

— Authentication, which is used to establish subject identity.

— Authorization, which is used to limit subject access to a network.

The following section describes authentication, and the section on "Authorization and Network Filtering" describes authorization.

Network Authentication

Authentication is used to establish a subject's identity in a network. A subject can be a computer user, a computer system, a network device, or an application. It is important to separate the concept of identification, in which a subject *presents* its identity, from authentication, in which a subject *proves* its identity. For example, to log on to a resource, a user might be identified by a username and authenticated by a secret password.

Key Point: Authentication

Authentication, or the proving of identity, is traditionally based on one (or more) of the following three proofs:

- **Something the subject knows**—This usually involves knowledge of a unique secret, which the authenticating parties usually share. To a user, this secret appears as a classic password (or personal identification number [PIN]) or a private cryptographic key.

- **Something the subject has**—This usually involves physical possession of an item that is unique to the subject. Examples include password token cards, Smartcards, and hardware keys.

- **Something the subject is**—This involves verification of a subject's unique physical characteristic, such as a fingerprint, retina pattern, voice, or face.

To achieve high assurance in authentication, many trusted systems require *two-factor authentication* (also known as *strong authentication*); that is, they require a subject to include at least two types of proofs of identity. For example, an access control system might require a Smartcard and a password. With two-factor authentication, a compromise of one factor does not lead to a system compromise. In the example, a password might become known, but it is useless without the Smartcard. Conversely, if the Smartcard is stolen, it cannot be used without the password.

In a network, authentication is required to access sensitive network resources and when a subject wants to connect to the network. In environments where access to the network media is open, authentication is only necessary to allow authorized subjects to become part of the network. Figure 9-9 illustrates examples of where authentication can take place in the Enterprise Network, including the following locations:

- Dialup access points, where any subject can establish a dial connection to the network; authentication is necessary to distinguish between trusted and untrusted subjects. Well-known authentication protocols include Point-to-Point Protocol (PPP), Password Authentication Protocol (PAP), Challenge Handshake Authentication Protocol (CHAP), and Extensible Authentication Protocol (EAP). Those authentication protocols have different security properties: PAP sends the secret password over the link in clear text and should therefore only be used over trusted links or with one-time passwords; CHAP uses a challenge-response mechanism, which defeats password snooping on untrusted links; EAP is the next-generation authentication protocol that can support many authentication methods and is carried within one authentication framework.

- WAN and Virtual Private Network (VPN) infrastructure, where network devices can authenticate each other on WAN or VPN links, thereby mitigating the risk of infrastructure compromise or misconfiguration. WAN peer authentication usually involves PPP mechanisms and routing protocol authentication. In a VPN, authentication is embedded in the VPN security protocols—most often IPSec and Internet Key Exchange (IKE).

- Local-area network (LAN) access, where a network device (switch) authenticates the user before allowing access to the switched network. A standardized LAN authentication protocol is the Institute of Electrical and Electronics Engineers (IEEE) 802.1x (port-based network access control).

- Wireless access, where only authenticated users can establish an association with a wireless access point (IEEE 802.1x). (The "Wireless Security" section of this chapter further discusses wireless security.)

- Firewall authentication, where users must prove their identity when entering a sensitive network that is protected by a firewall.

NOTE   The IEEE 802.1X standard defines a client/server-based access control and authentication protocol that restricts unauthorized clients from connecting to a LAN through publicly accessible ports. An authentication server (such as a Remote Authentication Dial-In User Service [RADIUS] server) authenticates each client that is connected to a switch port before making any services available that are offered by the switch or the LAN.

You can find additional information about IEEE 802.1x at standards.ieee.org/getieee802/802.1.html.

Figure 9-9 *Authentication in the Enterprise Network*

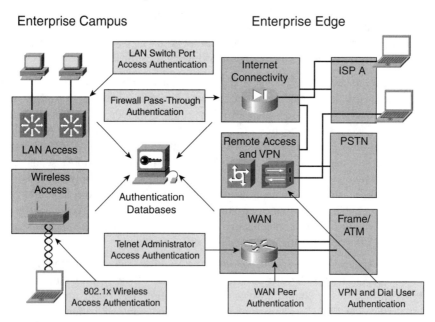

A network should also authenticate management access to its infrastructure; for example, network devices should require authentication for administrators. Telnet, SSH, and SNMP are examples of management protocols that have authentication capabilities, from simple clear text passwords (such as Telnet and SNMPv2) to digital signatures and secure fingerprints (such as SSH and SNMPv3).

Network Authentication Guidelines

It is important to select the appropriate authentication methods, depending on the context, for authentication design and implementation. Stronger (and more reliable) authentication is required for authenticating access to sensitive resources. Examples include direct access to the corporate network from external or untrusted networks (such as the Internet or PSTN) that use remote-access VPN, or terminal access to network devices (using Telnet or SSH). In these instances, an enterprise will probably choose a two-factor authentication for its users.

Authentication should be user-friendly so that users do not willingly compromise it. An example of an unfriendly method is a system that enforces a user password with extremely restrictive rules about password randomness. In many cases, the users do not remember their passwords, so they write them down; the passwords might then be stolen. A more user-friendly alternative is a One Time Password generator (token card) that displays the current password to the user, does not rely on the user to remember anything, and generally generates random passwords. Although such a system might be simple, it can require significant investment in its technology and operations. To lower authentication costs, some enterprises standardize one or a few authentication databases and methods and reuse them for several systems.

For example, consider an organization that must deploy remote-access services to its network from the Internet. It has implemented remote-access VPN technology and requires proper user authentication before users enter the protected network. The organization has had negative experiences using normal passwords and wishes to deploy a very secure yet simple system. One Time Password generators (token cards) for remote users might be the ideal solution because they are secure (they have a two-factor authentication) and simple to use (because the user does not have to remember a complex password).

Authorization and Network Filtering

Authorization mechanisms limit a subject's access to resources based on subject identity. Authorization is most often performed using general access control lists that enumerate subjects and their access rights for each resource. An example is a router packet filtering access control list (ACL) that specifies the clients that can connect to a sensitive server in a network. Another example is when network administrators are restricted to perform only a subset of configuration commands on a router.

In terms of network security, authorization mechanisms on a network can be divided into the following two categories:

- **Authorization of changes to network infrastructure**—Network devices are protected against unauthorized setting (configuration) changes by their operating-system authorization controls.

- **Access to network resources authorization**—Network controls a subject's network settings (such as the IP address) and limits its connectivity (such as filtering of sessions).

Figure 9-10 illustrates an example of device configuration authorization. When multiple administrators manage a network, it is good practice to limit their rights to include only the permissions that are necessary to perform their tasks; in security, this is often called the *least privilege concept*. Some very trusted administrators might require full access to a device, while other administrators might only require monitoring rights and perhaps some special rights for resolving common problems.

Figure 9-10 *Enforcing Network Configuration Authorization*

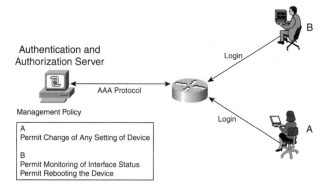

Figure 9-11 illustrates an example of how a network enforces client settings to simplify access control and manage the threat of identity spoofing. In the remote dial access scenario, the access server enforces a particular IP address to the remote user and verifies the user's Caller ID. The same applies to remote-access VPN setup, in which the VPN concentrator configures the remote client with a particular IP address and enforces the use of a personal firewall on the client system. The assigned IP addresses in both scenarios are used by other access control mechanisms, such as firewalls in the enterprise network, to control the subject's access rights.

Figure 9-11 *The Network Has Control over Client Settings*

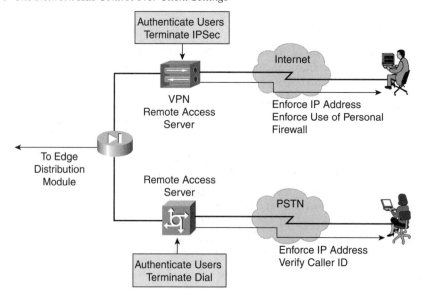

Figure 9-12 illustrates the use of a network firewall to control (or filter) access; this is the most common network authorization application. An enterprise network is usually divided into separate security perimeters (or zones)—such as the untrusted Internet zone, the perimeter of the trusted enterprise campus, perimeters of public and semi-public servers, and so forth—to allow a network firewall to control all traffic that passes between the perimeters. Because all traffic must pass through the network firewall, it enforces the network's access and authorization policy effectively by specifying which connections are permitted or denied between security perimeters.

Figure 9-12   *A Firewall Can Filter Network Sessions*

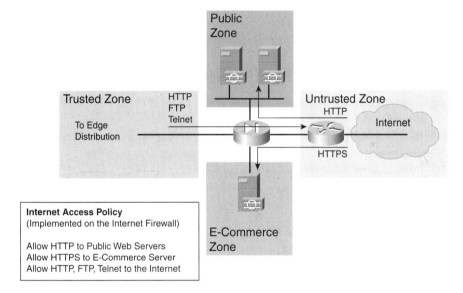

Network Authorization Guidelines

Use the following guidelines to design and implement access authorization:

- **Principle of least privilege**—This principle is based on the practice by which each subject is given only the minimal rights that are necessary (access permissions) to perform their tasks. For example, if a user needs to access a particular web server, the firewall should allow that user to access only the specified web server. In reality, enterprises often introduce lenient rules that allow subjects further access than they require. This can result in deliberate or accidental confidentiality and integrity breaches.

- **Principle of defense in depth**—This principle suggests that security mechanisms should be fault-tolerant; that is, a security mechanism should have a backup security mechanism. This is called the *belt-and-suspenders approach*—both the belt and suspenders are used to ensure that the trousers stay up. An example includes using a dedicated firewall to limit access to a resource, and then using a packet filtering router to add another line of defense.

- **Enforce but do not trust client-supplied settings**—This principle suggests that all networking parameters must be controlled centrally. For example, the client must not be relied upon to configure a proper IP address for remote dial-in; rather, the access server should push those settings to the client.

For example, consider an organization that must present some data on the Internet for its partners. A policy has been developed that requires that all access to that data is properly authorized. An Internet application has been developed that resides on a general-purpose server, and the server must be connected to the Internet. The following network authorization mechanisms must be implemented to ensure protection:

- A firewall system filters all traffic, except the minimal necessary access (this is the *principle of least privilege*), to the server.

- A firewall does not allow any connection from the server; this contains an attacker if a server break-in occurs.

- An access router protects the server with additional filtering, thereby replicating the firewall rules (this is the *principle of defense in depth*).

As discussed throughout this chapter, beyond network authorization, numerous additional application-specific protection mechanisms should be used to protect sensitive data on the server.

Transmission Confidentiality

Transmission confidentiality protects data as it is transported over unsafe networks.

When connecting trusted and untrusted networks—for example, connecting a corporate network with the Internet—data can be transmitted among trusted subjects over untrusted networks. Untrusted networks do not allow implementation of classic access control mechanisms because a corporation does not have control over users and network resources in an untrusted network. Therefore, the transmitted data must be protected to ensure that no one in the untrusted network can view (violate the confidentiality of) or change (violate the integrity of) it. Modern network security relies on cryptography to provide confidentiality and integrity for transmitted data. The following sections introduce guidelines for selecting transmission confidentiality methods and their impact on the overall security design.

Encryption

Key Point: Encryption

Cryptography provides confidentiality through encryption, which is the process of disguising a message to hide its original content.

With encryption, plain text (the readable message) is converted to cipertext (the unreadable, disguised message); decryption reverses this process. The purpose of encryption is to guarantee confidentiality; only authorized entities can encrypt and decrypt data. With most modern algorithms, successful encryption and decryption require knowledge of the appropriate cryptographic keys. An example of data encryption is using encryption algorithms to hide the payload of IP packets using IPSec security protocols.

The network in Figure 9-13 shows a connection of two sites over an untrusted network: the Internet. To provide data confidentiality, a VPN technology that supports encryption creates a secured point-to-point association of the sites over the Internet. All packets that leave one site are encrypted, forwarded through the untrusted network, and decrypted by a device on the remote site. Anyone who eavesdrops on the untrusted network should not be able to decrypt the packet payloads to read sensitive data.

Figure 9-13 *Transmission Confidentiality Provided by Encryption*

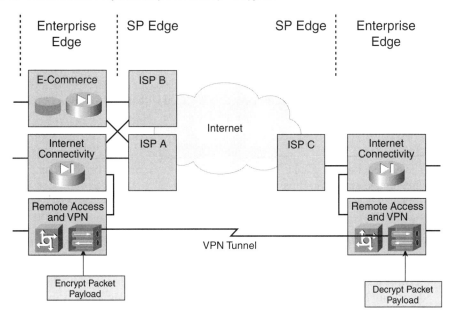

Transmission Confidentiality Guidelines

Following are some specific cryptography guidelines to consider when designing and implementing a solution for transmission confidentiality:

- Cryptography can become a performance bottleneck, and careful analysis is required for determining where data should be protected. In general, if confidential or sensitive data travels over a network where an attacker could easily intercept communications (such as a network outside of the organization's physical control or a network where device compromises are likely), communications must be protected as the security policy defines.

- Modern cryptography can be exported, subject to controls that have recently been relaxed, and can perform well in most scenarios. Therefore, you should use the strongest available cryptography to provide sufficient protection. Be cautious, however; some cryptographic algorithms allow specification of extremely long key lengths, which, at some point, do not provide worthwhile confidentiality improvements.

- Only use well-known cryptographic algorithms, because only well-known algorithms that have been tested and analyzed are considered trustworthy. In general, do not trust any algorithms that claim to represent a security breakthrough; these are often extremely weak and easily broken.

- Do not forget that encryption only provides confidentiality, and most organizations consider data integrity and authenticity equally important security elements. If possible, use both confidentiality- and integrity-guaranteeing cryptographic algorithms.

For example, to lower communication costs, a health insurance company decides to connect some of its branch offices to its headquarters over the Internet. Because the company must protect patient record confidentiality and attackers on the Internet can intercept communications, the company implements a VPN using the strongest possible encryption algorithms to guarantee data confidentiality. In the event of interception, it is unlikely that the attacker can decrypt messages that are protected with modern cryptographic algorithms, such as triple data encryption standard (3DES) or RC4.

NOTE The data encryption standard (DES) uses a 56-bit key. Triple DES (3DES) encrypts the data three times, with up to three different keys.

Maintaining Data Integrity

Data integrity mechanisms use cryptography to protect data that is in transit over untrusted networks. Cryptographic protocols, such as secure fingerprints and digital signatures, can detect any integrity violation of sensitive data. Cryptographic integrity techniques often guarantee data authenticity and protect against replay attacks.

Key Point: Secure Fingerprints

Secure fingerprints attach a cryptographically strong checksum to data. This checksum is generated and verified using a secret key that only authorized subjects know.

By verifying the checksum of received data, an authorized subject can verify data integrity. For example, a method of secure fingerprints known as a Hash-based Message Authentication Code (HMAC) is implemented in the IPSec standard to provide packet integrity and authenticity in IP networks. The HMAC method is very fast and suitable for real-time traffic protection (for both integrity and authentication).

Key Point: Digital Signing

Digital signing of data uses a cryptography method that attaches a digital signature to sensitive data. This signature is generated using a unique signature generation key that is known only to the signer, not all authorized subjects. Other parties can use the signer's signature verification key to verify the signature.

The cryptography behind digital signing guarantees the data's authenticity and the fact that the data has not been modified since it was signed. In the financial world, digital signatures also provide nonrepudiation of transactions, in which a subject can prove to a third party that a transaction has indeed occurred. Digital signature protocols are based on public-key cryptography and, because of their performance limitations, are not used for bulk protection.

Figure 9-14 illustrates a connection between two network sites over the Internet. To provide data integrity, a VPN that supports secure fingerprinting is used to create a secured point-to-point association over the Internet. All packets that leave one site are imprinted with a secure digital fingerprint (similar to a very strong checksum) that uniquely identifies the data at the sender's side. The packets are forwarded onto the untrusted network, and a device on the remote site verifies the secure fingerprint to ensure that no one has tampered with the packet. Anyone who eavesdrops on the untrusted network should not be able to change the packet payloads; therefore, they should not be able to change sensitive data without being detected.

Figure 9-14 *Secure Fingerprints Ensure Data Integrity*

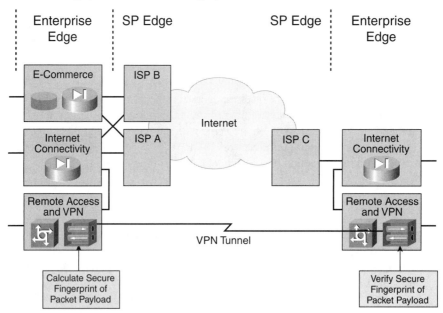

Transmission Integrity Guidelines

Following are some guidelines for using integrity cryptographic mechanisms, which are similar to those for confidentiality mechanisms:

- Carefully evaluate the need for integrity and enforce only where justified by potential threats.

- Use the strongest available mechanisms for integrity, but take the performance effects into account.

- Only use established and well-known cryptographic algorithms.

For example, consider an organization that must transmit stock market data over the Internet. Confidentiality is not its main concern; rather, its primary risk lies in the possibility of an attacker changing data in transit and presenting false stock market data to the organization. Because e-mail is the organization's preferred data exchange application, it decides to implement digital signatures of all e-mail messages when exchanging data among partners over the Internet.

Secure Management and Reporting

Network and security management can use many of the authentication and authorization mechanisms discussed in this chapter to authenticate administrator access to devices and authorize configuration changes. This section documents the importance of secure network management and security management practices and provides guidelines for their design.

Key Point: Secure Management

A secured network must be managed securely. Network managers must use well-defined operational practices, and network management protocols must be protected.

Audit Trails and Intrusion Detection

An important task of security management is the creation and analysis of an *audit trail*, which tracks the activities of a network's users and systems. An audit trail consists of the following:

- **Logging data**—Systems and applications audit exceptional events for analysis.
- **Accounting data**—Systems and applications audit user actions.

In a network, the resulting audit trail records are examined for various purposes, including the following:

- To detect and respond to unauthorized actions that endanger sensitive data (security monitoring).
- To identify new risks.
- To collect usage statistics for the purpose of contingency planning and billing (accounting).

Detecting and responding to unauthorized actions are primary security-related tasks that provide information about how effectively the security policy is enforced, and what attacks are being launched against the network. Compare this information to the risk profile that is defined by the security policy. Such monitoring is generally called *intrusion detection* and can be performed in real time or by using offline analysis.

Intrusion detection systems (IDSs) can range from basic (such as displaying attack statistics) to very complex (such as correlating events from multiple sources over a long period of time). Modern IDSs include the following systems:

- **Host Intrusion Detection Systems (HIDSs)**—Installed on network servers and provide detection and protection against attacks within the host operating system.

- **Network Intrusion Detection Systems (NIDSs)**—Installed on the network, where they search for potential attacks by capturing and analyzing network traffic. In Cisco's case, an NIDS is a sensor appliance (a purpose-built device) that is installed passively on the network so as not to impede or introduce any delay or overhead on the network traffic itself.

Figure 9-15 illustrates a sample network that contains some intrusion detection systems.

Figure 9-15 *Intrusion Detection Systems Identify, Log, and Respond to Attacks*

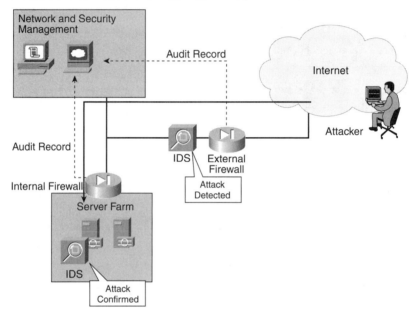

In this sample network, an attacker on the Internet attempts to connect to a server in the enterprise network and perhaps copy some confidential data. The Internet firewall permits the connection, and the syslog protocol sends a log of the connection to the central logging server. The intrusion detection system behind the Internet firewall detects an attempted breach of security and reports it to its management station. The external IDS might also be configured to respond and possibly stop the attacker immediately. The intranet firewall also permits the connection and sends a syslog audit record to the log repository. The intrusion detection system that runs on the target host confirms the security breach and responds by disallowing the attacker further access. The security manager receives several alerts, correlates them, assesses the damage, and prepares a structured response to the attack.

NOTE   Device and policy management systems are used to configure security devices according to appropriate policies.

Secure Management and Monitoring Guidelines

You can use the following guidelines while designing and implementing network and security management and monitoring:

- Network management personnel must be aware of secure management techniques and operations. To prevent accidental damage, they must be trained in the correct change control and monitoring procedures.

- Network and security management channels must be secure. This is usually accomplished by using either a separate management network (such as a separate VLAN) or cryptography to protect management protocols (such as SSH for terminal access or IPSec protocols to protect SNMP traffic).

- You must implement change control for configuration and software changes. All device configurations must be audited, and perhaps versioned, and device software maintained according to corporate standards.

- Results of the auditing process (for example, logs and traps) must be centrally stored and analyzed for monitoring purposes. In addition to classic logging, which is usually performed using the syslog protocol, intrusion detection systems can provide automatic correlation and in-depth visibility into complex security events. This saves administrators a considerable amount of time.

- IDSs should be deployed where the best security visibility is required—usually on the most important network segments (for example, where high-value servers reside or near external connections) and hosts. Host and network intrusion detection should complement each other to provide the best probability of detection and allow the security administrator to respond to an incident quickly and reliably.

Consider an organization that must manage a remote router at its branch office, for example. The security policy requires that the management channel be secured against eavesdropping and strong authentication for managers. A local branch office administrator must have limited access to the router to check its interface status. The solution is to implement secure management practices using only encrypted terminal sessions (using SSH) to the router, One Time Passwords to authenticate administrators, and configuration control to provide different levels of access to different administrators.

Selecting Security Solutions within Network Modules

This section introduces the Cisco SAFE Blueprint and provides information on best practices for designing and implementing secure networks. It describes the security threats that are identified in each network module of the Enterprise Composite Network and assesses possible security solutions. The emphasis is on external threats: network perimeter security (for example, in the E-commerce module, the Internet Connectivity module, the Remote Access and VPN module, and the WAN module) and the Server Farm and Network Management modules of the Enterprise Campus. This section also discusses IP telephony security and concludes with an introduction to the CiscoWorks Auto Update Server, an innovative tool for configuring Cisco PIX firewalls.

Cisco SAFE Blueprint

To assist network designers and security architects, Cisco has developed the SAFE Blueprint for providing guidelines for implementing security mechanisms within the network infrastructure and beyond. The intent of SAFE is to provide information regarding best practices for designing and implementing secure networks. The SAFE security design follows a modular approach, in which each of the network modules is analyzed to determine the threats, assess the severity of risks, and suggest best-practice guidelines for design and implementation. SAFE often exceeds pure network security because it relies on the concept of *defense in depth*, in which the failure of one security system is unlikely to lead to the compromise of network resources.

Cisco's SAFE Blueprint

SAFE emulates the functional requirements of today's enterprise networks as closely as possible. Implementation decisions vary depending on the required network functionality. However, the following design objectives (listed in order of priority) guide the decision-making process:

— Security and attack mitigation based on policy

— Security implementation throughout the infrastructure (not just on specialized security devices)

— Secure management and reporting

— Authentication and authorization of users and administrators to critical network resources

— Intrusion detection for critical resources and subnets

— Support for emerging networked applications

First and foremost, SAFE is a security architecture. It must prevent most attacks from successfully affecting valuable network resources. The attacks that succeed in penetrating the first line of defense or that originate from inside the network must be accurately detected and quickly contained to minimize their effect on the rest of the network. However, when secure, the network must continue to provide critical services that users expect. Proper network security and good network functionality can be provided at the same time. The SAFE architecture is not a revolutionary way of designing networks, but merely a blueprint for making networks secure.

SAFE is also resilient and scalable. Resilience in networks includes physical redundancy to protect against a device failure, whether through misconfiguration, physical failure, or network attack.

At many points in the network design process, you must choose between using integrated functionality in a network device versus using a specialized functional appliance. The integrated functionality is often attractive because you can implement it on existing equipment, and because the features can interoperate with the rest of the device to provide a better functional solution. Appliances are often used when the required depth of functionality is very advanced, or when performance needs require specialized hardware. Most critical security functions migrate to dedicated appliances because of large enterprise networks' performance requirements.

This information was adapted from Cisco's SAFE Blueprint, which is available at www.cisco.com/go/safe.

The SAFE Blueprint uses the Enterprise Composite Network modular view of the network infrastructure, which we introduced in Chapter 3, "Structuring and Modularizing the Network." By using a modular approach, a security designer reviews the security policy and then focuses on individual modules of the enterprise network to address the relevant risks. However, it is important to understand that SAFE does not apply to every network in the same way. Some networks might already have protection mechanisms in place and therefore cannot be redesigned to support SAFE designs; SAFE generally assumes that the network is being designed securely from the beginning. In this case, SAFE can provide suggestions for how to improve existing security methods and introduce ideas about additional measures to provide defense in depth.

For example, the network diagram in Figure 9-16 illustrates how SAFE guidelines can be applied to the enterprise network's Remote Access and VPN module. SAFE provides general design suggestions and selected configuration guideline recommendations for increasing security and complying with the risk management strategies the security policy suggests.

Figure 9-16 *Sample SAFE Guidelines for Remote Access and VPN Module*

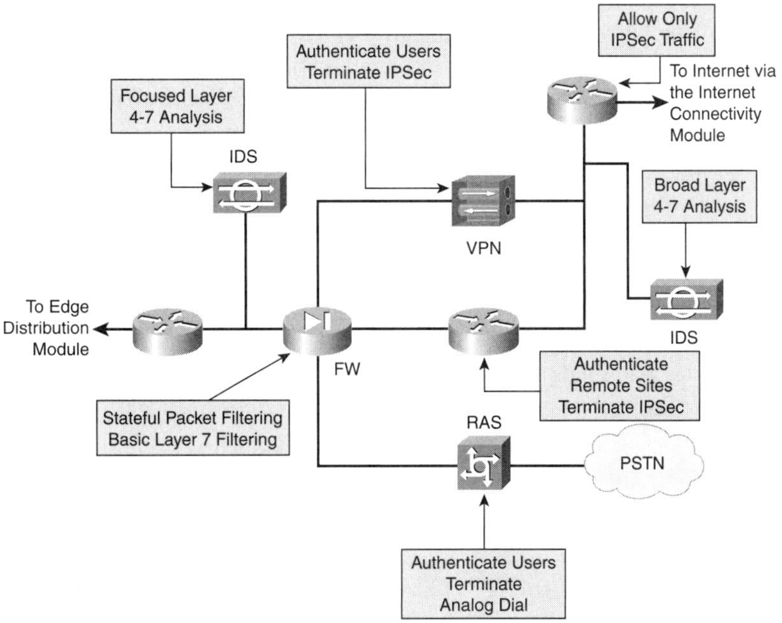

The following sections provide guidelines for securing the various modules in the Enterprise Composite Network.

Securing the Internet Connectivity Module

The Internet Connectivity module directly or indirectly connects all other network modules to the Internet, thereby establishing potential contact with the most dangerous external network where attackers can gain network access most easily, and where the attackers are difficult to trace. Public servers, such as an enterprise network's web and mail relay servers, are traditionally connected in this module, thereby exposing them to the Internet. Historically, the majority of IP networks were strengthened at this point; this was reasonable because of the involved risks. However, this philosophy often relaxed security in other parts of the network. The SAFE blueprint enables all parts of the network to be included in a systematic security design, with each part secured according to the organization's policy.

Risks at the Internet Connectivity Module

Common risks associated with the Internet Connectivity module include the following:

- Reconnaissance threats from the Internet, in which an attacker attempts to probe the network and its hosts in an effort to map the network in order to discover reachable networks, hosts, and services that are running on exposed hosts. An example of such mapping is an attempt to ping all systems in the enterprise's IP address range.

- The compromise of exposed hosts and their applications, which can lead directly to confidentiality breaches and integrity violations for data that is processed by exposed servers (such as a web server or a mail relay server). An example is an attacker who breaks into the mail relay server and can view or change all mail messages that pass between the enterprise and the Internet.

- The compromise of other hosts from compromised hosts in the module. This enables an attacker to first compromise a host in the Internet Connectivity module and, from that host, compromise a host on another network, such as the Enterprise Campus. An example is an attacker who breaks into a public web server and, from there, into the internal database server.

- DoS attacks that are directed at exposed hosts in this module. An example is an attacker who sends a storm of connection requests (also known as a *SYN flood*) to the public Web server, thereby disabling its services.

- DoS attacks that are directed at network links, such as the enterprise network's Internet connection. For example, an attacker could send a multigigabit stream of ICMP messages toward the enterprise network, thereby congesting its link to the Internet.

- Introduction of malicious code (for example, viruses, Trojan horses, and malicious mobile code in Internet browsers) over supported services, such as e-mail and Internet access. A well-known example is an e-mail message with an executable attachment that contains a Trojan horse program; when executed, this program sends the local user's passwords to the attacker.

Guidelines for Securing Internet Connectivity Module

To manage the risks that are associated with the Internet Connectivity module, well-known and accepted solutions exist and are defined by the Cisco SAFE blueprint. These solutions include the following:

- To manage the risk of network mapping attempts, the routers and first-line firewall devices should block all incoming connections except those that are necessary for the exposed hosts in the module. This prevents network mapping applications from reaching other hosts and networks. Configuring access control lists on routers and firewalls is an example of a tool that can be used to filter connections.

- To manage the risk of compromising an exposed host, the usual solution is to configure network firewalls to permit only the minimal required connections to exposed servers, and then secure the exposed server applications. Then, network and host intrusion detection systems monitor individual hosts and subnets to detect signs of attack or malicious network activity and identify potential successful breaches.

- To manage the risk of compromising other hosts from already compromised hosts, a common solution is to build a demilitarized zone (DMZ) network within the module. DMZ networks are connected to a leg of a firewall and contain one or more servers. The purpose of a DMZ network is to contain an attacker who has compromised a host so that the firewall again filters all access from the potentially compromised host. This allows the enforcement of an extremely strict connection policy that denies all connections from public servers by default, and prevents connectivity to hosts outside the DMZ network. If multiple hosts are located in the same DMZ, LAN switch-based security access control mechanisms such as private VLANs can also effectively restrict communications among such hosts. Hardening of the other hosts (running reliable and up-to-date operating systems and applications) presents another defense in depth technique. Intrusion detection systems detect further break-in attempts from compromised hosts.

- DoS attacks that are directed at hosts are managed by running reliable and up-to-date (patched) operating systems and applications, and by using all available host DoS protection tools on a firewall (such as connection rate limiting).

- Devices that are connected to potentially critical resources manage DoS attacks that are directed at networks. For example, the Internet router can limit the rate of specific traffic types over links to make flooding more difficult.

- Application code that is transferred between the Enterprise Campus and the Internet is often filtered using special application filtering servers in the Internet Connectivity module. Such servers examine the content of the application protocol by scanning and possibly eliminating dangerous content, such as viruses or mobile code.

Table 9-1 summarizes the guidelines for securing the Internet Connectivity module.

Table 9-1   *Guidelines for Securing the Internet Connectivity Module*

Risk	Managed By
Network mapping attempts	Network access control using firewalls, routers, and network IDS
Compromise of exposed hosts	Network access control using firewalls, host hardening, network and host IDS
Compromise of other hosts from compromised hosts	DMZ networks, network access control using firewalls, host hardening, LAN switch access control, network and host IDS
DoS directed at hosts	Host hardening, firewalls
DoS directed at links	Network IDS, quality of service (QoS) mechanisms
Introduction of malicious code	Application filtering

Figure 9-17 illustrates some risk management techniques and their positions within the Internet Connectivity module.

Figure 9-17   *Securing the Internet Connectivity Module*

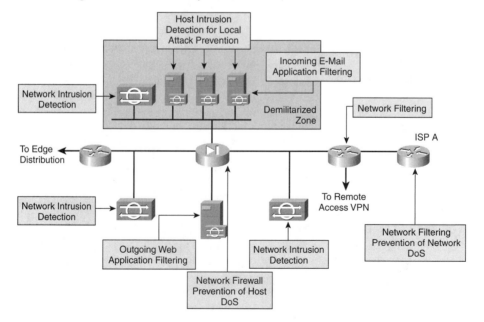

E-commerce Module Security

The E-commerce module hosts application servers that serve e-commerce applications to Internet users. (Internet connectivity is available through the Internet Connectivity module, which already provides security mechanisms to manage risks, such as network DoS.)

Risks in the E-commerce Module

Specific security risks in the E-commerce module include the following:

- Compromise of exposed e-commerce hosts and applications, a risk that is also present in the Internet Connectivity module. However, because the E-commerce module usually hosts high-profile servers that process highly confidential and sensitive data, a compromise could result in a more substantial loss.

- Compromise of other hosts, including other e-commerce servers, from compromised e-commerce servers in this module.

- DoS attacks which are directed at E-commerce server's operating systems or applications.

Guidelines for Securing the E-commerce Module

To manage the risks to the E-commerce module, the following techniques are recommended:

- Host and application protection is managed through tight network filtering on firewalls and through good host hardening and secure applications.

- To manage the risk of compromising other hosts from compromised e-commerce servers, similar techniques are used as in the Internet Connectivity module. E-commerce applications are often multitiered and run on multiple servers. For example, an E-commerce application front-end web server accepts encrypted sessions from Internet clients, processes the requests, and queries a database server that contains sensitive data. Separating the multitiered server systems into their own DMZ networks ensures that there is a firewall system between them to protect more secure servers in the event of front-end compromise. Firewalls generally restrict connections from exposed e-commerce servers, so the compromise of any other host is less likely. LAN switch access control mechanisms (such as private VLANs) can separate hosts on the same segment. Network and host intrusion detection systems can monitor individual hosts and subnets to detect signs of attacks and confirm potential successful breaches.

- The same risk management mechanisms apply for host-directed DoS attacks as for the Internet Connectivity module—specifically, running reliable and up-to-date (patched) operating systems and applications (host hardening), deploying host intrusion detection software, and using all available host DoS protection tools on a firewall.

Table 9-2 summarizes the guidelines for securing the E-commerce module.

Table 9-2 *Guidelines for Securing the E-commerce Module*

Risk	Managed By
Compromise of exposed hosts and applications	Network access control using firewalls, host hardening, secure programming of applications, intrusion detection
Compromise of other hosts from compromised hosts	DMZ networks, access control using network firewalls, intrusion detection, LAN switch access control
DoS directed at exposed hosts	Host hardening, access control using network firewalls, intrusion detection

Figure 9-18 illustrates risk management techniques and their positioning within the E-commerce module.

Figure 9-18 *Securing the E-commerce Module*

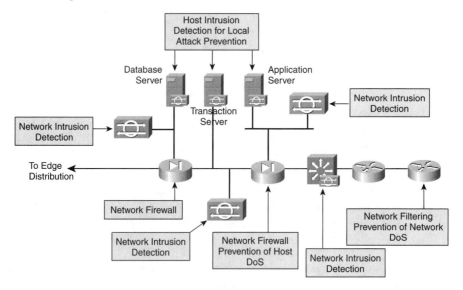

Observe the multiple-DMZ network concept in Figure 9-18; it separates multitiered E-commerce application servers in their own segments, which are separated by firewalls.

For example, an enterprise sets up an E-commerce server farm that consists of an application web server and a back-end database server, which replicates data from internal production servers. A good firewall design places both servers in separate DMZ networks with firewalls in between and allows only the necessary e-commerce application connections. Moreover, the application itself can be developed using high-level languages and security awareness, and an outside verification agency can check the code. Intrusion detection on both hosts and network intrusion detection in most segments are used to detect attack attempts and perhaps respond to some of the attacks automatically. This design could be simplified with a single, multilegged firewall rather than multiple firewall devices that separate all of these segments. Multiple firewall devices are often used to distribute access rules to multiple devices, thereby making them simpler to understand and lessening the impact of firewall misconfiguration or potential firewall code bugs, which hopefully impact only one of many devices.

Remote Access and VPN Module Security

The Remote Access and VPN module hosts dialup access servers, remote-access VPN concentrators, and site-to-site VPN gateways. Internet connectivity is available through the Internet Connectivity module, which already provides security mechanisms to manage some risks such as network DoS. Local connectivity to external dial networks, such as the PSTN, is also available.

Risks in the Remote Access and VPN Module

Specific risks in the Remote Access and VPN module include the following:

- **Identity spoofing of remote clients or sites**—Where an attacker can impersonate a legitimate client and log in to the remote-access VPN connection. This is possible if an attacker steals a legitimate user's credentials (such as a dialup username and password pair) or correctly guesses the authentication keys of a VPN connection, for example.

- **Compromise of data transmission confidentiality and integrity**—Because VPN and dialup connections are both transported over public networks (the Internet or PSTN), an attacker can access and change sensitive data by accessing the network media. For example, an attacker might break into an ISP or a Telco switch and eavesdrop on traffic.

- **Compromise of a client or remote site**—Where an attacker successfully attacks the protected network over the VPN or dialup connection through a legitimate client's system or a branch office. An example is a VPN client that has been compromised by a Trojan horse application. Such an application could turn the client system into a relay so that when the client is connected to the enterprise network via an Internet remote-access VPN, the attacker can connect to the client from the Internet, and from the client to the protected enterprise network over the VPN.

Guidelines for Securing the Remote Access and VPN Module

You can use the following security solutions to manage the risks that are associated with the Remote Access and VPN module:

- To manage the risk of identity spoofing and because external networks do not provide any trusted authentication by themselves, an organization should deploy strong authentication for access from an external network. Examples include token-card two-factor authentication for remote clients and public-key-based (certificate) authentication for VPN sites.

- Modern cryptography can be used to manage the risk of compromising transmission confidentiality and integrity over an unsafe network. Encryption algorithms provide confidentiality, while per-packet secure fingerprints provide data integrity and authenticity. The IPSec protocol suite is a well-known standard that provides confidentiality, integrity, and authenticity in an IP network. IPSec provides a secure path between remote users and the VPN concentrator, and between remote sites and the VPN site-to-site gateway. IPSec can also protect classic dialup users over the PSTN.

- To manage the risk of compromised clients and remote sites, enforce security standards on remote clients and sites and use network firewalls to limit access to the protected network. For example, a VPN concentrator might verify that the client is running a personal firewall and thus prevent communication with the Internet while connected to the VPN.

Table 9-3 summarizes the guidelines for securing the Remote Access and VPN module.

Table 9-3   *Guidelines for Securing the Remote Access and VPN Module*

Risk	Managed By
Client/site identity spoofing	Strong authentication mechanisms
Compromise of data transmission confidentiality and integrity	Strong cryptography (encryption and secure fingerprints of packets)
Compromised clients and remote sites	Personal firewalls, network firewalls, virus scanning

Figure 9-19 illustrates the implementation of risk management mechanisms in the Remote Access and VPN module.

Consider an organization that is migrating from a costly analog dialup access system to an Internet remote-access and VPN system. When using the dialup system, the organization accomplishes authentication by using plain passwords (something a user knows) and callback to a predefined telephone number (something a user is). When migrating to the Internet, the organization requires equivalent authentication strength and thus deploys One Time Password token cards. To guarantee confidentiality and integrity, the organization chooses the strong encryption and integrity guarantees of the IPSec protocol suite.

Figure 9-19 *Securing the Remote Access and VPN Module*

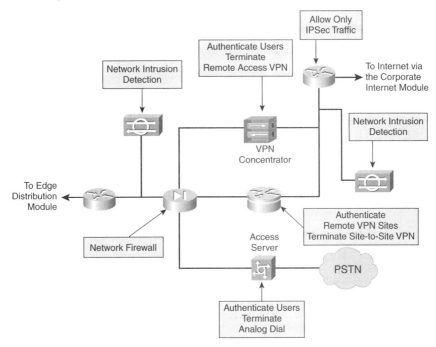

Wireless Security

This section describes wireless LANs (WLANs) and the 802.11b protocol and discusses the security aspects of these popular networks.

WLANs

Wireless networks have become one of the most interesting targets for today's hackers. Organizations are currently deploying wireless technology at a faster rate than most IT departments can keep up with. This rapid deployment is partially due to the low cost of the devices, the ease of deployment, and the large productivity gains. Because WLAN devices ship with all security features disabled, this wide deployment has attracted the hacker community's attention.

Most organizations' WLANs operate in a mode called *infrastructure,* in which all wireless clients connect through an access point (AP) for all communications. WLAN technology can be deployed in a mode called *ad hoc*, in which devices form an independent, peer-to-peer network. In an ad hoc WLAN, laptop or desktop computers that are equipped with compatible WLAN adapters and are within range of one another can share files directly, without using an AP. The security impact of ad hoc WLANs is significant. Many wireless cards ship with the ad hoc mode enabled by default. Any hacker who is also configured for ad hoc mode is immediately connected to PCs that use these cards and can attempt to gain unauthorized access.

Following are some basic recommendations that every WLAN device should follow:

- Access point security recommendations:
  - Enable user authentication for the management interface.
  - Choose strong community strings for SNMP and change them frequently.
  - If your management infrastructure allows it, consider using SNMP read-only mode.
  - Disable any insecure and nonessential management protocol provided by the manufacturer.
  - Utilize secure management protocols, such as SSH.
  - Limit management traffic to a dedicated wired subnet.
  - Isolate management traffic from user traffic and encrypt all management traffic, where possible.
  - Enable wireless frame encryption where available.
  - Physically secure the access point.
- Client security recommendations:
  - Disable ad hoc mode.
  - Enable wireless frame encryption where available.

Two additional practices that can help improve wireless security include the following:

- Turn off Service Set Identifiers (SSIDs) broadcast on the AP. The SSID is an identifier for the WLAN; to connect to the WLAN, a device must know the SSID.
- Enforce Media Access Control (MAC) authentication on the AP. However, this can be a complex solution because every AP would have to retain a list of all legitimate MAC addresses; maintaining this list would be very cumbersome.

The following section introduces the 802.11b WLAN protocol and its security features.

802.11b

Currently, 802.11b is the most widely deployed WLAN technology. The foundation of the security of 802.11b is based on a frame encryption protocol called Wired Equivalent Privacy (WEP).

WEP is a simple mechanism that protects the over-the-air transmission between WLAN access points and network interface cards (NICs). Working at the data link layer, WEP requires that all communicating parties share the same secret key (40- or 128-bit). However,

WEP can easily be cracked, in both 40- and 128-bit variants, by using off-the-shelf tools that are readily available on the Internet.

Changing WEP keys frequently is good practice for reducing the possibility of key exposure. Other solutions to the WEP problem include a network layer encryption approach based on IPSec, a mutual authentication-based key distribution method using 802.1X, and some proprietary improvements to WEP, which Cisco implemented recently. The following sections describe these solutions. Additionally, IEEE 802.11 Task Group "i" and the Wi-Fi Alliance compliance testing committee are working on standardizing WLAN authentication and encryption improvements.

IPSec in WLANs

IPSec is an open standards framework for ensuring secure private communications over IP networks. IPSec VPNs use the services that are defined within IPSec to ensure confidentiality, integrity, and authenticity of data communications across such public networks as the Internet. IPSec also has a practical application to secure WLANs by overlaying IPSec on top of clear text 802.11 wireless traffic.

In a WLAN environment, an IPSec client is installed on every PC that is connected to the WLAN, and users are required to establish an IPSec tunnel to route any traffic to the wired network. Filters prevent any wireless traffic from reaching any destination other than the VPN gateway (and the DNS and Dynamic Host Configuration Protocol [DHCP] servers).

802.1X and Extensible Authentication Protocol

An alternative WLAN security approach focuses on developing a framework for providing centralized authentication and dynamic key distribution. This approach is based on the IEEE 802.11 Task Group "i" end-to-end framework using 802.1X and EAP to provide this enhanced functionality. Cisco has incorporated 802.1X and EAP into its WLAN security solution (the Cisco Wireless Security Suite). (IEEE 802.1X is a standard for port-based network access control, as discussed in the "Network Authentication" section of this chapter.)

Following are the three main elements of an 802.1X and EAP approach:

- Mutual authentication between a client and a RADIUS authentication server
- Encryption keys dynamically derived after authentication
- Centralized policy control, where session time-out triggers reauthentication and new encryption key generation

When this approach is implemented, a wireless client that associates with an AP cannot access the network until the user performs a network logon—the client and the RADIUS server exchange EAP messages to perform mutual authentication, with the client verifying the RADIUS server credentials, and vice versa. Upon successful mutual authentication, the RADIUS server and client then derive a client-specific WEP key, which the client uses for the current logon session. User passwords and session keys are never transmitted in the clear over the wireless link.

Current EAP authentication methods available include

- EAP-Cisco Wireless (LEAP) (also called *Lightweight EAP*)
- EAP-Transport Layer Security (EAP-TLS)
- Protected EAP (PEAP)
- EAP-Tunneled TLS (EAP-TTLS)
- EAP-Subscriber Identity Module (EAP-SIM)

In the Cisco SAFE wireless architecture, LEAP, EAP-TLS, and PEAP were tested and documented as viable mutual authentication EAP protocols for WLAN deployments.

WEP Improvements

IEEE 802.11i includes the following two encryption enhancements in its draft standard for 802.11 security:

- Temporal Key Integrity Protocol (TKIP), a set of software enhancements to RC4-based WEP.
- Advanced Encryption Standard (AES), which is a stronger alternative to the RC4 encryption algorithm that is used in WEP.

Before the 802.11i standard was introduced, Cisco introduced TKIP support as a component of the Cisco Wireless Security Suite; this implementation is sometimes referred to as Cisco TKIP. In 2002, 802.11i finalized the TKIP specification, and the Wi-Fi Alliance announced that it was making TKIP a component of Wi-Fi Protected Access (WPA), which will become a requirement for Wi-Fi compliance before the end of 2003. The enterprise version of WPA also requires 802.1X for 802.11. Both Cisco TKIP and the WPA TKIP include per-packet keying (PPK) and message integrity check (MIC). WPA TKIP also includes an extension of the initialization vector, from 24 bits to 48 bits.

NOTE   Per-packet keying uses different keys per packet as a potential means of mitigating the attacks against WEP.

MIC protects WEP frames from tampering—the MIC is based on a seed value, destination MAC address, source MAC address, and payload (that is, any changes to these affects the MIC value). The WEP-encrypted payload includes the MIC.

Even with these protocols and improvements, many security threats are still associated with WLANs. The next section summarizes the risks that are inherent in a wireless network, and guidelines for reducing them.

Wireless Risks and Mitigation Strategies

Following are specific risks that are associated with wireless networks, and their mitigation strategies:

- **Wireless packet sniffers**—Wireless packet sniffers can take advantage of any of the known WEP vulnerabilities to derive the encryption key. WEP enhancements, key rotation using EAP, and IPSec encryption mitigate these threats.

- **Unauthenticated access**—Only authenticated users should be able to access the wireless and wired network. Optional access control on the Layer 3 switch limits wired network access.

- **Man-in-the-middle**—Combined with the MIC, the mutual authentication nature of several EAP authentication types prevents a hacker from inserting himself in the path of wireless communications. IPSec encryption can also mitigate this threat.

- **IP spoofing**—Hackers cannot perform IP spoofing without authenticating to the WLAN first. After authenticating, optional filtering on the Layer 3 switch restricts any spoofing to the local subnet range. If using IPSec, hackers can spoof traffic on the wireless LAN; however, only valid, authenticated IPSec packets ever reach the production wired network.

- **Address Resolution Protocol (ARP) spoofing**—ARP spoofing occurs when an attacker inserts its MAC address in the reply to an ARP request, allowing it to receive data that is destined for someone else. Hackers cannot perform ARP spoofing without authenticating to the WLAN first. After authenticating, ARP spoofing attacks can be launched in the same manner as in a wired environment to intercept other users' data.

- **Network topology discovery**—If they are unable to authenticate, hackers cannot perform network discovery. When authenticated via EAP, standard topology discovery can occur in the same way that is possible for the wired network. If using IPSec, only necessary protocols are allowed into the corporate network, thereby mitigating this risk.

- **Password attack**—These threats are mitigated by auditing selected passwords for weakness and adhering to a good password usage policy that limits the number of tries for a password before locking out the account. Some of the EAP types incorporate various methods, including tunneling user information and public key cryptography, to mitigate this risk.

WAN Module Security

The WAN module provides WAN connectivity among different parts of the enterprise network and usually connects campuses with branch offices. This section provides guidelines for implementing security mechanisms in the WAN module.

Risks in the WAN Module

Specific risks in the WAN module include the following:

- Compromise of data transmission confidentiality and integrity, whereby an attacker who obtains physical access to the network media or a service provider WAN switch can intercept WAN connections. An attacker might eavesdrop on any traffic or change data in transit.

- Accidental or deliberate misconfiguration of the WAN network that interconnects different enterprises. Some WAN protocols can establish automatic peering, and unwanted connectivity might become possible.

The following section provides guidelines for mitigating these risks.

Guidelines for Securing the WAN Module

To manage the risks in the WAN module, apply the following guidelines:

- The same technologies that are used with Internet VPNs can be used to protect WAN communications. Encryption algorithms provide confidentiality, and per-packet secure fingerprints provide data integrity and authenticity. For example, IPSec protocols are often deployed on enterprise WAN networks to protect sensitive data.

- To prevent the accidental WAN interconnection of different enterprises, WAN devices might require authentication of peers and routing protocols over WAN links. Therefore, the WAN devices might not accept data from an unknown device, even though they both use the same WAN protocol.

Table 9-4 summarizes the guidelines for securing the WAN module.

Table 9-4   *Guidelines for Securing the WAN Module*

Risk	Managed By
Compromise of data transmission confidentiality and integrity	Strong cryptography (encryption and secure fingerprints of packets), network firewalls for access control
Service provider WAN misconfiguration	WAN peer authentication

Figure 9-20 illustrates how risk management techniques can be deployed in the WAN module. Depending on the level of trust in the service provider's network, encryption and secure fingerprinting can be deployed in addition to basic filtering on WAN interfaces.

For example, a service provider leased-line network has failed several times in a year by mixing customer circuits and thereby accidentally interconnecting different enterprises. With address auto configuration (Serial Line Address Resolution Protocol [SLARP]) on some serial interfaces and with most enterprises running EIGRP over Frame Relay, the networks interconnected and accidentally interchanged traffic. As a result, most enterprises deployed PPP CHAP authentication on WAN links to manage the risk of rogue peers. Routing protocol authentication could also be deployed as an alternative.

Figure 9-20 *Securing the WAN Module*

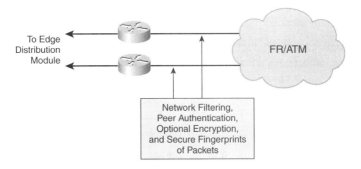

Securing the Network Management Module

The Network Management module provides network and security management functionality for the entire enterprise network. Its servers host extremely sensitive network and security device configuration data. Moreover, it is usually connected to many devices directly, over a separate management network, and sometimes provides a potential path around security mechanisms (such as firewalls).

The following sections detail the security risks in the Network Management module and strategies to mitigate those risks.

Risks in the Network Management Module

Specific risks in the Network Management module include the following:

- Impersonation of administrators, whereby an attacker might steal an administrator's credentials (usernames or passwords), log on to network devices, and change his configuration.

- Compromise of management protocols, whereby the attacker might send false management messages or listen to management protocol messages to obtain sensitive information.

- Accidental or deliberate misconfiguration of network or security devices—for example, by inexperienced administrators.

- Avoidance of responsibility among administrators, whereby an administrator might deny responsibility for certain actions that led to a security incident.

- Compromise of management hosts, whereby very sensitive configuration, security, and audit data can be hosted.

Guidelines for Securing the Management Module

The following techniques are recommended for managing risks in the Network Management module:

- To manage the risk of administrator impersonation, provide strong authentication mechanisms for administrators. A good example is a two-factor OTP system that is based on token cards.

- Use protocols with cryptographic protection to manage the risk of management protocol compromise. Examples include SSH for terminal access (instead of Telnet) and strongly authenticated SNMP instead of classic SNMP with basic authentication.

- Enforce authorization on configuration mechanisms to manage misconfiguration risks. You can accomplish this by using well-known methods of centralized change control and authorization servers that only permit specific changes by specific administrators.

- Prevent avoidance of responsibility with a good management audit trail that logs all management events into a centralized and secured audit record repository. In addition, good organization practices must be in place to respond to such events.

- To manage the risk of management host compromise, separate the management network from the rest of the networks and implement good host security on the management stations.

Table 9-5 summarizes the guidelines for securing the Network Management module.

Table 9-5   *Guidelines for Securing the Network Management Module*

Risk	Managed By
Administrator impersonation	Strong authentication in management protocols
Compromise of management protocols	Secure management protocols
Accidental or deliberate misconfiguration	Device configuration authorization
Responsibility avoidance	Configuration auditing
Management host compromise	Separate management networks, network firewalls for access control, intrusion detection

Figure 9-21 shows how different risk management mechanisms fit into the different elements of the Network Management module. A separate out-of-band management network exists, and another network for network management system (NMS) servers is created and separated from the rest of the campus by a firewall router. A terminal server provides console access to network devices in an emergency, and an additional switch connects the NMS server network to the out-of-band management network (device management network).

Figure 9-21 *Securing the Network Management Module*

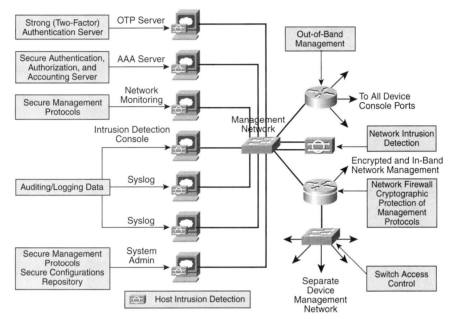

Consider an example in which an organization has experienced several incidents involving distrusted users on the campus network intercepting management traffic. To manage the risk, the organization has decided to move all management traffic to a separate VLAN (a separate management network) to isolate it from user traffic.

Securing the Server Farm Module

The Server Farm module hosts servers inside the main campus network and branch offices. Servers can contain the enterprise's most sensitive information and are accessed by a large number of users. Therefore, network performance is usually a critically important issue that sometimes limits the choice of protection mechanisms. The specific risks in the Server Farm module are similar to the risks in the E-commerce module, except that sensitivity of internal server data is usually critical. Specific risks include the compromise of exposed applications, unauthorized access to data, and the compromise of other hosts from compromised servers in this module.

Guidelines for Securing the Server Farm Module

Risk management in the Server Farm module involves the same mechanisms as in the E-commerce module, except that DoS attacks in the internal network are less common. The following guidelines apply:

- Use good host hardening and secure applications to manage host and application protection. If performance permits, use firewalls to allow only minimal connectivity to those servers.

- To manage the risk of compromise to other hosts from compromised servers, use network filtering to limit connectivity from the server. Separate the hosts on the same segment with LAN switch access control mechanisms, and use network and host intrusion detection systems to monitor individual hosts and subnets to detect signs of attacks and confirm potential successful breaches.

Table 9-6 summarizes the guidelines for securing the Server Farm module.

Table 9-6 *Guidelines for Securing the Server Farm Module*

Risk	Managed By
Compromise of exposed hosts and applications	Access control using network firewalls, host hardening, secure programming of applications, intrusion detection
Compromise of other hosts from compromised hosts	Access control using network firewalls, intrusion detection, LAN switch access control

Figure 9-22 outlines risk management techniques and their positioning within the Server Farm module.

Let's consider a sample organization that became concerned when a number of security vulnerabilities for one of their operating systems were published. The server management personnel were unable to patch the system quickly enough, and internal server compromises occurred. The enterprise quickly deployed a firewall to protect their most valuable servers and limited user access to most of its services. This resulted in hiding the majority of the unnecessary (not used by the organization) and possibly vulnerable server services from the campus, thus exposing the servers to fewer future vulnerabilities.

Figure 9-22 *Securing the Server Farm Module*

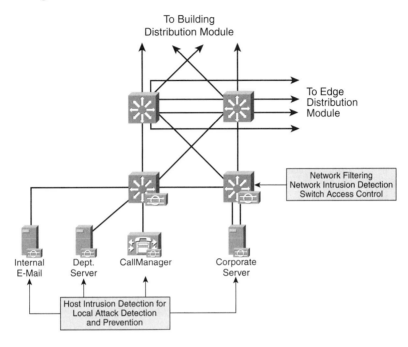

IP Telephony Security

As discussed in Chapter 8, "Designing Networks for Voice Transport," voice transport is becoming more popular in today's networks. This section explores the security aspects of IP telephony.

Voice Network Vulnerabilities and Solutions

Voice networks are interesting targets for hackers who have ulterior motives. The main issue with voice networks today is that they are generally wide open, and they require little or no authentication to gain access; this is because the model that was chosen for IP voice networks parallels that chosen for legacy voice systems.

IP-based telephony presents a means of providing telephony over the existing IP data network. However, for reasons including QoS, scalability, manageability, and security, deployment of IP telephony devices and IP data devices should occur on two logically disparate segments. Segmenting IP voice from the traditional IP data network greatly increases attack mitigation capability while still allowing use of the same access, core, and distribution layers. Although the segments should be disparate, they do not have to be on two separate IP infrastructures. Technologies such as VLANs, access control, and stateful firewalls provide the Layer 3 segmentation that is necessary for keeping the voice and data segments separate at the access layer.

A stateful firewall provides host-based DoS protection against connection starvation and fragmentation attacks, dynamic per-port granular access through the firewall when legitimate and necessary, spoof mitigation, and general filtering.

The phones that are used in IP telephony can be either PC-based or standalone IP phones. Because the deployment of PC-based IP phones provides a path for attacks against the voice segment, Cisco does not recommend their usage unless a stateful firewall brokers the data-voice interaction. By their nature, PC-based IP phones reside in the data segment and therefore require access to the voice segment in order to access call control, place calls to IP phones, and leave voice messages. PC-based IP phone hosts are more susceptible to attacks because of operating system (OS) vulnerabilities, application vulnerabilities, service vulnerabilities, worms, viruses, and so on. IP phones run custom OSs with limited service support and are less likely to have vulnerabilities. Also, because the PC-based IP phone resides in the data segment, it is susceptible to any attack against that entire segment—not only against the host itself. Because it mitigates many attacks against the IP telephony network, include user and device authentication whenever possible. The MAC address is the primary method for device authentication of IP phones. Some IP phones also support basic user authentication, which provides a facility for a user to log in to a phone.

Locking down the switched ports, segments, and services in the network provides attack mitigation for rogue devices. In addition, the following best practices provide mitigation details that are specific to IP telephony:

- DHCP is typically used for a scalable IP phone deployment; consider statically assigning IP addresses to known MAC addresses.

- Many call-processing managers provide an automatic phone registration feature that bootstraps an unknown phone with a temporary configuration and allows it to interact with the network. Turn this functionality off for normal day-to-day use.

- Consider using a utility like Arpwatch (available at www-nrg.ee.lbl.gov/nrg.html) to monitor the MAC addresses in your voice segment. Compared to the data segment, MAC addresses in the voice segment are more likely to be static; Arpwatch tracks the MAC addresses of all devices in the voice segments and logs any changes in MAC-to-IP address pairings.

- Filtering in all segments should limit devices in unknown segments from connecting to the call-processing manager.

- Deploy NIDS in front of the call-processing manager to detect attacks that are sourced from the data segment against its HTTP user service. Deploy NIDS between the voice and data segments to detect DoS attacks against the voice segment.

IP Telephony Risks and Mitigation Strategies

Following are some of the risks that are associated with IP telephony and ways to mitigate them:

- **Packet sniffers/call interception**—A switched infrastructure with VLANs limits the effectiveness of sniffing.

- **Unauthorized access**—The use of HIDS and application access control mitigates unauthorized access.

- **Caller identity spoofing**—Use a utility such as Arpwatch to notify the administrator of the unknown device.

- **Toll fraud**—Configure the call-processing manager to not allow unknown phones to be configured. Use access control to limit only known telephony networks from communicating with one another.

- **Repudiation**—Use call-processing manager call setup logs to provide some level of nonrepudiation, thereby reducing the likelihood of a denial that the call was placed.

- **IP spoofing**—Provide a stateful firewall and filtering on Layer 3 switches.

- **Application layer attack**—Operating systems, devices, and applications must be kept up-to-date with the latest security fixes, and HIDS should protect most servers.

- **Denial of service**—Separation of voice and data segments significantly reduces the likelihood of an attack. Stateful firewall controls limit exposure to the call-processing manager and proxy server.

- **Trust exploitation**—Use a restrictive trust model and private VLANs to limit trust-based attacks.

- **Virus and Trojan-horse applications**—Host-based virus scanning prevents most viruses and many Trojan horses.

Auto Update Server

This chapter has discussed many ways of mitigating the security risks that are associated with modern networks. However, configuring the security devices within networks and maintaining those configurations is a very complex task. The CiscoWorks Auto Update Server, described in this section, is an example of a new Cisco technology in security management evolution. For the first time, security devices, including Cisco PIX firewalls, can pull new configuration and operating system updates from the Auto Update Server.

The Auto Update Server is a component of the CiscoWorks VPN/Security Management Solution (VMS), an integral part of the SAFE Blueprint for network security that combines web-based tools for configuring, monitoring, and troubleshooting VPNs, firewalls, NIDSs, and host-based IDSs.

The CiscoWorks Auto Update Server allows users to implement a pull model for security and operating system management; Cisco PIX firewalls can periodically and dynamically contact the management station for any configuration, PIX Operating System, and PIX Device Manager (PDM) updates.

The CiscoWorks Management Center for Firewalls, which is included with the Auto Update Server in CiscoWorks VMS, provides an easy-to-use feature for configuring PIX Firewalls to use the Auto Update Server and can push configuration updates to the Auto Update Server.

Remote Cisco PIX firewalls can contact the Auto Update Server at boot time for periodic configuration and operating system refreshes, or dynamically any time the remote Cisco PIX firewall receives a new DHCP-assigned address. The Auto Update Server improves the security of remote networks, and increases the scalability and decreases the costs associated with remote PIX deployments.

Auto Update Server version 1.1 supports the following devices and software versions:

- Cisco PIX 501, 506, 506E, 515, 515E, 525, and 535 firewalls
- Version 6.2 of the Cisco PIX Operating System
- Versions 1.x, 2.x, and 3.x of Cisco PDM
- DHCP updates to configure all firewall and VPN IOS device configurations that are supported by VMS

NOTE   Additional information on the Auto Update Server and VMS is available at www.cisco.com/go/vms.

Some Cisco documentation refers to the Auto Update Server as *Auto Security.*

Summary

In this chapter, you learned about network security solutions.

Networks significantly increase both the benefits and the risks of computing. Network security is used to mitigate the risks to acceptable levels. It should provide data confidentiality (who can view), integrity (who can change), and availability (uninterrupted access).

A common example of a security threat is a DoS attack that aims to compromise the availability of a network, host, or application.

Risk assessment defines threats, their probability, and their severity. A network security policy enumerates risks that are relevant to the network and determines how to manage those risks. A network security design implements the security policy.

Network devices themselves must be secured to provide a secure network foundation.

Networks, as a whole, can be attacked; however, hosts and applications are often the ultimate targets of attacks.

Although physical security is often overlooked, physical access to a device or communications media can compromise network security.

Network authentication provides proof of user identity and is traditionally based on one (or more) of the following three proofs:

- Something the subject knows
- Something the subject has
- Something the subject is

Two-factor authentication requires a subject to include at least two types of proofs of identity.

Network authorization defines what an authenticated network user can do.

Cryptography provides data confidentiality through encryption, which is the process of disguising a message to hide its original content.

Secure fingerprints or digital signatures provide data integrity. Secure fingerprints attach a cryptographically strong checksum to data; this checksum is generated and verified using a secret key that only authorized subjects know. Digital data signing uses a cryptography method that attaches a digital signature to sensitive data. This signature is generated using a unique signature generation key that is known only to the signer rather than to all authorized subjects; other parties can use the signer's signature verification key to verify the signature.

Secure management and monitoring are needed for responding to security events and incidents. A secured network must be managed securely; network managers must use well-defined operational practices, and network management protocols must be protected.

The Cisco SAFE Blueprint provides a modular approach to building security into the network fabric. Each network module has its own unique risk profile; however, many security concepts and technologies can be reused to manage similar risks in different modules.

The Internet Connectivity module connects all other network modules to the Internet, thereby establishing potential contact with the most dangerous external network. Risks include reconnaissance threats, compromise of hosts, DoS attacks, and introduction of malicious code. Mitigation strategies include using firewalls, NIDS, host IDS, and DMZ networks.

The E-commerce and the Remote Access and VPN modules are partially secured through the Internet Connectivity module. Specific threats to the E-commerce module include the compromise of hosts and DoS attacks; mitigation strategies include using firewalls, intrusion detection systems, and DMZ networks. The Remote Access and VPN module is vulnerable to identity spoofing, compromise of transmitted data, and compromise of a client or remote site. Mitigation strategies include the use of strong authentication and cryptography mechanisms, firewalls, and virus protection.

The WAN module provides WAN connectivity among different parts of the enterprise network and usually connects campuses with branch offices. Threats to this module include compromise of transmitted data and misconfiguration of the WAN network; mitigation strategies include using cryptography, peer authentication, and firewalls.

The Network Management module sometimes provides a potential management path around security mechanisms. Risks in this module include impersonation of administrators, compromise of management protocols and hosts, misconfiguration, and avoidance of responsibility among administrators. Mitigation strategies include the use of device configuration authorization, configuration auditing, separate management networks, and firewalls.

The Server Farm module hosts servers inside the main campus network and branch offices. Specific risks include compromise of exposed applications, unauthorized access to data, and compromise of other hosts from compromised servers in this module. Mitigation strategies include the use of firewalls, intrusion detection, and switch access control.

The CiscoWorks Auto Update Server is a component of the CiscoWorks VMS which allows users to implement a pull model for security and operating system management.

References

For additional information, refer to the following resources:

- The Cisco SAFE: Extending the Security Blueprint to Small, Midsize, and Remote-User Networks white paper, also available at www.cisco.com/go/safe.

- The Cisco SAFE: IP Telephony Security in Depth white paper, also available at http://www.cisco.com/go/safe.

- The Cisco SAFE: A Security Blueprint For Enterprise Networks white paper, also available at www.cisco.com/go/safe.

- The Cisco SAFE: Wireless LAN Security in Depth—version 2 white paper, also available at www.cisco.com/go/safe.

- The CiscoWorks Auto Update Server, Version 1.1 Data Sheet, available at www.cisco.com/go/vms.

Review Questions

Answer the following questions and then refer to Appendix G, "Answers to Review Questions, Case Studies, and Simulation Exercises," for the answers.

1 Match the terms with the definitions:

Terms:

— Integrity violation

— Confidentiality breach

— Availability threat

Definitions:

— Result of a network's inability to handle an enormous quantity of data

— Attacker changes sensitive data

— Can be difficult to detect

2 What is a denial of service (DoS) attack?

3 How are risk assessment and security policy related?

4 What are some steps that can be taken to prevent network devices from being compromised?

5 What types of threats are directed at networks as a whole?

6 How can an organization defend against DoS attacks that flood the network with packets?

7 Why might a hacker launch a reconnaissance attack?

8 How can attacks against hosts and applications be mitigated?

9 What are some components of a typical security policy?

10 What are the processes in the security wheel?

11 How can a network security mechanism manage the risk of stolen laptops?

12 What are the three types of authentication (proof of identity)?

13 What is the difference between authentication and authorization?

14 What is the principle of least privilege?

15 Which two of the following attacks can be prevented using network filtering (for example, a firewall)?

- An attacker who has a legitimate account on a UNIX server uses locally available tools to obtain administrator privileges.

- An attacker attempts to connect to an organization's sensitive, nonpublic server from the Internet.

- An attacker steals a bank ATM to obtain its cryptographic keys.

- An attacker maps a company's network using network management tools.

- An attacker decrypts a sensitive e-mail message that was sent freely over the Internet.

16 Complete this sentence: Cryptography provides _____ through _____.

17 True or false: Cryptography can impact network performance.

18 Provide some examples of cryptographic mechanisms that ensure data integrity.

19 What is a Network Intrusion Detection System (NIDS)?

20 How can network management channels be secured?

21 What is the Cisco SAFE Blueprint?

22 Which type of attacks can generally be prevented using a demilitarized zone (DMZ)?

23 What are some of the risks associated with the Internet Connectivity module?

24 Why is a compromise in an e-commerce server generally riskier than in an Internet module server?

25 How do you manage the risk of a compromised e-commerce server that is compromising another host?

26 What are some of the security risks in the Remote Access and VPN module?

27 How can the risk of identity spoofing in the Remote Access and VPN module be managed?

28 How can enterprises protect against a risk of service provider misconfiguration?

29 What security risks are associated with the WAN module?

30 What security risks are associated with the Network Management module?

31 How can the risk of administrator impersonation be mitigated?

32 What are the differences in security risks associated with servers in the Server Farm versus those in the E-commerce module?

33 What are the common security risks in the Server Farm module?

34 What is the CiscoWorks Auto Update Server?

This chapter discusses network management design and contains the following sections:

- Network Management Protocols and Features
- Functional Areas of Network Management
- Managing Service Levels in a Network
- Summary
- Review Questions

Applying Basic Network Management Design Concepts

Service providers are under increasing pressure to ensure that their network technology operates efficiently and that it offers quality service to end users. Proper management is critical to an efficiently run network. Network management helps manage configuration changes in the network and determine faults and performance levels; it also provides security and accounting management for both individual and group usage of network resources. Controlled changes—such as configuration modifications, software updates, and cabling changes—and unexpected behaviors or failures affect a network. To maintain control, tools are required for tracking and monitoring all activity that might affect network performance.

This chapter begins with an introduction to network management protocols, explains the functional areas of network management in detail, and outlines design guidelines for each functional area. We conclude with an explanation of the service levels that are managed in modern networks.

After completing this chapter, you will be able to identify network management protocols and features, describe the functional areas of network management, and manage service levels in a network.

Network Management Protocols and Features

Network management is an important feature of modern networks. Network administrators need instruments for monitoring the functionality of the network devices and the connections between them. The Simple Network Management Protocol (SNMP) has become the de facto standard for use in network management solutions and is tightly connected with remote monitoring (RMON) and Management Information Bases (MIBs). Each managed device in the network is viewed as having several variables that quantify the state of the device. You can monitor managed devices by reading the values of these variables and control managed devices by writing values into these variables. Systematic presentation of these values shows the managed network's overall functionality.

The following sections introduce management protocols by describing the difference between SNMP versions 1, 2, and 3. We describe the role of MIBs in SNMP and RMON monitoring, and introduce Cisco's network discovery protocol (the Cisco Discovery Protocol [CDP]) and discuss its benefits and limitations. We conclude with a description of methods for gathering network statistics.

Network Management Architecture

Figure 10-1 shows a general network management architecture.

Figure 10-1 *Network Management Architecture*

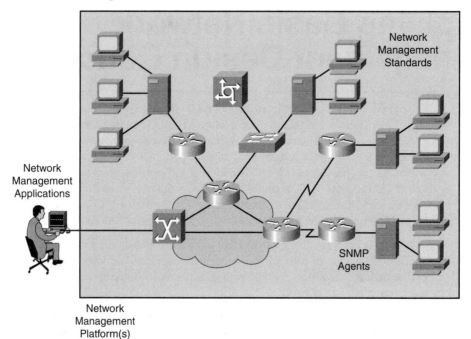

The network management architecture consists of the following:

- **Network management system (NMS)**—A system that executes applications that monitor and control managed devices. NMSs provide the bulk of the processing and memory resources that are required for network management.

- **Network management protocol**—A protocol that facilitates the exchange of management information between the NMS and managed devices.

- **Managed devices**—A device (such as a router) that is managed by an NMS.

- **Management agents**—Software on managed devices that collects and stores management information.

- **Management information**—Data that is of interest to a device's management.

Different network management applications can be used on a network management system; the choice depends on the network platform (such as the hardware or operating system).

The management information resides on network devices; management agents that reside on the device collect and store data in a standardized data definition structure, known as the *MIB*.

The network management application uses SNMP or other network management protocols to retrieve the data that the management agents collect. The retrieved data is typically processed and prepared for display with a graphical user interface (GUI), which allows the operator to use a graphical representation of the network to control managed devices and program the network management application.

Protocols and Standards

Several protocols are used within the network management architecture.

Key Point: Network Management Protocols and Standards

SNMP is the simplest network management protocol. The initial SNMP version 1 (SNMPv1) was extended to SNMP version 2 (SNMPv2) with its variants, which were further extended with SNMP version 3 (SNMPv3).

The MIB is a detailed definition of the information on a network device and is accessible through a network management protocol, such as SNMP.

RMON is an extension of the MIB. The MIB typically provides only static information about the managed device; the RMON agent has specific groups of statistics, which can be collected for long-term trend analysis.

The following sections discuss SNMP, MIB, and RMON in detail.

SNMP

SNMP has become the de facto standard for network management; because it is a simple solution that requires little code to implement, it enables vendors to build SNMP agents easily for their products. SNMP is a communication specification that defines how management information is exchanged between network management applications and management agents.

Figure 10-2 shows the terms that are used in SNMP; they are described as follows:

- **Manager**—The manager, a network management application in an NMS (such as CiscoWorks 2000), polls the SNMP agents that reside on managed devices and collects the data periodically, thereby enabling information to be displayed using a GUI on the NMS.

- **Protocol**—SNMP is a protocol for message exchange. It uses the Internet Protocol (IP) within the User Datagram Protocol (UDP) to transport the management data. SNMP allows for setting and retrieval of management information (such as MIB variables).

- **Managed device**—A device (such as a router) that is to be managed by the manager.

- **Management agents**—Management agents reside on managed devices to collect and store a range of information about the device and its operation, respond to the manager's requests, and generate traps to inform the manager about certain events.

- **MIB**—The management agent collects data and stores it locally in the MIB (a database of objects about the device). Community strings (which are similar to passwords) control access to the MIB. To access certain MIB variables, the user must specify a read or write community string; otherwise, access is denied.

Figure 10-2 *SNMP Is a Protocol for Management Information Exchange*

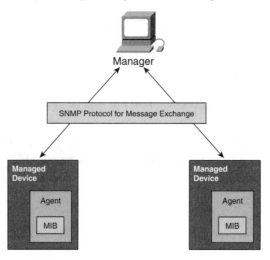

SNMP Message Types

SNMP's simplicity is apparent by the set of operations that are available in the protocol.

Figure 10-3 shows the following SNMP messages, which the manager uses to transfer data from agents that reside on managed devices:

- **Get request**—The manager requests the specific MIB variable from the agent.

- **Get next request**—Used after the initial get request to retrieve the next object instance from a table or list.

- **Set request**—Used to set an MIB variable on an agent.

- **Get response**—Used by an agent to respond to a manager's get request or get next request.

- **Trap message**—Used by an agent to transmit an unsolicited alarm to the manager. A trap message can be sent when a certain condition, such as a change in the state of a device, a device or component failure, or an agent initialization or restart, has occurred.

Figure 10-3 *SNMP Message Types*

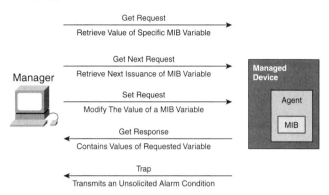

SNMP Version 2

SNMPv2 is a revised protocol that includes performance, security, confidentiality, and manager-to-manager communication improvements to SNMP.

SNMPv2 was introduced with the RFC 1441, *Introduction to version 2 of the Internet-standard Network Management Framework*, but members of the Internet Engineering Task Force (IETF) subcommittee could not agree upon several sections of the SNMPv2 specification (primarily the protocol's security and administrative needs). Several attempts to achieve acceptance of SNMPv2 have been made by releasing experimental modified versions, commonly known as SNMPv2*, SNMPv2, SNMPv2u, SNMPv1+, and SNMPv1.5, that do not contain the disputed parts.

NOTE	RFCs are available at www.cis.ohio-state.edu/cs/Services/rfc/index.html.

Community-based SNMPv2, or SNMPv2c, which is defined in RFC 1901, *Introduction to Community-based SNMPv2*, is referred to as SNMPv2 because it is the most common implementation. The "c" stands for community-based security because SNMPv2c uses SNMPv1 community strings for security (read and write access).

SNMPv2 changes include the introduction of the following two new message types:

- GetBulk message type, which is used for retrieving large amounts of data (for example, tables). This message reduces repetitive requests and replies, thereby improving performance.

- InformRequest, which is similar to the Trap message. A managed device sends an InformRequest to the NMS, which sends an acknowledgment by sending a Response message back to the managed device.

Another improvement of SNMPv2 over SNMPv1 is the addition of new data types with 64-bit counters, because 32-bit counters were quickly overflowed by fast network interfaces.

On Cisco routers, the Cisco IOS software release 11.3 and later versions implement SNMPv2.

SNMP Version 3

SNMPv3 is the latest SNMP version to become a full standard. Its introduction has moved SNMPv1 and SNMPv2 to historic status.

SNMPv3, which is described in RFCs 2571 through 2575, adds methods to ensure the secure transmission of critical data to and from managed devices. Table 10-1 lists these RFCs. (Note that these RFCs make RFCs 2271 through 2275 obsolete.)

Table 10-1 *SNMPv3 Proposed Standards Documents*

RFC Number	Title of RFC
2571	An Architecture for Describing SNMP Management Frameworks
2572	Message Processing and Dispatching for the Simple Network Management Protocol (SNMP)
2573	SNMP Applications
2574	User-based Security Model (USM) for Version 3 of the Simple Network Management Protocol (SNMPv3)
2575	View-based Access Control Model (VACM) for the Simple Network Management Protocol (SNMP)

NOTE   SNMPv3 was recently promoted to full standard, but the IETF has not yet assigned RFC numbers for documents.

SNMPv3 introduces the following three security levels:

*   **NoAuthNoPriv**—Without authentication and without privacy.
*   **AuthNoPriv**—With authentication, but without privacy (authentication is based on Hash-based Message Authentication Code-Message Digest 5 [HMAC-MD5] or HMAC-Secure Hash Algorithm [HMAC-SHA] algorithms).
*   **AuthPriv**—With authentication and privacy (uses the 56-bit Cipher-Block Chaining-data encryption standard [CBC-DES] encryption standard).

Security can be created per user or group of users via direct interaction with the managed device or via SNMP operations. Security levels determine which SNMP objects a user can access for reading, writing, or creating, and the list of notifications that users can receive.

NOTE   On Cisco routers, Cisco IOS software release 12.0 and later versions implement SNMPv3.

MIB

Key Point: MIB

An MIB is a collection of managed objects. An MIB stores the information, which is entered by the local management agent, on a managed device for later retrieval by a network management protocol.

Each object in an MIB has a unique identifier, which network management applications use to identify and retrieve a specific object. The MIB has a tree-like structure in which similar objects are grouped under the same branch of the MIB tree (for example, different interface counters are grouped under the MIB tree's interfaces branch).

Internet MIB Hierarchy

As shown in Figure 10-4, a tree hierarchy logically represents the MIB structure. The root of the tree is unnamed and splits into three main branches: Consultative Committee for International Telegraph and Telephone (CCITT), International Organization for Standardization (ISO), and joint ISO/CCITT.

These branches and those that fall below each category are identified with short text strings and integers. Text strings describe *object names*, while integers are used to form *object identifiers* that allow software to create compact, encoded representations of the names.

The *object identifier* in the Internet MIB hierarchy is the sequence of numeric labels on the nodes along a path from the root to the object. The Internet standard MIB is represented by the object identifier 1.3.6.1.2.1. It also can be expressed as iso.org.dod.internet.mgmt.mib.

Figure 10-4 *Internet MIB Hierarchy*

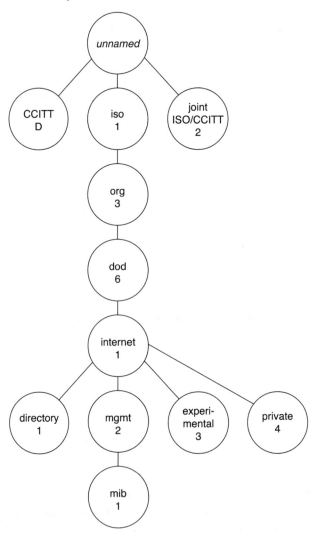

This information was adapted from the Cisco Management Information Base (MIB) User Quick Reference, which is available at www.cisco.com/univercd/cc/td/doc/product/ software/ios112/mbook/index.htm.

Standard MIBs are defined in different RFCs. For example, RFC 1213 (*Management Information Base for Network Management of TCP/IP-based internets: MIB-II*) defines the Transmission Control Protocol (TCP)/IP MIB; RFC 1231 (*IEEE 802.5 Token Ring MIB*) defines the Token Ring MIB; RFC 1243 (*AppleTalk Management Information Base*) defines the AppleTalk MIB, and so forth.

In addition to standard MIBs, there are vendor-specific MIB definitions. Vendors can obtain their own branch of the MIB subtree and create custom managed objects under that branch.

For example, a Cisco router's MIB tree has several defined standard managed objects , such as from the following groups:

- Interface group (including interface description, type, physical address, counts of incoming and outgoing packets, and so forth)
- IP group (including whether the device is acting as an IP gateway, the number of input packets, the number of packets discarded because of error, and so forth)
- ICMP group (including the number of ICMP messages received, the number of messages with errors, and so forth)

The router's private section of the MIB tree also contains private managed objects, which were introduced by Cisco, such as the following:

- Small, medium, large, and huge buffers
- Primary and secondary memory
- Proprietary protocols

MIB-II

MIB-II is an extension of the original MIB (which is now called MIB-I) and is defined by RFC 1213. MIB-II supports a number of new protocols and provides more detailed, structured information. It remains compatible with the previous version, which is why MIB-II retains the same object identifier as MIB-I (1.3.6.1.2.1).

The location of MIB-II objects is under the iso.org.dod.internet.mgmt subtree, where the top level MIB objects are defined as follows (definitions of these objects can be found in RFC 1213):

- System (1)
- Interfaces (2)
- Address Translation (3)
- IP (4)
- ICMP (5)
- TCP (6)

- UDP (7)
- EGP (8)
- Transmission (10)
- SNMP (11)

Although the MIB-II definition is an improvement over MIB-I, the following unresolved issues exist:

- MIB-II is still a device-centric solution, meaning that its focus is on individual devices, not the entire network or data flows.

- MIB-II is poll-based, meaning that data is stored in managed devices, and a management system must request (poll) it via the management protocol; the data is not sent automatically.

To use the private definitions of managed objects, the private definitions must be compiled into the NMS. This process is useful for operators because the results are outputs that are more descriptive; variables and events can be referred to by name.

Cisco MIB

Cisco's private MIB definitions are under the Cisco MIB subtree (1.3.6.1.4.1.9 or iso.org.dod.internet.private.enterprise.cisco). You can obtain Cisco MIB definitions that Cisco devices support at www.cisco.com/public/mibs.

The Cisco private MIB subtree contains the following three subtrees:

- Local (2)
- Temporary (3)
- CiscoMgmt (9)

The local (2) subtree contains MIB objects that were defined before Cisco IOS software release 10.2. These MIB objects are implemented in the SNMPv1 Structure of Management Information (SMI). (The SMI defines the structure of data that resides within MIB managed objects.) Beginning with Cisco IOS software release 10.2, however, Cisco MIBs are defined according to the SNMPv2 SMI.

MIBs that are defined with SNMPv2 SMI are placed in the ciscoMgmt subtree (9). Cisco is gradually phasing out MIBs that are currently defined in the local subtree and replacing them with new objects that are defined in the ciscoMgmt subtree.

The temporary subtree is equivalent to the experimental space that is defined in the SMI. The variables in this subtree are subject to change for each Cisco IOS software release.

MIB Example

Figure 10-5 depicts SNMP MIB variable retrieval in action.

Figure 10-5 *SNMP MIB Variable Retrieval*

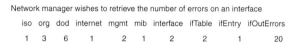

Network manager wishes to retrieve the number of errors on an interface

iso	org	dod	internet	mgmt	mib	interface	ifTable	ifEntry	ifOutErrors
1	3	6	1	2	1	2	2	1	20

The instance is the interface # (0 to max ports-1)

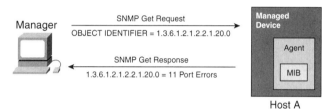

Manager

SNMP Get Request
OBJECT IDENTIFIER = 1.3.6.1.2.1.2.2.1.20.0

SNMP Get Response
1.3.6.1.2.1.2.2.1.20.0 = 11 Port Errors

Managed Device

Agent

MIB

Host A

In this example, the network manager wishes to retrieve the number of errors on an interface. The manager creates the SNMP Get Request message with the reference to the MIB variable 1.3.6.1.2.1.2.2.1.20.0, which represents interface outgoing errors on interface 0.

The agent creates the SNMP Get Response message in response to the manager's request. The response includes the value of the referenced variable. In the example, the agent returned value is 11, which indicates that there were 11 outgoing errors on that interface.

RMON

Key Point: RMON

RMON is an MIB that provides support for proactive management of local-area network (LAN) traffic.

The RMON standard allows for monitoring packet and traffic patterns on LAN segments. RMON tracks the following items:

- Number of packets
- Packet sizes
- Broadcasts

- Network utilization
- Errors and conditions, such as Ethernet collisions
- Statistics for hosts, including errors generated by hosts, the busiest hosts, and which hosts talk to each other

RMON features include historical views of RMON statistics that are based on user-defined sample intervals, alarms that are based on user-defined thresholds, and packet capture that is based on user-defined filters.

NOTE   RMON is defined as a portion of the MIB II database. RFC 1757, *Remote Network Monitoring Management Information Base*, defines the objects for managing remote network monitoring devices. RFC 1513, *Token Ring Extensions to the Remote Network Monitoring MIB*, defines extensions to the RMON MIB for managing 802.5 Token Ring networks.

Key Point: RMON and the MIB

Without RMON, an MIB could be used to check the device's network performance; however, this would lead to a large bandwidth requirement for management traffic. By using RMON, the managed device itself (via its RMON agent) collects and stores the data that would otherwise be retrieved from the MIB frequently.

RMON agents can reside in routers, switches, hubs, servers, hosts, or dedicated RMON probes. Because the RMON can collect a lot of data, dedicated RMON probes are often used on routers and switches instead of enabling RMON agents on these devices.

RMON can set performance thresholds and report only if the threshold is breached; this helps reduce management traffic. RMON provides effective network fault diagnosis, performance tuning, and planning for network upgrades.

RMON1

Key Point: RMON1

RMON1 works on the media access control (MAC) layer data and provides the aggregate LAN traffic statistics and analysis for remote LAN segments.

Because RMON agents must look at every frame on the network, they can cause performance problems on a managed device. The agent's performance can be classified based on processing power and memory.

NOTE   The RMON MIB is 1.3.6.1.2.16 (iso.ord.dod.internet.mgmt.mib.rmon).

RMON1 Groups

RMON agents gather nine groups of statistics (10 including Token Ring). The agents then forward this information to a manager upon request.

As summarized in Figure 10-6, RMON1 agents can implement some or all of the following groups:

- **Statistics**—Contains statistics (packets sent, bytes sent, broadcast packets, multicast packets, CRC errors, runts, giants, fragments, jabbers, collisions, and so forth) for each monitored interface on the device.
- **History**—Used to store periodic statistical samples for later retrieval.
- **Alarm**—Used to set specific thresholds for managed objects and to trigger an event upon crossing the threshold (this requires an Events group).
- **Host**—Contains statistics associated with each host that is discovered on the network.
- **Host top N**—Contains statistics for hosts that top a list ordered by one of their observed variables.
- **Matrix**—Contains statistics for conversations between sets of two addresses (packets or bytes exchanged between two hosts).
- **Filters**—Contains rules for data packet filters; data packets that are matched by these rules generate events or are stored locally in a Packet Capture group.
- **Packet capture**—Contains data packets that match rules set in the Filters group.
- **Events**—Controls the generation and notification of events from this device.
- **TokenRing**—Contains Token Ring Extensions:
  - **Ring station**—Provides detailed statistics on individual stations.
  - **Ring station order**—An ordered list of stations that are currently on the ring.
  - **Ring station configuration**—Configuration information and insert/removal data on each station.
  - **Source routing**—Statistics on source routing, such as hop counts.

Figure 10-6 *RMON1 Groups*

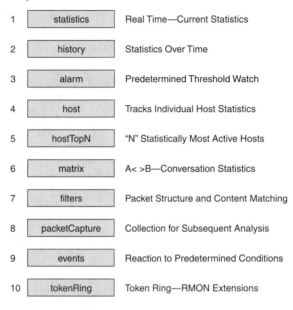

1	statistics	Real Time—Current Statistics
2	history	Statistics Over Time
3	alarm	Predetermined Threshold Watch
4	host	Tracks Individual Host Statistics
5	hostTopN	"N" Statistically Most Active Hosts
6	matrix	A< >B—Conversation Statistics
7	filters	Packet Structure and Content Matching
8	packetCapture	Collection for Subsequent Analysis
9	events	Reaction to Predetermined Conditions
10	tokenRing	Token Ring—RMON Extensions

RMON1 and RMON2

RMON1 only provides visibility into the data link and the physical layers; potential problems that occur at the higher layers still require other capture and decode tools.

Because of RMON1's limitations, RMON2 was developed to extend functionality to upper layer protocols. As illustrated in Figure 10-7, RMON2 provides full network visibility from the network layer through to the application layer.

Figure 10-7 *RMON2 is an Extension of RMON1*

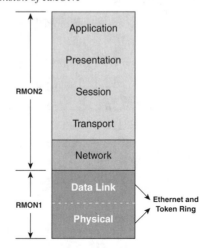

RMON2

Key Point: RMON2

RMON2 is not a replacement for RMON1, but an extension of it. RMON2 extends RMON1 by adding nine more groups that provide the visibility of the upper layers.

With visibility into the upper layer protocols, the network manager can monitor any upper layer protocol traffic for any device or subnet, in addition to the MAC layer traffic. RMON2 also provides the end-to-end view of network conversations per protocol.

As illustrated in Figure 10-8, RMON2 allows the collection of statistics beyond a specific segment's MAC layer. The network manager can view conversations at the network and application layers; therefore, traffic generated by a specific host or even a specific application on that host can be observed (for example, a Telnet client or a web browser).

Figure 10-8 *RMON2 Provides Visibility Through to the Application Layer*

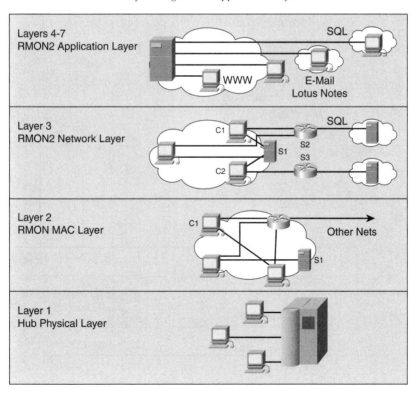

Figure 10-9 illustrates the RMON groups that were added when RMON2 was introduced. They include

- **Protocol directory**—Provides the list of protocols that the device supports.
- **Protocol distribution**—Contains the traffic statistics for each supported protocol.
- **Address mapping**—Contains network layer to MAC layer address mappings.
- **Network layer host**—Contains statistics for the network layer traffic to or from each host.
- **Network layer matrix**—Contains network layer traffic statistics for conversations between pairs of hosts.
- **Application layer host**—Contains statistics for the application layer traffic to or from each host.
- **Application layer matrix**—Contains application layer traffic statistics for conversations between pairs of hosts.
- **User history collection**—Contains periodic samples of user-specified variables.
- **Probe configuration**—Provides a standard way of remotely configuring probe parameters, such as trap destination and out-of-band management.

Figure 10-9 *RMON2 Groups Extend RMON1 Groups*

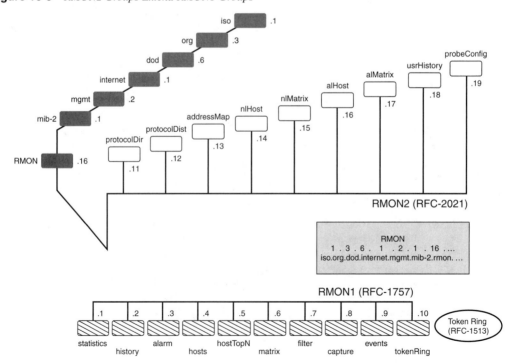

CDP

Key Point: CDP

CDP is a Cisco proprietary protocol that runs between Cisco devices over the data link layer. CDP enables systems that support different network layer protocols to communicate and enables the discovery of other Cisco devices on the network. CDP provides a summary of directly connected switches, routers, and other Cisco devices.

CDP is a media and protocol-independent protocol that is enabled on each supported interface of a Cisco device (routers, access servers, and switches) by default. (The physical media must support subnetwork access protocol [SNAP] encapsulation.)

Figure 10-10 illustrates the relationship between CDP and other protocols.

Figure 10-10 *CDP Runs at the Data Link Layer and Allows the Discovery of Directly Connected Cisco Devices*

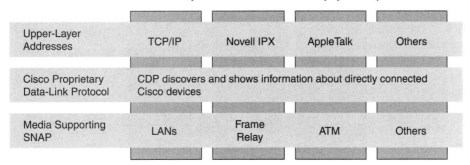

CDP Information

Following is the information that Cisco devices exchange in the CDP frame:

- **Device ID**—The name of the neighbor device and either the MAC address or the serial number of the device.

- **Local interface**—The local interface that is connected to the discovered neighbor.

- **Holdtime**—The remaining amount of time (in seconds) the current device holds the CDP advertisement from a sending device before discarding it.

- **Capability list**—The type of device that is discovered (R—Router, T—Trans Bridge, B—Source Route Bridge, S—Switch, H—Host, I—IGMP, r—Repeater).

- **Platform**—The device's product type.

- **Port identifier (ID)**—The port number on the discovered neighbor.

- **Address list**—All the network layer protocol addresses that have been configured on the interface (or, in the case of protocols that are configured globally, on the box).

NOTE   Cisco IOS software release 10.3 introduced the first version of CDP; the second version of CDP is available in Cisco IOS software release 12.0 and later.

How CDP Works

As Figure 10-11 shows, CDP information is only sent between directly connected Cisco devices; a Cisco device never forwards a CDP frame. In this figure, the person who is connected to Switch A can see the router and two switches that are directly attached to Switch A; other devices are not visible via CDP. For example, the person would have to log on to Switch B to see Router C with CDP.

Figure 10-11   *CDP Provides Information About Neighboring Cisco Devices*

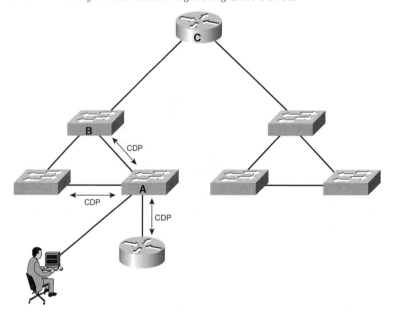

Key Point: CDP Frames

Cisco devices never forward a CDP frame.

CDP is a hello-based protocol, and all Cisco devices that run CDP periodically advertise their attributes to their neighbors using a multicast address. These frames advertise a time-to-live value (the holdtime, in seconds), which indicates the length of time the information must be retained before it can be discarded. CDP frames are sent with a time-to-live value that is nonzero after an interface is enabled. A time-to-live value of 0 is sent immediately, before an interface is shut down. Sending a CDP frame with time-to-live value of 0 allows quicker discovery of lost neighbors.

Cisco devices receive CDP frames and cache the received information. This cached information is available for network management. If any information changes from the last received frame, the new information is cached and the previous information is discarded, even if its time-to-live value has not yet expired.

NOTE   CDP should *not* be run in the following cases:

     — Do not run CDP on links that you do not want discovered, such as Internet connections.

     — Do not enable CDP on links that do not go to Cisco devices.

NOTE   More information on CDP can be found at www.cisco.com/en/US/tech/tk648/tk362/tk100/ tech_protocol_home.html.

NetFlow

The *Cisco NetFlow* is a measurement technology that measures flows that pass through Cisco devices.

NetFlow provides the measurement base that is required for recording network and application resource utilization, and for Cisco's Internet and enterprise quality of service (QoS) initiatives. NetFlow captures the traffic classification (or precedence) that is associated with each flow, thereby enabling differentiated charging based on QoS.

Key Point: Network Flow

A *network flow* is defined as a unidirectional sequence of packets between source and destination endpoints. Network flows are highly granular; both IP address and transport layer application port numbers identify flow endpoints. NetFlow also identifies the flows by IP protocol type, class of service (CoS), and the input interface identifier.

With separate serial tasks for switching, security services, and traffic measurements that are applied to each packet, non-NetFlow enabled switching handles incoming packets independently. Processing is applied only to a flow's first packet with NetFlow-enabled switching security (Access Control List [ACL]); information from the first packet is used to build an entry in the NetFlow cache. Subsequent packets in the flow are handled via a single, streamlined task that handles switching, security services, and data collection concurrently.

Therefore, NetFlow services capitalize on the network traffic's flow nature to provide detailed data collection with minimal impact on router performance, and to efficiently process access lists for packet filtering and security services.

NetFlow enables several key customer applications, including the following:

- **Accounting and billing**—Because flow data includes details such as IP addresses, packet and byte counts, timestamps, CoS, and application ports, NetFlow data provides fine-grained metering for highly flexible and detailed resource utilization accounting. Service providers can use this information to migrate from single fee, flat rate billing to more flexible charging mechanisms based on time of day, bandwidth usage, application usage, QoS, and so forth. Enterprise customers can use the information for departmental cost recovery or cost allocation for resource utilization.

- **Network planning and analysis**—NetFlow data provides key information for sophisticated network architecture tools to optimize both strategic planning (such as whom to peer with, backbone upgrade planning, and routing policy planning) and tactical network engineering decisions (such as adding resources to routers or upgrading link capacity). This has the benefit of minimizing the total cost of network operations while maximizing network performance, capacity, and reliability.

- **Network monitoring**—NetFlow data enables extensive near-real-time network monitoring. To provide aggregate traffic or application-based views, flow-based analysis techniques can be used to visualize traffic patterns that are associated with individual routers and switches on a network-wide basis. This analysis provides network managers with proactive problem detection, efficient troubleshooting, and rapid problem resolution.

- **Application monitoring and profiling**—NetFlow data enables network managers to gain a detailed, time-based view of application usage over the network. Content and service providers can use this information to plan and allocate network and application resources (such as web server sizing and location) to meet customer demands.

- **User monitoring and profiling**—NetFlow data enables network managers to understand customer and user network utilization and resource application. This information can be used to plan efficiently; allocate access, backbone, and application resources; and detect and resolve potential security and policy violations.

- **NetFlow data warehousing and data mining**—In support of proactive marketing and customer service programs, NetFlow data or the information derived from it can be warehoused for later retrieval and analysis (for example, to determine which applications and services are being used by internal and external users and target them for improved service). This is especially useful for service providers because NetFlow data enables them to create a wider range of offered services. For example, the service provider can easily determine the traffic characteristics of various services and, based on this data, provide new services to the users. An example of such a service could be voice over IP (VoIP), which requires QoS adjustment; the service provider might charge users for this service.

NetFlow Activation and Data Collection Strategy

NetFlow should be deployed on the edge or distribution router interfaces for service providers, or on WAN access router interfaces for enterprises.

Cisco recommends a carefully planned NetFlow deployment that has NetFlow services activated on strategically located routers. Rather than being deployed on every router on the network, NetFlow can be deployed incrementally (interface by interface) and strategically (on select routers).

NetFlow Infrastructure

The NetFlow services infrastructure has a three-tiered architecture. Figure 10-12 illustrates three components: NetFlow Data Export on routing devices, the NetFlow FlowCollector (NFC), and the Network Data Analyzer (NDA). The following describes these components:

- **NetFlow Data Export**—Captures NetFlow accounting statistics for traffic on a networking device and uses UDP to export the data to a collection device. NetFlow allows you to aggregate NetFlow data on the routing device before exporting it to a collection device, thereby resulting in lower bandwidth requirements for NetFlow data and reduced platform requirements for the NetFlow data collection devices.

- **NetFlow FlowCollector**—Provides scalable and economical data collection from multiple NetFlow-enabled devices. The NFC is a UNIX application that is supported on Solaris and HP-UX platforms. The NFC provides the following functionality:

  — Consumes flows from multiple NetFlow-enabled devices.

  — Performs data volume reduction through selective filtering and aggregation.

  — Stores flow information in flat files on disk for post-processing by NetFlow data consumers, third-party billing applications, and traffic analysis tools.

- **Network Data Analyzer**—A NetFlow-specific network traffic analysis tool that combines a graphical user interface with other companion modules. Together, these modules enable the user to retrieve, display, and analyze NetFlow data that has been collected from NFC flat files. The NDA provides several major functionality categories, including the following:

    — NetFlow data visualization policies (such as what to display and how to display it)

    — Graphical data display that is based on the specified visualization policies

    — Data export to external applications (such as Microsoft Excel spreadsheets) for reporting purposes

Figure 10-12 *Netflow Infrastructure*

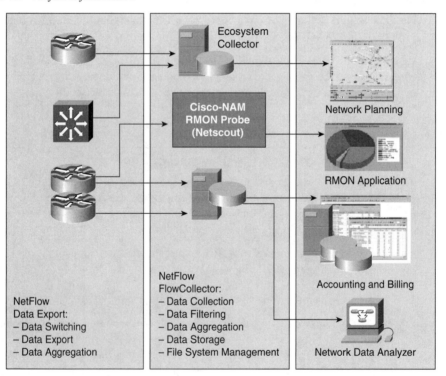

This information was adapted from the NetFlow Services Solutions Guide, which is available at www.cisco.com/en/US/customer/products/sw/netmgtsw/ps1964/ products_implementation_design_guide09186a00800d6a11.html.

NetFlow Versus RMON Information Gathering

NetFlow can be configured on individual interfaces, thereby providing information on traffic that passes through those interfaces and collecting the following types of information:

- Source and destination interfaces and IP addresses
- Input and output interface numbers
- TCP/UDP source port and destination ports
- Number of bytes and packets in the flow
- Source and destination autonomous system numbers (for the Border Gateway Protocol [BGP])
- Time of day
- IP CoS

Compared to a simple solution using SNMP with RMON MIB, NetFlow information gathering benefits include greater detail about collected data, data time stamping, support for various data per interface, and greater scalability (to a large number of interfaces; RMON is also limited by the size of its memory table). NetFlow's performance impact is much lower than RMON's, and external probes are not required.

Syslog Accounting

A system message and error reporting service is an essential component of any operating system. The system message service provides a means for the system and its running processes to report system state information to a network manager.

Cisco devices produce syslog messages as a result of network events. Every syslog message contains a timestamp (if enabled), severity level, and facility.

Example 10-1 shows samples of syslog messages produced by the Cisco IOS software. The most common messages are those that a device produces upon exiting configuration mode, and the link up and down messages. If ACL logging is configured, the device generates syslog messages when packets match the access list condition.

Example 10-1 *Syslog Messages*

```
20:11:31: %SYS-5-CONFIG_I: Configured from console by console

20:11:57: %LINK-5-CHANGED: Interface FastEthernet0/0, changed state to
administratively down
20:11:58: %LINEPROTO-5-UPDOWN: Line protocol on Interface FastEthernet0/0, changed
state to down

20:12:04: %LINK-3-UPDOWN: Interface FastEthernet0/0, changed state to up
20:12:06: %LINEPROTO-5-UPDOWN: Line protocol on Interface FastEthernet0/0, changed
state to up
```

continues

Example 10-1 *Syslog Messages (Continued)*

```
20:13:53: %SEC-6-IPACCESSLOGP: list internet-inbound denied udp 66.56.16.77(1029) -
> 63.78.199.4(161), 1 packet
20:14:26: %MLS-5-MLSENABLED:IP Multilayer switching is enabled
20:14:26: %MLS-5-NDEDISABLED:Netflow Data Export disabled
20:14:26: %SYS-5-MOD_OK:Module 1 is online
20:15:47: %SYS-5-MOD_OK:Module 3 is online
20:15:42: %SYS-5-MOD_OK:Module 6 is online
20:16:27: %PAGP-5-PORTTOSTP:Port 3/1 joined bridge port 3/1
20:16:28: %PAGP-5-PORTTOSTP:Port 3/2 joined bridge port 3/2
```

System error messages are structured as follows:

```
mm/dd/yy:hh/mm/ss:%FACILITY-SUBFACILITY-SEVERITY-MNEMONIC: Message-text
```

The following parameters are used in the system messages:

- **Facility**—Is a code that consists of two or more uppercase letters, which indicate the facility to which the message refers. A facility can be a hardware device, a protocol, or a module of the system software. The Cisco IOS software has more than 500 different facilities. Following are the most common syslog facilities:

  — IP

  — OSPF (Open Shortest Path First protocol)

  — SYS (operating system)

  — SEC (IP Security)

  — RSP (Route Switch Processor)

  — IF (interface)

  — LINK (data link messages)

  Other facilities include CDP, QoS, RADIUS, multicast (MCAST), Multilayer Switching (MLS), TCP, virtual trunk protocol (VTP), Telnet, and trivial file transfer protocol (TFTP). For more information, refer to www.cisco.com/univercd/cc/td/doc/product/software/ios122/122sup/122sems/index.htm.

- **Severity**—Is a single-digit code (from 0 to 7) that reflects the severity of the condition. The lower the number, the more serious the situation. Syslog defines the following severity levels:

  — Emergency (Level 0, which is the highest level)

  — Alert (Level 1)

  — Critical (Level 2)

  — Error (Level 3)

  — Warning (Level 4)

  — Notice (Level 5)

    — Informational (Level 6)

    — Debugging (Level 7)

- **Mnemonic**—Is a code that uniquely identifies the error message.

- **Message-text**—Is a text string that describes the condition. This portion of the message sometimes contains detailed information about the event, including terminal port numbers, network addresses, or addresses that correspond to locations in the system memory address space.

Syslog Distributed Architecture

Figure 10-13 shows the syslog distributed architecture.

Figure 10-13 *Syslog Distributed Architecture*

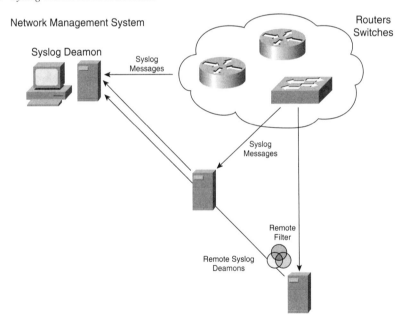

Network devices can be configured to send syslog messages directly to the NMS, or to a remote network host on which a syslog analyzer is installed. (Syslog messages are sent to console and Telnet sessions by default; a device must be configured with the NMS or another address to send syslog messages elsewhere.) A syslog analyzer is used to conserve bandwidth on WAN links because the analyzer usually applies different filters and sends only the predefined subset of all syslog messages that it receives. The analyzer filters and periodically forwards messages to the central NMS.

Upon receiving a syslog message, the NMS applies filters to remove unwanted messages. Filters can also be applied to perform actions based on the received syslog message, such as paging or e-mailing the network manager.

Functional Areas of Network Management

The International Organization for Standardization (ISO) network management model defines the following five functional areas of network management (abbreviated as FCAPS):

- **Fault management**—Detects, isolates, notifies, and corrects faults that are encountered in the network.

- **Configuration management**—Administers configuration aspects of network devices, such as configuration file management, inventory management, and software management.

- **Accounting management**—Provides usage information of network resources.

- **Performance management**—Monitors and measures various aspects of performance so that overall performance can be maintained at an acceptable level.

- **Security management**—Provides access to network devices and corporate resources to authorized individuals.

The following sections provide a high-level review of the functional areas of network management and present practical recommendations to increase the overall effectiveness of current management tools and practices. They also provide design guidelines for future implementation of network management tools and technologies.

Fault Management

Fault management, which is designed to handle error conditions that cause users to lose the full functionality of a network resource, is one of the most important ISO functional areas.

Fault management encompasses the activities of detection, isolation, and correction of abnormal network operation, and provides the means to receive and present a fault indication, determine the cause of a network fault, isolate the fault, and perform a corrective action.

Key Point: Fault Management

The goal of fault management is to keep the network running effectively by detecting, logging, notifying users about, and (to the extent possible) automatically fixing network problems.

Fault management is performed through the following five steps:

- **Fault determination**—Consists of detecting a fault and completing the steps that are necessary to begin fault diagnosis—such as isolating the fault to a particular subsystem.

- **Fault diagnosis**—Consists of determining the precise cause of the fault and the action that is required to solve it.

- **Fault bypass and recovery**—Consists of attempts to bypass the fault, either partially or completely. It provides only a temporary solution and relies on resolution to permanently solve the fault.

- **Fault resolution**—Consists of efforts to eliminate the fault. It usually begins after fault diagnosis is complete and often involves corrective action, such as the replacement of failed hardware or software.

- **Fault tracking and control**—Consists of tracking each fault until a final resolution is reached. Vital information that describes the fault is recorded in a fault database.

Fault management most commonly deals with events and traps as they occur on the network.

Fault Management Architecture

As shown in Figure 10-14, the fault management architecture consists of event generators and event collectors.

Figure 10-14 *Fault Management Includes Event Generators and Event Collectors*

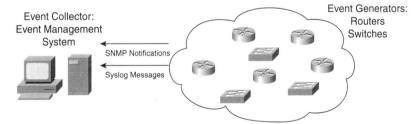

Event generators are typically network devices, such as routers, switches, and hosts. The events being generated are either SNMP notifications (traps, informs, or RMON alarms and notifications) or syslog messages. The event generators are configured with the event collector's address, thereby enabling them to forward events to the appropriate location.

Event collectors assemble the events that the event generators send and use predefined sets of rules to determine what events require what type of action.

Events

Events can be divided into two categories: state change events and performance events.

State change events are triggered when a network device changes state. For example, network devices can be configured to send state change events when a link or a neighbor goes down, or when the current OSPF designated router (DR) times out and a new DR is elected.

Performance events are generated when a network device detects a possible performance issue. Following are examples of performance events:

* A router CPU utilization exceeds 80%

* The number of errors on a link exceeds 50 per second

* A server's free disk space falls below 10%

Event Processing

Events that event generators produce are collected and processed by an event management system, which is typically part of the NMS. Event processing involves the following steps:

Step 1   Event collection

Step 2   Event normalization

Step 3   Event filtering

Step 4   Event correlation

Step 5   Event reporting

As discussed in the "Syslog Accounting" section of this chapter, syslog messages are sent with a facility code to which the message refers (the facility code can be a hardware device, a protocol, or a portion of the system software) and a severity level (priority). Event producers (such as a switch or router) are preconfigured to send messages with only certain priorities; therefore, only messages with critical information are sent to the collector. Other messages that are not crucial for network activity could be stored on a device to reduce collector and network utilization. Normalization of syslog messages is relatively easy because they are formalized and time stamped when they are received. The event collector can also filter syslog messages that contain certain facility or priority codes.

SNMP notifications are similar to syslog messages because the generator sends both of them to the event collector. SNMP notifications are more descriptive because of the detailed MIB definitions that supply the description of each SNMP notification. However, because SNMP notifications do not contain the event's priority, the event collector must maintain a table of different SNMP notifications and their priorities.

Event correlation identifies duplicate events so that only one action is taken.

Event reporting uses different methods to inform network engineers and operators about critical events in the network by displaying popup notifications, sending e-mails, or paging and telephoning network staff, for example.

Configuration Management

Configuration management is a collection of processes and tools that promote network consistency, track network changes, and provide up-to-date network documentation and visibility. By building and maintaining configuration management best practices, the network manager can expect several benefits, including improved network availability and lower costs.

Key Point: Configuration Management

Configuration management identifies, exercises control over, collects data from, and provides data to open systems for the purpose of preparing for, initializing, starting, providing for the continuous operation of, and terminating interconnection services.

Configuration management includes functions for performing the following operations:

- Set the parameters that control the open system's routine operation
- Associate names with managed objects and sets of managed objects
- Initialize and close down managed objects
- Collect information on demand about the open system's current condition
- Obtain announcements of significant changes in the open system's condition
- Change the open system's configuration

The goal of configuration management is to monitor network and system configuration information so that various versions of hardware and software elements can be tracked and managed.

The benefits of configuration management include the following:

- Lower support costs because of a decrease in reactive support issues
- Lower network costs because of device, circuit, and user tracking tools, and processes that identify unused network components
- Improved network availability because of a decrease in reactive support costs and improved time to resolve problems

A lack of configuration management can result in such issues as the following:

- The inability to determine the impact of network changes on the end user
- Increased reactive support issues
- Increased time to resolve problems
- Higher network costs because of unused network components

The following sections describe configuration management practices, standards, challenges, and tools.

Configuration Management Practices

Configuration management practices include the following:

- Configuration standards
- Configuration file management
- Inventory management
- Software management

The following sections describe each of these practices.

Configuration Standards

The greater the number of devices in a network, the more critical it is to accurately identify the location of each device. This location information should provide a detailed description that is meaningful to those who are tasked with dispatching resources when a network problem occurs. To expedite a resolution in the event of a network problem, you must have the contact information of the person or department who is responsible for the available devices. Contact information should include the person's name, telephone number, and department.

Starting from the device name to individual interfaces, naming conventions for network devices should be planned and implemented as part of the configuration standard. A well-defined naming convention provides personnel with the ability to provide accurate information when troubleshooting network problems. The naming convention for devices can use geographical location, building name, floor, and so forth. The interface naming convention can include such information such the segment to which a port is connected and the connecting hub's name. On serial interfaces, the naming convention should include the actual bandwidth, the local data-link connection identifier (DLCI) number (if Frame Relay), the destination, and the circuit ID or information that the carrier provides.

Configuration File Management

When adding new configuration commands on existing network devices, the commands must be verified for integrity before the actual implementation takes place. An improperly configured network device can have a disastrous effect on network connectivity and performance. Configuration command parameters must be checked to avoid mismatches and incompatibility issues. Schedule a thorough review of configurations with expert engineers on a regular basis.

Inventory Management

The discovery function of most network management platforms provides a dynamic listing of devices that are found in the network and should be used for the inventory management process.

An inventory database provides detailed configuration information on network devices. It details common information, including models of hardware, installed modules, software images, microcode levels, and so forth. This information is crucial to the completion of such tasks as software and hardware maintenance. The up-to-date listing of network devices collected by the discovery process is used as a master list for collecting inventory information using SNMP or scripting.

Software Management

A successful upgrade of software images on network devices requires a detailed analysis of the requirements such as memory, boot read-only memory (ROM), and microcode level. Usually the requirements are documented and made available on websites in the form of release notes and installation guides. The process of upgrading a network device that runs Cisco IOS software includes downloading a correct image from Cisco.com backing up the current image, ensuring that all hardware requirements are met, and then loading the new image into the device.

In some organizations, the window of opportunity for completing device maintenance is limited. In a large network environment with limited resources, it might be necessary to schedule and automate software upgrades after business hours. You can complete this procedure by using either a scripting language (such as Expect) or a specific application to perform this task.

To assist with the analysis phase when subsequent software maintenance is required, you should track changes to software, such as Cisco IOS software images and microcode versions in network devices. Using a modification history report minimizes the risk of loading incompatible images or microcodes into network devices.

Network Configuration Standards

Creating standards for network consistency reduces network complexity, the amount of unplanned downtime, and exposure to events that negatively impact the network. For optimal network consistency, follow these recommended standards:

- Software version control and management
- IP addressing standards and management
- Naming conventions and Domain Name System (DNS) and Dynamic Host Configuration Protocol (DHCP) assignments
- Standard configurations and descriptors
- Configuration upgrade procedures
- Solution templates

The following sections describe each of these standards.

Software Version Control and Management

Software version control is the practice of deploying consistent software versions on similar network devices. Version control improves the opportunity for validation and testing on selected software versions and limits the amount of software defects and interoperability issues in the network. Similar network devices should have the same software versions to reduce the risk of unexpected behavior with user interfaces, command or management output, upgrades, and features. This makes the environment less complex and easier to support. Overall, software version control improves network availability and helps to lower reactive support costs.

IP Addressing Standards and Management

IP address management is the process of allocating, recycling, and documenting IP addresses and subnets in a network. IP addressing standards define subnet size, subnet assignment, network device assignments, and dynamic address assignments within a subnet range. Recommended IP address management standards reduce the opportunity for overlapping or duplicate subnets, duplicate device IP address assignments, wasted IP address space, and unnecessary complexity.

Naming Conventions and DNS/DHCP Assignments

Consistent, structured use of naming conventions and DNS and DHCP for devices enables easier network management in the following ways:

- Creates a consistent access point for all network management information that is related to a device.

- Reduces the opportunity for duplicate IP addresses.

- Creates simple identification information, such as location, device type, and purpose.

- Improves inventory management by providing a simpler method by which to identify network devices.

Standard Configuration and Descriptors

Standard configurations should be created for each device classification, such as router, LAN switch, wide-area network (WAN) switch, or Asynchronous Transfer Mode (ATM) switch. Each standard configuration should contain the global, media, and protocol configuration commands that are necessary for maintaining network consistency. Media configuration includes ATM, Frame Relay, or Fast Ethernet configuration. Protocol configuration includes standard IP routing protocol configuration parameters, common QoS configurations, common access lists, and other required protocol configurations. Global configuration commands apply to all similar devices and include parameters such as service commands, IP commands, Terminal Access Controller Access Control System plus (TACACS+) commands, virtual terminal (vty) line, banners, SNMP configuration, and Network Time Protocol (NTP) configuration.

Descriptors are interface commands that describe an interface and are developed by creating a standard format that applies to each interface. The descriptor includes the purpose and location of the interface, other devices or locations connected to the interface, and circuit identifiers. Descriptors help a network support organization enable faster resolution and better understand the scope of the problems that are related to an interface.

Configuration Upgrade Procedures

Upgrade procedures help to ensure that software and hardware upgrades occur smoothly and with minimal downtime. Upgrade procedures include vendor verification, vendor installation references such as release notes, upgrade methodologies or steps, configuration guidelines, and testing requirements.

Upgrade procedures vary widely, depending on network types, device types, or new software requirements. Individual router or switch upgrade requirements can be developed and tested within an architecture group and referenced in any change documentation. Other upgrades that involve entire networks cannot be tested as easily. These upgrades might require more in-depth planning, vendor involvement, and additional steps to ensure success.

Update or upgrade procedures should be created in conjunction with new software deployment or identified standard release. The procedures should define all upgrade steps, reference vendor documentation related to updating the device, and provide testing procedures for validating the device after the upgrade. When upgrade procedures are defined and validated, the upgrade procedures should be referenced in all change documentation that is appropriate to the particular upgrade.

Solution Templates

Solution templates are used to define standard modular network solutions. For example, a network module can be a wiring closet, a remote office, or an access concentrator. In each case, the solution must be defined, tested, and documented to ensure that similar deployments can be implemented in exactly the same way. This ensures that future changes occur at a much lower risk level to the organization because the solution's behavior is well defined.

Configuration Challenges

In a world of increasingly complex networks, network administrators face many challenges in maintaining the configuration integrity of the network. As information systems have become more critical to the success of the business, it is even more important for network administrators to be able to guarantee the network's operation and performance, make changes easily, and locate and correct problems quickly.

To address these needs, network administrators require powerful, user-friendly tools that provide information on software and hardware profiles, allow them to manage and update device configurations, and track network changes.

Network managers face such challenges as managing remote devices, tracking changes, maintaining up-to-date network information, and implementing global changes quickly. The following sections outline these challenges.

Managing Remote Devices

In a large distributed network, network administrators are often responsible for devices in remote locations. Therefore, to troubleshoot problems efficiently, network managers require easy access to the devices for which they are responsible without having to be in the same physical location. At the same time, access to these devices must be controlled and should not jeopardize network and application security.

Tracking Changes and Maintaining Up-to-Date Network Information

Several people usually share responsibility for the network and its configuration. This makes it difficult to maintain accurate documentation on the most current network configuration and to document changes. To quickly locate the source of problems or plan for upgrades and expansion, network administrators need up-to-date information on device inventory, software versions that are running, and specific device configurations. If this information is not maintained in one central place, it is difficult to determine the current state of the network.

Implementing Global Changes Quickly

Performing software upgrades or updating configuration files manually on a large network with many devices can become cumbersome and time-consuming. If automated tools are not available to perform these tasks, updates can be prone to errors or result in a lot of network downtime. Because of the time-consuming nature of changing passwords and network administrators' limited time, security can also be jeopardized if passwords are not changed frequently.

Configuration Tools

Cisco realizes that, to efficiently maintain and troubleshoot a large network, network managers must have access to current network information and all troubleshooting tools in one integrated place on the desktop. Network managers must also have the ability to identify network changes and perform updates to multiple devices quickly.

The following sections introduce CiscoWorks 2000 and describe the protocols that configuration tools use.

Configuration Protocols

Standard protocols like SNMP, Telnet, and TFTP are used for collecting configuration data.

SNMP is used to collect inventory information because many devices have inventory data available in the MIB database. Some devices, such as Cisco IOS routers and Cisco Catalyst switches, also support configuration over SNMP and TFTP. SNMP usually initiates the transfer of configuration data to or from a device, while the actual file transfer uses TFTP. SNMP and TFTP are both unreliable transport mechanisms that run on top of UDP. These methods might not be an appropriate solution for network policies that require higher security. Telnet can be used as a reliable protocol for configuration management. Using the Secure Shell (SSH) protocol or enabling encryption using IP Security (IPSec) can increase security.

CiscoWorks 2000

As shown in Figure 10-15, CiscoWorks 2000 is a configuration tool that supports all of the aforementioned configuration protocols. All management data is stored centrally, thereby allowing the network manager to access information on remote network devices through any web browser. CiscoWorks 2000 can manage information about the devices' configuration, inventory, and software versions.

Figure 10-15   *CiscoWorks 2000 Provides Configuration Management*

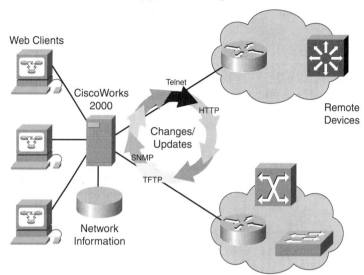

CiscoWorks 2000 maintains a database of network information and provides many reports that can be used for configuration and troubleshooting. When devices are added to the inventory, the network administrator can schedule tasks to periodically retrieve and update device information, such as hardware, software, and configuration files, to ensure that the most current network information is stored. In addition, CiscoWorks 2000 automatically records any network device changes, thereby making it easy to identify when changes are made and who makes them.

Accounting Management

Key Point: Accounting Management

The goal of accounting management is to measure network utilization parameters so that individual or group use of the network can be regulated.

Such regulation minimizes network problems (because network resources can be apportioned based on resource capacities) and maximizes the network access fairness across all users.

As with performance management, the first step toward achieving appropriate accounting management is to measure the utilization of all important network resources. Analyzing the results provides insight into current usage patterns, thereby enabling the establishment of usage quotas. Adjustments are often necessary to achieve optimal access practices. Going forward, measuring resource use can yield billing information and information that can be used to assess continued fair and optimal resource utilization.

Accounting Tools

The following three major accounting options are available:

- **IP accounting**—Used to collect the information about the number of packets and bytes that are transferred between any pair of IP endpoints.

- **The accounting part of authentication, authorization, and accounting (AAA)**— Typically used to time and log events, such as users dialing into and disconnecting from networks.

- **NetFlow accounting**—Similar to IP accounting, except that it provides more granularity by monitoring flows rather than pairs of IP addresses.

The following sections describe each of these options.

IP Accounting

IP accounting can be used to measure the amount of traffic that different IP hosts or subnets generate. With IP accounting enabled, a router holds the following traffic information between a pair of IP endpoints:

- Source IP address
- Destination IP address
- Number of packets
- Number of bytes

Optional IP accounting features include accounting for the following:

- Packets to and from devices, based on MAC addresses
- Packets that are based on IP precedence values
- ACL violations

Key Point: The Server Polls IP Accounting Data

IP accounting information must be transferred from the router to an accounting server. The server must initiate the transfer; in other words, the server polls the router. Accounting data can be lost if the polling is not frequent enough.

Accounting data can be collected using Cisco IOS software commands or SNMP.

Figure 10-16 illustrates the polling process that is periodically initiated by the accounting server. First, the server freezes the accounting database on the router (by issuing the **clear ip accounting** command) and then downloads the accounting information (by issuing the **show ip accounting checkpoint** command).

Figure 10-16 *IP Accounting in Action*

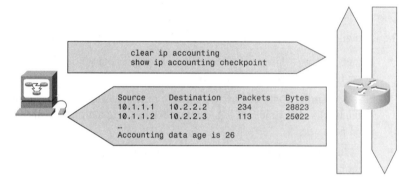

Accounting Using the AAA Framework

As users of modern access technologies have sought a way to authenticate, authorize, and initiate accounting records for billing user time on their networks, AAA has changed dramatically.

Secure network access and the ability to dynamically define a user's profile in order to access network resources have been requirements since dialup was the only means of network access. AAA network security services provide the primary framework through which a network administrator can establish access control on network points of entry or network access servers (which is usually the function of a router or access server).

Key Point: AAA Services

Authentication identifies a user, *authorization* determines what that user can do, and *accounting* monitors the duration of the user's network usage for billing purposes.

AAA information is typically stored in an external database or remote server, such as a RADIUS or TACACS+ server. This information can also be stored locally on the access server or router. Remote security servers such as RADIUS and TACACS+ assign specific privileges to users by associating attribute-value (AV) pairs that define a user's access rights. All authorization methods must be defined through AAA.

Figure 10-17 shows how AAA authenticates and maintains accounting records for a dial-in Point-to-Point Protocol (PPP) user. In this implementation, a user dials a telephone number that corresponds to a port on a network access server (NAS) that resides at the edge of the network. The server queries the user's ID and password locally at the NAS database or pre-configured RADIUS server to determine whether to permit or deny network access. If the user is permitted, the RADIUS server typically sends a configuration or AV pair to the NAS, thereby determining the type of access and service granted.

Figure 10-17 *AAA Accounting Data Is Sent To the NMS*

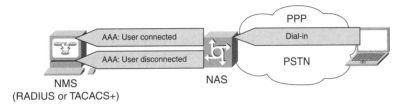

Key Point: AAA Accounting Data

The router pushes AAA accounting data to the management server; the server does not poll for the data.

NetFlow Accounting

As previously described in the "NetFlow" section of this chapter, NetFlow services provide network administrators with access to IP flow information from their data networks. Exported NetFlow data can be used for a variety of purposes, including network management and planning, enterprise accounting and departmental cost charges, Internet service provider (ISP) billing, data warehousing, and data mining for marketing purposes.

Figure 10-18 shows the NetFlow service's three-tiered architecture, which includes the following three tiers:

- **NetFlow-capable Layer 3 device**—Captures NetFlow accounting statistics for unicast ingress traffic on networking devices and exports the data to a collection device.

- **NetFlow collector**—Provides scalable and economical data collection from multiple NetFlow-enabled devices. The NetFlow collector provides the following functionalities:
  - Consumes flows from multiple NetFlow-enabled devices
  - Performs data volume reduction through selective filtering and aggregation
  - Stores flow information in flat files on a disk for post-processing by NetFlow data consumers, third-party billing applications, and traffic analysis tools
- **Accounting and billing application**—Enables the network's administrator to retrieve, display, and generate bills based on NetFlow data collected by NetFlow collector files.

Figure 10-18 *NetFlow Accounting Contains Three Tiers*

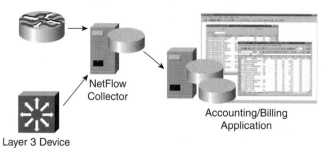

NetFlow accounting and billing options provide detailed metering (for example, IP addresses, packet and byte counts, timestamps, CoS, and application ports) for highly flexible and detailed resource usage accounting. Service providers can use this information to migrate from single-fee, flat-rate billing to more flexible charging mechanisms that are based on time of day, bandwidth usage, application usage, QoS, and so on. Enterprise customers can use the information for departmental cost recovery or cost allocation for resource usage.

Performance Management

Key Point: Capacity Planning and Performance Management

Capacity planning is the process of determining the network resources that are required for preventing a performance or availability impact on business-critical applications. *Performance management* is the practice of managing network service response time, consistency, and quality for individual and overall services.

The goal of performance management is to measure various aspects of network performance and provide the information to network administrators to maintain an acceptable level of internetwork performance. Performance management aims to do the following:

- Ensure that the data network remains as accessible and uncongested as possible.
- Reduce network overcrowding and inaccessibility.
- Provide a consistent level of service to the network user.
- Determine utilization trends to isolate and solve performance problems.

NOTE   Performance problems are usually related to capacity. Applications are slower because bandwidth and data must wait in queues before being transmitted through the network. In voice applications, problems such as delay and jitter directly affect voice call quality.

Most organizations already collect capacity-related information and work consistently to resolve problems, plan changes, and implement new capacity and performance functionality. However, organizations do not routinely perform *trending* and *what-if analysis*. What-if analysis is the process of determining the impact of a network change. Trending is the process of capturing network capacity baselines and performance issues to identify network trends for future upgrade requirements. Capacity and performance management also includes exception management (where issues are identified and resolved before users call in) and QoS management (where network administrators plan, manage, and identify individual service performance issues).

The following items limit capacity and performance management:

- CPU
- Backplane or input/output (I/O) speed
- Memory and buffers
- Interface and pipe sizes
- Queuing, latency, and jitter
- Speed and distance
- Application characteristics

Some references to capacity planning and performance management mention the *data plane* and the *control plane*. The data plane refers to capacity and performance issues that are involved with data traversing the network. The control plane refers to resources that are required to maintain proper functionality of the data plane. Control plane functionality includes overhead services such as routing, spanning tree, interface keepalives, and device management via SNMP. Like the traffic that traverses the network, these control plane requirements use CPU, memory, buffering, queuing, and bandwidth. Many of the control plane requirements are essential to the system's overall functionality. The network could fail if the control plane requirements do not have the proper resources.

Performance Practices

When network operators want to measure performance, they can select from many different approaches or techniques that are based on many factors. This section discusses the following factors:

- Service level management
- Network and application what-if analysis
- Baselining and trending
- Exception management
- QoS management

Service Level Management

Capacity planning is an important issue for network managers. *Service level management (SLM)* is a proven methodology that helps network managers resolve resource issues by defining and regulating capacity and performance management processes in a cost-effective manner. This can be accomplished in one of the following two ways:

- By establishing a service level agreement (SLA) between the network users and the network service provider. The SLA includes capacity and performance management objectives and identifies reports and recommendations for maintaining service quality. (The "Managing Service Levels in a Network" section of this chapter further discusses SLAs.)

- The network administrator defines capacity and performance management service requirements and then attempts to fund the service and upgrades on a case-by-case basis. (First, the network organization defines a capacity planning and performance management service that describes its current capability and future requirements.) A complete service would include a what-if analysis for network changes and application changes, baseline and trend analysis for defined performance variables, exception management for defined capacity and performance variables, and QoS management.

Network and Application What-if Analysis

A network and application what-if analysis is performed to determine the outcome of a planned change. Without what-if analysis, organizations not only risk the success of the change, but also risk overall network availability. In many cases, a network change has resulted in increased traffic on the network, causing network collapse and many hours of production downtime.

Baselining and Trending

Baselining and trending allows network administrators to plan and complete network upgrades before a capacity problem causes network downtime or performance problems. This process compares resource utilization during successive time periods and stores the information in a database. Therefore, baselining and trending allows planners to view resource utilization parameters for the previous hour, day, week, month, and year. To be useful, this information must be reviewed on a regular (weekly, biweekly, or monthly) basis. One issue with baselining and trending in large networks is the overwhelming amount of information that is produced for review.

Many network management solutions provide information and graphs about capacity resource variables. Unfortunately, this data is often used to provide reactive support for an existing problem rather than proactive support for potential problems, which is the purpose of baselining and trending.

Exception Management

Exception management is a valuable methodology for identifying and resolving capacity and performance issues. The network administrator or manager receives notification of capacity and performance threshold violations, thereby enabling an immediate investigation. For example, a network administrator might receive an alarm about high CPU utilization on a router. The network administrator can log into the router to determine why the CPU utilization is so high. The administrator can then perform a remedial configuration that reduces the CPU usage or create an access list that prevents the traffic that is causing the problem, particularly if the traffic is not business-critical.

QoS Management

QoS management involves creating and monitoring specific traffic classes within the network. QoS provides more consistent performance for specific application groups (defined within traffic classes). Traffic shaping features provide significant flexibility in the prioritizing and traffic shaping of specific classes of traffic. These features include capabilities such as committed access rate (CAR), weighted random early detection (WRED), and class-based weighted fair queuing (CBWFQ). Traffic classes are usually created based on performance SLAs for more business-critical applications and specific application requirements, such as voice. Because less-critical traffic is controlled, it cannot affect higher-priority applications and services.

Performance Data Reporting

It is important to develop an information collection plan within each area of performance practice. For network or application what-if analysis, tools are used to mimic the network environment and simulate the impact of the change relative to potential resource issues within the device control or data plane. Snapshots of devices and links that show current resource utilization are required for baselining and trending. Network administrators review this data in order to understand potential upgrade requirements and properly plan upgrades before capacity or performance problems arise. When problems occur, exception management alerts the network administrators so they can tune the network or fix the problem.

The process for developing a performance information collection plan can be divided into the following five steps:

Step 1 Determine networking requirements

Step 2 Define a process

Step 3 Define capacity areas

Step 4 Define capacity variables

Step 5 Interpret data

The following sections detail these steps.

Determine Networking Requirements

Developing a capacity and performance management plan requires identifying what information is required and identifying the purpose of that information. A network administrator must determine what resources and tools are available, what gaps exist, and what is required for correct performance monitoring.

Define a Process

You need a process for ensuring that the performance measurement tools are used successfully and consistently. Process improvements can be required to define how network administrators should react when threshold violations occur, or what process to follow for baselining, trending, and upgrading the network. When you have determined the requirements and resources for successful capacity planning, you can consider the appropriate methodology.

Define Capacity Areas

Capacity planning should include a definition of *capacity areas*, which are areas of the network that can share a common capacity planning strategy—such as the corporate backbone, remote offices, critical WAN sites, and dial-in access. Defining different areas is helpful for the following reasons:

- Different network areas might have different thresholds. For example, LAN bandwidth is less expensive than WAN bandwidth; therefore, utilization thresholds should be lower.

- Different areas might require the monitoring of different MIB variables. For example, forward explicit congestion notification (FECN) and backward explicit congestion notification (BECN) counters in Frame Relay are critical to understanding Frame Relay capacity problems.

- Network upgrades that are required because of capacity shortage can be performed in smaller areas rather than on the complete network. This is particularly important for areas in which business processes demand high network availability and flexibility.

Define Capacity Variables

The next important step is to define the variables to monitor and the threshold values that require action. Defining the capacity variables depends significantly on the devices and media that are used within the network. In general, parameters such as CPU, memory, and link utilization are valuable. However, other variables might be important for specific technologies or requirements; these variables include queue depths, performance, Frame Relay congestion notification, backplane utilization, buffer utilization, NetFlow statistics, broadcast volume, and RMON data. Careful selection of a meaningful collection interval is useful and should not cause excessive overhead.

Interpret Data

Understanding the collected data is critical for providing high quality of service. For example, many organizations do not fully understand peak and average utilization levels.

Performance Collection Challenges

As information systems continue to grow in size, scope, and strategic importance, network managers face numerous challenges in managing mission-critical networks that have become an integral component of the business. The ability to measure network response time, determine device availability, resolve connectivity issues, analyze response time patterns, and provide critical reports (both real-time and historical) have taken on an even higher priority.

Tools are needed to address these challenges, which include both real-time and historical analysis. Network managers require tools to isolate performance problems, locate bottlenecks, diagnose latency, and perform trend analysis in multiprotocol networks. Rapid problem diagnostic capabilities can lead to higher network availability by allowing network managers to alleviate performance bottlenecks quickly.

Following are some challenges that network managers face:

- **Pinpointing network response time and availability problems**—In a large distributed network, network managers often spend much of their time identifying network problems in a reactive mode. For example, network managers must identify not only that a network delay exists, but also where in a network path the traffic is being delayed. To diagnose problems quickly, performance measurements are needed for an entire path and for each hop within the path.

- **Pinpointing the source of the problem**—When problems with networked applications arise, network managers can spend much of their time determining whether the problem resides in the network or the server. In enterprises that have different groups administering the network and servers, this diagnosis must be made quickly to ensure a rapid resolution to the problem.

  Enterprises often rely on services from multiple service providers to run mission-critical networked applications. For example, a telecommunications company can provide wide-area connectivity between an enterprise's central office and its remote sites. An ISP connects the enterprise to the Internet; another service provider can supply virtual private networks (VPNs) between enterprises. As a result, during a network outage, it can be extremely difficult for a network manager to pinpoint both where in the network the problem occurred and which service provider is responsible for the problem.

Performance Information Collection Solutions

Performance information collection solutions include the following:

- Internet Control Message Protocol (ICMP) ping
- Network analyzers or probes
- NetFlow

ICMP Ping

Ping is a common and user-friendly troubleshooting technique for network professionals. Ping is a utility that uses the ICMP echo request and reply protocol to test for connectivity to an IP address. Pinging a device from a station provides a quick view of device reachability and response time from the station to the target IP device. However, using ping from a station to a remote node might not identify *where* a problem is located because the measurement might be occurring over a different network path or over multiple hops. In addition, using ICMP to measure response time does not accurately reflect an application's response time. An apparently healthy network (for example, one with quick ping responses or low utilization) can still mask potential response time problems because the problem might reside in the upper layers of the protocol stack.

Network Analyzers or Probes

Network analyzers, or *probes*, are tools that are commonly used for monitoring and troubleshooting response time. A probe is generally a dedicated hardware device that is used to monitor a network segment's performance. For example, an RMON2 probe can analyze the existing network traffic and report on the connected segment's utilization, top talkers, and conversations; each of these reports is broken out by upper-layer protocols. Probes can capture packets and analyze packet header information for an in-depth analysis of a network segment's activity.

A probe's report on segment utilization and error counts might assist the network professional in pinpointing network delays or problems. However, numerous probes are needed along each hop of the application path to detect where in the network the delay resides. Although a network analyzer or probe can yield valuable information, it might not be a cost-effective solution when solving response time and availability issues. Dedicated probes are a better fit when baselining a network or trending link, protocol, and application utilization, and when characterizing and identifying the top talkers and conversations.

NetFlow

Cisco IOS NetFlow technology, which collects and measures data as it enters specific routers or switch interfaces, is an integral part of Cisco IOS software.

By analyzing NetFlow data, a network manager can identify the cause of congestion, determine the CoS for each user and application, and identify traffic's source and destination network. NetFlow allows extremely granular and accurate traffic measurements and high-level aggregated traffic collection. Because it is a component of Cisco IOS software, NetFlow enables Cisco product-based networks to perform IP traffic flow analysis without purchasing custom probes, thereby making traffic analysis economical on large IP networks.

Performance Solution Tools

To determine where network performance lacks, you must measure response time and availability end-to-end, measure hop-by-hop (network device-to-device), and be warned of long delays. A hop-by-hop path analysis then assists a network manager in isolating the network's trouble spots.

In addition, it is important to measure business application traffic performance directly. Using only ping to measure response time problems might not be enough. Measuring the delay of voice data and other upper layer protocols such as TCP, UDP, DNS, DHCP, can provide important information for optimizing a network.

Cisco's service assurance agents (SAAs), embedded in Cisco routers or Catalyst Layer 3 switches along with the Internetwork Performance Monitor (IPM) application, can accomplish these objectives. A dedicated hardware probe is not necessary for measuring and monitoring network performance statistics. Performance tools such as IPM and SAA help network managers trace and identify performance degradation in a network.

NOTE   The "Managing Service Levels in a Network" section of this chapter further discusses SAA and IPM.

Security Management

The purpose of security management is to support security policy application, including the creation, deletion, and control of security services and mechanisms; the distribution of security-relevant information; and the reporting of security-relevant events. Security management controls access to network resources and prevents network sabotage (intentional or unintentional) and unauthorized access to sensitive information.

Security management assists administrators in creating a secure network environment. This includes partitioning network resources into authorized and unauthorized areas, mapping groups of users to those areas, and monitoring, policing, and logging user access to resources in those areas.

The following protocols can be used for router or switch security management:

- **Telnet**—Typically used to make ad-hoc changes to router or switch configurations. Authentication is in clear text and is therefore not the most secure. As an alternative, using the SSH protocol or enabling encryption using IPSec can increase security. Authentication should be offloaded to a centralized authentication server (an AAA server) that can also use a One Time Password (OTP) approach to increase the level of security.

- **SNMP**—Typically used to manage and monitor routers and switches. Depending on which version of SNMP is used, different security mechanisms are available. (Information on IPSec and SNMP support is available in *IPSec—SNMP Support*, at www.cisco.com/univercd/cc/td/doc/product/software/ios121/121newft/121limit/121e/121e4/dtipmib.htm.)

- **Hypertext Transfer Protocol (HTTP)**—Also supported by routers and switches. A similar approach can be used as with Telnet (for example, use an AAA server with an optional OTP system or IPSec for confidentiality).

- **Remote Shell/Remote Shell Command Execution (RSH/RCMD)**—Can be used to modify configurations but is not recommended because of its lack of security.

- **SSH**—A protocol that provides strong authentication and encryption of the management session but that not all devices might support.

Key Point: Security Management Protocols

Telnet and SNMP are the most common management protocols. Only one management protocol is required; all others should be disabled. Use the same management approach on all network devices.

To ensure enterprise network security, you must first secure the network devices. The default authentication of routers and switches is based on password-only authentication, in which multiple administrators share the same password and it is impossible to identify who configured or misconfigured a router or a switch. The passwords must be configured on all routers and switches; therefore, they are difficult to change because they must be changed on every router in the network.

A solution to this problem is to use a username and password pair to identify individual administrators and a centralized user database to make security management more scalable. Use RADIUS or TACACS+ between a router or switch and an AAA server. Recall that routers and switches support centralized security management using the AAA approach: the first A stands for *authentication* (identifying the administrator), the second A for *authorization* (determining whether the authenticated administrator is allowed to perform a certain action), and the third A for *accounting* (logging of all actions). AAA supports optional OTP authentication.

Using IP filters to allow management sessions from a designated management network module (the management LAN) only can increase security.

Security Management Examples

Figure 10-19 illustrates the first line of defense, where management sessions are authorized based on source IP addresses. An access list is applied to either incoming packets on interfaces or the vty line. Subsequent authentication is necessary to defend against IP spoofing.

Figure 10-19 *Authorization of Management Workstations Is a Key First Line of Defense*

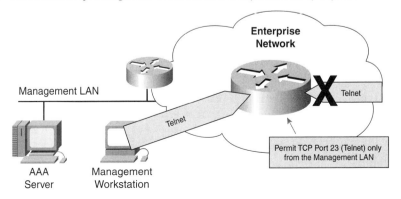

Figure 10-20 illustrates the steps the authentication process takes when an AAA server is used for storing the user database. When a user starts the management session (Telnet, in the example), the router asks the AAA server (by using the TACACS+ or RADIUS protocol) if this user is allowed to manage this router. The AAA server allows the router to grant access to the user if the credentials (username and password) match an entry in the user database. Using an additional server that verifies OTPs can strengthen authentication.

Figure 10-20 *Centralized Authentication of Users with an AAA Server*

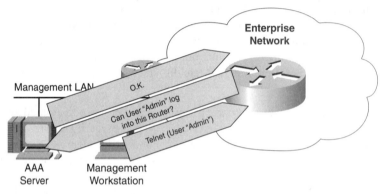

Figure 10-21 illustrates the next security level, in which the AAA server authorizes each user action. This allows for very detailed control over what actions users can perform on network devices.

Figure 10-21 *An AAA Server Can Authorize User Actions*

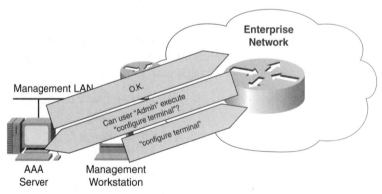

As illustrated in Figure 10-22, the final step is to account for all actions by logging the administrator's actions to an AAA server. This step is important for tracking changes to the network. Authorization identifies which commands users can use, while accounting identifies which commands users have used or misused.

Figure 10-22 *AAA Accounting of User Actions*

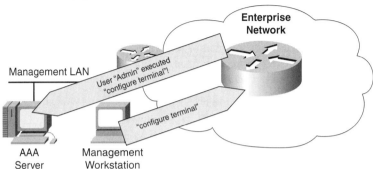

Managing Service Levels in a Network

Information technology providers are under increasing pressure to offer service level agreements to their customers. Whether the service provider is the enterprise IT department or a third-party vendor, such as an ISP, management must have contractual assurance that business objectives will be met. The SLA assures the end user that critical network applications and services will be available when needed. In many cases, an SLA is required before a company deploys new technology or services.

We begin with an explanation of what an SLA is, its importance and target customers, and the typical requirements found in the SLA. We also discuss service-level management, which is important for assuring end-to-end service. Finally, we describe the service assurance agent, which enables active response time measurements, and introduce network response and availability applications.

The Importance of SLAs

An SLA is a key component of a service level contract (SLC).

Key Point: SLC and SLAs

An SLC specifies connectivity and performance levels the service provider must meet for the end user.

SLAs define specific service performance measurements between device pairs, including routers, servers, workstations, and other equipment.

The service provider could be within the enterprise—such as an IT department providing services to internal network users—or an external company, such as an ISP providing wide-area or hosted application services.

SLAs are becoming an integral part of service delivery and are the cornerstones of providing differentiated service offerings. Businesses are relying on SLAs for mission-critical applications and processes.

An SLC typically includes multiple SLAs. A violation of any particular SLA could create a violation of the overall SLC. The SLM solution must manage all agreements in a way that constitutes a service provider contract. The SLM solution should enable the user to individually monitor multiple SLCs, examine SLA details, and monitor the percentage of SLA conformance for a given SLC.

Figure 10-23 illustrates an example of an SLC and constituent SLAs. The SLC for connectivity from remote building sites (numbered 1 and 2) to the Enterprise Edge might read, "Provide connections between the Enterprise Edge and all remote buildings at a latency of no greater than 50 milliseconds averaged over one hour, and with an availability of 99.9 percent." Following would be the constituent SLAs:

- Round-trip delay of no more than 50 ms averaged over one hour from remote Building 1 to the Enterprise Edge.

- Round-trip delay of no more than 50 ms averaged over one hour from remote Building 2 to the Enterprise Edge.

- Link availability of no less than 99.9 percent from remote Building 1 to the Enterprise Edge.

- Link availability of no less than 99.9 percent from remote Building 2 to the Enterprise Edge.

Figure 10-23 *A Service Level Contract and Constituent Service Level Agreements*

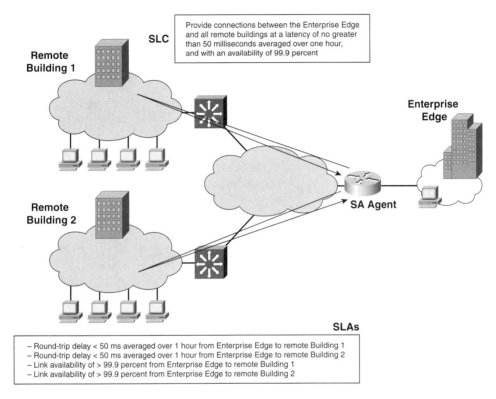

SLC

Provide connections between the Enterprise Edge and all remote buildings at a latency of no greater than 50 milliseconds averaged over one hour, and with an availability of 99.9 percent

Remote Building 1

Enterprise Edge

Remote Building 2

SA Agent

SLAs

– Round-trip delay < 50 ms averaged over 1 hour from Enterprise Edge to remote Building 1
– Round-trip delay < 50 ms averaged over 1 hour from Enterprise Edge to remote Building 2
– Link availability of > 99.9 percent from Enterprise Edge to remote Building 1
– Link availability of > 99.9 percent from Enterprise Edge to remote Building 2

SLA Requirements

As the trend to contract for services continues to increase both in numbers and strategic importance, network managers face new challenges in managing diverse, business-critical networks.

Challenges of Managing SLAs

Adoption of the e-business model and increased competition in the service provider market have forced service providers and large corporations to monitor and manage network resources more efficiently in order to win and maintain business. However, organizations or departments should monitor SLC compliance—enterprise customers should implement a means of validating that service levels are being met and should not rely solely on external service providers' reports for validation.

Management of any device or service requires the ability to collect measurement data from the device or devices that comprise the service. Monitoring a third-party vendor's provided services presents a unique challenge because individual service components are unknown to the customer, and, therefore, their data is unavailable (as illustrated in Figure 10-24). Conformance is determined by collecting service-level measurements from customer-owned and -controlled devices. Even though there is no visibility into the actual components of a particular service, the data collected must accurately represent and report on SLA conformance.

Figure 10-24   *Managing SLAs Can Be Challenging Because of the Invisibility of External Networks*

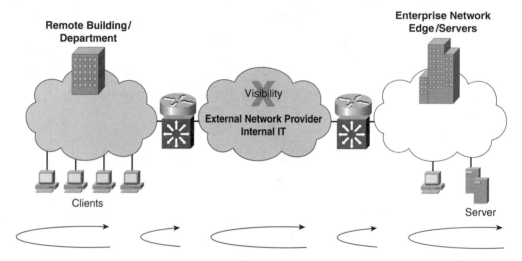

Of course, the provided service level is not always the source of trouble with an end-user application that relies on the service. The network manager must be able to view the service from an end-user perspective and demarcate where the problem is occurring.

In the corporate network, the department that receives the service signs the SLC with the corporate IT department, which controls and manages the enterprise network. The IT department must have tools for proactive traffic measurement on the enterprise network. The measurement equipment determines when the terms of the SLC are being violated, thereby enabling the IT department to respond with corrective action.

Requirements in SLAs

A key success factor for developing effective SLAs is ensuring that business objectives are translated accurately into SLAs, and that they have tangible service metrics that can be measured, reported, and validated. Long, complex, and unrealistic agreements contribute to service providers that fail to manage the service levels.

As SLAs become more popular, their requirements become more clearly defined. The enterprise customer usually requires the following:

- The ability to confirm that the provider meets SLAs, based on network connectivity and network applications responses. In the enterprise network, meeting the SLA parameters (and definitions) is important for users of business-critical applications over the corporate network. For instance, IP telephones might require low latency and low delay to any other IP telephones in the corporate network. The enterprise customer would therefore require an SLA with particular latency and delay parameters that suit the IP telephones' communication demands.

- The ability to identify SLA issues in detail. In the event of an SLA violation, the enterprise department managers want to know where and why the SLA was broken. For example, if an IP telephone call has poor voice quality, the department manager wants to know if the cause is related to the network or the IP telephone system.

- The ability to impose financial penalties for missed SLAs. Penalties might be required if business could not be conducted because of unavailable business services. If the correct SLA measurements have been applied, the location of the faulty equipment and the time of the event can be tracked.

- Business-level reports and detailed technical reports that can be enhanced and extended easily and incrementally. Reports identify the time of an SLA violation and show trends in network performance. Reports are useful tools for managers and stakeholders when SLAs or network specifications require adjustments.

- Validation that key business objectives are being met when deploying technologies. When networks are upgraded, the SLA plays an important role in monitoring the performance of newly introduced technology.

To provide all required information to the users and customers, a variety of metrics must be constantly monitored on the network; the following section discusses SLA metrics.

SLA Metrics

Service level management is critical when bringing diverse partners, suppliers, and consumers together. The adoption of the e-business model places pressure on service providers to deliver quantitative and qualitative measurements in SLAs. These expectations require the service provider to monitor and manage network resources more effectively and efficiently.

Enterprise customers need service management solutions that provide a means of validating that service levels are being met. Within an organization, departments that use network services can require an SLA with the IT department to support their business-critical traffic. Each service might place different demands on the network. These varying network demands require a variety of measurements, including the following:

- **Availability**—Constant polling of a selected device determines when there is no response from a device. Business-critical applications require constant availability of network devices and services. If the business-critical application cannot communicate, the point of failure must be located. An obvious cause of broken communication could be other services or devices that are unavailable and therefore not responding.

- **Latency (delay)**—Polling records the amount of time that is required for a packet to be sent and received. High latency numbers can indicate congestion on either an end device or a relaying device, such as a router or switch.

- **Packet loss**—Packet loss can indicate a bottleneck on the network. Hop-by-hop polling can isolate the point where this trouble is occurring.

- **Jitter (delay variation)**—Jitter on the network is becoming important with the introduction of new services such as voice and video. These services must be transported on a constant stream of data on the network. Jitter causes voice applications to become garbled, thereby making communication impossible.

Delivering the requested SLA means that the network operator must do the following:

- Actively monitor the network to verify SLA implementation and provide necessary changes to the network. The changes might only require minor network configuration adjustments, such as changing the policy-based parameters. However, network design changes might be required if the network runs low on resources. Proper measurement tools enable the network operator to detect in advance when and where the network will be congested.

- Maintain proactive notification systems. Because of unpredictable traffic flows in the network, monitoring and periodic report generation of SLA performance are not enough. Proactive notification informs network operators when network performance is not within SLA parameters.

SLM as a Key Component for Assuring SLAs

Guaranteeing a specific SLA requires SLM. While vendors might have different definitions and capabilities for managing service levels, only one definition and capability is meaningful to customers: end-to-end management of all aspects that relate to the connectivity, performance, and availability of the service or application. Thus, SLCs should include contracts between the end user or department and the network provider or IT department.

Cisco's focus is to provide an SLM solution that enables end-to-end visibility into all components of a service. Open-standard interfaces provide the ability to integrate the technologies of different vendors with true network visibility.

Managing service conformance to an SLC is important to the end users' overall satisfaction and can be driven by financial concerns. Services provided by third-party vendors, such as ISPs and application service providers (ASPs), are differentiated and priced according to various service guarantees (as defined in SLCs and SLAs).

Key Point: SLC and SLAs Ensure Network Performance

An SLC and encompassing SLAs ensure that the network provider satisfies the requests from the department or end user. In the event of a violation, the source of the problem is identified and properly rectified, and reports are provided.

End-to-End SLM Challenges

Delivering end-to-end SLM is extremely challenging because the solution must satisfy the following requirements:

- Leverage component management products from multiple vendors
- Work with clients and equipment that the customer does not own or control
- Adapt to new SLM metrics as new technologies are deployed
- Scale by orders of magnitude
- Collect the correct network and application SLM metrics at the appropriate times

SLA metrics vary widely, and the technologies for measuring those metrics also vary. In managing service levels end-to-end, it is necessary to measure and collect data at every level of the protocol stack—from the Layer 5, 6, and 7 client-to-server layers, to the Layer 3 and 4 network and network services layers, to the Layer 1 and 2 LAN and WAN layers. No one product or technology satisfies all these requirements. High-quality products from multiple vendors cover the client/server layers and the LAN and WAN layers, but little is available in the Layer 3 and Layer 4 spaces, and no product that measures the entire protocol stack.

High-level and Detailed Reporting

An SLA application should measure data against the requested metrics, print basic SLA reports, such as whether or not an SLA has been met, and provide network administrators with high-level management reports and detailed reports. This is a significant improvement over traditional reporting, in which tedious reports were only prepared for a specific group within an IT department.

With SLAs, business objectives are translated into service provider agreements. Department managers must be aware of their business needs so they can negotiate an SLA with the network provider. At the same time, the providers' reports must be detailed enough so department managers can understand how the SLAs are met.

The SLA management system must provide the level of technical information that is required by the day-to-day operations staff to help them resolve problems when SLAs are not being met.

The high-level reports must be web-accessible and include the following information:

- SLCs that are not in conformance
- Percentage of SLAs that are out of conformance for a given contract
- Business objects that are impacted
- Escalation procedures to resolve nonconformance of SLCs
- Performance of service levels over time: today, yesterday, this month, last month, this year, last year, and so on

The detailed reports should provide the following information:

- Device pairs that are related to an SLA
- Exceptions that occur and how often
- Round-trip latency and latency variations
- Mean time to repair and mean time to fail
- Link and device availability
- Throughput

SLM Example

Consider an example in which the enterprise illustrated in Figure 10-25 might require many SLCs from its network provider, each for a different service:

- Low latency for IP telephony in the complete network
- Constant access for business application server users from inside and outside the corporate boundary
- High availability of business application services such as HTTP

Developing a precise, thorough SLC or SLA is challenging. Creating the SLC or SLA entails not only signing documents between the provider and the user that explain measurements and numbers, but it also requires a thorough understanding of the network, services, applications, and other parameters that are involved in the network business application. Reports must be generated that provide useful information. Clear SLA parameters enable easy verification that SLA requirements are met. Management plans must be made for collecting all necessary parameters and adjusting the SLC or SLA accordingly.

Figure 10-25   *Example of an Enterprise Requiring Multiple SLCs*

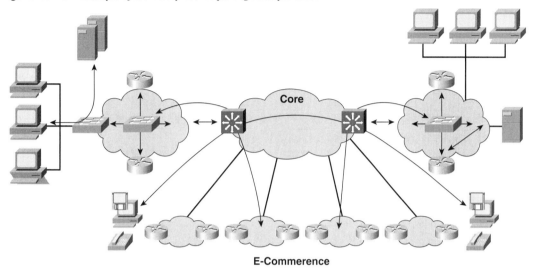

SLM Planning

Defining a network management plan assists the network manager in understanding the importance of business services and the range of network segments that services traverse. Having a network management plan in place eases the adjustment of performance monitoring tools. The network management plan should include at least the following:

- A description of the network topology, its components, and the services the network can handle.

- A list of business-critical services to assist the administrator in choosing the operations that should be generated and measured by proactive monitoring agents.

- An explanation of the end users for the services. Understanding the topology and the users of critical networked applications helps administrators choose the source routers and target devices for measurements.

- An explanation of who is responsible for the network upon which the services run. Businesses can rely on service providers to link people and information sources in various locations. Such outsourcing makes it difficult to troubleshoot poor response time and network connectivity. Proactive performance tools help to troubleshoot in this type of network.

- A description of the minimum acceptable response times for the protocols that these services use. If the minimum acceptable response time is unknown, proactive performance tools help to establish baselines. Useful sources for guidelines are either the results of current network response times or that of averaging the monthly or weekly values of those responses. If the users are satisfied with network response time, these values are used as thresholds for future performance. Network designers often define acceptable performance, which might not always match end user expectations.

Cisco's Service Assurance Agent is an application that is part of the Cisco IOS software. SAA, which is described in the following section, provides useful results for SLA measurement and notification.

Service Assurance Agent

The Service Assurance Agent, which was previously known as Response Time Reporter (RTR), is a Cisco IOS software feature that exists on some Cisco IOS platforms. The SAA allows users to monitor network performance between a Cisco router (or Layer 3 switch) and a remote device, which can be another Cisco device or an IP host.

Key Point: SAA

The SAA provides a way for a Cisco IOS device to be configured to perform tests in the network, to either end systems or other IOS devices. The results of these tests are used to validate the SLA.

SAA uses IP as the foundation protocol and overlays communication protocols, such as TCP, UDP, and ICMP, to generate test packets and measure the SLA parameters when the packets return.

Key Point: SAA Can Test TCP and UDP Services

A key value of the SAA is its ability to mark the test packets with the appropriate CoS value, thereby enabling network managers to observe various TCP and UDP services and performance when QoS is implemented.

SAA performance metrics include round-trip response time, connect time, packet loss, application performance, inter-packet delay variance (jitter), and more. SAA allows users to perform troubleshooting, problem analysis, and notification based on the statistics it collects.

SAA is accessible using the Cisco IOS command-line interface (CLI) and SNMP.

SAA's key capabilities include the following:

- The ability to define rising and falling thresholds to monitor SLAs, measure SAA-generated packet loss, and notify the network management system about threshold violations.
- The ability to measure ICMP, TCP, or UDP response times on a specific path.
- The ability to measure response times between endpoints for a specific QoS, using IP CoS bits.
- The ability to measure voice application traffic response using UDP jitter operations.
- The ability to measure HTTP service performance, including DNS lookup, TCP connect, and HTTP transaction time.
- The ability to schedule an operation in the future and store historical data collected by SAA services.

As illustrated in Figure 10-26, SAA can monitor and measure many metrics from the IP layer to the application layer, including the following:

- File transfer performance using the File Transfer Protocol (FTP) operation.
- Business-critical websites using the HTTP protocol to measure response time and availability of those sites.
- UDP jitter operation. SAA stores information such as jitter, round-trip delay, one-way latency, and packet loss. Jitter is an important parameter to monitor for voice service.
- Hop-by-hop measurements using the ICMP path echo protocol. This is essential if a view of the traffic over the complete network is required. More importantly, this information helps to isolate the troubled link quickly if problems occur.
- If QoS is implemented on the network, the SAA uses different CoS for any of the protocols (HTTP, FTP, ICMP, and so forth) to generate traffic that is used for proactive measurements.

Figure 10-26 *SAA Can Monitor a Variety of Metrics*

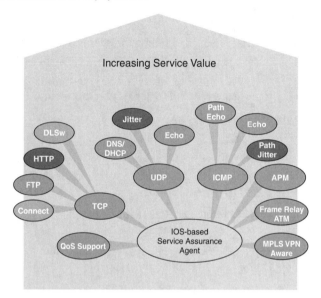

SAA Deployment

Figure 10-27 illustrates an sample of SAA deployment. The enterprise network structure is built using the three-layer network design model: the network is divided into a corporate headquarters (core), regional aggregation (distribution), and retail branches (access) modules. (Although Figure 10-27 shows routers, Layer 3 switches with SAA capabilities can also be used.)

Typical network management requirements include the availability of network devices (such as switches, servers, and workstations) and immediate notification if the end-to-end communication is broken or is not within the defined values. Additional requirements might include the availability of HTTP services in the campus server farm and low jitter for IP telephony running in the campus.

Testing for the availability of network devices can be initiated from almost any device and carried out with the IP **ping** command. The network management station, which generates ping packets, can only test connectivity from that point in the network. The benefit of initiating a ping on network devices is that it can be triggered from any point in the network to any destination. SAA also provides effective notification in the event of a device's unavailability.

Figure 10-27 *SAA Deployment Example*

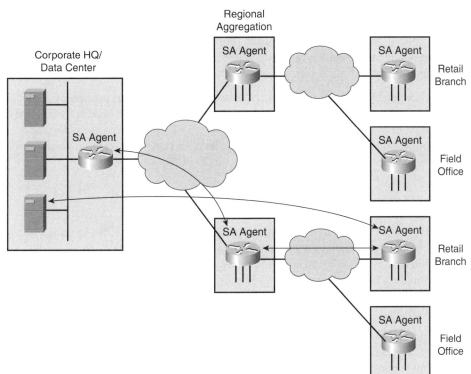

HTTP polling requires an understanding of the HTTP standard protocol, which works between a server and client. The SAA emulates the role of a web client for measuring purposes. The SAA device can be close to the servers, thereby allowing the service's availability to be checked. Because bottlenecks can exist in the network, a consideration might be to have the SAA with HTTP support located close to end users. Reports from SAA-capable devices can then identify where HTTP traffic is slow.

HTTP servers are usually located in the network's core so that the major HTTP traffic stream is from the user edge to the server edge. In contrast, IP telephony is an application that sends most of its traffic elsewhere on the network.

To avoid delay as much as possible when passing through Layer 3 devices, voice traffic should be assigned a higher priority in IP packets; voice also requires low jitter. Any IP device can reply to IP ICMP packets, but when testing connectivity of services that run on different TCP or UDP ports (such as voice and video) is required, typical network devices cannot respond. The SAA has the ability to measure the jitter for IP telephony by sending test packets as the source from one side of the network and responding as the destination of those packets on the other side of the network; the destination SAA accepts the packets, provides measurements, and responds to the source. The source SAA assesses the values in the reply packets and compares these values to the defined SLA. If the defined values are exceeded, the notification mechanism provides information to the management station, and the administrator can easily locate where disturbances might appear in the IP telephony application.

When establishing the SLC or SLA for an entire enterprise network, configuring and managing multiple devices might be challenging. Without the correct tools, some devices might be not be configured correctly, thereby resulting in inaccurate reports and notification. Other Cisco tools (some of which are covered in the next section) can assist the administrator in managing the SAA on Cisco IOS devices.

Network Response and Availability Applications

The SAA is an embedded agent that is available within Cisco IOS—specifically, within the Cisco IOS core technology. It can be configured to measure SLA metrics from a Cisco router to any other IP host or network device. The results of these measurements can be read from the CLI and through other protocols, such as SNMP. Because most devices have limited capability to store information, additional applications are needed to present results in graphical format and for longer periods.

Cisco and other vendors have used the SAA feature, and many management applications that support SAA are available today. Following is a partial list of these management applications:

- Within Cisco, the IPM and Service Management Solution (SMS) are CiscoWorks 2000 application modules for performance monitoring and SLM. The VPN Solutions Center is a comprehensive solution for managed VPN services.

- Outside of Cisco, many top management applications—such as those provided by Concord, Infovista, and Agilent— support SAA. In addition to the measurements provided by the vendors' elementary applications, they have incorporated Cisco SAA; this results in more detailed reports that better meet network operators' needs.

NOTE   Concord can be found at www.concord.com/. Infovista can be found at www.infovista.com/. Agilent can be found at www.agilent.com.

These applications receive measurement data from the SAA; they analyze the results and present the performance statistics through various reports. The following sections discuss IPM and SMS.

IPM

IPM is a network management application that allows the monitoring of the performance of multiprotocol networks.

Key Point: IPM

IPM measures the latency and availability of IP networks on a hop-by-hop (router-to-router) basis. It also measures latency between routers and the mainframe in Systems Network Architecture (SNA) networks.

IPM can perform the following tasks:

- Troubleshoot problems by checking the performance between devices.
- Send SNMP traps and SNA alerts when a user-configured threshold is exceeded, a connection is lost and reestablished, or a timeout occurs.
- Analyze potential problems before they occur by accumulating statistics, which are used to model and predict future network topologies.
- Monitor latency, availability, and errors between two network endpoints.
- Monitor jitter, availability, and errors between two network endpoints.

As shown in Figure 10-28, the IPM/SAA monitoring solution is composed of three parts: the IPM server application, the IPM client application, and the SAA feature of the Cisco IOS software. The IPM network management application includes the server and the client.

IPM is a client/server application. As illustrated in Figure 10-29, the user defines components, such as the source routers where the measurements are to begin, and uses the IPM client to identify possible target devices and typical synthetic traffic operations in the network. The network manager then defines the measurement methods (ICMP, TCP, UDP, and so forth). These definitions are stored in the IPM server's database and can be accessed by any other IPM client application.

After the components are defined, the IPM server configures the SAA in the source router to perform the operation at a specified interval. Each SAA takes measurements between the source router and target device using the specified traffic operation and repeating at the specified interval. The IPM server then extracts data from each source router and stores the data in the IPM database. The IPM client provides a real-time feature that allows an operator to display the collected data immediately. Together with Cisco IOS SAA, IPM provides reports on operation latency, device availability, and packet jitter between a source router and a target device for a specified operation.

Figure 10-28   *Internet Performance Monitor Components*

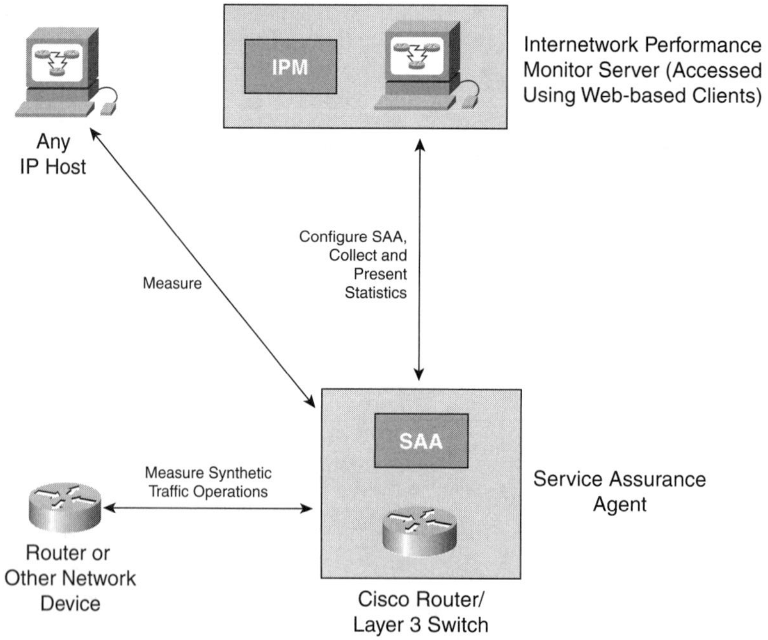

Internetwork Performance
Monitor Server (Accessed
Using Web-based Clients)

Any
IP Host

Configure SAA,
Collect and
Present
Statistics

Measure

Measure Synthetic
Traffic Operations

Service Assurance
Agent

Router or
Other Network
Device

Cisco Router/
Layer 3 Switch

Figure 10-29   *IPM Architecture*

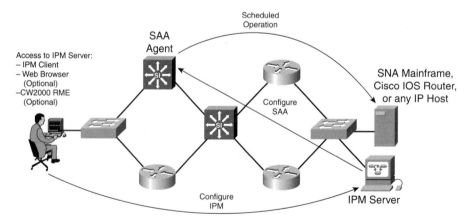

SAA
Agent

Scheduled
Operation

Access to IPM Server:
– IPM Client
– Web Browser
 (Optional)
–CW2000 RME
 (Optional)

SNA Mainframe,
Cisco IOS Router,
or any IP Host

Configure
SAA

Configure
IPM

IPM Server

The IPM provides various comprehensive reports. Figure 10-30 shows a sample report that
presents the "ICMP Path Echo" historical statistics. These statistics contain a list of the
paths the collector found between the source router and the target device. For each path

between the source and the target, the IPM user (network operator) can display the hops
(router host names or IP addresses), as shown on the left selection bar. The right side of the
figure displays a separate graph for each unique path to illustrate the end-to-end delay from
the source router to the target device using that path.

Figure 10-30   *Sample IPM Report*

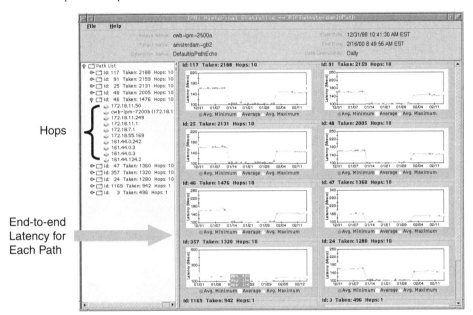

Key Point: IPM and SNMP

IPM uses SNMP to configure the SAA and read its data. Because SNMP is unreliable and
insecure, we do not encourage applying IPM beyond the boundaries of the corporate or
controlled network.

When communication between the database and SAA requires a more reliable protocol,
Cisco offers another solution: the Service Management Solution (SMS).

Service Management Solution

The SMS manages service levels between enterprises and internal or external service providers to ensure high-quality, economic delivery of converged network services. Working with the embedded Cisco IOS SAA, SMS defines and monitors SLAs by specifying traffic type, endpoints, and thresholds against key parameters such as latency, packet loss, and jitter. SMS sets real-time traps, thereby allowing prompt detection and correction of possible service degradation. Open programming interfaces enable full management of service levels through easy integration with in-house or third-party analysis and provisioning systems.

The SMS architecture was developed to provide scalability, resilience, and ease of integration with complementary third-party applications.

Key Point: SMS Communication Interfaces

All communication interfaces in the SMS architecture are industry standards, including SNMP and extensible markup language (XML)/HTTP, allowing for easy data sharing and integration with third-party vendor applications. The architecture uses a distributed independent network appliance to poll locally, via SNMP, for service metrics recorded on the SAA.

The SMS architecture has three main components: the SLM server, SLM collection managers, and SAAs. This SMS architecture is best explained by observing how an SLA is configured and how the resulting data is retrieved. Figure 10-31 illustrates this architecture and data flow.

The user or SLM application client uses a commercially available web browser to access the server. Using the SLM GUI, the SLM user (network administrator) defines SLCs or SLAs that are necessary for testing and verifying the performance of a provided service (for example, WAN and LAN connectivity and QoS parameters) using a simple format; no special knowledge of Cisco IOS commands is required. The resulting SLA requests, or jobs, are passed from the SLM server to the collection manager, which then takes care of configuring the SAA. (Communication between the SLM server and the collection manager is via HTTP and XML, as opposed to SNMP; this eases operation through a firewall.)

Figure 10-31 *SMS Architecture and Data Flow*

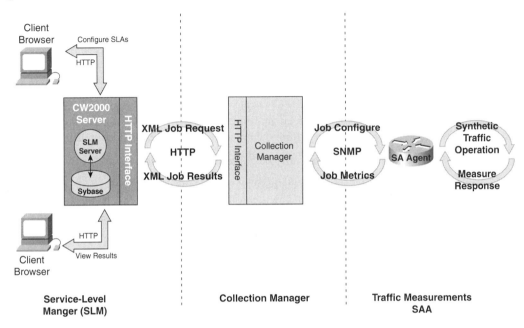

The SLM server periodically requests the results from the collection manager. The SLM server stores the retrieved results in a database and allows the SLM user (network operator) to view a variety of reports that are based on this data.

NOTE The SLM application is a performance tool, not a fault-management tool. The SLM application provides graphical results regarding the configured SLA or SLC, but has no option to configure proactive monitoring and notification of the operation. The IPM is a better tool for such requests.

Summary

In this chapter, you learned about network management design.

An NMS system executes applications that monitor and control managed devices. A managed device contains a management agent, which is software that collects and stores management information.

SNMP is the simplest network management protocol. An NMS sends SNMP requests to network devices, while network devices send unsolicited trap messages to inform the NMS of special events.

The MIB is a detailed definition of the information on a network device and is accessible through a network management protocol, such as SNMP.

RMON is an extension to the MIB. The MIB typically provides only static information about the managed device; the RMON agent contains specific groups of statistics, which can be collected for long-term trend analysis. RMON1 works on the MAC layer; RMON2 provides full network visibility from the network layer to the application layer.

CDP is used to discover and identify neighboring Cisco devices.

NetFlow provides the measurement base to record network and application resource utilization by measuring flows that pass through Cisco devices. A network flow is defined as a unidirectional sequence of packets between source and destination endpoints.

Syslog messages are used to provide reports on various system states, including errors. Every syslog message contains a timestamp (if enabled), severity level (0 through 7; 0 is an emergency), and facility (device, protocol, or module).

The ISO network management model defines the following five functional areas of network management, which are abbreviated as FCAPS:

- **Fault management**—Detects, isolates, notifies, and corrects faults that are encountered in the network.
- **Configuration management**—Administers configuration aspects of network devices, such as configuration file management, inventory management, and software management.
- **Accounting management**—Provides usage information of network resources.
- **Performance management**—Monitors and measures various aspects of performance so that overall performance can be maintained at an acceptable level.
- **Security management**—Provides network device and corporate resource access to authorized individuals.

AAA stands for authentication, authorization, and accounting. Authentication identifies a user, authorization determines what that user can do, and accounting monitors the duration of network usage (for billing purposes) and logs all actions.

SLM is a proven methodology that helps network managers resolve resource issues by defining and regulating capacity and performance management processes in a cost-effective manner. This can be accomplished by establishing an SLA with a network service provider, or by defining and funding the service and upgrades as required.

An SLC specifies connectivity and performance levels a service provider must meet for the service's end user. SLAs define specific service performance measurements between device pairs, including routers, servers, workstations, and other equipment. An SLC typically includes multiple SLAs.

Active monitoring of metrics such as availability, latency, packet loss, and jitter is required to verify that SLAs are being met.

The SAA in Cisco IOS software can proactively monitor the network. The SAA provides a way for a Cisco IOS device to be configured to perform tests in the network, to either end systems or other IOS devices. The results of these tests are used to validate the SLA. A key value of the SAA is its ability to mark the test packets with the appropriate CoS value, thereby enabling network managers to observe various TCP and UDP services and performance when QoS is implemented.

IPM measures the latency and availability of IP networks on a hop-by-hop (router-to-router) basis. The IPM/SAA monitoring solution is composed of three parts: the IPM server application, the IPM client application, and the SAA feature of the Cisco IOS software.

The SMS manages service levels between enterprises and internal or external service providers. All communication interfaces in the SMS architecture are industry standards, including SNMP and XML/HTTP. The architecture uses a distributed independent network appliance to poll locally, via SNMP, for service metrics that are recorded on the SAA.

References

For additional information, refer to these resources:

- Cisco Management Information Base (MIB) User Quick Reference, available at www.cisco.com/univercd/cc/td/doc/product/software/ios112/mbook/index.htm.
- Deploying Service-Level Management in an Enterprise Network Environment White Paper, available at www.cisco.com/en/US/partner/products/sw/cscowork/ps2428/products_white_paper09186a0080092498.shtml.

NOTE   You must be a registered user to access this document.

- Internetwork Performance Monitor product documentation, available at www.cisco.com/univercd/cc/td/doc/product/rtrmgmt/ipmcw2k/index.htm.
- Leinwand, F. and K. Fang. *Network Management*. Addison-Wesley, 1993.
- Network Management System: Best Practices White Paper, available at www.cisco.com/warp/public/126/NMS_bestpractice.html.
- Service Assurance Agent product page, available at www.cisco.com/go/saa.
- Service Level Management: Best Practices White Paper, available at www.cisco.com/warp/public/126/sla.htm.

- Service Level Manager product documentation, available at www.cisco.com/univercd/cc/td/doc/product/rtrmgmt/cw2000/slm/index.htm.
- Stallings, W. *SNMP, SNMPv2 and CMIP*. Addison-Wesley, 1993.
- White Paper: Service-Level Management: Defining and Monitoring Service Levels in the Enterprise, www.cisco.com/warp/public/cc/pd/wr2k/svmnso/prodlit/srlm_wp.htm.

Review Questions

Answer the following questions and refer to Appendix G, "Answers to Review Questions, Case Studies, and Simulation Exercises," for the answers.

1 What is a network management agent?

2 How does an SNMP manager request a list of data?

3 How does an SNMPv2 manager request a list of data?

4 What is the MIB structure?

5 How are private MIB definitions supported?

6 What are the RMON1 groups?

7 What groups were added by RMON2?

8 How does RMON simplify proactive network management?

9 At which layer does CDP work?

10 Two routers are connected via Frame Relay, but ping is not working between them. How could CDP help troubleshoot this situation?

11 Why is NetFlow superior to RMON?

12 What is a NetFlow network flow?

13 What are the syslog severity levels?

14 What syslog severity level does the first message show in Example 10-2?

Example 10-2 *Message for Question 14*

```
20:11:58: %LINEPROTO-5-UPDOWN: Line protocol on Interface FastEthernet0/0, changed
state to down
20:12:04: %LINK-3-UPDOWN: Interface FastEthernet0/0, changed state to up
```

15 What are the five functional areas of network management?

16 What does fault management event processing involve?

17 What are the two types of fault management devices?

18 Why is configuration management beneficial to a network administrator?

19 Which protocols are used for configuration management?

20 What are the three tiers of the NetFlow architecture?

21 Which accounting method should a network administrator use to measure the amount of time a dialup user is connected?

22 What are the data plane and the control plane?

23 What is the difference between SLM, an SLC, and an SLA?

24 What steps are involved in developing a performance information collection plan?

25 How can performance data be collected?

26 How is AAA used in security management?

27 Is Telnet considered a secure protocol?

28 How should an enterprise ensure that its network can meet its business needs?

29 How can an enterprise monitor conformance to an SLA with a third-party vendor?

30 What are some requirements that SLAs should meet?

31 What might high latency values in a network indicate?

32 Why might an end-to-end SLM be challenging?

33 An enterprise has implemented a web-based ordering application. Orders are processed from internal users or external partners. Which network services or levels must be monitored and reported to ensure that proper SLM is achieved?

34 How are acceptable response times for an SLA determined?

35 What additional devices are required in a network in order to run SAA?

36 How would SAA help determine if an SLA related to IP telephony in an enterprise is being met?

37 Which SAA feature would be useful in determining where network connectivity has failed?

38 What are the components of the IPM/SAA monitoring solution?

39 Which protocols do IPM and SMS use to read data?

40 Cisco equipment that supports SAA is used in a campus network. Web-based reports on SLA are required. Which Cisco application should be used?

This chapter contains a brief review of key topics in this book and culminates with a new case study that allows you to practice many of these topics. The chapter includes the following sections:

- Review of Key Topics
- Comprehensive Case Study: MCMB Corporation Network Redesign

CHAPTER **11**

Review and Case Study

This chapter reviews the key topics in this book and presents a comprehensive case study that applies the concepts to another real-world example.

Review of Key Topics

The following sections contain a brief review of the key topics covered in the previous chapters. For in-depth coverage of these topics, please refer to the appropriate chapters.

Applying Design Principles in Network Deployment

The Network Organizational architecture, shown in Figure 11-1, uses the corporate information infrastructure to leverage the advantages of networks.

Every organization uses various policies and procedures to achieve its organizational goals, which it can accomplish only by using the network infrastructure effectively.

Figure 11-1 *Network Organizational Architecture*

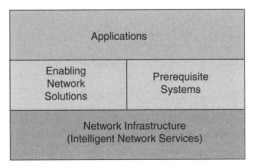

This architecture is divided into several layers, thereby making the organizational processes easier to implement or expand. The following list describes each layer of architecture, which has special tasks that contribute to the success of the organizational processes:

- **Applications**—Directly address organizational goals. They offer a discrete set of functions (accessed via the network) for authorized users such as employees, customers, suppliers, or partners.

- **Enabling network solutions (such as voice transport or content networking)**— Makes modern networks more intelligent so they can support applications.

- **Prerequisite systems**—Are combinations of structured data and business logic that are sometimes wrapped in an application that exposes information as requested or directed.

- **Network infrastructure**—Includes network platforms and links, coupled with intelligent network services that provide a highly available and secure network.

Cisco's Plan-Design-Implement-Operate-Optimize (PDIOO) methodology of network design reflects a network's life cycle. As illustrated in Figure 11-2, the PDIOO life cycle phases are separate, yet closely related.

Figure 11-2   *PDIOO Network Life Cycle Influences Design*

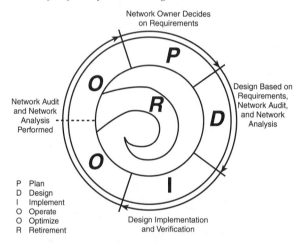

The following describes each PDIOO phase:

- **Plan phase**—This phase identifies the network requirements. These requirements are based on the goals, where the network will be installed, who will require which network services, and so forth. The output of this phase is a set of network requirements.

- **Design phase**—The initial requirements determined in the Plan phase drive the activities of the network design specialists, who design the network according to the initial requirements. They incorporate any additional data gathered during network analysis and network audit (when upgrading an existing network) or acquired through discussion with the managers and network users. The network design specification that is produced provides the basis for the implementation activities.

- **Implement phase** — Implementation begins after the design has been approved. The network is built according to the design specifications. Implementation also serves to verify the design.

- **Operate phase** — Operation is the final test of the design's appropriateness. The fault detection and correction and performance monitoring that occur in daily operations provide initial data for the Optimize phase of the network life cycle.

- **Optimize phase** — The Optimize phase is based on proactive network management. The goal of proactive management is to identify and resolve issues before any real problems arise. Reactive fault detection and correction (troubleshooting) are necessary when proactive management cannot predict and mitigate the failures.

- **Retirement** — When the network or a part of the network is recognized as being out-of-date, it can be taken out of production.

Although Design is one of the five PDIOO phases, all the other phases influence design decisions, and the Design phase interacts closely with them.

The design methodology presented here includes seven mandatory steps and one optional step. Each of these steps and their relationship to the PDIOO phases are described as follows:

Step 1   **Identify customer requirements** — The initial requirements are extracted from the information provided by the network's owner. This typically occurs during the PDIOO Plan phase.

Step 2   **Characterize the existing network** — Characterization of the existing network includes two substeps: the network audit and network analysis. During the network audit step, the existing network is thoroughly checked for integrity and quality. During the network analysis step, network behavior is analyzed (traffic analysis is performed, congestion points are determined, and so forth). This is typically done within the PDIOO Optimize phase.

Step 3   **Design the topology and network solutions** — During the PDIOO Design phase, this step undertakes the network's actual design. Decisions are made about network infrastructure (hardware, software, physical topology, routing protocols, high availability, and so on), intelligent network services (Quality of Service [QoS], security, network management, and so on), and network solutions (Voice over Internet Protocol [VoIP], content networking, and so on). The data for making these decisions is gathered during the first two steps.

Step 4   **Plan the implementation** — During this step, the implementation procedures are prepared in advance to expedite and clarify the actual implementation. Cost assessment is undertaken at this time. This step is done during the PDIOO Design phase.

Step 5 **Build a pilot network**—During this optional step, a pilot or prototype network can be constructed to verify the correctness of the design. This occurs either late in the PDIOO Design phase or early in the PDIOO Implement phase. The goal of this step is to identify any problems and correct them before implementing the entire network.

Step 6 **Document the design**—The actual design documents are written during this step. The design document includes information that is documented in all other steps. This step begins in the PDIOO Design phase, but it might not be completed until early in the Implement phase (for example, if a pilot is constructed, results of the pilot are included in the design documents).

Step 7 **Implement and verify the design**—By building a network, the design is actually implemented and verified. This step maps directly to the Implement phase of the PDIOO methodology.

Step 8 **Monitor and optionally redesign**—After the network is built, it is put into operation. During operation, the network is constantly monitored and checked for errors. If troubleshooting problems becomes too frequent or even impossible to manage, a network redesign might be required; hopefully this can be avoided if the previous steps have been completed properly. In fact, this step is a part of the Operate and Optimize phases of the PDIOO methodology.

Structuring and Modularizing the Network

This section presents two models for designing networks: the Hierarchical Network model and the Enterprise Composite Network Model.

The Hierarchical Network model (shown in Figure 11-3) uses the following layers to simplify the required internetworking tasks:

- **Access layer**—This layer provides local and remote workgroup or user access to the network.
- **Distribution layer**—This layer implements policy-based connectivity.
- **Core layer**—This layer provides high-speed data transport to satisfy the connectivity and transport needs of the distribution layer devices.

Figure 11-3   *The Three Layers of the Hierarchical Model*

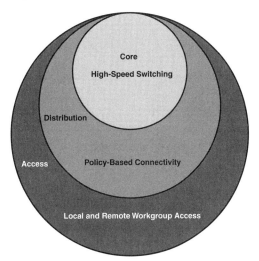

The Enterprise Composite Network model is a blueprint, or framework, for designing networks. Its built-in modularity allows flexibility in network design and facilitates implementation and troubleshooting.

The Enterprise Composite Network model is comprised of the following three major functional areas:

- **Enterprise Campus**—This area contains all of the network elements for independent operation within one campus location. This functional area does not provide remote connections or Internet access. An enterprise can have more than one campus.

- **Enterprise Edge**—This functional area aggregates the connectivity from the various elements at the edge of the Enterprise network. The Enterprise Edge functional area filters traffic from the edge modules and routes it into the Enterprise Campus. The Enterprise Edge contains all the network elements for efficient and secure communication between the Enterprise Campus and remote locations, business partners, mobile users, and the Internet.

- **Service Provider Edge**—The Service Provider Edge modules are included to enable communication with other networks that use different WAN technologies and with Internet service providers (ISPs).

Each of these functional areas is divided further; Figure 11-4 represents a more granular view of the modules within each functional area.

Figure 11-4   *The Functional Areas of the Enterprise Composite Network Model*

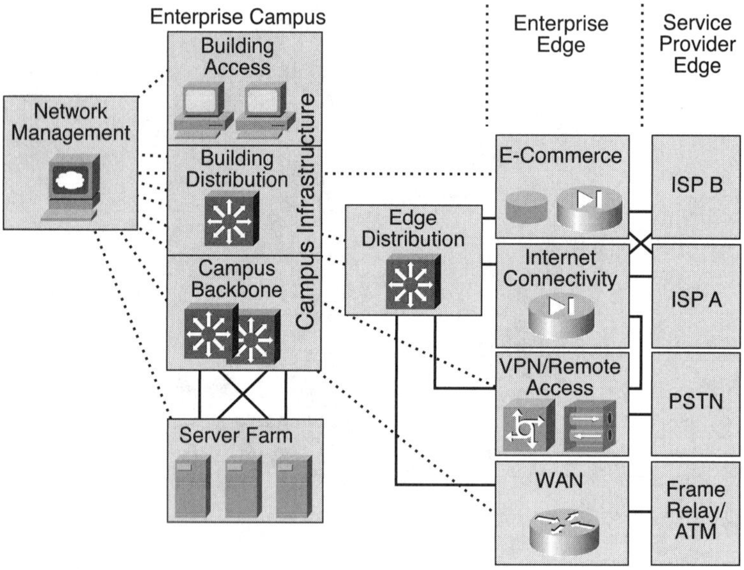

As shown in Figure 11-4, the Enterprise Campus functional area is further divided into four major modules:

- **Campus Infrastructure module**—The Campus Infrastructure module is composed of one or more buildings connected to a backbone. This module is comprised of three submodules: Building Access, Building Distribution, and Campus Backbone.

- **Network Management module**—The Network Management module supports end-to-end security, monitoring, logging, troubleshooting, and other common management features.

- **Server Farm module**—A high-capacity, centralized Server Farm module provides users with internal server resources.

- **Edge Distribution module**—The Edge Distribution module provides connectivity between the Enterprise Campus and the Enterprise Edge.

The Enterprise Edge functional area also comprises four modules, as follows:

- **E-commerce module**—The E-commerce module includes the devices and services necessary for an organization to provide E-commerce applications.

- **Internet Connectivity module**—The Internet Connectivity module provides Internet access for the enterprise users.

- **Virtual Private Network (VPN)/Remote Access module**—The VPN/Remote Access module terminates VPN traffic and dial-in connections from external users.

- **Wide-area Network (WAN) module**—The WAN module provides connectivity between remote sites and the central site over various WAN technologies.

The modules within the Service Provider Edge functional area are as follows:

- **Internet Service Provider module**—The Internet Service Provider module enables enterprise Internet Protocol (IP) connectivity to the Internet.

- **Public Switched Telephone Network (PSTN) module**—The PSTN module represents the dialup infrastructure for accessing the Enterprise network using ISDN, analog, and wireless telephony (cellular) technologies.

- **Relay/Asynchronous Transfer Mode (ATM) module**—The Frame Relay/ATM module covers all WAN technologies for permanent connectivity with remote locations.

Two important network design terms are *network service* and *network solution*. An intelligent network service is a supporting, but necessary, service. For example, security and QoS are not ultimate services within the network; they are necessary for enabling other services and applications. Therefore, security and QoS are not solutions, but intelligent network services. However, voice communication is a network solution because it is an ultimate goal of the network.

Basic Campus Switching Design Considerations

The multilayer approach to campus network design combines Layer 2 switching with Layer 3 switching to achieve robust, highly available campus networks.

You must consider the following factors when deploying the campus network:

- **Network geography**—The distribution of network nodes (hosts and network devices) and the distances between them significantly affect the campus solution, especially the physical transmission media.

- **Network applications**—In terms of bandwidth and delay, the application requirements place stringent requirements on a campus network solution. Four types of application communication are client-client, client-distributed server, client-Server Farm, and client-Enterprise Edge.

- **Data link layer technology—shared or switched**—The dedicated bandwidth solution of local-area network (LAN) switching is replacing the traditional approach, in which all devices share the available bandwidth using hubs.

- **Layer 2 versus Layer 3 switching**—The network devices and their features not only determine the flexibility of the network, but also contribute to the overall network delay. Layer 2 switching is based on media access control (MAC) addresses, and Layer 3 switching is based on network layer addresses (usually IP addresses).

- **Transmission media (physical cabling)**—Cabling is one of the biggest long-term investments in network deployment. Therefore, selection of transmission media not only depends on the required bandwidth and distances, but it must also take into consideration the emerging technologies that might be deployed over the same infrastructure in the future. Two major cabling options exist: copper-based media (for example, unshielded twisted pair [UTP]) and optical fiber. The choice of physical media depends on bandwidth and distance between devices.

Switched technology has many benefits over shared technology, such as higher bandwidth support, larger network diameter, additional Layer 2 and Layer 3 services, and high availability. Deciding whether to use Layer 2 or Layer 3 switching involves considering the network service capabilities, the size of the network segments, and the maximum network failure convergence time that can be tolerated.

The various modules within the Enterprise Campus have different switching requirements, including the following:

- The Building Access module aggregates the workstations or hosts on a Layer 2 device. The Building Distribution module aggregates the access layer and uses a combination of Layer 2 and Layer 3 switching to segment workgroups and isolate segments from failures and broadcast storms.

- The Campus Backbone and Server Farm modules require fast and resilient connectivity. Campus backbone switches are Layer 2 and Layer 3 switches that are focused primarily on wire-speed forwarding on all interfaces.

- The speed of switching is not as important as security is in the Edge Distribution module. Thus, Layer 3 switches are the key devices that are used in this module to aggregate edge connectivity and provide advanced services.

Designing WAN Networks

In the Enterprise Edge module, the role of the WAN is to reliably and efficiently connect distant sites over transmission facilities that are provided by service providers.

Traditional WAN technologies include the following:

- **Leased lines**—Point-to-point connections that are indefinitely reserved for transmissions, rather than only being available when transmission is required.

- **Circuit-switched networks**—A type of network that, for the duration of the connection, obtains and dedicates a physical path to a single connection between two network endpoints. Ordinary voice phone service over the PSTN is circuit-switched.

- **Packet and cell-switched networks**—A carrier creates permanent virtual circuits (PVCs) or switched virtual circuits (SVCs), which deliver packets of data among customer sites. Users share common carrier resources and can use different paths through the WAN. Examples of packet-switching networks are X.25, Frame Relay, and Switched Multimegabit Data Services (SMDS).

- **ATM**—A dedicated-connection cell switching technology. It organizes digital data into cell units of a fixed size (53 bytes) and transmits them over a physical medium using digital signal technology. Each ATM cell can be processed asynchronously (relative to other related cells), queued, and multiplexed over the transmission path.

In addition to traditional technologies, new technologies include the following:

- **Digital Subscriber Line (DSL)**—A technology that delivers high bandwidth over traditional telephone copper lines. The four most common varieties of DSL are Asymmetric DSL (ADSL), which is the most common, Symmetric DSL (SDSL), High-data-rate DSL (HDSL), and Very-high-data-rate DSL (VDSL). Since ADSL operates at frequencies (from 100 kilohertz [kHz] to 1.1 Megahertz [MHz]) that are above the voice channel (300 to 3400 hertz [Hz]), plain old telephone system (POTS) technology and ADSL can share the same line.

- **Long Reach Ethernet (LRE)**—Uses DSL coding and digital modulation techniques to enable the use of Ethernet over existing telephone-grade wire. LRE offers a maximum of 15 Megabits per second (Mbps) on a short distance symmetric channel. The channel's speed decreases with distance.

- **Cable**—A technology for data transport that uses a coaxial cable medium.

- **Wireless**—A term used to describe telecommunications in which electromagnetic waves, rather than a form of wire, carry the signal over the communication path. Some common examples of wireless equipment used today include cellular phones and pagers, Global Positioning System (GPS), cordless computer peripherals, satellite television, and wireless local-area networks (WLANs).

- **Multiprotocol Label Switching (MPLS)**—A technology that combines the advantages of Layer 3 routing with the benefits of Layer 2 switching. With MPLS, labels are assigned to each packet at the edge of the network. Rather than examining the IP packet header information, MPLS nodes use this label to determine how to process the data. This results in a faster, more scalable and flexible WAN solution.

An alternative to WAN connections is an Internet service provider's (ISP's) IP network that spans remote sites of an Enterprise network.

Planning and designing WAN networks involves trade-offs between application requirements, technical requirements, and cost. Table 11-1 evaluates various WAN technologies against the main aspects that influence technology selection.

Table 11-1   *WAN Characteristics*

WAN Type	BW	Latency	Jitter	Connection Time	Cost Per Time	Investment	Reliability	Availability
Analog modem	L	H	H	H	H	L	L	H
ISDN	L	M/H	H	M	H	L	M	H
P2P protocols over sync or async serial	L	M	M	L	M	M	M	H
X.25, FR	L	L	L	L	M	M	M	H
TDM	M	L	L	L	M	M	M	H
Ethernet over Fiber	M/H	L	L	L	M	M	M	M
Leased lines	M/H	L	L	L	M/H	H	H	L
POS and ATM over SONET/ SDH	H	L	L	L	M	M	H	M
ADSL, LRE	L/M	M/H	M/H	L	L	M	M	M
Cable modem	L/M	M/H	M/H	L	L	M	L	M
Wireless	L/M	M/H	M/H	L	L	M	L	L
MPLS	H	L	L	L	M	M	H	L

BW = bandwidth; L = low; M = medium; H = high

The implementation of a WAN includes selecting appropriate hardware components and software features, including the following:

- **Compression**—Compression is the reduction of data size to save transmission time.

- **Queuing**—Hardware queuing uses a first-in, first-out (FIFO) strategy, which is necessary for the interface drivers to transmit packets one by one. Software queuing schedules packets into the hardware queue based on their QoS requirements. There are three main types of software queuing: custom queuing (CQ), priority queuing (PQ), and weighted fair queuing (WFQ). Other types of queuing include Class-Based Weighted Fair Queuing (CBWFQ) and Low Latency Queuing (LLQ).

- **Traffic shaping and policing**—These are both mechanisms that inspect traffic and then take action based on the various characteristics of that traffic. Policing either discards or modifies some aspect of the packet, such as its IP Precedence, when it meets a given criteria. (The policing methods supported by Cisco include committed access rate [CAR], random early detection [RED], and weighted random early detection [WRED].) By comparison, traffic shaping attempts to adjust the transmission rate of packets that match a certain criteria. (Cisco supports the Generic Traffic Shaping (GTS) method.)

Different scenarios require different WAN solutions. Examples include the following:

- **Remote access**—Dialup services might be a cost-effective solution for connectivity across a WAN. Integrated Services Digital Network (ISDN) provides increased bandwidth, reduced call setup time, and reduced latency. For permanent connections, packet-switched networks traditionally offer more flexibility and use network bandwidth more efficiently than time-division multiplexing (TDM) networks because the network resources are shared dynamically.

- **Backup WAN**—A WAN backup can be implemented with dial backup routing, a permanent secondary WAN link, or a shadow PVC.

- **Dispersed sites**—A point-to-point link provides a pre-established WAN communication path from a customer's premises, through a carrier network, to a customer's remote network. Synchronous Optical Network (SONET) and Synchronous Digital Hierarchy (SDH) are alternatives to a point-to-point link.

- **IP connectivity**—IP users in geographically dispersed locations can use analog modem, ISDN, point-to-point protocols over synchronous or asynchronous serial links, X.25, Frame Relay, TDM, and Ethernet over fiber technologies, in addition to such emerging technologies as DSL, LRE, cable, wireless, and MPLS.

- **VPNs**—VPNs that are deployed on a shared infrastructure guarantee the same policies and performance as a private network. IP access through VPNs can be provided through overlay VPNs, Virtual Private Dialup Networks (VPDNs), or peer-to-peer VPNs.

Designing IP Addressing in the Network

IP version 4 (IPv4) addresses are hierarchical and consist of the following two parts:

- **Network**—The network portion identifies a specific network.

- **Host (or device, or node)**—The host portion identifies a specific device in a network.

IPv4

As shown in Figure 11-5, an IPv4 address is 32 bits long.

Figure 11-5 *IPv4 Address Structure*

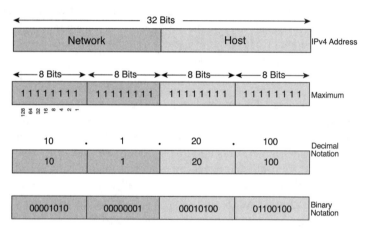

A subnet mask is used to interpret an IPv4 address. A subnet mask is 32 bits long and, much like the IPv4 address, is divided into four octets. When subnetting, some bits from the host part are used for the subnetwork part.

IPv4 addressing defines five address classes: A, B, C, D, and E. Only Classes A, B, and C are available for addressing devices; Class D is used for multicast groups, and Class E is reserved for experimental use. An address's first octet defines its class, as Table 11-2 illustrates for Class A, B, and C addresses (this is sometimes called the *first octet rule*). The bits that represent network and subnet information in an IP address are known as the *prefix*; the number of such bits is known as the *prefix length*. The Prefix Length column in Table 11-2 indicates the default prefix lengths for the three address classes.

Table 11-2 *IP Address Classes A, B, and C Are Available for Addressing Devices*

Class	Format (N = network number, H = host number)	Prefix Length	Higher-order Bit(s)	Address Range	Number of Hosts
Class A	N.H.H.H	8 bits	0	1.0.0.0 to 126.0.0.0	16,777,214
Class B	N.N.H.H	16 bits	10	128.0.0.0 to 191.255.0.0	65534
Class C	N.N.N.H	24 bits	110	192.0.0.0 to 223.255.255.0	254

The IPv4 address space is divided into public and private sections. Private addresses are reserved IPv4 addresses that are only to be used internally, within a company's network. The decision about when to use private and/or public addresses depends on the Internet connection, the number of publicly visible servers, and the size of the network. The private IPv4 addresses are as follows:

- 10.0.0.0/8 (10.0.0.0 to 10.255.255.255)
- 172.16.0.0/12 (172.16.0.0 to 172.31.255.255)
- 192.168.0.0/16 (192.168.0.0 to 192.168.255.255)

The IP addressing plan for a network depends on the network size, including the number and type of locations, and the number and type of devices located at each location.

A hierarchical addressing plan reduces routing overhead by allowing route summarization, or aggregation. With route summarization, one route in the routing table represents many other routes. Summarizing routes reduces the number of routes in the routing table, the routing update traffic, and overall router overhead.

A major network is a Class A, B, or C network. With Variable Length Subnet Masking (VLSM), subnet masks within a major network can be different sizes. VLSM should be used in modern networks to conserve the IP addresses.

Two IP address assignment strategies exist: static and dynamic. Dynamic address assignment, using Dynamic Host Configuration Protocol (DHCP), reduces administrative overhead. Static address assignment presents an extra burden for the administrator, who must configure the address on every end-system on the network.

The process of resolving a host name to an IP address can also be either static or dynamic. By using the Domain Names System (DNS), dynamic name resolution introduces more flexibility into the network and facilitates renumbering and renaming. Static name resolution means additional work because the administrator must configure manual entries on every host. It is prone to errors and omissions.

IPv6

IPv6, a successor to IPv4, has been designed to overcome IPv4's limitations.

Using 128-bit addresses, IPv6 has a larger address space. IPv6 addresses are represented as a series of 16-bit hexadecimal fields separated by colons (:) in the format x:x:x:x:x:x:x:x. To shorten IPv6 addresses, two colons (::) can be used to compress successive hexadecimal fields of 0s (the colons represent successive hexadecimal fields of 0s). The two colons can appear at the beginning, middle, or end of an IPv6 address, but is allowed only once in an address. For example, the IPv6 address 2031:**0000**:130F:**0000:0000:0**9C0:876A:130B can be written as 2031:**0**:130F::9C0:876A:130B.

As shown in Figure 11-6, the IPv6 packet header has eight fields, with a total length of 40 octets (320 bits). All fields are aligned to 64 bits, thereby enabling more efficient processing. If there are any extension headers, they follow the eight fields, which are followed by the data portion of the packet.

Figure 11-6 *IPv6 Datagram Structure Includes a 40-Octet Header*

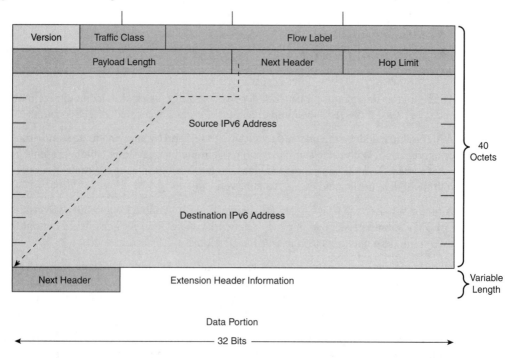

Data Portion

32 Bits

The three types of IPv6 addresses are unicast (one-to-one), anycast (one-to-nearest), and multicast (one-to-many). Unicast addresses are further broken down into global aggregatable, site-local, link-local, and IPv4-compatible IPv6 addresses.

Stateless autoconfiguration of IPv6 addresses allows hosts to automatically generate site-local and global addresses. Stateful dynamic address assignment using DHCPv6 gives more control than stateless autoconfiguration and can be used for renumbering nodes without any routers.

IPv6 dynamic name resolution requires DNS servers with IPv6 protocol stack support.

The IPv4 to IPv6 migration process uses IPv4 to IPv6 transition strategies, which include a dual stack, tunneling mechanisms, and translation mechanisms.

Currently available routing protocols for IPv6 are Routing Information Protocol new generation (RIPng), Integrated Intermediate System-Intermediate System version 6 (IS-ISv6), and Border Gateway Protocol 4+ (BGP4+). Open Shortest Path First version 3 (OSPFv3) is also available on some platforms.

Selecting Routing Protocols for a Network

Static routes are only used in very small networks, or for specific scenarios (such as dial-on-demand routing [DDR], stub networks, and so on). Dynamic routing protocols adapt to changes in the network and are much easier to configure than static routes.

On-demand Routing (ODR) is a Cisco proprietary alternative to static routes or dynamic routing protocols in hub-and-spoke networks. ODR provides IP routing while avoiding the overhead of a general, dynamic routing protocol and without incurring static routing's configuration and management overhead.

Distance vector protocols are easier to implement, but, in general, have limited scalability and slow convergence compared to link-state protocols.

Exterior gateway protocols are used for inter-autonomous system (AS) connectivity, whereas interior gateway protocols enable intra-AS connectivity.

Routing protocols use different methods for metric calculation, thus resulting in more or less optimal routing paths. RIP version 1 (RIPv1) and RIP version 2 (RIPv2) use hop count; OSPF uses a cost (related to bandwidth); Integrated IS-IS uses a metric (also related to bandwidth); the Interior Gateway Routing Protocol (IGRP) and Enhanced IGRP (EIGRP) use a formula that accounts for minimum bandwidth and accumulated delay, by default. BGP uses the AS-path attribute and indicates the number of autonomous systems in the path as part of its metric.

Routing protocols that enable a hierarchical design, such as EIGRP and OSPF, are adapted for deployment in large networks.

There is no best or worst routing protocol. The decision about which routing protocol to implement (or if, indeed, you should implement multiple routing protocols in a network) can only be made after the design goals have been carefully considered and the network's physical topology has been examined in detail. Table 11-3 summarizes some of the characteristics of IP routing protocols.

Table 11-3   *IP Routing Protocol Comparison*

Feature	RIPv1	RIPv2	IGRP	EIGRP	OSPF	IS-IS
Hierarchical				X	X	X
Flat	X	X	X	X		
Distance vector	X	X	X	X		
Link-state				X	X	X
Classless		X		X	X	X
Classful	X		X			
Multiaccess (LAN) support	X	X	X	X	X	X
Point-to-point support	X	X	X	X	X	X
NBMA point-to-multipoint (Frame Relay) support				X	X	

Some IP routing protocol characteristics are as follows:

- RIPv2 is suitable for deployment in small networks because it only uses hop count as its metric and allows a maximum of only 15 hops.

- OSPF is an open-standard protocol that was developed to overcome RIP's limitations. OSPF includes multiple areas inside an AS to reduce the amount of routing traffic and result in more scalable networks.

- EIGRP is a powerful Cisco proprietary routing protocol that includes a topology table to maintain all routes received from its neighbors; the best of these routes are put in the routing table. EIGRP's Diffusing Update Algorithm (DUAL) route calculation mechanism allows the backup routes that are stored in the topology table to be used in case of primary route failure. Because this procedure is local to the router, the switchover to the backup route is immediate and does not involve action in any other routers.

- Integrated IS-IS is a complex routing protocol that is derived from Open Systems Interconnection (OSI) IS-IS standards and is suitable for very large networks. Even if Integrated IS-IS is only being used for routing IP (and not for the OSI network layer protocol Connectionless Network Protocol [CLNP]), OSI protocols are used to form the neighbor relationships between the routers; therefore, OSI addresses must still be assigned so that Integrated IS-IS works.

- BGP is an exterior gateway protocol (EGP) that is used primarily for inter-AS routing. When BGP is running between routers within one AS, it is called *interior BGP (IBGP)*; when BGP is running between routers in different autonomous systems, it is called *exterior BGP (EBGP)*. BGP is a distance vector protocol that uses AS path metrics as a basis for routing decisions. BGP enhancements include several additional metric parameters, or path attributes, that allow administrators to influence routing decisions in BGP. Inter-AS routing involves numerous strategic routing policy decisions with which ISPs must comply.

For a network that uses multiple routing protocols, Cisco routers allow the exchange of routing information through a feature called *route redistribution*.

Route filtering allows the network administrator to prevent the advertisement of certain routes through the routing domain. Filtering can occur either on the routing domain boundary where redistribution occurs, or within the routing domain to isolate some parts of the network from other parts of the network.

Designing Networks for Voice Transport

Designing networks to transport voice requires knowledge of voice characteristics and considerations.

To obtain clear voice connections, analog speech must be converted to a digital format and sent over a digital network. The process of digitizing analog voice signals is called *pulse code modulation (PCM)* and involves filtering, sampling, and digitizing.

The primary task of a PSTN switch is to provide residential telephony. In contrast, a Private Branch Exchange (PBX) supports user telephones within an enterprise by providing business features such as call hold, call transfer, call forward, and so on. Enterprises install PBXs because the number of telephones is usually greater than the number of simultaneous calls to the PSTN network; therefore, the enterprise only needs the number of external lines (to the PSTN) to equal the maximum possible number of simultaneous calls.

As shown in Figure 11-7, the telephone infrastructure includes telephone lines, station lines, and various trunks.

Figure 11-7 *Local Loops, Trunks, and Interswitch Communication*

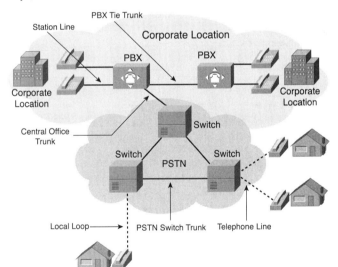

Some form of signaling mechanism is required for setting up and tearing down calls. Signaling methods include loop start, ground start, E&M (derived from a combination of recEive and transMit, and sometimes also known as *Ear and Mouth*), channel associated signaling (CAS), and common channel signaling (CCS). CCS signaling includes ISDN and Signaling System 7 (SS7).

A PSTN numbering plan governs the routing of voice calls within the PSTN. The North American Numbering Plan (NANP) is an example of a PSTN numbering plan. NANP numbers are 10 digits in length and occur in the following format: NXX-NXX-XXXX, where N is any digit 2–9 and X is any digit 0–9.

The PSTN offers the following services:

- **Centrex**—Centrex is a set of specialized business solutions in which the service provider owns and operates the equipment, which is therefore located on the service provider's premises.

- **Virtual private voice networks**—Virtual private voice networks interconnect corporate voice traffic among multiple locations over the PSTN.

- **Voice mail**—Voice messaging is an optional service for PSTN customers that provides the ability to divert incoming PSTN calls to a voice mailbox.

- **Call center**—A call center is a place of conducting business by telephone, combined with a centralized database that uses an automatic call distribution (ACD) system. Call centers require live agents to accept and handle calls.

- **Interactive voice response (IVR)**—IVR systems allow callers to exchange information over the telephone without a live intermediary agent.

Circuit-switched calls require a permanent duplex 64 kilobits per second (kbps) dedicated circuit between two telephones for the duration of a call, whether either caller is talking or not. During the call, no other party is permitted use the connection. Packet switched networking only uses bandwidth when it is required; this difference is a major benefit of packet-based voice networking.

Although the PSTN is effective, many business drivers are striving to change to an integrated voice and data network.

The H.323 standard provides a foundation for audio, video, and data communications across IP-based networks. H.323 defines four major components for a network-based communications system: terminals, gateways, gatekeepers, and multipoint control units (MCUs).

VoIP uses voice-enabled routers to convert analog voice from traditional telephones into IP packets, and to route those packets between corresponding locations. Often users do not notice that VoIP is implemented in the network; they use their traditional phones, connected to a PBX. However, the PBX is not connected to the PSTN or to another PBX, but to a voice-enabled router that is an entry point to VoIP.

In contrast, IP telephony replaces traditional phones with IP phones using Cisco CallManager (a server for call control and signaling). The IP phone itself performs voice-to-IP conversion, and the enterprise network does not require any voice-enabled routers. If connection to the PSTN is required, a voice-enabled router or other gateway must be added to forward calls to the PSTN. The IP telephony architecture includes four distinct components: infrastructure, call processing, applications, and clients. *Cisco CallManager* is the software-based call-processing component of the Cisco enterprise IP telephony solution. It performs much like the PBX in a traditional telephone network, including call setup and processing functions. Figure 11-8 depicts an Internet IP telephony design that uses the Internet for communication between distant locations.

Figure 11-8 *Internet IP Telephony Design*

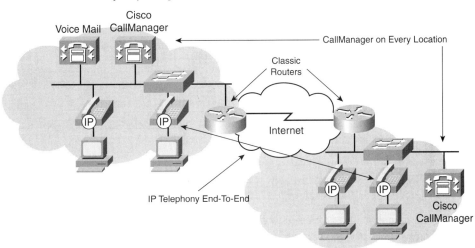

When an interface on a voice gateway carries voice data, it is referred to as a *voice port*. A voice port is a physical port that comes with a voice module, which is what makes a router voice-enabled. Dial peers are logical peers that are associated with physical voice ports; based on the configuration of dial peers, the voice gateway establishes a connection.

Overall voice quality is a function of many factors, including delay, jitter (the variable delay between packets), packet loss, and echo. Delay can be classified into two types: fixed network delay and variable network delay. Congested output queues on network interfaces are the most common sources of variable delay. The generally accepted limit for good-quality voice connection delay is 150 milliseconds (ms) one-way.

Compression is the method of reducing the amount of digital information below the traditional 64 kbps. Because of its relatively low bandwidth requirements (8 kbps) and high mean opinion score (MOS) of 3.92 (out of a possible 5), the ITU standard G.729 is a recommended voice codec for most WAN networks.

Voice communications over IP can be considered a mix of control signals and voice conversation. Control signals and data require reliable transport (using the transmission control protocol [TCP]) because the signals must be received in the order in which they were sent and cannot be lost. However, voice loses its value with time; if a voice packet is delayed, it might lose its relevance to the end user. Therefore, voice conversation uses the more efficient, unreliable transport (using the user datagram protocol [UDP]).

The following QoS mechanisms are available for voice:

- Bandwidth reduction
- Bandwidth reservation
- QoS classification
- Congestion avoidance
- Congestion management

If no congestion occurs on the WAN links, there is no reason to implement QoS mechanisms. It is important to remember that QoS does not create additional bandwidth; rather, it optimizes throughput and reduces network traffic delay.

LLQ is the preferred queuing mechanism for designing VoIP networks.

Voice over Frame Relay (VoFR) is intended for connecting existing PBXs; a voice-enabled router encodes the voice received from the PBX directly into Frame Relay frames and forwards those frames onto the Frame Relay network.

Variable bit rate (VBR) class of service with ATM adaptation L2 (AAL2)-based cells is the recommended implementation for voice over ATM (VoATM).

On-net calling refers to voice calls that are transmitted over private tie lines. If the private tie line is congested, voice gateways select an alternative path, which is usually the PSTN. This type of calling is referred to as *off-net calling*.

When implementing voice networks, one of the most important factors to consider is proper bandwidth capacity planning. WAN capacity planning depends on the sampling rate, codec, link type, header compression techniques, and the number of simultaneous voice calls.

The following three variables are involved in WAN capacity calculations:

- **Busy hour traffic (BHT) (in Erlangs)**—The number of hours of call traffic during the busiest hour of the telephone system's operation. One Erlang equals one full hour, or 3600 seconds, of telephone conversation. (Note that a centum call second [CCS] represents 1/36th of an Erlang.)

- **Blocking probability (the grade of service [GoS])**—The failure rate of calls resulting from an insufficient number of available lines. The GoS is written as a blocking factor, Pxx, where xx is the percentage of calls that are blocked for a traffic system.

- **Per-call bandwidth**—The amount of bandwidth (in kbps) required through an IP-based network to carry one voice call.

You can use the desired blocking probability, the BHT, and the traffic engineering Erlang tables to determine the number of required connections (circuits). Using the selected voice coding, header compression, sampling, and link type, you can calculate the required per-call bandwidth. To determine the required WAN capacity, multiply the number of circuits by the required per-call bandwidth.

A *digital signal processor* (DSP) is a hardware component that converts signal information from telephony-based protocols (such as DS0) to packet-based protocols (such as IP). The number of voice channels within one DSP can vary based on the codec complexity; medium complexity codecs (G.711, G.726, G.729a, G.729ab) allow the DSPs to process up to four voice calls per DSP, while high complexity codecs (G.728, G.723, G.729, and G.729b) allow the DSPs to process up to two voice calls per DSP.

Capacity planning is a critical process for enterprise IP telephony migration and overall success. IP telephony networks require three distinct capacity planning processes: Cisco CallManager processing requirements, network capacity and performance, and trunking capacity.

Evaluating Security Solutions for a Network

Networks significantly increase both the benefits and the risks of computing. Network security mitigates the risks to acceptable levels. The procedures and technologies deployed must guarantee the following network security points:

- **Confidentiality**—Determining who can view data
- **Integrity**—Determining who can change data
- **Availability**—Uninterrupted access to data

For example, if a denial of service (DoS) attack floods a public server with an enormous number of connection requests, it renders the server unresponsive to legitimate users. DoS attacks aim to compromise the availability of a network, host, or application.

Risk assessment defines threats, their probability, and their severity. A network security policy enumerates risks that are relevant to the network and how those risks are managed. A network security design implements the security policy.

Network devices themselves must be secured to provide a secure network foundation.

Networks, as a whole, can be attacked; however, hosts and applications are often the ultimate targets of attacks.

Although physical security is often overlooked, physical access to a device or communications media can compromise network security.

Network access control mechanisms are usually classified as either of the following:

- **Authentication**—Which provides proof of user identity and is traditionally based on one (or more) of the following three proofs:
    - Something the subject knows
    - Something the subject has
    - Something the subject is
- **Authorization**—Which defines what an authenticated network user can do.

Cryptography provides data confidentiality through *encryption*, which is the process of disguising a message to hide its original content. Secure fingerprints or digital signatures provide data integrity. Secure fingerprints attach a cryptographically strong checksum to data. This checksum is generated and verified using a secret key that is known only to authorized subjects. Digital signing of data uses a cryptography method that attaches a digital signature to sensitive data. This signature is generated using a unique signature generation key only the signer knows; other parties can verify the signature with the signer's signature verification key.

Secure management and monitoring are necessary for responding to security events and incidents. A secure network must also be managed securely; network managers must use well-defined operational practices, and network management protocols must be protected.

The Cisco SAFE Blueprint provides a modular approach to building security into the network fabric. Each network module has its unique risk profile; however, many security concepts and technologies can be reused in different modules to manage similar risks.

The Internet Connectivity module connects all other network modules to the Internet, thereby establishing potential contact with the most dangerous external network. Risks include reconnaissance threats, compromise of hosts, DoS attacks, and introduction of malicious code. Mitigation strategies include using firewalls, network intrusion detection systems (NIDSs), host intrusion detection systems (IDSs), and demilitarized zone (DMZ) networks. Figure 11-9 illustrates some risk management techniques and their positioning within the Internet Connectivity module.

Figure 11-9   *Securing the Internet Connectivity Module*

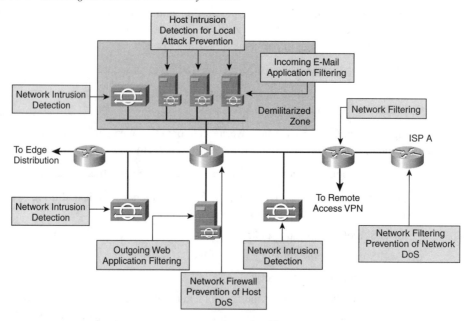

The E-commerce and Remote Access and VPN modules are partially secured through the Internet Connectivity module. Specific threats to the E-commerce module include the compromise of hosts and DoS attacks, and mitigation strategies include using firewalls, intrusion detection systems, and DMZ networks. The Remote Access and VPN module is vulnerable to identity spoofing, compromise of transmitted data, and compromise of a client or remote site. Mitigation strategies include using strong authentication and cryptography mechanisms, firewalls, and virus protection.

The WAN module provides WAN connectivity among different parts of the enterprise network and usually connects campuses with branch offices. Threats to this module include compromise of transmitted data and misconfiguration of the WAN network, and mitigation strategies include the use of cryptography, peer authentication, and firewalls.

The Network Management module sometimes provides a potential management path around security mechanisms. Risks in this module include impersonation of administrators, compromise of management protocols and hosts, misconfiguration, and avoidance of responsibility among administrators. Mitigation strategies include using device configuration authorization, configuration auditing, separate management networks, and firewalls.

The Server Farm module hosts servers inside the main campus network and branch offices. Specific risks include compromise of exposed applications, unauthorized access to data, and compromise of other hosts from compromised servers in this module. Mitigation strategies include using firewalls, intrusion detection, and switch access control.

Applying Basic Network Management Design Concepts

Network management helps determine faults and performance levels and manage configuration changes in the network; it also provides security and accounting management for both individual and group usage of network resources.

A network management system (NMS) executes applications that monitor and control managed devices. A managed device contains a management agent, which is software that collects and stores management information.

As its name implies, the Simple Network Management Protocol (SNMP) is the simplest network management protocol. An NMS sends SNMP requests to network devices, while network devices send unsolicited trap messages to inform the NMS of special events. Figure 11-10 illustrates the SNMP components.

Figure 11-10 *SNMP Is a Protocol for Management Information Exchange*

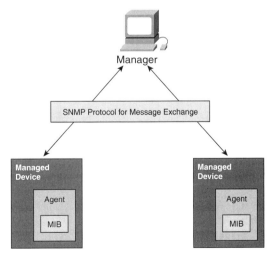

The *management information base (MIB)* is a detailed definition of the information on a network device that is accessible through a network management protocol such as SNMP. An MIB is a collection of managed objects that stores the information entered by the local management agent on a managed device.

Remote monitoring (RMON) is an extension of the MIB. The MIB typically provides only static information about the managed device; an RMON agent contains specific groups of statistics that can be collected for long-term trend analysis. RMON agents gather nine (10 with Token Ring) groups of statistics. The agents then forward this information to a manager, upon request. RMON2 added a further nine groups. RMON1 works on the MAC layer, while RMON2 provides full network visibility from the network layer to the application layer.

The *Cisco Discovery Protocol (CDP)* is a Cisco proprietary protocol that runs over the data link layer between Cisco devices and is used for discovering and identifying neighboring Cisco devices.

NetFlow provides the measurement base that is required for recording network and application resource utilization. A network flow is a unidirectional sequence of packets between source and destination endpoints. Flow endpoints are identified both by IP address and transport layer application port numbers. NetFlow also identifies the flows by IP protocol type, class of service (CoS), and the input interface identifier. As illustrated in Figure 11-11, the NetFlow services infrastructure has a three-tiered architecture.

Syslog messages are used to provide reports on various system states, including errors. Every syslog message contains a timestamp (if enabled), severity level (0 through 7; 0 being an emergency), and facility (device, protocol, or module).

The ISO network management model defines the following five functional areas of network management, which are abbreviated as FCAPS:

- **Fault management**—Detects, isolates, notifies, and corrects faults encountered in the network.

- **Configuration management**—Administers configuration aspects of network devices, such as configuration file management, inventory management, and software management.

- **Accounting management**—Provides usage information about network resources.

- **Performance management**—Monitors and measures various aspects of performance so that overall performance can be maintained at an acceptable level.

- **Security management**—Provides access to network devices and corporate resources to authorized individuals.

Figure 11-11 *Netflow Infrastructure*

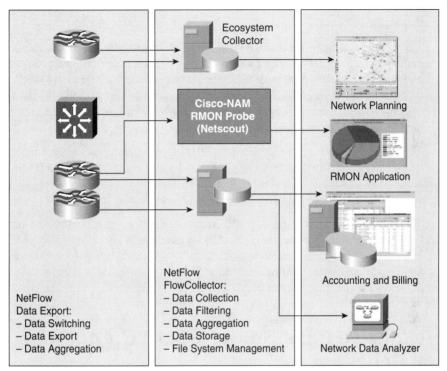

Authentication, authorization, and accounting (AAA) has changed dramatically as modern access technologies users have sought a way to authenticate, authorize, and initiate accounting records for billing user time on their networks. *Authentication* identifies a user, *authorization* determines what that user can do, and *accounting* monitors the duration of network usage for billing purposes.

Performance management is the practice of managing network service response time, consistency, and quality for individual and overall services.

Service-level management (SLM) is a proven methodology that helps network managers resolve resource issues by defining and regulating capacity and performance management processes in a cost-effective manner. You can accomplish this methodology by establishing a service level agreement (SLA) with a network service provider, or by defining and funding the service and upgrades as required.

A *service level contract (SLC)* specifies connectivity and performance levels to be met by the service provider for the service's end-user. SLAs define specific service performance measurements between device pairs, including routers, servers, workstations, and other equipment. An SLC typically includes multiple SLAs. Active monitoring of metrics—such as availability, latency (delay), packet loss, and jitter (delay variation)—is required to verify that SLAs are being met.

The service assurance agent (SAA) in the Cisco IOS software can proactively monitor the network. The SAA provides a way to configure a Cisco IOS device to perform network tests on either end-systems or other IOS devices. The results of these tests are used to validate the SLA. A key value of the SAA is the ability to mark the test packets with the appropriate CoS value, thus enabling network managers to observe various TCP and UDP services and performance when QoS is implemented.

The *Internetwork Performance Monitor (IPM)* application measures the latency and availability of IP networks on a hop-by-hop (router-to-router) basis. The IPM/SAA monitoring solution is composed of three parts: the IPM server application, the IPM client application, and the Cisco IOS software's SAA feature.

The *Service Management Solution (SMS)* manages service levels between enterprises and internal or external service providers. All communication interfaces in the SMS architecture are industry standards, including SNMP, extensible markup language (XML), and Hypertext Transfer Protocol (HTTP). The architecture uses a distributed independent network appliance to poll locally, via SNMP, for service metrics recorded on the SAA.

Comprehensive Case Study: MCMB Corporation Network Redesign

This section presents a comprehensive case study of a small to mid-sized network. In this case study, you will evaluate the existing network and, based on findings and customer requirements, propose a new network design.

Case Study General Instructions

Use the scenarios, information, and parameters provided at each task of the case study. If you encounter ambiguities, make reasonable assumptions and proceed. For all tasks, use the initial customer scenario and build on the solutions provided thus far.

You can use any and all documentation, books, white papers, and so on.

In each task, you act as a network design consultant. Make creative proposals to accomplish the customer's business needs. Justify your ideas when they differ from the provided solutions.

Use any design strategies and internetworking technologies you feel are appropriate.

The final goal for each case study is a paper solution; you are not required to provide the specific product names.

Appendix G, "Answers to Review Questions, Case Studies, and Simulation Exercises," provides a solution for each task based on assumptions made. There is no claim that the provided solution is the best or only solution. Your solution might be more appropriate for the assumptions you made. The provided solution helps you understand the author's reasoning and offers a way for you to compare and contrast your solution.

Scenario: MCMB Corporation Network Redesign

This case study involves analyzing the network infrastructure of MCMB Corporation, a fictitious manufacturer of tractor tires. The company has provided you with a short description of its current situation and future plans. As a network designer, it is your task to identify the customer requirements that allow you to provide the most effective solution.

Company Facts

MCMB Corporation, a leading manufacturer of tractor tires, is an international company with headquarters in Lyon, France and offices around the world. Demand for the company's product is constantly increasing; therefore, the company must tighten the integration of its customers and partners into its information infrastructure.

The company employs approximately 8000 people across 75 sites. These sites are located globally and vary in size from a single part-time person working from a small office/home office (SOHO) to 100 regular office staff. The company's headquarters consists of three buildings that contain approximately 1500 employees, 500 in each building. The headquarters also houses four major departments—development, technical support, marketing, and sales—that are dispersed across all three buildings.

The company has one international office and many smaller remote offices in each country where it is present. All larger remote offices (those that have more than five employees) within each country are permanently connected to the international office, while smaller offices (those with fewer than five employees) are connected on-demand via Integrated Services Digital Network (ISDN). Each international office provides connectivity to the headquarters for all sites within that country.

Most of the time, the employees use universal software that covers all the company's business workflows and runs on a mainframe. The e-mail server runs on a separate platform.

Current Situation

MCMB Corporation's WAN is a typical hierarchical, three-tier aggregation network that uses serial lines. The links vary from low bandwidth (64 kbps to 128 kbps) between the larger remote offices and the international office to higher bandwidth (up to 2 Mbps) between the international offices and the headquarters. All remote locations that have more than five employees are Layer 2 switched, while smaller locations use Ethernet hubs.

The current network does not provide any redundancy or backup strategy. Therefore, in the event of link or network equipment failures, the employees cannot perform their daily work; this results in lower productivity.

Internet connectivity with the maximum throughput of 1 Mbps is provided via a central firewall that is located next to the mainframe.

All internal servers (e-commerce, e-mail, and so on) are located at the headquarters in one of the three buildings, as shown in Figure 11-12. Usually (approximately 75% of the time), employees are accessing these servers; the remainder of the traffic is from the Internet. The entire campus network at the headquarters is switched using Layer 2 switches with 10/100 Mbps ports for connecting users and Gigabit Ethernet (GE) ports for the servers. Every building contains access and distribution switches. The distribution switches are connected to the core switch, which builds the campus backbone. Currently, no redundancy is implemented in the LAN.

Figure 11-12 shows the existing campus switching configuration.

Figure 11-12 *The MCMB Corporation Headquarters Campus Switching Configuration*

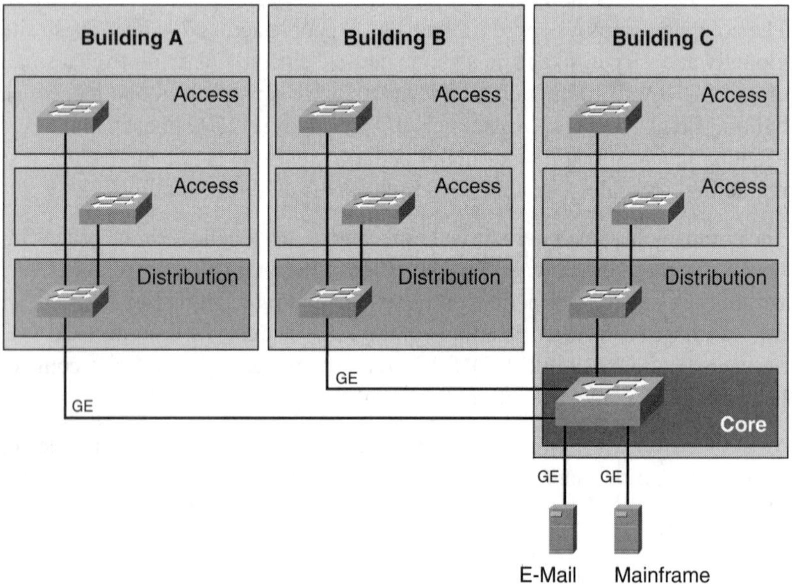

Users repeatedly report low response times; monitoring of the campus backbone switch does not show any serious congestions or high CPU utilizations. Furthermore, the average WAN utilization between the headquarters and the international offices is approximately 30% and rarely exceeds 80%. The WAN utilization between international offices and remote offices is even lower and does not seem to be the issue. The administrators are concerned about this problem and believe that it must be resolved soon.

The network is IP-based and uses EIGRP as the routing protocol. One Class C network from the range 192.168.x.x is allocated to each LAN and WAN link. In locations where more than 252 IP addresses are required, an additional Class C network is added. Route summarization is not implemented on any router. Connections to small remote offices with ISDN connections are implemented with static routes that are redistributed into the routing protocol at the international offices.

The data traffic is predominantly HTTP and e-mail because the company has implemented an intranet.

Figure 11-13 illustrates MCMB's network with three international offices.

Figure 11-13   *MCMB Corporation Network*

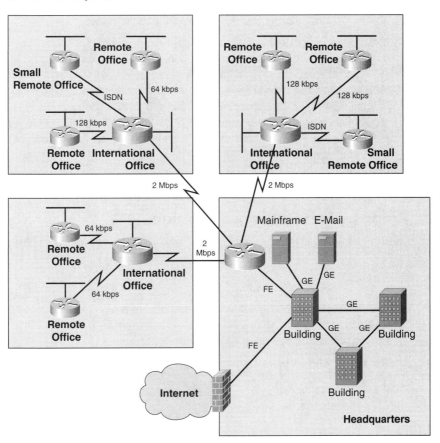

Plans and Requirements

The company urgently needs to resolve the low response time issue and is open to any potential solution.

The following are other things that MCMB would like to accomplish with its network:

- To minimize investment costs, MCMB would like to include redundancy while retaining the existing equipment. Redundancy should be implemented in the headquarters' LAN and on all WAN links. The company is aware of potential business risks that periodic network outages might cause during the solution implementation.

- MCMB would like to optimize its IP addressing because it understands the disadvantages of its network's current IP addressing scheme. The company would like a scalable and manageable solution that would allow for expansion to new markets by simply adding new remote locations to the system.

- MCMB would like to separate the four departments in the headquarters campus and possibly deploy security policies among them in the future.

- MCMB wants to offer extranet functionality to its partners and resellers to simplify its business. It's considering various connectivity options, including leased line, ISDN, ADSL, and the Internet. MCMB wants to provide secure and invulnerable access to its external servers, which should be separated from the internal servers. The internal mainframe should securely upload and download the data from the external server. This solution must be universal, regardless of what connectivity option the partners choose. The company expects that approximately 50 partners and customers will use the extranet at the beginning. The application requires about 64 kbps of bandwidth on the WAN for acceptable response times.

Exercise: Propose Your Network Redesign

The following sections are intended to guide you through this customer's network redesign.

Campus Redesign

1 Propose a campus redesign that solves the current problems reported by the users. Consider redundancy when redesigning the LAN. Write an overview of your redesign and articulate why you selected that solution.

Use Figure 11-14 to create your proposed campus switching topology.

Figure 11-14 *Your MCMB Campus Redesign*

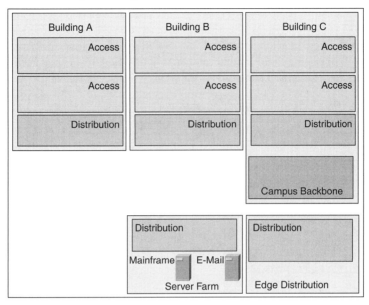

WAN Backup Design

2 Propose a WAN backup design to improve network reliability. Write an overview of your design and articulate why you selected that solution. Use Figure 11-15 to create your proposed WAN backup topology.

Figure 11-15 *Your MCMB WAN Backup Redesign*

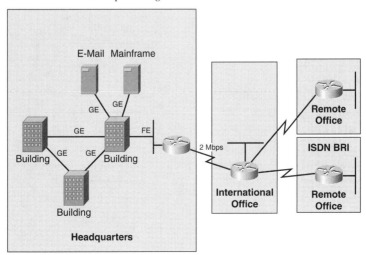

IP Addressing Redesign

   3 Propose an IP addressing redesign that optimizes IP addressing and IP routing (including the use of IP address summarization). Write an overview of your redesign and articulate why you selected that solution. Use Figure 11-16 to show the proposed IP addressing in the campus and WAN, including the backup links. Also include IP address summarization on this diagram.

Figure 11-16 *Your MCMB IP Addressing and Summarization Redesign*

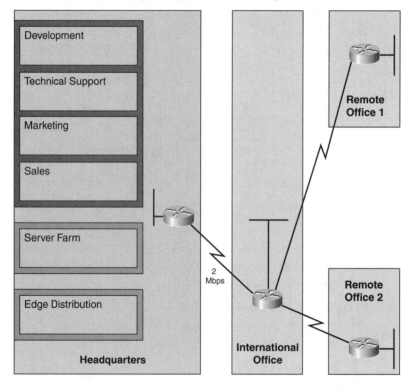

Routing Campus Redesign

   4 If the existing routing protocol does not fulfill all the requirements, propose a new one to meet the customer's needs. If a new routing protocol is not required, outline any modifications that are required for the existing routing protocol. Write an overview of your redesign and articulate why you selected that solution.

Extranet Design

5 Propose an extranet design that will enable secure access to the external servers for MCMB's customers and partners, regardless of the connectivity option they choose. Consider all possible solutions and propose the one that is appropriate for all customers who have a reasonable investment in network equipment and monthly costs. Write an overview of your design that articulates why you selected that solution, and create a diagram that depicts the proposed solution.

This appendix contains job aids for the following topics:

- IPv4 Addresses and Subnetting
- Decimal-to-Binary Conversion Chart
- IPv4 Addressing Review
- IPv4 Access Lists
- Review Questions

IPv4 Addressing Job Aids

The job aids in this appendix are provided to give you some background information on IP addressing.

The information in the "IPv4 Addressing Review" section and the "IPv4 Access Lists" section should serve as a review of the fundamentals of IP addressing and the concepts and configuration of access lists, respectively.

NOTE   In this appendix, the term Internet Protocol (IP) refers to IP version 4 (IPv4).

IPv4 Addresses and Subnetting

Figure A-1 is a job aid intended to help you with various aspects of IP addressing, including how to distinguish address classes, the number of subnets and hosts available with various subnet masks, and how to interpret IP addresses.

Figure A-1   *IP Addresses and Subnetting Job Aid*

Class	Net Host	First Octet	Standard Mask Binary
A	N.H.H.H	1–126	1111 1111 0000 0000 0000 0000 0000 0000
B	N.N.H.H	128–191	1111 1111 1111 1111 0000 0000 0000 0000
C	N.N.N.H	192–223	1111 1111 1111 1111 1111 1111 0000 0000

Address	172.16.5.72		1010 1100 0001 0000 0000 0101 0100 1000
Subnet Mask	255.255.255.192		1111 1111 1111 1111 1111 1111 1100 0000

First octet
(172 – Class B)
defines network
portion.

```
1010 1100 0001 0000 0000 0101 0100 1000
1111 1111 1111 1111 1111 1111 1100 0000
```

Of the part that
remains, the subnet
mask bits define the
subnet portion.

```
0000 0101 0100 1000
1111 1111 1100 0000
```

Whatever bits
remain define the
host portion.

```
00 1000
00 0000
```

Network

Subnet

Host

Subnet Bits	Subnet Mask	# Subnets	# Hosts
Class B			
2	255.255.192.0	4	16382
3	255.255.224.0	8	8190
4	255.255.240.0	16	4094
5	255.255.248.0	32	2046
6	255.255.252.0	64	1022
7	255.255.254.0	128	510
8	255.255.255.0	256	254
9	255.255.255.128	512	126
10	255.255.255.192	1024	62
11	255.255.255.224	2048	30
12	255.255.255.240	4096	14
13	255.255.255.248	8192	6
14	255.255.255.252	16384	2
Class C			
2	255.255.255.192	4	62
3	255.255.255.224	8	30
4	255.255.255.240	16	14
5	255.255.255.248	32	6
6	255.255.255.252	64	2

SUBNETTING

Decimal-to-Binary Conversion Chart

Table A-1 can be used to convert from decimal to binary, and from binary to decimal.

Table A-1   *Decimal-to-Binary Conversion Chart*

Decimal	Binary	Decimal	Binary	Decimal	Binary	Decimal	Binary
0	00000000	64	01000000	128	10000000	192	11000000
1	00000001	65	01000001	129	10000001	193	11000001
2	00000010	66	01000010	130	10000010	194	11000010
3	00000011	67	01000011	131	10000011	195	11000011
4	00000100	68	01000100	132	10000100	196	11000100
5	00000101	69	01000101	133	10000101	197	11000101
6	00000110	70	01000110	134	10000110	198	11000110
7	00000111	71	01000111	135	10000111	199	11000111
8	00001000	72	01001000	136	10001000	200	11001000
9	00001001	73	01001001	137	10001001	201	11001001
10	00001010	74	01001010	138	10001010	202	11001010
11	00001011	75	01001011	139	10001011	203	11001011
12	00001100	76	01001100	140	10001100	204	11001100
13	00001101	77	01001101	141	10001101	205	11001101
14	00001110	78	01001110	142	10001110	206	11001110
15	00001111	79	01001111	143	10001111	207	11001111
16	00010000	80	01010000	144	10010000	208	11010000
17	00010001	81	01010001	145	10010001	209	11010001
18	00010010	82	01010010	146	10010010	210	11010010
19	00010011	83	01010011	147	10010011	211	11010011
20	00010100	84	01010100	148	10010100	212	11010100
21	00010101	85	01010101	149	10010101	213	11010101
22	00010110	86	01010110	150	10010110	214	11010110
23	00010111	87	01010111	151	10010111	215	11010111
24	00011000	88	01011000	152	10011000	216	11011000
25	00011001	89	01011001	153	10011001	217	11011001
26	00011010	90	01011010	154	10011010	218	11011010
27	00011011	91	01011011	155	10011011	219	11011011

Table A-1   *Decimal-to-Binary Conversion Chart (Continued)*

Decimal	Binary	Decimal	Binary	Decimal	Binary	Decimal	Binary
28	00011100	92	01011100	156	10011100	220	11011100
29	00011101	93	01011101	157	10011101	221	11011101
30	00011110	94	01011110	158	10011110	222	11011110
31	00011111	95	01011111	159	10011111	223	11011111
32	00100000	96	01100000	160	10100000	224	11100000
33	00100001	97	01100001	161	10100001	225	11100001
34	00100010	98	01100010	162	10100010	226	11100010
35	00100011	99	01100011	163	10100011	227	11100011
36	00100100	100	01100100	164	10100100	228	11100100
37	00100101	101	01100101	165	10100101	229	11100101
38	00100110	102	01100110	166	10100110	230	11100110
39	00100111	103	01100111	167	10100111	231	11100111
40	00101000	104	01101000	168	10101000	232	11101000
41	00101001	105	01101001	169	10101001	233	11101001
42	00101010	106	01101010	170	10101010	234	11101010
43	00101011	107	01101011	171	10101011	235	11101011
44	00101100	108	01101100	172	10101100	236	11101100
45	00101101	109	01101101	173	10101101	237	11101101
46	00101110	110	01101110	174	10101110	238	11101110
47	00101111	111	01101111	175	10101111	239	11101111
48	00110000	112	01110000	176	10110000	240	11110000
49	00110001	113	01110001	177	10110001	241	11110001
50	00110010	114	01110010	178	10110010	242	11110010
51	00110011	115	01110011	179	10110011	243	11110011
52	00110100	116	01110100	180	10110100	244	11110100
53	00110101	117	01110101	181	10110101	245	11110101
54	00110110	118	01110110	182	10110110	246	11110110
55	00110111	119	01110111	183	10110111	247	11110111
56	00111000	120	01111000	184	10111000	248	11111000
57	00111001	121	01111001	185	10111001	249	11111001

continues

Table A-1   *Decimal-to-Binary Conversion Chart (Continued)*

Decimal	Binary	Decimal	Binary	Decimal	Binary	Decimal	Binary
58	00111010	122	01111010	186	10111010	250	11111010
59	00111011	123	01111011	187	10111011	251	11111011
60	00111100	124	01111100	188	10111100	252	11111100
61	00111101	125	01111101	189	10111101	253	11111101
62	00111110	126	01111110	190	10111110	254	11111110
63	00111111	127	01111111	191	10111111	255	11111111

IPv4 Addressing Review

This section reviews the basics of IPv4 addresses, including the following:

- Converting IP addresses between decimal and binary
- Determining an IP address class
- Extending an IP classful address using subnet masks
- Calculating a subnet mask
- Calculating the networks for a subnet mask
- Using prefixes to represent a subnet mask

Converting IP Addresses Between Decimal and Binary

An *IP address* is a 32-bit, two-level hierarchical number. It is hierarchical because the first portion of the address represents the network, and the second portion of the address represents the node (or host).

The 32 bits are grouped into four octets, with 8 bits per octet. The value of each octet ranges from 0 to 255 decimal, or 00000000 to 11111111 binary. IP addresses are usually written in dotted-decimal notation—each of the four octets is written in decimal notation, and dots are placed between the octets. Figure A-2 illustrates how you convert an IP address' octet in binary to decimal notation.

It is important that you understand how this conversion is done because it is used when calculating subnet masks, a topic we discuss later in this section.

Figure A-3 shows three examples of converting IP addresses between binary and decimal.

Figure A-2   *Converting an Octet of an IP Address from Binary to Decimal*

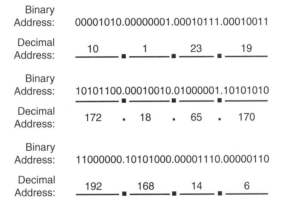

Now that you understand the decimal-to-binary and binary-to-decimal conversion processes, use the following sections to review address classes and the uses of subnet masks.

Determining an IP Address Class

To accommodate large and small networks, the 32-bit IP address is segregated into Classes A through E. The first few bits of the first octet determine an address' class; this then determines how many network bits and host bits are in the address. Figure A-4 illustrates this process for Class A, B, and C addresses. Each address class therefore allows for a certain number of network addresses and a certain number of host addresses within a network. Table A-2 shows the address range, the number of networks, and the number of hosts for each of the classes. (Note that Class D and E addresses are used for purposes other than addressing hosts.)

Figure A-4 *Determining an IP Address Class from the First Few Bits of an Address*

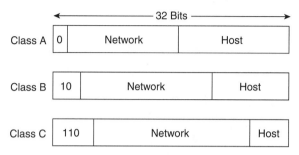

Table A-2 *IP Address Classes*

Class	Address Range	Number of Networks	Number of Hosts
Class A	1.0.0.0 to 126.0.0.0	128 (2^7)	16,777,214
Class B	128.0.0.0 to 191.255.0.0	16,386 (2^{14})	65,532
Class C	192.0.0.0 to 223.255.255.0	Approximately 2 million (2^{21})	254
Class D	224.0.0.0 to 239.255.255.254	Reserved for multicast addresses	—
Class E	240.0.0.0 to 254.255.255.255	Reserved for research	—

NOTE The network 127.0.0.0 (any address starting with decimal 127) is reserved for loopback.

Using classes to denote which portion of the address represents the network number and which portion represents the node or host address is referred to as *classful addressing*. Several issues must be addressed with classful addressing, however. First, the number of available Class A, B, and C addresses is finite. Another problem is that not all classes are useful for a midsize organization, as illustrated in Table A-2. As can be expected, the Class B range best accommodates the majority of today's organizational network topologies. Subnet masks were introduced to maximize the use of the IP addresses an organization receives, regardless of their class.

Extending an IP Classful Address Using Subnet Masks

RFC 950, *Internet Standard Subnetting Procedure*, available at www.cis.ohio-state.edu/cgi-bin/rfc/rfc0950.html, was written to address the IP address shortage. It proposed a procedure, called *subnet masking*, for dividing Class A, B, and C addresses into smaller pieces, thereby increasing the number of possible networks. A subnet mask is a 32-bit value that identifies which address bits represent network bits and which represent host bits. In other words, the router does not determine the network portion of the address by looking at the value of the first octet; rather, it looks at the subnet mask that is associated with the address. In this way, subnet masks enable you to extend the usage of an IP address. This is one way of making an IP address a three-level hierarchy, as shown in Figure A-5.

Figure A-5   *A Subnet Mask Determines How an IP Address Is Interpreted*

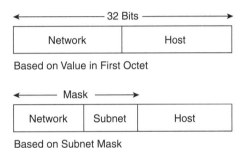

To create a subnet mask for an address, use a 1 for each bit that you want to represent the network or subnet portion of the address, and use a 0 for each bit that you want to represent the node portion of the address. Note that the 1s in the mask are contiguous. The default subnet masks for Class A, B, and C addresses are shown Table A-3.

Table A-3   *IP Address Default Subnet Masks*

Class	Default Mask in Binary	Default Mask in Decimal
Class A	11111111.00000000.00000000.00000000	255.0.0.0
Class B	11111111.11111111.00000000.00000000	255.255.0.0
Class C	11111111.11111111.11111111.00000000	255.255.255.0

Calculating a Subnet Mask

Because subnet masks extend the number of network addresses you can use by using bits from the host portion, you do not want to randomly decide how many additional bits to use for the network portion. Instead, you want to do some research to determine how many network addresses you need to derive from your given IP address. For example, consider that you have the IP address 172.16.0.0 and you want to configure the network shown in Figure A-6. To establish your subnet mask, do the following:

Step 1 Determine the number of networks (subnets) needed. In Figure A-6, for example, there are five networks.

Step 2 Determine how many nodes per subnet must be defined. This example has five nodes (two routers and three workstations) on each subnet.

Step 3 Determine future network and node requirements. For example, assume 100 percent growth.

Step 4 Given the information gathered in Steps 1 through 3, determine the total number of subnets required. For this example, 10 subnets are required. Refer to the "IPv4 Addresses and Subnetting" section of this appendix to select the appropriate subnet mask value that can accommodate 10 networks.

Figure A-6 *Network Used in Subnet Mask Example*

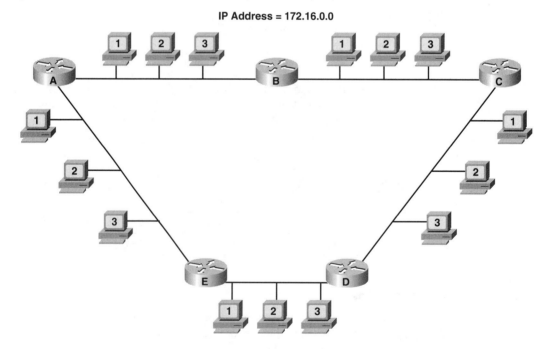

IP Address = 172.16.0.0

No mask accommodates exactly 10 subnets. Depending on your network growth trends, you might select 4 subnet bits, thereby resulting in a subnet mask of 255.255.240.0. The binary representation of this subnet mask is as follows:

11111111.11111111.11110000.00000000

The number of additional subnets given by n additional bits is 2^n. For example, the additional 4 subnet bits would give you $2^4 = 16$ subnets.

Calculating the Networks for a Subnet Mask

Refer to the example in Figure A-6. After you identify your subnet mask, you must calculate the 10 subnetted network addresses to use with 172.16.0.0 255.255.240.0. One way to do this is as follows:

Step 1   Write the subnetted address in binary format, as shown at the top of Figure A-7. If necessary, use the Decimal-to-Binary Conversion Chart, provided in Table A-1.

Step 2   On the binary address, draw a line between the 16th and 17th bits, as shown in Figure A-7. Then draw a line between the 20th and 21st bits. Now you can focus on the target subnet bits.

Step 3   Historically, it was recommended that you begin choosing subnets from highest (the leftmost bit) to lowest (to allow you to have more flexibility in the number of subnets used). However, this strategy does not allow you to adequately summarize subnet addresses, so the present recommendation is to choose subnets from lowest to highest (right to left).

When calculating the subnet address, all host bits are set to 0. To convert back to decimal, it is important to note that you must always convert an entire octet, or 8 bits. For the first subnet, your subnet bits are 0000, and the rest of the octet (all host bits) is 0000.

If necessary, use the Decimal-to-Binary Conversion Chart provided in Table A-1 and locate this first subnet number. The first subnet number would be 00000000, or decimal 0.

Step 4   (Optional) You should list each subnet in binary form to reduce the number of errors. This way, you will not forget where you left off in your subnet address selection.

Step 5   Locate the second-lowest subnet number. In this case, it would be 0001. When combined with the next 4 bits (the host bits) of 0000, this is subnet binary 00010000, or decimal 16.

Step 6   Continue locating subnet numbers until you have as many as you need— in this case, 10 subnets, as shown in Figure A-7.

Figure A-7 *Calculating the Subnets for the Example in Figure A-6*

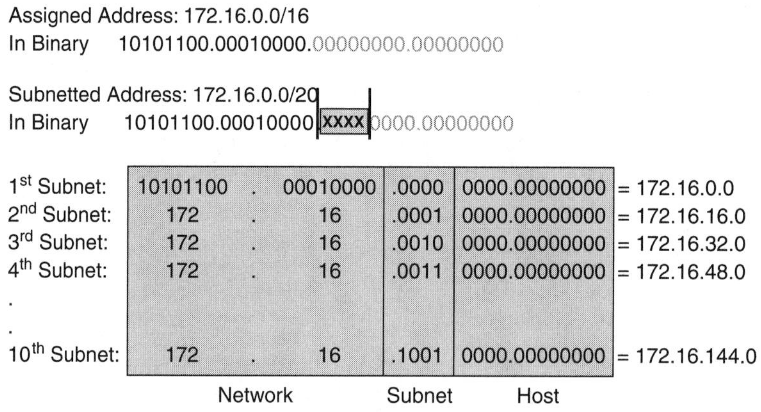

Assigned Address: 172.16.0.0/16
In Binary   10101100.00010000.00000000.00000000

Subnetted Address: 172.16.0.0/20
In Binary   10101100.00010000.xxxx0000.00000000

1st Subnet:	10101100	.	00010000	.0000	0000.00000000	= 172.16.0.0
2nd Subnet:	172	.	16	.0001	0000.00000000	= 172.16.16.0
3rd Subnet:	172	.	16	.0010	0000.00000000	= 172.16.32.0
4th Subnet:	172	.	16	.0011	0000.00000000	= 172.16.48.0
.						
.						
10th Subnet:	172	.	16	.1001	0000.00000000	= 172.16.144.0

Network   Subnet   Host

Using Prefixes to Represent a Subnet Mask

As previously discussed, subnet masks are used to identify the number of bits in an address that represent the network, subnet, and host portions of the address. Another way of indicating this is to use a prefix. A prefix is represented by a slash (/) followed by a numerical value that is the sum of the bits that represent the address' network and subnet portions. For example, if you were using a subnet mask of 255.255.255.0, the prefix would be /24 for 24 bits of subnet plus network.

Table A-4 shows some examples of the different ways you can represent a prefix and subnet mask.

Table A-4 *Representing Subnet Masks*

IP Address/Prefix	Subnet Mask in Decimal	Subnet Mask in Binary
192.168.112.0/21	255.255.248.0	11111111.11111111.11111000.00000000
172.16.0.0/16	255.255.0.0	11111111.11111111.00000000.00000000
10.1.1.0/27	255.255.255.224	11111111.11111111.11111111.11100000

It is important to know how to write subnet masks and prefixes because, as shown in Example A-1, Cisco routers use both. Typically, you will be asked to input a subnet mask when configuring an IP address, but the output generated using **show** commands typically displays an IP address with a prefix.

Example A-1 *Examples of Subnet Mask and Prefix Use on Cisco Routers*

```
p1r3#show run
<Output Omitted>
interface Ethernet0
 ip address 10.64.4.1 255.255.255.0
 !
interface Serial0
 ip address 10.1.3.2 255.255.255.0
<Output Omitted>

p1r3#show interface ethernet0
Ethernet0 is administratively down, line protocol is down
  Hardware is Lance, address is 00e0.b05a.d504 (bia 00e0.b05a.d504)
  Internet address is 10.64.4.1/24
<Output Omitted>

p1r3#show interface serial0
Serial0 is down, line protocol is down
  Hardware is HD64570
  Internet address is 10.1.3.2/24
<Output Omitted>
```

IPv4 Access Lists

This section reviews IPv4 access lists and includes the following topics:

- IP access list overview
- IP standard access lists
- IP extended access lists
- Restricting virtual terminal access
- Verifying access list configuration

IP Access List Overview

As illustrated in Figure A-8, packet filtering helps control packet movement through the network. Such control can help limit network traffic and restrict network use by certain users or devices. Cisco provides access lists to permit or deny packets from crossing specified router interfaces. An IP access list is a sequential collection of permit and deny conditions that apply to IP addresses or upper-layer IP protocols.

Figure A-8 *Access Lists Control Packet Movement Through a Network*

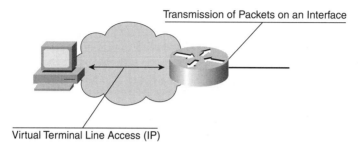

Table A-5 shows some of the available types of access lists on a Cisco router and their access list numbers.

Table A-5 *Access List Numbers*

Type of Access List	Range of Access List Numbers
IP standard	1 to 99
IP extended	100 to 199
Bridge type-code	200 to 299
IPX standard	800 to 899
IPX extended	900 to 999
IPX SAP	1000 to 1099

This section covers IP standard and extended access lists. For information on other types of access lists, refer to the technical documentation on Cisco's website at www.cisco.com.

WARNING Cisco IOS Release 10.3 introduced substantial additions to IP access lists. These extensions are backward-compatible. Migrating from existing releases to the Cisco IOS Release 10.3 or later image will convert your access lists automatically. However, previous releases are not upwardly compatible with these changes. Therefore, if you save an access list with the Cisco IOS Release 10.3 or later image and then use older software, the resulting access list will not be interpreted correctly. This incompatibility can cause security problems. Save your old configuration file before booting Cisco IOS Release 10.3 (or later) images in case you need to revert to an earlier version.

IP Standard Access Lists

Standard access lists permit or deny packets based only on the packet's source IP address, as shown in Figure A-9. The access list number range for standard IP access lists is 1 through 99. Standard access lists are easier to configure than extended access lists, their more robust counterparts.

Figure A-9   *Standard IP Access Lists Filter Based Only on the Source Address*

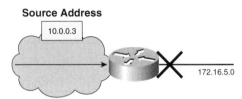

A standard access list is a sequential collection of permit and deny conditions that apply to source IP addresses. The router tests addresses against the conditions in an access list, one by one. The first match determines whether the router accepts or rejects the packet. Because the router stops testing conditions after the first match, the order of the conditions is critical. If no conditions match, the router rejects the packet.

Figure A-10 illustrates the processing of inbound standard access lists. After receiving a packet, the router checks the source address of the packet against the access list. If the access list permits the address, the router exits the access list and continues to process the packet. If the access list rejects the address, the router discards the packet and returns an Internet Control Message Protocol (ICMP) administratively prohibited message.

Figure A-10   *Inbound Standard IP Access List Processing*

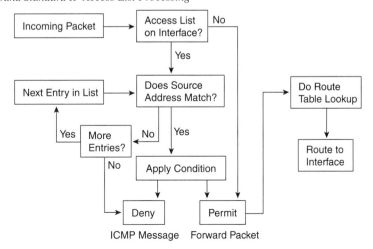

Note that, if no additional entries are found in the access list, the action taken is to deny the packet; this illustrates an important rule to remember when creating access lists. For example, consider what will happen if you create a list that simply denies traffic that you do not want to let into your network, and you configure this on an interface. If you forget about this rule, all of your traffic will be denied—the traffic explicitly denied by your list, and the rest of the traffic that is implicitly denied because the access list is applied to the interface.

Key Point: Implicit Deny Any

The last entry in an access list is known as an *implicit deny any*; all traffic not explicitly permitted will be implicitly denied.

Key Point: Order Is Important When Configuring Access Lists

When configuring access lists, order is important. Make sure that you list the entries from specific to general. For example, if you want to deny a specific host address and permit all other addresses, make sure that your entry about the specific host appears first.

Figure A-11 illustrates the processing of outbound standard IP access lists. After receiving and routing a packet to a controlled interface, the router checks the packet's source address against the access list. If the access list permits the address, the router transmits the packet. If the access list denies the address, the router discards the packet and returns an ICMP administratively prohibited message.

Figure A-11 *Outbound Standard IP Access List Processing*

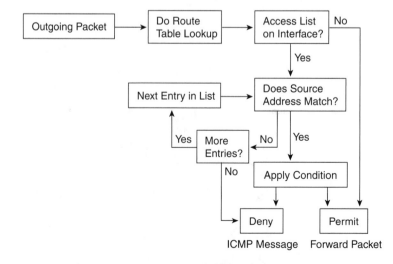

Both standard and extended IP access lists use a wildcard mask. Like an IP address, a wildcard mask is a 32-bit quantity written in dotted-decimal format. The wildcard mask tells the router which bits of the address to use in comparisons.

Key Point: Address Bits and Wildcard Mask Bits

Address bits corresponding to wildcard mask bits set to 1 are ignored in comparisons; address bits corresponding to wildcard mask bits set to 0 are used in comparisons.

An alternative way of thinking about the wildcard mask is as follows. If a 0 bit appears in the wildcard mask, the corresponding bit location in the access list address and the same bit location in the packet address must match (both must be 0 or both must be 1). If a 1 bit appears in the wildcard mask, the packet's corresponding bit location will match (whether it is 0 or 1), and that bit location in the access list address is ignored. For this reason, bits set to 1 in the wildcard mask are sometimes called *don't care bits*.

Remember that the order of the access list statements is important because the access list is not processed further after a match has been found.

Wildcard Masks

The concept of a wildcard mask is similar to the wildcard character used in DOS-based computers. For example, to delete all files on your computer that begin with the letter "f," enter:

delete f*.*

The * character is the wildcard; any files that start with "f," followed by any other characters, then a dot, and then any other characters, will be deleted.

Instead of using wildcard characters, routers use wildcard masks to implement this concept.

Table A-6 contains examples of addresses and wildcard masks, and what they match.

Table A-6   *Access List Wildcard Mask Examples*

Address	Wildcard Mask	Matches
0.0.0.0	255.255.255.255	Any address
172.16.0.0/16	0.0.255.255	Any host on network 172.16.0.0
172.16.7.11/16	0.0.0.0	Host address 172.16.7.11
255.255.255.255	0.0.0.0	Local broadcast address 255.255.255.255
172.16.8.0/21	0.0.7.255	Any host on subnet 172.16.8.0/21

Whether you are creating a standard or extended access list, you will need to complete the following two tasks:

Step 1   Create an access list in global configuration mode by specifying an access list number and access conditions.

Define a standard IP access list using a source address and wildcard, as shown later in this section.

Define an extended access list using source and destination addresses and optional protocol-type information for finer granularity of control, as shown in the "IP Extended Access Lists" section later in this appendix.

Step 2   Apply the access list in interface configuration mode to interfaces or terminal lines.

After an access list is created, you can apply it to one or more interfaces. Access lists can be applied on either outbound or inbound interfaces.

IP Standard Access List Configuration

As detailed in Table A-7, use the **access-list** *access-list-number* {**permit** | **deny**} {*source source-wildcard* | **any**} [**log**] global configuration command to create an entry in a standard traffic filter list.

Table A-7   *Standard IP* **access-list** *Command Description*

Parameter	Description
access-list-number	Identifies the list to which the entry belongs. A number from 1 to 99.
permit	**deny**	Indicates whether this entry allows or blocks traffic from the specified address.
source	Identifies the source IP address.
source-wildcard	(Optional) Identifies which bits in the address field must match. A 1 in a bit position indicates "don't care" bits, and a 0 in any bit position indicates that bit must strictly match. If this field is omitted, the wildcard mask 0.0.0.0 is assumed.
any	Use this keyword as an abbreviation for a source and source-wildcard of 0.0.0.0 255.255.255.255.
log	(Optional) Sends an informational logging message about the packet that matches the entry to the console. Exercise caution when using this keyword, because it consumes CPU cycles.

When a packet does not match any of the configured lines in an access list, the packet is denied by default because there is an invisible line at the end of the access list that is equivalent to **deny any**. (**deny any** is the same as denying an address of 0.0.0.0 with a wildcard mask of 255.255.255.255.)

An access list can also contain the keyword **host**, which causes the address that immediately follows it to be treated as if it were specified with a mask of 0.0.0.0. For example, configuring **host 10.1.1.1** in an access list is equivalent to configuring **10.1.1.1 0.0.0.0**.

Use the **ip access-group** *access-list-number* {**in** | **out**} interface configuration command to link an existing access list to an interface, as shown in Table A-8. Each interface can have both an inbound and an outbound IP access list.

Table A-8   **ip access-group** *Command Description*

Parameter	Description
access-list-number	Indicates the number of the access list to be linked to this interface.
in | **out**	Processes packets arriving on or leaving from this interface. The default is **out**.

Eliminate the entire list by entering the **no access-list** *access-list-number* global configuration command. Remove an access list from an interface with the **no ip access-group** *access-list-number* {**in** | **out**} interface configuration command.

Implicit Wildcard Masks

Implicit, or default, wildcard masks reduce typing and simplify configuration, but you must take care when relying on the default mask.

The access list line in Example A-2 is an example of a specific host configuration. For standard access lists, if no wildcard mask is specified, the wildcard mask is assumed to be 0.0.0.0. The implicit mask makes it easier to enter a large number of individual addresses.

Example A-2   *Standard Access List Using the Default Wildcard Mask*

```
access-list 1 permit 172.16.5.17
```

Example A-3 illustrates common errors found in access list lines.

Example A-3   *Standard Access List Using the Default Wildcard Mask*

```
access-list 1 permit 0.0.0.0
access-list 2 permit 172.16.0.0
access-list 3 deny any
access-list 3 deny 0.0.0.0 255.255.255.255
```

The first list in Example A-3—**permit 0.0.0.0**—would match the address 0.0.0.0 exactly and then permit it. In most cases, this address is illegal, so this list would prevent all traffic from getting through (because of the implicit **deny any** at the end of the list).

The second list in Example A-3—**permit 172.16.0.0**—is probably a configuration error. The intention is probably 172.16.0.0 0.0.255.255. The exact address 172.16.0.0 refers to the network and would never be assigned to a host. As a result, nothing would get through with this list, again because of the implicit **deny any** at the end of the list. To filter networks or subnets, use an explicit wildcard mask.

The next two lines in Example A-3—**deny any** and **deny 0.0.0.0 255.255.255.255**—are unnecessary to configure because they duplicate the function of the implicit deny that occurs when a packet fails to match all the configured lines in an access list. Although not necessary, you might want to add one of these entries for record-keeping purposes.

Configuration Principles

The following general principles help ensure that the access lists you create have the intended results:

- Top-down processing
  - Organize your access list so that more specific references in a network or subnet appear before more general ones.
  - Place more frequently occurring conditions before less frequent conditions.
- Implicit **deny any**
  - Unless you end your access list with an explicit **permit any**, it denies all traffic that fails to match any of the access list lines.
- New lines added to the end
  - Subsequent additions are always added to the end of the access list.
  - You cannot selectively add or remove lines when using numbered access lists, but you can when using IP named access lists (a feature that is available in Cisco IOS Release 11.2 and later).
- Undefined access list = **permit any**
  - If you apply an access list with the **ip access-group** command to an interface before any access list lines have been created, the result will be **permit any**. The list is live, so if you only enter one line, it goes from a **permit any** to a **deny** *most* (because of the implicit **deny any**) when you press Return. For this reason, you should create your access list before applying it to an interface.

Standard Access List Example

Figure A-12 shows an example network, and the configuration on Router X in that figure is shown in Example A-4.

Figure A-12 *Network Used for Standard IP Access List Example*

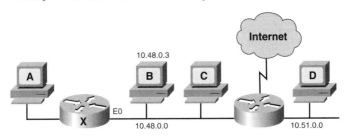

Example A-4 *Standard Access List Configuration of Router X in Figure A-12*

```
Router(config)#access-list 2 permit 10.48.0.3
Router(config)#access-list 2 deny 10.48.0.0 0.0.255.255
Router(config)#access-list 2 permit 10.0.0.0 0.255.255.255
Router(config)#!(Note: all other access implicitly denied)
Router(config)#interface ethernet 0
Router(config-if)#ip access-group 2 in
```

Consider which devices can communicate with Host A in this example:

- Host B can communicate with Host A. It is permitted by the first line of the access list, which uses an implicit host mask.

- Host C cannot communicate with Host A. Host C is in the subnet that is denied by the second line in the access list.

- Host D can communicate with Host A. Host D is on a subnet that is explicitly permitted by the access list's third line.

- Users on the Internet cannot communicate with Host A. Users outside of this network are not explicitly permitted, so they are denied by default with the implicit **deny any** at the end of the access list.

Location of Standard Access Lists

Access list location can be more of an art than a science, but Figure A-13 illustrates some general guidelines. An access list configuration for this network is shown in Example A-5. If the policy goal is to deny Host Z access to Host V on another network, and not to change any other access policy, determine on which interface of which router this access list should be configured.

Figure A-13 *Location of Standard IP Access List Example*

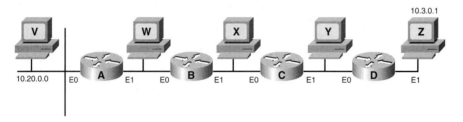

Example A-5 *Standard Access List to Be Configured on a Router in Figure A-13*

```
access-list 3 deny 10.3.0.1
access-list 3 permit any
```

The access list should be placed on Router A because a standard access list can only specify a source address. No hosts can connect beyond the point in the path at which the traffic is denied.

The access list could be configured as an outbound list on E0 of Router A; however, it would most likely be configured as an inbound list on E1 so that packets to be denied would not have to be routed through Router A first.

Consider the effect of placing the access list on other routers:

- **Router B**—Host Z could not connect with Host W (and Host V).
- **Router C**—Host Z could not connect with Hosts W and X (and Host V).
- **Router D**—Host Z could not connect with Hosts W, X, and Y (and Host V).

Key Point: Standard Access Lists Are Placed Close to the Destination

For standard access lists, the rule is to exercise the most control by placing them as close to the destination router as possible. However, this means that traffic is routed through the network, only to be denied close to its destination.

IP Extended Access Lists

Standard access lists offer quick configuration and low overhead while limiting traffic based on source addresses within a network. Extended access lists provide more control by enabling filtering based on the source and destination addresses, transport layer protocol, and application port number. These features make it possible to limit traffic based on the network's uses.

Extended Access List Processing

As shown in Figure A-14, every condition tested in an extended access list's line must match for the access list's line to match and the permit or deny condition to be applied. As soon as one parameter or condition fails, the next line in the access list is compared.

Figure A-14 *Extended IP Access List Processing Flow*

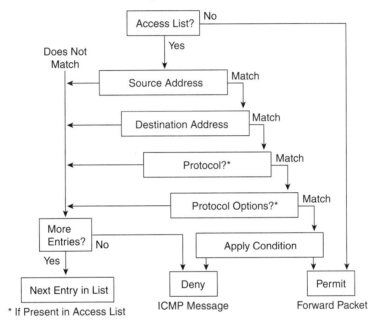

The extended access list checks source address, destination address, and protocol. Depending on the configured protocol, more protocol-dependent options might be tested. For example, a Transmission Control Protocol (TCP) port might be checked, thereby allowing routers to filter at the application layer.

Extended IP Access List Configuration

Use the **access-list** *access-list-number* {**permit** | **deny**} {*protocol* | *protocol-keyword*} {*source source-wildcard* | **any**} {*destination destination-wildcard* | **any**} [*protocol-specific options*] [**log**] global configuration command to create an entry in an extended traffic filter list. Table A-9 describes this command.

Table A-9 *Extended IP* **access-list** *Command Description*

Parameter	Description
access-list-number	Identifies the list to which the entry belongs (a number from 100 to 199).
permit | deny	Indicates whether this entry allows or blocks traffic.
protocol	**ip**, **tcp**, **udp**, **icmp**, **igmp**, **gre**, **igrp**, **eigrp**, **ospf**, **nos**, or a number from 0 to 255. Use the keyword **ip** to match any Internet protocol. As shown later in this section, some protocols allow more options that are supported by an alternate syntax for this command.
source and *destination*	Identifies the source and destination IP addresses.
source-wildcard and *destination-wildcard*	Identifies which bits in the address field must match. A 1 in a bit position indicates "don't care" bits, and a 0 in any bit position indicates that the bit must strictly match.
any	Use this keyword as an abbreviation for a source and source-wildcard, or a destination and destination-wildcard of 0.0.0.0 255.255.255.255.
log	(Optional) Sends to the console informational logging messages about a packet that matches the entry. Exercise caution when using this keyword, because it consumes CPU cycles.

The wildcard masks in an extended access list operate the same way as in standard access lists. The keyword **any** in either the source or the destination position matches any address and is equivalent to configuring an address of 0.0.0.0 with a wildcard mask of 255.255.255.255. Example A-6 shows an extended access list.

Example A-6 *Use of the Keyword* **any**

```
access-list 101 permit ip  0.0.0.0  255.255.255.255  0.0.0.0  255.255.255.255
! (alternate configuration)
access-list 101 permit ip any any
```

The keyword **host** can be used in either the source or the destination position; it causes the address immediately following to be treated as if it were specified with a mask of 0.0.0.0. Example A-7 shows an example.

Example A-7 *Use of the Keyword* **host**

```
access-list 101 permit ip  0.0.0.0  255.255.255.255  172.16.5.17  0.0.0.0
! (alternate configuration)
access-list 101 permit ip any host 172.16.5.17
```

Use the **access-list** *access-list-number* {**permit** | **deny**} **icmp** {*source source-wildcard* | **any**} {*destination destination-wildcard* | **any**} [*icmp-type* [*icmp-code*] | *icmp-message*] global configuration command to filter ICMP traffic. The protocol keyword **icmp** indicates that an alternate syntax is being used for this command and that protocol-specific options are available, as described in Table A-10.

Table A-10 *Extended IP* **access-list icmp** *Command Description*

Parameter	Description
access-list-number	Identifies the list to which the entry belongs (a number from 100 to 199).
permit | **deny**	Indicates whether this entry allows or blocks traffic.
source and *destination*	Identifies the source and destination IP addresses.
source-wildcard and *destination-wildcard*	Identifies which bits in the address field must match. A 1 in a bit position indicates "don't care" bits, and a 0 in any bit position indicates that the bit must strictly match.
any	Use this keyword as an abbreviation for a source and source-wildcard, or a destination and destination-wildcard of 0.0.0.0 255.255.255.255.
icmp-type	(Optional) Packets can be filtered by ICMP message type. The type is a number from 0 to 255.
icmp-code	(Optional) Packets that have been filtered by ICMP message type can also be filtered by ICMP message code. The code is a number from 0 to 255.
icmp-message	(Optional) Packets can be filtered by a symbolic name representing an ICMP message type, or by a combination of ICMP message type and ICMP message code. Table A-11 provides a list of these names.

Cisco IOS Release 10.3 and later versions provide symbolic names that simplify configuration and the reading of complex access lists. With symbolic names, understanding the meaning of the ICMP message type and code (for example, message eight and message zero can be used to filter the **ping** command) is no longer critical. Instead, the configuration can use symbolic names (for example, the **echo** and **echo-reply** symbolic names can be used to filter the **ping** command), as shown in Table A-11. (You can use the Cisco IOS context-sensitive help feature by entering **?** when entering the **access-list** command to verify the available names and proper command syntax.)

Table A-11 *ICMP Message and Type Names*

Administratively-prohibited	Information-reply	Precedence-unreachable
Alternate-address	Information-request	Protocol-unreachable
Conversion-error	Mask-reply	Reassembly-timeout

continues

Table A-11 *ICMP Message and Type Names (Continued)*

Dod-host-prohibited	Mask-request	Redirect
Dod-net-prohibited	Mobile-redirect	Router-advertisement
Echo	Net-redirect	Router-solicitation
Echo-reply	Net-tos-redirect	Source-quench
General-parameter-problem	Net-tos-unreachable	Source-route-failed
Host-isolated	Net-unreachable	Time-exceeded
Host-precedence-unreachable	Network-unknown	Timestamp-reply
Host-redirect	No-room-for-option	Timestamp-request
Host-tos-redirect	Option-missing	Traceroute
Host-tos-unreachable	Packet-too-big	TTL-exceeded
Host-unknown	Parameter-problem	Unreachable
Host-unreachable	Port-unreachable	

Use the **access-list** *access-list-number* {**permit** I **deny**} **tcp** {*source source-wildcard* I **any**} [*operator source-port* I *source-port*] {*destination destination-wildcard* I **any**} [*operator destination-port* I *destination-port*] [**established**] global configuration command to filter TCP traffic. The protocol keyword **tcp** indicates that an alternate syntax is being used for this command and that protocol-specific options are available, as described in Table A-12.

Table A-12 *Extended IP **access-list tcp** Command Description*

Parameter	Description
access-list-number	Identifies the list to which the entry belongs (a number from 100 to 199).
permit I **deny**	Indicates whether this entry allows or blocks traffic.
source and *destination*	Identifies the source and destination IP addresses.
source-wildcard and *destination-wildcard*	Identifies which bits in the address field must match. A 1 in a bit position indicates "don't care" bits, and a 0 in any bit position indicates that the bit must strictly match.
any	Use this keyword as an abbreviation for a source and source-wildcard, or a destination and destination-wildcard of 0.0.0.0 255.255.255.255.
operator	(Optional) A qualifying condition. Can be **lt**, **gt**, **eq**, or **neq**.
source-port and *destination-port*	(Optional) A decimal number from 0 to 65535, or a name that represents a TCP port number.
established	(Optional) A match occurs if the TCP segment has the ACK or RST bits set. Use this if you want a Telnet or another activity to be established in only one direction.

established Keyword in Extended Access Lists

When a TCP session is started between two devices, the first segment that is sent has the synchronize (SYN) code bit set; however, the segment header does not have the acknowledge (ACK) code bit set because it is not acknowledging any other segments. All subsequent segments that are sent do have the ACK code bit set because they are acknowledging previous segments sent by the other device. This is how a router can distinguish between a segment from a device that is attempting to start a TCP session and a segment of an ongoing already established session. The reset (RST) code bit is set when an established session is being terminated.

When you configure the **established** keyword in a TCP extended access list, it indicates that that access list statement should match only TCP segments in which the ACK or RST code bit is set. In other words, only segments that are part of an already *established* session will be matched; segments that are attempting to start a session will not match the access list statement.

Table A-13 is a list of TCP port names that can be used instead of port numbers. Port numbers corresponding to these protocols can be found by entering **?** in place of a port number, or by looking at RFC 1700, *Assigned Numbers*. (This RFC is available at www.cis.ohio-state.edu/cgi-bin/rfc/rfc1700.html.)

Table A-13 *TCP Port Names*

Bgp	Hostname	Syslog
Chargen	Irc	Tacacs-ds
Daytime	Klogin	Talk
Discard	Kshell	telnet
Domain	Lpd	Time
Echo	nntp	Uucp
Finger	Pop2	Whois
ftp control	Pop3	www
ftp-data	Smtp	
Gopher	Sunrpc	

Other port numbers can also be found in RFC 1700, *Assigned Numbers*. Table A-14 shows a partial list of the assigned TCP port numbers.

Table A-14   *Some Reserved TCP Port Numbers*

Port Number (Decimal)	Keyword	Description
7	ECHO	Echo
9	DISCARD	Discard
13	DAYTIME	Daytime
19	CHARGEN	Character generator
20	FTP-DATA	File Transfer Protocol (data)
21	FTP-CONTROL	File Transfer Protocol
23	TELNET	Terminal connection
25	SMTP	Simple Mail Transfer Protocol
37	TIME	Time of day
43	WHOIS	Who is
53	DOMAIN	Domain name server
79	FINGER	Finger
80	WWW	World Wide Web HTTP
101	HOSTNAME	NIC host name server

Use the **access-list** *access-list-number* {permit | **deny**} **udp** {*source source-wildcard* | **any**} [*operator source-port* | *source-port*] {*destination destination-wildcard* | **any**} [*operator destination-port* | *destination-port*] global configuration command to filter User Datagram Protocol (UDP) traffic. The protocol keyword **udp** indicates that an alternate syntax is being used for this command and that protocol-specific options are available, as described in Table A-15.

Table A-15   *Extended IP **access-list udp** Command Description*

Parameter	Description
access-list-number	Identifies the list to which the entry belongs (a number from 100 to 199).
**permit	deny**	Indicates whether this entry allows or blocks traffic.
source and *destination*	Identifies the source and destination IP addresses.
source-wildcard and *destination-wildcard*	Identifies which bits in the address field must match. A 1 in a bit position indicates "don't care" bits, and a 0 in any bit position indicates that bit must strictly match.

continues

Table A-15   *Extended IP* **access-list udp** *Command Description (Continued)*

Parameter	Description
any	Use this keyword as an abbreviation for a source and source-wildcard, or a destination and destination-wildcard of 0.0.0.0 255.255.255.255.
operator	(Optional) A qualifying condition. Can be **lt**, **gt**, **eq**, or **neq**.
source-port and *destination-port*	(Optional) A decimal number from 0 to 65535, or a name that represents a UDP port number.

Table A-16 is a list of UDP port names that can be used instead of port numbers. Port numbers corresponding to these protocols can be found by entering **?** in place of a port number, or by looking at RFC 1700, *Assigned Numbers*.

Table A-16   *UDP Port Names*

Biff	Nameserver	Syslog
Bootpc	NetBios-dgm	Tacasds-ds
Bootps	NetBios-ns	Talk
Discard	Ntp	Tftp
Dns	Rip	Time
Dnsix	Snmp	Whois
Echo	Snmptrap	Xdmcp
Mobile-ip	Sunrpc	

Other port numbers can also be found in RFC 1700, *Assigned Numbers*. Table A-17 shows a partial list of the assigned UDP port numbers.

Table A-17   *Some Reserved UDP Port Numbers*

Port Number (Decimal)	Keyword	Description
7	ECHO	Echo
9	DISCARD	Discard
37	TIME	Time of day
42	NAMESERVER	Host name server
43	WHOIS	Who is
53	DNS	Domain name server
67	BOOTPS	Bootstrap protocol server

continues

Table A-17 *Some Reserved UDP Port Numbers (Continued)*

Port Number (Decimal)	Keyword	Description
68	BOOTPC	Bootstrap protocol client
69	TFTP	Trivial File Transfer Protocol
123	NTP	Network Time Protocol
137	NetBIOS-ns	NetBIOS Name Service
138	NetBIOS-dgm	NetBIOS Datagram Service
161	SNMP	SNMP
162	SNMPTrap	SNMP Traps
520	RIP	RIP

Extended Access List Examples

In the example shown in Figure A-15, Router A's interface Ethernet 1 is part of a Class B subnet with the address 172.22.3.0, Router A's interface Serial 0 is connected to the Internet, and the e-mail server's address is 172.22.1.2. Example A-8 shows the access list configuration that is applied to Router A.

Figure A-15 *Network Used for Extended IP Access List Example*

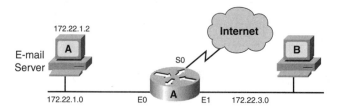

Example A-8 *Configuration on Router A in Figure A-15*

```
access-list 104 permit tcp any 172.22.0.0 0.0.255.255 established
access-list 104 permit tcp any host 172.22.1.2 eq smtp
access-list 104 permit udp any any eq dns
access-list 104 permit icmp any any echo
access-list 104 permit icmp any any echo-reply
!
interface serial 0
  ip access-group 104 in
```

In Example A-8, access list 104 is applied inbound on Router A's Serial 0 interface. The keyword **established** is only used for the TCP protocol to indicate an established connection. A match occurs if the TCP segment has the ACK or RST bits set, indicating that the packet belongs to an existing connection. If the session is not already established (the ACK bit is not set and the SYN bit is set), someone on the Internet is attempting to initialize a session and the packet is therefore denied. This configuration also permits Simple Mail Transfer Protocol (SMTP) traffic from any address to the e-mail server. UDP domain name server (DNS) packets and ICMP echo and echo-reply packets are also permitted from any address to any other address.

Figure A-16 shows another similar example, and Example A-9 shows the access list configuration that is applied to Router A.

Figure A-16 *Extended IP Access List Example with Many Servers*

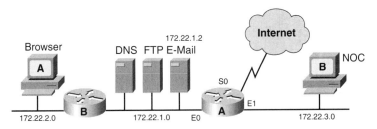

Example A-9 *Configuration on Router A in Figure A-16*

```
access-list 118 permit tcp any 172.22.0.0  0.0.255.255 eq www established
access-list 118 permit tcp any host 172.22.1.2 eq smtp
access-list 118 permit udp any any eq dns
access-list 118 permit udp 172.22.3.0  0.0.0.255 172.22.1.0 0.0.0.255 eq snmp
access-list 118 deny icmp any 172.22.0.0  0.0.255.255 echo
access-list 118 permit icmp any any echo-reply
!
interface ethernet 0
  ip access-group 118 out
```

In Example A-9, access list 118 is applied outbound on Router A's Ethernet 0 interface. With the configuration shown in Example A-9, replies to queries from the Client A browser to the Internet will be allowed back into the corporate network (because they are established sessions). Browser queries from external sources are not explicitly allowed and will be discarded by the implicit **deny any** at the end of the access list.

The access list in Example A-9 also allows e-mail (SMTP) to be delivered exclusively to the mail server. The name server is permitted to resolve DNS requests. The 172.22.1.0 subnet is controlled by the network management group located at the Network Operations Center (NOC) server (Client B), so network-management queries (Simple Network

Management Protocol [SNMP]) will be allowed to reach these devices in the server farm. Attempts to ping the corporate network from outside, or from subnet 172.22.3.0, will fail because the access list blocks the echo requests. However, the replies to echo requests generated from within the corporate network will be allowed to re-enter the network.

Location of Extended Access Lists

Because extended access lists can filter on more than source address, location is no longer the constraint it was when considering the location of a standard access list. Policy decisions and goals are frequently the driving forces behind extended access list placement.

If your goal is to minimize traffic congestion and maximize performance, you might want to push the access lists close to the source to minimize cross-traffic and administratively prohibited ICMP messages. If your goal is to maintain tight control over access lists as part of your network security strategy, you might want them to be more centrally located. Notice how changing network goals affects access list configuration.

Some things to consider when placing extended access lists include the following:

- Minimize the distance traveled by traffic that will be denied (and ICMP unreachable messages).
- Keep denied traffic off the backbone.
- Select the router to receive CPU overhead from access lists.
- Consider the number of interfaces affected.
- Consider access list management and security.
- Consider network growth impacts on access list maintenance.

Restricting Virtual Terminal Access

This section discusses how standard access lists can be used to limit virtual terminal access.

Standard and extended access lists block packets from going through the router. They are not designed to block packets that originate within the router. An outbound Telnet extended access list does not prevent router-initiated Telnet sessions by default.

For security purposes, users can be denied virtual terminal (vty) access to the router, or they can be permitted vty access to the router but denied access to destinations from that router. Restricting virtual terminal access is less of a traffic-control mechanism than a technique for increasing network security.

Because vty access is accomplished using the Telnet protocol, there is only one type of vty access list.

How to Control vty Access

Just as a router has physical ports or interfaces such as Ethernet 0 and Ethernet 1, it also has virtual ports. These virtual ports are called virtual terminal lines. By default, there are five such virtual terminal lines, numbered vty 0 through 4. These are shown in Figure A-17.

Figure A-17 *A Router Has Five Virtual Terminal Lines (Virtual Ports) by Default*

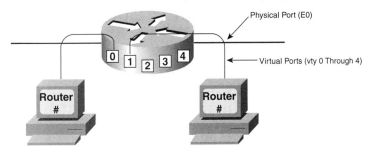

You should set identical restrictions on all virtual terminal lines because you cannot control on which virtual terminal line a user will connect.

NOTE   Some experts recommend that you configure one of the vty terminal lines differently than the others. This gives you a back door into the router.

Virtual Terminal Line Access Configuration

Use the **line vty** {*vty-number* | *vty-range*} global configuration command to place the router in line configuration mode, as described in Table A-18.

Table A-18   **line vty** *Command Description*

Parameter	Description
vty-number	Indicates the number of the vty line to be configured.
vty-range	Indicates the range of vty lines to which the configuration will apply.

Use the **access-class** *access-list-number* {**in** | **out**} line configuration command to link an existing access list to a terminal line or range of lines, as described in Table A-19.

Table A-19   **access-class** *Command Description*

Parameter	Description
access-list-number	Indicates the number of the standard access list to be linked to a terminal line. This is a decimal number from 1 to 99.
in	Prevents the router from receiving incoming connections from the addresses in the access list.
out	Prevents someone from initiating a Telnet to addresses that are defined in the access list.

NOTE   When using the **out** keyword in the **access-class** command, the addresses in the specified standard access list are treated as destination addresses rather than source addresses.

In the example configuration in Example A-10, any device on network 192.168.55.0 is permitted to establish a virtual terminal (Telnet) session with the router. Of course, the user must know the appropriate passwords for entering user mode and privileged mode.

Example A-10 *Configuration to Restrict Telnet Access to a Router*

```
access-list 12 permit 192.168.55.0 0.0.0.255
!
line vty 0 4
  access-class 12 in
```

Notice that, in this example, identical restrictions have been set on all virtual terminal lines (0 to 4) because you cannot control on which virtual terminal line a user will connect. (Note that the implicit **deny any** still applies to this alternate application of access lists.)

Verifying Access List Configuration

As described in Table A-20, use the **show access-lists** [*access-list-number* | *name*] privileged EXEC command to display access lists from all protocols. If no parameters are specified, all access lists will be displayed.

Table A-20   **show access-lists** *Command Description*

Parameter	Description
access-list-number	(Optional) Number of the access list to display
name	(Optional) Name of the access list to display

The system counts how many packets match each line of an extended access list; the **show access-lists** command displays the counters.

Example A-11 illustrates an example output from the **show access-lists** command. In this example, the first line of the access list has been matched three times, and the last line has been matched 629 times. The second line has not been matched.

Example A-11 *Output of the* **show access-lists** *Command*

```
P1r1#show access-lists
Extended IP access list 100
    deny tcp host 10.1.1.2 host 10.1.1.1 eq telnet (3 matches)
    deny tcp host 10.1.2.2 host 10.1.2.1 eq telnet
    permit ip any any (629 matches)
```

Use the **show ip access-list** [*access-list-number | name*] EXEC command to display IP access lists, as described in Table A-21. If no parameters are specified, all IP access lists will be displayed.

Table A-21   **show ip access-list** *Command Description*

Parameter	Description
access-list-number	(Optional) Number of the IP access list to display
name	(Optional) Name of the IP access list to display

Use the **clear access-list counters** [*access-list-number | name*] EXEC command to clear the counters for the number of matches in an extended access list, as described in Table A-22. If no parameters are specified, the counters will be cleared for all access lists.

Table A-22   **clear access-list counters** *Command Description*

Parameter	Description
access-list-number	(Optional) Number of the access list for which to clear the counters
name	(Optional) Name of the access list for which to clear the counters

Use the **show line** [*line-number*] EXEC command to display information about terminal lines. The *line-number* is optional and indicates the absolute line number of the line for which you want to list parameters. All lines are displayed if a line number is not specified.

Review Questions

Answer the following questions and then refer to Appendix G, "Answers to the Review Questions, Case Studies, and Simulation Exercises," for the answers.

1 You need to design an IP network for your organization. Your organization's IP address is 172.16.0.0. Your assessment indicates that the organization needs at least 130 networks with no more than 100 nodes in each network.

   As a result, you have decided to use a classful subnetting scheme based on the 172.16.0.0/24 scheme. Write any four IP addresses that are part of the range of subnetwork numbers, and write the subnet address and subnet mask for these addresses. An example is the address 172.16.1.0/24, which can also be written as 172.16.1.0 255.255.255.0.

2 Your network has the address 172.16.168.0/21. Write eight IP addresses in this network.

3 Write the four IP addresses in the range described by the 192.168.99.16/30 address.

4 Of the four addresses in question 3, which two could you use as host addresses in a point-to-point connection?

5 Figure A-18 shows the network for this question.

   Create an access list and place it in the proper location to satisfy the following requirements:

   — Prevent all hosts on subnet 172.16.1.0/24, except host 172.16.1.3, from accessing the web server on subnet 172.16.4.0. Allow all other hosts, including from the outside world, to access the web server.

   — Prevent the outside world from pinging subnet 172.16.4.0.

   — Allow all hosts on all subnets of network 172.16.0.0 (using subnet mask 255.255.255.0) to send queries to the DNS server on subnet 172.16.4.0. The outside world is not allowed to access the DNS server.

   — Prevent host 172.16.3.3 from accessing subnet 172.16.4.0 for any reason.

   — Prevent all other access to the 172.16.4.0 subnet.

Figure A-18 *Network for Review Question 5*

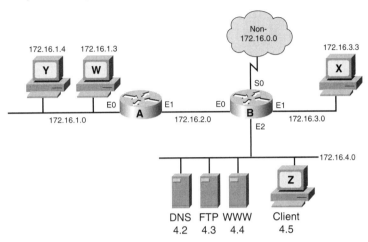

In your configuration, be sure to include the router name (A or B), interface name (E0, E1, or E2), and access list direction (in or out).

6 What do bits set to 1 in a wildcard mask indicate when matching an address?

7 By default, what happens to all traffic in an access list?

8 To save network resources, where should an extended access list be placed?

9 Using the keyword **host** in an access list is a substitute for using a wildcard mask of what value?

References

This appendix lists the websites and other external readings referred to throughout this book. They are listed by chapter or appendix..

NOTE The website references in this book were correct when this book was written. However, they might change. If you cannot find the document referenced, you might try searching for the information using either the Cisco website search facility or a general search engine.

NOTE This list does not include RFCs , which are all listed in Appendix E, "Common Requests For Comments."

Table B-1 lists referenced books.

Table B-1   *Books Referenced in Chapters and Appendixes*

Location	Book
Overview	McQuerry, Steve. *CCNA Self-Study: Interconnecting Cisco Network Devices.* Cisco Press, 2000
Chapter 1	Chappell, Laura. *Introduction to Cisco Routers.* Cisco Press, 1999
Chapter 3	Paquet, Catherine. *Building Cisco Remote Access Networks (BCRAN).* Cisco Press, 1999
	Oppenheimer, Priscilla. *Top-Down Network Design: A Systems Analysis Approach to Enterprise Network Design.* Cisco Press, 1999
Chapter 6	Comer, Douglas E. and David L. Stevens. *Internetworking with TCP/IP.* Prentice-Hall, 1991
	Bradner, Scott O. and Allison Mankin. *IPng Internet Protocol Next Generation.* Addison-Wesley, 1995
Chapter 7	Paquet, Catherine and Diane Teare. *CCNP Self-Study: Building Scalable Cisco Internetworks (BSCI).* Cisco Press, 2004
	McQuerry, Steve. *CCNA Self-Study: Interconnecting Cisco Network Devices.* Cisco Press, 2000
Chapter 8	Davidson, Jonathan, James Peters, and Brian Gracely. *Voice over IP Fundamentals.* Cisco Press, 2000
Chapter 10	Stallings, W. *SNMP, SNMPv2 and CMIP.* Addison-Wesley, 1993
	Leinwand, F. and K. Fang. *Network Management.* Addison-Wesley, 1993
Appendix D	McQuerry, Steve. *CCNA Self-Study: Interconnecting Cisco Network Devices.* Cisco Press, 2000

Table B-2 lists other readings.

Table B-2 *Other Readings*

Location	Title	Reference Information
Chapter 2	Network Based Application Recognition (NBAR)	www.cisco.com/en/US/customer/products/sw/iosswrel/ps1839/ products_feature_guide09186a0080087cd0.html (Note: You must be a registered user to access this document.)
	NetFlow Switching Overview	www.cisco.com/en/US/customer/products/sw/iosswrel/ps1831/ products_configuration_guide_chapter09186a00800ca6cb.html (Note: You must be a registered user to access this document.)
	FlowCollector Overview	www.cisco.com/en/US/customer/products/sw/netmgtsw/ps1964/ products_installation_and_configuration_guide_chapter09186a0080 080e4a.html (Note: You must be a registered user to access this document.)
	Network Data Analyzer Overview	www.cisco.com/en/US/customer/products/sw/netmgtsw/ps1974/ products_installation_guide_chapter09186a008007fb79.html (Note: You must be a registered user to access this document.)
Chapter 3	SAFE White Paper: A Security Blueprint for Enterprise Networks	www.cisco.com/go/safe
	"Internetworking Design Basics" chapter of *Cisco Internetwork Design Guide*	www.cisco.com/univercd/cc/td/doc/cisintwk/idg4/nd2002.htm
	SAFE: Extending the Security Blueprint to Small, Midsize, and Remote-user Networks	www.cisco.com/go/safe
	Cisco Architecture for Voice, Video and Integrated Data White Paper	www.cisco.com/warp/public/cc/so/neso/vvda/iptl/avvid_wp.htm
	Cisco Enterprise Solutions: Cisco Content Delivery Networks	www.cisco.com/en/US/netsol/ns110/ns49/net_solution_home.html
Chapter 4	Implementing Quality of Service Policies with DSCP	www.cisco.com/en/US/tech/tk543/tk757/ technologies_tech_note09186a00800949f2.shtml
	Introduction to Gigabit Ethernet	www.cisco.com/warp/public/cc/techno/media/lan/gig/tech/ gigbt_tc.htm
	Gigabit Campus Network Design—Principles and Architecture	www.cisco.com/warp/public/cc/so/neso/lnso/cpso/gcnd_wp.htm

Table B-2   *Other Readings (Continued)*

Location	Title	Reference Information
	SAFE: A Security Blueprint for Enterprise Networks	www.cisco.com/go/safe
	LAN Design Guide for the Midmarket	www.cisco.com/warp/public/cc/pd/si/casi/ca3500xl/prodlit/lan_dg.htm
	Recovering From errDisable Port State on the CatOS Platforms	www.cisco.com/en/US/tech/tk389/tk214/technologies_tech_note09186a0080093dcb.shtml
	Configuring RGMP	www.cisco.com/en/US/products/hw/switches/ps708/products_configuration_guide_chapter09186a008007e6f8.html
	Securing Networks with Private VLANs and VLAN Access Control Lists	www.cisco.com/en/US/products/hw/switches/ps700/products_tech_note09186a008013565f.shtml
Chapter 5	DSL frequently asked questions (FAQs) and their answers	www.cisco.com/en/US/partner/netsol/ns110/ns10/ns11/ns55/netqa09186a00800a3764.html (Note: You must be a registered user to access this document.)
	Cisco Product Documentation	www.cisco.com/univercd
	IT-related definitions and acronyms	www.whatis.com/
	Virtual Private Networks	www.cisco.com/warp/public/779/largeent/learn/technologies/VPNs.html
	Managed VPN Services	www.cisco.com/warp/public/779/servpro/services/vpn/
	DOCSIS Radio Frequency (RF) Interface Specification	www.cablemodem.com/downloads/specs/SP-RFIv2.0-I03-021218.pdf
Chapter 6	ABCs of IP Version 6	www.cisco.com/warp/public/732/abc/docs/abcipv6.pdf
	Designing Large-scale IP Internetworks	www.cisco.com/univercd/cc/td/doc/cisintwk/idg4/nd2003.htm
	Subnetting an IP Address Space	www.cisco.com/univercd/cc/td/doc/cisintwk/idg4/nd20a.htm
	Cisco IP Version 6 Solutions	www.cisco.com/univercd/cc/td/doc/cisintwk/intsolns/ipv6_sol/index.htm
	Cisco IOS IPv6	www.cisco.com/warp/public/732/Tech/ipv6
	Cisco IOS Software Release Specifics for IPv6 Features	www.cisco.com/univercd/cc/td/doc/product/software/ios123/123cgcr/ipv6_c/ftipv6s.htm
Chapter 7	Configuring Large-scale Dial-out	www.cisco.com/en/US/partner/products/sw/iosswrel/ps1835/products_configuration_guide_chapter09186a00800ca6ef.html (Note: You must be a registered user to access this document.)

continues

Table B-2   *Other Readings (Continued)*

Location	Title	Reference Information
	IGRP Metric	www.cisco.com/warp/public/103/3.html
	Designing Large-scale IP Internetworks	www.cisco.com/univercd/cc/td/doc/cisintwk/idg4/nd2003.htm
	OSPF Incremental SPF	www.cisco.com/univercd/cc/td/doc/product/software/ios120/ 120newft/120limit/120s/120s24/ospfispf.htm
	IP Summary Address for RIPv2	www.cisco.com/en/US/products/sw/iosswrel/ps1830/ products_feature_guide09186a0080087ad1.html
Chapter 8	Telephony Signaling	www.cisco.com/pcgi-bin/Support/browse/ index.pl?i=Technologies&f=775
	Voice Network Signaling and Control	www.cisco.com/warp/public/788/signalling/net_signal_control.html
	Waveform Coding Techniques	www.cisco.com/warp/public/788/signalling/ waveform_coding.html#subfirstsix
	Voice—Understanding How Inbound and Outbound Dial Peers are Matched on Cisco IOS Platforms	www.cisco.com/warp/public/788/voip/in_dial_peer_match.html
	Architecture for Voice, Video, and Integrated Data White Paper	www.cisco.com/warp/public/cc/so/neso/vvda/iptl/avvid_wp.htm
	Understanding Codecs: Complexity, Support, MOS, and Negotiation	www.cisco.com/warp/public/788/voip/codec_complexity.html
	Voice over IP (VoIP) and Frame Relay (VoFR) and ATM (VoATM)	www.cisco.com/pcgi-bin/Support/browse/ index.pl?i=Technologies&f=1533
	Understanding Delay in Packet Voice Networks	www.cisco.com/warp/public/788/voip/delay-details.html
	QoS Features for Voice	www.cisco.com/univercd/cc/td/doc/product/software/ios121/ 121cgcr/qos_c/qcprt7/qcdvoice.htm
	Configuring Quality of Service for Voice	www.cisco.com/univercd/cc/td/doc/product/software/ios122/ 122cgcr/fvvfax_c/vvfqos.htm
	Traffic Analysis for VoIP	www.cisco.com/univercd/cc/td/doc/cisintwk/intsolns/voipsol/ ta_isd.htm
	Echo Analysis for VoIP	www.cisco.com/en/US/partner/tech/tk652/tk701/ technologies_white_paper09186a00800d6b68.shtml

(Note: You must be a registered user to access this document.) |

Table B-2   *Other Readings (Continued)*

Location	Title	Reference Information
	CallManager Product Literature	www.cisco.com/warp/public/cc/pd/nemnsw/callmn/prodlit/index.shtml
	Quality of Service Deployments: Cisco AutoQoS	www.cisco.com/warp/public/732/Tech/qos/docs/autoqos_datasheet.pdf
	CiscoWorks QoS Policy Manager 3.0	www.cisco.com/en/US/products/sw/cscowork/ps2064/ps4622/index.html
Chapter 9	Configuring TCP Intercept (Preventing Denial-of-Service Attacks)	www.cisco.com/en/US/partner/products/sw/iosswrel/ps1831/products_configuration_guide_chapter09186a00800d9818.html (Note: You must be a registered user to access this document.)
	Cisco SAFE: A Security Blueprint for Enterprise Networks White Paper	www.cisco.com/go/safe
	Cisco SAFE: Wireless LAN Security in Depth, Version 2 White Paper	www.cisco.com/go/safe
	Cisco SAFE: IP Telephony Security in Depth White Paper	www.cisco.com/go/safe
	Cisco SAFE: Extending the Security Blueprint to Small, Midsize, and Remote-user Networks White Paper	www.cisco.com/go/safe
	Secure Shell Version 1 Support	www.cisco.com/univercd/cc/td/doc/product/software/ios120/120newft/120limit/120s/120s5/sshv1.htm
	Auto Update Server and VMS Information	www.cisco.com/go/vms
Chapter 10	Cisco Management Information Base (MIB) User Quick Reference	www.cisco.com/univercd/cc/td/doc/product/software/ios112/mbook/index.htm
	NetFlow Services Solutions Guide	www.cisco.com/en/US/customer/products/sw/netmgtsw/ps1964/products_implementation_design_guide09186a00800d6a11.html (Note: You must be a registered user to access this document.)
	Cisco IOS System Error Messages	www.cisco.com/univercd/cc/td/doc/product/software/ios122/122sup/122sems/index.htm
	Network Management System: Best Practices White Paper	www.cisco.com/warp/public/126/NMS_bestpractice.html

continues

Table B-2 *Other Readings (Continued)*

Location	Title	Reference Information
	Service Level Management: Best Practices White Paper	www.cisco.com/warp/public/126/sla.htm
	Service-Level Management: Defining and Monitoring Service Levels in the Enterprise White Paper	www.cisco.com/warp/public/cc/pd/wr2k/svmnso/prodlit/srlm_wp.htm
	Internetwork Performance Monitor product documentation	www.cisco.com/univercd/cc/td/doc/product/rtrmgmt/ipmcw2k/index.htm
	Service Level Manager product documentation	www.cisco.com/univercd/cc/td/doc/product/rtrmgmt/cw2000/slm/index.htm
	Deploying Service-level Management in an Enterprise Network Environment White Paper	www.cisco.com/en/US/partner/products/sw/cscowork/ps2428/products_white_paper09186a0080092498.shtml (Note: You must be a registered user to access this document.)
	IPSec—SNMP Support	www.cisco.com/univercd/cc/td/doc/product/software/ios121/121newft/121limit/121e/121e4/dtipmib.htm
	Cisco Discovery Protocol (CDP)	www.cisco.com/en/US/tech/tk648/tk362/tk100/tech_protocol_home.html
	Cisco IOS Quality of Service Solutions Configuration Guide	www.cisco.com/univercd/cc/td/doc/product/software/ios122/122cgcr/fqos_c/index.htm
	QoS Features for Voice	www.cisco.com/univercd/cc/td/doc/product/software/ios122/122cgcr/fqos_c/fqcprt7/qcfvoice.htm
Appendix F	Product Bulletin No. 792 Cisco IOS Network Address Translation (NAT) Packaging Update	www.cisco.com/warp/public/cc/pd/iosw/ioft/ionetn/prodlit/792_pp.htm

Table B-3 lists other website references.

Table B-3   *Website References*

Chapter	Item	Location/Reference Information
Chapter 2	Opera browser	www.opera.com/
	HP OpenView	www.openview.hp.com/
	Microsoft Visio Enterprise Network Tools	www.microsoft.com/office/visio/evaluation/indepth/network.asp
	NetZoom	www.altimatech.com/home/index.php
	IBM Tivoli	www.tivoli.com
	Whatsup Gold	www.ipswitch.com/Products/WhatsUp/index.html
	SNMPc	www.castlerock.com/
	MRTG	www.mrtg.org/
	Net Inspector Lite	www.mg-soft.si/netinsp-lite.html
	Sniffer	www.sniffer.com/
	Active Network Monitor	www.protect-me.com/anm/
	EtherPeek	www.wildpackets.com/
	Converged Network Investment Calculator (CNIC)	www.cisco.com/cgi-bin/front.x/roi/cnicHome.pl (Note: You must be a registered user to access this document.)
Chapter 6	Internet Assigned Numbers Authority (IANA)	www.iana.org/
Chapter 8	Erlang information from Westbay Engineers Limited	www.erlang.com
	Erlang table calculator	www.erlang.com/calculator/erlb/
Chapter 9	IEEE 802.1x	standards.ieee.org/getieee802/802.1.html
	Arpwatch utility	www-nrg.ee.lbl.gov/nrg.html
Chapter 10	Cisco MIB definitions	www.cisco.com/public/mibs
	Concord	www.concord.com/
	Infovista	www.infovista.com/
	Agilent	www.agilent.com
	Service Assurance Agent product page	www.cisco.com/go/saa

This appendix contains information on the Open System Interconnection (OSI) Reference Model. It includes the following sections:

- Characteristics of the OSI Layers
- Protocols
- OSI Model and Communication Between Systems
- OSI Model's Physical Layer
- OSI Model's Data Link Layer
- OSI Model's Network Layer
- OSI Model's Transport Layer
- OSI Model's Session Layer
- OSI Model's Presentation Layer
- OSI Model's Application Layer
- Information Formats

Open System Interconnection (OSI) Reference Model

The *Open System Interconnection (OSI)* reference model describes how information from a software application in one computer moves through a network medium to a software application in another computer. The OSI reference model is a conceptual model that is composed of seven layers, each specifying particular network functions. The International Organization for Standardization (ISO) developed the model in 1984. It is now considered the primary architectural model for intercomputer communications. The OSI model divides the tasks involved with moving information between networked computers into seven smaller, more manageable task groups. A task or group of tasks is assigned to each of the seven OSI layers. Each layer is reasonably self-contained so that the tasks assigned to each can be implemented independently. This enables the solutions offered by one layer to be updated without adversely affecting the other layers. The following list details the OSI reference model's seven layers:

- Layer 7—Application layer
- Layer 6—Presentation layer
- Layer 5—Session layer
- Layer 4—Transport layer
- Layer 3—Network layer
- Layer 2—Data link layer
- Layer 1—Physical layer

Figure C-1 illustrates the seven-layer OSI reference model.

Figure C-1   *The OSI Reference Model Contains Seven Independent Layers*

7	Application
6	Presentation
5	Session
4	Transport
3	Network
2	Data link
1	Physical

Characteristics of the OSI Layers

The OSI reference model's seven layers can be divided into two categories: upper layers and lower layers.

The upper layers contend with application issues and are generally only implemented in software. The highest layer, the application layer, is closest to the end user. Both users and application layer processes interact with software applications that contain a communications component. The term *upper layer* is sometimes used to refer to any layer above another layer in the OSI model.

Terminology: Upper Layers

Generally speaking, the term *upper layers* is often used to refer to Layers 5, 6, and 7; however, this terminology is relative.

The OSI model's *lower layers* handle data transport issues. The physical layer and the data link layer are implemented in hardware and software. The other lower layers are generally only implemented in software. The lowest layer, which is the physical layer, is closest to the physical network medium (for example, the network cabling) and is responsible for actually placing information on the medium.

Terminology: Lower Layers

Generally speaking, the term *lower layers* is often used to refer to Layers 1 through 4; however, this terminology is relative.

Figure C-2 illustrates the division between the upper and lower OSI layers.

Figure C-2   *Two Sets of Layers Comprise the OSI Layers*

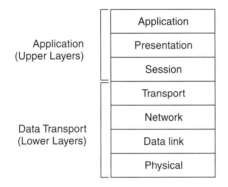

Application
(Upper Layers)

| Application |
| Presentation |
| Session |

Data Transport
(Lower Layers)

| Transport |
| Network |
| Data link |
| Physical |

Protocols

Although the OSI model provides a conceptual framework for communication between computers, the model itself is not a method of communication. Actual communication is made possible through communication protocols. In the context of data networking, a *protocol* is a formal set of rules and conventions that governs how computers exchange information over a network medium. A protocol implements the functions of one or more OSI layers. A wide variety of communication protocols exist, but they all tend to fall into one of the following groups: LAN protocols, WAN protocols, network protocols, or routing protocols. *LAN protocols* operate at the physical and data link layers of the OSI model and define communication over the various LAN media. *WAN protocols* operate at the lowest three layers of the OSI model and define communication over the various wide-area media. *Routing protocols* are network-layer protocols that are responsible for path determination and traffic switching. Finally, *network protocols* are the various upper-layer protocols that exist in a given protocol suite.

OSI Model and Communication Between Systems

When information is transferred from a software application in one computer system to a software application in another computer system, it must pass through each of the OSI layers. For example, if a software application in System A has information to transmit to a software application in System B, the application program in System A passes its information to System A's application layer (Layer 7). Next, the application layer passes the information to the presentation layer (Layer 6), which relays the data to the session layer (Layer 5), and so on, down to the physical layer (Layer 1). At the physical layer, the information is placed on the physical network medium and sent across the medium to

System B. System B's physical layer removes the information from the physical medium. Its physical layer then passes the information up to the data link layer (Layer 2), which passes it to the network layer (Layer 3), and so on, until it reaches System B's application layer (Layer 7). Finally, System B's application layer passes the information to the recipient application program to complete the communication process.

Interaction Between OSI Model Layers

A given OSI layer generally communicates with three other OSI layers: the layer directly above it, the layer directly below it, and its peer layer in other networked computer systems. For example, System A's data link layer communicates with System A's network layer, System A's physical layer, and System B's data link layer. Figure C-3 illustrates this interaction example.

Figure C-3   *An OSI Model Layer Communicates with Three Other Layers*

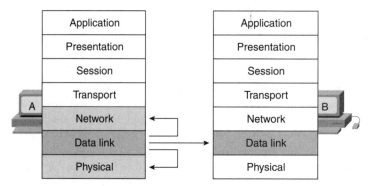

OSI Layer Services

One OSI layer communicates with another layer to make use of the services provided by the second layer. The services provided by adjacent layers help a given OSI layer communicate with its peer layer in other computer systems. Layer services involves three basic elements: the service user, the service provider, and the service access point (SAP).

In this context, the *service user* is the OSI layer that requests services from an adjacent OSI layer. The *service provider* is the OSI layer that provides services to service users. OSI layers can provide services to multiple service users. The *SAP* is a conceptual location at which one OSI layer can request the services of another OSI layer.

Figure C-4 illustrates how these three elements interact at the network and data link layers.

Figure C-4   *Service Users, Providers, and SAPs Interact at the Network and Data Link Layers*

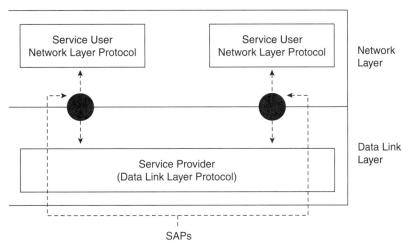

OSI Model Layers and Information Exchange

The seven OSI layers use various forms of control information to communicate with their peer layers in other computer systems. This control information consists of specific requests and instructions that are exchanged between peer OSI layers.

Control information typically takes one of two forms: headers and trailers. *Headers* are prepended to data that has been passed down from upper layers. *Trailers* are appended to data that has been passed down from upper layers. An OSI layer is not required for attaching a header or trailer to data from upper layers.

Depending on the layer that analyzes the information unit, headers, trailers, and data are relative concepts. An information unit, for example, consists of a Layer 3 header and data at the network layer. At the data link layer, however, all the information passed down by the network layer (the Layer 3 header and the data) is treated as data.

In other words, the data portion of an information unit at a given OSI layer can potentially contain headers, trailers, and data from all the higher layers. This is known as *encapsulation*. Figure C-5 illustrates how the header and data from one layer are encapsulated to become the data of the next lowest layer.

Figure C-5   *Headers and Data Are Encapsulated During Information Exchange*

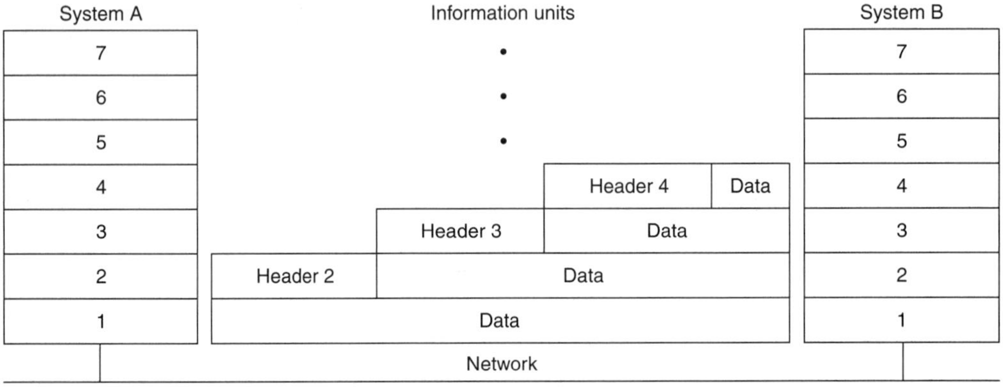

Information Exchange Process

The information exchange process occurs between peer OSI layers. Each layer in the source system adds control information to data, and each layer in the destination system analyzes and removes the control information from that data.

If System A sends data from a software application to System B, the data is passed to the application layer. System A's application layer then communicates any control information required by System B's application layer by prepending a header to the data. The resulting information unit (a header and the data) is passed to the presentation layer, which prepends its own header that contains control information intended for System B's presentation layer.

The information unit grows in size as each layer prepends its own header (and, in some cases, a trailer), which contains control information to be used by its peer layer in System B. At the physical layer, the entire information unit is placed on the network medium.

System B's physical layer receives the information unit and passes it to the data link layer. Next, System B's data link layer reads the control information contained in the header that was prepended by System A's data link layer. Next, the data link layer removes the header and passes the remainder of the information unit to the network layer. Each layer performs the same actions: the layer reads the header from its peer layer, strips it off, and passes the remaining information unit to the next highest layer. After the application layer performs these actions, the data is passed to System B's recipient software application in exactly the form in which it was transmitted by the application in System A.

OSI Model's Physical Layer

The *physical layer* defines the electrical, mechanical, procedural, and functional specifications for activating, maintaining, and deactivating the physical link between communicating network systems. Physical layer specifications define characteristics such as voltage levels, timing of voltage changes, physical data rates, maximum transmission distances, and physical connectors. Physical layer implementations can be categorized as either LAN or WAN specifications. Figure C-6 illustrates some common LAN and WAN physical layer implementations.

Figure C-6   *Physical Layer Implementations Can Be LAN or WAN Specifications*

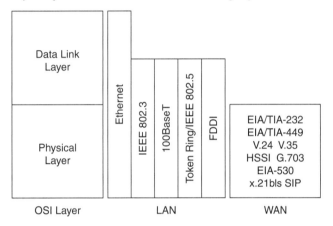

Physical Layer Implementations

OSI Model's Data Link Layer

The *data link layer* reliably transits data across a physical network link. Different data link layer specifications define different network and protocol characteristics, including physical addressing, network topology, error notification, frame sequencing, and flow control. Physical addressing (as opposed to network addressing) defines how devices are addressed at the data link layer. Network topology consists of the data link layer specifications that often define how devices are to be connected physically, such as in a bus or ring topology. Error notification alerts upper-layer protocols that a transmission error has occurred, and the sequencing of data frames reorders frames that are transmitted out of sequence. Finally, flow control moderates data transmission so that the receiving device is not overwhelmed with more traffic than it can handle at one time.

The Institute of Electrical and Electronics Engineers (IEEE) has subdivided the data link layer into two sublayers: Logical Link Control (LLC) and Media Access Control (MAC). Figure C-7 illustrates the data link layer's IEEE sublayers.

Figure C-7 *The Data Link Layer Contains Two Sublayers*

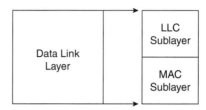

The data link layer's LLC sublayer manages communications between devices over a single network link. LLC, which is defined in the IEEE 802.2 specification, supports both connectionless and connection-oriented services used by higher-layer protocols. IEEE 802.2 defines a number of fields in data link layer frames that enable multiple higher-layer protocols to share a single physical data link. The data link layer's MAC sublayer manages protocol access to the physical network medium. The IEEE MAC specification defines MAC addresses, thereby enabling multiple devices to uniquely identify each other at the data link layer.

OSI Model's Network Layer

The *network layer* provides routing and related functions that enable multiple data links to be combined into an internetwork. This is accomplished by the logical addressing (as opposed to the physical addressing) of devices. The network layer supports both connection-oriented and connectionless service from higher-layer protocols. Routing protocols, routed protocols, and other types of protocols are implemented at the network layer. Some common routing protocols include *Border Gateway Protocol (BGP)*, which is an Internet interdomain routing protocol; *Open Shortest Path First (OSPF)*, which is a link-state, interior gateway protocol developed for use in Transmission Control Protocol/Internet Protocol (TCP/IP) networks; and *Routing Information Protocol (RIP)*, which is an Internet routing protocol that uses hop count as its metric.

OSI Model's Transport Layer

The *transport layer* implements optional, reliable internetwork data transport services that are transparent to upper layers. Transport layer functions can include flow control, multiplexing, virtual circuit management, and error checking and recovery.

Flow control manages data transmission between devices so that the transmitting device does not send more data than the receiving device can process. Multiplexing enables the tranmission of data from several applications to a single physical link. The transport layer establishes, maintains, and terminats virtual circuits. Error checking involves creating various mechanisms for detecting transmission errors, while error recovery involves taking an action, such as requesting that data be retransmitted, to resolve any errors.

Some transport layer implementations include *TCP*, which is the protocol in the TCP/IP suite that provides reliable transmission of data; *Name Binding Protocol (NBP)*, the protocol that associates AppleTalk names with addresses; and *OSI transport protocols*, which are a series of transport protocols in the OSI protocol suite.

OSI Model's Session Layer

The *session layer* establishes, manages, and terminates communication sessions between presentation layer entities. Communication sessions consist of service requests and service responses that occur between applications that are located in different network devices. Protocols that are implemented at the session layer coordinate these requests. Some examples of session layer implementations include *Zone Information Protocol (ZIP)*, which is the AppleTalk protocol that coordinates the name binding process; and *Session Control Protocol (SCP)*, which is the DECnet Phase IV session layer protocol.

OSI Model's Presentation Layer

The *presentation layer* provides a variety of coding and conversion functions that are applied to application layer data. These functions ensure that information sent from one system's application layer is readable by another system's application layer. Some examples of presentation layer coding and conversion schemes include common data representation formats, conversion of character representation formats, common data compression schemes, and common data encryption schemes.

Common data representation formats, or the use of standard image, sound, and video formats, enable different computer systems to interchange application data. Conversion schemes are used to exchange information with systems by using different text and data representations, such as EBCDIC and ASCII. Standard data compression schemes enable data that is compressed at the source device to be properly decompressed at the destination. Standard data-encryption schemes enable data that is encrypted at the source device to be properly deciphered at the destination.

Presentation layer implementations are not typically associated with a particular protocol stack. Some well-known standards for video include QuickTime and Motion Picture Experts Group (MPEG). *QuickTime* is an Apple Computer specification for video and audio, and *MPEG* is a standard for video compression and coding.

Among the well-known graphic image formats are Graphics Interchange Format (GIF), Joint Photographic Experts Group (JPEG), and Tagged Image File Format (TIFF). *GIF* is a standard for compressing and coding graphic images. *JPEG* is another compression and coding standard for graphic images. Finally, *TIFF* is a standard coding format for graphic images.

OSI Model's Application Layer

The *application layer* is the OSI layer that is closest to the end user; this means that both the OSI application layer and the user interact directly with the software application.

This layer interacts with software applications that implement a communicating component. Such application programs fall outside the scope of the OSI model. Application layer functions typically include identifying communication partners, determining resource availability, and synchronizing communication.

When identifying communication partners, the application layer determines the identity and availability of communication partners for an application that has data to transmit. When determining resource availability, the application layer must decide whether sufficient network resources for the requested communication exist. In synchronizing communication, all communication between applications requires cooperation that the application layer manages.

TCP/IP applications and OSI applications are two key types of application layer implementations. *TCP/IP applications* are protocols, such as Telnet, File Transfer Protocol (FTP), and Simple Mail Transfer Protocol (SMTP), that exist in the Internet Protocol suite. *OSI applications* are protocols, such as File Transfer, Access, and Management (FTAM), Virtual Terminal Protocol (VTP), and Common Management Information Protocol (CMIP), that exist in the OSI suite.

Information Formats

The data and control information that is transmitted through internetworks takes various forms. The terms used to refer to these information formats are not used consistently in the internetworking industry, but are sometimes are used interchangeably. Common information formats include the following:

- Frames
- Packets
- Datagrams
- Segments
- Messages
- Cells
- Data units

A *frame* is an information unit whose source and destination are data link layer entities. A frame is composed of the data link layer header (and possibly a trailer) and upper-layer data. The header and trailer contain control information that is intended for the destination system's data link layer entity. The data link layer header and trailer encapsulate data from upper-layer entities. Figure C-8 illustrates the basic components of a data link layer frame.

Figure C-8   *Data from Upper-Layer Entities Comprises the Data Link Layer Frame*

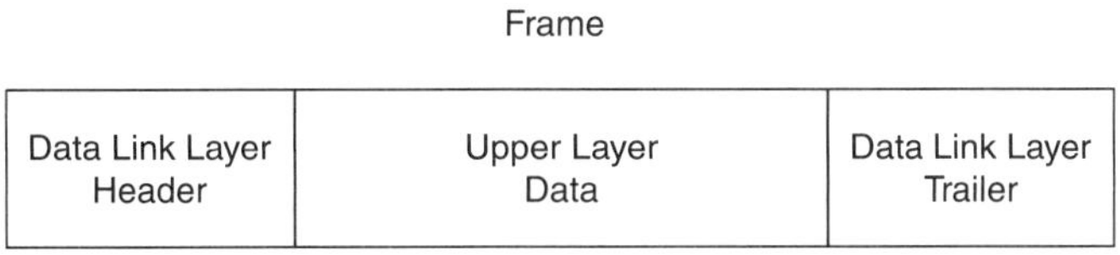

Frame

Data Link Layer Header	Upper Layer Data	Data Link Layer Trailer

A *packet* is an information unit whose source and destination are network layer entities. A packet is composed of the network layer header (and possibly a trailer) and upper-layer data. The header and trailer contain control information that is intended for the destination system's network layer entity. The network layer header and trailer encapsulate data from upper-layer entities. Figure C-9 illustrates the basic components of a network layer packet.

Figure C-9   *Three Basic Components Comprise a Network Layer Packet*

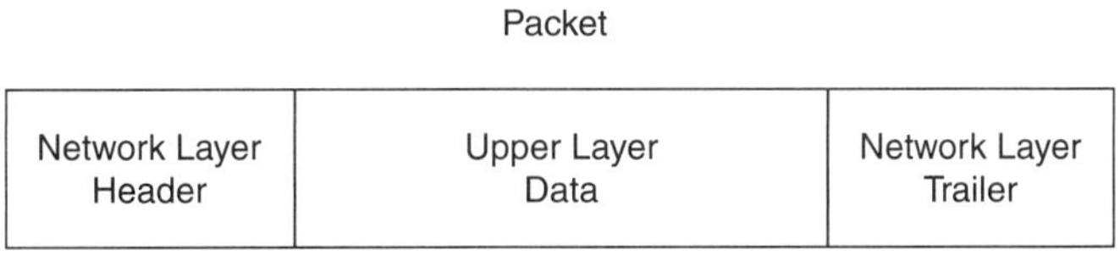

Packet

Network Layer Header	Upper Layer Data	Network Layer Trailer

The term *datagram* refers to an information unit whose source and destination are network layer entities that use connectionless network service.

The term *segment* refers to an information unit whose source and destination are transport layer entities.

A *message* is an information unit whose source and destination entities exist above the network layer (often in the application layer).

A *cell* is an information unit of a fixed size whose source and destination are data link layer entities. Cells are used in switched environments, such as Asynchronous Transfer Mode (ATM) and Switched Multimegabit Data Service (SMDS) networks. A cell is composed of the header and payload. The header contains control information that is intended for the destination data link layer entity and is typically 5 bytes long. The payload contains upper-layer data that is encapsulated in the cell header and is typically 48 bytes long.

The length of the header and the payload fields are always exactly the same for each cell. Figure C-10 depicts a typical cell's components.

Figure C-10 *Two Components Comprise a Typical Cell*

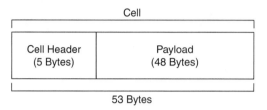

Data unit is a generic term that refers to a variety of information units. Some common data units include service data units (SDUs), protocol data units (PDUs), and bridge protocol data units (BPDUs). *SDUs* are information units from upper-layer protocols that define a service request to a lower-layer protocol. *PDU* is OSI terminology for describing the data unit at a given layer; for example, the Layer 3 PDU is also known as a packet, and the Layer 4 PDU is also known as a segment. *BPDUs* are used as hello messages by the spanning-tree algorithm.

This appendix is organized into the following sections:

- Summary of ICND Router Commands
- Summary of ICND Switch IOS Commands

Summary of ICND Router and Switch Commands

This appendix contains a listing of some of the Cisco router IOS, Catalyst 1900, and Catalyst 2950 Switch IOS commands you might find in the Cisco Interconnecting Cisco Network Devices (ICND) course and in Cisco Press's *CCNA Self-Study: Interconnecting Cisco Network Devices* (Steve McQuerry, 2000). The commands are organized into various categories.

NOTE   Only the commands are listed here; parameters are not included. For details on the parameters and how each command works, please see the *Command Reference Manuals* on the Cisco documentation CD-ROM or on Cisco's website at www.cisco.com.

NOTE   In the tables in this appendix, words within angled brackets (<>) are single keys that should be pressed, not command words that should be entered. A plus sign (+) between keys indicates that the keys should be pressed simultaneously. For example, **<Ctrl>(+)<a>** indicates that the Ctrl key and the "a" key should be pressed at the same time.

Summary of ICND Router Commands

This section contains a listing of some of the Cisco router IOS commands.

General Commands

Table D-1 lists general Cisco router EXEC IOS commands.

Table D-1   *General Commands*

Command	Meaning
?	Help.
<ctrl>+<a>	Moves to the beginning of the command line.
<ctrl>+<b>	Moves backward one character.
<ctrl>+<c>	Aborts from setup mode.

continues

Table D-1   *General Commands (Continued)*

Command	Meaning
\<ctrl\>+\<e\>	Moves to the end of the command line.
\<ctrl\>+\<f\>	Moves forward one character.
\<ctrl\>+\<n\> or \<down arrow\>	Returns to more recent commands in the history buffer after recalling commands with **\<ctrl\>+\<p\>** or **\<up arrow\>**. Repeat the key sequence to successively recall more recent commands.
\<ctrl\>+\<p\> or \<up arrow\>	Recalls commands in the history buffer, beginning with the most recent command. Repeat the key sequence to recall successively older commands.
\<ctrl\>+\<Shift\>+\<6\> \<x\>	The escape sequence, which is used to suspend a Telnet session.
\<ctrl\>+\<r\>	Redisplays a line.
\<ctrl\>+\<u\>	Erases a line from the beginning of the line.
\<ctrl\>+\<w\>	Erases a word.
\<ctrl\>+\<z\>	Exits from configuration mode back to privileged EXEC mode.
\<esc\>+\<b\>	Moves to the beginning of the previous word.
\<esc\>+\<f\>	Moves forward one word.
\<backspace\>	Removes one character to the left of the cursor.
\<enter\> or \<return\>	Resumes the last suspended Telnet session.
\<tab\>	Completes the keyword.
clear counters	Resets the show interface counters to zero.
clear line	Disconnects a Telnet session from a foreign host.
clock set	Sets the router's clock.
configure terminal	Enters configuration mode.
connect	Logs on to a host that supports Telnet, rlogin, or Local-Area Transport (LAT).
copy flash tftp	Copies a file from Flash memory to a Trivial File Transfer Protocol (TFTP) server.
copy running-config startup-config	Copies configuration from Random Access Memory (RAM) to Nonvolatile RAM (NVRAM) (overwrites).
copy running-config tftp	Copies configuration from RAM to TFTP server (overwrites).
copy startup-config running-config	Executes configuration from NVRAM into RAM (executes line by line; merges; does not overwrite).
copy startup-config tftp	Copies configuration from NVRAM to TFTP server (overwrites).
copy tftp flash	Copies a file from a TFTP server to Flash memory.

Table D-1   *General Commands (Continued)*

Command	Meaning
copy tftp running-config	Executes configuration from a TFTP server into RAM (executes line by line; in other words, it merges the commands—it does not overwrite).
copy tftp startup-config	Copies configuration from a TFTP server to NVRAM (overwrites).
debug	Starts the console display of the events on the router.
disable	Exits privileged EXEC mode.
disconnect	Disconnects a Telnet session.
enable	Enters privileged mode.
erase startup-config	Erases the configuration in NVRAM.
exit	Closes an active terminal session and terminates the EXEC. (Also used to exit any level in configuration mode.)
logout	Closes an active terminal session and terminates the EXEC.
ping	Sends an echo and expects an echo reply. The extended **ping** command, accessed by entering **ping** followed by <CR>, also allows ping for protocols other than IP.
reload	Reloads the operating system.
resume	Resumes a suspended Telnet session.
setup	Enters a prompted dialog to establish an initial configuration.
show access-lists	Displays the contents of all configured access lists.
show cdp entry	Displays a single cached Cisco Discovery Protocol (CDP) entry; use **show cdp entry** * to display cached information about all neighbors.
show cdp interface	Displays values of CDP timers and CDP interface status.
show cdp neighbors	Displays a summary of CDP information received from neighbors.
show cdp neighbors detail	Displays detailed CDP information received from neighbors.
show cdp traffic	Displays information about interface CDP traffic.
show clock	Displays the system clock.
show controller	Displays the Layer 1 information about an interface (including cable type and data circuit-terminating equipment/data terminal equipment [DCE/DTE] status for serial interfaces).
show flash	Displays information about Flash memory.
show history	Displays the list of recorded command lines during the current terminal session.

continues

Table D-1   *General Commands (Continued)*

Command	Meaning
show interfaces	Displays information about interfaces or an interface, including the state of the interface.
show processes	Displays the CPU utilization for each process.
show running-config	Displays the active configuration (in RAM).
show sessions	Displays a list of hosts to which you have established Telnet connectivity.
show startup-config	Displays the backup configuration (in NVRAM).
show terminal	Displays the current terminal settings.
show users	Displays a list of all active users on the router.
show version	Displays configuration of system hardware, software version, and configuration register value.
telnet	Connects to a host.
terminal editing	Re-enables advanced editing (use **no terminal editing** to disable advanced editing features). Advanced editing is enabled by default.
terminal history size	Changes the number of command lines the system records during the current terminal session.
terminal monitor	Forwards debug and error output to your Telnet session (use **terminal no monitor** to turn this off).
traceroute	Traces the route that packets are taking through the network. (Note that the **traceroute** command appears in the Cisco IOS documentation as **trace**; however, **traceroute** is the full command on the routers.)
undebug	Turns off debugging (also use **no debug**).

Comparison of Configuration File Commands

With Cisco IOS Release 12.0, commands used to copy and transfer configuration and system files have changed to conform to IOS File System (IFS) specifications. The old commands continue to perform their normal functions in the current release, but support for these commands will cease in a future release. Table D-2 contains the old and new commands used for configuration file movement and management.

Table D-2   *Comparison of Configuration File Commands*

Old Command	New Command
configure network (pre-IOS release 10.3)	**copy ftp: system:running-config**
copy rcp running-config	**copy rcp: system:running-config**
copy tftp running-config	**copy tftp: system:running-config**

Table D-2   *Comparison of Configuration File Commands (Continued)*

Old Command	New Command
configure overwrite-network (pre-IOS release 10.3) **copy rcp startup-config** **copy tftp startup-config**	**copy ftp: nvram:startup-config** **copy rcp: nvram:startup-config** **copy tftp: nvram:startup-config**
show configuration (pre-IOS release 10.3) **show startup-config**	**more nvram:startup-config**
write erase (pre-IOS release 10.3) **erase startup-config**	**erase nvram:**
write memory (pre-IOS release 10.3) **copy running-config startup-config**	**copy system:running-config** **nvram:startup-config**
write network (pre-IOS release 10.3) **copy running-config rcp** **copy running-config tftp**	**copy system:running-config ftp:** **copy system:running-config rcp:** **copy system:running-config tftp:**
write terminal (pre-IOS release 10.3) **show running-config**	**more system:running-config**

General Configuration Commands

Table D-3 contains some Cisco IOS configuration commands.

Table D-3   *General Configuration Commands*

Command	Meaning
<ctrl>+<z>	Exits from configuration mode back to privileged EXEC mode.
banner	Specifies a banner for the router (can be a **motd**, **idle**, or **exec** banner).
boot system	Specifies the source of IOS images.
cdp run	Enables CDP on a router. (CDP is enabled by default; use **no cdp run** to disable it.)
config-register	Sets the 16-bit configuration register.
enable password	Specifies the enable password for the router.
enable secret	Specifies the enable secret password for the router.
end	Exits from configuration mode.
exec-timeout 0 0	Sets the timeout for a line EXEC session to zero, preventing the session from timing out and disconnecting.

continues

Table D-3   *General Configuration Commands (Continued)*

Command	Meaning
exit	Exits any level in configuration mode.
history size	Specifies the number of command lines the system records on a line.
hostname	Specifies the router's name.
interface	Enters interface configuration mode (**ethernet**, **serial**, **loopback**, and so on); also used to enter subinterface configuration mode. The first time this command is used for a specific virtual interface (**loopback**, **tunnel**, **dialer**, and so on), it creates that virtual interface.
line	Enters line configuration mode (**console**, **aux**, **vty**).
login	Enables password checking on a line.
logging synchronous	Used on a line (**console**, **aux**, **vty**); causes input to be redisplayed on a single display line at the end of each console message that interrupts the input.
password	Specifies the password for a line.
service password-encryption	Specifies that any passwords set subsequent to this command will be encrypted. Use **no service password-encryption** after all such passwords have been set.
service timestamps	Adds a time stamp to debug or log messages.

General Interface Configuration Commands

Table D-4 contains some Cisco IOS interface configuration commands.

Table D-4   *General Interface Configuration Commands*

Command	Meaning
bandwidth	Sets interface bandwidth (used by some routing protocols, including Open Shortest Path First [OSPF], Interior Gateway Routing Protocol [IGRP], and Enhanced IGRP [EIGRP]; also used for load calculations). Note that this command does not change the speed of the interface; it simply changes the number used in calculations.
cdp enable	Enables CDP on an interface. (CDP is enabled by default; use **no cdp enable** to disable it.)
clock rate	Sets clock rate in bits per second (used if interface is DCE); note that **clockrate** also works.
description	Adds a text description to the interface.
encapsulation dot1q	Defines the data-link encapsulation as 802.1q.

Table D-4   *General Interface Configuration Commands (Continued)*

Command	Meaning
encapsulation isl	Defines the data-link encapsulation as Inter-switch Link (ISL) and defines a virtual local-area network (VLAN) number for a subinterface. Used for inter-VLAN routing on a Fast Ethernet subinterface.
interface	Enters interface configuration mode (or subinterface mode, if already in interface mode).
media-type	Selects the media-type connector for the Ethernet interface (for example, use **10baset** for RJ-45 connectors) on Cisco routers with more than one connector for an Ethernet interface.
shutdown	Administratively shuts down an interface. (Use **no shutdown** to bring up the interface.)

General Internet Protocol (IP) Commands

Table D-5 contains some Cisco IOS EXEC commands that are related to IP.

Table D-5   *General IP Commands*

Command	Meaning
clear ip nat translation	Clears dynamic address translation entries from the Network Address Translation (NAT) table.
debug eigrp neighbors	Starts the console display of the EIGRP neighbor interaction.
debug ip eigrp	Starts the console display of the IP EIGRP advertisements and changes to the IP routing table.
debug ip igrp	Starts the console display of the IP IGRP-related transactions or events on the router.
debug ip ospf events	Starts the console display of OSPF-related events, such as adjacencies, flooding information, designated router selection, and SPF calculation on the router.
debug ip ospf packet	Starts the console display about each OSPF packet received.
debug ip rip	Starts the console display of the IP Routing Information Protocol (RIP)-related events on the router.
debug ip nat	Starts the console display of NAT translations.
show hosts	Displays the cached list of host names and addresses (both static and those that are obtained from a DNS server).
show ip access-list	Displays the IP access lists that are configured.
show ip eigrp neighbors	Displays the neighbors discovered by IP EIGRP.

continues

Table D-5 *General IP Commands (Continued)*

Command	Meaning
show ip eigrp topology	Displays the IP EIGRP topology table. Use the **all** keyword to display the entire topology table, including those routes that are not feasible successors.
show ip eigrp traffic	Displays the number of IP EIGRP packets sent and received.
show ip interface	Displays IP-specific information about an interface, including whether access lists are applied.
show ip ospf interface	Displays details of the OSPF protocol on the interfaces, including the area, state, timers, neighbors, router ID, and network type.
show ip ospf neighbor	Displays the list of OSPF neighbors. Use the **detail** keyword to display more details about each neighbor (including priority and state).
show ip protocols	Displays the IP routing protocols that are running.
show ip route	Displays the IP routing table. Use other keywords to display specific parts of the routing table.
show ip route eigrp	Displays the current EIGRP entries in the IP routing table.
show ip nat statistics	Displays NAT translation statistics.
show ip nat translations	Displays active NAT translations.
term ip netmask-format	Specifies the format of how network masks are shown for the current session (bit count, decimal, or hexadecimal).

IP Configuration Commands

Table D-6 contains some Cisco IOS configuration commands that are related to IP.

Table D-6 *IP Configuration Commands*

Command	Meaning
access-class	Activates an access list on a line (**console**, **aux**, **vty**) to restrict incoming and outgoing connections.
access-list	Defines access lists: IP standard = numbers 1 to 99; IP extended = numbers 100 to 199, or 2000 to 2699.
ip access-group	Activates an access list on an interface.
ip access-list	Defines a named access list in Cisco IOS 11.2 or later.
ip address	Assigns an IP address and subnet mask to an interface.

Table D-6   *IP Configuration Commands (Continued)*

Command	Meaning
ip classless	Specifies that if a packet is received with a destination address within an unknown subnet of a directly attached network, the router matches it to the default route and forwards it to the next hop the default route specifies.
ip domain-lookup	Turns on name service (DNS) lookups. (Use **no ip domain-lookup** to turn off DNS lookups.)
ip host	Defines a static host name to IP address mapping.
ip name-server	Defines one or more (up to six) hosts that supply host name information (DNS).
ip nat	Defines the NAT parameters (inside and outside addresses, pools of addresses, and access lists).
ip netmask-format	Specifies how network masks are shown (bit count, decimal, or hexadecimal) for a specific line (**con, aux, vty**).
ip route	Defines a static route to an IP destination.
network	Defines the networks on which the routing protocol runs (for RIP, OSPF, IGRP, and EIGRP). Starts up the routing protocol on all interfaces in that network and allows the router to advertise that network. For OSPF, this command also defines the area in which the interface resides.
router eigrp	Defines EIGRP as an IP routing protocol and enters configuration mode for that protocol.
router igrp	Defines IGRP as an IP routing protocol and enters configuration mode for that protocol.
router ospf	Defines OSPF as an IP routing protocol and enters configuration mode for that protocol.
router rip	Defines RIP as an IP routing protocol and enters configuration mode for that protocol.
traffic-share	Defines how traffic is distributed among multiple unequal cost routes for the same destination network (for IGRP and EIGRP).
variance	Defines unequal cost load balancing when using IGRP or EIGRP.

General Internetwork Packet Exchange (IPX) Commands

Table D-7 contains some Cisco IOS EXEC commands that are related to IPX.

Table D-7   *General IPX Commands*

Command	Meaning
debug ipx routing activity	Starts the console display of the IPX routing-related events on the router.
debug ipx sap activity	Starts the console display of the IPX Service Advertisement Protocol (SAP)-related events on the router.
ping ipx	Sends an echo and expects an echo reply.
show ipx access-list	Displays the IPX access lists that are configured.
show ipx interface	Displays IPX-specific information about an interface, including whether access lists are applied.
show ipx route	Displays the IPX routing table.
show ipx servers	Displays the IPX server list.
show ipx traffic	Displays statistics on IPX traffic.

IPX Configuration Commands

Table D-8 contains some Cisco IOS configuration commands that are related to IPX.

Table D-8   *IPX Configuration Commands*

Command	Meaning
access-list	Defines access lists: IPX standard = numbers 800 to 899; IPX extended = numbers 900 to 999; IPX SAP = numbers 1000 to 1099.
ipx access-group	Activates an IPX standard or extended access list on an interface.
ipx delay	Defines the delay tick metric to associate with an interface.
ipx input-sap-filter	Activates an IPX SAP access list input on an interface.
ipx maximum-paths	Enables round-robin load sharing over multiple equal metric paths.
ipx network	Assigns IPX network number and encapsulation type to an interface or subinterface.
ipx output-sap-filter	Activates an IPX SAP access list output on an interface.
ipx routing	Enables IPX routing on the router.

General AppleTalk Commands

Table D-9 contains some Cisco IOS EXEC commands that are related to AppleTalk.

Table D-9　　*General AppleTalk Commands*

Command	Meaning
debug appletalk routing	Starts the console display of the AppleTalk routing-related events on the router.
show appletalk globals	Displays information and settings regarding the router's global AppleTalk configuration parameters.
show appletalk interface	Displays AppleTalk-specific information about an interface, including whether access lists are applied.
show appletalk route	Displays the AppleTalk routing table.
show appletalk zone	Displays the AppleTalk zone information table.

AppleTalk Configuration Commands

Table D-10 contains some Cisco IOS configuration commands that are related to AppleTalk.

Table D-10　　*AppleTalk Configuration Commands*

Command	Meaning
appletalk cable-range	Assigns an AppleTalk cable-range to an interface (for phase 2 or extended addressing).
appletalk discovery	Enables an interface to learn a cable-range and zone name (or use **appletalk cable-range 0-0).**
appletalk protocol	Selects an AppleTalk routing protocol (Routing Table Maintenance Protocol [RTMP], EIGRP, or AppleTalk Update Routing Protocol [AURP]).
appletalk routing	Enables AppleTalk routing on the router.
appletalk zone	Assigns an AppleTalk zone name to an interface.

General WAN Commands

Table D-11 contains some Cisco IOS EXEC commands that are related to WAN interfaces.

Table D-11　　*General WAN Commands*

Command	Meaning
clear frame-relay-inarp	Clears dynamically created Frame Relay maps, which are created by the use of Inverse Address Resolution Protocol (ARP).

continues

Table D-11   *General WAN Commands (Continued)*

Command	Meaning
debug dialer	Starts the console display of dialer events, including the number the interface is dialing.
debug frame-relay lmi	Starts the console display of Local Management Interface (LMI) packets between the router and the Frame Relay switch.
debug isdn q921	Starts the console display of data link layer (Layer 2) access procedures that are taking place at the router on the D channel (using the link access procedure for D channel [LAPD]) of its ISDN interface.
debug isdn q931	Starts the console display of call setup and teardown of ISDN network connections (Layer 3).
debug ppp authentication	Starts the console display of the Point-to-Point Protocol (PPP) authentication–related events on the router.
debug ppp error	Starts the console display of errors related to PPP on the router.
debug ppp negotiation	Starts the console display of the PPP negotiation-related events on the router.
show dialer	Displays the current status of an interface that is configured for dial-on-demand routing (DDR).
show frame-relay lmi	Displays the LMI traffic statistics.
show frame-relay map	Displays the route maps (between network layer addresses and data link connection identifiers [DLCIs]), both static and dynamic.
show frame-relay pvc	Displays the status of each configured PVC and traffic statistics (including the number of backward explicit congestion notification [BECN] and forward explicit congestion notification [FECN] messages).
show frame-relay traffic	Displays Frame Relay traffic statistics.
show dialer	Displays the current status of a dialer link, including the amount of time the link has been connected.
show isdn active	Displays the current call information, including the called number and the time until the call is disconnected.
show isdn status	Displays the status of an ISDN interface.

WAN Configuration Commands

Table D-12 contains some Cisco IOS configuration commands that are related to WAN interfaces.

Table D-12   *WAN Configuration Commands*

Command	Meaning
bandwidth	Defines the bandwidth (in kilobits per second) of the interface (used in routing protocol calculations and load calculations). Note that this command does not change the interface's speed; it simply changes the number used in calculations.
controller	Enters controller configuration mode. Use when configuring a Primary Rate Interface (PRI).
dialer idle-timeout	Defines the number of seconds of idle (no interesting data) time before the circuit is disconnected.
dialer load-threshold	Enables the router to place another call to the same destination (if channels are available), based on the load on the line.
dialer map	Defines how to reach a destination, maps protocol addresses to the destination's phone number, and defines options, including broadcast, speed, and name of remote device.
dialer pool	Specifies the pool of physical interfaces that are available for the dialer interface.
dialer pool-member	Defines the physical interface as a member of a particular dialer pool.
dialer string	Specifies the destination's phone number on a dialer interface.
dialer-group	Assigns a dialer list to an interface to determine when to trigger a call.
dialer-list list	Defines a dialer list to trigger a call based on an access list. (Used only for IP or IPX.)
dialer-list protocol	Defines a dialer list to trigger a call based on a protocol type or an access list.
encapsulation	Defines the data-link encapsulation for an interface (**ppp**, **hldc**, **x25** [**dte** is the default; can use **dce**], **frame-relay**, **smds**, and so on).
frame-relay interface-dlci	Assigns a DLCI to the subinterface. (Used only on subinterfaces that are defined by the **interface** *type.subinterface number* [**point-to-point** | **multipoint**] command.)
frame-relay inverse-arp	Enables Inverse ARP on an interface. (Necessary only if it was disabled at some point; the default is enabled.)

continues

Table D-12   *WAN Configuration Commands (Continued)*

Command	Meaning
frame-relay lmi-type	Defines the Local Management Interface (LMI) format (to match the Frame Relay switch).
frame-relay map	Defines how an interface reaches a destination, maps protocol addresses to the DLCI to the destination, and defines options, including broadcast.
framing	Defines the framing type on the interface controller; entered in controller configuration mode.
isdn spid1	Sets a B-channel service profile identifier (SPID) (required by many service providers/ISDN switches).
isdn spid2	Sets a B-channel SPID for the second B channel (required by many service providers/ISDN switches).
isdn switch-type	Specifies the ISDN switch to which the router is connected; can be done as a global or interface command from Cisco IOS 11.3 onward.
linecode	Defines the interface controller's line coding; entered in controller configuration mode.
ppp authentication	Sets password authentication on an interface (using challenge handshake authentication protocol [CHAP] or password authentication protocol [PAP]).
pri-group	Defines the interface controller as PRI; entered in controller configuration mode.
username	Defines a host name and password for verification (used in PAP or CHAP).

Summary of ICND Switch IOS Commands

This section contains a listing of some of the Catalyst 1900 and Catalyst 2950 Switch IOS commands.

General Switch Commands

Table D-13 contains some general Catalyst switch IOS commands.

Table D-13   *General Switch Commands*

Command	Meaning
?	Help.
<ctrl>+<a>	Moves to the beginning of the command line.

Table D-13   *General Switch Commands (Continued)*

Command	Meaning
\<ctrl\>+\<b\>	Moves backward one character.
\<ctrl\>+\<e\>	Moves to the end of the command line.
\<ctrl\>+\<f\>	Moves forward one character.
\<ctrl\>+\<n\> or \<down arrow\>	Returns to more recent commands in the history buffer after recalling commands with **\<ctrl\>+\<p\>** or **\<up arrow\>**. Repeat the key sequence to recall successively more recent commands.
\<ctrl\>+\<p\> or \<up arrow\>	Recalls commands in the history buffer, beginning with the most recent command. Repeat the key sequence to recall successively older commands.
\<ctrl\>+\<r\>	Redisplays a line.
\<ctrl\>+\<u\>	Erases a line from the beginning of the line.
\<ctrl\>+\<w\>	Erases a word.
\<ctrl\>+\<z\>	Exits from configuration mode and returns to privileged EXEC mode.
\<esc\>+\<b\>	Moves to the beginning of the previous word.
\<esc\>+\<f\>	Moves forward one word.
\<backspace\>	Removes one character to the left of the cursor.
\<tab\>	Completes the keyword.
configure terminal	Enters configuration mode.
copy nvram tftp://{host}/{file}	Copies switch configuration to a TFTP server (overwrites). (Catalyst 1900)
copy startup-config tftp:// {host}/{file}	Copies switch configuration to a TFTP server (overwrites). (Catalyst 2950)
copy tftp://{host}/{file} nvram	Copies switch configuration from a TFTP server (overwrites). (Catalyst 1900)
delete nvram	Erases the configuration in NVRAM. (Catalyst 1900)
delete vtp	Resets the VTP configuration to factory defaults, including the revision number. Also resets the system, but only VTP configurations are changed.
disable	Exits privileged EXEC mode.
enable	Enters privileged mode.
erase startup-config	Erases the startup configuration in memory. (Catalyst 2950)
ping	Sends an "echo" and expects an "echo reply."

continues

Table D-13 *General Switch Commands (Continued)*

Command	Meaning
show CDP interface	Displays values of CDP timers and CDP interface status.
show CDP neighbors	Displays a summary of CDP information received from neighbors.
show CDP neighbors detail	Displays detailed CDP information received from neighbors.
show history	Displays the list of recorded command lines during the current terminal session.
show ip	Displays IP information about the switch, including the IP address and subnet mask settings.
show interfaces	Displays information about interfaces or an interface, including the state of the interface, errors that have occurred, and duplex mode.
show interface vlan 1	Displays the switch IP address information. (Catalyst 2950)
show interface switchport	Displays the interface's trunk parameters. (Catalyst 2950)
show mac-address-table	Displays the MAC address table contents.
show mac-address-table secure	Displays the port security configuration. (Catalyst 2950)
show mac-address-table security	Displays the port security configuration. (Catalyst 1900)
show port security	Displays port security settings. (Catalyst 2950)
show running-config	Displays the active configuration.
show spanning-tree vlan	Displays STP configuration status for a particular VLAN. (Catalyst 2950)
show spantree	Displays the switch's spanning-tree configuration status. (Catalyst 1900)
show trunk	Displays an interface's trunk configuration. (Catalyst 1900)
show version	Displays system hardware's software version, uptime, and configuration.
show vlan	Displays the parameters of a VLAN, including the number, name, and ports.
show vlan brief	Displays the VLAN assignment and membership type for all switch ports. (Catalyst 2950)
show vlan-membership	Displays the VLAN assignment and membership type for all switch ports. (Catalyst 1900)
show vtp	Displays the VTP configuration information. (Catalyst 1900)
show vtp domain	Displays VTP domain information.
show vtp status	Displays the VTP configuration information. (Catalyst 2950)

General Switch Configuration Commands

Table D-14 contains some general Catalyst switch IOS configuration commands.

Table D-14 *General Switch Configuration Commands*

Command	Meaning
<ctrl>+<z>	Exits from configuration mode back to privileged EXEC mode.
address-violation	Specifies the action for a port address violation (suspend, disable, ignore). (Catalyst 1900)
end	Exits from configuration mode.
hostname	Specifies the switch's name.
interface	Enters interface configuration mode.
interface vlan 1	Enters interface configuration mode for VLAN1 to set the switch management IP address. (Catalyst 2950)
ip address	Specifies the switch's IP address and subnet mask.
ip default-gateway	Specifies the default gateway the switch uses to send traffic to a different IP network than that on which its own address resides.
login	Sets the login identifier on the console or virtual terminal ports. (Catalyst 2950)
mac-address-table permanent	Specifies a permanent address that is associated with a particular switched port. Permanent addresses do not age out. (Catalyst 1900)
mac-address-table restricted static	Specifies a restricted static address. The address is associated with a particular switched port, and only devices on specified interfaces can send data to it. Restricted static addresses do not age out. (Catalyst 1900)
mac-address-table secure	Specifies a secure static address. (Catalyst 2950)
mac-address-table static	Specifies a static address that is associated with a particular switched port. Permanent addresses do not age out. (Catalyst 2950)
password	Assigns a password to the console or to virtual terminal ports. (Catalyst 2950)
snmp-server	Configures the SNMP server in VLAN configuration mode. (Catalyst 2950).
vlan	Specifies the number and name of a VLAN that is being created or modified.
vlan database	Enters VLAN configuration mode. (Catalyst 2950)
vtp	Specifies the VTP operating mode, domain name, password, whether traps are generated, and whether pruning is enabled. (This is done in VLAN configuration mode on Catalyst 2950.)

General Switch Interface Configuration Commands

Table D-15 contains some general Catalyst switch IOS interface configuration commands.

Table D-15 *General Switch Interface Configuration Commands*

Command	Meaning
cdp enable	Enables CDP on an interface (CDP is enabled by default; use **no cdp enable** to disable it).
duplex	Enables a duplex mode on an interface.
port secure	Enables addressing security. (Catalyst 1900)
port secure max-mac-count	Specifies the number of devices on a secured port; the default is 132. (Catalyst 1900)
port security	Enables addressing security. (Catalyst 2950)
port security action	Specifies the action to take when an address violation occurs (shutdown, trap). The default is shutdown. (Catalyst 2950)
port security max-mac-count	Specifies the number of devices on a secured port; the default is 132. (Catalyst 2950)
shutdown	Administratively shuts down an interface (use **no shutdown** to bring the interface up).
switchport access	Specifies the VLAN to which an interface belongs. (Catalyst 2950)
switchport mode	Specifies the interface's 802.1Q trunk mode. (Catalyst 2950)
trunk	Specifies the interface's ISL trunk mode (on, off, desirable, auto, or nonegotiate).
vlan-membership	Specifies the VLAN to which an interface belongs, or specifies dynamic VLAN membership. (Catalyst 1900)

Common Requests For Comments

The Internet Requests for Comments (RFCs) documents are the written definitions of the Internet's protocols and policies.

RFCs Information

The following information about RFCs was adapted from RFC 1594, *FYI on Questions and Answers—Answers to Commonly asked "New Internet User" Questions:*

The Internet Architecture Board (IAB) is concerned with technical and policy issues involving the evolution of the Internet architecture. All decisions of the IAB are made public. The principal vehicle by which IAB decisions are propagated to the parties interested in the Internet and its TCP/IP protocol suite is the RFCs note series and the Internet Monthly Report.

RFCs are the working notes of the Internet research and development community. A document in this series can be on essentially any topic related to computer communication, and can be anything from a meeting report to the specification of a standard. Submissions for RFCs can be sent to the RFC Editor (RFC-EDITOR@ISI.EDU).

Most RFCs are the descriptions of network protocols or services, often giving detailed procedures and formats for their implementation. Other RFCs report on the results of policy studies or summarize the work of technical committees or workshops. All RFCs are considered public domain unless explicitly marked otherwise.

While RFCs are not refereed publications, they do receive technical review from the task forces, individual technical experts, or the RFC Editor, as appropriate. Currently, most standards are published as RFCs, but not all RFCs specify standards.

Anyone can submit a document for publication as an RFC. Submissions must be made via e-mail to the RFC Editor. Please consult RFC 1543, *Instructions to RFC Authors*, for additional information.

Once a document is assigned an RFC number and is published, that RFC is never revised or reissued with the same number. There is never a question of having the most recent version of a particular RFC. However, a protocol (such as File Transfer Protocol [FTP]) can be improved and redocumented many times in several different RFCs. It is important to verify that you have the most recent RFC on a particular protocol. The "Internet Official Protocol Standards" memo is the reference for determining the correct RFC to which to refer for the current specification of each protocol.

RFCs are available online at several repositories around the world.

Table E-1 lists some common RFCs. A complete list and the documents themselves can be found at www.cis.ohio-state.edu/cs/Services/rfc/index.html.

Table E-1 *RFCs*

RFC	Title
2766	Network Address Translation—Protocol Translation (NAT-PT)
2740	OSPF for IPv6
2575	View-based Access Control Model (VACM) for the Simple Network Management Protocol (SNMP)
2574	User-based Security Model (USM) for Version 3 of the Simple Network Management Protocol (SNMPv3)
2573	SNMP Applications
2572	Message Processing and Dispatching for the Simple Network Management Protocol (SNMP)
2571	An Architecture for Describing SNMP Management Frameworks
2547	BGP/MPLS VPNs
2545	Use of BGP-4 Multiprotocol Extensions for IPv6 Inter-domain Routing
2460	Internet Protocol, Version 6 (IPv6)
2439	BGP Route Flap Damping
2385	Protection of BGP Sessions via TCP MD5 Signature Option
2373	IP Version 6 Addressing Architecture
2370	The OSPF Opaque LSA Option
2329	OSPF Standardization Report
2328	OSPF Version 2
2283	Multiprotocol Extensions for BGP-4
2236	Internet Group Message Protocol (IGMP), Version 2
2226	IP Broadcast over ATM Networks
2200	Internet Official Protocol Standards (obsoletes RFC 2000, RFC 1920, RFC 1880, RFC 1800, RFC 1780, RFC 1720, RFC 1610, RFC 1600, RFC 1540, RFC 1500, RFC 1410, RFC 1360, RFC 1280, RFC 1250, RFC 1200, RFC 1140, RFC 1130, RFC 1100, and RFC 1083)
2185	Routing Aspects of IPv6 Transition
2178	OSPF Version 2 (made obsolete by RFC 2328)

Table E-1 *RFCs (Continued)*

RFC	Title
2136	Dynamic Updates in the Domain Name System (DNS UPDATE)
2131	Dynamic Host Configuration Protocol (DHCP)
2105	Cisco Systems' Tag Switching Architecture Overview
2080	RIPng for IPv6
2050	Internet Registry IP Allocation Guidelines
2042	Registering New BGP Attribute Types
2018	TCP Selective Acknowledgment Options
1998	Application of the BGP Community Attribute in Multi-home Routing
1997	BGP Communities Attribute
1994	PPP Challenge Handshake Authentication Protocol (CHAP)
1990	The PPP Multilink Protocol (MP)
1983	Internet Users' Glossary
1966	BGP Route Reflection—An Alternative to Full-mesh IBGP
1965	AS Confederations for BGP
1932	IP over ATM: A Framework Document
1930	Guidelines for Creation, Selection, and Registration of an Autonomous System (AS)
1918	Address Allocation for Private Internets
1901	Introduction to Community-based SNMPv2
1863	A BGP/IDRP Route Server Alternative to a Full-mesh Routing
1850	OSPF Version 2 Management Information Base
1817	CIDR and Classful Routing
1812	Requirements for IP Version 4 Routers
1793	Extending OSPF to Support Demand Circuits
1774	BGP-4 Protocol Analysis
1773	Experience with the BGP-4 Protocol
1772	An Application of BGP in the Internet

continues

Table E-1   *RFCs (Continued)*

RFC	Title
1771	A Border Gateway Protocol 4 (BGP-4)
1765	OSPF Database Overflow
1757	Remote Network Monitoring Management Information Base
1700	Assigned Numbers
1663	PPP Reliable Transmission
1661	The Point-to-Point Protocol (PPP)
1631	The IP Network Address Translator (NAT)
1613	Cisco Systems X.25 over TCP (XOT)
1594	FYI on Questions and Answers—Answers to Commonly asked "New Internet User" Questions
1587	OSPF NSSA Option
1586	Guidelines for Running OSPF over Frame Relay Networks
1583	OSPF Version 2 (made obsolete by RFC 2178)
1570	PPP LCP Extensions
1548	The Point-to-Point Protocol (PPP)
1519	Classless Inter-domain Routing (CIDR): An Address Assignment and Aggregation Strategy
1518	An Architecture for IP Address Allocation with CIDR
1513	Token Ring Extensions to the Remote Network Monitoring MIB
1490	Multiprotocol Interconnect over Frame Relay
1467	Status of CIDR Deployment in the Internet
1441	Introduction to Version 2 of the Internet-standard Network Management Framework
1350	The TFTP Protocol (Revision 2)
1305	Network Time Protocol (Version 3) Specification, Implementation
1256	ICMP Router Discovery Messages
1247	OSPF Version 2 (made obsolete by RFC 1583)
1246	Experience with the OSPF Protocol
1245	OSPF Protocol Analysis

Table E-1   *RFCs (Continued)*

RFC	Title
1243	AppleTalk Management Information Base
1231	IEEE 802.5 Token Ring MIB
1219	On the Assignment of Subnet Numbers
1213	Management Information Base for Network Management of TCP/IP-based internets: MIB-II
1144	Compressing TCP/IP Headers for Low-speed Serial Links
1058	Routing Information Protocol
1042	Standard for the Transmission of IP Datagrams over IEEE 802 Networks
1020	Internet Numbers
951	Bootstrap Protocol
950	Internet Standard Subnetting Procedure
903	Reverse Address Resolution Protocol
821	Simple Mail Transfer Protocol
793	Transmission Control Protocol
792	Internet Control Message Protocol
791	Internet Protocol

This appendix contains information about the Cisco Network Address Translation (NAT) that was obtained from the Cisco website and from some Cisco courses. It includes the following sections:

- Why Use NAT?
- NAT Operation
- Configuring NAT
- Verifying NAT
- Implementation Considerations

Network Address Translation

IP address depletion is a key problem facing the Internet. To assist in maximizing the use of your registered IP addresses, Cisco IOS Release 11.2 and later versions include software that implements Network Address Translation (NAT). This feature, which is the Cisco implementation of RFC 1631, *The IP Network Address Translator* (available at www.cis.ohio-state.edu/cgi-bin/rfc/rfc1631.html), provides a method for using the same IP addresses in multiple internal stub networks, thereby reducing the need for registered IP addresses.

Why Use NAT?

Use NAT in the following situations:

- **When you want to connect to the Internet, but not all hosts have globally unique IP addresses**—NAT technology enables private IP internetworks that use nonregistered IP addresses to connect to the Internet. A NAT router is placed on the border of a stub domain (referred to as the *inside network*) and a public network, such as the Internet (referred to as the *outside* network). It translates the internal local addresses into globally unique IP addresses before sending packets to the outside network.

    NAT takes advantage of the fact that relatively few hosts in a stub domain communicate outside of the domain at any given time. As a result, only a subset of the IP addresses in a stub domain must be translated into globally unique IP addresses when outside communication is necessary.

- **When you need to modify your internal addresses because you are changing Internet service providers (ISPs)**—NAT can be used to translate the appropriate addresses. This enables you to change addresses incrementally, without changing hosts or routers other than those that border stub domains.

- **When you want to do basic load sharing**—You can map outside IP addresses to inside IP addresses using the Transmission Control Protocol (TCP) Load Distribution feature.

NAT Terminology

When using NAT, the terms inside and outside networks are used, as shown in the example in Figure F-1. The terminology for NAT, as used in Figure F-1, is defined in Table F-1.

Figure F-1   *Network Address Translation Is Used to Translate Addresses Between the Inside and Outside Networks*

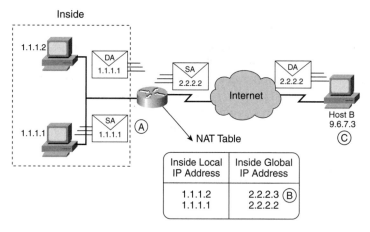

Table F-1   *NAT Terminology*

Term	Definition
Inside Local IP Address (A)	The IP address assigned to a host on the inside network. The address was globally unique, but obsolete, allocated from RFC 1918 (*Address Allocation for Private Internet Space*) or randomly picked.
Inside Global IP Address (B)	A legitimate IP address (typically assigned by a service provider) that represents one or more inside local IP addresses to the outside world. The address was allocated from a globally unique address space that is typically provided by the Internet Service Provider (ISP).
Outside Global IP Address (C)	The IP address that was assigned to a host on the outside network by its owner. The address was allocated from a globally routable address space.
Outside Local IP Address (not shown)	The IP address of an outside host as it appears to the inside network. The address was allocated from address space that is routable on the inside, or possibly from RFC 1918, for example.
Simple Translation Entry	A translation entry that maps one IP address to another. The NAT table in Figure F-1 shows this type of entry.
Extended Translation Entry (not shown)	A translation entry that maps one IP address and port pair to another.

Supported Features

NAT supports the following features:

- **Static address translation**—Establishes a one-to-one mapping between inside local and global addresses.

- **Dynamic source address translation**—Establishes a dynamic mapping between the inside local and global addresses by associating the local addresses to be translated with the pool of addresses from which to allocate global addresses. The router creates translations as needed.

- **Address overloading**—Can conserve addresses in the inside global address pool by allowing source ports in TCP connections or User Datagram Protocol (UDP) conversations to be translated. When different inside local addresses map to the same inside global address, each inside host's TCP or UDP port numbers are used to distinguish between them.

- **TCP load distribution**—A dynamic form of destination translation that can be configured for some outside-to-inside traffic. Once a mapping is defined, destination addresses that match an access list are replaced with an address from a rotary pool. Allocation is completed on a round-robin basis, and only when a new connection is opened from the outside to the inside. All non-TCP traffic is passed untranslated (unless other translations are in effect).

NAT Operation

NAT can be used to perform several functions. This section discusses the operation of the following NAT functions:

- Translating inside local addresses
- Overloading inside global addresses
- Handling overlapping networks
- TCP load distribution

Translating Inside Local Addresses

Figure F-2 illustrates NAT operation when NAT is used to translate addresses from inside your network to destinations outside of your network.

Figure F-2   *Translating Inside Local Addresses*

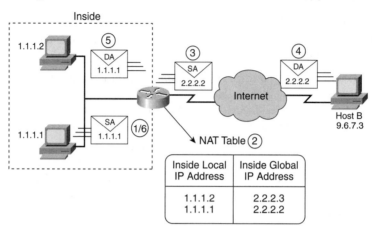

The following list describes this process of translating inside local addresses:

Step 1   The user at Host 1.1.1.1 opens a connection to Host B.

Step 2   The first packet that the router receives from Host 1.1.1.1 causes the router to check its NAT table.

   If a translation is found because it has been statically configured, the router continues to Step 3.

   If no translation is found, the router determines that address 1.1.1.1 must be translated. The router allocates a new address and sets up a translation of the inside local address 1.1.1.1 to a legal global address from the dynamic address pool. This type of translation entry is referred to as a *simple entry.*

Step 3   The router replaces Host 1.1.1.1's inside local IP address with the selected inside global address (2.2.2.2) and forwards the packet.

Step 4   Host B receives the packet and responds to Host 1.1.1.1 using the inside global IP address 2.2.2.2.

Step 5   When the router receives the packet with the inside global IP address, the router uses the inside global address as a reference to perform a NAT table lookup. The router then translates the address to Host 1.1.1.1's inside local address and forwards the packet to Host 1.1.1.1.

Step 6   Host 1.1.1.1 receives the packet and continues the conversation. For each packet, the router performs Steps 2 through 5.

Overloading Inside Global Addresses

Figure F-3 illustrates NAT operation when a single inside global address can represent multiple inside local addresses simultaneously.

Figure F-3   *Overloading Inside Global Addresses*

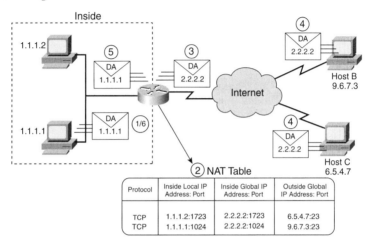

The following list describes the process of overloading inside global addresses, as depicted in Figure F-3:

Step 1   The user at Host 1.1.1.1 opens a connection to Host B.

Step 2   The first packet the router receives from Host 1.1.1.1 causes the router to check its NAT table.

Step 3   If no translation is found, the router determines that address 1.1.1.1 must be translated. The router allocates a new address and sets up a translation of the inside local address 1.1.1.1 to a legal global address (2.2.2.2). If overloading is enabled and another translation is active, the router reuses the global address from that translation and saves enough information (the port number) to distinguish it from the other translation entry. This type of entry is called an *extended entry*.

Step 4   The router replaces Host 1.1.1.1's inside local IP address with the selected inside global address (2.2.2.2) and forwards the packet.

Step 5   Host B receives the packet and responds to Host 1.1.1.1 using the inside global IP address 2.2.2.2.

When the router receives the packet with the inside global IP address, the router uses the inside global address and port number and the outside address and port number as references to perform a NAT table lookup. The router then translates the address to Host 1.1.1.1's inside local address and forwards the packet to Host 1.1.1.1.

Step 6   Host 1.1.1.1 receives the packet and continues the conversation. For each
packet, the router performs Steps 2 through 5.

Handling Overlapping Networks

Figure F-4 illustrates NAT operation when addresses in the inside network overlap with
addresses that are in the outside network.

Figure F-4   *Handling Overlapping Networks*

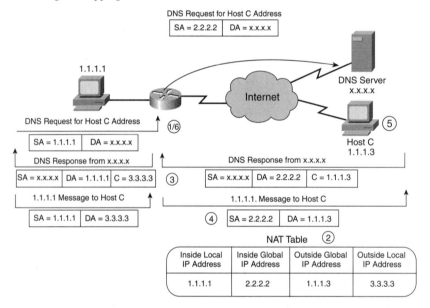

The following list describes this process of handling overlapping addresses:

Step 1   The user at 1.1.1.1 opens a connection to Host C (1.1.1.3), causing
1.1.1.1 to perform a name-to-address lookup to a Domain Name Service
(DNS) server.

Step 2   If there is an overlap, the router intercepts the DNS reply and translates
the returned address. In this case, 1.1.1.3 overlaps with an inside address.
To translate the return address of Host C, the router creates a simple
translation entry that maps the overlapping address 1.1.1.3 to an address
from a separately configured outside local address pool. In this example,
the address is 3.3.3.3.

Step 3   The router then forwards the DNS reply to Host 1.1.1.1. The reply has
Host C's address as 3.3.3.3. At this point, 1.1.1.1 opens a connection to
3.3.3.3.

Step 4 When the router receives the packet for Host C (3.3.3.3), it sets up a translation that maps the inside local and global addresses and the outside global and local addresses by replacing the source address of 1.1.1.1 with the inside global address 2.2.2.2 and replacing the destination address of 3.3.3.3 with Host C's outside global address 1.1.1.3.

Step 5 Host C receives a packet and continues the conversation.

Step 6 For each packet sent between Host 1.1.1.1 and Host C, the router performs a lookup, replaces the destination address with the inside local address, and replaces the source address with the outside local address.

TCP Load Distribution

Figure F-5 illustrates NAT operation when NAT is used to map one virtual host to several real hosts.

Figure F-5 *TCP Load Distribution*

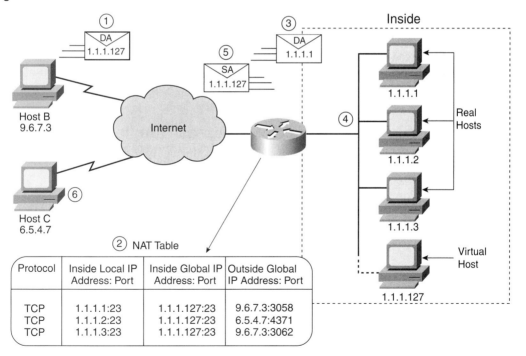

Protocol	Inside Local IP Address: Port	Inside Global IP Address: Port	Outside Global IP Address: Port
TCP	1.1.1.1:23	1.1.1.127:23	9.6.7.3:3058
TCP	1.1.1.2:23	1.1.1.127:23	6.5.4.7:4371
TCP	1.1.1.3:23	1.1.1.127:23	9.6.7.3:3062

The following list describes the process of TCP load distribution, as depicted in Figure F-5:

Step 1   The user on Host B (9.6.7.3) opens a TCP connection to the virtual host at 1.1.1.127.

Step 2   The router receives the connection request and creates a new translation, thereby allocating the next real host (1.1.1.1) for the inside local IP address.

Step 3   The router replaces the destination address with the selected real host address and forwards the packet.

Step 4   Host 1.1.1.1 receives the packet and responds.

Step 5   The router receives the packet and performs a NAT table lookup using the inside local address (1.1.1.1) and port number and the outside address (9.6.7.3) and port number as the key. The router then translates the source address to the virtual host's address and forwards the packet.

Step 6   The next connection request causes the router to allocate 1.1.1.2 for the inside local address.

Configuring NAT

This section describes how to configure various NAT capabilities.

Configuring NAT for Basic Local IP Address Translation

The following procedure enables basic local IP address translation:

Step 1   At a minimum, IP routing and appropriate IP addresses must be configured on the router.

Step 2   If you are performing static address translations for inside local addresses, define the addresses using the following command:

```
Router(config)#ip nat inside source static local-ip global-ip
```

Step 3   If you are performing dynamic translations, define a standard IP access list for the inside network.

Step 4   If you are performing dynamic translations, define an IP NAT pool for the inside network using the following command:

```
Router(config)#ip nat pool name start-ip end-ip {netmask netmask |
   prefix-length prefix-length}
```

This command defines a pool of contiguous addresses from the start address to the end address, using the netmask or prefix length. These addresses are allocated as needed.

Step 5 If you are performing dynamic translations, define a map between the access list and the IP NAT pool using the following command:

```
Router(config)#ip nat inside source list access-list-number pool name
```

Step 6 Enable NAT on at least one inside and one outside interface using the following command:

```
Router(config-if)#ip nat {inside | outside}
```

Step 7 Only packets moving between "inside" and "outside" interfaces can be translated. For example, if a packet is received on an "inside" interface but is not destined for an "outside" interface, it is not translated.

Example F-1 shows a sample configuration of basic inside local address translation. This example uses a pool of addresses named *net-2* to translate inside local addresses 1.1.1.x to inside global addresses 2.2.2.x.

Example F-12 *An Example of Basic Inside Local Address Translation*

```
ip nat pool net-2 2.2.2.1 2.2.2.254 netmask 255.255.255.0
ip nat inside source list 1 pool net-2
!
interface Serial0
  ip address 171.69.232.182 255.255.255.240
  ip nat outside
!
interface Ethernet0
  ip address 1.1.1.254 255.255.255.0
  ip nat inside
!
access-list 1 permit 1.1.1.0 0.0.0.255
```

Configuring Inside Global Address Overloading

The following procedure configures inside global address overloading:

Step 1 At a minimum, IP routing and appropriate IP addresses must be configured on the router.

Step 2 Configure dynamic address translation, as described in the "Configuring NAT for Basic Local IP Address Translation" section.

When you define the mapping between the access list and the IP NAT pool, add the **overload** keyword to the commands:

```
Router(config)#ip nat inside source list access-list-number pool name
  overload
```

Step 3 Enable NAT on the appropriate interfaces with the following command:

```
Router(config-if)#ip nat {inside | outside}
```

Example F-2 shows a sample configuration of inside global address overloading. This example uses a pool of addresses named *net-2* to translate inside local addresses 1.1.1.x to inside global addresses 2.2.2.x. Inside global addresses will be overloaded.

Example F-13 *An Example of Inside Global Address Overloading*

```
ip nat pool net-2 2.2.2.1 2.2.2.254 netmask 255.255.255.0
ip nat inside source list 1 pool net-2 overload
!
interface Serial0
  ip address 171.69.232.182 255.255.255.240
  ip nat outside
!
interface Ethernet0
  ip address 1.1.1.254 255.255.255.0
  ip nat inside
!
access-list 1 permit 1.1.1.0 0.0.0.255
```

Configuring NAT to Translate Overlapping Addresses

Following is the procedure used to configure overlapping address translation:

Step 1   At a minimum, IP routing and appropriate IP addresses must be configured on the router.

Step 2   Define the standard IP access list for the inside network, as previously discussed.

Step 3   Define an IP NAT pool for the inside network, as previously discussed, using the following command:

> Router(config)#**ip nat pool** *name start-ip end-ip* {**netmask** *netmask* |
> **prefix-length** *prefix-length*}

Step 4   Define an IP NAT pool (with a different name) for the outside network using the following command:

> Router(config)#**ip nat pool** *name start-ip end-ip* {**netmask** *netmask* |
> **prefix-length** *prefix-length*}

Step 5   Define the mapping between the access list and the inside global pool, as previously discussed, using the following command:

> Router(config)#**ip nat inside source list** *access-list-number* **pool** *name*
> [**overload**]

Step 6   Define the mapping between the access list and the outside local pool using the following command:

> Router(config)#**ip nat outside source list** *access-list-number* **pool** *name*

Step 7   Enable NAT on the appropriate interface, as previously discussed, using the following command:

> Router(config-if)#**ip nat {inside | outside}**

Example F-3 shows a sample configuration of translating overlapping addresses. This example uses a pool of addresses named *net-2* to translate inside local addresses 1.1.1.x to inside global addresses 2.2.2.x. It also uses a pool of addresses named *net-10* to translate outside global addresses 1.1.1.x to outside local addresses 10.0.1.x.

Example F-14 *An Example of Translating Overlapping Addresses*

```
ip nat pool net-2 2.2.2.1 2.2.2.254 prefix-length 24
ip nat pool net-10 10.0.1.1 10.0.1.254 prefix-length 24
ip nat inside source list 1 pool net-2
ip nat outside source list 1 pool net-10
!
interface Serial0
  ip address 171.69.232.182 255.255.255.240
  ip nat outside
!
interface Ethernet0
  ip address 1.1.1.254 255.255.255.0
  ip nat inside
!
access-list 1 permit 1.1.1.0 0.0.0.255
```

Configuring TCP Load Distribution

The following procedure configures TCP load distribution:

Step 1   At a minimum, configure IP routing and appropriate IP addresses on the router.

Step 2   Define a standard IP access list with a **permit** statement for the virtual host.

Step 3   Define an IP NAT pool for the real hosts, ensuring that it is a rotary-type pool, using the following command:

```
Router(config)#ip nat pool name start-ip end-ip {netmask netmask |
   prefix-length prefix-length} type rotary
```

Step 4   Use the following command to define a mapping between the access list and the real host pool:

```
Router(config)#ip nat inside destination list access-list-number pool
   name
```

Step 5   Enable NAT on the appropriate interface, as previously discussed, using the following command:

```
Router(config-if)#ip nat {inside | outside}
```

Example F-4 shows a sample configuration of TCP load distribution. This example uses an access list to translate the virtual server address 1.1.1.127 (the inside global address) to a pool of real host addresses from a pool named real-hosts.

Example F-15 *An Example of TCP Load Distribution*

```
ip nat pool real-hosts 1.1.1.1 1.1.1.126 prefix-length 24 type rotary
ip nat inside destination list 2 pool real-hosts
!
interface Serial0
  ip address 192.168.1.129 255.255.255.240
  ip nat outside
!
interface Ethernet0
  ip address 1.1.1.254 255.255.255.0
  ip nat inside
!
access-list 2 permit 1.1.1.127
```

Verifying NAT

This section lists **show** and **clear** commands that are used to verify NAT operation.

show Commands

Table F-2 presents the commands that can be used to verify NAT operation.

Table F-2   **show** *Commands to Verify NAT Operation*

Command	Description
show ip nat translations [verbose]	Shows active translations
show ip nat statistics	Shows translation statistics

Example F-5 shows a sample verification output for basic IP address translation.

Example F-16 *A Sample Verification Output for Basic IP Address Translation*

```
router#show ip nat trans
Pro  Inside global      Inside local     Outside local     Outside global
---   2.2.2.2            1.1.1.1          ---               ---
---   2.2.2.3            1.1.1.2          ---               ---
```

Example F-6 shows a sample verification output for IP address translation with overloading.

Example F-17 *A Sample Verification Output for IP Address Translation with Overloading*

```
router#show ip nat trans
Pro  Inside global    Inside local     Outside local      Outside global
udp  2.2.2.2:1220     1.1.1.1:1220     171.69.2.132:53    171.69.2.132:53
tcp  2.2.2.2:11012    1.1.1.2:11012    171.69.1.220:23    171.69.1.220:23
tcp  2.2.2.2:1067     1.1.1.1:1067     171.69.1.161:23    171.69.1.161:23
```

Clearing NAT Translation Entries

If you need to clear a dynamic translation entry, use the commands shown in Table F-3.

Table F-3   *Commands to Clear NAT Translation Entries*

Command	Description
clear ip nat translation *	Clears all translation entries.
clear ip nat translation inside *global-ip local- ip* [**outside** *local-ip global-ip*]	Clears a simple translation entry that contains an inside translation or both an inside and outside translation.
clear ip nat translation outside *local-ip global-ip*	Clears a simple translation entry that contains an outside translation.
clear ip nat translation *protocol* **inside** *global-ip global-port local-ip local-port* [**outside** *local-ip local-portglobal-ip global-port*]	Clears an extended entry (in its various forms).

Examples F-7 and F-8 provide two sample outputs using the **clear** commands.

Example F-18 *Clearing NAT Translation Example 1*

```
router#show ip nat trans
Pro  Inside global     Inside local     Outside local     Outside global
udp  2.2.2.2:1220       1.1.1.1:1220     171.69.2.132:53   171.69.2.132:53
tcp  2.2.2.2:11012      1.1.1.2:11012    171.69.1.220:23   171.69.1.220:23
tcp  2.2.2.2:1067       1.1.1.1:1067     171.69.1.161:23   171.69.1.161:23
router#clear ip nat translation *
router#show ip nat trans
router#
```

Example F-19 *Clearing NAT Translation Example 2*

```
router#show ip nat trans
Pro  Inside global     Inside local     Outside local     Outside global
udp  2.2.2.2:1220       1.1.1.1:1220     171.69.2.132:53   171.69.2.132:53
tcp  2.2.2.2:11012      1.1.1.2:11012    171.69.1.220:23   171.69.1.220:23
tcp  2.2.2.2:1067       1.1.1.1:1067     171.69.1.161:23   171.69.1.161:23
router#clear ip nat translation udp inside 2.2.2.2 1220 1.1.1.1 1220 outside
    171.69.2.132 53 171.69.2.132 53
router#show ip nat trans
Pro  Inside global     Inside local     Outside local     Outside global
tcp  2.2.2.2:11012      1.1.1.2:11012    171.69.1.220:23   171.69.1.220:23
tcp  2.2.2.2:1067       1.1.1.1:1067     171.69.1.161:23   171.69.1.161:23
```

Troubleshooting NAT

If you need to use a trace on a NAT operation, use the **debug ip nat [list | detailed]** command, which displays a line of output for each packet that is translated.

Example F-9 shows sample output using the **debug ip nat** command.

Example F-20 *Tracing NAT Operations with* **debug ip nat**

```
router#debug ip nat
NAT:  s=1.1.1.1->2.2.2.2, d=171.69.2.132       [6825]
NAT:  s=171.69.2.132,     d=2.2.2.2->1.1.1.1   [21852]
NAT:  s=1.1.1.1->2.2.2.2, d=171.69.1.161       [6826]
NAT*: s=171.69.1.161,     d=2.2.2.2->1.1.1.1   [23311]
NAT*: s=1.1.1.1->2.2.2.2, d=171.69.1.161       [6827]
NAT*: s=1.1.1.1->2.2.2.2, d=171.69.1.161       [6828]
NAT*: s=171.69.1.161,     d=2.2.2.2->1.1.1.1   [23313]
NAT*: s=171.69.1.161,     d=2.2.2.2->1.1.1.1   [23325]
```

The debug output in Example F-9 can be decoded as follows (using the fourth line of output):

- The asterisk next to NAT indicates that the translation is occurring in the fast path. The first packet in a conversation always goes through the slow path (that is, it is process-switched). The remaining packets go through the fast path if a cache entry exists.

- s=171.69.1.161 is the source address.

- d=2.2.2.2 is the destination address.

- 2.2.2.2->1.1.1.1 indicates that the address was translated.

- The value in brackets is the IP identification number. This information might be useful for debugging because it enables you to correlate with other packet traces, such as from protocol analyzers.

Implementation Considerations

Some things to consider before implementing NAT include the following:

- Translation introduces delays into the switching paths.

- NAT makes some applications that use IP addresses difficult or impossible to use. For example, public World Wide Web pages that have links expressed using local IP addresses rather than DNS names are not usable by outside hosts. A list of traffic types that are supported and not supported by NAT is available in the "Product Bulletin - No. 792 Cisco IOS Network Address Translation (NAT) Packaging Update" document on the Cisco website, at www.cisco.com/warp/public/cc/pd/iosw/ioft/ionetn/prodlit/792_pp.htm.

- NAT hides the hosts' real identity.
- All packets that need to be translated must go through the NAT router, which may place limitations on the network design.

Answers to Review Questions, Case Studies, and Simulation Exercises

This appendix provides our internetworking experts' solutions (listed by chapter) to the review questions, case study questions, and simulation exercise questions in each chapter.

A solution is provided for each of the case study and simulation tasks based on assumptions made. There is no claim that the provided solution is the best or only solution. Your solution might be more appropriate for the assumptions you made. The provided solution allows you to understand the author's reasoning and offers a means of comparing and contrasting your solution.

The answers appear in bold.

Chapter 2: Applying Design Principles in Network Deployment

Case Study

Step 2   Document any information that you think is missing from the scenario and that you consider necessary for the design. Write down these items and provide a brief comment for each.

Answer: The missing information necessary for the design but not presented by the customer is listed in Table G-1. Before beginning the detailed design, you should extract this information from the customer.

Table G-1   *Some Missing Information in the DJMP Case Study*

Missing Item	Comments
Current WAN type	There is no information about whether the WAN links to regional offices are leased lines or some type of public network such as Frame Relay.
Current bandwidth of the links to the regional offices and to the Internet	Knowing the existing bandwidths is necessary for evaluating the effect of the new applications and for planning new capacities.
WAN backup	There is no information about whether WAN links are backed up. The information is necessary for designing resilience in the network.
Current IP addressing scheme	Although the information says that a flat addressing scheme is implemented, this is not sufficient information. At a minimum, the address range and address class are required.
Technical constraints (availability of certain WAN services at the regional offices; availability of the Internet at the planned new remote offices)	Although it is a designer's job to determine the availability of the WAN and Internet connectivity options, you should discuss the current situation with the customer to try to extract this information.
Budget available for new solutions	The customer has not provided any information about the available budget. The available budget affects the proposed solution; at least some hints about the budget are extremely helpful to the designer.
Responsible people	The customer has not supplied any contacts. You should at least determine a project's technical and business contacts.
Business constraints	The customer has not mentioned any business constraints. The current network equipment vendor is unknown, no preferences are given, and so on. You should extract these constraints in the initial phases of the design.

Step 3   Outline the major design areas you must address while designing the solution for the given customer scenario; provide a brief comment for each.

Answer: Table G-2 lists the major design areas that you must address in your design project, according to the given scenario. For each area, your task is to evaluate possible solutions and propose the most optimal one based on the customer requirements.

Table G-2   *Major Design Areas in the DJMP Case Study*

Major Design Areas	Comments
Redesign IP addressing	The flat addressing scheme and the use of RIP as the routing protocol are certainly not features of scalable growing networks. New hierarchical addressing is required.
Redesign Campus LAN	The current campus LAN is shared and interconnects two buildings. The campus must be entirely redesigned, including the placement of servers, because there is no redundancy in the LAN.
Upgrade WAN links	Upgrade of the WAN links is essential because, according to the customer, the current bandwidth seems insufficient. The introduction of new applications will result in a higher load because the existing applications remain.
Select new routing protocol	The customer is aware of the drawbacks of RIP. You should replace it with a routing protocol that is more scalable, and that fits into the planned hierarchical addressing scheme more comfortably.
Integrate international offices into the company network	The two international offices, which are scheduled to open soon, will likely use Internet and VPN implementation. Additionally, a voice solution must be proposed for these two offices.

Step 4   Assume that you just purchased an extremely powerful network simulation tool. Decide how it can help you in making your design decisions. Write down some possible scenarios in which you could evaluate the effects of the new design by using the simulation tool.

Answer: Depending on the major design areas your design project addresses, you could use your simulation tool to evaluate the solutions listed in Table G-3. The simulation tool allows you to simplify the prototype or pilot for this project.

Table G-3   *Possible Simulation Scenarios for DJMP Case Study*

Possible Simulation	Comments
Effect of new applications on the existing links	Based on the applications' mix and the information you have about their users, you could simulate the load on the WAN links. Before the simulation, you must determine the current bandwidths of the links.
Comparison of shared versus switched LAN	Because the customer wants some proof of the benefits that the switched LAN will bring, you could simulate both scenarios and compare the results.

continues

Table G-3   *Possible Simulation Scenarios for DJMP Case Study (Continued)*

Possible Simulation	Comments
Switched campus LAN solution	You plan to completely redesign the campus LAN and introduce a switching solution that includes redundancy. You can use a simulation tool to check the effects of redundancy and link usage in the campus solution.
Routing convergence	Because of your plan to replace RIP with a hierarchical protocol (possibly OSPF), you could examine the convergence of the protocol in the new campus. You could compare various campus scenarios, including Layer 3 switching throughout or only in some parts. You can also examine the load sharing options.
Voice over IP	For the international offices, you can simulate the effect of adding voice on top of the data traffic.

Simulation Exercise

1 Observe the directions in which the load was higher. What can you determine from the results?

Answer: The utilization of the WAN links exceeded the predefined threshold in the direction of the headquarters, toward the regional offices. The traffic was light in the opposite direction. These results indicate that the regional offices access the central servers, and that the responses represent the majority of the traffic. A certain amount of traffic also results from accessing the Internet via the central site.

2 What can you determine from the simulation results? Compare the planned number of users and applications for each of the regional offices. In which direction are the links saturated?

Answer: The results show that, with an increased number of applications and their respective users, the amount of traffic increases and leads to saturation on the San Jose – Houston link, in the outbound direction.

3 Comparing the results from the initial traffic simulation with the results from the simulations using the new applications, you observe that the traffic from Denver to the Headquarters is also significant now. Why is this?

Answer: The users in Denver are mainly engineers, and from their profiles, it is evident that FTP is the major application they use. The heavy load in the outbound direction from Denver to the Headquarters is probably the result of uploading files to the central location.

4 What can you determine from the graphs?

Answer: The graphs show that the response time exceeded 10 seconds for approximately 25 percent of all web pages.

5 What do you observe from the graphs?

Answer: The link utilization in the outbound direction was jittering at approximately the 60 percent mark. The response time for over 90 percent of all web pages (HTTP requests) was below 10 seconds. The response time was below 5 seconds for approximately 75 percent of all HTTP requests.

Review Questions

1 List three characteristics of a corporation that uses a traditional organizational model.

Answer: Three characteristics of a corporation that uses a traditional organizational model include

— **The organization is integrated vertically.**

— **Partnering is difficult and costly.**

— **Most of the production is done internally.**

2 Describe the characteristics of a horizontally integrated organization.

Answer: An organization that is integrated horizontally partners with other organizations that have the expertise required to help them produce their product or service in a more efficient and effective manner. Sharing information, both internally and externally, is key to these modern organizations.

3 What are the four components of the Network Organizational Model architecture?

Answer: The four components of the Network Organizational Model architecture are applications, enabling network solutions, prerequisite systems, and network infrastructure.

4 List four guidelines to follow when implementing the Network Organizational Model.

Answer: The four guidelines to follow when implementing the Network Organizational Model are

— **Incremental integration.**

— **Develop an architecture that reflects the logical structure and the processes conducted within the organization and its ecosystem.**

— **Solicit constant input from users.**

— **Include manageability and control on all levels of the network architecture.**

5 What are the two categories of organizational policies?

Answer: Organizational policies fall into two categories:

— **Common legal and regulatory policies**

— **Organizationally specific policies**

6 True or false? Organizational structure and procedures influence the organization's network design.

Answer: True

7 Name some network features that must be understood in order to achieve organizational goals.

Answer: Organizational goals cannot be achieved without a full understanding and integration of the following networking features:

— **Functionality**

— **Scalability**

— **Availability**

— **Performance**

— **Manageability**

— **Efficiency**

8 Match the PDIOO network lifecycle phases with their correct descriptions.

Phases:

a. Plan phase

b. Design phase

c. Implement phase

d. Operate phase

e. Optimize phase

f. Retirement

Descriptions:

1. Network is built

2. Produces a network design specification

3. Includes fault detection and correction and performance monitoring

4. Network requirements are identified

5. Network is removed from production

6. Based on proactive management of the network

Answer:

a. 4

b. 2

c. 1

d. 3

e. 6

f. 5

9 During which PDIOO phase is the initial design verification performed?

Answer: The initial design verification is performed during the Implement phase.

10 What are the eight steps of the design methodology?

Answer: The eight steps of the design methodology are as follows:

Step 1   **Identify customer requirements**

Step 2   **Characterize the existing network**

Step 3   **Design the topology and network solutions**

Step 4   **Plan the implementation**

Step 5   **Build a pilot network**

Step 6   **Document the design**

Step 7   **Implement and verify the design**

Step 8   **Monitor and optionally redesign**

11 List some determinants of the scope of a design project.

Answer: Some determinants of the scope of a design project are as follows:

— **If the design is for a new network, or if it is a modification of an existing network**

— **If the design is for an entire enterprise network, a subset of the network, or simply a single segment or module**

— **The OSI protocol layers involved**

12 What information is required before a network design can begin?

Answer: The following information is required before a network design can begin:

— **Organizational goals**

— **Organizational constraints**

— **Planned applications and network services**

— **Technical goals**

— **Technical constraints**

13 What are some typical organizational goals?

Answer: Typical goals include

— **Increased revenue**

— **Shorter development cycles**

— **Improved customer support**

— **Open the organization's information infrastructure**

14 Corporation X is currently spending $7,000 per month for telephony services provided by its local phone company. The new IP telephony equipment costs $40,000, and the operating costs are $2,000 per month. Determine when the introduction of IP telephony will pay for itself.

a. After eight months

b. After five months

c. After one year

d. It will not pay for itself

Answer:

a. After eight months

b. After five months

c. After one year

d. It will not pay for itself

15 List some common organizational constraints.

Answer: Typical organizational constraints include

— **Budget**

— **Availability of personnel**

— **Policies**

— **Schedule**

16 Explain why a schedule might be a design constraint.

Answer: The new network design is often driven by the introduction of new network applications; the implementation time frames for new applications are often tightly connected and therefore influence the available time for network design.

17 Corporation X is planning to introduce new systems for its employees, including e-learning, videoconferencing, and an alternative telephone service to reduce its operational costs. Which are two planned applications?

   a. E-mail

   b. IP multicast

   c. IP/TV

   d. IP Telephony

   e. Quality of service (QoS)

   Answer:

   a. E-mail

   b. IP multicast

   c. IP/TV

   d. IP Telephony

   e. Quality-of-service (QoS)

18 Users typically think of network performance in terms of what?

   a. Throughput

   b. Responsiveness

   c. Resource utilization

   Answer:

   a. Throughput

   b. Responsiveness

   c. Resource utilization

19 What suggestion do you have for mitigating the bandwidth constraint?

   Answer: The corporation should consider looking for an alternate service provider.

20 What is the Converged Network Investment Calculator?

   Answer: The CNIC helps calculate a customer's ROI for Cisco IP telephony solutions by providing a framework for gathering the necessary data, analyzing the various costs and benefits, and calculating the ROI.

21 How does traffic analysis help in the characterization of a network?

   Answer: Traffic analysis provides information about the applications and protocols used in the network and might reveal some shortcomings in the network.

22 A Layer 2 topology map includes which two of the following features:

    a. Routers

    b. Switches

    c. IP Addressing Scheme

    d. Logical WAN Links

    e. Media type

    Answer:

    a. Routers

    b. Switches

    c. IP Addressing Scheme

    d. Logical WAN Links

    e. Media type

23 The auditing process should never require any changes in the network: true or false?

    Answer: False. The auditing process might require minor (temporary) changes in the network.

24 List some tools that can be used in the network audit process.

    Answer: Cisco Works and many third-party tools such as HP OpenView, IBM Tivoli, MRTG, and NetZoom can be used for network auditing.

25 Which command can be used to determine memory usage on a Cisco router?

    a. show processes memory

    b. show processes cpu

    c. show memory utilization

    d. show version

    Answer:

    a. show processes memory

    b. show processes cpu

    c. show memory utilization

    d. show version

26 Which command displays packet size distribution and activity by protocol on a Cisco router?

    a. show ip nbar protocol-discovery

    b. show ip interface

    c. show version

    d. show ip cache flow

Answer:

    a. show ip nbar protocol-discovery

    b. show ip interface

    c. show version

    d. show ip cache flow

27 What is the difference between a saturated Ethernet segment and a saturated WAN link?

Answer: An Ethernet segment is considered saturated at 40 percent network utilization, while a WAN link is not considered saturated until 70 percent network utilization.

28 Fill in the missing item: The network health summary report includes recommendations that _____.

    a. relate the existing network and the customer requirements

    b. are based on the customer requirements

    c. are used to sell more boxes

Answer:

    a. relate the existing network and the customer requirements

    b. are based on the customer requirements

    c. are used to sell more boxes

29 What information is used for understanding an existing network?

Answer: All existing sources, such as RFP/RFI documents, existing documentation, direct customer input, and network audits and analysis are used for understanding an existing network.

30 With a top-down design: (choose 3)

   a. The design adapts the physical infrastructure to the requirements.

   b. The design adapts the requirements to the physical infrastructure.

   c. Network devices are chosen after requirement analysis.

   d. Network devices are selected first.

   e. The risk of having to redesign the network is high.

   f. The risk of having to redesign the network is low.

   Answer:

   a. The design adapts the physical infrastructure to the requirements.

   b. The design adapts the requirements to the physical infrastructure.

   c. Network devices are chosen after requirement analysis.

   d. Network devices are selected first.

   e. The risk of having to redesign the network is high.

   f. The risk of having to redesign the network is low.

31 What are the layers in the three-layer hierarchical structure?

   a. Core, distribution, and desktop

   b. Core, distribution, and access

   c. Core, routing, and access

   d. Backbone, routing, and access

   Answer:

   a. Core, distribution, and desktop

   b. Core, distribution, and access

   c. Core, routing, and access

   d. Backbone, routing, and access

32 What types of tools can be used during the network design process?

Answer: The following tools can be used during the network design process:

— **Network modeling tools**

— **Strategic analysis tools**

— **Decision tables**

— **Simulation and verification tools or services**

33 What items should be included in the documentation for a network design implementation plan?

Answer: The documentation of each step in the implementation plan should contain

— **A description of the step.**

— **References to design documents.**

— **Detailed implementation guidelines.**

— **Detailed rollback guidelines, in case of failure.**

— **The estimated time needed for implementation.**

34 What is the difference between a pilot and a prototype?

Answer: A pilot network tests and verifies the design before the network is launched, or it is a subset of the existing network in which the design is tested.

A prototype network tests and verifies a redesign in an isolated network before it is applied to the existing network.

35 What sections are included in a typical final design document?

Answer: A typical final design document includes the following sections:

— **Introduction**

— **Design requirements**

— **Existing network infrastructure**

— **Design**

— **Proof of concept**

— **Implementation plan**

— **Appendixes**

36 Why is the network designer involved in the implementation phase?

Answer: The designer is involved in the implementation phase to assist in the design verification and to take remedial actions, if necessary.

37   What might necessitate a redesign of the network?

Answer: A network redesign might be required if troubleshooting problems becomes too frequent or even impossible to manage. Hopefully this scenario can be avoided if all previous design steps have been completed properly.

Chapter 3: Structuring and Modularizing the Network

Review Questions

1   Figure 3-26 presents a sample hierarchically-structured network. Some of the devices are marked with letters. How should you map the marked devices to the access, distribution, and core layers in Figure 3-26?

Answer:

Access layer: Devices A, B, E, and F

Distribution layer: Devices A, B, D, and F

Core layer: Device C

2   Describe the role of each layer in the hierarchical network model.

Answer: The role of each layer in the hierarchical network model is as follows:

— **The access layer provides local and remote workgroup or user access to the network.**

— **The distribution layer provides policy-based connectivity.**

— **The core (or backbone) layer provides high-speed transport.**

3   True or False? Each layer in the hierarchical network model must be implemented with distinct physical devices.

Answer: False. The layers do not need to be implemented as distinct physical entities. The layers are defined to aid successful network design and to represent functionality that must exist in a network; the actual manner in which the layers are implemented depends on the needs of the network that is being designed. Each layer can be implemented in routers or switches, represented by physical media, or combined in a single device. A particular layer can be omitted altogether, but hierarchy should be maintained for optimum performance.

4 What features of a Layer 3 switch could be used in the access layer?

Answer: Some Layer 3 features that are useful to the access layer include

— **Routing between broadcast domains (including VLANs)**

— **Access to remote offices using various wide-area technologies**

— **Route propagation**

— **Packet filtering**

— **Authentication and security**

— **Quality of Service (QoS)**

— **Dial-on-demand routing (DDR) and static routing**

5 Which two statements are true?

a. UplinkFast immediately unblocks a blocked port after root port failure.

b. PortFast immediately puts a port into the forwarding state.

c. UplinkFast immediately puts a port into the forwarding state.

d. PortFast immediately unblocks a blocked port after root port failure.

Answer: A and B.

6 Which layer in the hierarchical model provides media translation?

Answer: The distribution layer.

7 What are three roles of the hierarchical model's core layer?

a. Provide fast and efficient data transport

b. Provide maximum availability and reliability

c. Provide access to the corporate network via some wide-area technology

d. Implement policies regarding security

e. Delineate broadcast domains

f. Implement scalable routing protocols

Answer: A, B, and F.

8 Why might the distribution layer need to redistribute between routing protocols?

Answer: The distribution layer can redistribute between bandwidth-intensive access-layer routing protocols (such as RIP) and optimized core routing protocols (such as OSPF). Redistribution allows the access and core layers to share routing information.

9 What is a benefit of using Layer 3 switching in the core network layer?

Answer: Using Layer 3 allows use of all of the redundant links (since spanning-tree blocking is only done in Layer 2 switches). Along with load balancing, this results in faster convergence in the event of a failure.

10 What are the functional areas in the Enterprise Composite Network model?

Answer: The three functional areas include are

— **Enterprise Campus**

— **Enterprise Edge**

— **Service Provider Edge**

11 What are the modules and submodules within the Enterprise Campus functional area?

Answer: The Enterprise Campus functional area is composed of the following four major modules:

— **Campus Infrastructure module, which contains the following submodules:**

  • **Building Access**

  • **Building Distribution**

  • **Campus Backbone**

— **Network Management module**

— **Server Farm module**

— **Edge Distribution module**

12 The Enterprise Edge functional area includes which modules?

Answer: The Enterprise Edge functional area is comprised of the following four modules:

— **E-commerce module**

— **Internet Connectivity module**

— **VPN/Remote Access module**

— **WAN module**

13 The Service Provider Edge functional area is composed of which modules?

Answer: The modules within the Service Provider Edge functional area include

— **Internet Service Provider module**

— **PSTN module**

— **Frame Relay/ATM module**

14 Which module of the Enterprise Composite model would include wireless connectivity to remote locations?

Answer: The Frame Relay/ATM module covers all WAN technologies for connectivity with remote locations, including wireless.

15 What is an advantage of using the Enterprise Composite Network model?

Answer: This model allows network designers to focus only on a selected module and its functions at one time. Each network solution and intelligent network service can be described on a per-module basis and validated as part of the complete enterprise network design.

16 What is the Campus Backbone submodule's role?

Answer: The Campus Backbone submodule interconnects the Building Access and Distribution submodules with the Server Farm, Network Management, and Edge Distribution modules.

17 Indicate which types of devices would be found in each of these modules (note that some devices are found in more than one module):

Modules:

— E-commerce module

— Internet Connectivity module

— Remote Access and VPN module

Devices:

— Web servers

— SMTP mail servers

— Firewall

— Network Intrusion Detection System (NIDS) appliances

— DNS servers

— VPN concentrators

— Public FTP servers

Answer:

E-commerce module: Web servers, Firewall, Network Intrusion Detection System appliances

Internet Connectivity module: SMTP mail servers, Firewall, Public FTP servers, DNS servers

Remote Access and VPN module: VPN concentrators, Network Intrusion Detection System appliances, Firewall

18 What is the role of the Service Provider functional area?

Answer: The modules in the Service Provider functional area are not implemented by the enterprise itself; however, they are necessary for enabling communication with other networks using different WAN technologies and with Internet Service Providers (ISPs).

19 Classify each of the following as a network service or a network solution:

- — Network management
- — Voice over IP
- — Storage networking
- — Security
- — High availability
- — QoS
- — Content networking

Answer:

Network Services:

- **— Network management**
- **— Security**
- **— High availability**
- **— QoS**
- **— Network solutions**
- **— Voice over IP**
- **— Storage networking**
- **— Content networking**

20 Which functions that support security are the responsibility of the Enterprise Composite Network model's Network Management module?

Answer: The Network Management module's security functions include

- **— syslog**
- **— Authentication, authorization, and accounting (AAA)**
- **— One Time Passwords (OTP)**

21 High availability from end to end is only possible when _____ is deployed throughout the internetwork.

Answer: High availability from end to end is only possible when <u>redundancy</u> is deployed throughout the internetwork.

22 What is the purpose of designing route redundancy in a network?

Answer: Designing redundant routes

— **Minimizes the effect of link failures**

— **Minimizes the effect of an internetworking device failure**

— **Allows load balancing to take place when all routes are up**

23 A full mesh design is ideal for connecting a _____ number of devices.

a. small

b. large

Answer:

a. small

b. large

24 True or false: Back-up links can use different technologies.

Answer: True.

25 What components are required for IP telephony?

Answer: The following components are required for IP telephony:

— **IP phones (replacing traditional phones) to perform voice-to-IP conversion**

— **Switches with inline power (for the IP phones)**

— **Cisco CallManager, a server for call control and signaling**

— **If connection to the PSTN is required, a voice-enabled router or other gateway must be added in the Enterprise Edge, where calls are forwarded to the PSTN.**

26 What role does the Building Access submodule play in voice transportation?

Answer: The Building Access submodule is where IP phones and user computers are attached to Layer 2 switches. Switches provide power to the IP phones. They also provide packet classification, which is essential for proper voice packet manipulation through the network.

27 What should be considered when evaluating the existing data infrastructure for IP telephony?

Answer: When evaluating the existing data infrastructure for IP telephony, consider the following:

— **Performance**

— **Availability**

— **Features**

— **Capacity**

28 Why is Content Networking important in modern networks?

Answer: The goal of CN is to ensure that, transparent to the user, the network serves content with optimal resource usage. The large amount of data and its variety requires that the modern network be content-aware—in other words, be aware of the content that is carried across it in order to handle that content optimally.

29 Which content networking function directs a user request to the optimal resource within a global network based on user-defined policies?

Answer: Content routing

30 Which modules can contain content switches?

Answer: Content switches can be installed in front of the servers or cache devices in any Server Farm module, E-commerce module, or Internet Connectivity module.

Chapter 4: Basic Campus Switching Design Considerations

Case Study

Step 2 Propose the optimal campus design that addresses the scenario requirements (switched solution, redundancy, servers in a separate segment, and so on).

Answer: DJMP Industries' existing campus consists of two buildings that are located in San Jose. The customer has already decided to improve the performance of the campus LAN by introducing LAN switching. A simulation tool is used to prove the benefits of a switched versus a shared solution.

Because of requirements for increased reliability and performance, you propose a redundant switched design with servers placed in a separate LAN (Server Farm). Figure G-1 illustrates this proposed high-level solution.

Figure G-1   *Proposed Campus Design for DJMP Industries*

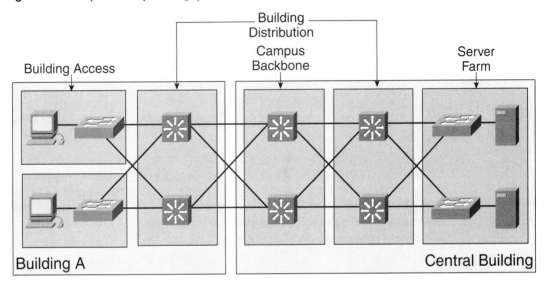

The proposed campus backbone and building distribution consists of Layer 3 switches, which are all redundantly interconnected to ensure high availability and load sharing capabilities.

The building access in both buildings consists of Layer 2 switches that are redundantly connected to upstream distribution switches.

All the servers are placed in the Server Farm module and are attached to access switches.

NOTE	The design currently does not address the high availability of workstations or servers. If this is a future requirement, it can easily be achieved by connecting dual-attached transceivers to the two access switches.

To increase high availability at the access layer, the distribution layer switches could be configured with Cisco Hot Standby Router Protocol (HSRP).

> **To achieve load sharing between the access layer switches and the distribution layer, VLANs must be configured on the access switches and the Spanning-Tree Protocol (STP) must be tuned per VLAN so that both upstream links to the distribution switches are utilized.**

Simulation Exercise

1 What can you observe from the graphs in Figures 4-23 and 4-24?

Answer: The HTTP response times are very low and consistent because the network is not loaded.

Answer:

2 What can you determine from the results? What is the reason for the delayed HTTP responses?

Answer: The overall Ethernet utilization substantially increased compared to the unloaded network. The HTTP response averages are within the expected values, but occasionally some significant delays also decrease the probability of prompt responses (the majority of the response times are below 150 ms). These delays are the result of collisions on the significantly loaded Ethernet and subsequent retransmission of the frames that carry the HTTP requests.

3 You concluded that the introduction of the Layer 2 switch represents a significant improvement in this case. How did you determine this from the previous graphs?

Answer: The graphs are comparable to the graphs that resulted from an unloaded shared network. The HTTP responses do not have any significant delays, and the probability of prompt (below 20 ms) responses is very high.

4 Does the traffic immediately start using the original path once the link or node has fully recovered?

Answer: No. The STP needs some time to recalculate the graph of best paths.

5 Examining the results in Figure 4-35, you might notice that no load sharing occurs in building A's access layer. Is this a result of the default routing on the workstations using distribution switch DS_A for the primary exit point, or a result of the attached Layer 2 switch placing the secondary port in the blocking mode?

Answer: The reason AS_F2 does not use the secondary Layer 3 switch DS_B is because of the way in which default routing is performed on the workstations; they both use DS_A as their default route. There is no need for the STP when the switch is attached to the routed ports.

6 In Figure 4-39, why is the return path completely bypassing the CS_A switch?

Answer: The return path completely bypasses the CS_A switch because the DC_A Layer 3 switch, which is used as a default gateway for the attached LAN, knows that the CS_A switch is down.

7   What is the load distribution ratio on DS_A → CS_A versus the DS_A → CS_B link in Figure 4-41? Explain.

Answer: The ratio is 1:1. The load is evenly shared among symmetric equal-cost paths, all the way to destination.

8   The workstation WS_B is not running any routing protocol; rather, it depends on the default routing. What is a proper next-hop address?

Answer: The proper next-hop address is the network address of the attached interface of the AS_F1 Layer 3 switch.

9   Running a routing protocol is one way to force the server to forward packets to both distribution-layer switches. Can you think of any other option?

Answer: Another option would be to use two equal-cost default routes, pointing to the interface network addresses of both distribution layer switches. However, note that this results in a serious disruption to the packet forwarding process if any of these interfaces or nodes fail.

Review Questions

1   What factors must be considered when designing a campus network?

Answer: You must consider five factors when deploying the campus network:

— **Network geography**

— **Network applications**

— **Data link layer technology—shared or switched**

— **Layer 2 versus Layer 3 switching**

— **Physical cabling**

2   A company keeps all its servers and workstations within one building. What geographical design structure should be chosen?

Answer: An intra-building structure should be chosen for the design.

3   What are some of the differences between inter-building and distant remote network geographical structures?

Answer: The differences include

— **Media—Inter-building uses MM or SM fiber, whereas distant remote uses SM fiber because of the distances involved.**

— **Importance of availability—Availability is important within a building, and it decreases with distance; it is therefore of medium importance for inter-building, and for distant connections it is of lower importance.**

— **Required throughput**—The throughput requirements increase close to the core of the network and close to the sites where the servers reside. Thus, for inter-building it is high, and for distant connections it is less.

4 The Engineering department has requirements to use a bandwidth- and processor-intensive research application. What type of application communication should it use?

Answer: It should use client-distributed server communication. Each segment would have its own servers, known as distributed servers, for its application. Servers and users are located in the same virtual LAN (VLAN).

5 What are some of the benefits of using LAN switches over hubs?

Answer: Some of the benefits of using LAN switches over hubs include the following:

— **Increased bandwidth**

— **Longer range**

— **Use of intelligent services**

— **High availability**

— **Similar cost per port**

6 Some users in a department use an application that generates many broadcast frames, which results in up to 10 Mbps bandwidth utilization. Which of the following solutions is the most optimal in this case?

a. Provide 100 Mbps or higher connections to all users in a domain

b. Limit the number of broadcast frames in a domain for all department users

c. Optimize the application

d. Put the application users into a separate broadcast domain

Answer:

a. Provide 100 Mbps or higher connections to all users in a domain

b. Limit the number of broadcast frames in a domain for all department users

c. Optimize the application

d. Put the application users into a separate broadcast domain

7 What type of cable would you recommend for connecting two switches that are 115 m apart?

Answer: MM optical cable is recommended.

8 What is the intended result of the application characterization process?

Answer: The application characterization process should result in information about network bandwidth usage and response times for critical applications. These parameters influence the selection of the transmission medium and desired bandwidth.

9 With default Spanning Tree Protocol parameters, how long could it take before the redundant link is available when the currently active link fails?

Answer: The time it takes for a redundant path to be activated depends on whether the failure is direct (a port on the same switch) or indirect (a port on another switch). Direct failures take 30 seconds because the switch bypasses the 20-second Maximum Age Timer (and associated Blocking State for the port) and moves straight to the listening state (for 15 seconds) and then the learning state (for 15 seconds). For indirect failures, the switch port must first wait 20 seconds (Maximum Age Timer) before it can transition to the listening state and then the learning state, for a total of 50 seconds. Thus, when a link fails, it might take up to 50 seconds before another link is available.

10 Compare the range and bandwidth specifications of UTP, MM fiber, and SM fiber.

Answer: The specifications are compared in Table G-4.

Table G-4   *Transmission Media Types Bandwidth and Range Characteristics*

Parameter	Twisted-Pair	MM Fiber	SM Fiber
Distance (range)	**Up to 100 meters**	**Up to 2 km (Fast Ethernet) Up to 550 m (Gigabit Ethernet)**	**Up to 40 km Up to 100 km (Gigabit Ethernet)**
Speed (bandwidth)	**Up to 1 Gpbs**	**Up to 1 Gbps**	**10 Gbps**

11 What are the benefits of using Layer 3 switches over Layer 2 switches?

Answer: Layer 3 switches provide better control over the policy domain, allowing QoS and ACLs to be applied at higher OSI layers. Layer 3 switches can provide load sharing based on IP addresses, and they typically have shorter convergence times. Layer 3 switches also reduce broadcast domains and therefore provide better network resource management.

12 The users in an organization are divided along their workgroup lines into VLANs. Workgroup servers are located within these workgroup VLANs. The organization has also placed mail and web servers, to which all corporate users have access, in a separate VLAN. What is the expected traffic flow in this organization?

Answer: Most of the traffic is expected to be local.

13 A company is using video on demand, which utilizes IP multicast as part of its distance-learning program. The routers are configured for IP multicast. Taking into account that the majority of the LAN switches are Layer 2 switches, which protocol should be enabled on the LAN switches to reduce flooding?

Answer: CGMP should be enabled on the LAN switches. CGMP allows switches to communicate with a router to determine whether any users who are attached to them are part of a multicast group.

14 Which Enterprise Campus modules typically have both high availability and high performance requirements?

Answer: The Campus Backbone and Server Farm modules typically have both high availability and high performance requirements.

15 What is the difference between the 80/20 rule and the 20/80 rule?

Answer: The conventional 80/20 rule underlies traditional network design models. The 80/20 rule refers to the goal of containing at least 80 percent of the traffic within the local segment.

Many new and existing applications now use distributed data storage and retrieval. The traffic pattern is moving toward what is now referred to as the 20/ 80 rule. With the 20/80 rule, only 20 percent of traffic is local to the workgroup LAN, and 80 percent of the traffic leaves the workgroup.

16 A link between the building distribution and campus backbone is oversubscribed, yet carries mission-critical data along with Internet traffic. How would you ensure that the mission-critical applications are not adversely affected by the bandwidth limitations?

Answer: One solution is to simply provide sufficient bandwidth on the link. However, an alternative is to implement a QoS mechanism to classify and police the traffic on the distribution switch.

17 What are two uses of redundant paths?

Answer: Redundant paths can be used for failover and load balancing.

18 A corporate network is spread over four floors. There is a Layer 2 switch on each floor, each with more than one VLAN. One connection from each floor leads to the basement, where all WAN connections are terminated and all servers are located. Traffic between VLANs is essential. What type of device should be used in the basement?

Answer: A Layer 3 switch should be used as the distribution layer in the basement to route between the VLANs, route to the WANs, and take advantage of the intelligent network services, such as QoS and traffic filtering, which must be supported at the distribution layer.

19 What applications might require the network to handle multicast traffic?

Answer: Videoconferencing, corporate communications, distance learning, distribution of software, stock quotes, and news are some applications that take advantage of IP multicast traffic to deliver source traffic to multiple receivers.

20 What functions does the Building Distribution submodule provide?

Answer: The Building Distribution submodule of the Campus Infrastructure module aggregates the access layer and uses a combination of Layer 2 and Layer 3 switching to segment workgroups and isolate segments from failures and broadcast storms. This layer implements several policies based on access lists and QoS settings.

21 What is the main focus of the campus backbone?

Answer: Campus backbone switches are Layer 2 and Layer 3 switches that focus primarily on wire-speed forwarding on all interfaces. Backbone switches are differentiated by the level of performance achieved per port, rather than by high port densities.

22 An organization requires a highly available core network and uses IP telephony for all of its voice communication, both internal and external. Which devices and topology would you recommend for the campus backbone design?

Answer: A Layer 3 switched backbone with redundant devices and redundant links to the backbone from each distribution layer switch is recommended.

23 A company has mission-critical applications hosted on common servers that are accessible to selected employees throughout the company's multiple buildings. Where and how would you recommend that these servers be placed within the network?

Answer: The company should create a Server Farm to host the centralized servers. Because of probable high traffic load, the servers should be Fast Ethernet-attached, Fast EtherChannel-attached, or even Gigabit Ethernet-attached. Intelligent Layer 3 switches should be used to provide scalability, availability, responsiveness, throughput, and security for the mission-critical applications, as required.

24 What is the function of the Edge Distribution module?

Answer: The Edge Distribution module connects the Enterprise Campus functional area with the Enterprise Edge functional area and filters and routes traffic into the campus backbone.

Chapter 5: Designing WANs

Case Study

Step 2   Propose the optimal WAN upgrade and WAN backup scenario, including for the international offices.

Answer: During the initial redesign phase, the current WAN bandwidths on links to all regional offices were determined to be 64 kbps. The links are leased lines. The simulation of new applications showed that the immediate upgrade was needed on the San Jose–Houston link, and that 128 kbps would be sufficient. Because of expected heavy load on other links as well, upgrading the entire WAN to 128 kbps is recommended.

Taking into account that the existing routers support higher speeds, Frame Relay could be considered an option over the leased lines. In the future, FR's flexibility would allow an increase in bandwidth (in terms of Committed Information Rate [CIR]) as demand grows.

You must perform a cost analysis before you decide whether to recommend a leased line upgrade or FR. Because the existing equipment supports both of these technologies, cost and flexibility are the decision factors.

ISDN is the most suitable option for a WAN backup because the existing WAN bandwidths are low, and the 64 kbps on an ISDN B channel is ideal in the current situation. The equipment installed on regional offices already supports ISDN for remote office connectivity. One of the available ISDN B channels, or an additional Basic Rate Interface (BRI), would be sufficient. The backup will always be triggered from the regional offices.

While one BRI interface would be sufficient for the three regional offices, the central router at the Headquarters should be upgraded with an additional slot that contains multiple BRI interfaces.

A VPN implementation is proposed for the international offices in London and Singapore that are opening soon. DJMP Industries already connects to the Internet at San Jose, and the new offices will also connect to the Internet. An IPSec implementation is suggested because the VPN implementation must be secure.

In case the international offices require redundancy, Generic Route Encapsulation (GRE) tunnels with IPSec are recommended. This requires an additional address block to be reserved and routing to be turned on in the GRE tunnels.

Figure G-2 illustrates the new WAN with the backup option and the integration of the international offices.

Figure G-2   *Proposed WAN Network of DJMP Industries*

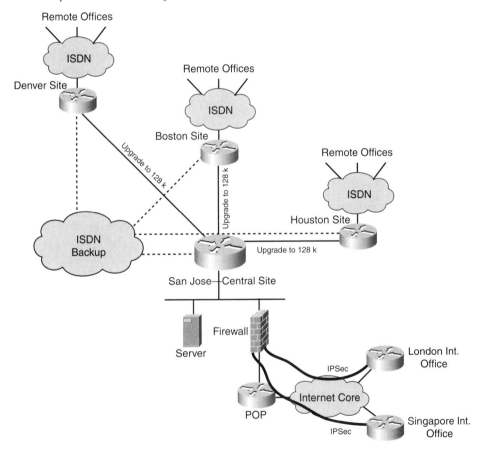

Review Questions

1 What type of cable is used for each of the following?

— ADSL

— VDSL

— Cable

— LRE

Answer:

ADSL: copper twisted pair

VDSL: copper twisted pair

Cable: coaxial cable

LRE: copper twisted pair

2 What is the definition of a WAN?

Answer: A WAN is a data communications network that covers a relatively broad geographic area and uses the transmission facilities provided by service providers.

3 What advantages do the emerging WAN technologies bring to a network?

Answer: The emerging WAN technologies either offer a new means of transport (such as wireless) or convert an existing medium into a data-enabled system (for example, ADSL using POTS lines).

4 What is a WAN's objective in the Enterprise Edge?

Answer: A WAN provides the Enterprise Edge network with access to the outside world and concentrates all WAN connections in a single functional area.

5 Compare the response time and throughput requirements of a file transfer and an interactive application.

Answer: A file transfer is a high-volume traffic application, but it is not susceptible to response time delays. Interactive applications are typically low-volume and therefore have low throughput requirements. However, interactivity involves users, and users have very stringent response time requirements (typically within 1 second).

6 Which technologies are suitable for WAN connections over 50 Mbps?

Answer: Fast Ethernet, Gigabit Ethernet, ATM over SONET/SDH, DWDM, and POS are suitable for WAN connections over 50 Mbps.

7 What can be done if WAN links are constantly congested?

Answer: If WAN links are constantly congested, either greater bandwidth or compression is required. QoS mechanisms, including queuing, do not relieve constant congestion. If WAN links are never congested, queuing is unnecessary.

8 Match the terms with their definitions:

Terms:

— Compression

— Bandwidth

— Response time

— Window size

— Throughput

Definitions:

— The amount of data transmitted or received per unit time

— The number of frames that can be sent before the sender must wait for an acknowledgement

— Percentage of bits that contain errors relative to the total number of bits received in a transmission

— The amount of data successfully moved from one place to another in a given time period

— Reduction of data size for the purpose of saving transmission time

— The time between a command or keystroke entry and the host system's command execution or response delivery

Answer:

— **Compression: Reduction of data size for the purpose of saving transmission time**

— **Bandwidth: The amount of data transmitted or received per unit time**

— **Response time: The time between a command or keystroke entry and the host system's command execution or response delivery**

— **Window size: The number of frames that can be sent before the sender must wait for an acknowledgment**

— **Throughput: The amount of data successfully moved from one place to another in a given time period**

9 Why is ISDN better than POTS for data connections?

Answer: Connectivity over ISDN offers the network designer increased bandwidth, reduced call setup time, reduced latency, and lower signal/noise ratios.

10 How do X.25 and Frame Relay technologies compare?

Answer: X.25 is a legacy technology that some environments still use; however, it is being replaced by faster and more efficient technologies, such as FR.

FR typically operates over WAN facilities that offer more reliable connection services and a higher degree of reliability than the media for which X.25 was designed.

FR is a Layer 2 protocol, whereas X.25 also provides services at Layer 3 (the network layer). This enables FR to offer higher performance and greater transmission efficiency than X.25 and makes FR suitable for current WAN applications such as LAN interconnection.

11 Why are fully meshed networks not always appropriate?

Answer: The key rationale for creating a fully meshed network is to provide a high level of redundancy; however, this might not be appropriate for large networks. Key issues include the following:

— The large number of virtual circuits required (one for every connection between routers)

— Problems associated with the requirement for large numbers of packet and broadcast replications

— The configuration complexity for routers in the absence of multicast support in nonbroadcast environments

12 What is the difference between dial backup and dial-on-demand routing?

Answer: For dial backup, the router is configured so that it initiates the dial backup line when a failure is detected on the primary circuit.

Dial-on-demand routing is a technique whereby a router initiates a call on a switched circuit, only when it needs to send data.

13 What is the difference between SONET and SDH?

Answer: SONET is an American National Standard Institute (ANSI) specification. SDH is the SONET-equivalent specification proposed by the International Telecommunications Union (ITU). While European carriers use SDH widely, North American and Asia/Pacific Rim carriers more frequently use SONET.

14 What is Packet over SONET/SDH (POS)?

Answer: POS sends native IP packets directly over SONET/SDH frames.

15 Identify the key ADSL devices shown in Figure 5-21.

Layer 3 concentrator

Layer 2 concentrator—DSLAM

Splitter

ADSL CPE

Answer:

D is the Layer 3 concentrator

A is the Layer 2 concentrator—DSLAM

C is the splitter

B is the ADSL CPE

16 What different roles does the ADSL CPE have for PPPoA and PPPoE?

Answer: In the PPPoA architecture, the CPE acts as an Ethernet-to-WAN *router*, **and the PPP session is established between the CPE and the NSP.**

In the PPPoE architecture, the CPE acts as an Ethernet-to-WAN *bridge*, **and the PPP session is established between the end user's PC or PPPoE router and the NSP.**

17 Which of the following two statements do not describe the operation of cable networks?

  a. The cable modem termination system (CMTS) enables the coax users to connect with either the PSTN or the Internet.

  b. The actual bandwidth for Internet service over a cable TV line is shared 2.5 Mbps on the download path to the subscriber, with about 27 Mbps of shared bandwidth for interactive responses in the other direction.

  c. All cable modems can receive from and send signals to the CMTS and other cable modems on the line.

  d. The cable backbone network is usually a SONET ring that runs on optical fiber.

  Answer:

  a. The cable modem termination system (CMTS) enables the coax users to connect with either the PSTN or the Internet.

  b. **The actual bandwidth for Internet service over a cable TV line is shared 2.5 Mbps on the download path to the subscriber, with about 27 Mbps of shared bandwidth for interactive responses in the other direction.**

  c. **All cable modems can receive from and send signals to the CMTS and other cable modems on the line.**

  d. The cable backbone network is usually a SONET ring that runs on optical fiber.

18 For what purpose is broadband fixed wireless used?

Answer: Broadband fixed wireless is designed to connect two or more networks, which are typically located in different buildings, at high data rates for data-intensive, line-of-sight applications.

19 What are some of the benefits of using a wireless network?

Answer: Following are the main benefits of using wireless technologies:

  — Completes the access technology portfolio

  — Goes where cable and fiber cannot

— Involves reduced time to revenue because a wireless system can be assembled and brought online in as little as two to three hours

— Comparable (or reduced) costs compared to copper

20 What is an MPLS Forwarding Equivalence Class?

Answer: An MPLS FEC is a grouping of packets; packets that belong to the same FEC receive the same treatment in the network. Various parameters, including source or destination IP address or port numbers, IP protocol, or IP precedence can determine FEC.

21 How many bits are in the MPLS label field?

Answer: An MPLS label is a 32-bit field that is placed between a packet's data link layer and its IP header. Following are the components of an MPLS label:

— **Label value: A 20-bit value. A label of 0 indicates that the label stack must be popped (removed), and the forwarding of the packet must then be based on the IP header. Label values 1 through 15 are reserved for other purposes.**

— **Exp: A 3-bit experimental field.**

— **S: A 1-bit field. When the S bit is set to 1, it indicates that this label is the bottom of the label stack.**

— **Time to Live (TTL): An 8-bit field. Because LSRs do not examine IP headers, the label field includes the TTL field to support TTL functionality.**

22 True or false: Packets sent from Device A to Device B through an MPLS network always take the same path through the network.

Answer: False. Packets sent between the same endpoints can belong to different FECs and can therefore flow through different network paths.

23 What is the difference between an overlay VPN and VPDN?

Answer: With overlay VPNs, the provider's infrastructure provides virtual point-to-point links between customer sites. From the Layer 3 perspective, the provider network is invisible. The provider is not aware of customer routing and does not have any information about customer routes.

With VPDNs, the customers use a provider's dial-in infrastructure for their private dialup connections. The ISP agrees to forward the company's traffic from the ISP's point of presence to a company-run home gateway. Network configuration and security remain in the client's control.

24 What is the most appropriate method for an Internet connection to be a secure backup solution for an Enterprise WAN link?

Answer: The use of IPSec tunnels is the most appropriate solution.

25 Define downstream and upstream.

Answer: Downstream refers to data that travels from the Internet to the end-user computer.

Upstream refers to data that travels from the end-user computer to the Internet.

26 What is the difference between ADSL and SDSL?

Answer: With ADSL, traffic can move upstream and downstream at different speeds. ADSL also allows PSTN telephony services concurrently on the same line.

With SDSL, traffic in either direction travels at the same speed, up to 1.54 Mbps. However, unlike ADSL, SDSL does not allow PSTN telephony services concurrently on the same line.

27 Is the goal of the wireless network to broaden the connectivity options or to increase the access speed?

Answer: The goal of the wireless network is to broaden the connectivity options. Higher speed wired networks are available.

Chapter 6: Designing IP Addressing in the Network

Case Study

Step 2 Propose the optimal IP addressing plan for the given network scenario. Take into account that you must also use a new routing protocol and ensure some WAN backup. The future campus will be completely restructured and more granular.

Answer: The IP addressing plan of the DJMP Industries network proposed here assumes the use of 10.0.0.0/8 private IP addresses. The address space is hierarchically designed and allows advanced routing design, including route summarization. Each location is assigned a /16 address block from the 10.0.0.0/8 address pool. Each address block is further subnetted to address specific network segments, and offers enough addresses for possible future growth. Table G-5 lists the proposed IP address space assignment by location.

Table G-5 *IP Address Allocation*

Location	IP Address Space
Headquarters in San Jose	10.1.0.0/16
Denver Regional Office	10.2.0.0/16
Boston Regional Office	10.3.0.0/16
Houston Regional Office	10.4.0.0/16
London International Office	10.5.0.0/16
Singapore International Office	10.6.0.0/16

The assigned IP address space at each location is divided into two blocks with /17 network masks. The first block is intended for LAN networks. The second block is intended for various WAN connections, both primary links and backup connections. Both IP address blocks provide enough IP address space for future growth. The point-to-point connections are assigned /30 network masks for optimal IP address assignment use. The LAN networks are assigned /24 network masks to leave enough IP addresses for possible new users.

San Jose Headquarters

The proposed IP addressing allocation for the San Jose headquarters (10.1.0.0/16) is divided into a 10.1.0.0/17 address block for LAN networks and a 10.1.128.0/17 address block for WAN connections. Currently, one LAN network and three WAN connections (to regional offices in Denver, Boston, and Houston) exist. There is also a backup connection for each of the WAN connections. Table G-6 shows the details of the San Jose address allocation.

Table G-6 *San Jose Headquarters IP Address Allocation*

Connection Type	Network
San Jose Headquarters LAN network	10.1.0.0/24
Headquarters to Denver WAN connection	10.1.128.0/30
Headquarters to Boston WAN connection	10.1.128.4/30
Headquarters to Houston WAN connection	10.1.128.8/30
Headquarters to London VPN tunnel (optional)	10.1.128.12/30
Headquarters to Singapore VPN tunnel (optional)	10.1.128.16/30

Table G-6   *San Jose Headquarters IP Address Allocation (Continued)*

Connection Type	Network
Headquarters to Denver backup connection	10.1.129.0/30
Headquarters to Boston backup connection	10.1.129.4/30
Headquarters to Houston backup connection	10.1.129.8/30

NOTE   For the international offices, a VPN implementation is planned and address space is also reserved for the tunnels, in case GRE tunnels are used. The VPN implementation details are explained in the section "Case Study: WAN Upgrade and Backup" in Chapter 5, "Designing WANs."

The proposed IP addressing plan for LAN networks allows the introduction of VLANs. Table G-7 lists a possible IP addressing scheme for VLANs at the San Jose headquarters and the planned Server Farm LAN.

Table G-7   *San Jose Headquarters VLANs and LAN*

VLAN or LAN Name	Network
Server Farm (LAN)	10.1.0.0/24
E-commerce	10.1.2.0/24
Administration	10.1.3.0/24
The Next VLAN	10.1.4.0/24

Regional/International Offices

Table G-8 describes the proposed IP addressing allocation for the Denver, Boston, and Houston Regional Office areas, including the remote offices, and the London and Singapore International Offices. Because the proposed IP address assignment is hierarchical, it enables route summarization toward the San Jose headquarters, thereby resulting in smaller routing tables.

Table G-8   *Regional/International Office IP Address Allocation*

Connection Type	Network
Denver Regional Office LAN network	10.2.0.0/24
Denver to Remote Office 1 connection	10.2.128.0/30
Denver to Remote Office 2 connection	10.2.128.4/30
Denver to Remote Office 3 connection	10.2.128.8/30

continues

Table G-8   *Regional/International Office IP Address Allocation (Continued)*

Connection Type	Network
Remote Office 1 LAN network	10.2.129.0/24
Remote Office 2 LAN network	10.2.130.0/24
Remote Office 3 LAN network	10.2.131.0/24
Boston Regional Office LAN network	10.3.0.0/24
Boston to Remote Office 1 connection	10.3.128.0/30
Boston to Remote Office 2 connection	10.3.128.4/30
Remote Office 1 LAN network	10.3.129.0/24
Remote Office 2 LAN network	10.3.130.0/24
Houston Regional Office LAN network	10.4.0.0/24
Houston to Remote Office 1 connection	10.4.128.0/30
Houston to Remote Office 2 connection	10.4.128.4/30
Houston to Remote Office 3 connection	10.4.128.8/30
Remote Office 1 LAN network	10.4.129.0/24
Remote Office 2 LAN network	10.4.130.0/24
Remote Office 3 LAN network	10.4.131.0/24
London International Office LAN network	10.5.0.0/24
Singapore International Office LAN network	10.6.0.0/24

Step 3   Propose possible methods of IP address assignment.

> **Answer: DHCP or manual configuration IP address assignment methods are suitable for the DJMP Industries network. We propose the following:**
>
> — **DHCP for the San Jose headquarters location. There are already 200 users and future growth can be expected, so manual configuration is not an option.**
>
> — **DHCP for the regional offices in Denver, Boston, and Houston. The current number of users is between 35 and 50 at each office.**
>
> — **DHCP for the international offices in London and Singapore. Approximately 10 users are expected in each office, and future growth can be expected.**
>
> — **Manual configuration for the remote offices with up to five users.**

Review Questions

1 For the address 172.17.7.245/28:

— What is the mask?

— What class is the address?

— What is the host part?

— What is the network part?

— How many hosts can reside on this subnet?

Answer:

— **What is the mask? 255.255.255.240**

— **What class is the address? Class B**

— **What is the host part? .5**

— **What is the network part? 172.17.7.240**

— **How many hosts can reside on this subnet? $2^4-2 = 14$**

2 What information must reside collected to determine the size of the network?

Answer: Information that must be collected to determine the size of the network includes the number and type of locations and number and type of devices in each location (such as workstation, server, IP phones, and so on).

3 Approximately how much reserve in the number of network devices should be included for future growth purposes?

Answer: Usually up to 20% of reserve in the number of network devices is added for future growth purposes. (Depending on the circumstances, more reserve might be required.)

4 Which of the following IPv4 addresses cannot be used in public networks?

a. 172.167.20.1/24

b. 192.168.1.200/28

c. 172.30.100.33/24

d. 172.32.1.1/16

Answer:

a. 172.167.20.1/24

b. 192.168.1.200/28

c. 172.30.100.33/24

d. 172.32.1.1/16

5 In what situation would both private and public IPv4 addresses be required?

Answer: Both private and public IPv4 addresses might be required in a network that requires Internet connectivity but does not make all of its end systems publicly accessible.

6 What type of routing protocol can support VLSM?

Answer: Classless routing protocols support VLSM.

7 What are some disadvantages of a flat IP addressing scheme?

Answer: Some disadvantages of a flat IP addressing scheme include the following:

— **Excess routing traffic consumes bandwidth**

— **Constant routing table recalculation**

— **Routing loops and black-hole routing**

8 What are some advantages of a hierarchical IP addressing scheme?

Answer: A hierarchical IP addressing scheme allows route summarization, which reduces routing overhead and required bandwidth.

9 What is the difference between classless and classful routing protocols?

Answer: With classful routing, routing updates do not carry the subnet mask; with classless routing, routing updates carry the subnet mask.

10 What are the advantages of using DHCP versus static address assignment?

Answer: DHCP relieves the administrator of the task of manually assigning an address to every device, and makes it easier to reconfigure addresses.

11 What are the three DHCP address allocation mechanisms?

Answer:

— **Manual—The network administrator assigns the IPv4 address to a specific MAC address. DHCP is simply used to dispatch the assigned address to the host.**

— **Automatic—DHCP assigns a permanent IPv4 address to a host.**

— **Dynamic—DHCP assigns an IPv4 address to a host for a limited time (called a lease) or until the host explicitly releases the address. This mechanism allows automatic address reuse when the host to which it has been assigned no longer needs the address.**

12 What is the advantage of using dynamic name resolution versus static name resolution?

Answer: Dynamic name resolution reduces administrative overhead.

13 Describe the process that is used when DNS resolves a URL, such as www.cisco.com.

Answer:

— **A user wants to browse www.cisco.com. The host queries the DNS server because it does not know the IP address of that site.**

— **The DNS server responds with the appropriate IP address for www.cisco.com.**

— **The host establishes the connection to the appropriate IP address (site).**

14 How many bits are in an IPv6 address?

Answer: 128

15 How long is the IPv6 packet header?

Answer: 40 octets, or 320 bits

16 What field of the IPv6 packet header is analogous to the IPv4 TTL field?

Answer: Hop limit

17 Which IPv6 packet header field is used to label sequences of packets?

Answer: Flow label

18 One-to-many IPv6 addresses are called _____.

Answer: One-to-many IPv6 addresses are called <u>multicast</u>.

19 What types of IPv6 unicast addresses must not be forwarded to the Internet by a router?

Answer: Site-local and link-local IPv6 addresses must not be forwarded to the Internet by a router.

20 How many bits are used for interface ID in an IPv6 unicast address?

Answer: 64

21 What IPv6 prefix would be used to connect devices on the same network?

Answer: FE80::/10, which is the prefix for link-local addresses, would be used to connect devices on the same network.

22 What are the three address assignment strategies that are available in IPv6?

Answer: Address assignment with DHCP, static, and stateless autoconfiguration.

23 How does the IPv6 stateless autoconfiguration work?

Answer: A router on the link advertises, either periodically or upon the host's request, its site-local and global prefixes and its willingness to function as the link's default router. Hosts can automatically generate site-local and global IPv6 addresses without manual configuration or a server (such as a DHCP server) by using the prefixes in these router messages.

24 What feature allows DNS to support IPv6?

Answer: The A6 record, which is an address record for an IPv6 host, allows DNS to support IPv6.

25 Can a host support IPv4 and IPv6 simultaneously?

Answer: Yes. This is called a dual-stack host.

26 What are three mechanisms for transitioning from IPv4 to IPv6?

Answer: Dual-stack, tunneling, and translation are three mechanisms for transitioning from IPv4 to IPv6.

27 Which operating systems support both IPv4 and IPv6?

Answer: Some operating systems that support the IPv6 stack are FreeBSD, Linux, Sun Solaris, NT 4, and Windows 2000/XP.

28 Describe how 6to4 tunneling works.

Answer: The 6to4 tunnel treats the IPv4 network as a virtual link. Each 6to4 edge router contains an IPv6 address with a /48 prefix, which is the concatenation of 2002::/16 and the IPv4 address of the edge router; 2002::/16 is a specially assigned address range for the purpose of 6to4. The edge routers automatically build the tunnel using the IPv4 addresses that are embedded in the IPv6 addresses.

When the edge router receives an IPv6 packet that has a destination address in the range of 2002::/16, it determines from its routing table that the packet must pass through the tunnel. The router extracts the IPv4 address that is embedded (in the third to sixth octets, inclusive) in the IPv6 next-hop address, the address of the router at the other end of the tunnel, and encapsulates the IPv6 packet in an IPv4 packet with the destination edge router's extracted IPv4 address . This IPv4 address is that of the 6to4 router at the destination site. The packet then passes through the IPv4 network. The destination edge router de-capsulates the IPv6 packet from the received IPv4 packet and forwards the IPv6 packet to its final destination. (A 6to4 relay router, which offers traffic forwarding to the IPv6 Internet, is required for reaching a native IPv6 Internet.)

29 Which IPv6 routing protocols do Cisco routers currently support?

Answer: Cisco routers currently support BG4+, IS-ISv6, and RIPng. Some routers support OSPFv3.

30 What is the multicast address that is used for RIPng?

Answer: FF02::9.

Chapter 7: Selecting Routing Protocols for a Network

Case Study

Step 2 Propose the most suitable routing protocol and explain major deployment issues.

Answer: OSPF is the new IP routing protocol choice for the DJMP Industries network. Following are the reasons for choosing the OSPF as the routing protocol:

— **OSPF is a standardized protocol for routing IP traffic and can therefore be used with multivendor equipment.**

— **OSPF has fast convergence. Slow convergence is one of the primary reasons for RIP replacement.**

— **It supports VLSM, thereby allowing the IP address space to be used more economically.**

— **It supports multiple area design and manual summarization, which reduce the routing table size and overhead.**

— **It supports dialup (and ISDN) connections with the OSPF Demand Circuit feature. In the DJMP Industries network, ISDN connections are used as backup links to provide a redundant connection from regional offices.**

OSPF Area Design

Figure G-3 shows the OSPF area design. The underlying IP address plan hierarchy maps to the OSPF routing protocol hierarchical structure. The OSPF Area 0 (the backbone area) resides in the San Jose headquarters and includes LAN networks. Currently there are three nonbackbone areas, which include WAN connections to the regional offices and LAN networks from those locations. All non-backbone areas are OSPF not-so-stubby areas (NSSAs) to allow the route redistribution from non-OSPF routing domains. The backup links, shown as dashed lines in Figure G-3, are in the same area as the primary links to the regional offices.

Figure G-3 *DJMP OSPF Area Design*

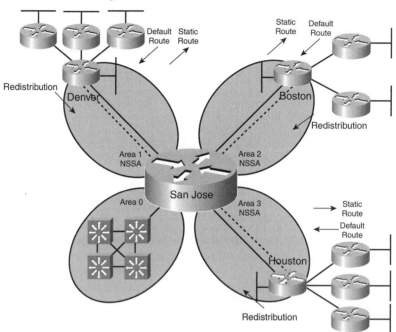

Table G-9 shows the networks in each of the areas.

Table G-9 *Networks in DJMP OSPF Areas*

Location	OSPF Area	Networks in the Area
Headquarters in San Jose	Area 0 (backbone area)	10.1.0.0/17
Denver Regional Office	Area 1	10.1.129.0/30, 10.1.128.0/30, 10.2.0.0/24
Boston Regional Office	Area 2	10.1.129.4/30, 10.1.128.4/30, 10.3.0.0/24
Houston Regional Office	Area 3	10.1.129.8/30, 10.1.128.8/30, 10.4.0.0/24

Redistribution is used to inject information about the remote offices'
LAN networks. The remote offices do not have to run the OSPF
routing protocol; instead, a default route is used in the remote offices
to reach the other networks. A static route is used on the regional
office side to reach the remote office LAN network. In the case where
PPP encapsulation with authentication is used, the route can either
be manually configured or installed by the AAA server.

Route Summarization

> The underlying IP addressing plan allows efficient route
> summarization. The manual summarization of routes is performed
> on area borders. As shown in Figure G-4, networks that are assigned
> to each location are summarized into one summary route, which is
> then announced to the backbone area. The summarization is:
>
> — **10.2.0.0/16 from Area 1**
>
> — **10.3.0.0/16 from Area 2**
>
> — **10.4.0.0/16 from Area 3**

Figure G-4   *DJMP OSPF Area Summarization*

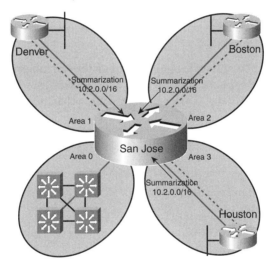

> The external routes (remote office LAN networks) that are injected
> into the OSPF area at the regional office routers are also
> summarized.
>
> Implementing route summarization narrows the scope of routing
> update propagation when a link that is internal to the area fails.

Simulation Exercise

1 The outage that occurred because of the primary link loss can be explained as the
   consequence of the STP recalculation. What is the reason for the second delay, after
   the primary path has physically recovered?

   **Answer: After the primary path has physically recovered, the Layer 2 switches
   must perform the STP recalculation again because the topology has changed.
   The second delay is a result of the STP protocol recalculating the graph of best
   paths, based on the new circumstances.**

2 Why do the link and node incidents impose the same disruption times before network recovery?

Answer: With this network topology, the STP protocol reacts equally to both disruptions because, from the path perspective, losing CS_A is the same as losing the CS_A to DC_A link.

3 If you chose RIP instead of OSPF, the convergence time would change significantly under a link or node failure. Why does this occur?

Answer: The speed of network convergence depends heavily on the routing protocol's reaction speed. Even with flash updates implemented, distance vector protocols utilize features such as invalid timer and hold-down timer, which extend the protocol's convergence time.

4 From the simulation log, it appears that the switchover to the primary path takes a long time—approximately 50 seconds. Why?

Answer: The routers are going through the startup process on the link, including sending hello packets, participating in the Designated Router (DR)/Backup Designated Router (BDR) election, and exchanging routing information.

Review Questions

1 In what situations is static routing preferred over dynamic routing?

Answer: Static routing might be preferred over dynamic routing in the following situations:

— **Dial-in networks**

— **Stub networks**

— **Dial-on-demand routing (DDR)**

2 What must dynamic routing protocols do in order to be effective?

Answer: Dynamic routing protocols should do the following to be effective:

— **Find sources from which routing information can be received (usually neighboring routers)**

— **Select best paths toward all reachable destinations based on received information**

— **Maintain this routing information**

— **Have a means of verifying routing information (periodical updates or refreshes)**

3 How do distance vector and link-state routing protocols differ?

Answer: Link-state routing protocols flood routing information to all nodes in the internetwork (this might be constrained to an area, depending on how the protocol is configured). However, each router sends only the portion of the routing table that describes the state of its own links.

Distance vector protocols call for each router to send all or some portion of its routing table, but only to its neighbors.

4 What are triggered updates?

Answer: Triggered updates are updates that are sent only when a change happens (the link goes down or comes up, or link parameters that affect routing are changed—for example, a bandwidth change).

5 Which type of routing protocol is used for interconnecting autonomous systems?

Answer: Exterior gateway protocols (EGPs) are used to interconnect autonomous systems.

6 Do IGPs or EGPs typically have faster convergence?

Answer: IGPs have faster convergence.

7 What parameters do the following routing protocols use in their metric calculation?

RIP

EIGRP

OSPF

IGRP

BGP

IS-IS

Answer:

RIP: Hop count

EIGRP: Bandwidth, delay, reliability, loading, MTU

OSPF: Cost

IGRP: Bandwidth, delay, reliability, loading, MTU

BGP: AS-path

IS-IS: Metric

8 What is convergence?

Answer: A network is converged when all routing tables are synchronized and each contains a usable route to each destination network.

9 How does the speed of convergence affect the network?

Answer: A network is not completely operable until the network has converged. Therefore, short convergence times are required for routing protocols.

10 What is an advantage of a hierarchical network versus a flat network?

Answer: Advantages of hierarchical networks include less routing traffic overhead, which results in higher scalability and isolation of network instabilities, and improved convergence time.

11 A large organization has decided to connect all of its regional offices to their appropriate branch offices. Each regional office has a minimum of two and a maximum of five branch offices to connect. The branch offices use low-end routers that are directly connected to the regional office router via Frame Relay permanent virtual circuit (PVC) links, which effectively creates a hub and spoke topology (star network). No physical connections exist between the branch office routers. The protocol that runs between the regional and branch offices does not need to be the same as in the rest of the network where OSPF is run. What are the two best options for establishing IP connectivity?

a. Deploy EIGRP both ways.

b. Deploy IS-IS both ways.

c. Deploy RIPv2 with a default route for branch office connectivity to the rest of the network.

d. Use static routing both ways with a default static route from each branch to the regional office, and static routes on each regional router toward the branch networks.

Answer:

a. Deploy EIGRP both ways.

b. Deploy IS-IS both ways.

c. Deploy RIPv2 with a default route for branch office connectivity to the rest of the network.

d. Use static routing both ways with a default static route from each branch to the regional office, and static routes on each regional router towards the branch networks.

12 On-demand routing (ODR) is best suited for what network topology?

Answer: ODR is best suited for hub and spoke or stub networks.

13 What Cisco protocol does ODR use?

Answer: ODR uses the Cisco discovery protocol (CDP).

14 What are the advantages of RIPv2 over RIPv1?

Answer: The advantages of RIPv2 over RIPv1 include

— **VLSM support**

— **Multicast**

— **Manual summarization (for dialup clients)**

— **Authentication**

— **Flash updates**

15 A network consists of links with varying bandwidths. Would RIPv2 be a good routing protocol choice in this network? Why or why not?

Answer: No, because it only uses hop count as its metric; it does not take the links' bandwidth into account.

16 What are some features of EIGRP that make it an appropriate choice for a core routing protocol?

Answer: Following are some EIGRP features that make it an appropriate core routing protocol:

— **Fast convergence with the DUAL algorithm**

— **Improved scalability with manual summarization**

— **Use of VLSM**

— **Reduced bandwidth usage with triggered updates**

— **Multiple network layer protocol support**

17 What is a feasible successor?

Answer: A feasible successor is a neighbor that is downstream with respect to the destination, but is not the least cost path and is therefore not used for forwarding data. In other words, it is a backup route to the destination.

18 Does OSPF support manual route summarization on all routers?

Answer: No, manual route summarization is only supported on Area Border Routers (ABRs) and Autonomous System Boundary Routers (ASBRs).

19 What is an OSPF link-state advertisement (LSA)?

Answer: An LSA describes the state of links on specific routers and is propagated, unchanged, over one area.

20 What is the OSPF metric?

Answer: The OSPF metric is cost, which is inversely proportional to link bandwidth.

21 For what network layer protocols does Integrated IS-IS provide support?

Answer: Integrated IS-IS can route IPv4 and CLNP.

22 What is the difference between an IS-IS backbone and an OSPF backbone?

Answer: In Integrated IS-IS the backbone (Level-2 and Level-1/Level-2) routers are not part of a special backbone area, as is the case in OSPF. Level-2 routers belong to Level-1 areas and only form adjacencies with other Level-2 (and Level-1/Level-2) routers. An IS-IS Level-2 backbone resembles a chain of Level-2 (and Level-1/Level-2) routers that winds its way through Level 1 areas.

23 Why might Integrated IS-IS be better than OSPF in a very large network?

Answer: In a very large network, Integrated IS-IS might be better than OSPF because its Partial Route Calculation (PRC) provides faster convergence and allows easier extension of the backbone.

24 What is BGP multi-homing?

Answer: BGP multi-homing is connectivity to multiple autonomous systems.

25 Why is BGP used for inter-AS routing?

Answer: BGP allows administrators to influence routing decisions, and it can handle larger amounts of routing data.

26 Which routing protocols are likely to be used in the core layer?

Answer: EIGRP, OSPF, and IS-IS are likely to be used in the core layer.

27 Is IS-IS typically a good choice of routing protocol for the access layer?

Answer: No. IS-IS requires extensive knowledge to configure and is not suitable for dialup networks.

28 What is route redistribution?

Answer: Route redistribution is the passing of routing information from one routing protocol to another routing protocol.

29 Which parts of the Enterprise Composite Network model are likely to implement redistribution?

Answer: The parts of the Enterprise Composite Network that are likely to implement redistribution include

— **The distribution layer in the Building Distribution submodule**

— **The Internet connectivity module**

— **The VPN/Remote Access module**

30 What is route filtering?

Answer: Route filtering allows the network administrator to prevent the advertisement of certain routes through the routing domain.

31 When is route filtering required?

Answer: Filtering is primarily used with route redistribution to prevent suboptimal routing and routing loops that might occur when routes are redistributed at multiple redistribution points. Route filtering is also used to prevent routes about certain networks, such as a private IP address space, to be sent to or received from remote sites.

32 Why does the EBGP next-hop address have to be announced by the IGP into a network that runs IBGP?

Answer: The EBGP next-hop address needs must be announced by the IGP into a network that runs IBGP so that the route is installed in the routing table; all routers can then reach the next-hop address and, therefore, the routes being advertised through it.

33 What is route summarization and why would a network need it?

Answer: Route summarization, (also called route aggregation or supernetting) can reduce the number of routes that a router must maintain because it is a method of representing a series of network numbers in a single summary address. Summarization is used to reduce the routing overhead—for example, it results in smaller routing tables—and to improve the stability of routing.

34 What is the best summary route for the following networks?

- 172.16.168.0/24
- 172.16.169.0/24
- 172.16.170.0/24
- 172.16.171.0/24
- 172.16.172.0/24
- 172.16.173.0/24
- 172.16.174.0/24
- 172.16.175.0/24

Answer: To determine the summary route, the router determines the number of highest-order (leftmost) bits that match in all the addresses. As shown in Figure G-5, the leftmost 21 bits match in all of these addresses. Therefore, the best summary route is 172.16.168.0/21 (or 172.16.168.0 255.255.248.0).

Figure G-5   *Summarizing Within an Octet*

172.16.168.0/24 =	10101100	. 00010000	. 10101	000 .	00000000
172.16.169.0/24 =	172	. 16	. 10101	001 .	0
172.16.170.0/24 =	172	. 16	. 10101	010 .	0
172.16.171.0/24 =	172	. 16	. 10101	011 .	0
172.16.172.0/24 =	172	. 16	. 10101	100 .	0
172.16.173.0/24 =	172	. 16	. 10101	101 .	0
172.16.174.0/24 =	172	. 16	. 10101	110 .	0
172.16.175.0/24 =	172	. 16	. 10101	111 .	0

Number of Common Bits = 21
Summary: 172.16.168.0/21

Number of
Noncommon
Bits = 11

Chapter 8: Designing Networks for Voice Transport

Case Study Simulation

1 What is the maximum value for end-to-end delay that is still acceptable in a voice session?

Answer: The maximum acceptable value is approximately 150 milliseconds.

2 Why does the jitter disturb the voice session?

Answer: Jitter introduces a variation in delay, to which voice is very sensitive.

3 How can QoS mechanisms improve the data propagation in congested networks?

Answer: QoS mechanisms can make data traffic more predictable in congested networks.

Review Questions

1 What steps are involved in converting analog signals to digital signals?

Answer: Several steps are involved in converting an analog signal into PCM digital format, including the following:

— **Filtering—Filters out the signal's non-speech frequency components.**

— **Sampling—Samples the filtered input signal at a constant sampling frequency.**

— **Digitizing—Digitizes the samples in preparation for transmission over a telephony network.**

2 What is pulse amplitude modulation?

Answer: PAM uses the original analog signal to modulate the amplitude of a pulse train that has a constant amplitude and frequency.

3 What is pulse code modulation?

Answer: The process of digitizing analog voice signals is called pulse code modulation. PCM takes the PAM process one step further by encoding each analog sample using binary code words.

4 Match the following terms with their definitions:

Terms:

— Filtering

— Quantization

— Companding

— Logarithmic compression

Definitions:

— Converting analog sample to a digital code word

— Compression increases as sample signal increases

— Removing non-speech components

— Compressing and coding signals

Answer:

Filtering: Removing non-speech components

Quantization: Converting analog sample to a digital code word

Companding: Compressing and coding signals

Logarithmic compression: Compression increases as sample signal increases

5 What are some of the call features provided by PBXs?

Answer: A PBX provides many call features, including call hold, transfer, forward and park, conferencing, music on hold, call history, and voice mail.

6 What are some differences between a PBX and a PSTN switch?

Answer:

— **A PBX is used in the private sector, while a PSTN is used in the public sector.**

— **A PBX scales to thousands of phones, while a PSTN scales to hundreds of thousands of phones.**

— **A PBX uses proprietary protocols to control phones, while a PSTN uses open standard protocols between switches and phones.**

7 How does having a PBX save on communication costs?

Answer: Enterprises install PBXs because the number of telephones is usually greater than the number of simultaneous calls to the PSTN network. Only a small percentage of telephones are active at one time. Companies with a PBX only need the number of external lines (to the PSTN) to equal the maximum possible number of simultaneous calls. Local calls between telephones within the PBX or group of PBXs are free of charge.

8 Match the following terms with their definitions:

Terms:

— Local loop

— Telephone line

— Station line

— Trunk

— Tie trunk

— CO trunk

— PSTN trunk

Definitions:

— Communication between CO switch and home telephone

— Connects CO switches to PBXs

— Physical cabling

— Communication between two telephony systems

— Connects PBXs

— Interconnects CO switches

— Communication between PBX and business telephone

Answer:

Local loop: Physical cabling

Telephone line: Communication between CO switch and home telephone

Station line: Communication between PBX and business telephone

Trunk: Communication between two telephony systems

Tie trunk: Connects PBXs

CO trunk: Connects CO switches to PBXs

PSTN trunk: Interconnects CO switches

9 Which signaling method is used between PSTN switches?

Answer: SS7 is the signaling method that is used between PSTN switches.

10 Which signaling method allows standardized communication between PBXs?

Answer: QSIG allows standardized communication between PBXs.

11 What is the difference between CAS and CCS?

Answer: CAS sends its signal for call setup in the same channel as voice, while CCS uses a separate channel for call setup.

12 What is the difference between subscriber and trunk signaling?

Answer: Subscriber signaling is between a PSTN or PBX switch and subscriber (telephone). Trunk signaling is between PSTN switches, between a PSTN switch and PBX, or between PBX switches.

13 Describe how a telephone call is routed from location A to location B through the PSTN using NANP.

Answer: The phone at location A dials the phone number of location B. A PSTN switch forwards the signal as soon as it receives enough digits to send the call to the next switch. The last switch in the series receives all the digits and rings the destination telephone.

14 Match the following terms with their definitions:

Terms:

- Centrex
- Virtual private voice networks
- Voice mail
- Call center
- Interactive voice response

Definitions:

- Interconnect corporate voice traffic among multiple locations over the PSTN
- Does not require live agents
- Provides customers with the facility to divert their incoming PSTN calls
- A set of specialized business solutions in which the service provider owns and operates the equipment that provides both call control and service logic functions
- Requires live agents

Answer: Centrex: A set of specialized business solutions in which the service provider owns and operates the equipment that provides both call control and service logic functions

Virtual private voice networks: Interconnect corporate voice traffic among multiple locations over the PSTN

Voice mail: Provides customers with the facility to divert their incoming PSTN calls

Call center: Requires live agents

Interactive voice response: Does not require live agents

15 What is automatic call distribution?

Answer: Using ACD, callers are greeted by a customized announcement and then queued until their call can be answered.

16 What is TDM?

Answer: TDM is a digital transmission technique for simultaneously carrying multiple signals over a single trunk line by interleaving bits of each signal into different time slots.

17 What are the advantages of using packet-switched networks for voice traffic?

Answer: Packet-switched networks only use bandwidth when it is required. Call routing, control, and applications can be widely distributed and based on industry standards; enterprises can mix and match equipment from multiple vendors and geographically deploy these systems wherever they are needed.

18 What is the difference between VoIP and IP telephony?

Answer: With VoIP, voice traffic is converted to IP packets and directed over IP data networks through voice-enabled routers.

With IP telephony, IP phones themselves convert voice into IP packets. A dedicated network server that runs specialized software replaces the PBX. IP telephony implementations do not use telephone cabling; instead, they send all signals over standard network cabling.

19 What is the difference between an H.323 gateway and an H.323 gatekeeper?

Answer: A gateway is an optional element in the voice network and can be a voice-enabled router or switch. Gateways provide many services, such as translating between H.323 endpoints and other non-H.323 devices, which allow H.323 endpoints and non-H.323 endpoints to communicate.

A gatekeeper manages H.323 endpoints by allowing them to register with the gatekeeper, locate another H.323 endpoint or gatekeeper, and thus establish a call. A gatekeeper is usually used in larger, more complex networks.

20 What role does an H.323 terminal play in voice networks?

Answer: Terminals are client endpoints on the LAN that provide real-time, two-way H.323 communications.

21 What does Cisco CallManager do?

Answer: Cisco CallManager is the Cisco enterprise IP telephony solution's software-based call-processing component. CallManager provides a scalable, distributable, and highly available enterprise IP telephony call processing solution. CallManager performs much like a PBX in a traditional telephone network, including call setup and processing functions.

22 What are the four components of IP telephony architecture?

Answer: The IP telephony architecture includes four distinct components: infrastructure, call processing, applications, and clients.

23 How does IP telephony lower costs?

Answer: IP telephony lowers costs in the following ways:

— **Reduced long distance costs—Long distance costs should be lower than when using traditional telephony. This can be accomplished by utilizing the public Internet or private IP networks for routing telephone calls.**

— **Lower cost of ownership—IP telephony should offer lower total ownership cost and greater flexibility than traditional telephony.**

— **Reduced operational and equipment costs—Data and telephony network consolidation should lead to savings in operational and equipment costs.**

24 What is a voice port?

Answer: A voice port is a voice gateway interface that carries voice data. It is a physical port that comes with a voice module, which is what makes a router voice-enabled.

25 What is a dial peer?

Answer: Dial peers are logical peers that are associated with physical voice ports. The voice gateway establishes a connection based on the configuration of dial peers.

26 Describe how a voice call is processed in a voice gateway.

Answer: Unless otherwise configured, when a call arrives on the voice gateway, the gateway presents a dial tone to the caller and collects digits until it can identify the destination dial peer. After the dial peer has been identified, the call is forwarded through the next call leg, to the destination.

27 Complete the following sentence:

Dejitter buffers are used on the _____ side(s) of the network to smooth out delay variability.

a. originating

b. receiving

c. all

Answer: Dejitter buffers are used on the <u>receiving</u> side(s) of the network to smooth out delay variability.

28 What is Link Fragmentation and Interleaving (LFI)?

Answer: LFI is a solution for queuing delay situations. With LFI, large packets are fragmented into smaller frames and interleaved with small voice packets. Thus, a voice packet does not have to wait until the entire data packet is sent. LFI reduces and ensures a more predictable voice delay.

29 What is the acceptable one-way delay limit for good quality voice?

Answer: 150 ms is the acceptable one-way delay limit for good-quality voice.

30 Match the following terms with their definitions:

Terms:

— Processing delay

— Propagation delay

— Jitter

— Echo

Definitions:

— Variation in the delay of received packets

— Audible leak of the caller's voice into the receive (return) path

— Length of time it takes to travel the distance between the sending and receiving endpoints

— Time the DSP takes to compress a block of PCM samples

Answer:

Processing delay: Time the DSP takes to compress a block of PCM samples

Propagation delay: Length of time it takes to travel the distance between the sending and receiving endpoints

Jitter: Variation in the delay of received packets

Echo: Audible leak of the caller's voice into the receive (return) path

31 Match the following coding standards with their bandwidth requirements.

Coding standards:

— G.711

— G.729

— G.726

— G.723

— G.728

Bandwidth requirements:

— Required bandwidth 5.3 kbps

— Required bandwidth 64 kbps

— Required bandwidth 24 kbps

— Required bandwidth 8 kbps

— Required bandwidth 16 kbps

Answer:

G.711: Required bandwidth 64 kbps

G.729: Required bandwidth 8 kbps

G.726: Required bandwidth 24 kbps

G.723: Required bandwidth 5.3 kbps

G.728: Required bandwidth 16 kbps

32 Which ITU voice coding standard results in the highest mean opinion score (MOS)?

Answer: G.711, with a MOS of 4.1.

33 What protocols are used to transport voice conversation traffic?

Answer: RTP, UDP, and IP are used to transport voice conversation traffic.

34 Will a voice packet loss always be audible?

Answer: No. For packet losses as small as one packet, the DSP interpolates the conversation with what it thinks the audio should be, and the packet loss is not audible.

35 Match the following terms with their definitions:

Terms:

— H.225 channel

— H.245 channel

— RAS

— RTCP

Definitions:

— Used only if a gatekeeper is present

— Uses Q.931 to establish a connection between two terminals

— Monitors quality for hosts that communicate with voice traffic

— Carries control messages that govern voice operation

Answer:

H.225 channel: Uses Q.931 to establish a connection between two terminals

H.245 channel: Carries control messages that govern voice operation

RAS: Used only if a gatekeeper is present

RTCP: Monitors quality for hosts that communicate with voice traffic

36 What does voice activity detection do?

Answer: VAD suppresses packets of silence.

37 What does compressed RTP do?

Answer: cRTP offers significant bandwidth savings by compressing the headers to 2 or 4 bytes. cRTP is sometimes referred to as RTP header compression.

38 Which of these codecs have relatively more IP header overhead compared to the payload? Arrange them in descending order.

G.729

G.711

G.728

Answer:

G.729: 1

G.711: 3

G.728: 2

G.729 has the most compression of the payload, but the IP header is a constant 40 bytes. Therefore, G.729 has more IP overhead relative to its payload.

39 Which queuing mechanism is recommended for most VoIP designs?

Answer: LLQ, which is a combination of CBWFQ and PQ, is recommended. Strict priority queuing allows delay-sensitive data, such as voice, to be dequeued and sent first (before packets in other queues are dequeued), giving delay-sensitive data preferential treatment over other traffic.

40 What QoS mechanisms are available for voice?

Answer: The following QoS mechanisms are available for voice:

— **Bandwidth reduction**

— **Bandwidth reservation**

— **QoS classification**

— **Congestion avoidance**

— **Congestion management**

41 What is the difference between AutoQoS and QPM?

Answer: AutoQoS provides QoS provisioning for individual routers and switches, thereby simplifying deployment and reducing human error. CiscoWorks QPM provides centralized QoS design, administration, and traffic monitoring that scales to large QoS deployments. While AutoQoS allows a user to configure QoS at the device level, enterprises use QPM to cost-effectively manage QoS in their IP network.

42 Why would a hub and spoke topology be beneficial compared to a fully meshed topology for VoFR?

Answer: A hub and spoke topology reduces network costs and reduces the number of PVCs.

43 What is the difference between static and dynamic VoFR?

Answer: With static FRF.11 trunks, the VoFR system provides transportation of the voice connection channels, but does not provide telephone call switching based on dial plan information. PBXs perform all telephone call switching.

With dynamic VoFR calls, the dial plan information is contained within dial-peer entries on every VoFR router in the path.

44 What is the preferred ATM class of service for VoATM transport?

Answer: Variable bit rate (VBR) is the preferred ATM class of service for VoATM transport.

45 Which is the preferred ATM adaptation type for VoATM?

Answer: AAL2 is the preferred ATM adaptation type for VoATM.

46 Match the following terms with their definitions:

Terms:

— On-net calling

— Off-net calling

— Least-cost routing

Definitions:

— Voice calls that are transmitted over the PSTN

— Voice calls that are transmitted over private interlocation tie lines

— Calls going to the PSTN at a point that is closest to the destination

Answer: On-net calling: Voice calls that are transmitted over private interlocation tie lines

Off-net calling: Voice calls that are transmitted over the PSTN

Least-cost routing: Calls going to the PSTN at a point that is closest to the destination

47 How does a user know that he has reached the PSTN during a manually selected off-net call?

Answer: When the call reaches the PSTN, a second dial tone can usually be heard.

48 How many centum call seconds (CCS) equals five Erlangs?

Answer: 5*36 = 180 CCS

49 What does a GoS of P05 mean?

Answer: There is a 5% probability that a call will be blocked.

50 Which two parameters are mandatory for trunk capacity calculation?

Answer: The acceptable GoS and the traffic volume in the busiest hour are mandatory parameters.

51 If your call logger says that 290 calls are made on a trunk group in an hour and the average call duration is 180 seconds, what is the busy hour traffic (in Erlangs)?

Answer: The calculation is as follows:

— **BHT = Average call duration (seconds) * calls per hour/3600**

— **BHT = 180 * 290/3600**

— **BHT = 14.5 Erlangs**

52 What is the difference between medium and high complexity codecs?

Answer: Medium complexity codecs allow the DSPs to process up to four voice calls per DSP. High complexity codecs allow the DSPs to process up to two voice calls per DSP.

53 Which codecs are high complexity?

Answer: High complexity codecs include G.728, G.723, G.729, and G.729b.

54 Which parameters are required for WAN capacity planning to support IP telephony?

Answer: WAN capacity planning for voice and data transport depends on a number of parameters, including the number of simultaneous voice calls, sampling rate, codec, link type, header compression techniques, and use of VAD.

55 What is the purpose of the Call Admission Control mechanism?

Answer: CAC protects voice traffic from being negatively affected by other voice traffic and keeps excess voice traffic off the network.

56 What steps are involved in planning for network capacity and performance in an IP telephony implementation?

Answer: The steps are as follows:

Step 1 Determine the current traffic load and the data traffic requirements for a combined IP telephony and data architecture.

Step 2 Determine IP telephony traffic overhead in required sections of the network based on busy hour estimates, gateway capacities, and Cisco CallManager capacities.

Step 3 Determine minimum bandwidth requirements by combining the busy hour data traffic and busy hour voice traffic.

Step 4 Determine the required design changes and QoS requirements based on IP telephony design recommendations and voice bandwidth requirements.

Step 5 Before implementation, validate baseline IP telephony performance with a performance baseline to determine voice readiness.

57 Why is Cisco CallManager processing requirements planning necessary?

Answer: Cisco CallManager processing requirements planning helps ensure that the Cisco CallManager servers have sufficient resources for normal call processing, voice conferencing, and other IP telephony services. This planning process typically leads to an improved network design that can better support the organization's requirements.

Chapter 9: Evaluating Security Solutions for the Network

Review Questions

1 Match the terms with the definitions:

Terms:

— Integrity violation

— Confidentiality breach

— Availability threat

Definitions:

— Result of a network's inability to handle an enormous quantity of data

— Attacker changes sensitive data

— Can be difficult to detect

Answer: Integrity violation: Attacker changes sensitive data

Confidentiality breach: Can be difficult to detect

Availability threat: Result of a network's inability to handle an enormous quantity of data

2   What is a denial of service (DoS) attack?

Answer: A DoS attack occurs when the attacker compromises the availability of a service. It might be the result of a failure to handle exceptional conditions or vast quantities of data.

3   How are risk assessment and security policy related?

Answer: Risk assessment defines threats, their probability, and their severity. A network security policy enumerates risks that are relevant to the network and determines how to manage those risks. A network security design implements the security policy.

4   What are some steps that can be taken to prevent network devices from being compromised?

Answer: The following can help prevent network devices from being compromised:

— **Use clearly defined security management procedures**

— **Enable only necessary services on devices**

— **Provide secure device management channels using strong authentication, session encryption, and change control**

— **Patch the device software so its security recommendations and identified security issues remain up-to-date**

5   What types of threats are directed at networks as a whole?

Answer: Threats directed at networks include the following:

— **Reconnaissance attacks, in which the network is searched for possible targets.**

— **DoS attacks, in which connectivity to an entire network is compromised.**

— **Traffic attacks, in which data flowing over a network is compromised— for example, the reading and changing of data in transit.**

6 How can an organization defend against DoS attacks that flood the network with packets?

Answer: Defending against these attacks requires a mixture of the following:

— **Heuristic-based defense mechanisms, which try to assess what data is malicious and discard it before it overwhelms a service.**

— **Buying more resources than necessary.**

— **Having plenty of backup options.**

7 Why might a hacker launch a reconnaissance attack?

Answer: Reconnaissance is usually the prelude to a more focused attack against a particular target; it is used to determine what subnets, hosts, and services are available as potential targets.

8 How can attacks against hosts and applications be mitigated?

Answer: Host and application protection methods include the following:

— **Network access control methods, which only allow access to minimal services and select users.**

— **Strong host security policies, which protect the operating system and its services from compromise.**

— **If it is used properly, cryptography can provide data confidentiality, integrity, and authenticity guarantees.**

— **Application access controls, coupled with secure programming, are the most significant cornerstones of application security.**

9 What are some components of a typical security policy?

Answer: Components might include an acceptable use policy, incident handling guidelines, security management policy, and an access control policy.

10 What are the processes in the security wheel?

Answer: The security wheel is the complete process of initial risk assessment, developing the initial security policy, implementing network security, monitoring and testing the security, and reassessing the risks.

11 How can a network security mechanism manage the risk of stolen laptops?

Answer: This risk is managed by not keeping encryption keys on the laptop and by having the ability to revoke credentials.

12 What are the three types of authentication (proof of identity)?

Answer: Authentication is traditionally based on one of the following three proofs:

— **Something the subject knows**

— **Something the subject has**

— **Something the subject is**

13 What is the difference between authentication and authorization?

Answer: Authentication is used to establish subject identity. Authorization is used to limit subject access to a network.

14 What is the principle of least privilege?

Answer: The principle of least privilege is based on the practice by which each subject is only given the minimal rights that are necessary to perform their tasks.

15 Which two of the following attacks can be prevented using network filtering (for example, a firewall)?

— An attacker, who has a legitimate account on a UNIX server, uses locally available tools to obtain administrator privileges.

— An attacker attempts to connect to an organization's sensitive, nonpublic server from the Internet.

— An attacker steals a bank ATM machine to obtain its cryptographic keys.

— An attacker maps a company's network using network management tools.

— An attacker decrypts a sensitive e-mail message that was sent freely over the Internet.

Answer:

— An attacker, who has a legitimate account on a UNIX server, uses locally available tools to obtain administrator privileges.

— **An attacker attempts to connect to an organization's sensitive, nonpublic server from the Internet.**

— An attacker steals a bank ATM machine to obtain its cryptographic keys.

— **An attacker maps a company's network using network management tools.**

— An attacker decrypts a sensitive e-mail message that was sent freely over the Internet.

16 Complete this sentence: Cryptography provides _____ through _____.

Answer: Cryptography provides <u>confidentiality</u> through <u>encryption</u>.

17 True or false: Cryptography can impact network performance.

Answer: True

18 Provide some examples of cryptographic mechanisms that ensure data integrity.

Answer: Digital signatures and secure fingerprints are examples of cryptographic mechanisms that ensure data integrity.

19 What is a Network Intrusion Detection System (NIDS)?

Answer: NIDSs are installed on the network, where they search for potential attacks by capturing and analyzing network traffic.

20 How can network management channels be secured?

Answer: Network management channels are usually secured by using either a separate management network (for example, a separate VLAN) or cryptography to protect management protocols (for example, SSH for terminal access or IPSec protocols to protect SNMP traffic).

21 What is the Cisco SAFE Blueprint?

Answer: To assist network designers and security architects, Cisco developed the SAFE Blueprint to provide guidelines for implementing security mechanisms within the network infrastructure and beyond. The intent of SAFE is to provide information regarding best practices for designing and implementing secure networks.

22 Which type of attacks can generally be prevented using a demilitarized zone (DMZ)?

Answer: A DMZ is a common solution for managing the risk of compromising other hosts from hosts that are already compromised.

23 What are some of the risks associated with the Internet Connectivity module?

Answer: Common risks associated with the Internet Connectivity module include the following:

— **Reconnaissance threats from the Internet, whereby an attacker attempts to probe the network and its hosts in an effort to map the network. It does this to discover reachable networks, hosts, and services running on exposed hosts.**

— **The compromise of exposed hosts and their applications, which can lead directly to confidentiality breaches and integrity violations for data that is processed by exposed servers.**

— **The compromise of other hosts from compromised hosts in the module. First, an attacker compromises a host in the Internet Connectivity module and, from that host, compromises a host on another network perimeter, such as the Enterprise Campus.**

— **DoS attacks that are directed at exposed hosts in this module.**

— **DoS attacks that are directed at network links, such as the enterprise network's Internet connection.**

— **Introduction of malicious code over supported services such as e-mail and Internet access.**

24 Why is a compromise in an e-commerce server generally riskier than in an Internet module server?

Answer: The E-commerce module usually hosts high-profile servers that process highly confidential and sensitive data; therefore, a compromise could result in a more substantial loss.

25 How do you manage the risk of a compromised e-commerce server that is compromising another host?

Answer: E-commerce applications are often multi-tiered and run on multiple servers. Separating the multi-tiered server systems into their own DMZ networks ensures that there is a firewall system between them to protect more secure servers in the event of front-end compromise. Firewalls generally restrict connections from exposed e-commerce servers, so the compromise of any other host is less likely. Hosts on the same segment can be separated by LAN switch access control mechanisms (such as private VLANs). Network and host intrusion detection systems can monitor individual hosts and subnets to detect signs of attacks and confirm potential successful breaches.

26 What are some of the security risks in the Remote Access and VPN module?

Answer: Specific risks in the Remote Access and VPN module include the following:

— **Identity spoofing of remote clients or sites, whereby an attacker can impersonate a legitimate client and log in to the remote-access VPN connection.**

— **Compromise of data transmission confidentiality and integrity, whereby an attacker can access the network media to obtain access to and change sensitive data.**

— **The compromise of a client or remote site, whereby an attacker successfully attacks the protected network over the VPN or dialup connection through a legitimate client's system or a branch office.**

27 How can the risk of identity spoofing in the Remote Access and VPN module be managed?

Answer: To manage the risk of identity spoofing, and because external networks alone do not provide any trusted authentication, an organization should deploy very strong authentication for access from an external network.

28 How can enterprises protect against a risk of service provider misconfiguration?

Answer: To prevent accidental WAN interconnection of different enterprises, WAN devices might require authentication of peers and routing protocols over WAN links. The WAN devices might not accept data from an unknown device even though they both use the same WAN protocol.

29 What security risks are associated with the WAN module?

Answer: Specific risks to the WAN module include the following:

— **Compromise of data transmission confidentiality and integrity, whereby an attacker who obtains physical access to the network media or to a service provider WAN switch can intercept WAN connections.**

— **Accidental or deliberate misconfiguration of the WAN network that interconnects different enterprises.**

30 What security risks are associated with the Network Management module?

Answer: Specific risks to the Network Management module include the following:

— **Impersonation of administrators, whereby an attacker might steal an administrator's credentials, log on to network devices, and change the device's configuration.**

— **Compromise of management protocols, whereby the attacker might send false management messages or listen to management protocol messages to obtain sensitive information.**

— **Accidental or deliberate misconfiguration of network or security devices.**

— **Avoidance of responsibility among administrators, whereby an administrator might deny responsibility for certain actions that led to a security incident.**

— **Compromise of management hosts, whereby very sensitive configuration, security, and audit data can be hosted.**

31 How can the risk of administrator impersonation be mitigated?

Answer: To manage the risk of administrator impersonation, provide strong authentication mechanisms for administrators. A good example is a two-factor OTP system that is based on token cards.

32 What are the differences in security risks associated with servers in the Server Farm versus those in the E-commerce module?

Answer: The specific risks in the Server Farm module are similar to those in the E-commerce module, except that sensitivity of data on internal servers is usually critical.

33 What are the common security risks in the Server Farm module?

Answer: Specific risks in the Server Farm module include direct compromise of exposed applications and unauthorized access to data, and compromise of other hosts from compromised servers in this module.

34 What is the CiscoWorks Auto Update Server?

Answer: A component of the CiscoWorks VMS, the Auto Update Server allows users to implement a pull model for security and operating system management; Cisco PIX firewalls can periodically and dynamically contact the management station for any configuration, PIX Operating System, and PIX Device Manager updates. Remote Cisco PIX firewalls can contact the Auto Update Server at boot time, for periodic configuration and operating system refreshes, or dynamically any time the remote Cisco PIX firewall receives a new DHCP-assigned address.

Chapter 10: Applying Basic Network Management Design Concepts

Review Questions

1 What is a network management agent?

Answer: A network management agent is software on a managed device that collects and stores management information.

2 How does an SNMP manager request a list of data?

Answer: First, the manager sends a get request to request the specific MIB variable from the agent. Then, get next request messages are used to retrieve the next object instance from a table or a list.

3 How does an SNMPv2 manager request a list of data?

Answer: An SNMPv2 manager sends a GetBulk message to request a list of data. (This new SNMPv2 message reduces the repetitive requests and replies, thereby improving performance while retrieving large amounts of data.)

4 What is the MIB structure?

Answer: Each object in an MIB has a unique identifier, which network management applications use to identify and retrieve a specific object. The MIB structure is a tree-like structure in which similar objects are grouped under the same branch of the MIB tree (for example, different interface counters are grouped under the MIB tree's interfaces branch).

5 How are private MIB definitions supported?

Answer: To use the private definitions of managed objects, the private definitions must be compiled into the NMS.

6 What are the RMON1 groups?

Answer: Following are the RMON1 groups:

— **Statistics**

— **History**

— **Alarm**

— **Host**

— **Host top N**

— **Matrix**

— **Filters**

— **Packet capture**

— **Events**

— **TokenRing**

7 What groups were added by RMON2?

Answer: Following are the RMON groups that were added with the introduction of RMON2:

— **Protocol directory**

— **Protocol distribution**

— **Address mapping**

— **Network layer host**

— **Network layer matrix**

— **Application layer host**

— **Application layer matrix**

— **User history collection**

— **Probe configuration**

8 How does RMON simplify proactive network management?

Answer: Without RMON, an MIB could be used to check each machine's network performance; however, this would lead to large amounts of required bandwidth for management traffic. By using RMON, the managed device itself collects and stores the data (via its RMON agent) that would otherwise be retrieved from the MIB frequently.

9 At which layer does CDP work?

Answer: CDP works at the data link layer.

10 Two routers are connected via Frame Relay, but ping is not working between them. How could CDP help troubleshoot this situation?

Answer: If CDP frames are being received, the Frame Relay connection (the data link layer) is running. Because ping does not work, the problem is likely with the IP addresses that are configured on the interfaces. CDP shows the IP addresses that are configured on neighboring devices; thus, CDP information can be used to determine where the IP addressing problem resides.

11 Why is NetFlow superior to RMON?

Answer: NetFlow information-gathering benefits include the greater detail of data collected, time stamping of the data, support for various data per interface, and greater scalability. NetFlow's performance impact is much lower than that of RMON, and external probes are not required. NetFlow services capitalize on the flow nature of traffic in the network to provide detailed data collection with minimal impact on router performance and to process access lists efficiently for packet filtering and security services.

12   What is a NetFlow network flow?

Answer: A network flow is defined as a unidirectional sequence of packets between source and destination endpoints. Network flows are highly granular; flow endpoints are identified both by IP address and transport layer application port numbers. NetFlow also identifies the flows by IP protocol type, class of service, and the input interface identifier.

13   What are the syslog severity levels?

Answer: Syslog defines the following severity levels:

— **Emergency (level 0, which is the highest level)**

— **Alert (level 1)**

— **Critical (level 2)**

— **Error (level 3)**

— **Warning (level 4)**

— **Notice (level 5)**

— **Informational (level 6)**

— **Debugging (level 7)**

14   What syslog severity level does the first message show in Example 10-2?

Answer: This message is severity level 5, a notice.

15   What are the five functional areas of network management?

Answer: The following are the five functional areas of network management (abbreviated as FCAPS):

— **Fault management**

— **Configuration management**

— **Accounting management**

— **Performance management**

— **Security management**

16   What does fault management event processing involve?

Answer: Event processing involves the following steps:

— **Event collection**

— **Event normalization**

— **Event filtering**

— **Event correlation**

— **Event reporting**

17 What are the two types of fault management devices?

Answer: The fault management architecture consists of event generators and event collectors.

18 Why is configuration management beneficial to a network administrator?

Answer: The benefits of configuration management include the following:

— **Lower support costs because of a decrease in reactive support issues.**

— **Lower network costs because of device, circuit, and user tracking tools and processes that identify unused network components.**

— **Improved network availability because of a decrease in reactive support costs and improved time to resolve problems.**

19 Which protocols are used for configuration management?

Answer: SNMP, TFTP, and Telnet.

20 What are the three tiers of the NetFlow architecture?

Answer: Following are the three tiers of NetFlow:

— **NetFlow-capable Layer 3 device**

— **NetFlow collector**

— **Accounting and billing application**

21 Which accounting method should a network administrator use to measure the amount of time a dialup user is connected?

Answer: A network administrator should use the accounting portion of AAA to measure the amount of time a dialup user is connected.

22 What are the *data plane* and the *control plane*?

Answer: The data plane refers to capacity and performance issues that are involved with data traversing the network. The control plane refers to resources that are required to maintain proper functionality of the data plane.

23 What is the difference between SLM, an SLC, and an SLA?

Answer: SLM is a proven methodology that helps network managers to resolve resource issues by defining and regulating capacity and performance management processes in a cost-effective manner.

An SLC specifies connectivity and performance levels the service provider must meet for the service's end user.

SLAs define specific service performance measurements between device pairs, including routers, servers, workstations, and other equipment.

24 What steps are involved in developing a performance information collection plan?

Answer: The process for developing a performance information collection plan can be divided into the following five steps:

— **Determine networking requirements**

— **Define a process**

— **Define capacity areas**

— **Define capacity variables**

— **Interpret data**

25 How can performance data be collected?

Answer: Performance information can be collected using the following methods:

— **ICMP ping**

— **Network analyzers or probes**

— **NetFlow**

26 How is AAA used in security management?

Answer: Routers and switches support centralized security management using the AAA approach: the first A stands for authentication (identifying the administrator), the second A stands for authorization (determining whether the authenticated administrator is allowed to perform a certain action), and the third A stands for accounting (logging of all actions). AAA supports optional OTP authentication.

27 Is Telnet considered a secure protocol?

Answer: No. Telnet authentication is in clear text and therefore is not secure.

28 How should an enterprise ensure that its network can meet its business needs?

Answer: It should sign an SLC, containing SLAs that define its network requirements.

29 How can an enterprise monitor conformance to an SLA with a third party vendor?

Answer: Monitoring a third-party vendor's provided services presents a unique challenge because individual components of the service are unknown to the customer and their data is therefore unavailable. Conformance is determined by collecting service-level measurements from customer-owned and -controlled devices. Even though there is no visibility into the actual components and -controlled a particular service, the collected data must accurately represent and report on SLA conformance.

30 What are some requirements that SLAs should meet?

Answer: SLA requirements include the following:

— **The ability to confirm that the provider meets SLAs, based on network connectivity and network application responses.**

— **The ability to identify SLA issues in detail.**

— **The ability to impose financial penalties for missed SLAs.**

— **Business-level reports and detailed technical reports that can be enhanced and extended easily and incrementally.**

— **Validation that key business objectives are being met when deploying technologies.**

31 What might high latency values in a network indicate?

Answer: High latency numbers can indicate congestion on either an end device or a relaying device, such as a router or switch.

32 Why might an end-to-end SLM be challenging?

Answer: An end-to-end SLM might be challenging because the solution must satisfy the following requirements:

— **Leverage component management products from multiple vendors**

— **Work with clients and equipment that the customer does not own or control**

— **Adapt to new SLM metrics as new technologies are deployed**

— **Scale by orders of magnitude**

— **Collect the correct network and application SLM metrics at the appropriate times**

33 An enterprise has implemented a web-based ordering application. Orders are processed from internal users or external partners. Which network services or levels must be monitored and reported to ensure that proper SLM is achieved?

Answer: Corporate devices and servers and Internet connectivity must be monitored and reported on.

34 How are acceptable response times for an SLA determined?

Answer: If the minimum acceptable response time is unknown, proactive performance tools help establish baselines. Useful sources for guidelines are either the results of current network response times or the results of averaging the monthly or weekly values of those responses. If the users are satisfied with the network response time, these values are used as thresholds for future performance.

35 What additional devices are required in a network in order to run SAA?

Answer: None. SAA is an integral part of Cisco IOS software.

36 How would SAA help determine if an SLA related to IP telephony in an enterprise is being met?

Answer: The SAA can measure the jitter for IP telephony by sending test packets as the source from one side of the network and responding as the destination of those packets on the other side of the network; the destination SAA accepts the packets, provides measurements, and responds to the source. The source SAA assesses the values in the reply packets and compares these values to the defined SLA. If the defined values are exceeded, the notification mechanism provides information to the management station, and the administrator can easily locate where disturbances in the IP telephony application might appear.

37 Which SAA feature would be useful in determining where network connectivity has failed?

Answer: Hop-by-hop measurements using the ICMP path echo protocol help isolate the troubled link quickly.

38 What are the components of the IPM/SAA monitoring solution?

Answer: The IPM/SAA monitoring solution is composed of three parts: the IPM server application, the IPM client application, and the SAA feature of the Cisco IOS software. The IPM network management application includes the server and the client.

39 Which protocols do IPM and SMS use to read data?

Answer: IPM uses SNMP; SMS uses HTTP and XML.

40 Cisco equipment that supports SAA is used in a campus network. Web-based reports on SLA are required. Which Cisco application should be used?

Answer: SMS should be used.

Chapter 11: Review and Case Study

Comprehensive Case Study

1 Propose a campus redesign that solves the current problems reported by the users. Consider redundancy when redesigning the LAN. Write an overview of your redesign and articulate why you selected that solution.

Answer:

A possible reason for the users' reported low response times is the number of broadcasts generated by the network's stations. These broadcasts are flooded throughout the Layer 2 switched network because Layer 2 switches do not stop broadcasts.

The administrators did not detect any congestion on the backbone switch because of its high bandwidth; however, the same broadcasts cause serious problems on 100 megabits per second (Mbps) and 10 Mbps user ports.

The only solution for this issue is to divide the campus into smaller networks and route between them. Layer 3 functionality, provided by routers or Layer 3 switches, limits the broadcasts within the network and therefore relieves end-user stations from processing broadcast requests.

Figure G-6 shows the proposed campus redesign.

Figure G-6   *MCMB Proposed Campus Redesign*

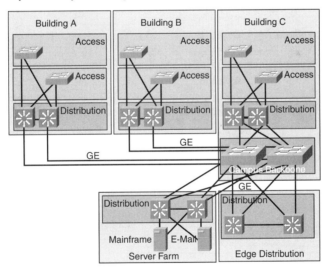

This design proposes Layer 3 switching in the building distribution layer, while the building access and the campus backbone keep Layer 2 switching. In the campus backbone, a second Layer 2 switch is recommended to provide redundancy.

Using Layer 2 switches, the building access layer supports virtual local-area networks (VLANs) and has redundant trunk uplinks to the building distribution Layer 3 switches. All routing between department VLANs and between buildings is performed there. The campus backbone does not perform any routing and is dedicated to fast packet switching.

Layer 3 switching is also proposed for the Server Farm and Edge Distribution modules. The Server Farm comprises all the internal servers, and the Edge Distribution module connects the campus network with remote locations and the Internet. Because most of the traffic flows from the mainframe toward the users and can cause a possible bottleneck, the number of Gigabit Ethernet (GE) ports between the campus backbone and the Server Farm should also be considered. In Figure G-6, two GE uplinks are provided between the Server Farm and the campus backbone.

To equalize all links between switches, the Spanning Tree Protocol (STP) must be tuned per VLAN. The Cisco per-VLAN Spanning Tree Protocol permits a separate instance of STP to be configured independently for each VLAN. For example, the root port can be selected independently for each VLAN, thereby making load balancing over redundant links possible.

2 Propose a WAN backup design to improve network reliability. Write an overview of your design and articulate why you selected that solution.

Answer: Figure G-7 shows the proposed backup scenario.

Figure G-7 *MCMB Proposed WAN Backup Redesign*

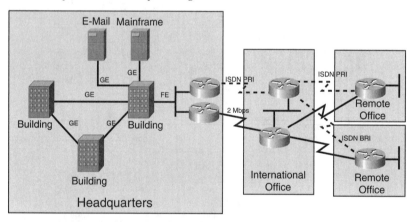

The proposed wide-area network (WAN) backup design assumes that all WAN links should have Integrated Services Digital Network (ISDN) backup. Because the headquarters connects to each international office with 2-Mbps links, the ISDN backup links should be the same size. Therefore, at least one ISDN primary rate interface (PRI) should be allocated in the headquarters and each international office. The number of ISDN PRI links in the headquarters should be considered; if the customer requires full WAN redundancy, the number of PRIs should equal the number of WAN links from the headquarters. If full WAN redundancy is not required, the number of ISDN PRIs can be smaller. Because the distance between international offices and the headquarters is large and the ISDN calls are international, the designer must also consider whether the backup link should have the same bandwidth as the primary WAN link. Usually, the backup link has a slightly lower bandwidth, especially on expensive international calls. The bandwidth-on-demand feature can achieve the variable bandwidth and consequential dialup connection savings.

The proposed ISDN backup on international-to-remote office connections is based on ISDN BRI with one or two B channels, with a corresponding bandwidth of 64 or 128 kbps. Again, the designer must consider either a full or partial backup scenario. In the full backup scenario, the number of available ISDN B channels in the international office should be equal to or larger than the number of connected remote offices.

All backup links should be implemented with floating static routes, which enable dynamic use of the backup route when a destination route is not reachable through the primary links. In the absence of dynamic routes, the static route (which has a higher administrative distance than the primary dynamic route) that points over the dialup link is used. This scenario enables smooth and efficient routing, regardless of the WAN connection technique used. In this design, we propose default routes to the dialup links, with an administrative distance of 200 (because this is bigger than the administrative distance of any of the interior routing protocols) for all upstream connections and remote locations. These default routes must be advertised through the routing protocol to the downstream routers; usually only the WAN link is utilized.

3 Propose an IP addressing redesign that optimizes IP addressing and IP routing (including the use of IP address summarization). Write an overview of your redesign and articulate why you selected that solution.

Answer: The proposed IP addressing redesign is shown in Figure G-8.

Figure G-8 *MCMB Proposed IP Addressing and Summarization Redesign*

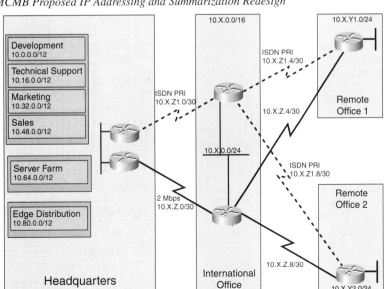

The proposed IP addressing plan assumes the use of 10.0.0.0/8 private IP addresses. The address space is hierarchically designed, which enables route summarization.

The /9 address block is assigned in the headquarters. This block is further divided into /12 blocks for each department and /16 for each building-department combination. A /16 address block is used for each country (international office with multiple remote offices). This block is then divided into /24 blocks for international office and remote office local-area networks (LANs). All WAN links from the international office use /30 subnets from one of the international /24 blocks. The ISDN backup links also use /30 subnets from another /24 address block.

Table G-10 shows the proposed IP address space assignment by typical locations.

Table G-10   *MCMB IP Address Allocation*

Location	IP Address Space	
Headquarters	10.0.0.0/9	
Headquarters—Development VLAN	**10.0.0.0/12**	
Headquarters—Development VLAN—Building 1	10.1.0.0/16	
Headquarters—Development VLAN—Building 2	10.2.0.0/16	
Headquarters—Development VLAN—Building 3	10.3.0.0/16	
Headquarters—Technical Support VLAN	**10.16.0.0/12**	
Headquarters—Technical Support VLAN—Building 1	10.16.0.0/16	
Headquarters—Technical Support VLAN—Building 2	10.17.0.0/16	
Headquarters—Technical Support VLAN—Building 2	10.18.0.0/16	
Headquarters—Marketing VLAN	**10.32.0.0/12**	
Headquarters—Marketing VLAN—Building 1	10.32.0.0/16	
Headquarters—Marketing VLAN—Building 2	10.33.0.0/16	
Headquarters—Marketing VLAN—Building 3	10.34.0.0/16	
Headquarters—Sales VLAN	**10.48.0.0/12**	
Headquarters—Sales VLAN—Building 1	10.48.0.0/16	
Headquarters—Sales VLAN—Building 2	10.49.0.0/16	
Headquarters—Sales VLAN—Building 3	10.50.0.0/16	
Headquarters—Server Farm	**10.64.0.0/12**	

Table G-10   *MCMB IP Address Allocation (Continued)*

Location	IP Address Space	
Headquarters—Edge Distribution	**10.80.0.0/12**	
International network	10.X.0.0/16	x > 127
International Office LAN network	10.X.0.0/24	x > 127
Remote Office 1 LAN network	10.X.Y1.0/24	x > 127, Y1 > 0
Remote Office 2 LAN network	10.X.Y2.0/24	x > 127, Y2 > 0, Y2 <> Y1
International Office to Headquarters WAN connection	10.X.Z.0/30	x > 127, Z <> Y
International Office to Remote Office 1 WAN connection	10.X.Z.4/30	x > 127, Z <> Y
International Office to Remote Office 2 WAN connection	10.X.Z.8/30	x > 127, Z <> Y
International Office to Headquarters ISDN backup	10.X.Z1.0/30	x > 127, Z1 <> Y, Z1 <> Z
International Office to Remote Office 1 ISDN backup	10.X.Z1.4/30	x > 127, Z1 <> Y, Z1 <> Z
International Office to Remote Office 2 ISDN backup	10.X.Z1.8/30	x > 127, Z1 <> Y, Z1 <> Z

Deploying different security policies becomes very simple if you use VLANs for each department within the campus and between buildings. All packets between different VLANs must pass through the distribution layer switch, where security policies are implemented.

This proposed IP address assignment is hierarchical and enables route summarization. The goal of route summarization is to have small and easily-manageable routes in the routing table, and to relieve small routers in the international offices from calculating a large number of routes (which can be a fairly CPU-intensive task). Figure G-9 shows the proposed route summarization.

Figure G-9 *MCMB Proposed IP Address Summarization*

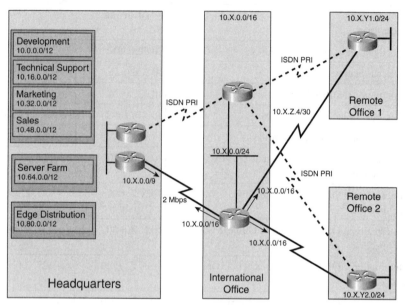

International routers summarize the network 10.X.0.0/16 toward the
headquarters and downstream, to the remote offices. The headquarters router
summarizes the network 10.0.0.0/9 toward all international offices. If the default
route is required (for accessing the Internet when the firewall does not contain a
proxy), the 0.0.0.0/0 network should also be advertised via the routing protocol.
The floating static routes between remote locations that point to the dialup
interfaces should not be more specific than the received summarized addresses;
otherwise, most of the traffic will flow through the dialup links.

4 If the existing routing, protocol does not fulfill all the requirements, propose a new
one to meet the customers needs. If a new routing protocol is not required, outline any
modifications that are required for the existing routing protocol. Write an overview of
your redesign and articulate why you selected that solution.

**Answer: The existing routing protocol, the Enhanced Interior Gateway Routing
Protocol (EIGRP), supports fast convergence and does not have any major
disadvantages compared to other routing protocols. Therefore, EIGRP will be
kept in this design. Summarization will also be implemented to reduce routing
tables and simplify the network.**

Extranet Design

5 Propose an extranet design that will enable secure access to the external servers for MCMB's customers and partners, regardless of the connectivity option they choose. Consider all possible solutions and propose the one that is appropriate for all customers who have a reasonable investment in network equipment and monthly costs. Write an overview of your design that articulates why you selected that solution, and create a diagram that depicts the proposed solution.

Answer: Figure G-10 illustrates the proposed extranet design.

Figure G-10 *MCMB Proposed Extranet Design*

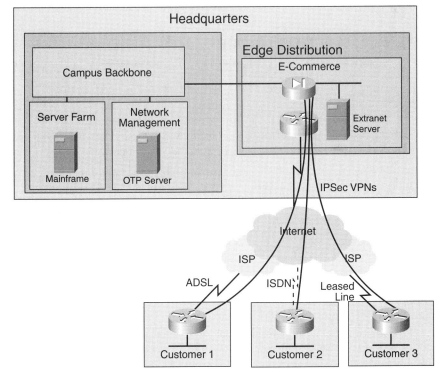

The extranet design is based on the assumption that partners and customers can choose any connectivity option they want; the only requirement is that the connection must be secure because of the nature of the transferred data. In this case, the natural choice is a secure virtual private network (VPN) with Internet Protocol Security (IPSec) and triple data encryption standard (3DES) encryption to provide data confidentiality and integrity. In addition, every user who accesses the application through the VPN tunnel must be authenticated. In this design, user authentication is provided using token-cards with one-time passwords.

The VPN tunnels are terminated on the PIX firewall in the E-commerce module, where the extranet servers are also located. The E-commerce module is connected to the campus network through the Edge Distribution module.

Because of the large number of connectivity options (ISDN, asymmetric digital subscriber line [ADSL], leased line, and so on), the access was outsourced to a service provider, and access to the E-commerce module is provided through the Internet. This solution requires a PIX firewall that has adequate performance characteristics and an Internet connection that has enough bandwidth. 50 partners and customers are expected to use the extranet with an application that requires 64 kbps of bandwidth; therefore, 50 * 64 kbps = 3.2 Mbps would allow everyone to access the application at the same time. You can make assumptions about the number of partners that would require access at the same time and reduce this bandwidth requirement.

Appendix A: IPv4 Addressing Job Aids

Review Questions

1 You need to design an IP network for your organization. Your organization's IP address is 172.16.0.0. Your assessment indicates that the organization needs at least 130 networks with no more than 100 nodes in each network.

As a result, you have decided to use a classful subnetting scheme based on the 172.16.0.0/24 scheme. Write any four IP addresses that are part of the range of subnetwork numbers, and write the subnet address and subnet mask for these addresses. An example is the address 172.16.1.0/24, which can also be written as 172.16.1.0 255.255.255.0.

Answer: Four addresses in this subnet are as follows:

IP Address	Subnet Address and Mask
172.16.2.9/24	172.16.2.0 255.255.255.0
172.16.3.11/24	172.16.3.0 255.255.255.0
172.16.4.12/24	172.16.4.0 255.255.255.0
172.16.255.2/24	172.16.255.0 255.255.255.0

2 Your network has the address 172.16.168.0/21. Write eight IP addresses in this network.

Answer: Eight addresses in this network are as follows:

— **172.16.168.1**

— **172.16.168.255**

— **172.16.169.1**

— **172.16.175.253**

— **172.16.168.2**

— **172.16.169.0**

— **172.16.169.2**

— **172.16.175.254**

3 Write the four IP addresses in the range described by the 192.168.99.16/30 address.

Answer: Four addresses in this range are as follows:

— **192.168.99.16**

— **192.168.99.17**

— **192.168.99.18**

— **192.168.99.19**

4 Of the four addresses in question 3, which two could you use as host addresses in a point-to-point connection?

Answer: The following two addresses could be used as host addresses: 192.168.99.17 and 192.168.99.18.

5 Figure A-18 shows the network for this question.

Create an access list and place it in the proper location to satisfy the following requirements:

— Prevent all hosts on subnet 172.16.1.0/24, except host 172.16.1.3, from accessing the web server on subnet 172.16.4.0. Allow all other hosts, including from the outside world, to access the web server.

— Prevent the outside world from pinging subnet 172.16.4.0.

— Allow all hosts on all subnets of network 172.16.0.0 (using subnet mask 255.255.255.0) to send queries to the DNS server on subnet 172.16.4.0. The outside world is not allowed to access the DNS server.

— Prevent host 172.16.3.3 from accessing subnet 172.16.4.0 for any reason.

— Prevent all other access to the 172.16.4.0 subnet.

Figure A-18   *Network for Review Question 5*

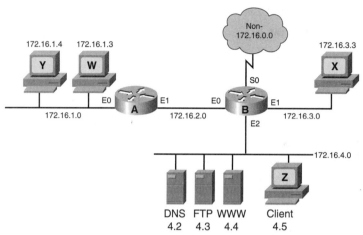

In your configuration, be sure to include the router name (A or B), interface name (E0, E1, or E2), and access list direction (in or out).

Answer: Global commands: Configuration for Router B

```
access-list 104 deny ip host 172.16.3.3 172.16.4.0 0.0.0.255
access-list 104 permit tcp host 172.16.1.3 172.16.4.0 0.0.0.255 eq 80
access-list 104 deny tcp 172.16.1.0 0.0.0.255 172.16.4.0 0.0.0.255 eq 80
access-list 104 permit tcp any any eq 80
access-list 104 permit udp 172.16.0.0 0.0.255.255 172.16.4.0 0.0.0.255 eq dns
```

Interface commands:

```
interface e2
ip access-group 104 out
```

6   What do bits set to 1 in a wildcard mask indicate when matching an address?

Answer: Bits set to 1 in a wildcard mask indicate that the corresponding bits in the address are ignored when matching an address in a packet to the address in the access list.

7   By default, what happens to all traffic in an access list?

Answer: By default, an access list denies all traffic.

8   To save network resources, where should an extended access list be placed?

Answer: To save network resources, an extended access list should be placed close to the source.

9   Using the keyword **host** in an access list is a substitute for using a wildcard mask of what value?

Answer: The keyword host is a substitute for a wildcard mask of 0.0.0.0.

This glossary assembles and defines terms and acronyms that are used in this book and in the internetworking industry. Many terms have several meanings; multiple definitions and acronym expressions are included where they apply. Many of these terms are also described in the Cisco Internetworking Terms and Acronyms resource, which is available at www.cisco.com/univercd/cc/td/doc/cisintwk/ita/.

NUMERICS

3DES   Triple data encryption standard. 3DES encrypts data three times with up to three different keys.

A

AAA   Authentication, authorization, and accounting. Pronounced "triple A." Authentication identifies a user, authorization determines what that user can do, and accounting monitors the duration of the user's network usage for billing purposes.

AAL   ATM adaptation layer, which is the service-dependent sublayer of the data link layer. The AAL accepts data from different applications and presents it to the ATM layer in the form of 48-byte ATM payload segments.

AAL1   ATM adaptation Layer 1. One of four AALs recommended by the ITU-T. AAL1 is used for connection-oriented, delay-sensitive services that require constant bit rates, such as uncompressed video and other isochronous traffic.

AAL2   ATM adaptation Layer 2. One of four AALs recommended by the ITU-T. AAL2 is used for connection-oriented services that support a variable bit rate, such as some isochronous video and voice traffic.

AAL5   ATM adaptation Layer 5. One of four AALs recommended by the ITU-T. AAL5 supports connection-oriented variable bit rate services and is predominantly used for the transfer of classical IP over ATM and LANE traffic.

ABR

1   Area border router. Router that is located on the border of one or more OSPF areas and connects those areas to the backbone network. ABRs are considered members of both the OSPF backbone and the attached areas. Therefore, they maintain routing tables that describe both the backbone topology and the topology of the other areas.

2   Available bit rate. QoS class that is defined by the ATM Forum for ATM networks. ABR is used for connections that do not require timing relationships between source and destination.

access layer   The layer in a hierarchical network that provides workgroup/user access to the network.

access list   Routers keep this list to control access to or from the router for a number of services (such as preventing packets with a certain IP address from leaving a particular interface on the router).

access method   Generally, the way in which network devices access the network medium.

access server   A communications processor that connects asynchronous devices to a LAN or WAN through a network and terminal emulation software. Performs both synchronous and asynchronous routing of supported protocols. It is sometimes called a network access server.

accounting management   One of the five network management categories that ISO defines for OSI network management. Accounting management subsystems are responsible for collecting network data that relates to resource usage. *See also* configuration management, fault management, performance management, and security management.

accuracy   The percentage of useful traffic that is correctly transmitted on the system, relative to total traffic, including transmission errors.

ACD   Automatic call distribution. Using ACD, callers are greeted by a customized announcement and then queued until their call can be answered. The ACD system generally offers inbound call routing.

ACELP   Algebraic Code Excited Linear Prediction. The process by which analog voice samples are encoded into high-quality digital signals.

ACK

   1   Acknowledgment bit in a TCP segment.

   2   *See also* acknowledgment.

acknowledgment   Notification sent from one network device to another to acknowledge that some event (such as receipt of a message) has occurred. Sometimes abbreviated ACK.

ACL   Access Control List. *See* access list.

address   A data structure or logical convention used to identify a unique entity, such as a particular process or network device.

address mapping   A technique that allows different protocols to interoperate by translating addresses from one format to another. For example, when routing IP over X.25, the IP addresses must be mapped to the X.25 addresses so the X.25 network can transmit IP packets. *See also* address resolution.

address resolution   Generally, a method for resolving differences between computer addressing schemes. Address resolution usually specifies a method for mapping network layer (Layer 3) addresses to data link layer (Layer 2) addresses. *See also* address mapping.

adjacency   A relationship formed between selected neighboring routers and end nodes for the purpose of exchanging routing information. Adjacency is based on the use of a common media segment.

administrative distance   A routing information source's trustworthiness rating. The higher the value, the lower the trustworthiness rating.

ADPCM   Adaptive Differential Pulse Code Modulation. The process by which analog voice samples are encoded into high-quality digital signals.

ADSL   Asymmetric Digital Subscriber Line, which is one of four DSL technologies. ADSL is designed to deliver more bandwidth downstream (from the central office to the customer site) than upstream. Downstream rates range from 1.5 to 9 Mbps, while upstream bandwidth ranges from 16 to 640 kbps. ADSL transmissions work at distances up to 18,000 feet (5488 meters) over a single copper twisted pair. *See also* HDSL, SDSL, and VDSL.

AES   Advanced Encryption Standard, which is a strong encryption algorithm that is part of the IEEE 802.11i standard.

agent

1   Generally, software that processes queries and returns replies on behalf of an application.

2   In NMSs, a process that resides in all managed devices and reports the values of specified variables to management stations.

aggregation   *See* route summarization.

alarm   A message that notifies an operator or administrator about a network problem. *See also* event and trap.

A-law   ITU-T companding standard used for converting between analog and digital signals in PCM systems. A-law is used primarily in European telephone networks and is similar to the North American u-law standard.

ALG   Application Level Gateway. An ALG translates between the IPv4 and IPv6 DNS requests and responses.

algorithm   A well-defined rule or process for arriving at a solution to a problem. In networking, algorithms are commonly used to determine the best traffic route from a particular source to a particular destination.

AM   Amplitude Modulation. A modulation technique whereby information is conveyed through the carrier signal's amplitude.

analog transmission   Signal transmission, over wires or through the air, in which information is conveyed through a variation of some combination of signal amplitude, frequency, and phase.

ANSI   American National Standards Institute. A voluntary organization comprised of corporate, government, and other members who coordinate standards-related activities, approve U.S. national standards, and develop positions for the United States in international standards organizations. ANSI helps develop international and U.S. standards relating to communications and networking, among other things.

anti-replay   Security service in which the receiver can reject old or duplicate packets to protect itself against replay attacks. IPSec provides this optional service by using a sequence number combined with data authentication.

AP   Access Point. When WLANs operate in infrastructure mode, all wireless clients connect through an AP for all communications.

API   Application programming interface. A specification of function-call conventions that defines an interface to a service.

APPC   Advanced Program-to-Program Communication. IBM SNA system software that allows high-speed communication between programs on different computers in a distributed computing environment.

AppleTalk   A series of communications protocols designed by Apple Computer. Two phases currently exist. Phase 1, the earlier version, supports a single physical network that can have only one network number and reside in one zone. Phase 2, the more recent version, supports multiple logical networks on a single physical network and allows networks to reside in more than one zone. *See also* zone.

application layer   Layer 7 of the OSI reference model. This layer provides services to application processes (such as e-mail, file transfer, and terminal emulation) that reside outside of the OSI model. The application layer identifies and establishes the availability of intended communication partners (and the resources that are required to connect with them), synchronizes cooperating applications, and establishes agreement on procedures for error recovery and control of data integrity.

APPN   Advanced Peer-to-Peer Networking. An enhancement to the original IBM SNA architecture, APPN handles session establishment between peer nodes, dynamic transparent route calculation, and traffic prioritization for APPC traffic. *See also* APPC.

APS   Automatic protection switching. A method that allows transmission equipment to automatically recover from failures, such as a cut cable.

area   A logical set of network segments and their attached devices. Areas are usually connected to other areas via routers, making up a single autonomous system. *See also* AS.

ARP   Address Resolution Protocol. An Internet protocol that is used to map an IP address to a MAC address. Defined in RFC 826. *Compare with* RARP.

AS   Autonomous system. A collection of networks, under a common administration, that shares a common routing strategy. Autonomous systems can be subdivided into areas.

ASBR   Autonomous system boundary router. An ABR that is located between an OSPF autonomous system and a non-OSPF network. ASBRs run both OSPF and another routing protocol, such as RIP. ASBRs must reside in a non-stub OSPF area. *See also* ABR, non-stub area, and OSPF.

ASP   Application service provider. An enterprise that hosts applications used by other organizations.

asynchronous transmission   Digital signals that are transmitted without precise clocking. Such signals generally have different frequencies and phase relationships. Asynchronous transmissions usually encapsulate individual characters in control bits (called start and stop bits), which designate the beginning and end of each character. *Compare with* synchronous transmission.

ATM

1 Asynchronous Transfer Mode. An international standard for cell relay in which multiple service types (such as voice, video, or data) are conveyed in fixed-length (53-byte) cells. Fixed-length cells allow cell processing to occur in hardware, thereby reducing transit delays. ATM is designed to take advantage of high-speed transmission media, such as E3, SONET, and T3.

2 Automated teller machine. A device used by financial institutions as a replacement for live tellers.

ATU-R　ADSL terminating unit router. A router that is used in customer premises to connect to an ADSL network.

authentication　Verification of the identity of a person or process.

autonomous switching　An incoming packet matches an entry in the autonomous-switching cache, which is located on the interface processor. It is only available on Cisco 7000 series routers and in AGS+ systems that have high-speed network controller cards.

AV　Attribute-value. Remote security servers, such as RADIUS and TACACS+, assign specific privileges to users by associating AV pairs that define a user's access rights.

availability　The amount of time during which the network is operational, sometimes expressed as: (Mean Time Between Failures [MTBF] / (MTBF+Mean Time to Repair [MTTR]).

AVVID　Cisco Architecture for Voice, Video, and Integrated Data. An Internet business solutions framework that includes network platforms, infrastructure, service control, and Internet business integrators.

B

backbone　The part of a network that acts as the primary path for traffic that is most often sourced from and destined for other networks.

BackboneFast　A feature on the switch that reduces the link convergence time from 50 seconds to 20 to 30 seconds.

bandwidth　The difference between the highest and lowest frequencies that are available for network signals. The term is also used to describe a given network medium or protocol's rated throughput capacity.

bandwidth domain   Includes all devices that share the same bandwidth. Known as a collision domain for Ethernet LANs.

bandwidth reservation   A process of assigning bandwidth to users and applications that are served by a network. It involves assigning priority to different traffic flows based on how critical and delay-sensitive they are. This makes the best use of available bandwidth, and lower-priority traffic can be dropped if the network becomes congested. Sometimes called bandwidth allocation.

baseband   A characteristic of a network technology that uses only one carrier frequency. Ethernet is an example of a baseband network. Also called narrowband. *Compare with* broadband.

B channel   Bearer channel. In ISDN, a full-duplex, 64-kbps channel used to send user data. *Compare with* D channel.

Bc   Committed Burst. Negotiated tariff metric in Frame Relay internetworks. The maximum amount of data (in bits) that a Frame Relay internetwork is committed to accept and transmit at the CIR. *See also* Be and CIR.

BDR   Backup designated router in OSPF. The BDR is elected as a backup to the DR; if the DR goes down, the BDR takes over the DR's responsibilities. *See also* DR.

Be   Excess Burst. Negotiated tariff metric in Frame Relay internetworks. The number of bits a Frame Relay internetwork attempts to transmit after Bc is accommodated. In general, Be data is delivered with a lower probability than Bc data because the network can mark it as DE. *See also* Bc and DE.

bearer channel   *See* B channel.

BECN   Backward explicit congestion notification. A bit set by a Frame Relay network in frames traveling in the opposite direction of frames encountering a congested path. DTE-receiving frames with the BECN bit set can request that higher-level protocols take flow control action when appropriate. *Compare with* FECN.

Bellman-Ford routing algorithm   *See* distance vector routing algorithm and DBF.

BER   Bit error rate. Ratio of received bits that contain errors.

best-effort delivery   Delivery in a network system that does not use a sophisticated acknowledgment system to guarantee reliable delivery of information.

BGP   Border Gateway Protocol. An interdomain routing protocol that replaces EGP, BGP exchanges reachability information with other BGP systems. It is defined in RFC 1163. *See also* BGP4 and EGP.

BGP4   BGP Version 4. Version 4 of the predominant interdomain routing protocol used on the Internet. BGP4 supports CIDR and uses route aggregation mechanisms to reduce the size of routing tables. *See also* BGP and CIDR.

BHT   Busy hour traffic. The number of hours of call traffic during the busiest hour of telephone system operation.

BIA   Burned-in address, which is another name for a MAC address.

binary   A numbering system that uses 1s and 0s (1 = on; 0 = off).

bit   A binary digit used in the binary numbering system. Can be 0 or 1.

BOOTP   Bootstrap Protocol. A protocol that a network node uses to determine its Ethernet interfaces' IP address in order to affect network booting.

BPDU   Bridge protocol data unit. A Spanning-Tree Protocol hello packet that is sent out at configurable intervals to exchange information among bridges in the network. *See also* PDU.

bps   Bits per second. Used in measurement of network throughput.

BRI   Basic Rate Interface. An ISDN interface composed of two B channels and one D channel for circuit-switched communication of voice, video, and data. *Compare with* PRI. *See also* ISDN.

bridge   A device that connects and passes packets between two network segments that use the same communications protocol. Bridges operate at the data link layer (Layer 2) of the OSI reference model. In general, a bridge filters, forwards, or floods an incoming frame based on the frame's MAC address.

broadband   A transmission system that multiplexes multiple independent signals onto one cable. In telecommunications terminology, any channel that has a bandwidth greater than a voice-grade channel (4 kHz). In LAN terminology, a coaxial cable on which analog signaling is used. Also called wideband. *Compare with* baseband.

broadcast   A data packet that is sent to all nodes on a network. Broadcasts are identified by a broadcast address. *Compare with* multicast and unicast. *See also* broadcast address.

broadcast address   A special address reserved for sending a message to all stations. Generally, a broadcast address is a MAC destination address of all 1s. *Compare with* multicast address and unicast address. *See also* broadcast.

broadcast domain   The set of all devices that receive broadcast frames that originate from any device within the set. Because they do not forward broadcast frames, routers typically bound broadcast domains.

broadcast storm   An undesirable network event in which many broadcasts are simultaneously sent across all network segments. If there is redundancy in the network, this could result in broadcasts continuously circling the network. A broadcast storm uses substantial network bandwidth and typically causes network time-outs.

BSCI   Building Scalable Cisco Internetworks.

buffer   A storage area used for handling data in transit. Buffers are used in internetworking to compensate for differences in processing speed between network devices. Bursts of data can be stored in buffers until slower processing devices can handle them. Sometimes referred to as a packet buffer.

bus   A common physical signal path composed of wires or other media, across which signals can be sent from one part of a computer to another. Sometimes called highway. *See* bus topology.

bus topology   A linear LAN architecture in which transmissions from network stations propagate the length of the medium and are received by all other stations.

byte   A series of consecutive binary digits that are operated on as a unit (for example, an 8-bit byte).

C

CA   Certification Authority. Used in IPSec, a CA is a third party that the receiver explicitly trusts to validate identities and create digital certificates. Each device is enrolled with a CA. When two devices attempt to communicate, they exchange certificates and digitally sign data to authenticate each other. *See also* IPSec and IKE.

CAC   Call Admission Control. A voice QoS category that is a base for handling oversubscribed calls off-net.

caching   A form of replication in which information learned during a previous transaction is used to process later transactions.

Call leg   Discrete segment of a voice call connection. A call leg is a logical connection between the router and either a telephony endpoint over a bearer channel or another endpoint using H.323 protocol.

CAR   Committed Access Rate. The CAR service limits the input or output transmission rate on an interface or subinterface, based on a flexible set of criteria.

CAS   Channel associated signaling. The transmission of signaling information within the voice channel. CAS signaling is often referred to as *robbed-bit signaling* because the network robs user bandwidth for other purposes.

CAT 5   *See* Category 5 cabling.

Category 1 cabling   One of five grades of UTP cabling that are described in the EIA/TIA-586 standard. Category 1 cabling is used for telephone communications and is not suitable for transmitting data.

Category 2 cabling   One of five grades of UTP cabling that are described in the EIA/TIA-586 standard. Category 2 cabling is capable of transmitting data at speeds of up to 4 Mbps.

Category 3 cabling   One of five grades of UTP cabling that are described in the EIA/TIA-586 standard. Category 3 cabling is used in 10BaseT networks and can transmit data at speeds of up to 10 Mbps.

Category 4 cabling   One of five grades of UTP cabling that are described in the EIA/TIA-586 standard. Category 4 cabling is used in Token Ring networks and can transmit data at speeds of up to 16 Mbps.

Category 5 cabling   One of five grades of UTP cabling that are described in the EIA/TIA-586 standard. Category 5 cabling can transmit data at speeds of up to 100 Mbps.

CATV   Cable television. A communication system in which multiple channels of programming material are transmitted to homes using broadband coaxial cable. Formerly called Community Antenna Television.

CBC-DES   Cipher-Block Chaining-data encryption. A 56-bit encryption standard.

CBR   Constant bit rate. The ATM Forum for ATM networks defines this QoS class. CBR is used for connections that depend on precise clocking to ensure undistorted delivery.

CBWFQ   Class-Based Weighted Fair Queuing. Extends the standard WFQ functionality to provide support for user-defined traffic classes.

CCDA   Cisco Certified Design Associate. This certification is the first in the Network Design certifications path; it is a prerequisite to the CCDP certification.

CCDP   Cisco Certified Design Professional. This certification is a follow-up to the CCDA certification.

CCITT   Consultative Committee for International Telegraph and Telephone. An international organization that is responsible for the development of communications standards. Now called the ITU-T. *See* ITU-T.

CCM   Cisco CallManager. The software-based call processing component of the Cisco enterprise IP telephony solution; Cisco AVVID enables this product. Cisco CallManager software extends enterprise telephony features and capabilities to packet telephony network devices such as IP phones, media processing devices, VoIP gateways, and multimedia applications.

CCNA   Cisco Certified Network Associate. This certification is a prerequisite to the CCNP certification.

CCNP   Cisco Certified Network Professional. This certification is a follow-up to the CCNA certification.

CCO   Cisco Connection Online. Cisco's website.

CCS

1   Common channel signaling. Signaling system used in telephone networks that separates signaling information from user data. A specified channel is exclusively designated to carry signaling information for all other channels in the system.

2   Centum Call Second. A CCS represents 1/36th of an Erlang.

CCSI   Cisco Certified Systems Instructor. An instructor who is certified by Cisco to teach Cisco authorized courses.

CDP Cisco Discovery Protocol. A Cisco proprietary protocol that runs over the data link layer between Cisco devices. CDP enables systems that support different network layer protocols to communicate, and enables the discovery of other Cisco devices on the network.

CDR Call detail record. A record about a phone call in the CallManager or network accounting system.

CD-ROM Compact Disc-Read Only Memory. A compact disc for storing data that can later be read by a computer.

CEF Cisco Express Forwarding. A scalable, distributed, Layer 3 switching solution in Cisco IOS.

CELP Code Excited Linear Prediction compression. Compression algorithm used in low bit-rate voice encoding. Used in ITU-T Recommendations G.728, G.729, and G.723.1.

Centrex A local exchanged carrier service that provides local switching applications similar to those provided by an onsite PBX. With Centrex, there is no onsite switching; all customer connections go back to the CO.

CEO Chief Executive Officer. Top executive in an enterprise; reports to the Board that controls the company.

CES Circuit emulation service. Enables users to multiplex or concentrate multiple circuit emulation streams for voice and video with packet data on a single high-speed ATM link without a separate ATM access multiplexer.

CET Cisco Encryption Technology. Provides packet-level encryption that enables you to protect the confidentiality and integrity of network data that travels between cooperating (peer) encrypting routers.

CGMP Cisco Group Management Protocol. A protocol that allows switches to participate in multicast groups by communicating to a router that runs IGMP. *See also* IGMP.

channel

1 A communication path. Multiple channels can be multiplexed over a single cable in certain environments.
2 In IBM, the specific path between large computers (such as mainframes) and attached peripheral devices.

channelized E1   An access link operating at 2.048 Mbps that is subdivided into 30 B channels and one D channel. Supports DDR, Frame Relay, and X.25. *Compare with* channelized T1.

channelized T1   An access link operating at 1.544 Mbps that is subdivided into 24 channels (23 B channels and 1 D channel) of 64 kbps each. The individual channels or groups of channels connect to different destinations. Supports DDR, Frame Relay, and X.25. Also referred to as fractional T1. *Compare with* channelized E1.

CHAP   Challenge Handshake Authentication Protocol. A security feature that is supported on lines using PPP encapsulation and that prevents unauthorized access. CHAP does not itself prevent unauthorized access; it merely identifies the remote end. Then, the router or access server determines whether that user is allowed access. *Compare with* PAP.

CIDR   Classless interdomain routing. A mechanism developed to help alleviate the problem of IP address exhaustion. The idea behind CIDR is that multiple Class C addresses can be combined, or aggregated, to create a larger (that is, more hosts allowed) classless set of IP addresses. Several IP networks appear to networks outside the group as a single, larger entity. *See also* BGP4.

CIR   Committed information rate. The rate at which a Frame Relay network agrees to transfer information under normal conditions, averaged over a minimum increment of time. CIR, which is measured in bits per second, is one of the key negotiated tariff metrics. *See also* Bc.

circuit   A communications path between two or more points.

circuit switching   A switching system in which a dedicated physical circuit path must exist between sender and receiver for the duration of the call. Used heavily in the telephone company network.

classful routing protocols   Routing protocols that do not transmit any information about the prefix length. Examples include RIP and IGRP.

classless routing protocols   Routing protocols that include the prefix length with routing updates; routers running classless routing protocols do not have to determine the prefix themselves. Classless routing protocols support VLSM. *See also* VLSM.

CLI   Command Line Interface. An interface that allows the user to interact with the operating system by entering commands and optional arguments. *Compare with* GUI.

client   A node or software program that requests services from a server. *See also* server.

client-server model   A common way to describe network services and their model user processes (programs). Examples include the nameserver/nameresolver paradigm of DNS and fileserver/file-client relationships, such as NFS and diskless hosts.

CLNP   Connectionless Network Protocol. The OSI network layer protocol that does not require that a circuit be established before data is transmitted.

CM   Cable modem. A device that connects a PC to a local cable TV line and receives data at much higher rates than ordinary telephone modems or ISDN. A cable modem can be added to or integrated with a set-top box, thereby enabling Internet access via a television set. In most cases, cable modems are furnished as part of the cable access service and are not purchased directly or installed by the subscriber.

CMTS   Cable Modem Termination System, such as a router or a bridge, that is typically located at the cable headend. Any DOCSIS-compliant headend cable router, such as the Cisco uBR7246.

CN   Content Networking. An essential ingredient for optimizing web content delivery, proactively distributing cacheable content from origin servers to content servers at the edges of the network, and keeping content fresh.

CNG   Comfort noise generation. A feature of DSPs that is used with VAD. The far end supports CNG for toll-quality voice.

CNIC   Converged Network Investment Calculator. The CNIC helps calculate a customer's ROI for Cisco IP telephony solutions.

CO   Central office. A local telephone company office to which all local loops in a given area connect, and in which circuit switching of subscriber lines occurs.

codec

1 Coder-decoder. A device that typically uses PCM to transform analog signals into a digital bit stream, and digital signals back into analog.

2 In Voice over IP, Voice over Frame Relay, and Voice over ATM, a DSP software algorithm that is used to compress/decompress speech or audio signals.

3 Compress/Decompress. An algorithm used to compress/decompress data.

collision   In Ethernet, the result of two nodes transmitting simultaneously. The frames from each device impact and are damaged when they meet on the physical media. *See also* collision domain.

collision domain   In Ethernet, the network area within which frames that have collided are propagated. Repeaters and hubs propagate collisions; LAN switches, bridges, and routers do not. *See also* collision.

communications line   The physical link (such as wire or a telephone circuit) that connects one or more devices to one or more other devices.

community   In SNMP, a logical group of managed devices and NMSs in the same administrative domain.

community string   A text string that acts as a password and is used to authenticate messages sent between a management station and a router that contains an SNMP agent. The community string is sent in each packet between the manager and the agent.

companding   Contraction derived from the opposite processes of compression and expansion. Part of the PCM process whereby analog signal values are rounded logically to discrete scale-step values on a nonlinear scale. The decimal step number then is coded in its binary equivalent before transmission. At the receiving terminal, the process is reversed using the same nonlinear scale.

compression   The running of a data set through an algorithm that reduces the space required to store the data set, or the bandwidth required to transmit the data set. *Compare with* expansion.

concentrator   *See* hub.

configuration management   One of five categories of network management that ISO defines for OSI network management. Configuration management subsystems are responsible for detecting and determining a network's state. *See also* accounting management, fault management, performance management, and security management.

congestion   Traffic in excess of network capacity.

connectionless   Data transfer that occurs without the existence of a virtual circuit. *Compare with* connection-oriented. *See also* VC.

connection-oriented   Data transfer that requires the establishment of a virtual circuit. A Layer 4 protocol that creates, with software, a virtual circuit between devices to provide guaranteed data transport. *See also* connectionless and VC.

content cache   Accelerates content delivery for end users by transparently caching frequently accessed content and then locally fulfilling content requests rather than traversing the Internet/intranet to a distant server.

convergence   The speed and capability of a group of internetworking devices that run a specific routing protocol to arrive at a consistent understanding of an internetwork's topology after a change in that topology.

core layer   The layer in a hierarchical network that provides optimal transport between sites.

CoS   Class of service. An indication of how an upper-layer protocol requires a lower-layer protocol to treat its messages.

cost   An arbitrary value that is typically based on hop count, media bandwidth, or other measures and that a network administrator assigns and uses to compare various paths through an internetwork environment. Routing protocols use cost values to determine the most favorable path to a particular destination: the lower the cost, the better the path. Sometimes called path cost. *See also* routing metric.

CPE   Customer premises equipment. Terminating equipment, such as terminals, telephones, and modems, that is supplied by the telephone company, installed at customer sites, and connected to the telephone company network.

CPU   Central Processing Unit. The main processor in a device, such as a computer or router.

CQ   See *custom queuing*.

cRTP   RTP header compression. Compresses the voice headers from 40 bytes to 2 or 4 bytes, which offers significant bandwidth savings. cRTP is also referred to as Compressed Real-Time Transfer Protocol.

CS-ACELP   Conjugate Structure-Algebraic Code Excited Linear Prediction compression. CELP voice compression algorithm providing 8 kbps, or 8:1 compression, standardized in ITU-T Recommendation G.729.

CSMA/CD   Carrier sense multiple access collision detect. Media-access mechanism wherein devices that are ready to transmit data first check the channel for a carrier. A device can transmit if no carrier is sensed for a specific time period. If two devices transmit at once, a collision occurs and is detected by all colliding devices. This collision subsequently delays retransmissions from those devices for a random length of time. Ethernet and IEEE 802.3 use CSMA/CD access.

CSU   Channel service unit. A digital interface device that connects end-user equipment to the local digital telephone loop. Together with DSU, often referred to as CSU/DSU. *See also* DSU.

CUG   Closed User Group. A Centrex feature in which a telephone call can be placed to all telephones within the group using only four to five digits, regardless of geographical location. The telephones within the group can be located at many distant locations, but within the system they appear to be in a single location.

custom queuing   A method of queuing that guarantees bandwidth for traffic by assigning queue space based on protocol, port number, or other criteria. Custom queuing handles the queues in a round-robin fashion. *Compare with* priority queuing and WFQ.

D

D channel   Data channel. Full-duplex, 16-kbps (BRI), or 64-kbps (PRI) ISDN channel. *Compare with* B channel.

dark fiber   Refers to unused fiber-optic cable.

datagram   A logical grouping of information sent as a network layer unit over a transmission medium without prior establishment of a virtual circuit. IP datagrams are the primary information units in the Internet.

data link layer   Layer 2 of the OSI reference model. This layer provides reliable transit of data across a physical link. The data link layer is concerned with physical addressing, network topology, line discipline, error notification, ordered delivery of frames, and flow control. The IEEE has divided this layer into two sublayers: the MAC sublayer and the LLC sublayer. Sometimes simply called the link layer.

DBF   Distributed Bellman-Ford algorithm; distance-vector protocols are mainly based on variations of DBF.

DC   Demand Circuit. OSPF can be adjusted for usage over dialup connections by suppressing the Hello protocol. This mode of OSPF operation is called OSPF DC.

DCE   Data communications equipment (EIA expansion) or data circuit-terminating equipment (ITU-T expansion). A communications network's devices and connections that comprise the network end of the user-to-network interface. The DCE provides a physical connection to the network, forwards traffic, and provides a clocking signal that is used to synchronize data transmission between DCE and DTE devices. Modems and interface cards are examples of DCE. *Compare with* DTE.

DDoS   Distributed denial of service attack. DDoS works by causing tens or hundreds of machines to simultaneously send spurious data to an IP address—the goal of such an attack is generally not to shut down a particular host, but to render the entire network unresponsive.

DDR   Dial-on-demand routing. A technique whereby a Cisco router can automatically initiate and close a circuit-switched session as transmitting stations demand.

DE   Discard eligible. A bit in a Frame Relay frame that, when set, indicates that the frame is eligible to be discarded because it contains data that is being transmitted in excess of the CIR. *See also* Be and CIR.

decapsulation   The unwrapping of data from a particular protocol header. For example, when data is received on an Ethernet, the Ethernet header is removed so the data can be processed. *Compare with* encapsulation.

decryption   The reverse application of an encryption algorithm to encrypted data, thereby restoring that data to its original, unencrypted state. *See also* encryption.

dedicated line   A communications line that is indefinitely reserved for transmissions, rather than switched as transmission is required. *See also* leased line.

default route   A routing table entry that is used to direct frames for which a next hop is not explicitly listed in the routing table.

default router   The router to which frames are directed when the routing table does not explicitly list a next hop. Also called a default gateway.

dejitter buffer   Used at the receiving end to smooth delay variability and allow time for decoding and decompression. It helps provide smooth playback of voice traffic on the first talk spurt.

delay   The time between a sender's initiation of a transaction and the first response the sender receives. Also, the time required to move a packet from source to destination over a given path.

delay-sensitive traffic   Traffic that requires timeliness of delivery and varies its rate accordingly.

DES   Data Encryption Standard. A standard cryptographic algorithm developed by the U.S. National Bureau of Standards.

DES key   Data Encryption Standard key. A temporary session key used in CET to encrypt data during the encrypted session. *See also* CET and DH.

designated bridge   The bridge that incurs the lowest path cost when forwarding a frame from a segment to the root bridge.

designated router   *See* DR.

destination address   The address of a network device that is receiving data. *See also* source address.

DH   Diffie-Hellman. In CET, DH numbers are exchanged in the connection messages and are used to compute a common DES session key. *See also* CET and DES.

DHCP   Dynamic Host Configuration Protocol. DHCP provides a mechanism for dynamically allocating IP addresses so addresses can be reused when hosts no longer need them.

dial peer   Addressable call endpoint. In Voice over IP, there are two kinds of dial peers: POTS and VoIP. Dial peers are logical peers that are associated with physical voice ports. The voice gateway establishes a connection based on the configuration of dial peers.

dialup line   A communications circuit that a switched-circuit connection establishes using the telephone company network.

digital certificate   Used in IPSec. It contains information for identifying a user or device, such as the name, serial number, company, or IP address. It also contains a copy of the device's public key. The certificate is itself signed by a Certification Authority (CA). *See also* CA, IKE, and IPSec.

digital signature   Value that is computed with a cryptographic algorithm and appended to a data object in such a way that any can use the signature to verify the data's origin and integrity.

distance vector routing algorithm   A class of routing algorithms that calls for each router to send all or some portion of its routing table, but only to its neighbors. Also called Bellman-Ford routing algorithm and DBF. *See also* DBF link state routing algorithm and SPF.

Distribution layer   Layer in a hierarchical network that provides policy-based connectivity.

DLCI   Data-link connection identifier. A value that identifies a PVC or SVC in a Frame Relay network. In the basic Frame Relay specification, DLCIs are locally significant (connected devices might use different values to specify the same connection). In the LMI extended specification, DLCIs are globally significant (DLCIs specify individual end devices).

DLSw   Data-link switching. An interoperability standard described in RFC 1434 that provides a method for forwarding SNA and NetBIOS traffic over TCP/IP networks using data link layer switching and encapsulation.

DLSw+   Data-link switching plus. Cisco's implementation of the Data Link Switching standard.

DMZ   Demilitarized zone. A buffer between the corporate internetwork and the outside world. Also called an isolation LAN.

DNS   Domain Name Service, or Domain Name System. A protocol used on the Internet for translating names of network nodes into addresses.

DOCSIS   Data over Cable Service Interface Specification. Defines technical specifications for equipment at both subscriber locations and cable operators' headends. Adoption of DOCSIS accelerates the deployment of data-over-cable services and ensures interoperability of equipment throughout system operators' infrastructures.

domain

1 On the Internet, a portion of the naming hierarchy tree that refers to general groupings of networks based on organization type or geography.

2 In Windows networking, a domain has security and administrative properties. Each domain must have at least one NT server.

DoS   Denial of Service. A DoS attack is an incident in which a user or organization is deprived of a resource's services that they would usually expect to have. Typically, the loss of service is the inability of a particular network service, such as e-mail, to be available, or the temporary loss of all network connectivity and services.

DPNSS   Digital Private Network Signaling System. A standards-based signaling protocol that enables interoperability between different vendors' PBXs. Another standard is QSIG.

DR   Designated Router. An OSPF router that generates LSAs for a multiaccess network and has other special responsibilities running OSPF. Instead of each router exchanging updates with every other router on the segment, every router will exchange the information with the DR and BDR. The DR and BDR relay the information to the other routers. *See also* BDR.

DS-0   Digital signal level 0. A framing specification used for transmitting digital signals over a single channel at 64 kbps on a T1 facility. *Compare with* DS-1 and DS-3.

DS-1   Digital signal level 1. A framing specification used for transmitting digital signals at 1.544 Mbps on a T1 facility (in the United States), or at 2.108 Mbps on an E1 facility (in Europe). *Compare with* DS-0 and DS-3.

DS-3   Digital signal level 3. A framing specification used for transmitting digital signals at 44.736 Mbps on a T3 facility. *Compare with* DS-0 and DS-1. *See also* E3 and T3.

DSCP   Differentiated Services Code Point. The 6 most signification bits of the ToS byte in the IPv4 header are now called the DiffServ field. IP precedence uses 3 bits, while DSCP, an extension of IP precedence, uses 6 bits to select the per-hop behavior for the packet at each network node.

DSL   Digital subscriber line. Public network technology that delivers high bandwidth over conventional copper wiring at limited distances. There are four common types of DSL: ADSL, HDSL, SDSL, and VDSL. All are provisioned via modem pairs, with one modem located at a central office and the other at the customer site. Because most DSL technologies do not use the entire twisted pair bandwidth, there is room remaining for a voice channel. *See also* ADSL, HDSL, SDSL, and VDSL.

DSLAM   Digital subscriber line access multiplexer. A device that connects many digital subscriber lines to a network by multiplexing the DSL traffic onto one or more network trunk lines.

DSP   Digital signal processor. A DSP segments the voice signal into frames and stores them in voice packets.

DSS   Digital Signature Standard. A standard used in CET for generating public and private keys that are used to authenticate peer routers. *See also* CET.

DSU   Data service unit. A device used in digital transmission that adapts the physical interface on a DTE device to a transmission facility, such as T1 or E1. The DSU is also responsible for functions such as signal timing. Together with CSU, often referred to as CSU/DSU. *See also* CSU.

DTE   Data terminal equipment. A device that resides at the user end of a user-network interface and serves as a data source, destination, or both. DTE connects to a data network through a DCE device (such as a modem) and typically uses clocking signals that are generated by the DCE. DTE includes devices such as computers, protocol translators, and multiplexers. *Compare with* DCE.

DTMF   Dual-tone multifrequency. Tones that are generated when a button is pressed on a telephone; primarily used in the United States and Canada.

DUAL   Diffusing Update Algorithm. A convergence algorithm used in EIGRP that provides loop-free operation at every instant throughout a route computation. Allows routers that are involved in a topology change to synchronize at the same time, while not involving routers that are unaffected by the change. *See also* EIGRP.

DWDM   Dense Wavelength Division Multiplexing. Optical transmission of multiple signals over closely-spaced wavelengths in the 1550 nm region. (Wavelength spacing is usually 100 GHz or 200 GHz, which corresponds to 0.8 nm or 1.6 nm.)

dynamic routing   Routing that adjusts automatically to network topology or traffic changes. Also called adaptive routing.

E

E1   A wide-area digital transmission scheme that is predominantly used in Europe and carries data at a rate of 2.048 Mbps. E1 lines can be leased for private use from common carriers. *Compare with* T1. *See also* DS-1.

E3   A wide-area digital transmission scheme that is predominantly used in Europe and carries data at a rate of 34.368 Mbps. E3 lines can be leased for private use from common carriers. *Compare with* T3. *See also* DS-3.

E&M   Derived from a combination of recEive and transMit; sometimes also known as Ear and Mouth. E&M is the most common analog trunk signaling method.

EAP   Extensible Authentication Protocol. A framework that supports multiple, optional authentication mechanisms for PPP, including clear text passwords, challenge-response, and arbitrary dialog sequences.

EAP-SIM   EAP-Subscriber Identity Module. An EAP authentication protocol.

EAP-TLS   EAP-Transport Layer Security. An EAP authentication protocol.

EAP-TTLS   EAP-Tunneled TLS. An EAP authentication protocol.

EBGP   Exterior BGP. BGP is called EBGP when it is used between autonomous systems.

echo   Telephony-audible and unwanted leak-through of one's own voice into one's own receive (return) path. Hence, signal from the transmission path is returning to one's ear through the receive path.

e-commerce   Electronic commerce. The buying and selling of goods and services on the Internet.

efficiency   The measurement of how much effort is required to produce a certain amount of data throughput.

EGP

1   Exterior Gateway Protocol. An Internet protocol used for exchanging routing information between autonomous systems. Documented in RFC 904. EGP is an obsolete protocol that has been replaced by BGP. *See also* BGP.

2   Exterior gateway protocol. A general term for protocols used between autonomous systems.

EIA   Electronic Industries Association. A group that specifies electrical transmission standards. The EIA and TIA have developed numerous well-known communications standards, including EIA/TIA-232 and EIA/TIA-449. *See also* TIA.

EIA-530   Refers to two electrical implementations of EIA/TIA-449: RS-422 (for balanced transmission) and RS-423 (for unbalanced transmission). *See also* RS-422, RS-423, and EIA/TIA-449.

EIA/TIA-232   Developed by EIA and TIA, a common physical layer interface standard that supports unbalanced circuits at signal speeds of up to 64 kbps. Formerly known as RS-232.

EIA/TIA-449   A popular physical layer interface developed by EIA and TIA. Essentially, a faster (up to 2 Mbps) version of EIA/TIA-232 that is capable of longer cable runs. Formerly called RS-449. *See also* EIA-530.

EIA/TIA-586   A standard that describes the characteristics and applications for various grades of UTP cabling. *See also* Category 1 cabling, Category 2 cabling, Category 3 cabling, Category 4 cabling, Category 5 cabling, and UTP.

EIGRP   Enhanced Interior Gateway Routing Protocol. An advanced version of IGRP developed by Cisco. Provides superior convergence properties and operating efficiency, and combines the advantages of link state protocols with those of distance vector protocols. *Compare with* IGRP. *See also* IGP, OSPF, and RIP.

electronic mail   A widely used network application in which mail messages are transmitted electronically between end users over various types of networks using various network protocols. Often called e-mail.

e-mail   *See* electronic mail.

encapsulation   The wrapping of data in a particular protocol header. For example, Ethernet data is wrapped in a specific Ethernet header before network transit. *Compare with* decapsulation. *See also* tunneling.

encryption   Applying a specific algorithm to data so as to alter its appearance, thereby making the data incomprehensible to those who are not authorized to see the information. *See also* decryption.

Erlang   One of the most common measurements of voice traffic. One Erlang equals one full hour, or 3600 seconds, of telephone conversation. Erlang tables combine offered traffic, number of circuits, and grade of service (GoS).

ES   End system. A nonrouting host or node in an OSI network.

Ethernet   A baseband LAN specification invented by Xerox Corporation and developed jointly by Xerox, Intel, and Digital Equipment Corporation. Ethernet networks use CSMA/CD and run over a variety of cable types at 10 Mbps. Ethernet is similar to the IEEE 802.3 series of standards. *See also* IEEE 802.3.

EUI-64   Extended universal identifier 64-bit. The EUI-64 format interface ID for IPv6 is derived from the 48-bit link-layer MAC address by inserting the hex number FFFE between the upper 3 bytes and the lower 3 bytes of the link-layer address. To make sure that the chosen address is from a unique MAC address, the seventh bit in the high-order byte is set to 1 to indicate the uniqueness of the 48-bit address.

event   A network message that indicates operational irregularities in a network's physical elements, or a response to the occurrence of a significant task—typically, the completion of a request for information. *See also* alarm and trap.

expansion   The process of running a compressed data set through an algorithm that restores the data set to its original size. *Compare with* compression.

exterior gateway protocol   Any internetwork protocol used to exchange routing information between autonomous systems. Not to be confused with Exterior Gateway Protocol (EGP), which is a particular instance of an exterior gateway protocol. *See also* BGP.

F

Fast EtherChannel   Grouping multiple Fast Ethernet interfaces into a single logical transmission path to deliver higher-speed connections.

Fast Ethernet   Any of a number of 100-Mbps Ethernet specifications. Fast Ethernet offers a speed increase 10 times that of the 10BaseT Ethernet specification, while preserving qualities such as frame format, MAC mechanisms, and MTU. Such similarities allow the use of existing 10BaseT applications and network management tools on Fast Ethernet networks. Based on an extension of the IEEE 802.3 specification. *Compare with* Ethernet.

fast switching   A Cisco feature whereby a route cache is used to expedite packet switching through a router. *Compare with* process switching.

fault management   One of five categories of network management that are defined by ISO for managing OSI networks. Fault management attempts to ensure that network faults are detected and controlled. *See also* accounting management, configuration management, performance management, and security management.

FCAPS   Fault Management, Configuration Management, Accounting Management Performance Management, Security Management; five functional areas of network management.

FDDI   Fiber Distributed Data Interface. A LAN standard, defined by ANSI X3T9.5, that specifies a 100-Mbps token passing network using fiber-optic cable, with transmission distances of up to 2 km. FDDI uses a dual-ring architecture to provide redundancy.

FDDI ring operations   When the FDDI ring becomes active from an inoperable state.

FDM   Frequency division multiplexing. A way of combining multiple signals on a single line by assigning different frequencies to each signal.

FDMA   Frequency division multiple access. FDMA means that multiple RF channels are assigned. With FDMA, a CM transmits on a single RF channel.

FEC

  1 Fast EtherChannel. A group of several parallel links between LAN switches into a channel; seen as a single link from the Layer 2 perspective.

  2 Forwarding Equivalence Class. In MPLS, a flow of packets (for example, voice traffic between two nodes) identified by a label. An FEC is a grouping of packets; packets that belong to the same FEC receive the same treatment in the network.

FECN   Forward explicit congestion notification. A bit set by a Frame Relay network to inform the DTE receiving the frame that the path experienced congestion from source to destination. DTE-receiving frames with the FECN bit set can request that higher-level protocols take flow-control action when appropriate. *Compare with* BECN.

fiber-optic cable   A physical medium that is capable of conducting modulated light transmission. Compared with other transmission media, fiber-optic cable is more expensive; however, it is not susceptible to electromagnetic interference, and it is capable of higher data rates. Sometimes called optical fiber.

FIFO   First-in, first-out. Refers to a buffering scheme in which the first byte of data entering the buffer is the first byte that the CPU retrieves. In telephony, FIFO refers to a queuing scheme in which the first calls received are the first calls processed.

filter   Generally, a process or device that screens network traffic for certain characteristics, such as source address, destination address, or protocol, and determines whether to forward or discard that traffic based on the established criteria. *See also* access list.

firewall   A router or access server (or several routers or access servers) designated as a buffer between any connected public networks and a private network. A firewall router uses access lists and other methods to ensure the security of the private network. A firewall protects one network from another, untrusted network. This protection can be accomplished in many ways, but in principle, a firewall is a pair of mechanisms: one blocks traffic, and the other permits traffic.

flash update   A routing update that is sent asynchronously in response to a change in network topology. *Compare with* routing update.

floating static route   A static route that has a higher administrative distance than a dynamically learned route so that dynamically-learned routing information can override it.

flooding   A traffic-passing technique used by switches and bridges in which traffic received on an interface is sent out of all of that device's interfaces, except the interface on which the information was originally received.

FLSM   Fixed Length Subnet Masking. A major network is a Class A, B, or C network. FLSM is when all subnet masks in a major network must be the same size.

FM   Frequency Modulation. A modulation technique whereby information is conveyed through the frequency of the carrier signal.

FQDM   Fully Qualified Domain Name. The FQDN is a system's full name, rather than simply its host name. For example, aldebaran is a host name, and aldebaran.interop.com is an FQDN.

FR   *See* Frame Relay.

fractional T1   *See* channelized T1.

fragmentation   The process of breaking a packet into smaller units for transmission over a network medium that cannot support the packet in its original size. *See also* reassembly.

frame   A logical grouping of information that is sent as a data link layer unit over a transmission medium. Often refers to the header and trailer, used for synchronization and error control, which surround the user data contained in the unit.

Frame Relay   An industry-standard, switched data-link layer protocol that handles multiple virtual circuits using HDLC encapsulation between connected devices. Frame Relay is more efficient than X.25, the protocol for which it is generally considered a replacement. *See also* X.25.

Frame Relay traffic shaping   Rate enforcement, generalized BECN support, and priority/custom queuing support on a per-VC basis. *See also* traffic shaping.

FRR   Fast reroute. An MPLS service that allows extremely fast recovery from node or link failure, thereby preventing applications from timing out and losing data.

FTP   File Transfer Protocol. An application protocol—part of the TCP/IP protocol stack—that is used for transferring files between network nodes. RFC 959 defines FTP.

full duplex   The capability for simultaneous data transmission between a sending station and a receiving station. *Compare with* half duplex and simplex.

full mesh   A network in which devices are organized in a mesh topology, with each network node having either a physical circuit or a virtual circuit connecting it to every other network node. *See also* partial mesh.

FXO   Foreign Exchange Office. An FXO interface connects to the PSTN central office; it is the interface that is offered on a standard telephone. Cisco's FXO interface is an RJ-11 connector that allows an analog connection at the PSTN's central office or to a station interface on a PBX.

FXS   Foreign Exchange Station. An FXS interface directly connects to a standard telephone and supplies ring, voltage, and dial tone. Cisco's FXS interface is an RJ-11 connector that allows connections to basic telephone service equipment, keysets, and PBXs.

G

G.711 Describes the 64-kbps PCM voice coding technique. In G.711, encoded voice is already in the correct format for digital voice delivery in the PSTN or through PBXs. Described in the ITU-T standard in its G-series recommendations.

G.723 Describes a compression technique that can be used for compressing speech or audio signal components at a very low bit rate as part of the H.324 family of standards. Two bit rates are associated with this codec: 5.3 and 6.3 kbps. The higher bit rate is based on ML-MLQ technology and provides a somewhat higher sound quality. The lower bit rate is based on CELP and provides system designers with additional flexibility. The ITU-T standard describes it in its G-series recommendations.

G.729 Describes CELP compression where voice is coded into 8-kbps streams. There are two variations of this standard (G.729 and G.729 Annex A) that differ primarily in computational complexity; both provide speech quality that is similar to 32-kbps ADPCM. The ITU-T standard describes it in its G-series recommendations.

GAAP Generally Accepted Accounting Principles.

gatekeeper

1 The component of an H.323 conferencing system that performs call address resolution, admission control, and subnet bandwidth management.

2 Telecommunications: H.323 entity on a LAN that provides address translation and control access to the LAN for H.323 terminals and gateways. The gatekeeper can provide other services, such as bandwidth management and locating gateways, to the H.323 terminals and gateways. A gatekeeper maintains a registry of devices in the multimedia network. The devices register with the gatekeeper at startup and request admission to a call from the gatekeeper.

gateway In the IP community, an older term that refers to a routing device. Today, the term router is used to describe nodes that perform this function, and gateway refers to a special-purpose device that performs an application layer conversion of information from one protocol stack to another. *Compare with* router.

Gbps Gigabits per second.

GE *See* Gigabit Ethernet.

GHz Gigahertz.

Gigabit EtherChannel Bundling multiple Gigabit Ethernet links that appear as one logical interface.

Gigabit Ethernet Standard for a high-speed Ethernet; approved by the IEEE 802.3z standards committee in 1996.

GMRP Generic Multicast Registration Protocol. A protocol that addresses the problem of multicast frames in a switched environment, GMRP is used between the switch and the host.

GoS Grade of Service. The probability that a call will be blocked while attempting to seize circuits during the busiest hour. It is written as a decimal fraction, Pxx, blocking factor or blockage, where xx is the percentage of calls that are blocked for a traffic system.

GPRS General Packet Radio Service. The European Telecommunication Standards Institute defined and standardized this service. GPRS is an IP packet-based data service for Global System Mobile Communications networks.

GPS Global Positioning System. A grouping of satellites orbiting the Earth that allow ground receivers to determine their geographic location.

GRE Generic Routing Encapsulation. A tunneling protocol developed by Cisco that can encapsulate a wide variety of protocol packet types inside IP tunnels, thereby creating a virtual point-to-point link to Cisco routers at remote points over an IP internetwork.

ground-start signaling A method of signaling that is primarily used on CO trunk lines to PBXs. A ground is placed on one side of the two-wire line to indicate that it is in use so that the other side of the two-wire interface does not attempt to use the line.

GSM Global System for Mobile communication. A second-generation (2G) mobile wireless networking standard defined by ETSI, GSM is deployed widely throughout the world. GSM uses TDMA technology and operates in the 900-MHz radio band.

GTS Generic Traffic Shaping. Cisco supports this traffic-shaping method, which is used to limit the traffic flow's full bandwidth potential.

GUI Graphical user interface. A user environment that uses pictorial and textual representations of the input and output of applications, and the hierarchical or other data structure in which information is stored.

H

H.323 H.323 allows dissimilar communication devices to communicate with each other via a standardized communication protocol. H.323 defines a common set of codecs, call setup and negotiating procedures, and basic data transport methods.

half duplex The capability for data transmission in only one direction at a time between a sending station and a receiving station. *Compare with* full duplex and simplex.

HDLC High-level Data Link Control. A bit-oriented synchronous data link layer protocol developed by ISO, HDLC specifies a data encapsulation method on synchronous serial links using frame characters and checksums.

HDSL High-data-rate Digital Subscriber Line. One of four DSL technologies. HDSL delivers 1.544 Mbps of bandwidth each way over two copper twisted pairs. Because HDSL provides T1 speed, telephone companies use HDSL to provision local access to T1 services whenever possible. HDSL's operating range is limited to 12,000 feet (3658.5 meters), so signal repeaters are installed to extend the service. HDSL requires two twisted pairs, so it is primarily deployed for PBX network connections, digital loop carrier systems, interexchange POPs, Internet servers, and private data networks. *Compare with* ADSL, SDSL, and VDSL.

headend The endpoint of a broadband network. All stations transmit toward the headend, which then transmits toward the destination stations.

header Control information placed before data when encapsulating that data for network transmission.

HEHO Head End Hop On. A call originates at sites that are connected via the PSTN and terminates in the private network. Also called off-net to on-net calling.

hello packet A multicast packet that routers use for neighbor discovery and recovery. Hello packets also indicate that a client is still operating and network-ready.

Hello protocol   A protocol OSPF systems use for establishing and maintaining neighbor relationships.

HFC   Hybrid Fiber Coaxial. Technology the cable TV industry is developing to provide two-way, high-speed data access to the home using a combination of fiber optics and traditional coaxial cable.

HIDS   Host-based Intrusion Detection System. An IDS resident on a host device.

HMAC   Hash-based Message Authentication Code. HMAC is a mechanism for message authentication using cryptographic hash functions.

holddown   A state into which a route is placed so that routers neither advertise the route nor accept advertisements about the route for a specific length of time (the holddown period), thereby allowing the entire network to learn about the change. Holddown is used to flush bad information about a route from all network routers. A route is typically placed in holddown when a link in that route fails.

hop   The passage of a data packet between two network nodes (for example, between two routers). *See also* hop count.

hop count   A routing metric used to measure the distance between a source and a destination. IP RIP uses hop count as its sole metric. *See also* hop and RIP.

host   A computer system on a network. Similar to the term node, except that host usually implies a computer system and node generally applies to any networked system, including access servers and routers. *See also* node.

HSRP   Hot Standby Router Protocol. Provides a way for IP workstations to continue communicating on the internetwork even if their default router becomes unavailable, thereby providing high network availability and transparent network topology changes.

HTML   Hypertext Markup Language. A simple hypertext document formatting language that uses tags to indicate how a viewing application, such as a WWW browser, should interpret part of a document.

HTTP   Hypertext Transfer Protocol. The TCP/IP protocol used to send hypertext documents.

hub

  1 Generally, a device that serves as the center of a star-topology network.

2 A hardware or software device that contains multiple independent but connected modules of network and internetwork equipment. Hubs can be active (where they repeat signals that are sent through them) or passive (where they do not repeat, but merely split, signals that are sent through them).

3 In Ethernet and IEEE 802.3, an Ethernet multiport repeater, sometimes referred to as a concentrator.

Hz Hertz. A measure of frequency; synonymous with cycles per second.

I

IAB Internet Architecture Board. A board of internetwork researchers who discuss issues that are pertinent to Internet architecture. Responsible for appointing a variety of Internet-related groups, such as IANA. *See also* IANA.

IANA Internet Assigned Numbers Authority. An organization operated under the auspices of ISOC as a part of IAB. IANA delegates authority for IP address-space allocation and domain-name assignment to the NIC and other organizations. *See also* IAB and NIC.

IBGP Interior BGP. When BGP is used within an autonomous system, it is called IBGP.

ICMP Internet Control Message Protocol. A network layer Internet protocol that reports errors and provides other information that is relevant to IP packet processing. Documented in RFC 792.

ICND Interconnecting Cisco Network Devices. A Cisco Press book and a Cisco course detailing how Cisco routers and switches work.

ID Identifier.

IDS Intrusion Detection System. Security service that monitors and analyzes system events for the purpose of finding (and providing a real-time, or near real-time, warning about) attempts to access system resources in an unauthorized manner.

IDSL ISDN Digital Subscriber Line. A form of DSL that is similar to ISDN; it is always on, it can reach speeds of 144 kbps, and it is very capable, through compression, of reaching speeds of 512 kbps.

IEEE   Institute of Electrical and Electronics Engineers. A professional organization whose activities include the development of communications and network standards. IEEE LAN standards are the predominant LAN standards today.

IEEE 802.1d   An IEEE specification that describes an algorithm that prevents bridging loops by creating a spanning tree. Digital Equipment Corporation invented the algorithm. The Digital algorithm and the IEEE 802.1 algorithm are not exactly the same, nor are they compatible. *See also* spanning tree, spanning-tree algorithm, and Spanning Tree Protocol.

IEEE 802.2   An IEEE LAN protocol that specifies an implementation of the LLC sublayer of the data link layer. IEEE 802.2 handles errors, framing, flow control, and the network layer (Layer 3) service interface. Used in IEEE 802.3, IEEE 802.5, and FDDI LANs. *See also* IEEE 802.3 and IEEE 802.5.

IEEE 802.3   An IEEE LAN protocol that specifies an implementation of the physical layer and the MAC sublayer of the data link layer. IEEE 802.3 uses CSMA/CD access at a variety of speeds over a variety of physical media. Extensions to the IEEE 802.3 standard specify implementations for Fast Ethernet. Physical variations of the original IEEE 802.3 specification include 10Base2, 10Base5, 10BaseF, 10BaseT, and 10Broad36. Physical variations for Fast Ethernet include 100BaseT, 100BaseT4, and 100BaseX.

IEEE 802.5   An IEEE LAN protocol that specifies an implementation of the physical layer and MAC sublayer of the data link layer. IEEE 802.5 uses token passing access at 4 or 16 Mbps over STP cabling and is similar to IBM Token Ring. *See also* Token Ring.

IETF   Internet Engineering Task Force. A task force that consists of more than 80 working groups that are responsible for developing Internet standards.

IF   Intermediate Frequency. Intermediate electromagnetic frequencies generated by a superheterodyne radio receiver.

IFS   IOS File System. The system of naming devices and files within the IOS.

IGMP   Internet Group Management Protocol. A protocol used by IP hosts to report their multicast group memberships to an adjacent multicast router. *See also* multicast router.

IGP   Interior Gateway Protocol. An Internet protocol used to exchange routing information within an autonomous system. Examples of common Internet IGPs include IGRP, OSPF, and RIP. *See also* IGRP, OSPF, and RIP.

IGRP   Interior Gateway Routing Protocol. An IGP developed by Cisco to address the problems associated with routing in large, heterogeneous networks. *Compare with* EIGRP. *See also* IGP, OSPF, and RIP.

IKE   Internet Key Exchange Protocol. Used in IPSec to exchange digital certificates with the CA. *See also* CA, digital certificate, and IPSec.

ILEC   Incumbent local exchange carrier. A telephone company in the United States that was providing local service when the Telecommunications Act of 1996 was enacted.

Integrated IS-IS   Routing protocol based on the OSI routing protocol IS-IS, and includes support for IP and other protocols. Integrated IS-IS implementations send only one set of routing updates, making it more efficient than two separate implementations. Formerly called Dual IS-IS.

intelligent network services   Allow for application awareness within the network. Intelligent network services essentially add intelligence to the network infrastructure, beyond just moving a datagram between two points. Examples of intelligent network service include: Network Management, Security, High Availability, QoS, and IP Multicasting.

interface

1   A connection between two systems or devices.

2   In routing terminology, a network connection.

3   In telephony, a shared boundary defined by common physical interconnection characteristics, signal characteristics, and meanings of interchanged signals.

4   The boundary between adjacent layers of the OSI model.

interior routing protocols   Routing protocols used by routers within the same autonomous system, such as RIP, IGRP, and EIGRP.

Internet   The largest global internetwork, which connects tens of thousands of networks worldwide and that has a "culture" that focuses on research and standardization based on real-life use. Many leading-edge network technologies come from the Internet community.

internet   Short for internetwork. Not to be confused with the Internet. *See also* internetwork.

internetwork   A collection of networks interconnected by routers and other devices that generally functions as a single network. Sometimes called an internet, which is not to be confused with the Internet.

internetworking   The industry that has risen around the problem of connecting networks. The term can refer to products, procedures, and technologies.

intranet   A network that is internal to an organization, based on Internet and World Wide Web technology, that delivers immediate, up-to-date information and services to networked employees.

intrusion detection   Security service that monitors and analyzes system events for the purpose of finding (and providing a real-time or near-real-time warning about) attempts to access system resources in an unauthorized manner.

I/O   Input/output. Typically used when discussing ports on a device where data comes in or goes out.

IOS   Cisco's Internetwork Operating System. The software in Cisco routers and some Cisco switches.

IP   Internet Protocol. A network layer protocol in the TCP/IP stack that offers a connectionless internetwork service. IP provides features for addressing, type-of-service specification, fragmentation and reassembly, and security and is documented in RFC 791.

IP address   A 32-bit address assigned to hosts using TCP/IP. An IP address belongs to one of five classes (A, B, C, D, or E) and is written as four octets that are separated with periods (dotted decimal format). Each address consists of a network number, an optional subnetwork number, and a host number. The network and subnetwork numbers are used together for routing, and the host number is used to address an individual host within the network or subnetwork. A subnet mask is used to extract network and subnetwork information from the IP address. Also called an Internet address. *See also* IP and subnet mask.

IP datagram   Fundamental unit of information that is passed across the Internet. Contains source and destination addresses, along with data and several fields that define such things as the length of the datagram, the header checksum, and flags to indicate whether the datagram can be (or was) fragmented.

IP multicast   A routing technique that allows IP traffic to be propagated from one source to a number of destinations, or from many sources to many destinations. Rather than sending one packet to each destination, one packet is sent to a multicast group that is identified by a single IP destination group address.

IP phone   Devices that allow communication across the IP network. The Cisco CallManager centrally manages IP telephones, which are powered through Ethernet connections.

IP precedence   Part of the IP specification and provides prioritization. It is used in the routed networks to make a more informed decision about routing the generated IP packets.

IP spoofing   An IP spoofing attack occurs when an attacker outside your network pretends to be a trusted user, either by using an IP address that is within the range of IP addresses for your network, or by using an authorized external IP address that you trust and to which you wish to provide access to specified resources on your network. Should an attacker obtain access to your IPSec security parameters, that attacker can masquerade as a remote user who is authorized to connect to the corporate network.

IP telephony   Internet Protocol telephony. The transmission of voice and fax phone calls over data networks that uses the Internet Protocol (IP). IP telephony is the result of the transformation of the circuit-switched telephone network to a packet-based network that deploys voice-compression algorithms and flexible and sophisticated transmission techniques, and delivers richer services using only a fraction of traditional digital telephony's usual bandwidth.

IPM   Internetwork Performance Monitor. A network management application that allows monitoring of multiprotocol network performance.

IPSec   Internet Protocol Security. A framework of open standards developed by the IETF. IPSec provides security for the transmission of sensitive information over unprotected networks, such as the Internet. IPSec acts at the network layer.

IP/TV   Internet Protocol Television using one-way video traffic, streaming video.

IPv4   IP version 4. The correct name for the current version of IP.

IPv6   IP version 6. A replacement for the current version of IP (version 4), IPv6 includes support for flow ID in the packet header, which can be used to identify flows. Formerly called IPng (IP next generation).

IPX   Internetwork Packet Exchange. A NetWare network layer (Layer 3) protocol that is used for transferring data from servers to workstations.

IS

1   Information Systems. A broad term used to describe the use of information technology in organizations. This includes the movement, storage, and use of information.

2   Intermediate System. A routing node in an OSI network. *See also* IS-IS.

ISDN   Integrated Services Digital Network. A communication protocol offered by telephone companies that permits telephone networks to carry data, voice, and other source traffic. *See also* BRI and PRI.

IS-IS   Intermediate System-to-Intermediate System. An OSI link-state hierarchical routing protocol whereby ISs (routers) exchange routing information based on a single metric in order to determine network topology.

IS-ISv6   Intermediate System-to-Intermediate System version 6. An OSI routing protocol for IPv6.

ISL   Inter-Switch Link. A Cisco-proprietary protocol that maintains VLAN information as traffic flows between switches and routers.

ISO   International Organization for Standardization. An international organization that is responsible for a wide range of standards, including those that are relevant to networking. ISO developed the OSI reference model, which is a popular networking reference model.

ISP   Internet service provider. A company that provides Internet access to other companies and individuals.

IT   Information Technology. Computers, networking devices, and networks used to transport, store, and manage information.

ITU-T   International Telecommunication Union Telecommunication Standardization Sector. An international body that develops worldwide standards for telecommunications technologies. The ITU-T carries out the functions of the former CCITT. *See also* CCITT.

ITV   Interactive television. ITV is television that allows the viewer to interact with the television set in ways other than by simply controlling the channel and volume and handling videotapes. Typical interactive TV uses are selecting a video film to view from a central bank of films, playing games, voting, providing other immediate feedback through the television connection, banking from home, and shopping from home.

IVR Interactive voice response. Term used to describe systems that provide information in the form of recorded messages over telephone lines, in response to user input in the form of spoken words or, more commonly, DTMF signaling. Examples include banks that allow you to check your balance from any telephone and automated stock quote systems.

J–K

jitter

1 Interpacket delay variance; that is, the difference between interpacket arrival and departure. Jitter is an important QoS metric for voice and video applications.

2 Analog communication line distortion caused by the variation of a signal from its reference timing positions. Jitter can cause data loss, particularly at high speeds.

kbps Kilobits per second.

KHz Kilohertz.

L

L2 Layer 2. Refers to OSI Layer 2: the data link layer.

L2F Layer 2 Forwarding Protocol. Protocol that supports the creation of secure virtual private dialup networks over the Internet.

L2TP Layer 2 Tunneling Protocol. An IETF standard protocol defined in RFC 2661 that provides PPP tunneling. Based on the best features of L2F and PPTP, L2TP provides an industry-wide interoperable method of implementing VPDN.

L3 Layer 3. Refers to OSI Layer 3: the network layer.

LAC L2TP access concentrator. A node that acts as one side of an L2TP tunnel endpoint and is a peer to the LNS. The LAC sits between an LNS and a remote system and forwards packets to and from each. The connection from the LAC to the remote system is either local or a PPP link.

LACP Link Aggregation Control Protocol. Standard protocol for automatic EtherChannel formation, defined in IEEE 802.3ad.

LAN   Local-area network. A high-speed, low-error data network that covers a relatively small geographic area (up to a few thousand meters). LANs connect workstations, peripherals, terminals, and other devices in a single building or other geographically limited area. LAN standards specify cabling and signaling at the physical and data link layers of the OSI model. Ethernet, FDDI, and Token Ring are widely used LAN technologies. *Compare with* MAN and WAN.

LAN switch   A high-speed switch that forwards packets between data link segments. Most LAN switches forward traffic based on MAC addresses. This type of LAN switch is sometimes called a frame switch. Multilayer switches are an intelligent subset of LAN switches.

LANE   LAN Emulation. Technology that allows an ATM network to function as a LAN backbone.

LAPB   Link Access Procedure, Balanced. A data link layer protocol in the X.25 protocol stack. LAPB is a bit-oriented protocol derived from HDLC. *See also* HDLC and X.25.

LAPD   Link access procedure for D channel. Used on the ISDN D channel.

LAT   Local-Area Transport. A network virtual terminal protocol developed by Digital Equipment Corporation.

latency

1   The delay between the time a device requests access to a network and the time it is granted permission to transmit.

2   The delay between the time a device receives a frame and the time the frame is forwarded from the destination port.

LD-CELP   Low-Delay-Code Excited Linear Prediction compression. CELP voice compression algorithm that provides 16 kbps, or 4:1 compression. Standardized in ITU-T Recommendation G.728.

LDP   Label Distribution Protocol. An MPLS protocol used to communicate the label to use for each FEC with other nodes.

LEAP   Lightweight Extensible Authentication Protocol. A Cisco authentication type for wireless networks in which the RADIUS server sends an authentication challenge to the client.

leased line A transmission line reserved by a communications carrier for a customer's private use. A leased line is a type of dedicated line. *See also* dedicated line.

LED Light emitting diode. Semiconductor device that emits light produced by converting electrical energy. Status lights on hardware devices are typically LEDs.

LFI Link Fragmentation and Interleaving. A solution for queuing delay situations. With LFI, large packets are fragmented into smaller frames and interleaved with small voice packets.

link A network communications channel that consists of a circuit or transmission path and all related equipment between a sender and a receiver. Most often used to refer to a WAN connection. Sometimes referred to as a line or a transmission link.

link flapping Links going up and down, which means a link is intermittently nonoperational. Noise, misconfigurations or reconfigurations, or hardware failures can cause link flapping.

link-state routing algorithm A routing algorithm in which each router broadcasts or multicasts information about the cost of reaching each of its neighbors to all nodes in the internetwork. *Compare with* distance vector routing algorithm.

LIR Local Internet registry. ISPs obtain address allocations from an LIR, an NIR, or their appropriate RIR. The IANA is responsible for allocating addresses to the RIRs, according to their needs.

LLC Logical Link Control. The higher of the two data link layer sublayers defined by the IEEE. The LLC sublayer handles error control, flow control, framing, and MAC-sublayer addressing.

LLQ Low Latency Queuing. A feature that brings strict priority queuing to CBWFQ. Strict priority queuing allows delay-sensitive data, such as voice, to be dequeued and sent first (before packets in other queues are dequeued), thereby giving delay-sensitive data preferential treatment over other traffic.

LNS L2TP network server. A node that acts as one side of an L2TP tunnel endpoint and is a peer to the LAC. The LNS is the logical termination point of a PPP session that is being tunneled from the remote system by the LAC.

load balancing   In routing, the ability of a router to distribute traffic over all of its network ports that are the same distance from the destination address. Good load-balancing algorithms use both line speed and reliability information. Load balancing increases the utilization of network segments, thus increasing effective network bandwidth.

local loop   Line from the premises of a telephone subscriber to the telephone company CO.

loop-start signaling   A method of signaling in which a DC closure is applied to a phone line (loop); the start of DC current flow indicates a change from on-hook to off-hook.

LRE   Long Reach Ethernet. Enables the use of Ethernet over existing telephone-grade wire using DSL coding and digital modulation techniques.

LSA   Link-state advertisement. A broadcast packet, used by link-state protocols, that contains information about neighbors and path costs. Receiving routers use LSAs to maintain their routing tables.

LSP

1   Link-state packet. In IS-IS, used to distribute link-state information.

2   Label Switched Path. For each FEC, an LSP must be defined before packets can be sent.

LSR   Label Switched Router. Nodes within an MPLS network.

LZS   Lempel-Ziv Stack. A compression algorithm commonly referred to as the Stacker (STAC) or Predictor algorithm.

M

MAC   Media Access Control. The lower of the two sublayers of the data link layer defined by the IEEE. The MAC sublayer handles access to shared media, such as whether token passing or contention will be used. *See also* data link layer and LLC.

MAC address   A standardized data link layer address that is required for every port or device that connects to a LAN. Other devices in the network use these addresses to locate specific ports in the network and to create and update routing tables and data structures. MAC addresses are 6 bytes long and are controlled by the IEEE. Also known as a hardware address, a MAC-layer address, or a physical address. *Compare with* network address.

MAN   Metropolitan-area network. A network that spans a metropolitan area. Generally, a MAN spans a larger geographic area than a LAN, but a smaller geographic area than a WAN. *Compare with* LAN and WAN.

managed device   In network management, a managed device is a network device that can be managed by a network management protocol.

management database   A database that contains information about managed devices.

management entity   An entity within an NMS that manages the network using a network management protocol.

MB   Megabyte.

Mbps   Megabits per second.

MCAST   *See* multicast.

MCU   Multipoint control unit. An endpoint on the LAN that enables three or more terminals and gateways to participate in a multipoint H.323 conference.

MD5   Message Digest 5. An algorithm used for message authentication in SNMPv2. MD5 verifies the integrity of the communication, authenticates the origin, and checks for timeliness.

metric   A standard of measurement, such as performance, that is used for measuring whether network management goals have been met. *See also* routing metric.

MGCP   Media Gateway Control Protocol. A call control protocol in the packet-switching model's Open call control layer.

MHz   Megahertz.

MIB   Management Information Base. A management database used and maintained by a network management protocol such as SNMP. The value of an MIB object can be changed or retrieved using SNMP commands. MIB objects are organized in a tree structure that includes public (standard) and private (proprietary) branches.

MIC   Message Integrity Check. Protects WEP frames from tampering. The MIC is based on a seed value, destination MAC address, source MAC address, and payload (that is, any changes to these affect the MIC value).

millisecond   1/1000 of a second.

MISTP   Multi-Instance Spanning Tree Protocol. *See also* MSTP.

MLS   Multilayer Switching. Performing routing in hardware (thus, called switching). Also known as Layer 3 switching.

MM fiber   Multimode Fiber. A fiber-optic medium in which light travels in multiple modes.

modem   Modulator-demodulator. A device that converts digital signals to and from analog signals. Modems allow data to be transmitted over voice-grade telephone lines.

MOS   Mean opinion score. A common benchmark used to determine the quality of sound produced by specific codecs.

MPLS   Multiprotocol Label Switching. A switching method that uses a label to forward IP traffic. This label instructs the network's routers and switches where to forward the packets based on pre-established IP routing information.

MPPC   Microsoft Point-to-Point Compression. A software compression service provided by Microsoft.

MPPP   Multilink Point-to-Point Protocol. Defined in RFC 1717, a standard for aggregating multiple PPP links that allows for multivendor interoperability. MPPP defines a way of sequencing and transmitting packets over multiple physical interfaces and defines a method of fragmenting and reassembling large packets. Also called MLP.

ms   Milliseconds.

MSB   Most significant bit. The highest weighted bit, which is usually the left-most bit.

MSO   Multiple service operator. A cable service provider that provides additional services, such as data and/or voice telephony.

MSTP   Multiple STP, sometimes referred to as MISTP, or Multiple Instances of STP.

MTBF   Mean time between failures. The average time between a device's failures. Used as a standard for comparing the availability of devices.

MTU   Maximum transmission unit. The maximum packet size, in bytes, that a particular interface can handle.

multicast   Single packets copied by the network and sent to a specific subset of network addresses. These addresses are specified in the destination address field. *Compare with* broadcast and unicast.

multicast address   A single address that refers to multiple network devices; synonymous with group address. *Compare with* broadcast address and unicast address. *See also* multicast.

multicast group   A dynamically determined group of IP hosts identified by a single IP multicast address.

multicast router   A router used to send IGMP query messages on their attached local networks. Host members of a multicast group respond to a query by sending IGMP reports and noting the multicast groups to which they belong. The multicast router takes responsibility for forwarding multicast datagrams from one multicast group to all other networks that have members in the group. *See also* IGMP.

multilayer switch   A switch that filters and forwards packets based on MAC addresses and network addresses. A subset of a LAN switch.

MWI   Message waiting indicator. An indicator that a voice-mail message is waiting—for example, a flashing light, message display, special dial tone, or announcement.

N

NANP   North American Numbering Plan. The NANP is an example of a PSTN numbering plan for North America.

NAP   Network Access Provider. Provides ADSL line termination by using DSL access multiplexers.

NAS   Network Access Server. A Cisco platform (or collection of platforms) that interfaces between the packet world (for example, the Internet) and the circuit world (for example, the PSTN).

NAT   Network Address Translation. A Cisco router feature that enables you to translate private addresses into registered IP addresses only when needed, thereby reducing the need for registered IP addresses.

NAT-PT   Network Address Translation-Protocol Translation. An extension of NAT that also translates TCP port numbers.

NBAR   Network-Based Application Recognition. Cisco IOS software commands used for network traffic analysis.

NBMA   Nonbroadcast multiaccess. A multiaccess network that either does not support broadcasting (such as X.25), or in which broadcasting is not feasible (for example, an SMDS broadcast group or an extended Ethernet that is too large).

NDA   Network Data Analyzer. A NetFlow-specific network traffic analysis tool that combines a graphical user interface with other companion modules.

neigboring router   In OSPF, two routers that have interfaces to a common network.

NetFlow   Network Flow. A feature of some routers that allows them to categorize incoming packets into flows. Because packets in a flow often can be treated in the same way, this classification can be used to bypass some of the router's work and accelerate its switching operation.

network   A collection of computers, printers, routers, switches, and other devices that can communicate with each other over some transmission medium.

network address   A network layer address that refers to a logical, rather than a physical, network device. Also called a protocol address. *Compare with* MAC address.

network layer   Layer 3 of the OSI reference model. This layer provides connectivity and path selection between two end systems. The network layer is the layer in which routing occurs.

network management   Systems or actions that help maintain, characterize, or troubleshoot a network. *See also* NMS.

network management protocol   The protocol that management entities within NMSs use to communicate with agents in managed devices. The Simple Network Management Protocol (SNMP) is a well-known network management protocol.

NFC   NetFlow FlowCollector. An application that provides scalable and economical data collection from multiple NetFlow-enabled devices.

NIC

  1 Network interface card. A board that provides network communication capabilities to and from a computer system. Also called an adapter.

  2 Network Information Center. An organization that serves the Internet community by supplying user assistance, documentation, training, and other services.

NIDS   Network Intrusion Detection System. A security service that monitors and analyzes system events for the purpose of finding (and providing a real-time or near-real-time warning about) attempts to access system resources in an unauthorized manner.

NIR   National Internet Registry. ISPs obtain address allocations from an LIR, an NIR, or their appropriate RIR. The IANA is responsible for allocating addresses to the RIRs, according to their needs.

NIS   Network Information Services. A protocol developed by Sun Microsystems for the administration of network-wide databases. The service essentially uses two programs: one for finding an NIS server and one for accessing the NIS databases.

NLA   Next-Level Aggregator. Represents large providers and global corporate networks in IPv6.

NMS   Network management system. A system that is responsible for managing at least part of a network. An NMS is generally a reasonably powerful and well-equipped computer, such as an engineering workstation. NMSs communicate with agents to help keep track of network statistics and resources.

NMT   Network modeling tool. Tool that enables modeling of both simple and complex networks.

NOC   Network Operation Center. The organization that is responsible for maintaining a network.

node   An endpoint of a network connection or a junction that is common to two or more lines in a network. Nodes can be processors, controllers, or workstations. Nodes, which vary in routing and other functional capabilities, can be interconnected by links and serve as control points in the network. Node is sometimes used generically to refer to any entity that can access a network and is frequently used interchangeably with device. *See also* host.

non-stub area A resource-intensive OSPF area that carries a default route, static routes, intra-area routes, inter-area routes, and external routes. *Compare with* stub area. *See also* ASBR and OSPF.

NOS Network operating system. A generic term used to refer to what are actually distributed file systems. Examples of NOSs include NetWare, NFS, and VINES.

NSP Network Service Provider. Local access concentrator used for Layer 3 termination in ADSL.

NSSA Not-so-stubby area. In OSPF, a not-so-stubby area imports a limited number of external routes. The number of routes is limited to only those that are required for providing connectivity between backbone areas.

NTP Network Time Protocol. Protocol built on top of TCP that assures accurate local time keeping with reference to radio and atomic clocks that are located on the Internet.

O

ODR On-Demand Routing. A Cisco proprietary feature that provides IP routing with minimum overhead for stub networks.

OS Operating system.

OSI Open System Interconnection. An international standardization program created by ISO and ITU-T to develop standards for data networking that facilitate multivendor equipment interoperability.

OSI protocol stack Set of related communications protocols that operate together and, as a group, address communication at some or all of the seven layers of the OSI reference model. Not every protocol stack covers each layer of the model, and a single protocol in the stack often addresses a number of layers at once. TCP/IP is a typical protocol stack.

OSI reference model Open System Interconnection reference model. A network architectural model developed by ISO and ITU-T. The model consists of seven layers, each of which specifies particular network functions such as addressing, flow control, error control, encapsulation, and reliable message transfer. The highest layer (the application layer) is closest to the user; the lowest layer (the physical layer) is closest to the media technology. *See also* application layer, data link layer, network layer, physical layer, presentation layer, session layer, and transport layer.

OSPF   Open Shortest Path First. A link-state, hierarchical IGP routing algorithm proposed as a successor to RIP in the Internet community. OSPF features include least-cost routing, multipath routing, and load balancing. OSPF was derived from an early version of the IS-IS protocol. *See also* EIGRP, IGP, IGRP, IS-IS, and RIP.

OSPFv3   OSPF version 3. A new version of OSPF for IPv6.

OTP   One Time Password. OTP is a type of two-factor authentication. With OTP, you need a PIN and your token card to authenticate to a device or software application. A token card is a hardware or software device that generates new, seemingly random passwords at specified intervals (usually every 60 seconds). A user combines that random password with a PIN to create a unique password that only works for one instance of authentication.

OUI   Organizational Unique Identifier. Three octets assigned by the IEEE that are used in the 48-bit MAC addresses.

out-of-band signaling   Transmission that uses frequencies or channels outside the frequencies or channels that are normally used for information transfer. Out-of-band signaling is often used for error reporting in situations in which in-band signaling can be affected by whatever problems the network might be experiencing.

P

p2mp   Point-to-Multipoint. Communication between a series of receivers and transmitters to a central location. Cisco p2mp is typically set up in three segments to enable frequency reuse.

p2p   Point-to-Point. Communication between one receiver and one location. p2p has a higher bandwidth than p2mp; it has less overhead to manage the data paths, and there is only one receiver per transmitter.

packet   A logical grouping of information, including a header that contains control information and (usually) user data. Packets are most often used to refer to network layer units of data. *See also* PDU.

packet switching   A networking method in which nodes share bandwidth with each other when sending packets.

PagP Port Aggregation Control Protocol. Cisco proprietary protocol for automatic EtherChannel formation.

PAM Pulse Amplitude Modulation. Modulation scheme where the modulating wave is caused to modulate the amplitude of a pulse stream.

PAP

  1 Password Authentication Protocol. An authentication protocol that allows PPP peers to authenticate one another. The remote router attempting to connect to the local router is required to send an authentication request. Unlike CHAP, PAP passes the password and host name or username in the clear (unencrypted). PAP does not prevent unauthorized access, but merely identifies the remote end. Then, the router or access server determines whether that user is allowed access. PAP is only supported on PPP lines. *Compare with* CHAP.

  2 Printer-Access Protocol. AppleTalk protocol that allows client workstations to establish connections with servers—particularly printers.

partial mesh A network in which devices are organized in a mesh topology; some network nodes are organized in a full mesh, but others are connected to only one or two other nodes in the network. *See also* full mesh.

payload The portion of a frame that contains upper-layer information (data).

PBX Private branch exchange. Digital or analog telephone switchboard that is located on the subscriber premises and is used to connect private and public telephone networks.

PC Personal computer.

PCM Pulse code modulation. Technique of encoding analog voice into a 64-kbps data stream by sampling with 8-bit resolution at a rate of 8000 times per second.

PDIOO Plan-Design-Implement-Operate-Optimize. A design methodology with five phases that reflect the phases of a standard network's life cycle.

PDM

  1 Protocol-dependent modules that are located at the network layer in EIGRP.

  2 PIX Device Manager.

PDU   Protocol data unit, which is an OSI term for packet. A packet of data that consists of control information and user information that is to be exchanged between communicating peers in a network. In general, a PDU is a segment of data generated by a specific layer of a protocol stack; it usually contains information from the next higher layer, encapsulated with header and trailer information that is generated by the layer in question. *See also* BPDU and packet.

PE   Provider Edge. A PE router is located on the edge of a provider's network.

PEAP   Protected EAP. An EAP authentication protocol.

performance management   One of five categories of network management defined by ISO for OSI network management. Performance management subsystems are responsible for analyzing and controlling network performance, including network throughput and error rates. *See also* accounting management, configuration management, fault management, and security management.

physical layer   Layer 1 of the OSI reference model. The physical layer defines the electrical, mechanical, procedural, and functional specifications for activating, maintaining, and deactivating the physical link between end systems.

pilot   A pilot of a network is a scaled-down prototype that is used to demonstrate basic functionality and is typically used for smaller networks. *See also* prototype.

PIM   Protocol Independent Multicast. A multicast routing architecture that allows the addition of IP multicast routing on existing IP networks.

ping   Packet Internet groper. An ICMP echo message and its reply. Often used to test the reachability of a network device.

PIX   Cisco's Private Internet Exchange Firewall. *See also* firewall.

PKI   Public Key Infrastructure. System of CAs (and, optionally, RAs and other supporting servers and agents) that perform some set of certificate management, archive management, key management, and token management functions for a community of users in an application of asymmetric cryptography.

PLP   Packet level protocol. A network layer protocol in the X.25 protocol stack. Sometimes called X.25 Level 3 or X.25 Protocol. *See also* X.25.

PMD   Physical Media Dependent. Sublayer of the physical layer on some interfaces that interfaces directly with the physical medium and performs the most basic bit transmission functions of the network.

policy routing   A routing scheme that forwards packets to specific interfaces based on user-configured policies. Such policies might specify that traffic sent from a particular network should be forwarded out one interface, while all other traffic should be forwarded out another interface.

POP   Point of presence. A physical location in which an interexchange's carrier installed equipment to interconnect with a local exchange carrier.

port

1   An interface on an internetworking device, such as a router.

2   In IP terminology, an upper-layer process that receives information from lower layers.

3   To rewrite software or microcode so it runs on a different hardware platform or in a different software environment than that for which it was originally designed.

PortFast   STP feature used for switched ports where end-user stations are directly connected. There is no delay in passing traffic, because the switch immediately puts the port to the forward state.

POS   Packet-over-SONET. A technology that maps IP packets into SONET frames in hardware and transports them over the optical SONET network.

POTS   Plain Old Telephone System. *See also* PSTN.

PPK   Per-packet keying. An algorithm that uses different keys per packet as a potential way to mitigate attacks against WEP.

PPP   Point-to-Point Protocol. A successor to SLIP that provides router-to-router and host-to-network connections over synchronous and asynchronous circuits. *See also* SLIP.

pps   Packets per second. Used as a measurement of throughput and performance of networks and networking devices.

PPTP   Point-to-Point Tunneling Protocol.

PQ   See *priority queuing*.

PQ-CBWFQ   Priority Queuing-Class-Based Weighted Fair Queuing. Feature that brings strict priority queuing to CBWFQ. Strict priority queuing allows delay-sensitive data, such as voice, to be dequeued and sent first (before packets in other queues are dequeued), thereby giving delay-sensitive data preferential treatment over other traffic.

PRC   Partial Route Calculation. In Integrated IS-IS, when IP subnet information changes, only a PRC for the subnet in question is run on routers. This saves router resources and allows faster calculation.

presentation layer   Layer 6 of the OSI reference model. This layer ensures that information sent by the application layer of one system will be readable by the application layer of another. The presentation layer is also concerned with the data structures that are used by programs and therefore negotiates data transfer syntax for the application layer.

PRI   Primary Rate Interface. ISDN interface to primary rate access. Primary rate access consists of a single 64-kbps D channel plus 23 (T1) or 30 (E1) B channels for voice or data. *Compare with* BRI. *See also* ISDN.

priority queuing   A method of queuing that is used to guarantee bandwidth for traffic by assigning queue space based on protocol, port number, or other criteria. Priority queuing has four queues: high, medium, normal, and low; the high queue is always emptied first. *Compare with* custom queuing and WFQ.

private addresses   RFC 1918 defines these reserved IP addresses, which are only to be used internally to a company's network. The addresses are 10.0.0.0 to 10.255.255.255, 172.16.0.0 to 172.31.255.255, and 192.168.0.0 to 192.168.255.255.

process switching   An operation that provides full route evaluation and per-packet load balancing across parallel WAN links. Involves the transmission of entire frames to the router CPU, where they are repackaged for delivery to or from a WAN interface, with the router selecting a route for each packet. Process switching is the most resource-intensive switching operation that the CPU can perform.

protocol   The formal description of a set of rules and conventions that govern how devices on a network exchange information.

protocol stack   A set of related communications protocols that operate together and, as a group, address communication at some or all of the seven layers of the OSI reference model. Not every protocol stack covers each layer of the model, and often a single protocol in the stack addresses a number of layers at once. TCP/IP is a typical protocol stack.

protocol suite   *See* protocol stack.

prototype   An implementation of a portion of the network to prove that the design meets the requirements that are typically used for larger networks. *See also* pilot.

PSTN Public Switched Telephone Network. The variety of telephone networks and services that are in place worldwide.

PTT Post, Telephone, and Telegraph. A government agency that provides telephone services. PTTs exist in most areas outside of North America and provide both local and long-distance telephone services.

PVC Permanent virtual circuit. A virtual circuit that is permanently established. PVCs save bandwidth that is associated with circuit establishment and tear down in situations where certain virtual circuits must exist all the time. Called a permanent virtual connection in ATM terminology. *Compare with* SVC.

Q

Q.931 ITU-T specification for signaling to establish, maintain, and clear ISDN network connections.

QAM Quadrature Amplitude Modulation. Method for encoding digital data in an analog signal, in which each combination of phase and amplitude represents one of 16 4-bit patterns. This is required for fax transmission at 9600 bits per second.

QLLC Qualified Logical Link Control. Data link layer protocol defined by IBM; it allows SNA data to be transported across X.25 networks.

QoS Quality of service. A measure of performance for a transmission system; reflects its transmission quality and service availability.

QPPB QoS Policy Propagation on BGP. Feature that classifies packets by IP precedence based on BGP community lists, BGP autonomous system paths, and access lists.

QPSK Quadrature Phase Shift Keying. Digital frequency modulation technique used for sending data over coaxial cable networks. QPSK is a method of modulating digital signals onto a radio-frequency carrier signal using four phase states to code 2 digital bits. Because it is both easy to implement and fairly resistant to noise, QPSK is primarily used for sending data from the cable subscriber upstream to the Internet.

QSIG   Q Signaling; signaling at the ISDN model's Q point. Common channel signaling protocol based on ISDN Q.931 standards and used by many digital PBXs.

queue

1   Generally, an ordered list of elements that is waiting to be processed.

2   In routing, a backlog of packets that is waiting to be forwarded over a router interface.

queuing delay   Amount of time data must wait before it can be transmitted onto a statistically multiplexed physical circuit.

R

RADIUS   Remote Authentication Dial-In User Service. Database for authenticating modem and ISDN connections and for tracking connection time.

RAM   Random-access memory. Volatile memory that a microprocessor can read and write.

RARP   Reverse Address Resolution Protocol. A protocol in the TCP/IP stack that provides a method, based on MAC addresses, for finding IP addresses. *Compare with* ARP.

RAS   Registration, Admission, and Status protocol. Protocol that is used between endpoints and the gatekeeper to perform management functions. RAS signaling function performs registration, admissions, bandwidth changes, status, and disengage procedures between the VoIP gateway and the gatekeeper.

RDP   Router Discovery Protocol. Protocol that allows a workstation to learn a router's address.

RED   Random Early Detection. A congestion avoidance mechanism that takes advantage of TCP's congestion control mechanisms.

redistribution   Allowing routing information discovered through one routing protocol to be distributed in the update messages of another routing protocol. Sometimes called route redistribution.

redundancy   The duplication of devices, services, or connections so that, in the event of a failure, the redundant devices, services, or connections can perform the work of those that failed.

reliability   The ratio of expected to received keepalives from a link. If the ratio is high, the line is reliable. Used as a routing metric.

repeater   A device that regenerates and propagates electrical signals between two network segments. *See also* segment.

RF   Radio Frequency. An alternating current that, when input to an antenna, generates an electromagnetic field that is suitable for wireless communication.

RFC   Request for Comments. A document series used as the primary means of communicating information about the Internet. RFCs are available from numerous online sources.

RFI   Request for Information. A document that requests the submission of information for a project. The RFI is used for gathering information; this information can be used to create an RFP. *See also* RFP.

RFP   Request for Proposal. A formal document that invites proposals to be submitted for a project (for example, to perform a specific task or to sell a product). The RFP can specify the contents and format of the proposal and details of what is expected for the final project.

RGMP   Router-Port Group Management Protocol. RGMP reduces network congestion by forwarding multicast traffic to only those routers that are configured to receive it.

RIP

1   Routing Information Protocol. A distance vector IGP, RIP uses hop count as a routing metric. *See also* EIGRP, hop count, IGP, IGRP, OSPF, and RIPv2.

2   IPX Routing Information Protocol. A distance vector routing protocol for IPX.

RIPng   Routing Information Protocol next generation. A newer version of RIP for IPv6.

RIPv1   Routing Information Protocol version 1.

RIPv2   Routing Information Protocol version 2. A newer version of RIP for IP.

RIR   Regional Internet Registry. ISPs obtain address allocations from an LIR, an NIR, or their appropriate RIR. The IANA is responsible for allocating addresses to the RIRs according to their needs.

RMON Remote Monitoring. An MIB agent specification that defines functions for the remote monitoring of networked devices. The RMON specification provides numerous monitoring, problem detection, and reporting capabilities.

ROI Return on Investment. Used to compare investments an enterprise is considering. The return can include profit, cost savings, and other less tangible items (such as improved customer service, more knowledgeable staff, and so forth).

ROM Read-only memory. Nonvolatile memory that the microprocessor can read, but not write.

root bridge Exchanges topology information with designated bridges in a spanning-tree implementation to notify all other bridges in the network when topology changes are required. This prevents loops and provides a measure of defense against link failure.

route A path through an internetwork.

route summarization The consolidation of advertised addresses in a routing table. Summarizing routes reduces the number of routes in the routing table, the routing update traffic, and overall router overhead. Also called route aggregation.

routed protocol A protocol that can be routed by a router. A routed protocol contains enough network-layer addressing information for user traffic to be directed from one network to another network. Routed protocols define the format and use of a packet's fields. Packets that use a routed protocol are conveyed from end system to end system through an internetwork. Examples of routed protocols include AppleTalk and IP.

router A network layer device that uses one or more metrics to determine the optimal path along which network traffic should be forwarded. Routers forward packets from one network to another based on network layer information. Occasionally called a gateway (however, this definition of gateway is becoming increasingly outdated). *Compare with* gateway.

routing The process of finding a path to a destination host. Because of the many potential intermediate destinations a packet might traverse before reaching its destination host, routing is complex in large networks. Routing occurs at Layer 3, or the network layer.

routing metric   A standard of measurement, such as path length, that is used by routing algorithms to determine the optimal path to a destination. This information is stored in routing tables. Metrics include bandwidth, communication cost, delay, hop count, load, MTU, path cost, and reliability. Sometimes simply referred to as a metric. *See also* cost.

routing protocol   Supports a routed protocol by providing mechanisms for sharing routing information. Routing protocol messages move between the routers. A routing protocol allows the routers to communicate with other routers to update and maintain routing tables. Routing protocol messages do not carry end-user traffic from network to network. A routing protocol uses the routed protocol to pass information between routers. Examples of routing protocols include IGRP, OSPF, and RIP.

routing table   A table stored in a router or some other internetworking device that keeps track of routes to particular network destinations and metrics that are associated with those routes.

routing update   A message sent from a router to indicate network reachability and associated cost information. Routing updates are typically sent at regular intervals and after a network topology change. *Compare with* flash update.

RS-232   A popular physical layer interface. Now known as EIA/TIA-232. *See* EIA/TIA-232.

RS-422   A balanced electrical implementation of EIA/TIA-449 for high-speed data transmission. Now referred to collectively with RS-423 as EIA-530. *See also* EIA-530 and RS-423.

RS-423   An unbalanced electrical implementation of EIA/TIA-449 for EIA/TIA-232 compatibility. Now referred to collectively with RS-422 as EIA-530. *See also* EIA-530 and RS-422.

RS-449   A popular physical layer interface. Now known as EIA/TIA-449. *See* EIA/TIA-449.

RSH/RCMD   Remote Shell/Remote Shell Command Execution. A protocol that can be used to modify configurations; however, it is not recommended because of its lack of security.

RSP   Route/Switch Processor on Cisco 7500 series routers.

RST   Reset bit in a TCP segment.

RSTP   Rapid STP. RSTP provides rapid convergence of the spanning tree by assigning port roles and determining the active topology. The RSTP builds upon the IEEE 802.1d STP to select the switch with the highest switch priority as the root switch and then assigning the port roles (root, designated, alternate, backup, and disabled) to individual ports. These roles assist in rapid STP convergence, which can be extremely fast (within a second) because of the knowledge of the topology.

RSVP   Resource Reservation Protocol. A protocol that supports the reservation of resources across an IP network. Also known as Resource Reservation Setup Protocol.

RTCP   Real-time Transport Control Protocol. Provides a mechanism for hosts that are involved in an RTP session to exchange information about monitoring and controlling the session. RTCP monitors quality for such elements as packet counts, packet loss, and inter-arrival jitter.

RTMP   Routing Table Maintenance Protocol.

RTP   Real-time Transport Protocol. A protocol used for carrying packetized audio and video traffic over an IP network.

RTR   Response Time Reporter. Previous name for the SAA. *See* SAA.

S

SAA   Service Assurance Agent. A Cisco IOS software feature that allows users to monitor network performance between a Cisco router (or Layer 3 switch) and a remote device, which can be another Cisco device or an IP host.

SAFE   Cisco's Security Architecture for Enterprise blueprint.

S-CDMA   Synchronous code division multiple access. S-CDMA means that multiple CMs can transmit simultaneously on the same RF channel and during the same TDMA time slot using different codes.

SDH   Synchronous Digital Hierarchy. A standard technology for synchronous data transmission on optical media. It is the international equivalent of Synchronous Optical Network.

SDSL Single-line Digital Subscriber Line. Also known as Single-pair DSL and Symmetric DSL. One of four DSL technologies. SDSL delivers 1.544 Mbps both downstream and upstream over a single copper twisted pair. The use of a single twisted pair limits SDSL's operating range to 10,000 feet (3048.8 meters). *Compare with* ADSL, HDSL, and VDSL.

security management One of five categories of network management defined by ISO for OSI network management. Security management subsystems are responsible for controlling access to network resources. *See also* accounting management, configuration management, fault management, and performance management.

Segment

1 A section of a network that is bound by bridges, routers, or switches.

2 In a LAN using a bus topology, a continuous electrical circuit that is often connected to other such segments with repeaters.

3 In the TCP specification, a single transport layer unit of information.

server A node or software program that provides services to clients. *See also* client.

service level Various levels and quality of services defined for each service type. For example, the service type called quality of sound might have service levels defined for telephone, broadcast, and digital CD.

session A related set of communications transactions between two or more network devices.

session layer Layer 5 of the OSI reference model. This layer establishes, manages, and terminates sessions between applications and manages data exchange between presentation layer entities.

SGCP Simple Gateway Control Protocol. Controls Voice over IP gateways by an external call control element (called a call-agent). This has been adapted to allow SGCP to control switch ATM Circuit Emulation Service circuits (called endpoints in SGCP). The resulting system (call-agents and gateways) allows for the call-agent to engage in Common Channel Signaling over a 64-kbps CES circuit, thereby governing the interconnection of bearer channels on the CES interface.

shielded cable A cable that has a layer of shielded insulation to reduce electromagnetic interference.

simplex   The ability for data transmission in only one direction between a sending station and a receiving station. *Compare with* full duplex and half duplex.

SIP   Session Initiation Protocol. Protocol developed by the IETF MMUSIC Working Group as an alternative to H.323. SIP features are compliant with IETF RFC 2543, which was published in March 1999. SIP equips platforms to signal the setup of voice and multimedia calls over IP networks.

SLA

1   Service level agreement.

2   Site Level Aggregator.

SLARP   Serial Line Address Resolution Protocol. Upon power up, a router sends an SLARP request to determine its IP address from a router that is directly connected to it on a serial line.

SLC   Service Level Contract. An SLC specifies connectivity and performance levels for the service's end user that are to be met by the service provider.

SLIP   Serial Line Internet Protocol. A standard protocol for point-to-point serial connections using a variation of TCP/IP. A predecessor of PPP. *See also* PPP.

SLM   Service-level management. A methodology that helps network managers resolve resource issues by defining and regulating capacity and performance management processes in a cost-effective manner.

SM   Single-mode. Fiber that has a relatively low diameter, through which only one mode can propagate.

SMDS   Switched Multimegabit Data Service. A high-speed, packet-switched, datagram-based WAN networking technology offered by the telephone companies.

SMI   Structure of Management Information. A document (RFC 1155) that specifies rules for defining managed objects in the MIB. *See also* MIB.

SMS   Service Management Solution. An application module for performance monitoring and SLM in CiscoWorks 2000.

SMTP   Simple Mail Transfer Protocol. An Internet protocol that provides electronic mail services.

SNA Systems Network Architecture. A large, complex, feature-rich network architecture that IBM developed in the 1970s. Similar in some respects to the OSI reference model, except with several differences. SNA is essentially composed of seven layers.

SNMP Simple Network Management Protocol. A network management protocol used almost exclusively in TCP/IP networks. SNMP provides a means of monitoring and controlling network devices and managing configurations, statistics collection, performance, and security. *See also* SNMP communities and SNMPv2.

SNMP communities Authentication scheme that enables an intelligent network device to validate SNMP requests from sources such as the NMS. *See also* SNMP.

SNMPv1 SNMP version 1. The original version of SNMP.

SNMPv2 SNMP version 2. Version 2 of the popular network management protocol. SNMPv2 supports centralized and distributed network management strategies and includes improvements in SMI, protocol operations, management architecture, and security. *See also* SNMP.

SNMPv3 SNMP version 3. Described in RFCs 2571 through 2575, SNMPv3 adds methods to ensure the secure transmission of critical data to and from managed devices.

SNR Signal-to-noise ratio. A measure of signal strength relative to the strength of the background noise.

SOHO Small office/home office.

SONET Synchronous Optical Network. A high-speed (up to 2.5 Gbps) synchronous network specification developed by Bellcore and designed to run on optical fiber. Approved as an international standard in 1988.

source address The address of a network device that is sending data. *See also* destination address.

SP Service provider. A company that provides a communications service, such as a Frame Relay network.

spanning tree A loop-free subset of a network topology. *See also* spanning-tree algorithm and Spanning Tree Protocol.

spanning-tree algorithm An algorithm used by the Spanning Tree Protocol to create a spanning tree. Sometimes abbreviated STA. *See also* spanning tree and Spanning Tree Protocol.

Spanning Tree Protocol A bridge protocol that utilizes the spanning tree algorithm, thereby enabling a learning bridge to dynamically work around loops in a network topology by creating a spanning tree. Bridges exchange BPDU messages with other bridges to detect loops and then remove the loops by shutting down selected bridge interfaces. Refers to both the IEEE 802.1 Spanning Tree Protocol standard and the earlier Digital Equipment Corporation Spanning Tree Protocol on which it is based. The IEEE version supports bridge domains and allows the bridge to construct a loop-free topology across an extended LAN. The IEEE version is generally preferred over the Digital version. Sometimes abbreviated STP. *See also* BPDU, spanning tree, and spanning-tree algorithm.

SPF Shortest path first. A routing algorithm that iterates on length of path to determine a shortest-path spanning tree. Commonly used in link-state routing algorithms. Also called Dijkstra's algorithm. *See also* link state routing algorithm.

split horizon A routing rule that states that a router cannot send routing information about a network from the same interface from which it learned that information. A router knows the interface from which it learned information by looking in its routing table. Split-horizon updates are useful in preventing routing loops.

spoofing The act of a packet illegally claiming to be from an address from which it did not actually originate. Spoofing is designed to foil network security mechanisms, such as filters and access lists.

SPX Sequenced Packet Exchange. A reliable, connection-oriented protocol that supplements the datagram service provided by the IPX protocol. Novell derived this commonly used NetWare transport protocol from the SPP of the XNS protocol suite.

SS7 Signaling System 7. Standard CCS system used with BISDN and ISDN.

SSH Secure shell. A UNIX-based command interface and protocol for securely accessing a remote computer.

SSID Service Set Identifiers. SSID is broadcast on the AP. The SSID is an identifier for the WLAN; a device must know the SSID to connect to the WLAN.

STAC Stacker. A compression algorithm.

star topology   A LAN topology in which point-to-point links connect network endpoints to a common central switch.

static route   A route that is explicitly configured and entered into the routing table.

STP

1   Shielded twisted-pair. A two-pair wiring medium used in a variety of network implementations. STP cabling has a layer of shielded insulation to reduce EMI. *Compare with* UTP.

2   *See* Spanning Tree Protocol.

stub area   An OSPF area that carries a default route, intra-area routes, and inter-area routes, but does not carry external routes. *Compare with* non-stub area. *See also* ASBR and OSPF.

stub network   Part of an internetwork that can only be reached by one path; a network that has only a single connection to a router.

subinterface   One of a number of virtual interfaces on a single physical interface.

subnet   *See* subnetwork.

subnet address   A portion of an IP address that the subnet mask specifies as the subnetwork. *See also* IP address, subnet mask, and subnetwork.

subnet mask   A 32-bit number that is associated with an IP address; each bit in the subnet mask indicates how to interpret the corresponding bit in the IP address. In binary, a subnet mask bit of 1 indicates that the corresponding bit in the IP address is a network or subnet bit; a subnet mask bit of 0 indicates that the corresponding bit in the IP address is a host bit. The subnet mask then indicates how many bits have been borrowed from the host field for the subnet field. Sometimes simply referred to as a mask. *See also* IP address.

subnetwork   In IP networks, a network that shares a particular subnet address. Subnetworks are networks that are arbitrarily segmented by a network administrator to provide a multilevel, hierarchical routing structure while shielding the subnetwork from the addressing complexity of attached networks. Sometimes called a subnet. *See also* IP address, subnet address, and subnet mask.

SVC   Switched virtual circuit. A virtual circuit that is dynamically established on demand and is torn down when transmission is complete. SVCs are used in situations in which data transmission is sporadic. Called a switched virtual connection in ATM terminology. *Compare with* PVC.

switch

1 A network device that filters, forwards, and floods frames based on each frame's destination address. The switch operates at the data link layer of the OSI model.

2 An electronic or mechanical device that allows a connection to be established as necessary and terminated when there is no longer a session to support.

3 In telephony, a general term for any device, such as a PBX, that connects individual phones to phone lines. *See also* PBX and PSTN.

SYN

1 The synchronize bit in a TCP segment, used to indicate that the segment is a SYN segment (see Definition 2).

2 The first segment sent by the TCP protocol, used to synchronize the two ends of a connection in preparation for opening a connection.

SYN flood   A denial of service attack that sends more TCP SYN packets than the protocol implementation can handle.

synchronous transmission   Digital signals that are transmitted with precise clocking. Such signals have the same frequency, with individual characters encapsulated in control bits (called start bits and stop bits) that designate the beginning and end of each character. *Compare with* asynchronous transmission.

Syslog   A service that receives messages from applications on the local host or from remote hosts (such as a router or printer) that have been configured to forward messages. Syslog directs messages to a log file.

T

T1   A digital WAN carrier facility. T1 transmits DS-1-formatted data at 1.544 Mbps through the telephone-switching network. *Compare with* E1. *See also* DS-1.

T3   A digital WAN carrier facility. T3 transmits DS-3-formatted data at 44.736 Mbps through the telephone-switching network. *Compare with* E3. *See also* DS-3.

TA   Terminal adapter. A device used to connect ISDN BRI connections to existing serial interfaces such as EIA/TIA-232.

TACACS   Terminal Access Controller Access Control System. An authentication protocol that provides remote access authentication and related services, such as event logging. User passwords are administered in a central database rather than in individual routers, thus providing an easily scalable network security solution.

TCP   Transmission Control Protocol. A connection-oriented transport layer protocol that provides reliable full-duplex data transmission. TCP is part of the TCP/IP protocol stack. *See also* TCP/IP.

TCP/IP   Transmission Control Protocol/Internet Protocol. A common name for the suite of protocols the U.S. DoD (Department of Defense) developed in the 1970s to support the construction of worldwide internetworks. TCP and IP are the two best-known protocols in the suite. *See also* IP and TCP.

TDM   Time-Division Multiplexing. Technique in which information from multiple channels can be allocated bandwidth on a single wire based on pre-assigned time slots. Bandwidth is allocated to each channel regardless of whether the station has data to transmit.

TDMA   Time division multiplex access. Type of multiplexing in which two or more information channels are transmitted over the same link by allocating a different time interval ("slot" or "slice") for the transmission of each channel; that is, the channels take turns using the link. Some kind of periodic synchronizing signal or distinguishing identifier is usually required so that the receiver can distinguish one channel from another. For cable modems that use TDMA, multiple CMs share a given RF channel via the dynamic assignment of time slots.

TEHO   Tail End Hop Off. A call originates in a private network, is carried over private tie lines close to the call's destination, and is then connected to the PSTN. This is also referred to as on-net to off-net calling.

Telnet   A standard terminal emulation protocol in the TCP/IP protocol stack. Telnet is used for remote terminal connection to enable users to log in to remote systems and use resources as if they were connected to a local system. RFC 854 defines Telnet.

terminal   A simple device by which data can be entered into or retrieved from a network. Generally, a terminal has a monitor and a keyboard, but no processor or local disk drive.

TFTP   Trivial File Transfer Protocol. A simplified version of FTP that allows file transfer from one computer to another over a network.

throughput   The quantity of data that is successfully transferred between nodes per unit of time, usually seconds.

TIA   Telecommunications Industry Association. A communications and IT trade association that is involved in standards development. *See also* EIA.

tie-line   Connects enterprise PBXs without connecting to the CO (PSTN) switch.

TKIP   Temporal Key Integrity Protocol. A set of software enhancements to RC4-based WEP.

TLA   Top-level aggregator. IPv6 public transit points (exchanges) where long-haul providers establish peer connections.

Token Ring   A token-passing LAN developed and supported by IBM. Token Ring runs at 4 or 16 Mbps over a ring topology. Similar to IEEE 802.5. *See also* IEEE 802.5.

topology   The physical arrangement of network nodes and media within an enterprise networking structure.

ToS   Type of service. A field in an IP datagram that indicates how the datagram should be handled. It specifies reliability, precedence, delay, and throughput parameters.

traffic policing   Process used to measure the actual traffic flow across a given connection and compare it to the total admissible traffic flow for that connection. If congestion develops, traffic outside of the agreed-upon flow can be tagged and discarded en route. Traffic policing is used in ATM, Frame Relay, and other types of networks. Also known as admission control, permit processing, and rate enforcement.

traffic shaping   The use of queues to limit surges that can congest a network. Data is buffered and then sent into the network in regulated amounts to ensure that the traffic fits within the promised traffic envelope for the particular connection. Traffic shaping is used in ATM, Frame Relay, and other types of networks. Also known as metering, shaping, and smoothing. *See also* Frame Relay traffic shaping.

transport layer   Layer 4 of the OSI reference model. This layer is responsible for reliable network communication between end nodes. The transport layer provides mechanisms for the establishment, maintenance, and termination of virtual circuits, transport fault detection and recovery, and information flow control.

trap   A message sent by an SNMP agent to an NMS, console, or terminal to indicate the occurrence of a significant event, such as a specifically defined condition or a threshold that has been reached. *See also* alarm and event.

tree topology   A LAN topology that is similar to a bus topology, except that tree networks can contain branches with multiple nodes. Transmissions from a station propagate the length of the medium and are received by all other stations.

trunk

1   Physical and logical connection between two switches, across which network traffic travels. A backbone is composed of numerous trunks.

2   In telephony, a phone line between two COs or between a CO and a PBX.

TTL   Time To Live. A field in an IP header that indicates how long a packet is considered valid.

tunneling   An architecture that provides a virtual data link connection between two like networks through a foreign network. The virtual data link is created by encapsulating the network data inside the packets of the foreign network. *See also* encapsulation.

twisted pair   A relatively low-speed transmission medium that consists of two insulated wires arranged in a regular spiral pattern. The wires can be shielded or unshielded. Twisted pair is common in telephony applications and is increasingly common in data networks. *See also* STP and UTP.

U

UBR   Unspecified Bit Rate. QoS class defined by the ATM Forum for ATM networks. UBR allows any amount of data up to a specified maximum to be sent across the network, but there are no guarantees in terms of cell loss rate and delay.

uBR   Universal Broadband Router. Also referred to as the Cable Modem Termination System. *See* CMTS.

UDLD   Unidirectional Link Detection. A Layer 2 protocol for STP that works with the Layer 1 mechanisms to determine a link's physical status. If the port does not see its own device/port ID in the incoming UDLD packets for a specific duration of time, the link is considered unidirectional from the Layer 2 perspective. When UDLD detects the unidirectional link, the respective port is disabled and the error message is generated.

UDP   User Datagram Protocol. A connectionless transport layer protocol in the TCP/ IP protocol stack. UDP is a simple protocol that exchanges datagrams without acknowledgments or guaranteed delivery, thereby requiring that other protocols handle error processing and retransmission. RFC 768 defines UDP.

u-law   A companding technique commonly used in North America. u-law is standardized as a 64-kbps codec in ITU-T G.711.

UMTS   Universal Mobile Telephone Service. A 3G mobile wireless telecommunications system whose standards are being developed by the Third Generation Partnership Project (3GPP).

unicast   A message that is sent to a single network destination. *Compare with* broadcast and multicast.

unicast address   An address that specifies a single network device. *Compare with* broadcast address and multicast address. *See also* unicast.

UplinkFast   Enables a switch to put a redundant path (port) into active state within 1 second.

URL   Uniform Resource Locator. Type of formatted identifier that describes the access method and location of an information resource object on the Internet.

USM   User-based Security Model. A model developed for SNMPv3 that associates security information with users; defined in RFC 2574.

utilization   Percentage of the total capacity (bandwidth) of a network segment.

UTP   Unshielded twisted pair. A four-pair wire medium that is used in a variety of networks. Unlike coaxial-type connections, UTP does not require fixed spacing between connections. Following are the five types of UTP cabling that are commonly used: Category 1 cabling, Category 2 cabling, Category 3 cabling, Category 4 cabling, and Category 5 cabling. *Compare with* STP. *See also* twisted pair.

V

VACM   View-based Access Control Model. An access control model developed for SNMP; defined in RFC 2575.

VAD   Voice activity detection. When enabled on a voice port or dial peer, silence is not transmitted over the network—only audible speech. When VAD is enabled, the sound quality is slightly degraded, but the connection monopolizes much less bandwidth.

VBR   Variable Bit Rate. QoS class defined by the ATM Forum for ATM networks. VBR is subdivided into a real time (RT) class and non-real time (NRT) class. VBR (RT) is used for connections in which samples have a fixed timing relationship. VBR (NRT) is used for connections in which samples do not have a fixed timing relationship, but that still require a guaranteed QoS.

VC   Virtual circuit. A logical circuit created to ensure reliable communication between two network devices. A virtual circuit is defined by a VPI/VCI pair and can be either permanent (a PVC) or switched (an SVC). Virtual circuits are used in Frame Relay and X.25. In ATM, a virtual circuit is called a virtual channel. Sometimes abbreviated VC. *See also* PVC and SVC.

VDSL   Very-high-data-rate Digital Subscriber Line. One of four DSL technologies. VDSL delivers 13 to 52 Mbps downstream and 1.5 to 2.3 Mbps upstream over a single twisted copper pair. The operating range of VDSL is limited to 1000 to 4500 feet (304.8 to 1372 meters). *See also* ADSL, HDSL, and SDSL.

VLAN   Virtual LAN. A logical, rather than physical, grouping of devices. The devices are grouped using switch management software so that they can communicate as if they were attached to the same wire; in fact, they might be located on a number of different physical LAN segments. VLANs are extremely flexible because they are based on logical rather than physical connections.

VLSM   Variable length subnet mask. The capability to specify a different subnet mask for the same network number on different subnets. VLSM can help optimize available address space. Some protocols do not allow the use of VLSM. *See also* classless routing protocols.

VMS   CiscoWorks VPN/Security Management Solution. Part of the SAFE Blueprint for network security that combines web-based tools for configuring, monitoring, and troubleshooting VPNs, firewalls, NIDSs, and host-based IDSs.

VoATM   Voice over Asynchronous Transfer Mode. Voice over ATM enables a router to carry voice traffic (such as telephone calls and faxes) over an ATM network. When sending voice traffic over ATM, the voice traffic is encapsulated using a special AAL5 encapsulation for multiplexed voice.

VoD   Video on demand. A system that, when requested, uses video compression to supply video programs to viewers.

VoFR   Voice over Frame Relay. VoFR enables a router to carry voice traffic (such as telephone calls and faxes) over a Frame Relay network. When sending voice traffic over Frame Relay, the voice traffic is segmented and encapsulated for transit across the Frame Relay network using FRF.12 encapsulation.

VoIP   Voice over IP. The ability to carry normal telephony-style voice over an IP-based internet with basic telephone service-like functionality, reliability, and voice quality. VoIP enables a router to carry voice traffic (such as telephone calls and faxes) over an IP network. Voice packets are transported using IP, in compliance with ITU-T specification H.323.

VPDN   Virtual private dialup network. Also known as virtual private dial network. A VPDN is a network that extends remote access to a private network using a shared infrastructure. VPDNs use Layer 2 tunnel technologies (L2F, L2TP, and PPTP) to extend the Layer 2 and higher parts of the network connection from a remote user across an ISP network to a private network. VPDNs are a cost-effective method of establishing a long distance, point-to-point connection between remote dial users and a private network.

VPN   Virtual private network. Enables IP traffic to travel securely over a public TCP/IP network by encrypting all traffic from one network to another. A VPN uses tunneling to encrypt all information at the IP level. *See also* tunneling.

VRRP   Virtual Router Redundancy Protocol. VRRP provides redundancy over a VPN tunnel by dynamically assigning one of the VPN Concentrators on a LAN as the virtual router for the LAN; this is called the Master. The Master controls the IP addresses that are associated with the virtual router and forwards packets sent to those IP addresses. If the Master becomes unavailable, a backup VPN Concentrator takes its place.

VTP   VLAN Trunk Protocol. A Layer 2 messaging protocol that manages the addition, deletion, and renaming of VLANs.

vty   Virtual Type Terminal. Commonly used as virtual terminal lines.

W

WAN Wide-area network. A data communications network that serves users across a broad geographic area and often uses transmission devices that are provided by common carriers. Frame Relay, SMDS, and X.25 are examples of WANs. *Compare with* LAN and MAN.

weighted fair queuing *See* WFQ.

WEP Wired Equivalent Privacy. A frame encryption protocol that protects the over-the-air transmission between WLAN access points and network interface cards. Working at the data link layer, WEP requires that all communicating parties share the same secret key (40- or 128-bit). However, in both 40- and 128-bit variants, WEP can easily be cracked using off-the-shelf tools that are readily available on the Internet.

WFQ Weighted Fair Queuing. A method of queuing that prioritizes low-volume traffic over high-volume traffic to ensure satisfactory response time for common user applications. *Compare with* custom queuing and priority queuing.

wildcard mask A 32-bit quantity used in conjunction with an IP address to determine which bits in an IP address should be ignored when comparing that address with another IP address. A wildcard mask is specified when setting up access lists.

window The number of outstanding data segments the sender is allowed to have without receiving an acknowledgment.

windowing A method of controlling the amount of information transferred end-to-end, using different window sizes.

WLAN Wireless local-area network. A LAN that is implemented using wireless technology.

workgroup A collection of workstations and servers on a LAN that are designed to communicate and exchange data with one another.

WPA Wi-Fi Protected Access. A Wi-Fi Alliance specification for interoperable, standards-based wireless LAN security that is based on the IEEE 802.11i standard.

WRED   Weighted Random Early Detection. Queuing method that ensures that high-precedence traffic has lower loss rates than other traffic during times of congestion.

WWW   World Wide Web. A large network of Internet servers that provide hypertext and other services to terminals that run client applications, such as a WWW browser.

X–Y

X.25   An ITU-T standard that defines how connections between DTE and DCE are maintained for remote terminal access and computer communications. To some degree, Frame Relay has superseded X.25. *See also* Frame Relay.

xDSL   Group term used to refer to ADSL, HDSL, SDSL, and VDSL. All are digital technologies using the existing copper infrastructure that is provided by the telephone companies. xDSL is a high-speed alternative to ISDN.

XML   Extensible Markup Language. A standard maintained by the World Wide Web Consortium (W3C). It defines a syntax that allows you to create markup languages to specify information structures.

XNS   Xerox Network Systems. A protocol suite originally designed by the Palo Alto Research Center. Many PC networking companies, such as 3Com, Banyan, Novell, and UB Networks, used or currently use a variation of XNS as their primary transport protocol.

Z

zone   A collection of all terminals, gateways, and MCUs that are managed by a single gatekeeper. A zone includes at least one terminal, and can include gateways or MCUs. A zone has only one gatekeeper. It can be independent of LAN topology and comprised of multiple LAN segments that are connected using routers or other devices.

INDEX

Symbols

<backspace> command, 774
<down arrow> command, 774
<Enter> command, 774
<Return> command, 774
<Tab> command, 774
<up arrow> command, 774
? command, 773

Numerics

3DES (triple data encryption standard), 572
20/80 rule, 209
80/20 rule, 209
802.11b, 588
802.11i, 590
802.1X, 589

A

AAA, 705
    accounting management, 644
    overview, 151
AAL1, 504
AAL2, 503
AAL5, 503
access-class command, 746, 780
access control, 563
access layer (network hierarchy model), 120, 684
    designing Enterprise Campus networks, 216–217
    L2 and L3 switching, 121
    role of, 120
    route redistribution, 413
    routing protocols, 409
access-list command, 780-782
access lists, 726
    configuring, 746–747
    creating, 730

ensuring results, 732
extended, 735
    backwards compatibility, 726
    configuring, 735–739
    example, 742–743
    placement, 744
implicit deny any entries, 728
IP, 725, 728
standard, 727, 733
vty, 744
wildcard masks, 729-731
access servers, 8
accounting management tools, 642-643
    AAA framework, 644
    IP accounting, 643
    NetFlow, 645
ACD (automatic call distribution) systems, 459
ACF/VTAM (Advanced Communication Facility/Virtual Telecommunication Access Method), 26
acknowledgment, 272
activation and data collection, 627
Active Network Monitor, 79
active time, 410
adaptation (ATM), 503
Address mapping group (RMON2), 622
Address Resolution Protocol (ARP), 17, 157
address signaling, 450
addresses, 329
    host, 322
    IP
        assigning, 343–345
        converting between decimal and binary, 718
    IPv4, 319-320
addressing
    AppleTalk, 25
    classful, 720
    discovery
        ARP, 157
        explicit configuration, 157

HSRP, 158
routing protocols, 157
VRRP, 158
encapsulation, 4
IP, 21, 691
ANDing, 21–22
classes, 692
default gateway, 157
job aids, 715
octets, 18, 321
prefixes, 323, 692
private addresses, 329-331, 334, 692
route summarization, 334–335
subnets, 21
IPv4, 18
classes, 19, 323
subnets, 19
IPX, 25
MAC, 9
network layer, 9
address-violation command, 789
ADPCM (Adaptive Differential Pulse Code
Modulation) algorithm, 485
ADSL (Asymmetric DSL), 258, 291
architecture, 292
point-to-point protocol networks, 293
PPPoA implementation, 294
PPPoE implementation, 294
advanced distance vector routing protocols, 406
Advanced Encryption Standard (AES), 590
Advanced Peer-to-Peer Networking (APPN), 26
Advanced Program-to-Program Computing
(APPC), 26
advanced routing protocols, 16
AES (Advanced Encryption Standard), 590
aggregation, 162. *See also* channel aggregation
Alarm group (RMON1), 619
A-law companding, 443–444
algorithms, 15
compression, 270
routing, 15
security, 546

Spanning-Tree Protocol, 161
voice coding and compression, 485
always-on connections
FR vs. X.25, 281
TDM vs. packet switching, 280
analog signaling, 442, 451–452
companding, 443
converting to digital, 442–443
and, 11, 362
ANDing (IP addresses), 21–22
anycast addresses (IPv6), 354
APPC (Advanced Program-to-Program
Computing), 26
AppleTalk, 25
addressing, 25
configuration commands, 783
general commands, 783
phases, 25
appletalk cable-range command, 783
AppleTalk commands (table), 783
AppleTalk configuration commands (table), 783
appletalk discovery command, 783
appletalk protocol command, 783
appletalk routing command, 783
appletalk zone command, 783
application characterization, 185
application requirements, 189
client-client, 185
client-distributed server, 186
client-Enterprise Edge, 188
client-server farms, 187
application layer (OSI model), 768
application layer attacks, 152–153
Application layer host group (RMON2), 622
Application layer matrix group (RMON2), 622
application maps, 67
application requirements of WAN design, 262-
263
applications, 670–671, 674
analyzing in existing networks
example, 78
tools, 79

communication, 185
cost consideration, 191
high availability, 191
IP telephony, 471
Network Organizational Model, 36
security, 557-558
throughput, 190
APPN (Advanced Peer-to-Peer Networking), 26
architectures
distributed, 631
fault management, 633
IP telephony, 471
modern organizational model, 33
network management, 607-609
Network Organizational, 681
example, 35
layers, 682
OSI model, 3
voice networks, 460
ARP (Address Resolution Protocol), 17, 157
AS (autonomous systems)
connectivity, 695
IGRP (Interior Gateway Routing Protocol), 23
multi-homing, 405
routing protocols, 22
AS-path attribute, 385
assessing, 101
existing networks, 64, 67
customer input, 65
draft design documents, 85–86
examples, 66

network audits, 70–75
summary reports, 84
traffic analysis, 77–82
network health, 76
assigned TCP port numbers, 740
assigned UDP port numbers, 741
assigning
IP addresses, 343
DHCP servers, 346

guidelines for assignment, 345
IPv6, 358
static vs. dynamic, 344–345
private addresses, 329-331, 334, 692
Asymmetric DSL. *See* ADSL
ATM (Asynchronous Transfer Mode), 255, 258
adaptation types, 503
characteristics, 502
audit trails, 575
auditing existing networks, 70. *See also* assessing
manual commands, 72–75
third-part tools (Web sites), 72
tools, 70–71
audits (network assessment), 70
authentication, 563–564
EAP, 589
guidelines, 566
how to use, 565
IEEE 802.1X standard, 565
two-factor/strong, 564
authorization, 567
guidelines, 569
least privilege concept, 567
Auto Update Server
security, 599–600
Web site, 600
automatic call distribution (ACD) systems, 459
autonomous system connectivity. *See* AS
AutoQoS (Cisco), 497-498
availability threats, 548
AVVID (Cisco Architecture for Voice, Video and Integrated Data), 88

B

backbone, routing protocols, 408
BackboneFast, 197
<backspace> command, 774
Backup, 162
backup links, 268
backup serial lines, 7

backwards compatibility, IP access list
  extensions, 726
bandwidth
  cable networks, 297
  data compression, 269
  DWDM, 289
  E3, 143
  EIGRP, 397
  increasing with secondary links, 285
  IP telephony systems, 489
    reducing traffic, 490
    requirements, 490–491
  LANs, 265
  optimizing, 268
  shared vs. switched LAN technology, 193
  T3, 143
  WANs, 264
bandwidth command, 778, 785
bandwidth domains, 191
bandwidth metric, 382-383
bandwidth reduction QoS mechanism, 493
bandwidth reservation QoS mechanism, 493
banner command, 777
baselining, 649
Bellman-Ford algorithms, 16
BER (bit error rate), 263
best effort connections, 259
best-effort traffic, 24
BGP (Border Gateway Protocol), 23, 404
  AS-path attribute, 385
  external, 406
  implementation example, 405
  integrating interior routing protocols, 416–
    417
  internal, 406
  neighbors, 406
  next-hop attribute, 418
BGP4+, 367
BHT (busy hour traffic), 510
BIAs (burned-in addresses), 9
binary numbers
  decimal-to-binary conversion chart, 716-717

logically ANDing, 22
bit error rate (BER), 263
bits (IP addressing), 323, 692
blocking probability, 511
boot system command, 777
Border Gateway Protocol. *See* BGP
bottlenecks
  content caching, 169
  traffic shaping, 276
bottom-up design approach vs. top-down, 89
BPDU (Bridge Protocol Data Unit), 196
BPDU skew detection, 197
BRI (Basic Rate Interface), 8, 452
Bridge Protocol Data Unit (BPDU), 196
bridges, 10-12
bridging protocols, 11
broadband
  3G, 298
  fixed wireless network example, 298-299
broadcast domains, 191
broadcast storms, 12
broadcast transmission, 6
budgets, consideration in network design, 55
building access module, 226
Building Access submodule, 166
Building Distribution submodule, 166
building distribution module, 226
busy hour traffic (BHT), 510

C

c, 24
Cable Modem Termination System (CMTS), 295
cable networks, 258–259, 295
  CATV transmission, 297
  CM-to-CMTS interface, 297
  components, 295
  data flow, 296
  topology, 296
cabling, 182
  copper vs. fiber, 203–204
  MM, 202

SM, 202
  network installation example, 205
  unshielded twisted-pair, 201
CAC (Call Admission Control), 512, 518
caches, 171
calculating networks for subnet masks, 723
calculating subnet masks, 721–722
call centers, 459
call control functions, 489
call legs, 477
call progress signaling, 450
CallManager, 471, 522
campus backbone design, 221
  auxiliary VLAN feature, 226
  dual-path, 225
  Layer 3 switching, 223–224
  network management module integration,
    226
  Server Farms, 227
  servers directly attached, 227
  split Layer 2 design, 222
Campus Backbone module, 155
Campus Backbone submodule, 166
Campus Infrastructure, route redundancy, 160
Campus Infrastructure module, 132
  building blocks, 133
  Campus Backbone, 134
  guidelines, 136
campus networks, 181, 687
  redesign case study, 710
capacity areas, 651
capacity planning, 505
  Campus IP telephony, 519–521
  DSP resources, 514
  GoS, 508
    BHT, 510
    blocking probability, 511
    CSS, 509
    Erlang, 508
    Erlang tables, 509
    overview, 508
    trunk capacity calculation, 512

network migration, 507
on-net/off-net calling, 505–506
trunking, 521
WANs, 515
  CAC, 518
  call routing alternatives, 518
  capacity calculations, 516
  combining capacity calculations with
    GoS, 517
carrier sense multiple access collision detect. *See*
  CSMA/CD
CAS (channel associated signaling), 452
CAs (Certificate Authorities), 310
case studies
  MCMB network redesign, 706–707, 710
  network design, analyzing existing networks,
    101
  network upgrades, 105
Catalyst 1900 Switch, 786
Catalyst switches, 13, 789
  configuration commands, 789
  interface configuration commands, 790
CatOS, network auditing, 73
CATV transmission, 297
CBWFQ (Class-Based Weighted Fair Queuing),
  85 , 495
CCM, clustering, 165
CCS (centum call second), 509
CDN (Content Delivery Network), 168
CDP (Cisco Discovery Protocol), 393, 623
  functionality, 624
  information, 623
  Web site, 625
  when not to run, 625
cdp enable command, 778, 790
cdp run command, 777
cells, 769
cell-switched networks, 258
CELP (Code Excited Linear Prediction
  Compression) algorithm, 486
Centrex, 457, 698
centum call second (CSS), 509

CES (circuit emulation service), 504
CGMP (Cisco Group Management Protocol), 212
channel aggregation, 162
channel associated signaling (CAS), 452
characteristics (OSI model), 760
characterizing. *See* assessing
CIDR (Classless Inter-Domain Routing), 334
ciphertext, 571
circuit emulation service (CES), 504
circuit switched calls, 522
circuit switching, 7
circuit-switched networks, 257
Cisco
    CDP, 623
        functionality, 624
        information, 623
    NetFlow, 625
        activation and data collection, 627
        vs. RMON, 629
    SAA (service assurance agents), 653
    SAFE (Security Architecture for Enterprise)
      Blueprint. *See* SAFE Blueprint
Cisco Architecture for Voice, Video and
    Integrated Data. *See* AVVID
Cisco AutoQoS, 497–498
Cisco CallManager, 522
Cisco Converged Network Investment Calculator.
    See CNIC
Cisco Discovery Protocol (CDP), 393
Cisco Group Management Protocol (CGMP), 212
Cisco IOS, 268, 309, 777
    compression services, 270
    configuration file commands, 776
    configuring IP extended access lists, 737
    data software compression types supported,
      269
    EXEC commands, 779, 783
    Express RTP Header Compression feature,
      488
    interface configuration commands, 778
    IP access list extensions, backwards
      compatibility, 726

    IP configuration commands, 780
    ip tcp selective-ack global configuration
      command, 272
    IPX commands, 782
    network auditing, 73
    queuing mechanisms, 495
      custom queuing, 274
    show interface command, 384
    syslog accounting, 629
    TCP intercept feature, 556
    traffic shaping, 276
Cisco MIB, 616
Cisco NetFlow, 79
Cisco SAFE Blueprint, 702
Cisco Secure PIX firewalls, network auditing, 73
Cisco Secure Scanner, 72
CiscoWorks 2000, 642
class of service (CoS), 81
Class-Based Weighted Fair Queuing (CBWFQ),
    85, 495
classes
    IP addresses, 719–720
      prefix length, 323, 692
      subnetting, 21
    IPv4 addresses, subnetting, 19
classful addresses, 720-721
classful distance vector protocols, 388
classful routing, 341
Classless Inter-Domain Routing (CIDR), 334
classless routing, 342
clear counters command, 774
clear frame-relay-inarp command, 783
clear ip nat translation command, 779
clear line command, 774
clearing NAT entries, 811
client-client applications, 185, 190
client-distributed server applications, 186
client-Enterprise Edge applications, 188
client-server farm applications, 187
clock rate command, 778
clock set command, 774
clustering, 165

CMTS (Cable Modem Termination System), 295-296

CN (Content Networking), 168
    content delivery functions, 169
        content caching, 169–170
        content routing, 171
        content switching, 172
    example, 173

CNIC (Cisco Converged Network Investment Calculator), 63

CO trunks, 448

Code Excited Linear Prediction Compression (CELP) algorithm, 486

codecs, 466
    G.729, 489
    mean opinion score, 486
    voice coding and compression, 486-487

collision domains, 191

commands, 810
    access-class, 746
    AppleTalk (table), 783
    AppleTalk configuration (table), 783
    Catalyst 1900/Catalyst 2950 Switch IOS, 786
    Catalyst switch configuration, 789
    configuration
        Catalyst switch interface, 790
        WAN interfaces, 785
    ICND router, 773–774
    interface configuration (table), 778–779
    IP (table), 779–780
    ip access group, 731
    IPX, 782
    IPX configuration, 782
    line vty, 745
    response time, 262
    WAN configuration (table), 785–786

common channel signaling (CSS), 452

common Server Farms, 187

communication (applications), 185

communication protocols, 761

companding, 443–444

comparing configuration file commands, 776–777

compressed Real-Time Transport Protocol (cRTP), 490

compression, 269–270, 699
    affect on performance, 271
    dictionary, 270
    disabling, 271
    hardware-assisted, 271
    RTP, 271
    statistical, 270

compulsory tunnels (VPDN), 307

concatenation. *See* ANDing

confidentiality threats, 547

config-register command, 777

configuration commands, 789
    Catalyst switch interface, 790
    IP, 780
    WAN interfaces, 785

configuration file commands, 776–777

configuration management, 635
    configuration standards, 636
    configuration tools
        CiscoWorks 2000, 642
        protocols, 641
    functions and importance of, 635
    inventory, 637
    naming conventions, 638
    software, 637
    standard configuration and descriptors, 639
    upgrade procedures, 639

configure network command, 776

configure overwrite-network command, 777

configure terminal command, 774, 787

configuring
    access lists, 746–747
    extended IP access lists, 735–739
    IP access lists
        ensuring results, 732
        standard, 730
    NAT
        basic local IP address translation, 806
        inside global address overloading, 807

TCP load distribution, 809-810

translating overlapping addresses, 808

queuing, 273

congestion

dejitter buffers, 481

queuing, 272-274

traffic shaping, 276

congestion avoidance QoS mechanism, 494

congestion management QoS mechanism, 495

Conjugate Structure-Algebraic Code Excited Linear Prediction Compression (CS-ACELP) algorithm, 485

connect command, 774

connecting Enterprise Edge modules with outside world, 260

connection-oriented protocols, 25

connections

best efforts, 259

dark fiber, 290

remote access, 277

always-on connections, 280–281

backup solutions, 283–285

design as process, 283

dispersed Enterprise sites, 288, 290

evaluating parameters, 278–279

IP connectivity, 291–298, 300–302

on-demand connections, 280

packet switched topologies, 281–282

VPNs, 304–308

WANs, 259

connectivity

AS, 695

bridges, 10

hubs, 9

links, 161

media access, 6

multi-homing, 405

switches, 10

WANs, 7

consistency, 639

constituencies. *See* stakeholders

constraint assessment, 55-57

constraints (technical), 62

content caching (CN), 169-170

Content Delivery Network (CDN), 168

Content Networking. *See* CN

content routing (CN), 169-171

content switching (CN), 169, 172

contention access, 6

control information (OSI model), 763

control plane, 647

controller command, 785

controlling vty access, 744

converged networks, 463

convergence, 201

IS-IS, 402

OSPF, 399

RIPv2, 386

routing protocols, 385-387

STP, 196

converting

decimal-to-binary (chart), 716–717

IP addresses between decimal and binary, 718

copper cable

deployment area, 204

uses and limitations, 204

vs. fiber cables, 203

copy flash tftp command, 774

copy ftp: nvram:startup-config command, 777

copy ftp: system:running-config command, 776

copy nvram tftp://{host}/{file} command, 787

copy rcp running-config command, 776

copy rcp startup-config command, 777

copy rcp: nvram:startup-config command, 777

copy rcp: system:running-config command, 776

copy running-config rcp command, 777

copy running-config startup-config command, 774, 777

copy running-config tftp command, 774, 777

copy startup-config running config command, 774

copy startup-config tftp command, 774

copy startup-config tftp://{host}/{file} command, 787

copy system:running-config ftp: command, 777

copy system:running-config nvram:startup-config command, 777

copy system:running-config rcp: command, 777

copy system:running-config tftp: command, 777

copy tftp flash command, 774

copy tftp running-config command, 775–776

copy tftp startup-config command, 775, 777

copy tftp: nvram:startup-config command, 777

copy tftp: system:running-config command, 776

copy tftp://{host}/{file} nvram command, 787

core layer (network hierarchy model), 125, 684

    L2 vs. L3 switching, 126

    role of, 125

    route redistribution, 413

    routing protocols, 408–409

CoS (cost of service), 441

CoS (class of service), 81

cost

    applications, 191

    cabling, 205

    Centrex service (PSTN telephony), 457

    hierarchical network design models, 118

    off-net calculation, 512

    ROI, 63

    secondary links, 285

    shared vs. switched LAN technology, 194

    WANs, 265

CQ (custom queuing), 273, 495

creating

    access lists, 730

    design decision tables, 91

cRTP (compressed Real-Time Transport Protocol), 490

cryptography, 558, 571–573, 701

CS-ACELP (Conjugate Structure-Algebraic Code Excited Linear Prediction Compression) algorithm, 485

CSMA/CD (carrier sense multiple access collision detect), 6

CSS (common channel signaling), 452

CSU/DSU (channel service unit/digital service unit), 8

Ctrl+a command, 773

Ctrl+b command, 773

Ctrl+c command, 773

Ctrl+e command, 773

Ctrl+f command, 774

Ctrl+n command, 774

Ctrl+p command, 774

Ctrl+r command, 774

Ctrl+Shift+6 x command, 774

Ctrl+u command, 774

Ctrl+w command, 774

Ctrl+z command, 774, 777

cumulative delay metric, 382

current window, 271–272

custom queuing (CQ), 273-274, 495

cut-through switches, 12

D

dark fiber, 290

data

    compression, 269–270, 699

        disabling, 271

        encoding techniques, 270

        hardware assisted, 271

        performance, affect on, 271

        supported by Cisco IOS software, 269

    decapsulated/un-encapsulated, 5

    encapsulation, 4

    integrity, 572–574

    security, 310

    throughput, 262

    transmission confidentiality, 570

        encryption, 571

        guidelines, 572

    voice transport, 697

data flows, 23-24, 296

data gathering (design process)

    initial requirements, 51

    network requirements, 52

organizational constraints, 55-57
organizational goals, 53–55
planned applications and network services,
57-60
technical constraint identification, 62–63
technical goals, 60–62
data link layer (OSI model), 256, 765
frames, 768
OSI model, 5
Data Link Switching Plus (DLSw+), 27
data networks, migrating to an integrated
network, 507
data plane, 647
data terminating equipment (DTE), 8
data transmission, 6
acknowledgment, 272
packet loss, 263
WANs, 7
window size, 271–272
data units, 769–770
datagrams, 352, 769
data-link layer technologies, 191-193
data-link switching (DLSw), 26
DDoS attacks, 556
DDR (dial-on-demand routing), 7, 280
debug appletalk routing command, 783
debug command, 775
debug dialer command, 783
debug eigrp neighbors command, 779
debug frame-relay lmi command, 784
debug ip eigrp command, 779
debug ip igrp command, 779
debug ip nat command, 779, 812
debug ip ospf events command, 779
debug ip ospf packet command, 779
debug ip rip command, 779
debug ipx routing activity command, 782
debug ipx sap activity command, 782
debug isdn q921 command, 784
debug isdn q931 command, 784
debug ppp authentication command, 784
debug ppp error command, 784

debug ppp negotiation command, 784
decapsulated data, 5
decimal-to-binary conversion chart, 716–717
decision tables, 91
guidelines, 92
template, 93
dedicated-connection cell switching technologies,
258
default gateways, 157
defining organizational policies, 37–38
dejitter buffers, 481
delay metric, 382
delay-sensitive traffic, 24
delete nvram command, 787
delete vtp command, 787
delta frames, 24
demilitarized zone (DMZ) network, 581
Denial of Service attacks. *See* DoS attacks
Dense Wavelength Division Multiplexing. *See*
DWDM
deny conditions, 725
deploying SAA, 668
deployment area, copper vs. fiber cable, 204
description command, 778
descriptors, 639
design implementation, 95–96
design methodology, 268, 683
(Design phase (PDIOO), 682
designing
ADSL point-to-point protocol networks, 293
Enterprise Campus networks, 181, 206
application characterization, 185–188
data-link layer technologies, 191-193
design considerations, 182
Layer 2/Layer 3 switching, 194–195,
198–199
module requirements, 207
network geography, 182-184
transmission media, 201–202
IP addressing, 319, 322
assigning addresses, 343–345
case study, 370

determining network size, 325
dynamic IPv6 renumbering, 359
evaluating location size, 327–328
hierarchy criteria, 336
implementing hierarchy, 334
IPv4 compatible IPv6 addresses, 357
IPv6 address assignment, 358
IPv6 name resolution, 360
IPv6 overview, 355–356
IPv6 routing protocols, 366
name resolution, 347–349
network size, 328–329
network topology, 326–327
pitfalls, 338
public vs. private addresses, 331
route aggregation, 339
routing protocols, 341
subnet masking choice, 339
summarization groups, 336
transitioning between IPv4 and IPv6,
362-364
link redundancy, 161
networks, 117. *See also* Enterprise
Composite Network Model
applications and network services, 57–
60
assessing existing networks, 64–67, 70–
84
assessing organizational constraints,
55-57
campus, 687
customer requirements, 49
decision tables, 91–93
documentation, 97
draft design documents, 85–86
Enterprise Campus,
208–217, 219–226, 231
Enterprise Campus (case study), 234
Enterprise Campus/Enterprise Network
connectivity, 230
Enterprise Composite Network Model,
128, 684

Hierarchicical Network model, 118, 684
high availability, 155
implementation and verification, 98
importance of effective design, 33
IP telephony, 63, 472
methodology, 47–48
monitoring and redesigning, 99
network requirements, 52
network solutions, 163
OSI model, 49
PDIOO, 44–45
planning design implementation, 95–96
prototypes and pilots, 97
redesign case study, 706–707, 710
RFPs/RFIs, 50
scope, 49
security. *See* security
structured approach, 87
technical constraint identification,
62–63
technical goals, 60–62
telephony. *See* telephony systems
tools, 94
top-down approach, 87, 90
top-down approach vs. bottom-up, 89
understanding organizational goals, 53
understanding organizations'
procedures, 29
VoFR, 500
voice transport, 441, 697
WANs, 688
route redundancy, 159-160
WANs, 256
analyzing customer requirements, 261
application requirements, 262–263
characterizing the existing network, 261
cost effectiveness, 265
methodology, 260
remote access, 277–280
response time, 264
selecting technologies, 276
technical requirements, 263–264

topology and network solutions, 261
trade-offs, 261
determining, 719
devices, 18
bridges, 10-12
IP addressing, 21
IPX addressing, 25
LANs, 9
media access, 6
port numbers, 17
routers, 13–14
security
guidelines, 551
risks, 550
standard configuration, 639
switches, 10-12
WANs, 8
DHCP servers, assigning IP addresses, 346
dial backup, 7
dial backup routing, 284
dial peers, 476-477
dialer idle-timeout command, 785
dialer load-threshold command, 785
dialer map command, 785
dialer pool command, 785
dialer pool-member command, 785
dialer string command, 785
dialer-group command, 785
dialer-list list command, 785
dialer-list protocol command, 785
dial-on-demand routing (DDR), 7, 280
dialup services, 7
dictionary compression, 270
Diffusing Update Algorithm (DUAL), 23
digital certificates, 310
digital devices (CSU/DSU), 8
Digital Private Network Signaling System
(DPNSS), 445
digital signal processors (DSPs), 470, 700

digital signaling, 442, 452
ISDN, 452
SS7, 453
digital signatures, 572–573, 701
Digital Subscriber Line. *See* DSL
directed broadcasts, 192
disable command, 775, 787
disabling STP, 217
disconnect command, 775
discovery (address)
ARP, 157
explicit configuration, 157
HSRP (Hot Standby Router Protocol), 158
routing protocols, 157
VRRP, 158
dispersed sites, 691
distance vector protocols, 376
BGP, 404
example, 377–378
selection guidelines, 380
distance-vector routing algorithms, 16
distant remote building network structure, 184
Distribution layer (Hierarchical Network model),
684
controlling traffic, 124
designing Enterprise Campus networks, 216,
219–220
features, 125
role of, 123
routing protocols, 409
distribution switches, 219
DLS (data-link switching), 258
DLSw, 26
DLSw+ (Data Link Switching Plus), 27
DMZ (demilitarized zone) network, 581
DNS servers, IP address name resolution, 349
documentation
audit trails, 575
design implementation, 95
draft design documents, 85
network design, 97
security policies, 560

domains
  failure, 200
  policy, 200
  routing, intradomain vs. interdomain, 16
don't care bits, 729
DoS (Denial of Service) attacks, 152-153, 548–549, 553–554
  application targets, 557–558
  distributed DoS (DDOS) attacks, 554-556
  protection guidelines, 555
  TCP SYN-flooding, 556
dotted decimal notation, 18, 321
<down arrow> command, 774
downstream, 291
DPNSS (Digital Private Network Signaling System), 445
draft design documents, 85–86
DSL (Digital Subscriber Line), 255, 258
  asymmetric, 291-293
  Cisco's FAQs web site, 259
  remote access implications, 291
  symmetric, 291
  xDSL, 292
DSPs (digital signal processors), 470, 700
DSTM translation mechanism, 366
DTE (data terminating equipment), 8
DTMF (dual tone multifrequency), 460
DUAL (Diffusing Update Algorithm), 23
dual-path Layer 3 campus backbone design, 225
dual-stack transition mechanism, 362
duplex command, 790
DWDM (Dense Wavelength Division Multiplexing), 289
dynamic IP address assignment, 344–345
dynamic name resolution, 348, 360
dynamic routing, 375–376
dynamic routing algorithms, 15
dynamic switched VoFR calls, 499

E

E&M (ear and mouth) signaling, 451
E3, 143
EAP (Extensible Authentication Protocol), 589
EBGP (external BGP), 406, 417, 422, 696
echo, 483
E-commerce module, 139, 583
ecosystems, 31–32
Edge Distribution module (Enterprise Campus networks), 132, 135-136, 230-231
edge routing protocols, 409
EGPs (exterior gateway protocols), 380, 406
egress edge LSRs, 302
EIGRP (Enhanced Internet Gateway Routing Protocol), 23
  characteristics, 397
  convergence, 388
  features, 395–396
  metric calculation, 383–384
  terminology, 396
  when to use, 391
emerging WAN technologies
  cable, 259
  comparing, 267
  DSL, 258
  LRE, 259
  MPLS, 259
  wireless, 259
enable command, 775, 787
enable password command, 777
enable secret command, 777
encapsulation, 763
  bridging, 11
  OSI model, 4
encapsulation command, 785
encapsulation dot1q command, 778
encapsulation isl command, 779
encoding techniques (data compression), 270
encryption, 571, 701
  3DES, 572
  802.11i, 590

end command, 777
end system (ES), 400
Enhanced Internet Gateway Routing Protocol. *See*
    EIGRP
<Enter> command, 774
Enterprise Campus networks, 130, 685
    building internal security, 150
    connectivity to rest of Enterprise Network,
        230
    designing, 181, 206-208
        access and distribution layers, 216–220
        application characterization, 185–188
        campus backbone, 221–226
        case study, 234
        data-link layer technologies, 191-193
        design considerations, 182
        Layer 2/Layer 3 switching, 194–195,
            198–199
    Edge Distribution module, 230-231
    modules, 132, 686
        Campus Infrastructure, 133
        Edge Distribution, 135, 230-231
        example, 135
        guidelines, 136
        Network Management, 134
        requirements, 207
        Server Farm, 134
    multicast traffic considerations, 211–212
    network geography, 182-184
    network traffic patterns, 209–210
    QoS considerations, 213–214
    security threats, 149
    Server Farm module
        design guidelines, 228
        server connectivity, 229
        switches, 227
    server placement, 226
    transmission media, 201–202
Enterprise Composite Network Model,
    117, 163, 684
    benefits, 129
    E-commerce module, 583

Enterprise Campus, 132–134
    example, 135
    guidelines, 136
Enterprise Edge, 137–141, 255–256
evolution of enterprise networks, 128
functional areas, 130
goals of, 129
intelligent network services, 145
    example, 147
    overview, 146
    security, 149–151
Internet Connectivity module, 580
layers, 685
modules, 127, 130
network hierarchy, 117
    access layer, 120–121
    core layer, 125–126
    design layers, 118
    distribution layer, 123–125
    vs. OSI model, 120
Network Management module, 593–594
network solutions, 145, 163. *See also*
    network solutions
overview, 128
Remote Access and VPN module, 585–591
SAFE Blueprint, 579
security
    E-commerce module, 583
    Internet Connectivity module, 580
    Network Management module, 593–594
    Remote Access and VPN module,
        585–591
    Server Farm module, 595
    WAN module, 591–592
Server Farm module, 595
Service Provider Edge
    guidelines, 144
    modules, 141-143
WAN module, 591–592
Enterprise Edge functional area, 230
Enterprise Edge module, 166

Enterprise Edge networks, 255–256, 685
  connecting
      dispersed sites, 288-290
      with outside world, 260
  link redundancy, 162
  modules, 137, 686
      E-commerce, 139
      guidelines, 141
      Internet Connectivity, 139
      VPN/Remote Access, 140
      WAN, 140–141
  redundant links, 268
  remote access connections, 277
  WAN design methodology, 255
Enterprise Networks
  CN (Content Networking), 168
      content caching, 169–170
      content delivery functions, 169
      content routing, 171
      content switching, 172
      example, 173
  connectivity with Enterprise Campus, 230
  redundancy, 156
  voice transport, 164
      evaluating existing data infrastructure,
        167–168
      IP telephony, 164–165
      modules, 166
      network solution example, 166
erase nvram: command, 777
erase startup-config command, 775, 787
Erlangs, 508, 511
errors
  checking, 4, 766
  encapsulation, 4
  recovery, 766
  reporting, 629
ES (end system), 400
Esc+b command, 774
Esc+f command, 774
established keyword (IP extended access lists),
  739

Ethernet, 5, 191
EtherPeek, 79
EUI-64 format interface ID, 358
evaluating
  technical constraints of network design, 63
  technical goals of proposed network, 62
events (fault management), 634
Events group (RMON1), 619
exception management, 649
EXEC commands, 779
exec-timeout 0 0 command, 777
existing networks (case study), 101
exit command, 775, 778
explicit configuration, 157
Express RTP Header Compression feature, 488
extended access lists
  configuring, 735–739
  example, 742–743
  placement, 744
  process flow, 735
  wildcard masks, 729
extending IP addresses
  classful addresses, 721
  job aids, 716–718
Extensible Authentication Protocol (EAP), 589
exterior gateway protocols (EGPs), 380, 406
exterior routing protocols, 380
external security threats, 152
  application layer attacks, 153
  designing against, 154
  DoS attacks, 153
extranet VPN, 304

F

failure domain, 200
FAQs (frequently asked questions), 259
fast, 227
Fast EtherChannel (FEC), 204
Fast Ethernet, 5
fast switching, 286
fault

fault management, 632
  architecture, 633
  event processing, 634
  isolation (hierarchical network models), 118
  tolerance, 125
FCAPS, 632, 704
  accounting management, 642–645
  configuration management, 635
    configuration standards, 636
    configuration tools, 642
    functions and importance of, 635
    inventory, 637
    naming conventions, 638
    software, 637
    upgrade procedures, 639
  fault management, 632
    architecture, 633
    event processing, 634
  performance management, 646
    capacity areas, 651
    challenges, 651–652
    defining a process for, 650
    exceptions, 649
    goal of, 647
    performance data reporting, 650
    SLM, 648
    solutions, 652–653
    tools, 653
    what-if analysis, 648
  security management
    examples, 656
    protocols, 655
FDDI, token passing media access, 6
feasible successor, 397
FEC (Fast EtherChannel), 204
FEC (Fowarding Equivalence Class), 301
FIB (Forwarding Information Base), 287
fiber cable
  deployment area, 204
  vs. copper cables, 203
FIFO (first-in, first-out), 273
file-transfer activities, 262

filtering, 570
  packets, 725–726
  route, 414
Filters group (RMON1), 619
firewalls, authentication, 565
Fixed Length Subnet Masking (FLSM), 340
flash updates, 378
flat routing algorithms, 16
flat routing protocols, 388
floating static routes, 162
flooding, 212
flow control, 765–766
Flow Label field (IPv6), 352
flow specifications (RSVP), 23
FLSM (Fixed Length Subnet Masking), 340
Forward Delay timer (STP), 196
Forwarding Information Base (FIB), 287
forwarding unicast packets, 192
FQDNs (Fully Qualified Domain Names), 349
FR (Frame Relay), 255, 258
  always-on connections, 281
  remote access connections, 279
  traffic shaping, 276
Frame Relay/ATM module, 143
frame-relay interface dlci command, 785
frame-relay inverse-arp command, 785
frame-relay lmi-type command, 785
frame-relay map command, 785
frames, 11, 24, 768. *See also* packets
framing command, 786
full-mesh networks, 160, 281-282, 500
Fully Qualified Domain Names (FQDNs), 349
functional elements, 88
FX (foreign exchange) trunks, 448

G

G.729 codec, 489
GAAP (Generally Accepted Accounting
  Principles), 36
gatekeepers, 468
gateways, 467

general configuration commands (table), 777–778

general interface configuration commands (table), 778–779

General Packet Radio Service (GPRS), 298

Generally Accepted Accounting Principles (GAAP), 36

Generic Traffic Shaping (GTS), 494

Get next request message, 610

Get request message, 610

Get response message, 610

GetBulk messages, 611

Gigabit Ether Channel, 204

Gigabit Ethernet, 5

global addresses, 803–804

global aggregatable unicast addresses, 355

Global Positioning Systems (GPS), 259

Global System for Mobile (GSM), 298

goals (organizational), 54

GoS (Grade of Service), 505, 508

    BHT, 510

    blocking probability, 511

    combining calculations with WAN capacity calculations, 517

    CSS, 509

    Erlang tables, 508-509

    overview, 508

    trunk capacity calculation, 512

GPRS (General Packet Radio Service), 298

GPS (Global Positioning Systems), 259

GRE, 309

ground start signaling method, 451

groups (MIB), 615

GSM (Global System for Mobile), 298

GTS (Generic Traffic Shaping), 494

guaranteed bit-rate service, 24

guidelines for creating decision tables, 91

H

H.225 call signaling channel, 489

H.323 standard, 466, 698

    benefits, 466

    components, 467

    example, 470

H245 control channel, 489

hardware

    DSPs, 700

    queuing, 273, 690

    selecting for WANs, 268

    switches, 12

    WANs, 8

HDSL (High-data-rate DSL), 258

headers, 763, 768

health (networks), 76, 84

HFC (Hybrid Fiber Coaxial) topology, 296

HIDSs (Host Intrusion Detection Systems), 575

hierarchical addresses, 320

Hierarchical Network model, 118, 684

    design layers, 118

        access layer, 120–121

        core layer, 125–126

        distribution layer, 123–125

    vs. OSI model, 120

hierarchical routing algorithms, 16

hierarchical routing protocols, 389

hierarchies

    IP addressing

        criteria, 336

        implementing, 334

    MIB, 613

    networks, 117

    organizations, 39

high availability network services, 146, 191

    designing into networks, 155

    link redundancy, 161

    route redundancy, 159–160

    Server Farm module

        physical redundancy, 159

        high availability services, 156–157

    shared vs. switched LAN technology, 194

high-data-rate DSL (HDSL), 258

History group (RMON1), 619

history size command, 778

hold-down, 386

hop counts, 379, 382

horizontal integration, 31

host addresses, 22, 322

Host group (RMON1), 619

host-intelligent routing algorithms, 16

Host Intrusion Detection Systems (HIDSs), 575

Host top N group (RMON1), 619

hostname command, 778, 789

hosts, security

    concerns, 557

    guidelines, 558

    threats, 580

hosts per class (IP addresses), 719

HP OpenView, IBM Tivoli, 72

HSRP (Hot Standby Router Protocol), 158, 227

HTTP (Hyper Text Transfer Protocol), 654

hub and spoke topology (VoFR networks), 501

hubs, 9, 26

Hybrid Fiber Coaxial (HFC) topology, 296

hybrid interior gateway protocol, 377

hybrid routing algorithms, 16

Hyper Text Transfer Protocol (HTTP), 654

I

IANA (Internet Assigned Number Authority) web site, 324

IBGP (internal BGP), 406, 422, 696

IBM SNA (Systems Network Architecture), 26

ICMP (Internet Control Message Protocol), 17

    messages, 727

    ping, 652

ICMP group (MIB), 615

ICND router commands, 773–774

identifying devices, 9

IDSs, 150, 575

IETF standards, MPPP (Multilink Point-to-Point Protocol), 162

IGMP snooping, 212

IGPs (Interior Gateway Protocols), 380

    RIP (Routing Information Protocol), 22

    route filtering, 415

IGRP (Interior Gateway Routing Protocols)

    metric calculation, 383–384

    when to use, 391

IKE (Internet Key Exchange), 309

Implement phase (PDIOO), 682

implementing

    campus backbone, 221

    IP addressing hierarchy, 334-336

    network design, 95

    WANs, 268

implicit deny any entries (access lists), 728

implicit wildcard masks, 731

information exchange process (OSI model), 763–764

information flow (organizations), 40

information formats, 768–769

ingress edge LSRs, 302

initiating RSVP multicast sessions, 24

inside global IP addresses, 800, 803–804

inside local IP addresses, 800-801

integrated IS-IS, 696

integrated networks

    capacity planning, 505

        Campus IP telephony, 519–521

        DSP resources, 514

        GoS, 508–512

        network migration, 507

        on-net/off-net calling, 505–506

        trunking, 521

        WANs, 515–518

Integrated Services Digital Network (ISDN), 255

integrity threats, 547

intelligent network services, 59, 219

    example, 147

    high availability

        designing into networks, 155

        link redundancy, 161

        route redundancy, 159–160

        Server Farm module, 156–159

    network design stage, 59

    overview, 146

security
    AAA, 151
    external threats, 152–154
    IDS, 150
    OTPs, 151
    understanding threats, 149
  shared vs. switched LAN technology, 193
interactive voice response (IVR) systems.
  See IVR systems, 460, 698
inter-AS routing protocols, 380
inter-building network structure, 183
interdomain routing algorithms, 16
interface command, 778–779, 789
interface configuration commands (table),
  778–779
Interface group (MIB), 615
interface serial numbers (devices), 9
interface vlan 1 command, 789
interior gateway protocols. *See* IGPs
Interior Gateway Routing Protocol. *See* IGRP
interior routing protocols, 380
  integrating with BGP, 416–417
  selecting, 403–404
International Organization for Standardization
  (ISO), 3
Internet
  QoS, 23
  route redistribution, 414
  TCP/IP
    application layer, 18
    network layer, 16
    transport layer, 17
  as a WAN backup technology, 308–309
Internet Connectivity module, 139, 580, 702
Internet Control Message Protocol. *See* ICMP
Internet Key Exchange (IKE), 309
Internet Performance Monitor (IPM), 671
Internet Protocol. *See* IP
Internet Service Provider module, 142
Internet service providers (ISPs), 259, 324

internetworking, 31
  devices, 9-10
  LANs
    characteristics, 5
    circuit switching, 7
    data transmission, 6
    Ethernet, 5
    MAC addressing, 9
    network layer addressing, 9
  WANs
    characteristics, 6
    devices, 8
    dialup services, 7
    packet switching, 7
    provisioning, 8
    virtual circuits, 7
internetworks, 3
interswitch communications, 448
intra-AS routing protocols, 380-381
intradomain routing algorithms, 16
intranet VPN, 304
IP (Internet Protocol), 16, 259
  access lists, 725
    backwards compatibility, 726
    configuring, 728-730
    creating, 730
    ensuring results, 732
    implicit deny any entries, 728
    implicit wildcard masks, 731
    standard, 727
    verifying configuration, 746–747
  accounting, 643
  addresses, 691
    classes, 692
    converting between decimal and binary,
      718
    determining classes, 719
    private addresses, 692
  configuration commands, 780
  extended access lists
    configuring, 735–739
    example, 742–743
    placement, 744

H.323, 466
job aids, 715
precedence, 494
remote access options, 291–294
    cable networks, 295-297
    DSL, 291
    LRE technology, 294
    MPLS, 300–302
    wireless networks, 298-300
routing, 390, 696
security, 545
    algorithms, 546
    availability threats, 548
    confidentiality threats, 547
    devices as targets, 550-551
    DoS attacks, 554-556
    hosts and applications as targets, 557–558
    integrity threats, 547
    reconnaissance attacks, 553
    requirements, 546
    risk assessment, 549
ip access-group command, 731, 780
ip access-list command, 780
IP access lists, 726
    standard
        configuring, 730
        example, 733
        processing, 728
    wildcard masks, 729
ip address command, 780, 789
IP addressing, 21
    ANDing, 21–22
    classes, 323, 720
    configuration management, 638
    default gateway, 157
    depletion, 799
    designing, 319
        assigning addresses, 343–345
        case study, 370
        determining network size, 325
        evaluating location size, 327–328

hierarchy criteria, 336
implementing hierarchy, 334
name resolution, 347–349
network size, 328–329
network topology, 326–327
pitfalls, 338
route aggregation, 339
routing protocols, 341
subnet masking choice, 339
summarization groups, 336
dotted decimal notation, 18
EXEC commands (table), 779–780
extending, 716–718
hierarchical, 320
host addresses, 322
IPv4. *See* IPv4
IPv6, 350, 355. *See also* IPv6
    address assignment strategies, 358
    address scope types, 356
    dynamic renumbering, 359
    IPv4 compatible addresses, 357
    name resolution, 360
    routing protocols, 366
NAT
    configuration, 806
    configuring, 807–810
    entries, clearing, 811
    inside global addresses, overloading, 804
    overloading inside global addresses, 803
    TCP load distribution, 805
    terminology, 800
    translating inside local addresses, 801
    troubleshooting, 812
    verifying operation, 810
octets, 18, 321
overlapping networks, 804
prefixes, 323, 692
private addresses, 329-331, 334
route summarization, 334–335

subnet masks
    calculating, 721–722
    calculating networks for, 723
    prefixes, 724–725
    transitioning between IPv4 and IPv6,
      362-364
ip classless command, 781
IP configuration commands (table), 780–781
ip default-gateway command, 789
ip domain-lookup command, 781
IP extended access lists, 735
IP group (MIB), 615
ip host command, 781
IP multicasting network services, 146
ip name-server command, 781
ip nat command, 781
ip netmask-format command, 781
IP Network Address Translator, 799
IP networks, transporting SNA data, 26
IP phones, 165
ip route command, 781
IP RTP Priority queuing, 495
IP spoofing, 152
ip subnet-zero global configuration command, 20
ip summary-address rip command, 394
ip tcp selective-ack global configuration
    command, 272
IP telephony systems, 164, 698
    architecture, 471
    bandwidth, 489
      reducing traffic, 490
      requirements, 490–491
    capacity planning, 519–521
    centralized design, 473
    CNIC, 63
    components, 165
    design goals, 472
    implementation, 165
    Internet design, 474
    QoS and voice quality, 492
      AutoQoS, 497
      design considerations, 492
      mechanisms available, 493

security, 597
    best practices, 598
    risks, 599
single site design, 472
VoATM
    adaptation types, 503
    classes of services, 502
    design guidelines, 504
    overview, 502
VoFR, 498
    design guidelines, 500
    implementations, 499
voice coding and compression, 485
    codec design considerations, 487
    codec mean opinion score, 486
    codecs, 486
voice quality, 477
    echo, 483
    packet delays, 478–479
    variable network delays, 480-482
VoIP control and transport protocols, 487
    call control functions, 489
    RTP, 488
    UDP, 487
    vs. VoIP, 470
IPM (Internet Performance Monitor), 671
IPSec, 309-310, 589
IPv4, 715. *See also* IP
    addressing, 18, 319
      classes, 19
      hierarchical, 320
      host addresses, 322
      subnets, 19, 325
    IPv6 address backwards compatible, 357
    private/public addresses, 329-331, 334
    transitioning to IPv6, 362-364
    vs. IPv6, 361
IPv6, 693. *See also* IP
    addresses
      assignment strategies, 358
      format, 351
      scope types, 354–356

datagram structure, 352
dynamic renumbering, 359
features, 351
Flow Label field, 352
IPv4 compatible addresses, 357
name resolution, 360
overview, 350
routing protocols, 366
transitioning from IPv4, 362-364
vs. IPv4, 361
ipx access-group command, 782
IPX addressing, 25
IPX commands (table), 782
IPX configuration commands (table), 782
ipx delay command, 782
ipx input-sap-filter command, 782
ipx maximum-paths command, 782
ipx network command, 782
ipx output-sap-filter command, 782
ipx routing command, 782
irritation zones, 485
ISDN (Integrated Services Digital Network), 255
    digital signaling, 452
    remote access connections, 279
    TA (terminal adapter), 8
isdn spid1 command, 786
isdn spid2 command, 786
isdn switch-type command, 786
IS-IS
    characteristics, 402
    disadvantages, 403
    features, 400–401
    terminology, 400
    when to use, 392
IS-ISv6, 367
ISO (International Organization for Standardization), 3
ISO network management model
    functional areas, 632
        accounting management, 642–645
        configuration management, 635–639, 642

fault management, 632–634
performance management, 646–653
security management, 654–656
service levels
    challenges, 659
    constituent SLAs, 658
    management applications, 670–671, 674
    reporting, 664
    requirements, 660
    SAA, 666–667
    SLAs, 657
    SLM, 663–664
ISPs (Internet service providers), 259, 324
ITU, voice coding and compression standards, 486
IVR (interactive voice response) systems, 460, 698

J

jitter, 482
job aids, decimal-to-binary conversion chart, 716–717

K

key frames, 24

L

L2 switching, 121, 126
L3 switching, 121, 126
Label Distribution Protocol (LDP) , 301
Label Switched Paths (LSPs), 301
Label Switched Routers (LSRs), 301-302
LANs, 3
    authentication, 565
    bandwidth, 265
    bridges, 10

campus, 181
characteristics, 5
CSMA/CD, 6
data transmission, 6
devices
    routers, 13–14
    switches vs. bridges, 12
Ethernet, 5, 191
hubs, 9
MAC addressing, 9
network layer addressing, 9
protocols, 761
RMON, 617
shared vs. switched, 235
switched LAN technology, 192
switches, 10
    considerations, 194
    QoS, 214
technologies, 5
VLANs, 12–13
wireless, 298, 589
    802.11b, 588
    EAP, 589
    IPSec, 589
    security, 587
LAPB (Link Access Procedure Balanced) payload
  compression, 269
Layer 2 switching, 194, 221
  campus backbone design, 221
  load sharing, 198
  multicast aware, 209
  STP, 195
  vs. Layer 3 switching, 241
Layer 3 switching, 194–195
  campus backbone design, 223–224
  dual-path campus backbone design, 225
  load sharing, 198–199
  vs. Layer 2 switching, 241
Layer 3 tunnels, 308

layers
  Enterprise Composite Network model, 685
  Hierarchical Network model, 684
  Network Organizational architecture, 682
  OSI model, 4X, 25
  TCP/IP
    application layer, 18
    network layer, 16
    transport layer, 17
  upper layer protocols, 18. *See also*
    application layer
LD-CELP (Low-Delay-Code Excited Linear
  Prediction Compression) algorithm, 485
LDP (Label Distribution Protocol), 301
leased lines, 143, 257
leased WANs, 7, 266
least privilege concept, 567
LEDs (light emitting diodes), 202
legacy SNA (Systems Network Architecture), 26
Lempel-Ziv algorithm, 270
Lempel-Ziv Stack (LZS) algorithm, 269
line command, 778
line vty command, 745
linecode command, 786
Link Access Procedure Balanced (LAPB) payload
  compression, 269
link-local unicast addresses, 356
link redundancy, 161
links
  backup, 268
  optimizing performance, 263
  point-to-point, 7
  queuing to improve performance, 272
  redundancy, 161, 268
  serial lines, 7
  WANs, 285
  window size, 271–272
  WWW, 751–752, 757
link-state protocols, 377
  example, 379
  OSPF, 23
  selection guidelines, 380

link-state routing algorithms, 16
LLC (Logical Link Control), 765–766
LLQ (Low Latency Queuing), 495
load balancing, 159
load sharing, 198-200
local addresses, translating, 801
local loops, 448
logging synchronous command, 778
logical addresses, 9
logical ANDing, 21–22
logical networks, 18
login command, 778, 789
logout command, 775
Long Reach Ethernet (LRE), 258–259, 294
loop start signaling method, 451
Low-Delay-Code Excited Linear Prediction
    Compression (LD-CELP) algorithm, 485
Low Latency Queuing (LLQ), 495
lower layers (OSI model), 760
LRE (Long Reach Ethernet), 258–259, 294
LSPs (Label Switched Paths), 301
LSRs (Label Switched Routers), 301-302
LZS (Lempel-Ziv Stack) algorithm, 269

M

MAC (Media Access Control) addressing, 9,
    765–766
mac-address-table permanent command, 789
mac-address-table restricted static command, 789
mac-address-table static command, 789
MAC-layer addresses, 320
management, 118
    CDP, 623
        functionality, 624
        information, 623
    Cisco MIB, 616
    functional areas, 632
        accounting management, 642–645
        configuration management, 635–639,
            642
        fault management, 632–634
        performance management, 646–653
        security management, 654–656
    MIB, 613
        example, 617
        private managed objects, 615
        vendor-specific definitions, 615
    MIB-II, 615
    NetFlow, 625
        activation and data collection, 627
        functionality, 626
        vs. RMON, 629
    network, 607-609
    protocols, 607
    RMON, 617
        RMON1, 618–619
        RMON2, 620
    service levels
        challenges, 659
        constituent SLAs, 658
        management applications, 670–671, 674
        reporting, 664
        requirements, 660
        SAA, 666–667
        SLAs, 657
        SLM, 663–664
    SNMP, 609
        message types, 610
        SNMPv2, 611
        SNMPv3, 612
        SNMPv3 security, 612
    syslog accounting, 629
        distributed architecture, 631
        severity, 630
Management Information Base. See MIB
masks (subnets), 21
Matrix group (RMON1), 619
maximum Age timer (STP), 196
MCU (multipoint control units), 470
mean opinion score (MOS), 486
mean time between failure (MTBF), 191
media access (CSMA/CD), 6
media-type command, 779

memory, 9

message waiting indicator (MWI) services, 459

messages, 769

    error, 630

    ICMP, 727

    syslog, 629, 704

methodologies

    campus design, 181

    Network Organizational Model, 683

metrics, 15

    BGP, 385

    EIGRP, 384

    hop count, 379

    IGRP, 384

    routing protocols, 382–383

    variance, 160

    vectors, 23

MIB (Management Information Base), 613-614, 704

    Cisco MIB, 616

    example, 617

    MIB-II, 615

    private managed objects, 615

    RMON, 617

    vendor-specific definitions, 615

    Web site, 614

Microsoft Point-to-Point Compression (MPCC), 270

minimum bandwidth metric, 382

mobile wireless networks, 298

modems, 8

    cable, 295

    TA (terminal adapter), 8

Modern Organizational Ecosystem Model, 32

modern organizational model, 31

modular networks, 145

modularity, 69, 88, 118, 684

modules

    Enterprise Campus, 132–136, 207, 686

    Enterprise Composite Network Model, 127, 130

Enterprise Edge, 137, 141, 686

    E-commerce module, 139

    functional area, 230

    Internet Connectivity module, 139

    VPN/Remote Access module, 140

    WAN module, 140–141

Service Provider Edge, 141–144, 687

voice, 475

voice transport, 166

more nvram:startup-config command, 777

more system: running-config command, 777

MOS (mean opinion score), 486

MPCC (Microsoft Point-to-Point Compression), 270

MPLS (Multi-Protocol Label Switching), 258-259, 300

    egress edge LSRs, 302

    FEC, 301

    ingress edge LSRs, 302

    labels, 301

    packet flow, 302

    services provided, 303

    VPNs, 307

MPPP (Multilink Point-to-Point Protocol), 162

MRTG, 79

MSTP (Multiple STP), 198

MTBF (mean time between failure), 191

multicast addresses (IPv6), 354

multicast traffic, 211–212

multicast transmission, 6, 24

multihoming, 405

multilayer switching, 225

Multilink Point-to-Point Protocol (MPPP), 162

multimode (MM) fiber, 202

multipath routing algorithms, 15

Multiple STP (MSTP), 198

multiple-DMZ network example, 584

multiplexing, 766

multipoint control units (MCU), 470

Multi-Protocol Label Switching. *See* MPLS

MWI (message waiting indicator) services, 459

N

n, 6
name resolution
    designing IP addressing, 347
        DNS servers, 349
        static vs. dynamic, 348
    IPv6, 360
NANP (North American Numbering Plan), 455
NAT (Network Address Translation),
    332, 692, 799
    configuring
        for basic local IP address translation,
            806
        inside global address overloading, 807
        TCP load distribution, 809–810
        translating overlapping addresses, 808
    debug ip nat command, 812
    entries, clearing, 811
    implementation considerations, 812
    inside global addresses, 803–804
    inside local addresses, 801
    overlapping networks, address translation,
        804
    supported features, 801
    TCP load distribution, 805
    terminology, 800
    troubleshooting, 812
    uses for, 799
    verifying operation, 810
NAT-PT translation mechanism, 365
NBAR (network-based application recognition),
    79
neighbor table, 396
neighbors (BGP), 406
NetFlow, 77-79, 625-627
    accounting management, 645
    Data Export, 627
    FlowCollector, 627
    functionality, 626
    Network Data Analyzer, 628
    vs. RMON, 629

NetFlow Flow Collector application, 80
Network Address Translation. *See* NAT
network audits, 70
    manual commands, 72–75
    tools, 71
network-based application recognition (NBAR),
    79
network command, 781
Network Data Analyzer, 80
network geography, 182-184
Network Health Checklist, 76
Network Intrusion Detection Systems (NIDSs),
    575
network layer, 256
    addressing, 9
    IP addressing, 329-331, 334, 692
    OSI model, 5, 766
    packets, 768
Network layer host group (RMON2), 622
Network layer matrix group (RMON2), 622
Network Management module, 132, 134
    guidelines, 136
    integration, 226
    security
        guidelines, 594
        risks, 593
network management network services, 146
network management system (NMS), 608, 703
network modeling tools (NMTs), 94
network operating system (NOS), 24
network organizational architecture, 34
Network Organizational Model, 29, 84–86
    accomplishing organizational goals, 42
    applications and network services, 57–58, 60
    architecture, 34, 681
        example, 35
        layers, 682
    assessing existing networks, 64, 67, 70–75
        customer input, 65
        examples, 66
    assessing organizational constraints, 55-57
    benefits, 31

core assumptions, 31

design methodology, 44–48

flexibility, 31, 43

guidelines for implementation, 34

identifying

    customer requirements, 49

    network requirements, 52

methodology, 683

organizational hierarchy, 39

scope, 49

technical constraint identification, 62–63

technical goals, 60–62

traffic analysis, 77

    example, 78

    examples, 81–82

    tools, 79

understanding organizational goals, 53

network protocols, 761

network providers, tariffs, 256

network security policies, 549

network services, 687

    intelligent, 59

    security, 545

network solutions, 163, 687

    CN (Content Networking), 168

        content cachings, 169–170

        content delivery functions, 169

        content routing, 171

        content switching, 172

        example, 173

    examples, 163

    intelligent network services, 145

    voice transport, 164

        evaluating existing data infrastructure, 167–168

        example, 166

        IP telephony, 164–165

        modules, 166

networks, 597, 599

    accomplishing organizational goals, 42

    application characterization, 185

        application requirements, 189

        client-client, 185

        client-distributed server, 186

        client-Enterprise Edge, 188

        client-server farm, 187

    application maps, 67

    auditing, 71

    baselining, 649

    benefits, 32

    best practices, 598

    cable, 259, 295–297

    caches, 171

    campus, 181, 687

    CDN, 168

    cell-switched, 258

    converged, 463

    convergence, 385

    designing, 117. *See also* Enterprise Composite Network Model

        applications and network services, 57–58, 60

        assessing existing networks, 64–67, 70–84

        assessing organizational constraints, 55-57

        customer requirements, 49

        decision tables, 91–93

        documentation, 97

        draft design documents, 85–86

        Enterprise Campus, 181, 208–214, 216-226, 230-231, 234

        hierarchical network model, 118

        implementation and verification, 98

        IP telephony, 63

        methodology, 47–48

        monitoring and redesigning, 99

        network requirements, 52

        OSI model, 49

        PDIOO, 44–45

        planning design implementation, 95–96

        prototypes and pilots, 97

        redesign case study, 706–707, 710

        RFPs/RFIs, 50

scope, 49
structured approach, 87
technical constraint identification, 62–63
technical goals, 60–62
tools, 94
top-down approach, 87-90
understanding organizational goals, 53
VoFR, 500
voice transport, 441, 697
WANs, 688
devices, 9
bridges, 10
bridges vs. switches, 12
hubs, 9
routers, 13–14
switches, 10
dynamic routing, 375
enterprise, evolution of, 128
flexibility (example), 43
health summary report, 84
hierarchy, 117
infrastructure, 88
integrated IS-IS, 401
integrating voice and data, 461
internetworks, 3
IP
addressing, 691-692
security threats, 545
telephony, 472
transporting SNA data, 26
ISPs, 259
LANs
characteristics, 5
CSMA/CD, 6
data transmission, 6
Ethernet, 5
MAC addressing, 9
life cycles, 682
management, 607, 670, 703-705. *See also* management
masks, 322

modularizing, 69, 684
MPLS, 301
network organizational architecture, 34
OSI model, 3
overlapping, IP address translation, 804
packet switched, 258, 281–282, 464
peer-based, 26
performance, 60, 653
pilots or prototypes, 49
protocols (routing), 695
provisioning, 8
QoS (voice quality), 492–493, 497
remote access, 278–279
always-on connections, 280–281
backup solutions, 283–285
design as process, 283
dispersed Enterprise sites, 288-290
IP connectivity, 291–302
on-demand connections, 280
packet switched topologies, 281–282
VPNs, 304–305, 307–308
WANs, 277
routing
fast switching, 286
filtering, 696
process switching, 286
protocols, 403–404, 423
redistribution, 696
security, 545, 701. *See also* security
authentication, 563–566
authorization, 567–569
availability threats, 548
confidentiality threats, 547
data integrity, 572–574
device guidelines, 551
devices as targets, 550
DoS attacks, 554-556
external threats, 152–154
hosts and applications as targets, 557–558
integrity threats, 547
physical, 561–562

policies, 559–561
reconnaissance attacks, 553
requirements, 546
restricting vty access, 744
risk assessment, 549
SAFE Blueprint, 578
secure management and reporting, 575-577
transmission confidentiality, 570–572
understanding threats, 148
self-clocking, 272
static routing, 374
telephony. *See* telephony systems
traditional organizational, 42
traffic, upper-layer protocol transparency, 11
trending, 649
upgrades (case study), 105
VoFR, 498
voice quality, 477
voice transport, 441
PBXs, 444–447
PSTNs, 444
WANs, 256
characteristics, 6
circuit switching, 7
designing, 261
devices, 8
dialup services, 7
packet switching, 7
response time, 262
virtual circuits, 7
wireless, 259, 300
networks per class (IP addresses), 719
NetZoom, 72
NIDSs (Network Intrusion Detection Systems), 575
NMS (network management system), 608, 703
NMTs (network modeling tools), 94
nodes, 6, 182
North American Numbering Plan (NANP), 455
NOS (network operating system), 24
notation, dotted decimal, 321

Novel, Interware protocol suite, 24
numbering plans
North American, 455
PSTN, 454

O

octets, 18, 321
ODR (on-demand routing), 392-393, 695
off-net calling, 505–506, 512
on-demand connections, ISDN vs. analog modem, 280
One Time Passwords (OTPs), 151, 552
One Time Passwords authentication (OTP authentication), 134
on-net calling, 505–506, 700
Open Shortest Path First. *See* OSPF protocol
Open Systems Interconnection model. *See* OSI model
Operate phase (PDIOO), 683
Optimize phase (PDIOO), 683
optimizing
link performance, 263
WAN bandwidth, 268
organizations, 55, 57
accomplishing goals with networks, 42
architecture components, 33
benefits of networking, 32
ecosystems, 31–32
flexible network infrastructures, 43
goals
common examples, 53
data to be gathered from, 54
examples of, 54
template for assessment, 55
hierarchy, 39
information flow, 40
modern model, 31
networks
design methodology, 47–48
flexibility (example), 43
understanding goals, 53

policies, 36
  defining, 37–38
  levels of policy makers, 38
relationships with stakeholders, 31
structure, 39
traditional model, 30
ork, 25
OSI model (Open Systems Interconnection) , 3, 120, 256
  application layer, 768
  characteristics, 760
  communication between layers, 762
  control information, 763
  data link layer, 765
  information exchange process, 763–764
  LAN protocols, 5
  layer services, 762
  layers, 4
  lower layers, 760
  network layer, 766
  networks, 16
  physical layer, 765
  presentation layer, 767
  protocols, 16, 761
  relationship to IBM SNA, 26
  scope of project, 49
  transport layer, 23, 766
  upper layers, 760
  upper-layer protocols, 11
  vs. hierarchical network model, 120
OSPF (Open Shortest Path First) protocol, 23
  characteristics, 399
  features, 398
  hierarchical design, 398
  when to use, 391
OSPFv3, 367
OTPs (One Time Passwords), 134, 151, 552
OUI (Organizational Unique Identifier), 9
out keyword (access-class command), 746
outbound interfaces, queuing, 273
outside global IP addresses, 800
outside local IP, 800

overlapping networks, IP address translation, 804
overlay VPNs, 304
overloading inside global addresses, 803–804

P

Packet captu730re group (RMON1), 619
packet filtering, 725–727,
packet loss, 263
packet switched topologies, 258, 281, 464
  fully meshed, 282
  partially meshed, 282
  star, 282
packets, 768
  data transmission, 6
  dejitter buffers, 481
  delay from variable packet size, 482
  delays and losses in voice networks, 477
  fast switching, 286
  jitter, 482
  MPLS, 302
  network flow, 625
  process switching, 286
  processing delays, 479
  propagation delays, 478
  queuing delays, 480
  serialization delays, 479
  switching, 7
  unicast, forwarding, 192
Partial Route Calculation (PRC), 402
partially meshed topology, 281-282
password command, 778, 789
passwords
  attacks, 152
  OTPs, 552
PBXs (Private Branch Exchanges), 294
  features, 446–447
  vs. PSTNs, 444
PCM (pulse code modulation), 442-443, 697
PCM algorithm, 485
PDIOO (Plan-Design-Implement-Operate-Optimize), 44–45, 260, 682

PDUs, 770
peer-based networking, 26
peers, 406. *See also* neighbors
peer-to-peer VPNs, 307
performance, 60, 520. *See also* capacity planning
    assessing network health, 76
    bottlenecks, 276
    compression, affect on, 271
    distribution switches, 219
    evaluating for upgrade to voice network
        solutions, 167
    management, 646
        capacity areas, 651
        challenges, 651–652
        defining a process for, 650
        exceptions, 649
        goal of, 647
        performance data reporting, 650
        SLM, 648
        solutions, 652–653
        tools, 653
    voice networks, 477
    what-if analysis, 648
permanent virtual circuits (PVCs), 7, 258
permit conditions, 725
personnel, considerations in network design, 56
phantom routers, 158
physical layer (OSI model), 5, 256, 765
physical redundancy, 159
physical security
    guidelines, 562
    threats, 561
pilot networks, 97
PIM (Protocol Independent Multicast), 211
ping command, 652, 775, 787
ping ipx command, 782
PKI (Public Key Infrastructure), 309
placement
    extended access lists, 744
    standard access lists, 733
Plan phase (PDIOO), 682
Plan-Design-Implement-Operate-Optimize

(PDIOO), 260
planning design implementation, 95–96
points of presence (POPs), 258
point-to-point links, 7, 288
poisonous data, 555
policies
    consideration in network design, 56
    network security, 549
    organizational, 36-38
    policy domain, 200
    security, 559
        documentation, 560
        example, 561
        physical threats, 562
POPs (points of presence), 258
port names
    TCP, 740
    UDP, 741
port numbers, 17, 739
port secure command, 790
port secure max-mac-count command, 790
port security action command, 790
port security command, 790
port security max-mac-count command, 790
PortFast, 122, 196
POTS, 8
ppp authentication command, 786
PPPoA implementation, 294
PPPoE implementation, 294
PQ (Priority Queuing), 273-274, 495
PRC (Partial Route Calculation), 402
precedence (IP), 494
Predictor data compression algorithm, 270
prefixes, 323, 692, 724–725
presentation layer (OSI model), 767
PRI (Primary Rate Interface), 452
pri-group command, 786
Priority Queuing (PQ), 273–274, 495
private addresses, 329-331, 334, 692
    connectivity with public addresses, 332
    guidelines for use, 334
    requirements, 332

Private Branch Exchange. *See* PBX
private WANs, 266
privilege escalation, 557
Probe configuration group (RMON2), 622
process switching, 286
processing, 352, 728
processing delays, 479
propagation delays, 478
Protocol director group (RMON2), 622
Protocol distribution group (RMON2), 622
Protocol Independent Multicast (PIM), 211
protocol stacks, 16
protocols, 761
    AppleTalk protocol suite, 25
    ARP, router discovery, 157
    bridging, 11
    configuration, 641
    H.323, 466
        benefits, 466
        components, 467
        example, 470
    IP address assignment, 344
    LANs, 5
    management, 623–624
    NetWare protocol suite, 24
    network management architecture, 609
    OSI model, 3
    port numbers, 17
    routing, 3, 15, 695
        BGP, 23, 404-406
        case study, 423
        comparison of, 390
        convergence, 385-387
        distance vector, 376–380
        EIGRP, 23, 395–397
        features, 392
        flat, 388
        hierarchical, 389
        hierarchical network structure, 407
        hybrid interior gateway, 377
        IGRP, 391

        integrating interior routing protocols
            with BGP, 416–417
        IP addressing design, 341
        IPv6, 366
        IS-IS, 392, 400–401
        link-state, 377-379
        metrics, 382–383
        ODR, 392
        OSPF, 23, 391, 398
        RIPv1 or RIPv2, 390, 394
        route filtering, 414
        route redistribution, 411–413
        route summarization, 419–420
        selecting, 373, 389
        suites, 16
        TCP/IP, 22
    security, 655
    stacks, 16
    standardized, 3
    STP, 12
    switch security management, 654
    TCP/IP
        application layer, 18
        IP addressing, 21
        IPv4 addressing, 18–19
        network layer, 16
        transport layer, 17
    VoIP control and transport, 487
    WAN, 6
prototype networks, 49, 97
provisioning, 8
proxy ARP
    HSRP, 158
    router discovery, 157
PSTN module, 143
PSTNs (Public Switched Telephone Network),
    257
    features, 447
    numbering plans, 454
    services, 456
        call centers, 459
        Centrex, 457

interactive voice response (IVR), 460
virtual private voice networks, 458
voice mail, 459
switch trunks, 448
TDM, 461
vs. PBXs, 444
public addresses
connectivity with private addresses, 332
guidelines for use, 334
requirements, 332
Public Key Infrastructure (PKI), 309
Public Switched Telephone Networks. *See* PSTNs
pulse code modulation (PCM), 442-443, 697
PVCs (permanent virtual circuits), 7, 258

Q

Q Signaling (QSIG), 445
QoS (Quality of Service), 23, 79, 272
categories, 214
Cisco AutoQoS, 497
data flows, 23
design considerations (Enterprise Campus networks), 213–214
LAN switches, 214
Layer 2 switching support, 209
MPLS, 303
network services, 146
queuing strategies, 273
voice quality, 492
AutoQoS, 497
implementing, 492
mechanisms available, 493
voice transport, 699
VoIP example, 215
QoS classification mechanism, 493
QPPB (QoS Policy Propagation on BGP), 407
queuing, 272, 690
delays, 480
PQ, 274
types of, 273
WFQ, 273
quiet period, 410

R

R1/R2 signaling, 452
RA
route redistribution, 414
routing protocols, 410
RADIUS (Remote Authentication Dial-In User Service), 134
RAM, 9
random early detection (RED), 494
range, shared vs. switched LAN technology, 193
Rapid STP (RSTP), 197
RARP (Reverse Address Resolution Protocol), 17
rate-sensitive traffic, 24
Real-Time Transport Protocol (RTP), 271, 488
Recall, 321
receivers (RSVP sessions), 24
reconnaissance attacks, 553, 580
RED (random early detection), 494
redundancy
cost concerns, 155
Enterprise Networks, 156
link, 161, 268
physical, 159
route, 159–160
registered IP addresses, 329-331, 334, 692. *See also* private addresses
reliability (WAN design), 263
reload command, 775
Remote Access and VPN module security
802.11b, 588
guidelines, 586
risks, 585, 591
wireless LANs, 587, 590
remote access connections, 277, 303–309
always-on connections, 280–281
backup solutions, 283–285
design as process, 283
dispersed Enterprise sites, 288–290
establishing parameters, 278–279
IP connectivity, 291–302
on-demand connections, 280
packet switched topologies, 281–282

remote access networks, 308–309
remote monitoring. *See* RMON
Remote Shell/Remote Shell Command Execution
    (RSH/RCMD), 654
Request for Information (RIFs), 50
Request for Proposal (RFPs), 50
requires, 24
reserved TCP port numbers, 740
reserved UPD port numbers, 741
Response Time Reporter (RTR). *See* SAA
response times, 262-263
restricting vty access, 744
resume command, 775
retirement, 683
<Return> command, 774
Reverse Address Resolution Protocol (RARP), 17
RFC 1631, 799
RFC 1700, 739-741
RFC 1918, Address Allocation for Private
    Internets, 330
RFC 2080, RIPng for IPv6, 367
RFC 2283, Multiprotocol Extensions for BGP-4,
    367
RFC 2460, Internet Protocol, Version 6 (IPv6),
    350
RFCs (Requests for Comments), 793–797
RFIs (Request for Information), 50
RFPs (Request for Proposal), 50
RIP (Routing Information Protocol), 22
RIPng (RIP new generation), 366
RIPv1, 390, 394
RIPv2(RIP version 2), 22, 379, 390, 696
    convergence, 386
    features, 394
    snapshot routing, 390
risk assessment
    network security, 549
    security wheel, 559
RMON (remote monitoring), 607, 617–618, 704
    MIB, 618
    RMON1, 618-619

RMON2, 620
    vs. NetFlow, 629
ROM, 9
route aggregation, 334, 337-339, 419–420
route filtering, 696
route flaps, 419
route redistribution, 696
route redundancy, 159–160
route summarization, 334–335
routed networks, 286
routed protocols, 3, 15
router eigrp command, 781
router igrp command, 781
router ospf command, 781
router rip command, 781
routers, 13–14, 163
    Cisco, 411
    compression and its affects on performance,
        271
    DDR, 280
    LSRs, 301
    phantom, 158
    voice gateways, 165, 475
    voice-enabled. *See* voice gateways
routing, 15
    algorithms, 15
    classful, 341
    classless, 342
    DDR, 7
    dial backup, 284
    dynamic, 375–376
    floating static routes, 162
    IP, 696
    metrics, 15
    protocols. *See* routing protocols
    route filtering, 414, 696
    route redistribution, 412
    source routing, 16
    static, 374
    TCP/IP protocol
        IP addressing, 21
        IPv4 addressing, 18–19
        IPv4 subnets, 19

Routing Information Protocol (RIP), 22
routing protocols, 15, 761
    access layer, 409
    BGP, 23, 404
        external/internal, 406
        implementation example, 405
    case study, 423
    comparison of, 390
    convergence, 385-387
    core layer, 409
    deployment
        hierarchical network structure, 407
        integrating interior routing protocols
            with BGP, 416–417
        route filtering, 414
        route redistribution, 411–413
        route summarization, 419–420
    distance vector, 376
        example, 377–378
        selection guidelines, 380
    distribution layer, 409
    EIGRP, 23, 391
    features, 392
        EIGRP, 395–397
        IS-IS, 400–401
        ODR, 392
        OSPF, 398
        RIPv1 vs. RIPv2, 394
    flat, 388
    hierarchical, 389
    hybrid interior gateway, 377
    IGRP, 391
    interior, selecting, 403–404
    IPv6, 366
    IS-IS, 392, 403
    link-state, 377–380
    metrics, 160, 382–383
    OSPF, 391
    remote access, 410
    RIPv1 or RIPv2, 390
    router discovery, 157
    section criteria, 373
    selecting, 389
    suites, 16
    TCP/IP, 22
    vectors, 23
    vs. routed protocols, 15
routing tables, 15, 397
RSH/RCMD (Remote Shell/Remote Shell
    Command Execution), 654
RSTP (Rapid STP), 197
RSVP (Resource Reservation Protocol), 23-24
RTP (Real-Time Transport Protocol), 271, 488
RTR (Response Time Reporter). *See* SAA

S

SAA (service assurance agent), 653, 666, 706
    deployment, 668
    management applications, 670
        IPM, 670–671
        SMS, 674
    monitoring metrics, 667
SAFE (Security Architecture for Enterprise)
    Blueprint, 545
        Enterprise Composite Network
            E-commerce module, 583
            Internet Connectivity module, 580
            Network Management module, 593–594
            Remote Access and VPN module,
                585–591
            Server Farm module, 595
            WAN module, 591–592
        integrated functionality, 578
scalability
    EIGRP, 397
    IS-IS, 402
    OSPF, 399
S-CDMA mode, 297
scope
    IPv6 addresses, 354
    network device security breaches, 551
    organizational network design, 49
SDH (Synchronous Digital Hierarchy), 289

SDSL (Symmetric DSL), 258, 291
SDUs, 770
secure fingerprints, 572–573, 701
security, 545, 580, 583–595, 701
    algorithms, 546
    authentication, 563–564
        guidelines, 566
        how to use, 565
    authorization, 567
        guidelines, 569
        least privilege concept, 567
    Auto Update Server, 599–600
    Cisco Secure Scanner, 72
    data integrity, 572–574
    defense in depth concept, 578
    device guidelines, 551
    Edge Distribution module (Enterprise
        Campus networks), 230
    filtering, 570
    IP networks, 545
        availability threats, 548
        confidentiality threats, 547
        devices as targets, 550
        integrity threats, 547
        requirements, 546
        risk assessment, 549
    IP telephony systems, 597–599
    IPSec, 310
    management, 654
        examples, 656
        protocols, 655
    physical
        guidelines, 562
        threats, 561
    policies, 559
        documentation, 560
        example, 561
    restricting vty access, 744
    SAFE Blueprint, 578
    secure management and reporting
        audit trails, 575
        guidelines, 577
        IDSs, 575

    smurf attacks, 556
    SNMPv3, 612
    threats
        DoS attacks, 554-556
        hosts and applications as targets,
            557–558
        reconnaissance attacks, 553
    transmission confidentiality, 570
        encryption, 571
        guidelines, 572
    UTP concerns, 202
    wireless LANs, 587
Security Architecture for Enterprise Blueprint.
    See SAFE Blueprint
security network services, 146
    AAA, 151
    external threats, 152–153
        designing against, 154
        overview, 152
    IDSs, 150
    OTPs, 151
    understanding threats, 149
security wheel, 559
segments, 12, 769
selection guidelines, 380
self-clocking, 272
Sequenced Packet Exchange (SPX), 25
serial lines, dial backup, 7
serialization delays, 479
Server Farm module, 132-134
    guidelines, 136
    high availability, 155
    security, 595
    server connectivity, 229
    servers, 227
    voice network solutions, 166
Server Farms, 187, 227
servers
    access servers, 8
    Auto Update Server security, 599–600
    building distribution modules, 226
    common Server Farms, 187
    Enterprise Campus design, 226

service assurance agent. *See* SAA
service level contracts (SLCs), 657
Service Management Solution (SMS), 674
service password-encryption command, 778
Service Provider Edge, 685
    guidelines, 144
    modules, 141-143, 687
service providers (SPs), 259, 290
service timestamps command, 778
service-level contract (SLC), 657, 705
service-level management. *See* SLM
services
    MPLS, 303
    OSI model, 762
    queuing, 274
    RSVP, 24
sessions
    RSVP, 24
    TCP, 739
Set request message, 610
setup command, 775
shadow PVCs, 287
shared technology
    bandwidth, 193
    cost, 194
    high availability, 194
    intelligent services, 193
    range, 193
shared technology topology, 192
shared WANs, 266
shortest-path first routing algorithms, 16
show access-lists command, 775
show appletalk globals command, 783
show appletalk interface command, 783
show appletalk route command, 783
show appletalk zone command, 783
show cdp entry command, 775
show CDP interface command, 787
show cdp interface command, 775
show CDP neighbors command, 787
show cdp neighbors command, 775
show CDP neighbors detail command, 787

show cdp neighbors detail command, 775
show cdp traffic command, 775
show clock command, 775
show commands, 725, 810
show configuration command, 777
show controller command, 775
show dialer command, 784
show flash command, 775
show frame-relay lmi command, 784
show frame-relay map command, 784
show frame-relay pvc command, 784
show frame-relay traffic command, 784
show history command, 775, 787
show hosts command, 779
show interface command, 384
show interface switchport command, 788
show interface vlan 1 command, 788
show interfaces command, 776, 788
show ip access-list command, 779
show ip cache flow command, 81–82
show ip command, 787–788
show ip eigrp neighbors command, 779
show ip eigrp topology command, 779
show ip eigrp traffic command, 780
show ip interface command, 780
show ip nat statistics command, 780, 810
show ip nat translations command, 780
show ip nbar protocol-discovery command, 81
show ip ospf interface command, 780
show ip ospf neighbor command, 780
show ip protocols command, 780
show ip route command, 780
show ip route eigrp command, 780
show ipx access-list command, 782
show ipx interface command, 782
show ipx route command, 782
show ipx servers command, 782
show ipx traffic command, 782
show isdn active command, 784
show isdn status command, 784
show mac-address-table command, 788
show mac-address-table secure command, 788

show port security command, 788
show processes command, 776
show processes cpu command, 73
show processes memory command, 75
show running-config command, 776–777, 788
show sessions command, 776
show spanning-tree vlan command, 788
show spantree command, 788
show startup-config command, 776–777
show terminal command, 776
show trunk command, 788
show users command, 776
show version command, 776, 788
show versions command, 788
show vlan brief command, 788
show vlan command, 788
show vlan-membership command, 788
show vtp command, 788
show vtp domain command, 788
show vtp status command, 788
shutdown command, 779, 790
signaling, 697
    analog, 442
    digital, 442
    telephony systems, 449–450
        analog, 451–452
        digital, 452
        ISDN digital, 452
        PSTN numbering plans, 454
        PSTNs, 456–460
        SS7 digital, 453
signal-to-noise ratio (SNR), 443
signature verification key, 701
Simple Network Management Protocol. *See*
  SNMP
simple translation entry, 800
simulation tools, 94
single-mode (SM) fiber, 202
single-path routing algorithms, 15
site local unicast addresses, 356

SLAs
    challenges of management, 659
    constituent, 658
    reports, 664
    requirements, 660
    SLM, 663–664
SLCs (service-level contracts), 657, 705
SLM (service-level management) 648, 705
    challenges, 663
    example, 664
    planning, 665
SMDS (Switched Multimegabit Data Services),
  258
SMS (Service Management Solution), 674
smurf attacks, 556
SNA (Systems Network Architecture), 26
snapshot routing, 390
Sniffer, 79
SNMP (Simple Network Management Protocol),
  607-609
    message types, 610
    SNMPv2, 611
    SNMPv3, 612
    switch security management, 654
snmp-server command, 789
SNR (signal-to-noise ratio), 443
software
    bridges, 12
    Cisco IOS
        compression services, 270
        queuing services, 274
        traffic shaping, 276
    configuration management, 637
    queuing, 273
    selecting for WANs, 268
    version control, 638
SONET (Synchronous Optical Network), 289
source node, 6
source routing, 16
spanning-tree features of switches, 122
Spanning-Tree Protocol, 161

speed
    twisted-pair cable, 202
    WAN links, 268
split Layer 2 campus backbone design, 222
spoofing, 591
SPs (service providers), 259, 290
SPX (Sequenced Packet Exchange), 25
SR/TLB (source-route translational bridging), 11
SRB (source-route bridging), 11
SRT (source-route transparent bridging), 11
SS7 digital signaling, 453
SSH, 654
STAC compression algorithm, 270
stakeholders, 29-31
standard IP access lists, 727
    configuring, 730
    example, 733
    placement, 733
    processing, 728
    wildcard masks, 729
standards, 23
    network configuration, 636
    network management architecture, 609
star topologies, 281-282
static FRF.11 trunks, 499
static IP address assignment, 344–345
static name resolution, 348, 360
static routing, 162, 374
static routing algorithms, 15
statistical compression, 270
Statistics group (RMON1), 619
STP (Spanning-Tree Protocol), 12
    convergence enhancements, 197
    disabling on a device, 217
    error-reducing features, 197
    Forward Delay timer, 196
    Layer 2 switches, 195
    recent enhancements, 196
STP Loop Guard, 197
strategic analysis tools, 94
strong authentication, 564
structured approach to network design, 87

subnet masks, 19-21, 322
    calculating, 721–722
    calculating networks for, 723
    extending IP classful addresses, 721
    fixed vs. variable, 339
    prefixes, 724–725
subnets, 19, 325
successor, 397
suggested reading, 751–752, 757
summarization (routes), 419–420, 334–335
summary reports, 84
supernetting, 334, 419–420
supervision signaling, 450
SVCs (switched virtual circuits), 7, 258
switched LAN technology, 192
    cost, 194
    high availability, 194
    intelligent services, 193
    range, 193
Switched Multimegabit Data Services (SMDS), 258
switched virtual circuits (SVCs), 7, 258
switches, 8-11
    Catalyst, 13
    cut-through, 12
    distribution, 219
    effects of applications on performance, 229
    interswitch communications, 448
    IP telephony, 165
    Layer 2/Layer 3 comparison, 194–195
        cost, 201
        failure domain, 200
        load sharing, 198–199
    oversubscription, 228
    PBX, 446
    PSTN, 447, 697
    security management, 654
    Server Farm module (Enterprise Campus network), 227
    spanning-tree features, 122
    vs. bridges, 12

switching, 172
  L2, 121
  L3, 121
  modes, 286
  policy domains, 200
  vs. shared technology, 688
switchport access command, 790
switchport mode command, 790
Symmetric DSL (SDSL), 258, 291
SYN code bit set, 739
Synchronous Digital Hierarchy (SDH), 289
SYN-flooding attacks, 556
syslog accounting, 629
  severity, 630
  syslog distributed architecture, 631
syslog messages, 704
Systems Network Architecture (SNA), 26

T

T1 trunks, 446
T3, 143
TA (ISDN terminal adapter), 8
<Tab> command, 774
TACACS+ (Terminal Access Controller Access
  Control System Plus), 134
tariffs, 256
TCP (Transmission Control Protocol), 17, 666
  assigned port numbers, 740
  load distribution, 805
  port names, 739-740
  selective acknowledgment, 272
  sessions, 739
TCP intercept feature (Cisco IOS), 556
TCP/IP (Transmission Control Protocol/Internet
  Protocol), 270
  application layer, 18
  applications, 768
  IP addressing, 21
  IPv4 addressing, 18-19
  network layer, 16
  RIP, 22

routing protocols, 23
transport layer, 17
TDM (time-division multiplexing), 461
  always-on connections, 280
  remote access connections, 279
TDMA mode, 297
technical requirements of WAN design
  bandwidth, 264
  maximum offered traffic, 263
telephony systems, 448
  bandwidth, 489
    reducing traffic, 490
    requirements, 490–491
  call legs, 477
  integrating voice architectures, 460, 465
    converged networks, 463
    VoIP, 461, 469
  IP, 470
    architecture, 471
    centralized design, 473
    design goals, 472
    Internet design, 474
    single site design, 472
  PBX/PSTN comparison, 445
  PCM, 443
  PSTNs
    call centers, 459
    Centrex, 457
    features, 447
    interactive voice response (IVR), 460
    numbering plans, 454
    services, 456
    virtual private voice networks, 458
    voice mail, 459
  QoS and voice quality, 492
    AutoQoS, 497
    design considerations, 492
    mechanisms available, 493
  signaling, 449–450
    analog, 451–452
    digital, 452
    ISDN digital, 452

SS7 digital, 453
VoATM
    adaptation types, 503
    classes of services, 502
    design guidelines, 504
    overview, 502
VoFR, 498–500
voice coding and compression, 485
    codec design considerations, 487
    codec mean opinion score, 486
    codecs, 486
voice gateways, 476
voice quality, 477
    echo, 483
    packet delays, 478–479
    variable network delays, 480-482
voice routing, 454, 475
VoIP control and transport protocols, 487
    call control functions, 489
    RTP, 488
    UDP, 487
Telnet, 654
telnet command, 776
Temporal Key Integrity Protocol (TKIP), 590
term ip netmask-format command, 780
Terminal Access Controller Access Control
   System Plus (TACACS+), 134
terminal editing command, 776
terminal history size command, 776
terminal monitor command, 776
terminal servers, 134
terminals, 467
terminology (NAT), 800
testing
   prototype/pilot networks, 97
   TCP and UDP services, 666
testing services, 666
threats, 148. *See also* security
   external, 152–154
   Internet Connectivity module, 580
   physical, 561
three-way handshake, 17

throughput, 190, 262
tie-line emulation, 499
tie trunks, 448
time-division multiplexing. *See* TDM
tiport, 8
TKIP (Temporal Key Integrity Protocol), 590
token passing media access, 6
TokenRing group (RMON1), 619
top-down design approach, 87
   example, 90
   vs. bottom-up, 89
topologies
   assessing existing networks in design
     process, 66
   Ethernet, collision domains, 191
   Token Ring, token passing media access, 6
   WANs, 261
topology tables, 397
traceroute command, 776
traditional organizational model, 30
traditional WAN technologies, 257
traffic
   analyzing in existing networks, 77
     examples, 78, 81–82
     tools, 79
   attacks, 553
   best-effort, 24
   data flows, 23
   delay-sensitive, 24, 213–214
   downstream/upstream, 291
   flooding, 212
   flow specifications, 23
   interesting/uninteresting, 280
   IP extended access lists, 735
   monitoring, 617
   MPLS services, 303
   multicast, 211-212
   network patterns (Enterprise Campus
     networks), 209–210
   queuing services, 274
   queuing to avoid congestion, 272
   rate-sensitive, 24

reducing voice traffic, 490
routing, 15
shaping, 276
upper-layer protocol transparency, 11
voice, capacity planning, 505–518
Web, 172
traffic-share command, 781
trailers, 763, 768
translating
    inside local addresses, 801
    NAT, 332
    registered IP addresses to private addresses,
        692
translation transition mechanism, 365
translational bridging, 11
transmission confidentiality, 570
    encryption, 571
    guidelines, 572
Transmission Control Protocol/Internet Protocol.
    See TCP/IP
transmission media, 201
    bandwidth and range characteristics, 204
    cabling, 182
    copper vs. fiber, 203
    network example, 205
    optical cables, 202
    UTP, 201
transparency
    network interfaces (AppleTalk), 25
    upper-layer protocols, 11
transparent bridging, 11
transport layer
    OSI model, 4, 766
    RSVP (Resource Reservation Protocol), 23
    SPX, 25
Trap message, 610
trending, 649
triggered updates, 378
triple data encryption standard (3DES), 572
troubleshooting
    backup remote access solutions, 283
        dial backup routing, 284
        secondary WAN links, 285

bottlenecks, 169
echo, 484
NAT, 812
trunk command, 790
trunking capacity planning, 521
trunks, 448
tunneling transition mechanism, 363
tunnels
    GRE, 309
    layer 3, 308
two-factor authentication, 564

U

uBR (Universal Broadband Routers), 295
UDLD (Unidirectional Link Detection), 197
UDP (User Datagram Protocol), 17, 271
    assigned port numbers, 741
    IP telephony systems, 487
    port names, 741
    testing services, 666
udp protocol keyword, 740
u-law companding, 443–444
UMTS (Universal Mobile Telephone Service),
    298
undebug command, 776
un-encapsulated data, 5
unicast addresses, 354-356
unicast packet forwarding, 192
unicast transmission, 6, 24
Unidirectional Link Detection (UDLD), 197
Universal Broadband Routers (uBR), 295
Universal Mobile Telephone Service (UMTS),
    298
unshielded twisted-pair cables (UTP), 201
<up arrow> command, 774
upgrading
    configuration management, 639
    networks, 105
UplinkFast, 122, 197
upper layers (OSI model), 760. *See also*
    application layer

upper-layer protocols, 11, 18
    NetWare Protocol suite, 24-25
    transparency, 11
upstream, 291
User Datagram Protocol. *See* UDP
User history collection group (RMON2), 622
username command, 786
UTP (unshielded twisted-pair cables), 201

V

VAD (voice activity detection), 490
Variable Length Subnet Masking (VLSM), 21,
    349, 693
variance, 160
variance command, 781
VDSL (very-high-data-rate DSL), 258
vectors, 23
verification tools, 94
verifying
    access list configuration, 746–747
    NAT operation, 810
    pilot/prototype network implementation
        steps, 97
vertical integration, 31
very-high-data-rate DSL (VDSL), 258
virtual addresses, 9
virtual circuit management, 766
virtual circuits, 7
Virtual Private Networks. *See* VPNs
virtual private voice networks, 458
vlan command, 789
vlan database command, 789
vlan-membership command, 790
VLANs, 12–13, 197
VLSM (Variable Length Subnet Masking), 21,
    340, 693
VoATM
    adaptation types, 503
    classes of services, 502
    design guidelines, 504
    dial peer, 476
    overview, 502

VoFR, 498
    design guidelines, 500
    dial peer, 476
    implementations, 499
    vs. VoIP over Frame Relay, 499
voice activity detection (VAD), 490
voice data, integrating voice and data networks,
    461
voice-enabled routers, 165
voice gateways, 165, 475
    dial peers, 476
    echo, 484
    interfaces that support, 475
    jitter, 482
    VoATM networks, 504
    voice ports, 475
voice mail, 459
voice networks
    capacity planning, 505
        Campus IP telephony, 519–521
        DSP resources 514
        GoS, 508–512
        network migration, 507
        on-net/off-net calling, 505–506
        trunking, 521
        WANs, 515–518
voice over IP. *See* VoIP
voice ports, 475
voice routing, 454
voice transport, 164, 441, 697
    evaluating existing data infrastructure, 167–
        168
    IP telephony, 164-165
    modules, 166
    network solution example, 166
    PBXs, 444
        features, 446–447
        vs. PSTNs, 444
    PSTNs, 444
        features, 447
        vs. PBXs, 444
    QoS mechanisms, 699

VoIP (voice over IP), 261
   AutoQoS, 497
   bandwidth requirements, 490
   case study, 526
   control and transport protocols, 487
      call control functions, 489
      RTP, 488
      UDP, 487
   dial peer, 476
   DSPs, 470
   echo, 484
   gatekeepers, 469
   H.323, 467
   overview, 461
   QoS, 215
   vs. IP telephony, 470
voluntary tunnels (VPDN), 307
VPDNs, 306-307
VPN/Remote Access module, 140
VPNs (Virtual Private Networks), 255
   applications, 303
   authentication, 565
   benefits of, 308
   connectivity options, 304–307
   overlay, 304
   remote access options
      benefits of, 308
      connectivity, 304–307
      peer-to-peer, 307
VRRP, router discovery, 158
vtp command, 789
vty, denying access, 744

W

WAN commands (table), 783, 786
WAN configuration commands (table), 785–786
WAN module, 140–141
   security
      guidelines, 592
      risks, 591

WAN protocols, 761
WANs (wide-area networks), 3, 255-256
   authentication, 565
   backup links, 268
   bandwidth
      optimizing, 268
      ranges, 265
   capacity calculations, 700
   characteristics, 6
   circuit switching, 7
   Cisco IOS EXEC commands, 783
   comparing technologies, 267
   data compression, 269–270
   designing, 256, 688
      analyzing customer requirements, 261
      application requirements, 262–263
      characterizing the existing network, 261
      cost effectiveness, 265
      methodology, 260
      selecting technologies, 276
      technical requirements, 263–264
      topology and network solutions, 261
      trade-offs, 261
   devices, 8, 13–14
   dialup services, 7
   emerging technologies, 258
      cable, 259
      DSL, 258
      LRE, 259
      MPLS, 259
      vs. traditional technologies, 257
      wireless, 259
   Enterprise Composite Network Model, 256
   Enterprise Edge, connecting with outside
      world, 260
   G.729 codec, 489
   hardware, 268
   hubs, 9
   implementation, 268
   interconnections, 260

ISPs, 259
layers, 256
leased, 266
links
    permanent secondary, 285
    queuing to improve performance, 272
    redundancy, 161
ownership, 266
point-to-point links, 7
private, 266
provisioning, 8
queuing
    PQ, 274
    WFQ, 273
redundant links, 268
remote access
    always-on connections, 280–281
    backup solutions, 283–285
    design as process, 283
    dispersed Enterprise sites, 288-290
    establishing parameters, 278–279
    Internet as a backup, 308–309
    IP connectivity, 291–302
    on-demand connections, 280
    packet switched topologies, 281–282
    VPNs, 304–308
response time, 263
self-clocking, 272
service, 256
shared, 266
traditional technologies, 257
upgrading and backing up (case study), 313
virtual circuits, 7
voice data capacity planning, 515
    CAC, 518
    calculations, 516
    call routing alternatives, 518
    combining calculations with GoS, 517
window size, 271–272
war dialing, 553
war driving, 553
Watsup Gold, Net Inspector Lite, 72

Web sites, 367, 751–752, 757
    Auto Update Server, 600
    CDP, 625
    Cisco NetFlow technology, 80
    Erlang tables, 509
    MIB, 614
    NBAR, 80
    RFC 1918, Address Allocation for Private
        Internets, 330
    RFC 2080, RIPng for IPv6, 367
    RFC 2460, Internet Protocol, Version 6
        (IPv6), 350
    third-party network auditing tools, 72
    third-party traffic analysis tools, 79
web switching, 172
weighted random early detection (WRED), 494
WFQ (Weighted Fair Queuing), 273, 495
what-if analysis, 648
what-if tools, 94
wide-area networks. *See* WANs
wildcard masks, 729
    examples, 729–730
    implicit, 731
wireless LANs
    802.11b, 588
    802.1X, 589
    EAP, 589
    security, 587-589
wireless networks, 258–259
    benefits, 300
    broadband fixed, 298–299
    LANs, 298
    mobile, 298
wireless packet sniffers, 591
WLANs (wireless local area networks), 259
WRED (weighted random early detection), 494
write erase command, 777
write memory command, 777
write network command, 777
write terminal command, 777

X

X.25, 258
    always-on connections, 281
    remote access connections, 279
xDSL, 292

Y-Z

yields, 22

CISCO SYSTEMS

Cisco Press

SAVE UP TO 30%

Become a member and save at **ciscopress.com**!

Complete a **user profile** at ciscopress.com today to become a member and benefit from **discounts up to 30% on every purchase** at ciscopress.com, as well as a more customized user experience. Your membership will also allow you access to the entire Informit network of sites.

Don't forget to subscribe to the monthly Cisco Press newsletter to be the first to learn about new releases and special promotions. You can also sign up to get your first **30 days FREE on Safari Bookshelf** and preview Cisco Press content. Safari Bookshelf lets you access Cisco Press books online and build your own customized, searchable electronic reference library.

Visit **www.ciscopress.com/register** to sign up and start saving today!

The profile information we collect is used in aggregate to provide us with better insight into your technology interests and to create a better user experience for you. You must be logged into ciscopress.com to receive your discount. Discount is on Cisco Press products only; shipping and handling are not included.

Learning is serious business.
Invest wisely.

Cisco Press

Learning is serious business.

Invest wisely.

ciscopress.com

Wouldn't it be great
if the world's leading technical publishers joined forces to deliver their best tech books in a common digital reference platform?

They have. Introducing
InformIT Online Books
powered by Safari.

■ **Specific answers to specific questions.**
formIT Online Books' powerful search engine gives you relevance-nked results in a matter of seconds.

■ **Immediate results.**
/ith InformIt Online Books, you can select the book you want nd view the chapter or section you need immediately.

■ **Cut, paste and annotate.**
ste code to save time and eliminate typographical errors. ake notes on the material you find useful and choose whether not to share them with your work group.

■ **Customized for your enterprise.**
ustomize a library for you, your department or your entire rganization. You only pay for what you need.

Get your first 14 days **FREE!**
InformIT Online Books is offering its members a 10 book subscription risk-free for 14 days. Visit **http://www.informit.com/onlinebooks/cp** for details.

ciscopress.com